GW00363282

t

CEPHALOPODS
OF THE WORLD

Kir N. Nesis

CEPHALOPODS OF THE WORLD

Squids, Cuttlefishes, Octopuses, and Allies

Kir N. Nesis

Senior scientist, Department of Nekton, P. P. Shirshov Institute of Oceanology, USSR Academy of Sciences, Moscow.

Translated from Russian by B. S. Levitov

Edited by Lourdes A. Burgess

Title page: *Sepia officinalis* Linné. Photo by Gerhard Marcuse at Aquarium Berlin, German Democratic Republic.

Original Russian Edition: K. N. Nesis *Kratkiy opredelitel' golovonogikh molluskov Mirovogo okeana (Abridged key to the cephalopod mollusks of the World Ocean)*.

ISBN 0-86622-051-8

Distributed in the UNITED STATES by T.F.H. Publications, Inc., 211 West Sylvania Avenue, Neptune City, NJ 07753; in CANADA to the Pet Trade by H & L Pet Supplies Inc., 27 Kingston Crescent, Kitchener, Ontario N2B 2T6; Rolf C. Hagen Ltd., 3225 Sartelon Street, Montreal 382 Quebec; in CANADA to the Book Trade by Macmillan of Canada (A Division of Canada Publishing Corporation), 164 Commander Boulevard, Agincourt, Ontario M1S 3C7; in ENGLAND by T.F.H. Publications Limited, 4 Kier Park, Ascot, Berkshire SL5 7DS; in AUSTRALIA AND THE SOUTH PACIFIC by T.F.H. (Australia) Pty. Ltd., Box 149, Brookvale 2100 N.S.W., Australia; in NEW ZEALAND by Ross Haines & Son, Ltd., 18 Monmouth Street, Grey Lynn, Auckland 2 New Zealand; in SINGAPORE AND MALAYSIA by MPH Distributors (S) Pte., Ltd., 601 Sims Drive, #03/07/21, Singapore 1438; in the PHILIPPINES by Bio-Research, 5 Lippay Street, San Lorenzo Village, Makati Rizal; in SOUTH AFRICA by Multipet Pty. Ltd., 30 Turners Avenue, Durban 4001. Published by T.F.H. Publications Inc. Manufactured in the United States of America by T.F.H. Publications, Inc.

CONTENTS

To My Mother

Foreword

A continuous and rapid growth of interest in cephalopods—nautiluses, spirulas, squids, cuttlefishes, and octopuses—has been observed recently. There are various reasons for such interest. The cephalopods are an important and potentially valuable fishery resource. High nutritional qualities, short life span, and an extremely rapid growth (some tropical octopuses gain as much as 3 kg within 8 to 10 months) make them highly promising animals for mariculture. For neurophysiologists the squid is the most important subject for investigating the conductivity of nerve impulses. Physiologists are interested in cephalopods as invertebrates with a highly developed intelligence ("primates of the sea"). They are not of minor interest for ethologists. The most recent discoveries have shown that only a few sea animals can compete with the cephalopods as a source of important and promising biologically active substances (antishock, anesthetic, and antiparasitic drugs, powerful toxins and cytostatics, and so on). For paleontologists the study of recent cephalopods, particularly of the chambered nautiluses, is the key to the understanding of the mode of life and especially of the processes of fossilization and burial of nautiloids, ammonites, and belemnites.

This ever-growing flood of investigations encounters an obstacle of no small significance—the absence of taxonomic handbooks on the world cephalopods. Books on local faunas usually include only coastal species, and practically no books are available on the open-ocean species, whose significance has been growing during the last years. This concise handbook on the cephalopods of the world oceans is intended to fill this gap, at least partially. It includes all described genera and subgenera of Recent cephalopods and all species of nautiloids, cuttlefishes, neritic and oceanic squids and octopuses, except some Australian species of the genus *Sepia* that were described only on their shell and benthic octopuses belonging to the genera *Octopus* and *Benthoctopus*. These latter genera have not been revised, and it proved impossible to compose complete keys to all the species. I had to restrict myself to compilation of keys to the better-studied species of *Benthoctopus* and all species of Octopodinae of the Atlantic and North Pacific Oceans.

This book is an abridged manual, for it includes keys only and no detailed descriptions of each species. Such descriptions would have postponed publication for years but would also have made the book too bulky.

The keys are preceded by brief notes on morphology and anatomy of cephalopods. Stress is placed on descriptions of the dibranchiate (endocochleate) cephalopods, with a preference for such characters that are most important for identifying the species. Voluminous literature on particular problems in the study of recent cephalopod molluscs is not included in the bibliography, which contains only general works on this subject, keys to separate groups (orders, families, and genera) and local faunas (marked by*), modern catalogs, species lists for separate regions, and a few works specially cited in the text.

The author is indebted to his friends and colleagues who assisted in collecting the material, placed their collections to the author's disposal for study, read parts of the book, and expressed their opinions: V. E. Becker, G. M. Belyaev, T. N. Belyanina, O. D. Borodulina, R. N. Burukovsky, Yu. G. Chindonova, Yu. M. Chuvasov, T. S. Dubinina, B. I. Fedoryako, Yu. A. Filippova, Yu. M. Froerman, E. S. Karmovskaya, N. I. Kashkin, Ch. M. Nigmatullin, N. V. Parin, M. A. Pinchukov, T. S. Rass, Yu. I. Sazonov, G. A. Shevtsov, Yu. N. Shcherbachev, A. G. Tsokur, A. N. Vovk, and G. V. Zuev. The list of the Latin names has been compiled by I. V. Nikitina and L. V. Pereguda.

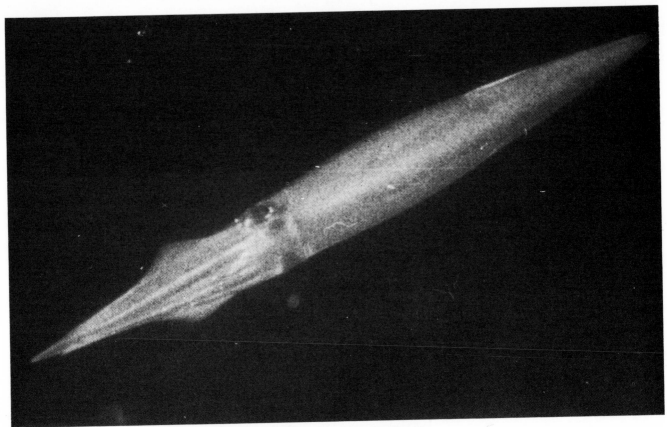

Todarodes sagittatus (Lamarck), the European arrow squid. Barents Sea near Murman Coast, in the fall of 1981. Depth of about 5 m. Photo from manned submersible *Sever 2*. Courtesy of Dr. Mikhail L. Zaferman, Polar Research Institute of Marine Fisheries & Oceanography, Murmansk, USSR.

Grimpoteuthis cf. *umbellata* (Fischer), a deep-sea cirrate octopod. August 1962. Reykjanes Ridge at 58°30′ N, depth 1300 m. Photo from manned submersible *Pisces*. Courtesy of Dr. Anatoly M. Sagalevich, P. P. Shirshov Institute of Oceanology, Academy of Sciences, USSR, Moscow.

Introduction

The cephalopod molluscs (chambered nautiluses, cuttlefishes, squids, vampyromorphs, and octopuses) belong to the highest class of the phylum Mollusca. Given below is the systematic position and subdivision of the class Cephalopoda.

Kingdom Animalia—animals
 Subkingdom Metazoa—multicellular animals
  Superdivision Enterozoa—enterozoans
   Division Bilateralia—bilaterally symmetrical animals
    Superphylum Trochozoa—animals with trochophore larva
     Phylum Mollusca—molluscs
      Subphylum Conchifera—shell-bearing molluscs
       Class Cephalopoda—cephalopods.

The class Cephalopoda comprises five subclasses containing numerous orders. The existing fauna is represented by two subclasses: Nautiloidea (tetrabranchiate cephalopods), with only the order Nautilida, family Nautilidae, and genus *Nautilus;* and Coleoidea (dibranchiate cephalopods). Coleoidea is divided into four orders: cuttlefishes, Sepiida, with suborders for *Spirula* (Spirulina) and cuttlefishes proper (Sepiina); squids, Teuthida, with suborders for neritic squids (Myopsida) and oceanic squids (Oegopsida); vampyromorphs, Vampyromorpha (the only species being *Vampyroteuthis infernalis*); and octopuses, Octopoda, with suborders for finned octopuses (Cirrata) and octopuses proper (Incirrata). The orders of cuttlefishes and squids are sometimes united into the group Decapoda. The general part of the book contains the characteristics of the dibranchiate cephalopods only. For the tetrabranchiate cephalopods refer to the treatment of Nautiloidea, subhead 1.

The keys utilize mainly external characters that do not require the dissection of specimens. As far as possible, the structural features of the immature and mature specimens of both sexes are taken into consideration. Unfortunately, this is not always possible since in many groups of the cuttlefishes, squids, and octopuses, especially those inhabiting the continental shelf, the species can be identified for certain in adult males only. The identification of the females and of immature specimens is extremely difficult in these groups and is sometimes practically impossible, so they may key only to genus or subgenus. It is also impossible to identify the larvae and the juveniles with the aid of the keys available in this book. Figures of the pelagic larvae and of the juveniles of the cephalopods are published in the *Field Manual of the Plankton*, vol. 3, issued by the Zoological Institute of the USSR Academy of Sciences in 1984.

GENERAL SECTION
General Characteristics of Cephalopod Molluscs

The class Cephalopoda is comprised of bilaterally symmetrical molluscs with external shell (in *Nautilus*), an internal shell represented by a calcareous plate (in true cuttlefishes, Sepiidae), by a coiled "ramshorn" shell (in *Spirula*), or by a thin transparent horny plate, the gladius (in squids); in some cuttlefishes and octopuses the shell is either reduced or entirely absent.

The body (Fig. 1) is covered by a muscular sac, the mantle, which is the main locomotory organ for fast (jet) swimming. The mantle encloses the organs of the mantle complex—the gills (one pair in dibranchiate cephalopods and two pairs in *Nautilus*) and the organs of the digestive, circulatory, genital, and excretory systems. The large head of a cephalopod is usually well separated from the body (except in some octopuses). It bears highly developed eyes (except in *Nautilus* and *Cirrothauma*, Fig. 74 C), a crown of appendages that surround the mouth, and the funnel. Dibranchiate cephalopods have 8 or 10 appendages. In squids and cuttlefishes there are always 10 (at least at the larval stage), 8 arms and 2 tentacles that are located between the ventrolateral and ventral arms and greatly differ from the arms in structure and armature. The vampyromorphs are equipped with 8 arms and a pair of slender filaments that are kept in special pockets between the dorsal and dorsolateral arms (Fig. 73). The octopuses are provided with only 8 arms. The limbs of dibranchiate cephalopods are equipped with suckers. In squids and cuttlefishes the suckers are armed with horny rings provided with teeth. The suckers of some oceanic squids are modified into hooks.

The head houses a large and most highly developed brain enclosed in a cartilaginous capsule. The optic lobes of the brain, which process the information obtained by the eyes, are particularly developed in the squids and cuttlefishes. An endocrine organ (optic gland) is also connected with the optic lobes. Situated on the underside of the head is the funnel, a conical, anteriorly narrowing tube. Through it the water is ejected from the mantle during respiration and jet-swimming, and the ink, urine, excrements, eggs, and the substance used for building the egg capsule are all ejected. The lateral edges of the funnel fuse with the mantle or are connected to it through locking cartilages functioning like a fastening knob. These cartilages are located on the right and left sides of the funnel and on the inner side of the mantle lateral to the median line near the anterior edge. At the occiput, the head is either connected to the mantle by a nuchal cartilage or fuses with it. The mouth is provided with a firm horny beak that resembles the beak of a parrot and which consists of lower and upper mandibles. In the mouth there is a radula (absent in *Spirula* and finned octopuses).

A pair of fins—the main propulsive organ for slow swimming—is located at the posterior end, middle, or along the margins of the mantle. There are no fins in the octopuses proper (Incirrata), although they are present during the embryonic stage. The smooth skin is beset by numerous pigment cells—chromatophores of various types and tiny "mirrors" (iridocytes) passively reflecting the light. In addition, many oceanic squids and some octopuses are equipped with luminous organs, the photophores.

The dibranchiate cephalopods have the following sense organs: the eyes; complicated statocysts—the organs of balance and of perception of linear and angular accelerations—located in the posterior part of the head capsule; the olfactory papillae or pits; and numerous chemo- and mechanoreceptors. Special extraocular photoreceptors are found in cuttlefishes and squids on the brain (parolfactory vesicles) and in octopuses are located in the inner side of the mantle on the stellate ganglion (epistellar bodies); in vampyromorphs the extraocular photoreceptors are in the anterior part of the mantle cavity.

The respiratory organs are represented by gills. The main organs of the circulatory system are the heart and a pair of accessory branchial hearts. The circulatory system is almost closed, hemocyanin being the main respiratory pigment. The excretory organs include a pair of renal sacs and the branchial heart appendages; excretory processes also take place in the gills and the appendages of the vena cava and digestive duct.

The organs of the digestive system include two pairs of salivary glands (the posterior gland often secretes toxins), an esophagus, a crop (in some octopuses and vampyromorphs), a stomach, a caecum (blind diverticulum of the stomach), a digestive gland commonly known as the liver, a digestive duct with appendages ("pancreatic gland"), and an intestine, into which the ink gland duct opens.

The cephalopods are bisexual animals. The primary organs of reproduction consist of an unpaired gonad (testis or ovary). In females, there is a paired or unpaired oviduct with additional glands—oviducal glands, nidamental glands, and accessory nidamental glands (not present in all cephalopods). Males, as a rule, possess an unpaired vas deferens with a complicated system of accessory glands wherein the spermatophores—special structures for preserving and transferring the sperm—are formed and a spermatophoric (Needham's) sac. For transferring the sperm to the female one or several arms of the male are modified either completely or only at the tip. The modified arm or part is known as the hectocotylus. The eggs are either shed into the water or laid on the bottom. As a rule, the eggs are surrounded by additional envelopes that form the egg capsule. The eggs are rich in yolk, and the cleavage is discoidal meroblastic. Development may be either pelagic (complete or reduced) or benthic (direct). In pelagic development a larva is hatched, and in benthic development a fully developed young cephalopod emerges.

The cephalopods may belong to a planktonic, nektonic, benthopelagic (planktonic near the bottom), nektobenthic or benthic life form.

The class Cephalopoda includes 600 to 650 species distributed from the Central Polar Basin to the Antarctic continent and from the intertidal to the ultra-abyssal depths, but only in seas and oceans of full salinity.

Size and Weight

The basic measurement of cephalopods is the dorsal mantle length. The octopuses are measured by the distance between the posterior end of the body and the line connecting the centers of the eyes. Cuttlefishes with heads fused to the mantle are measured from the posterior end of the body to the middle of the nuchal band (Fig. 13). In this book, the mantle length is always taken as described above. Other measurements such as the total length (up to the tip of the longest arm or of the extended tentacles) are occasionally given.

Listed below are the largest and the smallest species of squids, cuttlefishes, and octopuses. It is not always possible to define their exact size. Information on giant cephalopods has often turned out to be based on "fisherman's stories," and larvae and juveniles described as separate species are often erroneously mentioned among the smallest cephalopods. It also should be taken into consideration that the males of many squids and cuttlefishes mature considerably earlier than the females and that their maximum size may be half that of the females.

The largest squid, which is the largest of all invertebrates, is a giant squid *Architeuthis dux*. Its total length including the tentacles is up to 18 m, the mantle length up to 5 m, the weight (estimated) up to one metric ton. Average dimensions of the giant squids are: total length 6 to 13 m; mantle length 1.0 to 2.5 m; weight 50 to 300 kg.

The mantle length of the smallest squid among the Myopsida—*Pickfordiateuthis pulchella*—is up to 2.2 cm, and that of the smallest among the Oegopsida—*Pterygioteuthis giardi*—is up to 2.5 cm.

The largest cuttlefishes are the West African *Sepia officinalis hierredda* and *S. latimanus* of the Ryukyu Islands, both with mantle length up to 50 cm and weights of up to 10 to 12 kg. Somewhat smaller in size is the Australian *S. apama*, whose mantle length is up to 48 cm. The smallest of the true cuttlefishes (*Sepia*) is the South African *S. typica*, with the mantle length of a male up to 2 cm and a female up to 2.5 cm. Still smaller are the South African *S. robsoni* and *S. dubia* (up to 17 mm), but these species are known only from a few specimens. Extremely small are the cuttlefishes of the family Idiosepiidae, genus *Idiosepius*, with mantle length of a mature male 6 to 17 mm and of a female 8 to 22 mm. *Rondeletiola minor*, a sepiolid, reaches a mantle length of up to 15 mm. In the Halmahera Sea (Indonesia), the R/V *Vityaz* once caught an almost mature female of a new genus and species of Sepiolidae (not included in this book). Its mantle length is only 8.3 mm.

The largest of the finned octopuses is an undescribed abyssal *Cirroteuthis* species; its total length is up to 1.5 m. It is the largest abyssal invertebrate. Among the octopuses proper the record-holder is the giant North Pacific octopus, *Octopus dofleini*. According to unconfirmed data its

Fig. 1.

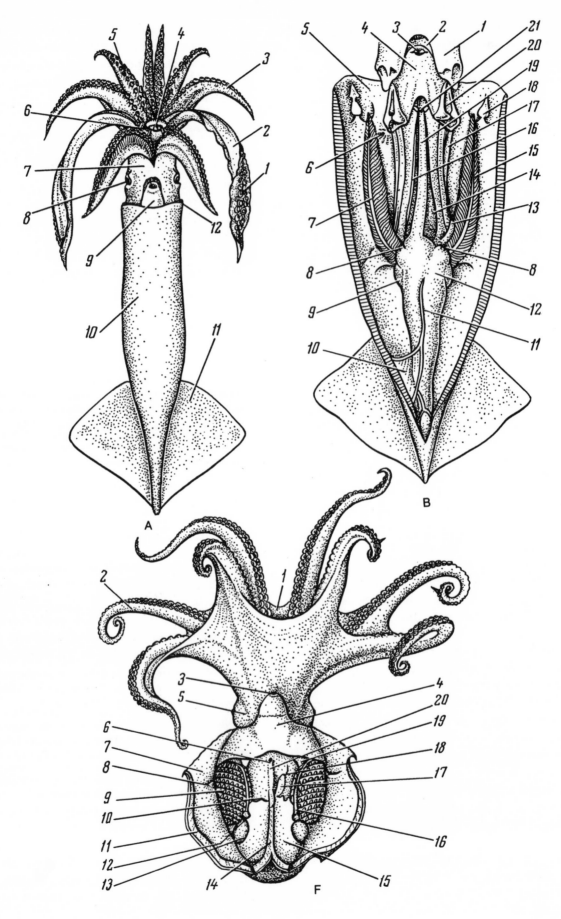

A

B

F

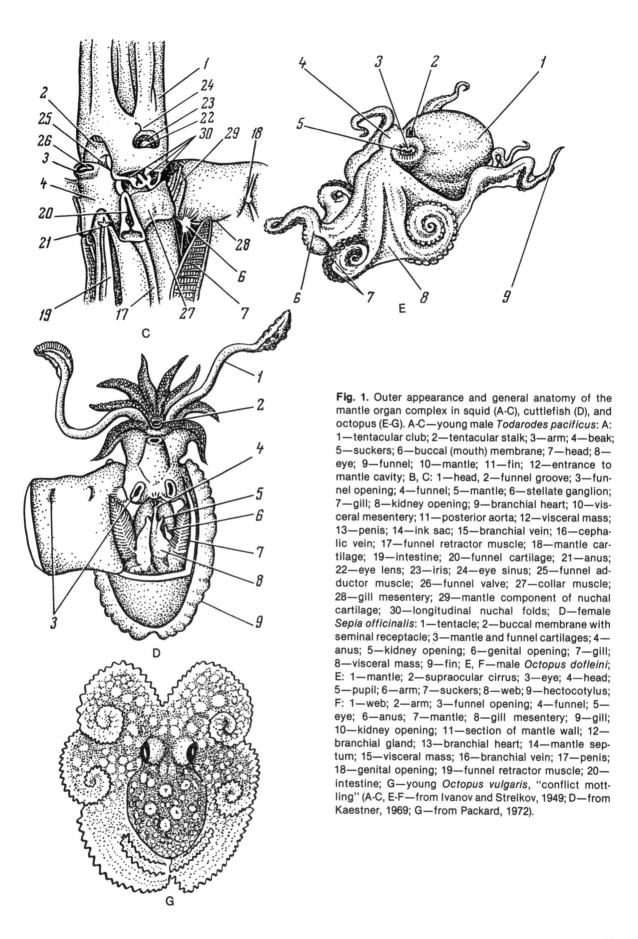

Fig. 1. Outer appearance and general anatomy of the mantle organ complex in squid (A-C), cuttlefish (D), and octopus (E-G). A-C—young male *Todarodes pacificus*: A: 1—tentacular club; 2—tentacular stalk; 3—arm; 4—beak; 5—suckers; 6—buccal (mouth) membrane; 7—head; 8—eye; 9—funnel; 10—mantle; 11—fin; 12—entrance to mantle cavity; B, C: 1—head, 2—funnel groove; 3—funnel opening; 4—funnel; 5—mantle; 6—stellate ganglion; 7—gill; 8—kidney opening; 9—branchial heart; 10—visceral mesentery; 11—posterior aorta; 12—visceral mass; 13—penis; 14—ink sac; 15—branchial vein; 16—cephalic vein; 17—funnel retractor muscle; 18—mantle cartilage; 19—intestine; 20—funnel cartilage; 21—anus; 22—eye lens; 23—iris; 24—eye sinus; 25—funnel adductor muscle; 26—funnel valve; 27—collar muscle; 28—gill mesentery; 29—mantle component of nuchal cartilage; 30—longitudinal nuchal folds; D—female *Sepia officinalis*: 1—tentacle; 2—buccal membrane with seminal receptacle; 3—mantle and funnel cartilages; 4—anus; 5—kidney opening; 6—genital opening; 7—gill; 8—visceral mass; 9—fin; E, F—male *Octopus dofleini*; E: 1—mantle; 2—supraocular cirrus; 3—eye; 4—head; 5—pupil; 6—arm; 7—suckers; 8—web; 9—hectocotylus; F: 1—web; 2—arm; 3—funnel opening; 4—funnel; 5—eye; 6—anus; 7—mantle; 8—gill mesentery; 9—gill; 10—kidney opening; 11—section of mantle wall; 12—branchial gland; 13—branchial heart; 14—mantle septum; 15—visceral mass; 16—branchial vein; 17—penis; 18—genital opening; 19—funnel retractor muscle; 20—intestine; G—young *Octopus vulgaris*, "conflict mottling" (A-C, E-F—from Ivanov and Strelkov, 1949; D—from Kaestner, 1969; G—from Packard, 1972).

total length reaches 9.6 m and its weight to 270 kg. The total length of actually measured specimens was 4.5 to 5 m with weights above 50 kg. The Californian *O. micropyrsus* has a male mantle length of 10 mm and female mantle length up to 25 mm. *O. nanus* of the Red Sea has a mantle length in a mature male of up to 13 mm, while a female is twice as large. These two species are the smallest octopuses. The mantle length of a mature male *O. stictochrus* from the Pacific coast of Panama is only 20 mm, and the females of the tropical western Atlantic *O. joubini* and eastern Pacific *O. chierchiae* mature at a mantle length of 2 to 2.5 cm and have total length of about 10 cm. Their weights are as low as 10 to 15 g.

The only species of the vampyromorphs, *Vampyroteuthis infernalis*, has a mantle length up to 13 cm and a total length to 37.5 cm.

External Structure

Head

The head of cuttlefishes and squids is well separated from the body by a neck (nuchal constriction). In some sepiolids (subfamily Sepiolinae and genera *Sepiolina, Stoloteuthis,* and *Iridoteuthis* of the subfamily Heteroteuthinae) and in Sepiadariidae (Figs. 28-32) the mantle dorsally fuses with the head and is connected to it by a narrow or wide cutaneous nuchal band. In the Idiosepiidae (Fig. 33) the mantle is not fused with the head but no nuchal cartilage is present. In the oceanic squids belonging to the families Promachoteuthidae and Cranchiidae the mantle is also fused with the head. In all the remaining squids and cuttlefishes the mantle is connected to the head by the nuchal cartilage.

In vampyromorphs and octopuses the head is poorly separated from the trunk. The nuchal constriction is clearly seen in some Octopodidae, but in the majority of the pelagic and in many benthic octopuses the head smoothly merges into the body. Usually the head is smaller than the mantle, but in the squids of the family Histioteuthidae (Figs. 53-56) it is much larger. In the finned octopus family Opisthoteuthidae (genus *Opisthoteuthis,* Fig. 76) the head and mantle form a hump on the top of the outstretched arms connected by a thick web.

The head of the squids and cuttlefishes may be wider, equal to, or narrower than the diameter of the mantle at its anterior edge. In the latter case, the head can be retracted into the mantle. A retractile head is peculiar to some oceanic squids, mainly at the early stages of development. The larvae of ommastrephids (*Todarodes, Ornithoteuthis,* and others), as well as of some cranchiids, are able to retract both head and arms into the mantle, so the squid may look like a small ball. The larvae of some Onychoteuthidae also retract the head into the mantle. The only species retaining this ability in adults is *Onychoteuthis banksi.* It retracts its head to the middle of the eyes or even farther. This is observed after a sudden irritation, for example during fixation of a specimen in alcohol or formalin. In some cuttlefishes the head may be partially retracted under a tongue-like projection on the dorsal side of the mantle. Those species with fused head and mantle cannot, of course, retract the head.

The width of the head is mainly the result of the size of eyes. In many squids and octopuses, especially in deepwater species the eyes are so big that they occupy almost the entire head and are nearly joined together at the middle. On the other hand, in such (also deepwater) pelagic octopuses as the *Eledonella* and *Vitreledonella* (Figs. 77 D; 86) the eyes are small but are placed far apart and are connected to the brain through long nerves—the optic tracts. In almost all cephalopods the eyes lie on the sides of the head, but in *Amphitretus* (Amphitretidae) and *Dorsopsis* (Bolitaenidae) they are closer together and are on top of the head (Fig. 77 I). In the *Amphitretus* and in the juveniles of some oceanic squids the eyes are almost cylindrical ("telescopic eyes"). The eyes of the larvae of Cycloteuthidae and of the larvae and juveniles of most Cranchiidae (except *Cranchia* and *Liocranchia*) are stalked, but with age they become flush with the head. The eye stalks of some cranchiids, and especially of *Bathothauma lyromma,* may be extremely long (Fig. 12 B). The eyes of the larvae and young of cranchiids and of the larvae of some Cycloteuthidae are elongated and extended dorsoventrally; sometimes they have a curved "rostrum" below and are shaped like a shoe (*Sandalops* and others). But the common shape of the eyes is circular, almost spherical. As a rule, both eyes are of similar shape and size, but in *Histioteuthis* (Figs 53-56) the left eye is much larger than the right one.

There are olfactory organs on the head. In squids, cuttlefishes, and vampyromorphs they are represented by papillae (olfactory papilla), while in octopuses there are olfactory pits. They are positioned on the sides of the head near the neck.

Arms and Tentacles

Normally the arms of dibranchiate cephalopods are conical in shape and are armed with one, two, or four (rarely more) rows of suckers. The arms are counted from the dorsal to the ventral pair: the first (1st) pair is the dorsal one, the second (2nd) is the dorsolateral pair, the third (3rd) is the ventrolateral pair, and the fourth (4th) is the ventral pair. The lengths of the arms differ from one pair to another. The relative lengths of the arms are expressed by the arm length formula, the length of the arms given in a decreasing order, for example: 4.3.2.1., i.e., 4 greater than 3 greater than 2 greater than 1. This is of significant taxonomic value, especially for octopuses. The right and the left arms of the same pair are usually equal in length except for the hectocotylized arm, which is frequently longer or shorter than the opposite arm. In some species of Sepiidae, Lycoteuthidae, Chiroteuthidae, Octopodidae, and others one or several pairs of arms may be very elongated or extended into a long, slender whip; this often occurs in adult males only.

The arms of the squids and cuttlefishes are attached to the outer lip surrounding the mouth by a cutaneous and muscular fringe—the buccal (mouth) membrane or funnel (Fig. 2 A). It is star-shaped and consists of 6,7 or 8 rays (lappets). There are initially 8 lappets, those going to the 1st and sometimes to the 4th arms may merge together. In a number of Loliginidae, Bathyteuthidae, and Ctenopterygidae the lappets of the buccal funnel are beset by minute suckers. The buccal funnel is attached to the arms by special supports (buccal connectives) extending from the tips of the buccal lappets. If the lappets running to the 1st or 4th arms merge, then the support is split into a fork. The buccal lappet supports are attached to the dorsal side of the 1st and 2nd arms, to the ventral side of the 3rd arms, and either to the dorsal or to the ventral side of the 4th arms. The latter is of a great taxonomic significance for squids: in all representatives of eight families of Oegopsida (Lycoteuthidae, Enoploteuthidae, Histioteuthidae, Psychroteuthidae, Bathyteuthidae, Neoteuthidae, Architeuthidae, and Ommastrephidae) the supports are attached to the 4th arms dorsally, while in all the remaining 15 families of the Oegopsida and Myopsida they are attached ventrally. These relations are expressed by a buccal attachment formula that indicates on what side, dorsal (D) or ventral (V), the buccal lappet supports are attached from the 1st to the 4th arms. The formula may be either DDVD (in the eight families mentioned above) or DDVV (in the remaining families). The only exception is *Enigmoteuthis* (Enoploteuthidae), where the ligaments are attached to all arms dorsally (DDDD). The main function of the buccal attachment is to hold the arms together in a cone during swimming. Vampyromorphs and octopuses have no buccal attachments, so they must expend muscular effort to prevent dangling of the arms that would otherwise impede their movement.

In cross-section the arms of squids and cuttlefishes are usually triangular: the inner (oral) sucker-bearing surface is flattened, while the outer (aboral) side is angular. Commonly there is a small ridge on top of the 1st arms. The 2nd and 3rd arms bear a sharp triangular keel—a swimming membrane. Its role is similar to that played by the tail assembly of an antiaircraft rocket, that is, to ensure horizontal stability in flight. The 4th arms are usually flattened and lack the external keel. The keels are commonly undeveloped in the slow-moving deepwater squids and cuttlefishes. The inner sucker-bearing surface of the arms is bordered laterally by protective membranes—thin cuticular films held up by supports (trabeculae) extending from the edge of the arm and usually alternating with the suckers. The degree of development of the protective membrane varies considerably. In the Thysanoteuthidae (Fig. 62 A) and in higher Ommastrephidae they are very wide and serve for catching small prey into the "basket" formed by the membranes. The ventral protective membrane of the lateral arms is usually wider than the dorsal one. In adult females of *Ommastrephes bartrami* it is extended into a huge triangular lobe.

In some species of *Histioteuthis* both protective membranes of the 1st to the 3rd arms merge together, thus forming a wide inner web (umbrella) as in octopuses (see below). The webs leading to the 4th arms are connected with the middle of the

Fig. 2.

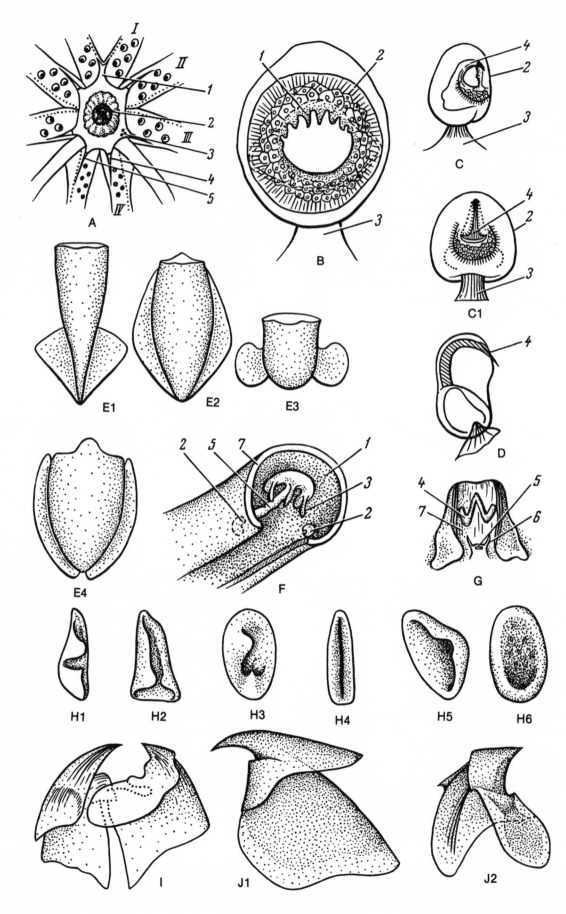

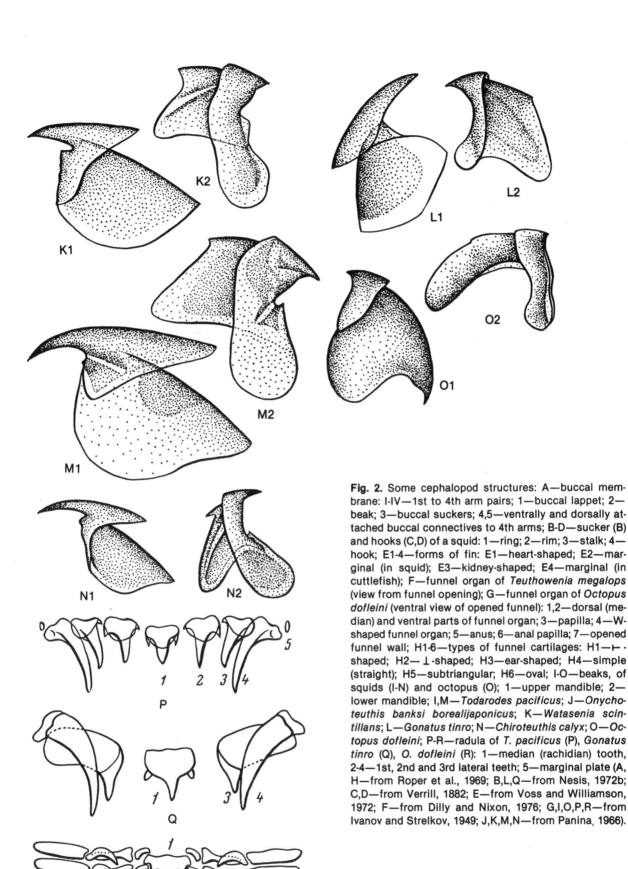

Fig. 2. Some cephalopod structures: A—buccal membrane: I-IV—1st to 4th arm pairs; 1—buccal lappet; 2—beak; 3—buccal suckers; 4,5—ventrally and dorsally attached buccal connectives to 4th arms; B-D—sucker (B) and hooks (C,D) of a squid: 1—ring; 2—rim; 3—stalk; 4—hook; E1-4—forms of fin: E1—heart-shaped; E2—marginal (in squid); E3—kidney-shaped; E4—marginal (in cuttlefish); F—funnel organ of *Teuthowenia megalops* (view from funnel opening); G—funnel organ of *Octopus dofleini* (ventral view of opened funnel): 1,2—dorsal (median) and ventral parts of funnel organ; 3—papilla; 4—W-shaped funnel organ; 5—anus; 6—anal papilla; 7—opened funnel wall; H1-6—types of funnel cartilages: H1—⊢-shaped; H2—⊥-shaped; H3—ear-shaped; H4—simple (straight); H5—subtriangular; H6—oval; I-O—beaks, of squids (I-N) and octopus (O); 1—upper mandible; 2—lower mandible; I,M—*Todarodes pacificus*; J—*Onychoteuthis banksi borealijaponicus*; K—*Watasenia scintillans*; L—*Gonatus tinro*; N—*Chiroteuthis calyx*; O—*Octopus dofleini*; P-R—radula of *T. pacificus* (P), *Gonatus tinro* (Q), *O. dofleini* (R): 1—median (rachidian) tooth, 2-4—1st, 2nd and 3rd lateral teeth; 5—marginal plate (A, H—from Roper et al., 1969; B,L,Q—from Nesis, 1972b; C,D—from Verrill, 1882; E—from Voss and Williamson, 1972; F—from Dilly and Nixon, 1976; G,I,O,P,R—from Ivanov and Strelkov, 1949; J,K,M,N—from Panina, 1966).

19

web between the 3rd arms, so the tentacles remain outside the umbrella and are free to move (Fig. 53 C). Such a web allows the squid to move in the manner of a jellyfish, partially compensating for the weakness of the mantle muscles. In *H. hoylei* a similar but shorter web embraces the arm bases not from within but from outside (Fig. 55 A,B).

The tentacles are always positioned between the 3rd and 4th arms. They are not connected with the buccal funnel. A tentacle consists of a circular or tetrahedral elastic stalk and an oval, usually widened club. The club is not widened in many species of cuttlefishes and oceanic squids, but it always differs from the stalk in armature. In cuttlefishes the tentacular stalk is highly elastic and the tentacles can be retracted into special pockets or covers (in Sepiadariidae). In squids the tentacles may extend or contract slightly, but they cannot retract entirely. The extension of the tentacles is caused by the contraction of the circular and transverse muscle fibers, while retraction is caused by the contraction of longitudinal muscle fibers. When the tentacular club is widened, it usually bears a keel on the dorsal side (opposite to the suckers) and protective membranes on both sides.

In Octopoteuthidae and some Gonatidae (*Gonatopsis*), Onychoteuthidae (*Chaunoteuthis*), and Lepidoteuthidae (*Lepidoteuthis*) the tentacles are present only at the larval stage. In the adult squids they are either absent or are represented only by rudimentary stalks (*Gonatopsis okutanii, Taningia danae*). The loss of tentacles can occur very rapidly, and they can break off like the tail of a lizard. The tentacles of *Mastigoteuthis* and (probably) of *Echinoteuthis* are cast off (autotomized) in the same way at the moment of the capture. The tentacles are also cast off in mature females of many squids, such as *Gonatus, Histioteuthis, Joubiniteuthis, Leachia, Taonius,* and *Sandalops. Grimalditeuthis* are also devoid of tentacles, but since their larvae have not been described, it is unknown when they are lost. The loss and autotomy of tentacles is mainly peculiar to semiplanktonic and planktonic deepwater and mid-depth oceanic squids, but it is not typical of neritic squids.

The arms of the vampyromorphs are circular in cross-section. They are interconnected to a considerable length by a web (umbrella) homologous with the protective membranes of squids and cuttlefishes. In finned octopuses the umbrella connects the arms almost up to the tips. In the majority of octopuses its depth is ¼ to ½ of the length of the longest arm. Three genera, *Froekenia, Argonauta,* and *Ocythoe*, have no web. Five sectors of the web are of different depths; the dorsal or the lateral sectors may be the deepest, while the ventral sector is the shallowest. The sectors are designated by the letters A, B, C, D, and E, starting from the dorsal side. The web depth is measured in the middle of the sectors with the web dilated and it is expressed by a formula similar to the arm length formula. For example, formula A. B. C. D. E. means that the sector between the 1st arms is the most developed, whereas the sector between the 4th arms is the least developed. In some Cirroteuthidae the web sectors are fused not with the lateral sides of the arms, as usual, but directly with one another, bypassing the arms on the outside and attaching to the dorsal side of arms through an auxiliary web, a secondary umbrella (Fig. 74). It allows spreading the arms maximally, and the octopus resembles an open umbrella. In most cases the webs of squids and octopuses are thin films, but in the Opisthoteuthidae it is thick and the arms connected by the web resemble a pancake or a flapjack (Fig. 76).

In the females of the pelagic octopuses *Tremoctopus* and *Argonauta* the tips of the 1st arms are greatly modified. In *Tremoctopus* they are a tool for intimidation and defense against enemies. In *Argonauta* they are used for building the shell wherein the female lives and broods her eggs (Figs. 87, 88).

Suckers

The suckers of squids and cuttlefishes are commonly stalked and have a hemispherical form (Fig. 2 B). The stalk is either short or long, slender or thick, sometimes with outgrowths in the middle (arm suckers of *Grimalditeuthis*, Fig. 68 H) or with an intermediate widening, forming a cup (tentacular suckers of *Chiroteuthis*, Fig. 65 M).

In squids and cuttlefishes the arm suckers are usually arranged in 2 but sometimes in 4 rows. The latter is peculiar to many Sepiidae, Sepiolidae, and (in squids) to Gonatidae. In *Spirula* the suckers are arranged in 4 rows in the median and distal parts of the arms and in 5 to 8 rows in the basal part. In some deepwater oegopsids the arm suckers are arranged in 4 to 6 rows (*Joubiniteuthis*) or in 2 rows in the basal part and in 4 to 6 rows in the distal part (*Ctenopteryx, Bathyteuthis*). Sometimes the number of suckers increases at the very tips of the arms; this may be peculiar to males alone (many Cranchiidae) or to both sexes (some Sepiolidae, *Abralia*). In some cases the suckers (especially on the 4th arms) are either rearranged into one row (*Pyroteuthis*), are entirely absent (*Pterygoteuthis*), or are present at the arm base only (*Valbyteuthis*). Frequently the 4th arms differ in armature from the other arms. Extremely different also is the armature of the hectocotylized arm. The largest suckers usually are found in the middle of the arms or near the base, the rest greatly diminishing to the tips of the arms.

The suckers of the tentacular club are commonly arranged in 4 rows, but in some oceanic squids, cuttlefishes, and *Spirula* are arranged in 6 to 8 or even more rows. In many Sepiolidae and Mastigoteuthidae the club is entirely covered by 20 to 30 or 50 rows of very minute suckers. The largest suckers are usually located in the central part of the club (manus), becoming smaller toward end of the club (dactylus). The number of sucker rows is often greater on the dactylus than in the central part (for example, in the *Illex* and *Histioteuthis*). In the carpal (nearest to the stalk) part of the club the suckers are also small and distributed irregularly.

A fixing apparatus that consists of several suckers with smooth rings and tubercles (knobs) is also present in the carpal part of the club. The tubercles of one fixing apparatus oppose the suckers of the opposite one. While the squid is swimming rapidly the tentacles are pressed against each other, ensuring a firm union. The fixing apparatus is present only in squids (though not in all) and has a very variable structure. The suckers and tubercles may be arranged in a circle and surrounded by a cuticular ridge (for example, in *Onychoteuthis* and Cranchiidae) or arranged in a row running along the club edge (Ommastrephidae) or along the stalk of the tentacle (*Gonatus*, many Cranchiidae). In *Todarodes sagittatus* (Fig. 59 Q) the carpal group of suckers runs almost along the entire stalk, and in the related species *Martialia hyadesi* (Fig. 60 F) two rows of cirri—the remnants of the reduced sucker stalks—are extended along the stalk. In juveniles of some squids (cranchiids, for example) the larval fixing apparatus occupies the entire tentacular stalk and is reduced with age. In the larvae and young of *Chiroteuthis* the club armature differs greatly from that in adults; the adult (definitive) club develops nearer to the stalk than the larval one, which is reduced or cast off later.

The suckers of squids and cuttlefishes are armed with horny rings. The edge of the ring is either smooth (on the arms of Onychoteuthidae and of many Cranchiidae and on tentacles of some Loliginidae) or armed with teeth. The teeth are longer and sharper on the distal edge of the ring than on the lateral edges and may be wholly absent or reduced to small denticles on the proximal edge. The teeth may sometimes be acuminate (conical or clawlike) or crenellate (blunt and square). Often the large teeth alternate with small ones (Loliginidae).

In some oceanic squids the suckers are modified into hooks (Fig. 2 C, D). The hooks are on the arms of most Gonatidae (on the 1st to 3rd arms only); in all Enoploteuthidae (sometimes only on the median parts of the arms or only on the 1st to 3rd arms); in Octopoteuthidae; in *Alluroteuthis*; and in the giant cranchiid *Mesonychoteuthis hamiltoni*. There are also hooks on the clubs of the Gonatidae (only subgenus *Gonatus* s. str.); in Enoploteuthidae (except *Pterygioteuthis*); in Onychoteuthidae; and in some cranchiids (*Belonella, Galiteuthis, Mesonychoteuthis*). The hooks always develop from suckers by the uneven elongation, bending, and longitudinal folding of the distal edge of the ring or by the sudden elongation of one or (rarely) two teeth (in *Belonella*, Fig. 71 I, J). The soft rim of the sucker transforms into an envelope that covers the hook so that only the tip protrudes outwardly. The hooks often develop at the late stage of ontogenesis. For example, in *Berryteuthis magister* the hooks develop on the arms only when the mantle length approaches 75 mm, and in *Galiteuthis phyllura* they develop on the club when the mantle length is about 40 mm long. The suckers that will become hooks are usually larger than the ordinary ones. Due to the gradual modification of suckers into hooks, the number of hooks in the young is less than in the adults. In the young *Galiteuthis* the club bears 5 to 7 pairs of hooks, whereas in the adults there are 13 to 16 pairs. In the young *Octopoteuthis* the tips of the arms bear suckers, while in adults the hooks are present to the very tips of the arms.

The arms of vampyromorphs and octopuses have only suckers. The suckers may be flat (commonly), urn-like, or almost spherical, but they have neither stalks nor horny rings. The inner cavity (infundibulum or funnel) of the sucker is lined with a thin pellicle that octopuses often cast off (suckers are said to be "shedding"). The suckers usually begin near the mouth, but in the vampyromorphs they begin a distance away from it (Fig. 73 C). The suckers are arranged in one row in vampyromorphs, finned octopuses, and many octopuses proper (Bolitaenidae, Amphitretidae, Idioctopodidae, Vitreledonellidae, and among the Octopodidae—in all Eledoninae and in some Bathypolypodinae). In the remaining Octopodidae and Argonautoidea they are in two rows. The size of the suckers usually rapidly increases from the mouth toward the distal part of the arm, reaching maximum size at approximately the end of the first third of the arm length, and then decreases gradually toward the tip. In some male *Octopus* a few suckers at the level of the edge of the web on all the arms or on the lateral arms only are greatly enlarged; this is characteristic of an adult male. The male displays these suckers to the female so that she will not attack him. In the males of some *Opisthoteuthis* and *Cirroteuthis* a few suckers are greatly enlarged at the very tips of the arms or at the basal part also. The structure of these suckers may differ radically from the others. The suckers of some Cirroteuthidae, including *Cirrothauma* (Fig. 74 B), are modified: they are fusiform, without a suction chamber, with a small infundibulum and minute orifice, and are incapable of use in catching the common prey.

The row of suckers on each arm of the vampyromorphs and finned octopuses is flanked on both sides by a row of small cirri. The cirri alternate with the suckers. In the vampyromorphs they start nearer to the mouth than does the first sucker (Fig. 73 C), but in finned octopuses they begin farther from the mouth. The cirri reach to the tips or almost to the tips of the arms. At the tips of the arms in vampyromorphs they merge into a low membrane. In the vampyromorphs and Opisthoteuthidae the cirri are short, but in some Cirroteuthidae (Fig. 74 E) they are very long and serve as tactile organs; they help to feel small prey such as copepods.

Mantle

The form of the mantle varies greatly. In the cuttlefishes the mantle is usually flattened and oval. In sepiolids it resembles the last joint of the thumb. In squids it is normally fusiform, but sometimes it is conical, cup-like, and even completely spherical, as in the young of *Cranchia* and *Liocranchia*. The mantle of the octopuses may be called egg-like or sac-like, and in *Opisthoteuthis* it is not much more than a hump. The structure of

the mantle in the nektonic squids and cuttlefishes is as follows: first comes the skin, then the external hypodermal coat (the tunic) with numerous collagenous fibers and a thin layer of longitudinal muscles, then the mantle proper—a muscular layer, a thin inner layer or tunic (also with fibers and a few longitudinal muscles), and a thin epidermal lining of the mantle cavity that, in contrast to the outer skin, is devoid of chromatophores, iridocytes, etc. The mantle proper, the main edible part in squids and cuttlefishes, is as much as 2 to 3 cm thick in nektonic species and about 0.5 to 1 cm thick in less agile ones. It consists of alternating rings of transverse (annular) and radial obliquely striated muscles. The muscle layers also contain elastic collagenous fibers. They are directed alternately to the right and to the left as if spirally coiled over the mantle, forming a structure of a "geodetic dome" type that stands up well against compression. The alternating contraction of the radial and annular muscles ensures the dilation and constriction of the mantle, i.e., the intake of water into the mantle cavity and its ejection through the funnel, whereas the elasticity of the collagenous fibers of the outer and the inner layer and of the muscle layer provides for the restoration of the mantle form after contraction of the muscles. The elastic fibers—the "mantle spring"—store part of the energy produced by the circular muscles during contraction and releases it during the refilling of the mantle cavity. This increases the utilization of the circular muscles potential almost to 100% and improves the locomotory performance of the squid.

Radically different is the mantle wall structure of semiplanktonic and planktonic cephalopods. Their muscles are reduced and saturated with water. In the extreme cases—such as the deepwater octopuses of the Cirroteuthidae, Bolitaenidae, Amphitretidae, and Vitreledonellidae or in *Tremoctopus gelatus*—the "muscular" layer of the mantle is a watery cellular matrix interspersed at some places by separate muscular and collagenous fibers. Such a mantle is almost transparent (it is possible to read a newspaper through the living body of such an octopod), and its consistency resembles the bell or umbrella of a jellyfish. The thick mantle wall of oceanic squids of the families Octopoteuthidae, Histioteuthidae, Lepidoteuthidae, Architeuthidae, and Chiroteuthidae (among others) is filled with vacuoles containing a solution of ammonium chloride. It is lighter than water so, as a whole, the buoyancy of these squids is neutral. The tissues of their arms and head are also filled with similar vacuoles, and only the fins and tentacle stalks remain muscular (there are no tentacles in the Octopoteuthidae). Such animals are, of course, not edible to humans, though they may satisfy the taste of the sperm whale.

Even more advanced in this way are the squids of the family Cranchiidae – the "bathyscaphoid squids" – where the ammonium chloride solution is kept in a spacious body cavity, the coelom, and the mantle has become firm and leatherly but not muscular. The presence of a spacious reservoir filled with a light liquid in the middle of the body (a "bathyscaphe float") makes impossible the rapid, frequent, and strong contractions of the mantle that enable nektonic squids to swim.

A normal cycle of jet-swimming runs as follows: first the longitudinal muscles of the mantle relax, the mantle becomes thinner and convex on the ventral side (the dorsal side is reinforced by a skeletal plate and its shape cannot be changed), slits between the mantle and the lateral sides of the head open widely, and the funnel aperture is locked. Water enters the mantle cavity and fills it. Then the muscles contract violently, the mantle becomes thicker, its ventral wall pulls up, the retractor muscles of the head and funnel slightly raise the head, locking the slits on the sides of the head, the funnel aperture opens widely, and the water is forced through a narrow "nozzle," thus giving the animal a jet push backward. Such pushes follow one another.

The muscles of the semiplanktonic and planktonic cephalopods are rather weak and their force is sufficient only for one or two violent pulses when it is necessary to escape from danger. One push of a young cranchiid moves the animal through a distance equal to 3 to 4 body lengths, which is not enough for escaping an active predator but quite sufficient to avoid an ambushing predator that is as muscleless and slow-moving as the victim itself. The mantle-and-funnel mechanism in these squids and octopods serves mainly for respiration. For swimming they use their fins, and those having a strongly developed web can also swim like a jellyfish.

Fins

The fins are always muscular even in the medusoid cephalopods. Five main types of fin shapes may be distinguished: marginal (fringing), rhomboidal or heart-shaped (cordate) fins, kidney-shaped (reniform) fins, round fins, and tongue-like fins (Fig. 2 E).

A marginal fin is a narrow band bordering the entire mantle or (rarely) only the posterior part of the body. Such fins are characteristic for true cuttlefishes (sepiids) and for the squids *Sepioteuthis* (Myopsida) and *Neoteuthis* (Oegopsida) (Figs. 35 I-K; 57 Q,R). Animals with such fins swim horizontally; they are fairly slow but highly maneuverable and agile.

The rhomboidal or heart-shaped fin is peculiar to the fast-swimming nektonic or nektobenthic squids of the families Loliginidae, Lycoteuthidae, Enoploteuthidae, Gonatidae, Onychoteuthidae, Brachioteuthidae, Psychroteuthidae, Ommastrephidae, Thysanoteuthidae, and Lepidoteuthidae. The fastest of them are equipped with rhomboidal fins. The squids with a heart-shaped fin are somewhat inferior in speed (a smaller area at an equal length) but they win in maneuverability. Usually such a fin occupies the posterior part of the mantle; its length is ⅓ to ⅔ of the mantle length, but in the Thysanoteuthidae it runs along the entire mantle. Some semiplanktonic squids, such as *Chaunoteuthis, Octopoteuthis,* and the Cycloteuthidae also have rhomboidal fins. They are also horizontal swimmers.

Kidney-shaped fins are mainly found to small animals, such as *Spirula,* Sepiolidae, Sepiadariidae, Idiosepiidae, Pickfordiateuthidae, Pyroteuthinae, Histioteuthidae, Bathyteuthidae, *Alluroteuthis,* and some Cranchiidae. Of the squids with such fins only the semiplanktonic Histioteuthidae and the planktonic Cranchiidae may reach dimensions measurable in decimeters – all the rest are smaller. The kidney-shaped fins have curved posterior edges. Sometimes such fins sit in the middle of the mantle (Rossiinae, Fig. 26) or are even shifted anteriorly (some Sepiolinae), but as a rule they are attached to the posterior part of the mantle and sometimes (*Spirula, Bathyteuthis,* Figs 16; 52 E-K) at an angle to the longitudinal axis of the body. The animals with such fins are more like "helicopters" than "planes" in their style of movement. For most of them the head-down position is the normal position of the body (*Spirula, Bathyteuthis*). They also can hover in such a position (*Histioteuthis,* Cranchiidae). The sepiolids use their fins for burrowing into the sand; they excavate the ground with the funnel, forming a pit and then covering their back by using the fins and arms. Pickfordiateuthidae and Idiosepiidae can maneuver between the stems of sea grasses.

The round (or elliptical) fin is peculiar to the slow-moving semiplanktonic and planktonic squids – Batoteuthidae, Chiroteuthidae, some Mastigoteuthidae, Grimalditeuthidae, Joubiniteuthidae, Promachoteuthidae, and many Cranchiidae (Cranchiinae and a part of Taoniinae). As a rule, the fin is attached to an extended rod-like gladius either wholly or partially at its posterior portion. Squids with such fins are able to keep themselves in any position – horizontally, vertically head down, and obliquely. The fin's function is to stabilize the body of the animal. Fins of this form are least muscular and, as a rule, are semi-transparent. In *Grimalditeuthis* (Fig. 68 F) and some Chiroteuthidae (*"Doratopsis" sagitta*) the round fin is followed by a second fin that is foliaceous or widely lanceolate, entirely transparent, and attached to a long needle-like end of the gladius. It is usually broken off in the young or when in danger (during capture, for example). Only in rare cases were squids with two fins captured.

A tongue- or paddle-like fin is peculiar to the vampyromorphs and finned octopuses. The tongue-like fin is of the same width almost through-out, while the paddle-like fin is narrowed at the base and widened in the middle, its anterior edge convex and the posterior edge almost straight. In *Opisthoteuthis* and the Cirroteuthidae the fins are attached on the edges of a saddle-like or horse-shoe-shaped skeletal cartilage (Fig. 76 K) that ensures a sufficient rigidity of structure for locomotion. Head-down is the common position of these animals, and they resort to a horizontal position only during fast swimming (flight reaction).

In the giant squids *Architeuthis*, large *Lepidoteuthis*, and *Mastigoteuthis* the shape of the fins is intermediate between the round and the rhomboidal form. The most diverse fin shapes are in the cranchiids, varying from tiny lobes in *Helicocranchia* to a long and narrow lancet in *Galiteuthis* or *Belonella*, a circle in *Mesonychoteuthis* or *Leachia*, and a narrow fringe in *Egea* (Figs. 69-72). In the cranchiids the fin is in most cases attached to the postero-lateral sides of the rhomboidally widened rear part of the gladius (the lanceola), but sometimes the fin's anterior part is attached directly to the lateral edges of the mantle (*Teuthowenia, Egea*), whereas in *Bathothauma* the lanceola is reduced and the fins are attached to the mantle far apart from one another.

The most uncommon type of fin is in *Ctenopteryx* – a squid with a "fish-like" or ribbed fin. In the adult *Ctenopteryx* the fin is a wide film-like lateral fringe running along the edge of the entire mantle and held erect by firm connective trabeculae closely resembling the soft rays of the fins of fishes (Fig. 52 A,B,D).

The fins are a propulsive organ when slowly swimming (when rapidly swimming they are firmly pressed to the body or envelop the mantle). A wave motion passing over the fin moves the cephalopod forward. If the fin is shaped like a long fringe or a lancet, more than one wave may be formed (the length of the wave is less than the length of the fin). If the fin is rhomboidal it may form a half or a full wave. In addition, the fin is able to generate a propulsive force by a violent downward stroke. Rhomboidal fins are best suited for this swimming method, and it is the only method of motion for the kidney-shaped fins. The animal waves both fins synchronously. The cirrate octopuses can flap their tongue- or paddle-like fins both synchronously and alternately; in the latter case the animal can hover over one place like a helicopter. Cuttlefishes (sepiids) can turn around by directing the wave forward on one fin and backward on the other.

During ontogenesis the shape of the squid's fin may change radically, whereas in the cuttlefishes and finned octopuses these changes are negligible. The fins of a newly hatched squid are minute and leaf-shaped. They are positioned at the posterior end of the body and are frequently not connected to one another. With age they elongate, shift forward, and assume the adult form. In many squids a long tail appears by the time of sexual maturation, so a fin initially positioned at the posterior part of the mantle is then located in the middle of the body (*Alloteuthis, Uroteuthis, Enoploteuthis, Ancistrocheirus*) and a fin once positioned in the middle is shifted to the anterior half (*Octopoteuthis*). If the fin extends onto the tail, then its relative length is rapidly increased in the process of sexual maturation (*Alloteuthis, Gonatus madokai*); if it does not, then it is decreased (*Ancistrocheirus*). In *Mastigoteuthis* and some other squids the fin stops growing in length at the beginning of sexual maturation while its width continues to increase, its shape changing correspondingly.

Funnel

The funnel is a conical tube widened posteriorly and narrowed anteriorly. It is positioned on the lower posterior portion the head parallel to the longitudinal axis of the body. In the squids and cuttlefishes the funnel is free over its entire length and lies in a special depression, the funnel groove. In octopuses it is partially or fully sunken in the head tissues, and often only its end remains free. The anterior part of the funnel groove is bordered in front of the funnel aperture by a cuticular ridge in many fast-swimming squids such as the Onychoteuthidae and Ommastrephidae. In some ommastrephids it is separated from the remaining part of the funnel groove by a skin fold, the foveola (Fig. 59 A).

The dorsal side of the funnel is connected with the head's lower side by a pair of adductor muscles (a "bridle"), and the postero-lateral sides are connected to the sac of the gladius or to the dorsal side of the mantle cavity by a pair of powerful, long retractor muscles. These muscles can pull the funnel backward and upward or turn it to the sides. A layer of circular muscles in the wall of the funnel itself allows the narrowing and widening of its diameter. The anterior end of the funnel is very flexible, and it may turn sideways or even backward, thus providing for turns and reverse movements of animal. It is true hinged nozzle.

In the cuttlefishes, vampyromorphs, and the great majority of squids there is inside the funnel a small rectangular or triangular valve in front of the aperture. The function of the valve is to strengthen the funnel wall when the aperture turns backward for jet-swimming with the head forward. There is no valve in octopuses and in some slow-moving oceanic squids (*Valbyteuthis* and almost all Cranchiidae except *Cranchia*, *Liocranchia*, *Megalocranchia*, and *Egea*). Another function of the valve is concerned with the ejection of the ink. When the ink is ejected with the valve lifted, it forms in the water a round or elongated drop slightly resembling the shape of the animal ("pseudomorph"). If the valve is lowered, then the ink forms a vast cloud (a "smoke screen") hanging in the water.

All dibranchiate cephalopods have a glandular structure—a funnel organ or Verrill's organ (Fig. 2 F, G)—on the dorsal side of the funnel slightly behind the valve. In the cuttlefishes and squids it consists of three parts, shaped like IΛI. In octopuses they either merge into a W-shaped band or are separated in the middle—VV, but sometimes the funnel organ consists of four parts—IIII. Outgrowths—lobes or papillae hanging in the space of the funnel (Figs. 55 G; 70 M)—develop on the limbs of the median part of the funnel organ in some species of Histioteuthidae and Cranchiidae. The structure of the funnel organ is of a great taxonomic importance, especially in the cranchiids and octopodids. Its function is not quite clear, but it has been supposed that the mucus secreted by the funnel organ helps to clean the funnel with a spray of water.

Mantle Aperture and Locking Apparatus

The mantle aperture, i.e., the entrance to the mantle cavity, is located around the neck. It is a space divided into three areas (on the occiput and posterolateral sides of the funnel) where the mantle is fused or connected with the head. Positioned in these places are, as a rule, the locking cartilages—the nuchal and the mantle-funnel cartilages. No nuchal cartilage is present in Sepiolinae, some Heteroteuthinae (*Sepiolina*, *Stoloteuthis*, *Iridoteuthis*), Sepiadariidae, Idiosepiidae, Cranchiidae, and some Promachoteuthidae. In two species of the Ommastrephidae—*Sthenoteuthis oualaniensis* and *Eucleoteuthis luminosa* (Fig. 61 L)—the mantle and funnel cartilages fuse on one or both sides (at the last larval stage), but they remain fairly developed and are shaped typically for the family. In *Sepiadarium*, *Grimalditeuthis* and Cranchiidae the mantle fuses with the funnel and no funnel cartilages are present.

In some of the cuttlefishes (Sepiolidae, Sepiadariidae, Idiosepiidae) and in all octopuses the ventral part of the visceral mass is connected to the inner surface of the ventral mantle wall by means of a short longitudinal muscular septum that divides the mantle cavity into right and left halves, but a passage remains in the anterior and posterior parts of the cavity. The septum can pull the ventral wall of the mantle up to the visceral mass, and at its contraction a shallow groove becomes conspicuous on the animal's belly. No septum is present in *Spirula*, Sepiidae, squids, and vampyromorphs, and here the mantle cavity lacks the longitudinal ventral partition.

The main passage of the water into the mantle cavity at "inhalation" lies along the lateral surfaces of the neck near the occipital area. In these areas the fast-swimming cephalopods, particularly the squids, have special guiding ridges, longitudinal and lateral nuchal crest folds. The longitudinal folds regulate the flow of water, and the lateral ones ensure a closer contact between the mantle edge and the head when the water is ejected. In addition, there is a set of longitudinal nuchal folds on both sides of the occipital area close to one another (Fig. 48 B) in some Onychoteuthidae.

In the vampyromorphs and octopuses the mantle fuses with the head but not with the funnel. The mantle aperture of octopuses (except the Argonautoidea) is commonly more or less narrowed. At times the aperture reaches the level of the middle or the upper edge of the eye, but sometimes it occupies only the underside of the head. The narrowest mantle aperture is in finned octopuses, Amphitretidae and Idioctopodidae. In the Opisthoteuthidae and most Cirroteuthidae the mantle aperture is reduced to a narrow slit surrounding the funnel base; in *Chunioteuthis* (Fig. 74 I) it is completely closed – the mantle edge fuses with the funnel base. In the Idioctopodidae and Amphitretidae the mantle also fuses with the funnel base but two slits remain on each side of the head (circular in *Amphitretus* and sausage-shaped in *Idioctopus*, Fig. 77 H, K).

The nuchal cartilage is an elongated rectangle or trapezoid with straight or slightly concave sides and, as a rule, with three longitudinal ridges running along the median line and along the sides. Its shape is not very variable.

Much more variable is the shape of the funnel cartilage, which is of great taxonomic importance, particularly for the oceanic squids. The following types of funnel cartilage structure are known: a simple (straight) cartilage; ⌐-like; ⊢-like; triangular; oval; and ear-like (Fig. 2 H). There are many variants of the main types. A simple funnel cartilage is a fairly elongated triangle with a straight, rarely slightly curved or posteriorly widened, groove that corresponds to a low ridge on the mantle. Such is (with a few variations) the form of the locking cartilages of *Spirula*, sepiolids, neritic squids, and the majority (14 out of 23 families) of the oceanic squids. The funnel cartilage of Sepiidae is a long oval with a deep groove; the mantle cartilage is oval in *Sepia* and triangular in *Sepiella* (Fig. 17 B, C). The distinctive ⌐-like funnel cartilage of Ommastrephidae is shaped like a triangle with two perpendicular gooves and two firm tubercles located at their crossing point. Their mantle cartilage is formed by two perpendicularly crossing ridges, but the vertical ridge is abruptly narrowing near the crossing point. The ⊢-shaped cartilage of Thysanoteuthidae is similar to that described above, but it is turned around 90°. A triangular funnel cartilage with a deep central pit and grooves running forward and backward from the pit is characteristic of Cycloteuthidae. In higher Chiroteuthidae and a few Mastigoteuthidae the ear-like funnel cartilage is an oval that encircles two protruding triangular tubercles; the larger lateral (ventral) tubercle is known as the tragus and the smaller rear (caudal) one as the antitragus. The mantle cartilage has the shape of a human nose (Figs. 65, 66). In lower Chiroteuthidae the funnel cartilage may be simple, posteriorly widened (bottle-shaped), or oval with or without an antitragus; in some Mastigoteuthidae it is oval, with or without the tragus, but in some species it is bottle-shaped (with two traguses and an antitragus). An oval funnel cartilage free of tubercles is also found in Joubiniteuthidae and Promachoteuthidae (Figs. 64; 67-68).

The highly specialized octopuses of the superfamily Argonautoidea also have a locking apparatus. It is primitive and represents in principle a hook-like structure: the postero-ventral free edge is greatly bent forward and is hooked to the anterior edge of the mantle. This type of simple structure is found in Alloposidae. In Tremoctopodidae an elongated depression is developed in the mantle that receives the bent edge of the funnel. In Ocythoidae the funnel edge is furled and looks like a helical knob that enters the corresponding pit on the mantle. Such a knob-like locking apparatus is still better developed in Argonautidae.

Mouth, Jaws, and Radula

The buccal aperture (mouth) is surrounded by outer and inner lips. The outer lip or the ventral part of the buccal membrane in the females of many species of squids and cuttlefishes bears a seminal receptacle. In the mouth there is a strong horny beak divided into upper and lower halves (mandibles). The upper mandible of the beak is shorter than the lower one, so the lower mandible overlaps the upper one. Both mandibles consist of lateral walls (pharyngeal plates) resembling a folded sheet and of a hood (frontal plate) covering the front part of the lateral walls like a roof or a tent. The lateral walls and the hood merge in the anterior part of the beak, forming the rostrum and cutting edges (shoulders) of the mandibles. The upper parts of the hood and of the lateral walls are ridged. The hood of the ventral mandible overlaps the edge of the lateral walls, thus forming wings. In all dibranchiate cephalopods the lateral walls of the ventral mandible are somewhat narrow and elongated, while those of the dorsal mandible are short and high. The general form, relative size, structure of the lateral walls and hood, the size of the rostrum, and presence or absence of an indentation in the cutting edge differ substantially among the cephalopods. The structure of the beak is in the whole characteristic of a family and, commonly, of a genus or even a species and sex, making it possible to identify the squids and cuttlefishes by their beaks (Fig. 2 I-N). The mandibles of octopuses are more uniform and are more difficult for species identification. The beaks of the octopuses are easily distinguished from the beaks of the squids and cuttlefishes by the short and blunt rostrum (Fig. 2 O).

The beaks of young cephalopods are semitransparent. They gradually darken with age, beginning from the wings, and in the adults they are completely black or brown. The period of the beak's rapid darkening coincides with sexual maturation.

Located in the buccal cavity on a muscular tongue-like projection, the odontophore, is the radula (Fig. 2 P-R). This is a long tooth-bearing band folded in half in the front part of the odontophore. New teeth are formed in the posterior and lower parts of the odontophore, while the old, gradually lost teeth are located in the upper anterior part. With the growth of the mollusc the width of its buccal cavity increases, so the width of the newer radular rows is correspondingly greater as compared to the old ones formed in the younger age.

The radula of the dibranchiate cephalopods usually consists of 7 longitudinal rows of teeth: a median (rhachidian) tooth and the 1st, 2nd, and 3rd lateral (or lateral, inner marginal, and outer marginal) teeth (Fig. 2 P). A marginal plate may be present on each edge. These plates are not present in all species—they are either reduced or absent in sepiolids and most oegopsids, but are highly developed in some octopuses. The radula is absent in *Spirula* and in finned octopuses. In some gonatids (genus *Gonatus* and subgenus *Gonatopsis*) the radula consists of 5 rows of teeth; the 1st lateral tooth is absent (Fig. 2 Q). In a few Octopodidae (*Thaumeledone, Vosseledone*) the radula is partially degenerated, the 1st lateral tooth inconspicuous and the 3rd tooth absent. In *Bentheledone* and in some *Graneledone* (among others) the radula is also partially degenerated. In squids, cuttlefishes, and vampyromorphs the rhachidian tooth has one or three cusps. In octopuses

it may have one, three, or five (sometimes to 7 to 11) symmetrical or asymmetrical cusps (Fig. 2 R). In some Octopodidae the shape of the rhachidian tooth varies in neighboring transverse rows, but it is exactly repeated in each third, fourth, or fifth row (seriation of the radula). The 1st lateral tooth in the dibranchiate cephalopods has one cusp with a wide heel or two cusps with the cusp that is nearer to the medial line the larger. In squids and cuttlefishes the 2nd and 3rd lateral (marginal) teeth are alike: a short base and a long saber-like or dagger-like cusp. In most octopuses the 2nd lateral tooth is, on the contrary, much like the 1st one, and only the 3rd tooth is saber-like. In the superfamily Bolitaenoidea (= Ctenoglossa, i.e., comb-toothed) the rhachidian and the 1st and 2nd lateral teeth are comb-like; the rhachidian tooth usually has seven cusps (*Idioctopus* has 9 to 11 cusps) and the lateral teeth have 4 to 7 cusps.

The radula in the squids, cuttlefishes, and Argonautoidea mainly serves for gripping the pieces of food bitten off by the beak and for transferring them into the pharynx. Therefore, the 2nd and the 3rd lateral teeth, which hold the pieces of food, are highly developed, whereas the rhachidian tooth, which serves to prevent the pieces from slipping along the radular band, is relatively weaker in development.

In the benthic octopuses the function of the radula is somewhat different: they use the rhachidian tooth for piercing the shells of the bivalves and gastropods and for scraping pieces of food out of crab legs. (The small teeth at the end of the salivary papilla, the so-called "second radula," take part in this process; the salivary enzymes soften the calcium salts in the shell.) Their rhachidian tooth is very large and strong. This also explains the great development of the marginal plates serving as a secure support for the teeth raised into a working position. However, the lateral teeth of octopuses, particularly the 1st one, are smaller. It is not known how the comb-like radula of Bolitaenoidea functions.

Skin and Chromatophores

The skin of the cephalopods is thin but is very complicated in structure. The upper layer—the epidermis—is formed by a single-layer cylindrical epithelium with numerous mucous cells. The mucus makes the body of the cephalopod slimy, which makes movement easier in water. Under the epidermis lies connective tissue containing muscular fibers, chromatophores, and iridocytes. This is followed by the outer tunic.

The skin surface may be completely smooth or rough, tuberculate and warty. The skin of most squids is smooth, but in Lepidoteuthidae scale-like bodies develop in the connective tissue layer (Fig. 62 I, L, N). These bodies are snugly fitted together like the blocks in paved road (*Tetronychoteuthis*), or overlap each other like fish scales (*Lepidoteuthis*, the "scaled squid"). On the skin of some Chiroteuthidae (*Asperoteuthis*), Mastigoteuthidae (*Echinoteuthis*), and Cranchiidae (Figs. 64, 67, 69) there are conical or stellate cartilaginous tubercles. In *Asperoteuthis, Echinoteuthis,* and *Cranchia* they cover almost the entire body (except fins and tentacles); in *Liocranchia, Leachia,* and *Drechselia* they lie along two to five hyaline cartilaginous strips on the mantle. In some Taoniinae (*Teuthowenia, Galiteuthis, Mesonychoteuthis*) they are fixed at the funnel-mantle or head-mantle fusion sites. The skin of some cuttelfishes (*Sepia tullbergi,* for example), some squids (*Mastigoteuthis cordiformis*), and most benthic octopuses is covered with tubercles, small warts, and papillae. Particularly large tubercles are located above the eyes (supraocular cirri or "ears") in octopuses. The papillae of some, mainly bathybenthic octopuses, may be very large and may cover the entire body. Such are, for example, the stellate warts of *Graneledone,* of some *Pareledone,* and of *Bathypolypus* (Figs. 80, 83, 85). Many octopuses and cuttlefishes are able to raise the papillae and tubercles or flatten them. This is a very good method of camouflage. There are areas of rough skin — the "skin suckers" (Figs. 19 E; 33) — on the ventral side of the mantle and on the 4th arms of some cuttlefishes (*Sepia tuberculata, S. papillata*) and on the dorsal side of the mantle of Idiosepiidae. Cuttlefishes use them to adhere to stones in the surf and tiny *Idiosepius* uses them to adhere to the leaves of seagrasses. Some sepiolids, for example *Euprymna,* are able to cause sand grains to adhere to their dorsal surface and thus create an effective camouflage. When the camouflage is no longer required the animal is able to release the adhering material instantly. The adhesion is caused by the secretion of epithelial goblet cells releasing a neutral polysaccharide, while release is caused by other type of epithelial cells, the ovate cells, that secrete a highly acidic mucoprotein-polysaccharide complex. The last secretion can cause the adhesive mucous layer together with sand to be lifted off from the skin surface (Singley, 1982).

Chromatophores, the pigment-containing organs (Fig. 3 A, B), are arranged in several layers. Discernable are the chromatophores proper (red, orange, and yellow) and melanophores (black or brown). The chromatophores contain at least three types of pigments belonging to the melanine (eumelanin, pheomelanines) and ommochrome groups. The same pigment may differ in color depending on the concentration of color components (ligands). Different types of chromatophores are distributed in independent layers. The melanophores usually form the upper layer, while the most lightly colored chromatophores form the lower. A chromatophore has a stellate form. It consists of a central container (sacculus) filled with pigment, muscle cells extending from it radially, and a net of supporting nervous and neuroglial cells. When the animal is quiet, the pigment is concentrated in the center of the sacculus and the chromatophore represents a color point ("freckle"). At excitation of the chromatophoric nerves the muscle fibers contract and dilate the pigment over the entire cell, thus forming a color spot shaped like an irregular polygon. The chromatophores are always under a dual nervous control: local and central (from the chromatophoric lobe of the brain). The nervous fibers of several neighboring chromatophores are interconnected, and such a group reacts to nervous signals as a whole (Fig. 3 C). The morphological units of coloration, for example, are minute ocellar spots (standard discoidal units) that form the general coloration background of most squids. Each unit is a dark point — the large chromatophore — surrounded by a clear ring that is in turn surrounded by a dark ring of many minute chromatophores. Separate units are controlled by different neurons, therefore at excitation color "waves" or "clouds" may pass over the body as one or another unit "flares up" or "goes out." Local control of the chromatophores is expressed by their excitation under the effect of local irritants. If a line is traced with a sharp stylus along the squid's body, then a dark line flares up along the track.

Iridocytes are the cells that contain laminar crystals readily reflecting and refracting the incident light. The crystals may be arranged parallel with the skin surface or at different angles, so they may function as tiny mirrors and prisms. Also recognizable are the iridocytes proper (iridophores), which give a yellow, green, and a light blue coloration due to the dispersion (differential reflection) followed by the interference of light rays, and leucophores, which reflect the waves of any length and, consequently, give a pure white color.

Thanks to multiple combinations of chromatophores and iridocytes—the elements of coloration—and to the speed of nervous control, the cephalopods can change their coloration very rapidly and camouflage themselves to any environment. They beautifully adapt their coloration to that of the substrate since the chromatophores create a generalized pattern, while the lateral leucophores act as tiny mirrors reflecting the coloration of the background.

In some cases the iridocytes lie not under the chromatophores but above them. In this case there appears an intense metallic iridescent coloration of a pure blue hue whose saturation and contrast may be changed by the mollusc. Such is the structure of the large ocellar spots of some octopuses and of the blue rings of the most beautiful and most dangerous octopus in the world, *Hapalochlaena maculosa* (Fig. 78 A, B). The ocellar spots of octopuses are situated on the umbrella between the 2nd and 3rd arms in front of the eyes. The diameter of the spots is about 1 to 2 cm (Fig. 82 C, W, Z). The spot is dark, round, and surrounded by consecutive light, dark, and light rings (sometimes the order is reversed). When in danger, the octopus spreads its arms, turns them inside, and exposes to the attacking fish two large, round eyes widely apart, which is quite sufficient to frighten any enemy.

The great ability to change the coloration and structure of the skin surface allows the cuttlefishes and, particularly, the benthic Octopodidae to assume various patterns—"to put on a mask" that may be protective, frightening, used for distracting an enemy, or used for attracting a female (Fig. 1 G). The "masks" are determined by the pattern of the light and dark spots and stripes on the body and arms in combination with the change of texture of the skin surface and with special poses and movements such as lifting, lowering, and spreading the arms, raising or retracting the head, moving the eyes, changing the outlines of the mantle, and accelerating or slowing the respiration. The masks differ greatly in the larvae, in the young, and in the adult animals, and also in males and females in many species. The main types of patterns are standard and similar in different but ecologically related genera, but the details of the particular "masks" are not only species-specific but are as individual as human fingerprints.

Loliginids in general have a little poorer pattern repertoire than benthic shelf octopuses and sepiids because they, as a rule, have neither a camouflage "mask" for benthic environment nor a fright "mask" (though some of them, for example *Sepioteuthis*, can assume disorienting coloration when lying on the bottom). Being gregarious animals, however, they have a wide range of signal patterns especially designed for visual communication. They include color changes, movement, and postures, some of them simple signals while other are ritualized displays. There are many such chromatic and postural signal patterns (unit components or combinations of units), and each has its own particular frequency and message and its own function roughly equivalent to the phonemes or morphemes of human language. As performed in context, these signals can convey information about the internal state of a performing animal and the external situation. They are somewhat analogous in most loliginids and some sepiids but are best developed in *Sepioteuthis*, where there is a real syntax and an opportunity for extended conversations (Corner & Moore, 1980; Hanlon, 1982; Moynihan & Rodaniche, 1982).

In pelagic oegopsid squids and epipelagic octopuses the repertoire of patterns is much poorer than in the benthic octopuses, sepiids, and loliginids. It is still poorer in the deeepwater cephalopods, some of which are transparent. The chromatophores of others (vampyromorphs, some deepwater squids and octopuses) are devoid of muscle elements and of central nervous innervation, so the coloration of these animals does not change.

Luminous Organs

Photophores are present in *Spirula, Vampyroteuthis*, and in a majority of oceanic squids: in all Lycoteuthidae, Enoploteuthidae, Octopoteuthidae, Ctenopterygidae, Bathyteuthidae, Histioteuthidae, Cycloteuthidae, Grimalditeuthidae, Cranchiidae, probably all Psychroteuthidae, most genera of Ommastrephidae, Chiroteuthidae, Mastigoteuthidae, some Onychoteuthidae (two genera), Gonatidae and Brachioteuthidae (one genus each), in 9 out of 14 genera of sepiolids, in many loliginids of the genera *Loligo* and *Uroteuthis*, in Bolitaenidae, and (doubtfully) in some species of sepiids (*Sepia australis*) and octopuses (*Octopus ornatus, Tremoctopus violaceus*).

Two types of luminescence are distinguished in cephalopods: symbiotic (bacterial) and intrinsic (intracellular) luminescence. In symbiotic luminescence the light is emitted by bacteria of the genus *Photobacterium* that live in the glands located on the ink sac on both sides of the gut. These organs are mainly present in sublittoral benthic cephalopods such as *Sepiola, Rondeletiola, Euprymna,* and *Semirossia;* the loliginids *Loligo* and *Uroteuthis;* and in semi-deepwater sepiolids of the subfamily Heteroteuthinae (Figs. 28 T; 29 K; 31 E; 39 M). The bacteria can glow from inside the gland. The mucus with the bacteria suspended in it also may be ejected to the outside through the funnel, forming a light cloud ("fire shooting"). It is supposed that *Spirula* also has bacterial luminescence, but no reliable proof has ever been obtained.

Intrinsic luminescence is caused by the oxidation of luciferin by atomic oxygen catalyzed by the enzyme luciferase. Chemistry of this process had been studied in the Japanese firefly squid *Watasenia scintillans* and was found fairly similar to the classic form of the luciferin-luciferase reaction peculiar to the crustacean *Cypridina* and to many other marine animals (coelenterates, ctenophores, polychaetes, decapod crustaceans, and fish). The formula of the *Watasenia* luciferin is $C_{26}H_{23}O_{10}N_3S_2$. Intrinsic luminescence is found mainly in the pelagic cephalopods, especially those distributed from the ocean surface down to the abyssopelagic zone.

In intracellular luminescence the light is emitted by special cells (photocytes) containing crystalloids probably built from luciferase. The light-emitting substance does not go out of the cell. Such are the photophores of oceanic squids, vampyromorphs and octopuses. The luminescence is triggered by the addition of oxygen, hydrogen peroxide, ATP (Adenosintriphosphate), or potassium or sodium ions in the presence of oxygen.

The position of photophores in cephalopods varies greatly (Fig. 4). Their number may range from one (*Spirula*) to many hundreds (Enoploteuthinae, Ancistrocheirinae, *Histioteuthis, Mastigoteuthis*) or thousands (Ommastrephinae). The most common locations of the photophores are at sites where a black sublayer—a pigment shield that allows directing of the light beams—is present or may appear easily. These locations include the ventral sides of the mantle, head, and arms, the eyeball, and the surface of the ink sac, but photophores also may be situated on the tips of the arms (*Abraliopsis, Octopoteuthis, Grimalditeuthis,* adult females of *Psychroteuthis,* and a number of cranchiids), on the tips of the tentacles (*Chiroteuthis*), on the dorsal side of the mantle (*Sthenoteuthis, Vampyroteuthis*), on the posterior end of the body (*Spirula*), on tentacular stalks (*Lycoteuthis*), around the mouth (females of Bolitaenidae), inside the mantle cavity on the viscera (Lycoteuthidae, Pyroteuthinae), on the nerve cords of the arms (for example, in Ommastrephinae), or even inside the gladius cone (Pyroteuthinae).

As a general rule, in cephalopods that swim horizontally the photophores are situated on the ventral side of the body. This helps the luminous cephalopods to mask themselves against predators attacking from above, as well as from enemies attacking from below (with the aid of ventral countershading, see below). If the photophores are located on the posterior end or on the dorsal side of the body, it means that the animal is either "not afraid" of enemies (*Sthenoteuthis*) or that it swims with its head down (*Spirula, Bathyteuthis, Vampyroteuthis,* Cranchiidae).

The structure of the photophores is as diverse (particularly in oceanic cephalopods) as is their location. The simplest type of photophore structure is found in Ommastrephidae and *Vampyroteuthis*. The photophores of the ommastrephids are minute oval or spherical yellowish bodies embedded in the layer of the skin connective tissue and dispersed over the entire animal except the tentacles and fins. Each body is an accumulation of photocytes penetrated by blood vessels and enveloped in vacuolized tissue. The bodies may be dispersed singly or collected in dense groups, as in the dorsal photophore of *Sthenoteuthis*. The structure of the photophores in *Vampyroteuthis* is nearly the same.

The most complicated type has developed independently in different families of oceanic squids. In photophores of this type the accumulation of photogenic tissue intimately penetrated by blood vessels is lined below by a thick layer of light-reflecting structures (chitin, collagen, and cytoplasm) and the reflector is often subdivided into two or three separate structures. It is surrounded by a pigment envelope. A large lens serving as an interference filter or a thick layer of light conducting fibers lies on the photogenic center. A transparent cover, a color filter, an upper reflector, or a pigment shield composed of chromatophores of different colors may be present still fur-

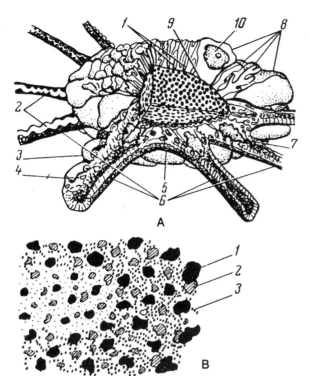

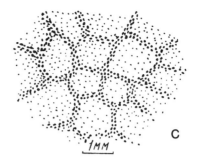

Fig. 3. Chromatophores of squids and octopuses: A—structure of chromatophore in *Loligo opalescens*: 1—supporting cells; 2—nerve endings; 3—glial cells; 4—axon; 5—muscle cells; 6—muscle fibers; 7—muscle cell nucleus; 8—folds of cellular membranes; 9—central pigment container (sacculus); 10—nucleus; B—distribution of black (1), yellow (2) chromatophores and iridocytes (3) in skin of octopus; C—reticulate skin pattern in *Octopus vulgaris* caused by distribution of patches with contracted black chromatophores (melanophores) and grooves with constantly expanded melanophores (A—from Cloney and Florey, 1978; B, C—from Packard, 1972).

Fig. 4.

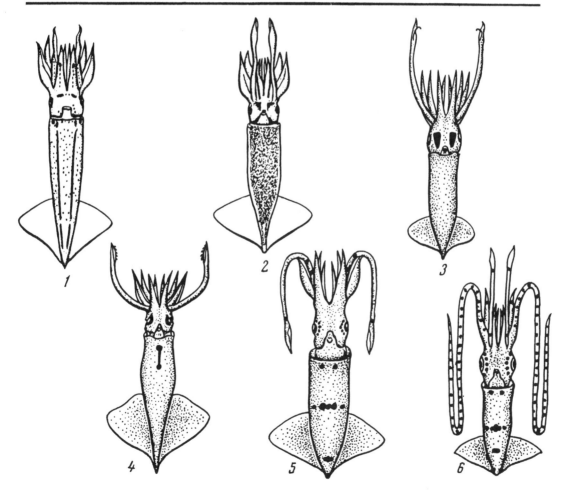

31

Fig. 4.

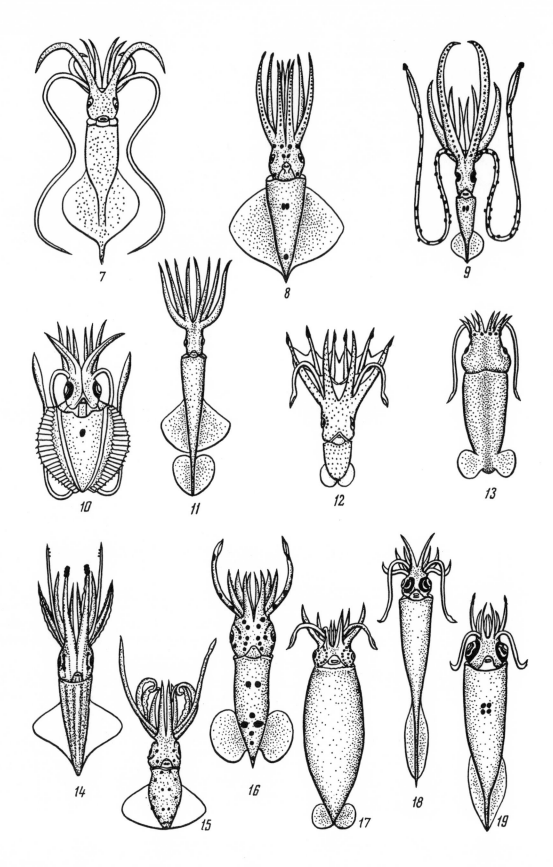

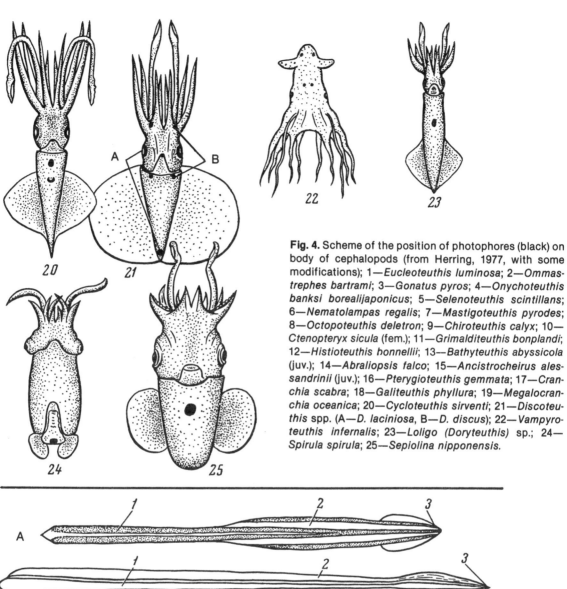

Fig. 4. Scheme of the position of photophores (black) on body of cephalopods (from Herring, 1977, with some modifications); 1—*Eucleoteuthis luminosa*; 2—*Ommastrephes bartrami*; 3—*Gonatus pyros*; 4—*Onychoteuthis banksi borealijaponicus*; 5—*Selenoteuthis scintillans*; 6—*Nematolampas regalis*; 7—*Mastigoteuthis pyrodes*; 8—*Octopoteuthis deletron*; 9—*Chiroteuthis calyx*; 10—*Ctenopteryx sicula* (fem.); 11—*Grimalditeuthis bonplandi*; 12—*Histioteuthis honnellii*; 13—*Bathyteuthis abyssicola* (juv.); 14—*Abraliopsis falco*; 15—*Ancistrocheirus alessandrinii* (juv.); 16—*Pterygioteuthis gemmata*; 17—*Cranchia scabra*; 18—*Galiteuthis phyllura*; 19—*Megalocranchia oceanica*; 20—*Cycloteuthis sirventi*; 21—*Discoteuthis* spp. (A—*D. laciniosa*, B—*D. discus*); 22—*Vampyroteuthis infernalis*; 23—*Loligo (Doryteuthis)* sp.; 24—*Spirula spirula*; 25—*Sepiolina nipponensis*.

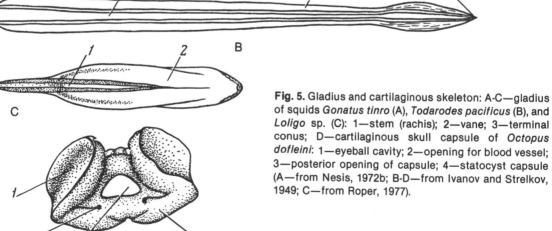

Fig. 5. Gladius and cartilaginous skeleton: A-C—gladius of squids *Gonatus tinro* (A), *Todarodes pacificus* (B), and *Loligo* sp. (C): 1—stem (rachis); 2—vane; 3—terminal conus; D—cartilaginous skull capsule of *Octopus dofleini*: 1—eyeball cavity; 2—opening for blood vessel; 3—posterior opening of capsule; 4—statocyst capsule (A—from Nesis, 1972b; B-D—from Ivanov and Strelkov, 1949; C—from Roper, 1977).

ther up. The details of photophore structure vary greatly—one species may have photophores of many types.

The photophores equipped with a lens (for example, the mantle photophores of Enoploteuthidae and Histioteuthidae) give a narrowly directed light beam. The photophores provided with light conductors, which distribute the light over the entire surface of the organ (some ocular photophores of Enoploteuthidae and Cranchiidae, pallial photophores of Lycoteuthidae, etc.), produce a dispersed luminescence. The light intensity also varies greatly, by as much as two or three orders of magnitude. For example, in *Watasenia scintillans* the light of the mantle photophores is almost inconspicuous, whereas the luminescence of the photophores on the tips of the ventral arms resembles the flash of a match struck in the darkness.

A photophore with bacterial luminescence in neritic squids and sepiolids is a gland communicating with the mantle cavity through a ciliated duct. Usually the gland is paired, but sometimes both glands fuse into one while the ducts remain paired. A reflector, a lens, and an abundant network of blood vessels are present. The ink sac surface, whereupon the photophore lies, plays the role of a pigment shield. The photophore of *Spirula* is unlike both those of sepiolids and of oegopsid squids.

The photophores of the epipelagic and deep-water (bathy- and abyssopelagic) cephalopods are the simplest in structure, and in the mid-depth (mesopelagic) species they are most complicated and variable. The greatest number of luminous species of cephalopods is also found in the mesopelagic zone.

Luminescence of all cephalopods, like that of the majority of marine animals, is greenish blue with a wave length of 470-480 nm. In some species, however, its color may be changed by color filters. In addition, in some migrating mesopelagic squids the color of the light depends on the temperature. In the daytime, when an animal lives in the depths at a low temperature, the luminescence is bluish, but at night, in the upper layers in warm water, it becomes greenish (Young & Mencher, 1980). The color of the photophores proper is determined by the relationship between the refraction and the reflection of the light in the light-reflecting, light-absorbing, and light-dispersing structures, and it may be various colors, including white, yellow, red, blue, violet, green, and metallic iridescent.

The bacteria emit the light continuously, but the visibility of the luminescence in a symbiotic photophore is controlled on the principle of a window blind. A thin layer of ink from the ink sac, upon which the photophore lies, covers it and absorbs the light, then the mollusc washes it off and the light emission is renewed. The intensity of light emission is regulated by intensifying and weakening the blood supply to the organ—a greater inflow of oxygen stimulates the luminescence.

In the animals with intracellular bioluminescence the light intensity may be controlled in three ways. Some photophores of complicated structure are innervated and, supposedly, are under direct nervous control (for example, in Enoploteuthidae). The majority of photophores, however, are not innervated but are richly supplied with blood vessels, and their light emission is controlled by intensifying and weakening the blood (and thus the oxygen) circulation. This method of regulation is rather slow. In the cases when rapid regulation of luminescence is necessary, chromatophoric pigment shields are put into action. They are provided with melanophores that can cover the photophore almost instantly and absorb the light completely. The large photophores on the tips of ventral arms in *Abraliopsis* and *Watasenia* are of this type.

The photophores on the arm tips of *Taningia* and Cranchiidae are equipped with special folds that cover the luminous surface like window shutters (Figs. 47 M; 69 N). The posterior photophores of *Vampyroteuthis* are equipped with a special "eyelid." Thus, cephalopods are able to emit light constantly with its periodic intensification and weakening or in short flashes; in a few instances flashes are observed against the background of general luminescence. The photophores that are either under direct nervous control or are equipped with the melanophoric shields emit the light in flashes; continuous luminescence that is alternately intensifying and weakening is characteristic of vascular regulation of luminescence.

It is supposed that luciferin is produced from food in the digestive gland and dispersed via the blood. In cephalopods with intrinsic luminescence its source is probably coelenterazine, $C_{23}H_{21}O_3N_3$, which emits light during oxidation. Due to its presence, many tissues of squids (organs of the digestive system, gills, kidneys, blood, etc.) may gleam when they are rubbed in the air. The digestive gland is luminous even in the young of the pelagic octopuses of the family Bolitaenidae, which have photophore only in adulthood (Young et al., 1979; Robison & Young, 1981).

There are a number of hypotheses concerning the function of luminescence in the cephalopods but only a few actual observations. It is clear only in sepiolids, which are capable of "shooting fire," thus blinding or frightening an attacking predator. In oceanic squids the supposed main function of the luminescence of the photophores located on the ventral side of the mantle, head and arms, on the ventral side of the eyes, and on the visceral organs is the camouflaging ventral counterillumination or countershading. If a nonluminous squid is looked at from below during daytime or at moonlit night, it would look like a dark silhouette against the background of the light sky; but it may become invisible if it emits a dim light.

R. Young and Roper (R. Young, 1973, 1977; Young et al., 1980; Young & Mencher, 1980; Young & Roper, 1976, 1977; Young, Roper & Walters, 1979) showed that species of Enoploteuthidae, *Octopoteuthis*, and *Histioteuthis* "switch them off" when in full darkness; they are able to match the intensity and (to a certain extent) the color of the luminescence with the intensity and color of the incident light (of the sun and the moon) within a fairly wide range of illumination intensity, completely "disappearing" in this case from the observer's eye. Such a method of camouflage is effective in depths from 350 to 400 m down to 750 to 800 m, which coincide with the common depths of the diurnal habitat of mesopelagic cephalopods. Such mechanisms must be designed as defense against some definite enemies, particularly against common, active, nektonic predators with vision as the main sense (mainly against fishes, of course) that hunt during the daytime and during the day inhabit the lower mesopelagic and the border between the meso- and bathypelagic zones. But most fishes—enemies of the cephalopods—do not meet these require-ments. They either hunt at night in the upper layers of water or lie in wait for prey, relying mainly not on vision but on other senses. Finally, their numbers may be so small that their pressure upon the squids could not be an effective factor in natural selection. Besides that, many squids have an absolutely different arrangement of photophores and inhabit different depths, while some of the mesopelagic species with a "suitable" arrangement of photophores (*Ancistrocheirus alessandrinii*, for example) emit the light in a different way. Obviously, countershading is not the only function of the luminous organs of oceanic squids.

The strict species specificity of photophores distribution over the body (in some species of Enoploteuthidae and Histioteuthidae the photophores are the only reliable character for distinguishing the species) brings up idea that an important, and perhaps the most important, function of the luminescence is the identification of specimens of one's own species, the partners in a school. The main functions of the photophores which develop at the time of sexual maturation or somewhat earlier (dorsal photophore in *Sthenoteuthis*, photophores on the arm tips in the females of *Psychroteuthis* and of some Cranchiidae, circumoral photophore in maturing and mature females of Bolitaenidae) are, apparently, the identification and attraction of a potential sexual partner and as a signal of readiness for mating. In addition, the photophores may be used for blinding and discouraging the enemy with a sudden bright flash of light (for example, some photophores of Pyroteuthinae: two pairs, one on the eyes and one on the viscera), disruption of the silhouette, and luring the prey (photophores on the tips of tentacles in *Chiroteuthis*). The same photophores may, probably, carry out different functions. Thus, if *Heteroteuthis hawaiiensis* is suddenly illuminated in a dark aquarium, it ejects a luminous cloud (blinding the enemy), darts over a some distance, emits constant light for a few minutes (ventral countershading), and then "extinguishes" itself (Young & Roper, 1976).

Internal Structure

Gladius

A gladius is a skeletal plate of the endocochleate cephalopods. It lies on the median line of the dorsal side of the body under a layer of skin or mantle muscles. In *Spirula* and sepiids it is a shell, i.e., a calcareous body with a system of isolated chambers divided by partitions—septae. It serves for regulating the buoyancy (a float). In primitive sepiolids (subfamilies Rossiinae and Sepiolinae), in the neritic and majority of oceanic squids (Fig. 5 A-C), and in vampyromorphs it is a proper gladius ("gladiator's sword"), lancet-like or needle-like horny (but mixed with chitin) plate shaped like a feather providing longitudinal rigidity for the body during swimming. In most finned octopuses it is a cartilaginous structure of a saddle-like, buckle-like or horseshoe-like shape that supports the bases of the fins. In benthic octopuses (Octopodidae) the gladius has been reduced to two slender cartilaginous rods lying in the layer of the mantle muscles on both sides of the median line of the body. In higher sepiolids (Heteroteuthinae), Sepiadariidae, Idiosepiidae, pelagic octopuses (Argonautoidea), and, probably, Promachoteuthidae the gladius is absent.

The shell of *Spirula* is a flat spiral coiled endogastrically (inward). In adults it consists of approximately 35 chambers. The shell, which occupies the posterior part of the body, is located in such a way that its plane coincides with the sagittal plane of the animal. At the posterior end of the body the shell is covered only with skin (Fig. 16). During fixation the mantle shrinks and the skin often breaks, exposing a part of the shell.

The shell of a true cuttlefish—the sepiids—is called a sepion. Its structure is distinctive for certain species or groups of species (Fig. 17 A). It is a thick, calcareous, oval or tongue-like plate covering the entire dorsal part of the animal's body or at least its middle part and covered above only by skin. The sepion consists of a multitude of thin plates—septae—arranged in a thick bundle and inclined posteriorly. The system of plates is called the phragmocone. The septae are interconnected by numerous "supporting poles" and pillars clearly visible on the ventral side of the sepion as thin stripes and sinuous lines. In tropical waters new septae are formed daily, so the number of lines corresponds roughly with age of the animal. In temperate waters two or three septae are formed each week in summer, but in winter their formation nearly stops. The anterior part of the sepion is not striated below. The relation between the smooth and the striated zones of the phragmocone is characteristic for many species but it may change seasonally. A longitudinal groove, sometimes flanked by two low ridges, usually runs in the middle of the ventral side of the sepion. The outlines of the groove and of the ridges affect the

pattern of the front stripes of the phragmocone striated zone. The dorsal side of the sepion is even but sometimes has a longitudinal keel. The sides of the phragmocone are fringed by a rim that usually is horny anteriorly and calcareous posteriorly. The front part of the phragmocone is usually convex, and its posterior part is concave, and the rear part of the rim surrounds it, forming an outer cone.

Between the inner side of the outer cone and the posterior end of the phragmocone there is (in species of the genus *Sepia*) a V-shaped or U-shaped narrow elevation in the form of a cord or of a small bent wall; this is the inner cone or fork. The limbs of the inner cone (the "fork prongs") extend anteriorly almost to the front end of the striated zone. At the very posterior end of the sepion dorsal to the outer cone there is a spine, the rostrum (not present in all cuttlefishes). In some species of *Sepia* the shell is somewhat decalcified and more or less reduced.

The gladius of squids and sepiolids consists of a firm column (rachis) usually having longitudinal ribs, of a thin pen (vane) present in many species of oceanic squids, and of a terminal cone formed by the furled edges of the posterior part of the pen. The shape of the gladius varies greatly, but it is strictly constant within one species. In general, its form is determined by the mode of life of the mollusc. Therefore, sometimes the gladii are often similar in the genera taxonomically far apart from one another, as for example in *Loligo* and *Histioteuthis*, *Rossia* and *Abralia*, *Sepiola* and *Brachioteuthis*. In fast-swimming oceanic squids with rhomboidal fins the gladius is a straight, nonflexible, slender rod with a narrow cone and a pen shifted posteriorly (Fig. 5 B). In slower but more maneuverable nektonic squids with cordate fins the pen is shifted to the middle of the gladius and the cone is elongated. Sometimes, however, the cone is not elongated but is replaced by a cartilaginous capping on the rear end of the gladius, also termed the rostrum (*Ancistroteuthis*, *Moroteuthis*, *Kondakovia*, Fig. 49 C, K, O), or the attenuated rear part of the fin rests not upon the gladius cone but on a firm muscular "tail" that is a continuation of the posterior end of the mantle (*Gonatus*). In semiplanktonic squids the gladius is usually provided with a wide pen. In horizontally swimming squids there is commonly a long cone, but in those swimming vertically or obliquely the cone is often reduced and the gladius is rounded posteriorly. Finally, in planktonic squids the gladius is a very slender penless rod with only a narrow rhomboidal widening and a long thin cone. The rachis itself is usually rigid but may be flexible, in which case the squid may be able to assume a spherical form (*Cranchia*, for example). In *Bathothauma* the posterior part of the gladius is reduced.

The gladius of neritic squids has a short rachis and a fairly wide pen with slender, convex and thin or straight and thickened edges (Fig. 5 C). There is no cone, but in *Alloteuthis* and *Uroteuthis* there is a small rostrum at the end of the gladius that resembles the rostrum in Onychoteuthidae. The shape of the gladius differs in the males and females of loliginids, the relative width of the vane being greater in the females.

The gladius of *Vampyroteuthis* differs greatly from the gladius of squids and sepiolids and resembles in shape the gladii of the fossil family Loligosepiidae. It is extremely slender and transparent, with a very wide stem without any ribs and with a wide pen with an intermediate constriction. Posteriorly the gladius is furled inward, forming a small cup-shaped cone sometimes with a tiny rudimentary rostrum.

In the finned octopuses *Cirroteuthis* and *Cirrothauma* the fin cartilage is saddle-like, laterally widened, and narrowed in the middle. In *Grimpoteuthis*, *Chunioteuthis*, and *Froekenia* it is horseshoe-like, buckle-like, or arc-shaped. In *Stauroteuthis* it is V-shaped, and in *Opisthoteuthis* it is either arc-shaped or almost straight.

The gladius of all endocochleate cephalopods lies free inside a closed epithelial sac that develops in the embryo as an invagination of the mantle. The gladius is produced by the epithelium of the shell sac. Therefore neither the muscles nor the cartilages are directly attached to the gladius: the retractor muscles of the funnel, the head, and the fins of Cirrata are attached to the outer side of the shell sac, but the gladius serves them as a reliable support.

Cartilaginous Skeleton

The major structure of the inner cartilaginous skeleton is the head capsule, which is of complicated form. It consists of three sections housing the brain and the statocysts (Fig. 5 D). The eyes and optic lobes of the brain are located in the concave sides of the head capsule. The eyes are also protected by small elongated cartilages joining the head capsule anteriorly. There are openings for the esophagus, nerves, and blood vessels. In addi-

tion, some cephalopods have cartilaginous structures in the bases of the arms and along the bases of the fins (for example, in sepiids and vampyromorphs). The locking cartilages and cartilaginous tubercles on the skin of some oceanic squids should not be forgotten either.

Organs of the Mantle Cavity (Fig. 6).

Coelom. The secondary body cavity of cephalopods is homologous with the coelomic cavities of the annelids, where its function is connected with the locomotion (hydrostatic skeleton), while in cephalopods it has different functions. The coelom of the cephalopods is divided into two sections, a pericardial and a visceral or genital coelom (Fig. 7 A). In chambered nautiluses, squids, cuttlefishes, and vampyromorphs the coelom is spacious and both sections communicate with each other through a gonopericardial duct. In *Nautilus* the genital section of the coelom forms a true body cavity: it contains the gonad, the stomach, and a part of the intestine and enters into the siphuncle. The pericardial section of coelom envelops only the heart and opens into the mantle cavity by two openings independent from the openings of the genital coelom (genital duct) and kidneys. The pericardial glands are situated outside the pericardial coelom, and there are no branchial hearts. In squids and cuttlefishes the spacious pericardial coelom contains the heart, branchial hearts, and pericardial glands and is connected with the renal sacs. The genital section of the coelom is also large and envelops the gonad and the stomach. The initial parts of the gonoducts belong to the coelom, but the terminal parts have a different origin—they are formed not by the mesoderm, like all the parts of the coelom, but by the ectoderm. The coelom of octopuses differs from that of other cephalopods by a greater reduction (Fig. 7 B). In octopuses the heart is positioned outside the coelom. The pericardial coelom is small and consists only of the branchial heart pockets and short ducts that connect them with aquiferous ducts through which the gonad cavity communicates with the renal sacs. In some octopuses the aquiferous ducts are either absent or are developed only on the side left (*Opisthoteuthis*), whereas the renopericardial ducts are always present. The genital section of the coelom surrounds only the gonad cavity.

The main functions of the coelom in dibranchiate cephalopods consist in the protection of the heart, excretion and salt metabolism, and removal of the genital products. In the course of evolution the excretory function of the coelom has been greatly improved, while the function of heart protection has been gradually lost.

The function of the coelom is different in cranchiids, where it is very large (up to 2/3 of the volume of the mantle cavity) and divided by a vertical membrane (mesentery) into right and left halves. The funnel depressor muscle has been modified into a thin horizontal membrane that extends through the entire mantle cavity, fusing laterally with its walls and above with the ventral side of the coelom. In the posterior part of the mantle cavity, behind the gills, the membrane ascends to the dorsal side, envelops the coelom from behind, and divides the mantle cavity into upper and lower halves. As a result, the anterior part of the body consists of five chambers: two halves of the coelom, two dorsal lateral chambers between the coelom and the mantle wall, and a ventral chamber below the horizontal membrane. The coelom is sealed and contains a considerable quantity of ammonium chloride, used to increase buoyancy. The lateral dorsal chambers communicate with the outer environment through slits on the sides of the neck that open at inhalation and close at exhalation. The ventral chamber communicates with the environment through the funnel. The dorsal lateral chambers are connected with the ventral chamber through two round openings, spiracles, situated directly above the gills, which are set apart on the sides.

The respiratory flow of water in cranchiids is not formed in the same way as in other cephalopods, but by correlated motions of the body cavity wall and of the horizontal membrane. At inhalation the anterior part of the horizontal membrane is retracted downward and the water runs in along the sides of the neck and enters the dorsal lateral chamber. At the same time the water, passing through the gills at previous inhalations, is pressed by the membrane through the funnel outward. Then posterior part of the membrane is moved upward, locking the openings on the sides of the neck. The wave of peristaltic contractions passes backward along the membrane, pressing the water through the spiracles and gills.

Circulatory System (Fig. 8 A). The circulatory system consists of the heart, branchial hearts, branchial glands, and blood vessels. The circulatory system of squids and cuttlefishes is almost closed. In octopuses there are vascular sinuses (cephalic, intestinal) where the blood passes between the organs. The blood of cephalopods is almost colorless but slightly bluish. The blood pigment is hemocyanin. In function it is similar to hemoglobin, but its structure is radically different: it contains an atom of copper instead of iron. The affinity between hemocyanin and oxygen is fairly lower than that between oxygen and hemoglobin, therefore the oxygen capacity of the blood in cephalopods is not high (3 to 5% of volume against 15 to 20% in mammals and birds), but the arterial pressure is high (the systolic pressure in the cephalic aorta of a giant Pacific octopus is 45 to 70 cm and in nektonic squids, 100 to 200 cm of water) and ensures intense circulation of the blood. The blood flow is provided for by the beating of the heart, branchial hearts, and possibly of the lateral vena cava. The heart beat frequency in *Octopus vulgaris* at a temperature of 22°C and at rest is 40 to 45 beats per minute. *Nautilus* has no branchial hearts and the blood flow is ensured by rhythmic contractions of the renal appendages and pericardial glands.

The heart consists of a ventricle and two (four in *Nautilus*) auricles. Two aortas, an anterior (cephalic) and posterior (ventral or mantle), leave the ventricle. The blood of the anterior aorta supplies the head, limbs, brain, buccal apparatus, funnel, the anterior part of the mantle, stomach, and liver. The posterior aorta supplies the mantle, fins, gonad, intestine, and ink sac. The venous blood from the anterior part of the body is collected into the cephalic vein and enters into a pair of vena cavae. The posterior part of the cephalic vein and the vena cavae are surrounded by the renal appendages that pertain to the excretory system but are closely connected with the circulatory system. The vena cavae lead into branchial vessels, and the latter into the branchial hearts. The venous blood and the blood from the posterior part of the body pass via the ventral veins into the branchial hearts. The branchial hearts are muscular thick-walled vesicles located at the bases of the gills. Besides the muscles, their walls contain glands. Contracting rhythmically, the branchial hearts force the blood into the gills. The vena cavae probably assist in this process. From the gills the blood, enriched by oxygen, goes into the auricles. The blood vessels, particularly the arteries, are provided with thick muscular walls that are very elastic and pulsate,

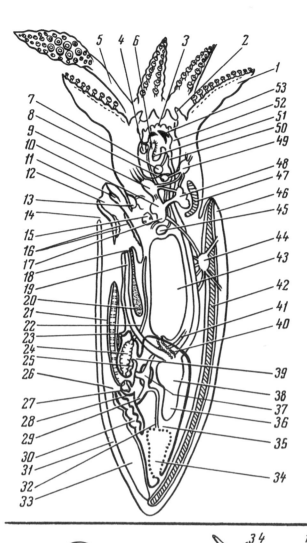

Fig. 6. General scheme of the arrangement of internal organs in a female squid: 1—arm; 2—buccal membrane; 3—lip; 4—sublingual salivary gland; 5—tentacle; 6—odontophore; 7—anterior salivary gland; 8-10—inferior buccal (8), brachial (9) and pedal (10) ganglia; 11—funnel valve; 12—funnel; 13—olfactory papilla; 14—mantle opening; 15—statocyst; 16—funnel organ; 17—pallioviseral ganglion; 18—ink sac duct; 19—intestine; 20—ink sac; 21—gill; 22—cephalic vein; 23—kidney opening; 24—renal appendages of vena cava; 25—kidney; 26—genital opening; 27—branchial heart; 28—pericardial cavity; 29—posterior aorta; 30—oviduct; 31—mantle; 32—genital artery; 33—mantle cavity; 34—ovary; 35—coelom (outlined by thick line); 36—cecum; 37—heart ventricle; 38—stomach; 39, 40—renopericardial and digestive ducts; 41—anterior aorta; 42—gladius; 43—digestive gland; 44—stellate ganglion; 45—posterior salivary gland; 46—anterior part of mantle; 47—cartilaginous skull capsule; 48—supraesophageal ganglia; 49—superior buccal ganglion; 50—esophagus; 51—radula; 52—buccal cavity; 53—beak (from Ivanov and Strelkov, 1949).

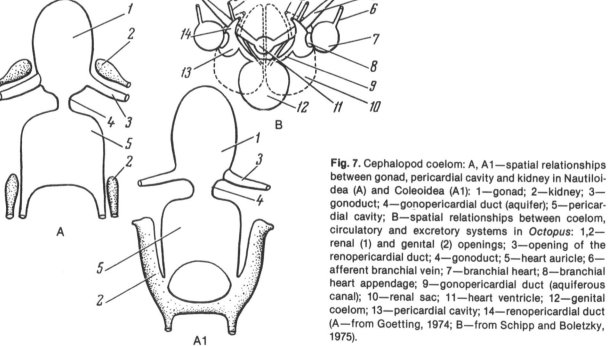

Fig. 7. Cephalopod coelom: A, A1—spatial relationships between gonad, pericardial cavity and kidney in Nautiloidea (A) and Coleoidea (A1): 1—gonad; 2—kidney; 3—gonoduct; 4—gonopericardial duct (aquifer); 5—pericardial cavity; B—spatial relationships between coelom, circulatory and excretory systems in *Octopus*: 1,2—renal (1) and genital (2) openings; 3—opening of the renopericardial duct; 4—gonoduct; 5—heart auricle; 6—afferent branchial vein; 7—branchial heart; 8—branchial heart appendage; 9—gonopericardial duct (aquiferous canal); 10—renal sac; 11—heart ventricle; 12—genital coelom; 13—pericardial cavity; 14—renopericardial duct (A—from Goetting, 1974; B—from Schipp and Boletzky, 1975).

helping the three hearts to pump the blood through the capillaries, which are particularly developed in the arms, tentacles, and posterior part of the mantle.

At swimming and other activities the octopus heartbeat frequency almost does not change, but the stroke volume of the blood (the amount of blood pumped over one contraction) may double. The heart contraction frequency increases substantially with the rise of the temperature.

The branchial gland extends along the gill at the site where the gill connects with the mantle. This gland is the place of hemocyanin synthesis. Hemocyanin is dissolved in the blood plasma. The blood cells in cephalopods are represented only by leucocytes—amoebocytes. They are synthesized in a special organ, the "white body" or Hensen gland, which is located in the head near the eyes (Fig. 12 A). The phagocytes of the reticulo-endothelial system are concentrated in this gland as well as in the salivary and branchial glands and gills.

Gills. The chambered nautilus has two pairs of gills, but all other living cephalopods have one pair. The gills are located on each side of the visceral mass (Fig. 8 A,B). One side of the gill is attached to the inner wall of the mantle by a thin membrane, whereas the opposite side is free. The elongated conical gills of squids, cuttlefishes, and vampyromorphs are positioned at an acute angle to the longitudinal axis of the body and diverge anteriorly. The gills of most octopuses are oval and parallel to the longitudinal axis of the body. In some finned octopuses the gills resemble a transverse cross-section of an orange and their axis is perpendicular to the longitudinal axis of the body.

The structure of the gills of cephalopods is similar to the structure of the ctenidia of other molluscs. They are bipinnulate and consist of an axis and filaments extending alternately from the axis to the right and left. Water circulates between the filaments. The number of filaments in squids and cuttlefishes is variable and great: from 20 to 80 on each side (in each demibranch). In benthic octopuses each demibranch usually consists of 6 to 13 filaments and their number is fairly constant within the species and serves as a taxonomic character. The gills of deepwater octopuses are small in size, the inner gill is often reduced, and the number of filaments drops to 3 to 5.

The gill filaments are plicate, which considerably increase their surface area. The blood vessels pass on both sides of the gill filaments. The venous blood (afferent vessels) flows on the side where the gill connects with the mantle; the arterial blood (efferent vessels) flows on the opposite side. During respiration the gills contract rhythmically, which also makes the blood flow easier.

The respiratory movements are the same as in jet-swimming: the water enters the mantle cavity at "inhalation" owing to the contraction of radial and or circular muscles, washes over the gill, and is then ejected through the funnel at exhalation, bypassing the gills. Frequency of the respiratory movements varies greatly in different species depending upon the mode of life and in the same species depending on the state of activity. In nektonic squids, cuttlefishes, and benthic shelf octopuses the breathing frequency is 20 to 30 movements per minute at rest; it is lower in cold-water semi-deepwater species (down to 10) and considerably higher in pelagic species (65 to 85 in young *Tremoctopus*, up to 200 in irritated *Argonauta*). In *Nautilus* it is 40 to 60 movements per minute at 18-20°C. During swimming the breathing frequency in squids is 120 to 180 per minute at slow swimming and 300 to 350 at fast swimming. Thus, the faster the squid swims, the more rapidly flows the water through its gills.

In benthic octopuses the oxygen consumption rises and falls with activity, and in nocturnal species it is higher by night than by day. It rises with the increase in weight of the animal to the power of 0.7-0.8. When the octopus moves along the bottom with ordinary speed, the oxygen consumption rises 2-2.5 times. Feeding also raises the metabolic rates, and in benthic animals sitting inactively during most of the day on the bottom or in the den, the oxygen cost of finding and capturing prey is less than the cost of ingesting and digesting it. But in active squids and cuttlefishes the metabolic cost of swimming is very high.

All cephalopods, the squids and pelagic octopuses particularly, are very sensitive to the oxygen content in water. When it is low they rapidly lose their strength, become flaccid, and die. The concentration of oxygen 2.5 ml/L is the threshold for *O. vulgaris*, since at this level the tissues completely remove the oxygen from the blood and the venous blood remains almost without oxygen. The affinity of hemocyanin to oxygen rises markedly when a cephalopod is subjected to hypoxic conditions.

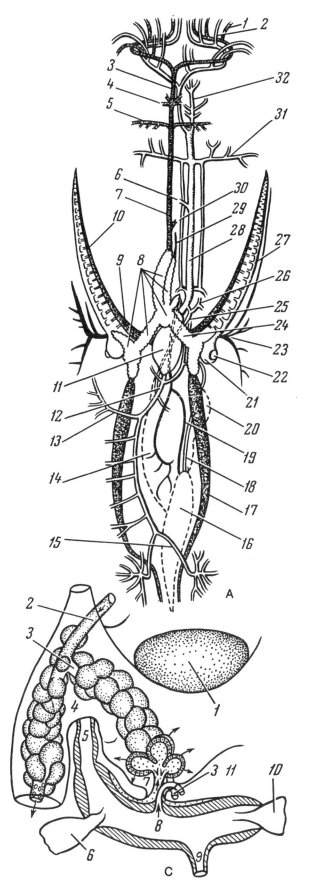

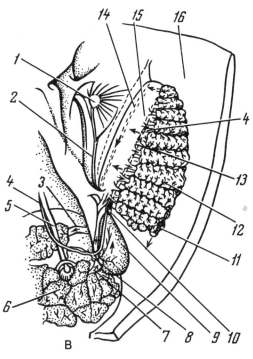

Fig. 8. Circulatory, excretory, and respiratory systems in cephalopods: A—circulatory system of *Todarodes pacificus* from ventral side (arteries are clear, veins are black): 1,2—veins and arteries of arms; 3—common brachial vein; 4,5—brain (4) and funnel (5) veins; 6—digestive gland (hepatic) artery; 7—cephalic vein; 8—renal appendages of vena cava; 9—auricle; 10—branchial vein; 11—ventricle; 12—posterior aorta; 13—mantle artery; 14—outline of cecum; 15—fin artery; 16—outline of gonad; 17—abdominal vein; 18—genital artery; 19—genital vein; 20—outline of stomach; 21—branchial heart; 22—branchial heart appendage; 23—mantle vein; 24—vena cava; 25—gastric artery; 26—pancreatic artery; 27—branchial artery; 28—anterior aorta; 29—intestinal vein; 30—hepatic vein; 31—anterior mantle artery; 32—buccal artery; B—excretory system of *Octopus vulgaris*: 1—stellate ganglion; 2—mantle vein; 3—genito-mesenteric vein; 4—branchial nerve; 5—oviduct; 6—kidney; 7—vena cava; 8—branchial ganglion; 9—branchial heart; 10, 11—afferent and efferent branchial vessels; 12—gill; 13—branchial artery; 14—branchial vein; 15—branchial gland; 16—mantle; C—renal appendages and heart of *Sepia officinalis*: 1—dorsal renal sac; 2—vena cava; 3—genito-mesenteric vein; 4—right ventral renal sac; 5—anterior aorta; 6—right auricle; 7—anterior renal artery; 8—genital artery; 9—posterior aorta; 10—left auricle; 11—viscero-pericardial coelom (A—from Ivanov and Strelkov, 1949; B—from Taki, 1964; C—from Schipp and Boletzky, 1975).

Excretory System. There are several excretory organs in cephalopods, and they are closely connected with the organs of the circulatory and respiratory systems (Fig. 8 C). The excretory system includes the renal sacs, pericardial glands (branchial heart appendages), renopericardial duct, renal appendages of the vena cava, and digestive duct appendages or pancreatic appendages (which are present only in cuttlefishes). The renal sacs of squids and cuttlefishes are spacious and are interconnected in a three-lobed formation composed of two ventral and one dorsal parts. The renal sacs of octopuses are a pair of completely isolated chambers corresponding to the ventral sacs of squids and cuttlefishes. The renal openings are on small papillae opening into the mantle cavity in front of the gill bases.

The pericardial glands (branchial heart appendages) are adjacent to the branchial hearts and intermingle with them through blood vessels. The branchial hearts and pericardial glands together form the organ of ultrafiltration, wherein under the pressure of the blood the substances dissolved in plasma that should be evacuated pass from the branchial heart into the cavity of the pericardial gland. In octopuses they then enter the renopericardial duct, where the reabsorption of salts, amino acids, sugars, and other small molecules important to the organism occurs. In squids and cuttlefishes the reabsorption is carried out in the renal appendages of the vena cava and partially in the gills. The renal appendages of the vena cava are really a true kidney, the main excretory organ. They also take part in osmoregulation. The pericardial gland is an additional secretory organ. In addition to the participation in digestion, the digestive duct appendages (pancreatic appendages) of cuttlefishes play the role of an additional organ of osmoregulation and of urine formation. An important role is played by the gills in the excretion of nitrogenous substances and in osmoregulation. The renal sacs are mainly the reservoirs for urine (urinary bladder), but they also perform a secretory function. Periodic pulsations of the renal appendages of the vena cava are transferred to the walls of the renal sacs, causing the urine to mix and dissolve the granules secreted by the epithelial glands of the renal sacs and appendages.

The cephalopods are ammoniotelic animals; the main component of their urine is ammonia or, more exactly, the ammonium ion, NH_4^+ (in contrast to the uricotelic animals, wherein the main component of urine is uric acid). Molecules of NH_3 diffuse from the blood into the primary urea, where in acid medium the reaction $NH_3 + H^+ \rightarrow NH_4^+$ takes place. A part of the ammonium ions is evacuated with the urine, another part through the gills. Excretion of a considerable amount of ammonia into the surrounding water is one of the main causes of poor survival of cephalopods in a closed space where the water is not changed: they poison themselves with ammonia.

In squids that are equipped with a liquid mechanism for neutral buoyancy, most of the ammonium is not excreted into the environment but is accumulated in the form of ammonium chloride. In cranchiids the amount of this light liquid is so great that the "float" of the body cavity contains up to 40% of the nitrogen excreted during the whole life of the squid.

The renal sacs of benthic octopuses (Cirrata and Octopodidae) and of cuttlefishes (Sepiidae, Sepiolidae) are inhabited by peculiar animals, the dicyemids, representatives of a separate class of Dicyemida (phylum Mesozoa) met with nowhere except the kidneys of cephalopods. In the shelf octopuses they are so common that an octopus without dicyemids is an exceptional rarity, but they are never met in the kidneys of pelagic cephalopods (among loliginids only the cuttlefish-like *Sepioteuthis* is infected). It was once thought that the dicyemids are typical though rather harmless parasites feeding on dissolved organic nutrients. However, a hypothesis was proposed by Lapan in 1975 that they are useful symbionts. Inhabiting the boundary between the renal appendages and the urine in the renal sacs, they acidify the medium, thus contributing to the transformation of ammonia molecules into ammonium ions.

Digestive System (Fig. 9). The digestive system consists of a buccal (mouth) complex with a beak and radula, esophagus, salivary glands, crop, stomach, digestive gland (liver), digestive duct appendages (pancreas), a blind diverticulum of the stomach (cecum), an intestine, and an anus. The ink sac is connected anatomically but not functionally with the digestive tract.

The esophagus in cephalopods is a slender tube connecting the buccal cavity with the stomach and passing anteriorly through the brain and posteriorly through the liver. Therefore, cephalopods need to chop the food into small pieces—prey swallowed whole may harm the vital organs. The crop is present only in some octopuses of the suborder Incirrata, where it serves for storing the chopped food until it enters the stomach.

There are three salivary glands (Fig. 9A): sublingual, anterior (paired), and posterior (paired or unpaired). The sublingual gland is present in all cephalopods; the posterior one is absent in *Spirula* and *Nautilus*. The function of the small sublingual gland is unclear. The anterior salivary glands are not large; their secretion obviously contains proteolytic enzymes. The posterior glands are very large in benthic octopuses, smaller in cuttlefishes, and still smaller in squids. Their function is dual: they are venom glands and at the same time the most important source of the digestive enzymes, especially of the proteolytic ones.

The saliva with its venomous secretion is discharged through a trunk-like salivary papilla or subradular organ (Fig. 9 B) located under the "tongue" (odontophore). This muscular "salivary proboscis" is very flexible and it may be thrust out of the mouth. The saliva is ejected under pressure; a small octopus can "spit" so that the spray of saliva covers a distance of 25 cm in the air. The tip of the salivary papilla of an octopus is armed with numerous small teeth that are used for drilling molluscan shells.

The venom of octopuses, genus *Octopus*, contains two toxins, α - and β - cephalotoxin. Both are fatal to crabs, lobsters, and other crustaceans, the usual food of octopuses. Such prey is paralyzed in a few minutes after being bitten. The venom is usually not harmful to man, except for the toxin of *Hapalochlaena maculosa*, but a bite from certain small octopuses (*O. fitchi*, *O. rubescens*, and *O. joubini*) sometimes causes a rather grave local reaction. A pain in the bitten arm, for example, may continue as long as 2-3 weeks, though usually it disappears after a few hours. The venom is effective only when it gets into the blood and it is harmless to the skin, eyes, etc.

The most venomous cephalopod is a small Australian octopus, *Hapalochlaena maculosa*, especially a female brooding the eggs. The venomous secretion of the glands contains two toxins: maculotoxin and hapalotoxin. The maculotoxin is similar to tetrodotoxin, a poison of a Japanese pufferfishes (fugu). The bite of an adult female of *H. maculosa* may be fatal. The poison paralyzes the nonstriated muscles and a person suffocates. Only continuous artificial respiration may prove helpful. The heart is not affected by the poison.

Large octopuses, including the giant Pacific oc-

topus *O. dofleini*, are not venomous.

The secretion of the posterior salivary gland of cuttlefishes also contains cephalotoxin, which is toxic to crustaceans but harmless to man. In squids this secretion does not contain toxins. The only venomous squid is *Onychoteuthis banksi banksi*. Its bite resembles the sting of a large wasp, but the pain disappears within an hour. The bite of the related *O. banksi borealijaponicus* is not venomous.

The cephalopod stomach is muscular and, like the esophagus, is lined with cuticle. It receives the chopped food and digestive juices from the mouth cavity, "liver," and "pancreas" (Fig. 9 C-E). The stomach musculature ensures constant mixing of the food with the digestive juices. The primary digestion of the food is performed in the stomach. Activity of the digestive enzymes in cephalopods is very high, therefore the food appears in the next sections of the digestive tract only as a formless mass. In connection with this, it is reasonable to dissect only the stomach (and the crop in octopuses) for the study of the cephalopod feeding. The digested food is not absorbed in the stomach. It is absorbed in the cecum, "liver," and "pancreas." The semidigested food, mixed with digestive juices, passes from the stomach and enters the cecum (blind diverticulum) in the form of a turbid emulsion. In cuttlefishes and in the majority of squids and octopuses, the cecum is a small spirally coiled sac. In loliginids it consists of two sections, a short spiral part and a long saccular part. Besides the cecum, some finned octopuses have an additional saccular diverticulum—the "third stomach." The stomach and cecum are usually positioned behind the liver, in the middle of the body; in loliginids the cecum extends almost to posterior part of the body. In *Amphitretus* and *Vitreledonella* the stomach and cecum are positioned in the anterior part of the body in front of the "liver." The inner surface of the cecum is lined with ciliated and mucous epithelium, and its spiral part bears numerous leaflets. The leaflets are covered with cilia, and the mucus passing through the grooves between them clears the emulsion of all suspended particles. In living squids—especially loliginids—the peristaltic waves pass over the saccular part of the cecum. Active contraction of the walls sometimes draws the emulsion into the cecum and then forces it back into the spiral part. In the cecum the digestion is completed and the absorption of fats, amino acids, and carbohydrates begins.

The digestive duct connecting the stomach with the digestive gland opens into the cecum near the duct connecting the stomach with the cecum and the intestine; the "pancreatic" duct also opens here. This complicated system of valves and grooves unilaterally directs the flow of liquids and emulsions. The food emulsion passes only from the stomach into the cecum. From the cecum it is directed into the digestive gland and intestine, but the large particles do not pass from the stomach into the cecum. First the food is digested in the stomach. Then the cecal valve, the sphincter of the digestive gland, and the digestive duct open and the digestive emulsion from the stomach and the enzymes from the "liver" and "pancreas" enter the cecum at the same time. After that, the valve, the sphincter, and the duct close up, and from this moment on the enzymes stop entering the cecum but enter the stomach, whose content is isolated from the cecum. From time to time the contents of the cecum pass through the digestive duct into the "liver" and "pancreas," where it is absorbed; in this case the enzymes are not secreted. At the end of the digestive period the food remnants start to enter the intestine.

The "liver" or digestive gland (the midgut gland) is a large, oval, brownish organ usually located before the stomach (except in *Amphitretus* and *Vitreledonella*, whose narrowly fusiform "liver" is located behind the stomach). The term "liver" is not an exact one, since numerous functions of this organ in cephalopods considerably exceed the functions of the liver in vertebrates. The digestive gland of cephalopods produces and secretes the digestive secretions, serves as a site of absorption of amino acids, serves as a storage site for reserve nutriments (fat), and takes part in the process of excretion. In octopuses and cuttlefishes the periods of digestive secretion are alternated with the periods of their synthesis, so the digestive gland functions like a pendulum; in squids both processes go on simultaneously, which considerably accelerates the digestion. The digestive gland is the main organ of food absorption; it absorbs 65 - 95% of the food. Vast resources of fat and carotenoids accumulated in the gland during fattening periods ensure the existence of the mollusc during periods of ripening and spawning of eggs. These reserves are also important in female octopuses during the periods of incubating eggs, too, since the quantity and activity of the digestive secretions are drastically reduced at this time and nourishment is either stopped or is decreased several times. Luciferin is also synthesized in the "liver."

The digestive duct appendage is often called the "pancreas," which is also incorrect, since it is not a secretory organ. This is a small, branched, light-colored gland that participates in the excretion, osmoregulation, and formation of urine, and in the absorption of carbohydrates and amino acids. In squids and particularly in cuttlefishes it is a dual organ consisting of an internal and external epithelium. Only the internal epithelium pertains to the digestive system, whereas the external one is a part of the excretory system. Only in octopuses does the "pancreas" entirely pertain to the digestive system as an organ of absorption.

The intestine, like the cecum, is lined with ciliated and mucous epithelium. It contracts peristaltically. The absorption that occurs in it is negligible, if any. The intestine is the main supplier of the mucus entering the stomach and enveloping the undigested remnants of food that bypass the cecum and enters the intestine. The mucous strings also come into the intestine from the cecum. Both are evacuated through the anus, a slit-like opening usually surrounded by two anal papillae or by anal lobes; in squids they resemble rabbit ears. There are no anal papillae in *Neorossia*. The ink sac duct enters the intestine somewhat posterior to the anus.

The rate or digestion in cephalopods depends upon the mode of life, water temperature, sex, age, and other factors. The higher the temperature, the faster the digestion of the food. The males of octopuses digest the food faster than the females, and the young faster than the adults. The rate of digestion in squids is considerably higher than that in the cuttlefishes and octopuses. Digestion in loliginids lasts from 4 to 6 hours at a temperature about 18°C; *Illex*, which lives in colder water (8-13°C), digests food in approximately 12 hours. The study of ommastrephids of tropical and temperate waters has shown that food eaten in the evening is fully digested by morning. In *Octopus vulgaris* and *O. cyanea* the duration of food digestion ranges 12 to 14 hours depending on the temperature. In *Sepia officinalis* and *Eledone cirrosa* it takes 15 to 20 hours at 15-20°C, and in *E. cirrosa* it is about 30 hours at 10°C (reviews: Bidder, 1950; Boucher-Rodoni & Mangold, 1977). Thus, octopuses and cuttlefishes mainly feed once a day and sometimes not every day (under low temperatures), while squids take food twice a day.

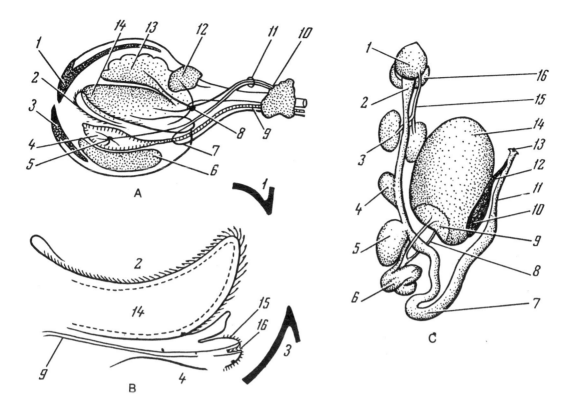

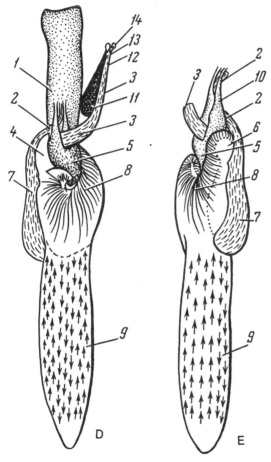

Fig. 9. Buccal (mouth) complex (A,B) and digestive system (C-E) of *Octopus vulgaris* (A-C) and *Loligo* sp. (D-E): A—general scheme of buccal complex; B—salivary papilla: 1—upper mandible; 2—radula; 3—lower mandible; 4—salivary papilla; 5—subradular ganglion; 6—sublingual salivary gland; 7—posterior salivary gland nerve; 8—inferior buccal ganglion; 9—posterior salivary gland duct; 10—superior buccal lobe; 11—interbuccal and cerebro-subradular connectives; 12—anterior salivary gland; 13—buccal palp; 14—muscular radula support; 15—salivary papilla teeth; 16—teeth on inverted end of salivary duct; C—digestive system, view from the side: 1—buccal mass; 2—esophagus; 3—posterior salivary gland; 4—crop; 5—stomach; 6—cecum; 7—anterior part of the intestine; 8—digestive duct; 9—digestive duct appendages; 10—ink sac; 11—posterior part of intestine; 12—ink sac duct; 13—anus; 14—digestive gland; 15—salivary duct; 16—anterior salivary gland; D,E—central part of the digestive system, view from the ventral (D) and left (E) side: 1—digestive gland; 2—esophagus; 3—intestine; 4—cecal appendix; 5—digestive duct appendages; 6—cecal valve; 7—stomach; 8,9—spiral (8) and saccular (9) parts of cecum; 10—digestive duct; 11—ink sac; 12— posterior part of the intestine; 13—anus; 14—anal papilla. Arrows—course of ciliary currents (A—from J. Young, 1965 after Boyle et al., 1979; B—from Nixon, 1980; C—from Ivanov and Strelkov, 1949; D,E—from Bidder, 1950).

Ink Sac. The ink sac is very characteristic of cephalopods. It is present in nearly all squids and cuttlefishes and in the majority of Incirrata. It is absent in chambered nautiluses, vampyromorphs, finned octopuses, *Promachoteuthis, Neorossia,* and Bathypolypodinae. All species lacking an ink sac live only or mainly in the depths of the ocean. In some deepwater or semi-deepwater forms the ink sac is poorly developed (*Spirula,* Bolitaenidae, *Idioctopus, Velodona*), but in the depths there also are inhabitants whose ink sac is developed normally.

The ink sac lies on the ventral side of the visceral mass on the dorsal side of the intestine. In some octopuses it is partially sunken into the tissue of the "liver" and is poorly visible from outside. It consists of an ink gland located on the inner side of the sac's dorsal wall, the ink sac proper (the reservoir for the ink liquid), and a long duct provided with two sphincters. The ink is secreted by the gland cells in the form of granules of melanin pigment suspended in a colorless liquid. A portion of ink ready for ejection is accumulated in the widened part of the duct between the sphincters. From the duct the ink liquid enters the intestine and then is ejected outward through the anus. When the duct is empty, it is filled by a new batch of ink liquid. The color of cephalopod ink ranges from brown to deep black.

The main function of the ink is to disorient the attacking enemy. After the ink is ejected the mollusc becomes very light in color, abruptly changes the trajectory of its movement, and disappears. The ink, very rich in tyrosinase, irritates the eyes and probably temporarily paralyzes the olfactory organs, thus impeding pursuit by the enemy. The human eye is also irritated by the ink. (If the eyes are affected they should be immediately washed with fresh water.)

The ink of cephalopods is one of the most stable dyes. If the ink of a squid or cuttlefish gets on clothes or on a ship's deck and then dries out, it is extremely difficult to get rid of it. In occasional specimens of fossil cephalopods the ink has been preserved for hundreds of millions of years. Long ago the cuttlefish ink sac was used for the production of high-quality brown paint—sepia. The dried contents of the ink sac were treated with potassium hydroxide to remove the organic components.

The function of the ink in the inhabitants of deep water may be only guessed. It should be recalled that the ink sacs of many squids and cuttlefishes is provided with luminous organs, for which it serves as a pigment shield. In *Heteroteuthis* the ink is sometimes ejected together with luminous liquid; it is not known whether the ink can be ejected without it.

Reproductive System (Fig. 10). In all cephalopods the sexes are separate. The sex is predetermined genetically. In Argonautoidea the male may be differentiated from the female even at the moment of hatching by the presence of 8 arms in females and only 7 in the males. In other cephalopods the secondary sex characters become conspicuous to the naked eye only in the young, though long before the beginning of maturation; it is possible to determine the sex of even a very young specimen by histological investigation.

The female reproductive system in cephalopods consists of an ovary, oviduct, and the oviducal, nidamental, and accessory nidamental glands (Fig. 10 A,B). The ovary resembles a bunch of grapes and is always unpaired. It occupies the posterior part of the mantle cavity. Its form is conical in squids, but mainly hemispherical in cuttlefishes and octopuses. A mature ovary is very large, often pushing all remaining organs of the mantle cavity anteriorly.

The oviduct is paired in oegopsids (except Pyroteuthinae), vampyromorphs, and Incirrata and is unpaired in *Pterygioteuthis* (only the right one present), *Pyroteuthis,* all cuttlefishes, myopsids, and finned octopuses (only the left one). Both oviducts are present in the females of Idiosepiidae, but the right one is not functional. In squids the gradually ripening eggs pass from the ovary into the oviduct (oviducts), wherein they are kept until spawning, so immediately before spawning the size of the oviduct may considerably exceed the size of the ovary. The oviducts of immature squids are bent and spirally coiled. In cuttlefishes and octopuses both the ripening and the ripe eggs are collected in the genital coelom up to the moment of spawning and their oviducts are not bent.

All cephalopods have oviducal glands, their number corresponding to the number of the oviducts. In squids and cuttlefishes the heart-shaped oviducal glands are joined to the oviduct near its end, except in Enoploteuthinae, whose oviducal glands are extremely large (larger than the oviduct itself), oval, and divided into two parts, a larger and a smaller. The annular oviducal glands of octopuses sit like a ring on a finger in the middle of the oviduct or near to its proximal end (Fig. 10 C). In some species there is an oviducal enlargement (the "vagina"), located somewhat more distally. The oviducal glands secrete a light adhesive substance that forms a third envelope for the eggs in squids and cuttlefishes (the first envelope is the egg membrane, the second is the chorion); in octopuses it forms the tip of the egg stalk and a cement that glues the egg to the substrate. There is a seminal receptacle inside the oviducal gland of Octopodinae. Sperm is preserved in the receptacle wherein fertilization takes place. In *Eledone* the sperm directly enters the oviduct. In squids, cuttlefishes, and vampyromorphs the sperm is preserved in the seminal receptacle outside the genital system (see below).

The nidamental glands are present in squids (except Enoploteuthinae) and cuttlefishes. In mature females they occupy the whole middle of the ventral side of the mantle cavity. The glands are tongue-like in squids and oval in cuttlefishes. They form a fourth envelope of the eggs, i.e., the external egg capsule in squids, wherein the eggs are located in mucus secreted by the oviducal glands. In cuttlefishes the fourth envelope forms a firm outer cover over the eggs. The secretion of the nidamental glands is usually denser than that of the oviducal glands, so the clutch of eggs is on the whole heavier than water (in species that shed their eggs on the bottom) or has a neutral buoyancy. The secretion of the nidamental glands is extremely adhesive, too, and it hardens rapidly in water. In loliginids it has a remarkable ability to supress the synchronous beating of the locomotory cilia of small metazoans and infusorians, saving the eggs from such small but dangerous enemies. The Enoploteuthinae, which do not have nidamental glands, shed separate eggs (like *Vampyroteuthis*) surrounded only by the secretion of the oviducal glands.

Small accessory nidamental glands are present in cuttlefishes and Myopsida. They are present in both sexes but are rudimentary in males. In immature females they are white but change their color in the course of maturation through yellow and orange to red in mature specimens. They consist of a multitude of small tubules inhabited by symbiotic white, yellow, and red bacteria. Each tube is of a different color. The color of the bacteria and the red color of the gland in mature females is explained by a special carotenoid pigment—sepiaxanthin—secreted by the bacteria. The bacteria may also live outside the squid's body, but they need special additives of animal origin for the synthesis of sepiaxanthin. Probably its synthesis is controlled by the secretory activity of the cells of the accessory nidamental gland (Bloodgood, 1977; Richard et al., 1979). Function of the accessory nidamental glands is puzzling.

In the study of the female maturation process it is necessary to differentiate the periods and phases of the development of oocytes, the stages of the development of the gonad, and the stages of the maturity of the reproductive system as a whole. R. N. Burukovsky et al. (1977) distinguish the following periods and phases of development of the oocytes in the squid *Sthenoteuthis pteropus* (applicable, to a certain degree to all cephalopods): 1) oogonia; 2) premeiotic oocytes; 3) period of protoplasmic growth (previtellogenesis)—with three phases: previtellogenesis, primary follicle, simple follicle (subphases of cup-like and formed follicle); 4) intercalary period—with two phases: complicated follicle and hydration; 5) period of trophoplasmic growth—with phases: vacuolization, yolk accumulation, expulsion of follicle and mature oocyte. In the course of this process the oocytes are growing and are being surrounded by the cells of the follicular epithelium. During the period of previtellogenesis the slightly differentiated follicular cells, the cells of the connective envelope (theca), and the capillaries envelop the entire oocyte from the outside and then began to proliferate into its surface. This results in the appearance of folds, and the oocyte seems reticulate when examined from outside. Within the vitellogenesis period (trophoplasmic growth) the follicular cells synthesize the yolk and supply it to the oocyte. At the end of vitellogenesis the oocyte folds are turned out and expelled from the cytoplasm. At the same time the cortical layer of the cytoplasm modifies into the primary envelope, while the follicular cells specialize to the formation of the secondary envelope—the chorion. A ripe oocyte, opaque and whitish earlier, becomes smooth and transparent, usually of amber color, and drops into the oviducal cavity.

Cephalopods (except chambered nautiluses) are characterized by continuous asynchrony of gonad development. A squid oviduct is a cluster of nests, as if representing separate small gonads, and each nest is a cluster of oocytes connected by capillaries, each with its own blood vessel. The network of vessels forms something like a tree. At any stage of the gonad development, oocytes of any stage of development may be found in each nest:

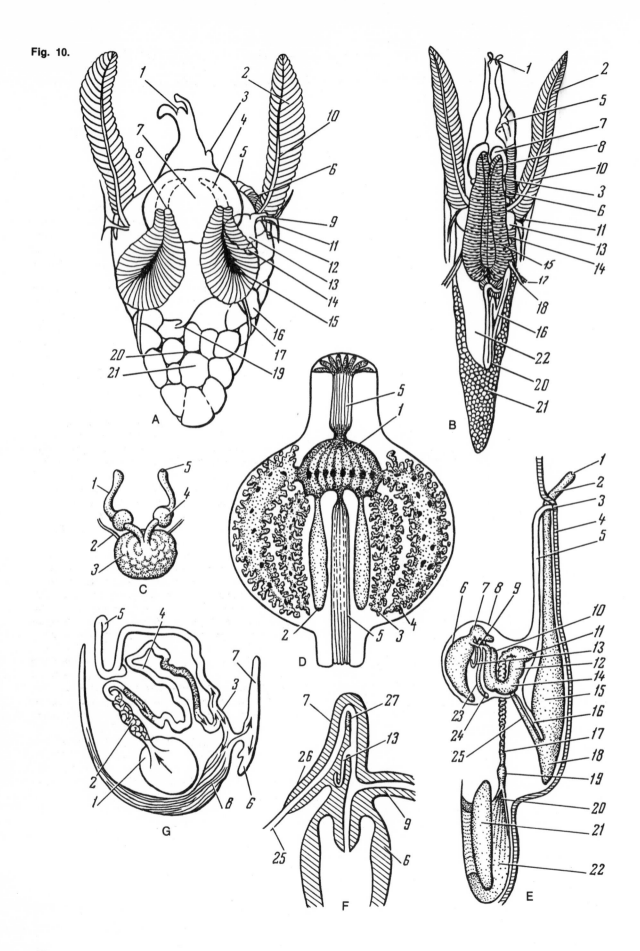

Fig. 10.

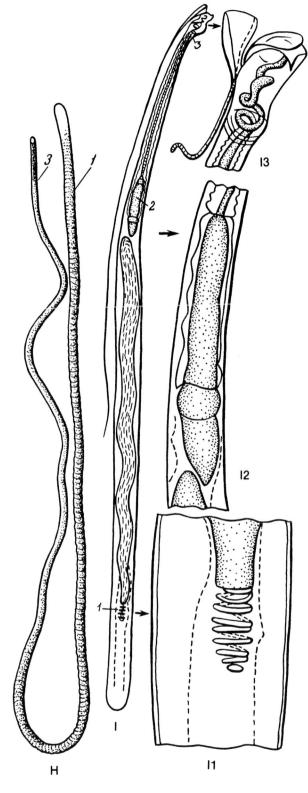

Fig. 10. Reproductive system of cephalopods: A,C—female reproductive system of *Sepia elegans* (A), *Loligo vulgaris* (B) and *Octopus dofleini* (C); A,B: 1—anus; 2—gill; 3—kidney opening; 4, 5—openings of accessory nidamental (4) and oviducal (5) gland; 6, 7—oviducal (6) and accessory nidamental (7) glands; 8—nidamental gland opening; 9—branchial artery; 10, 11—branchial (10) and mantle (11) veins; 12—gill base; 13—branchial heart; 14—branchial heart appendage; 15—nidamental gland; 16—oviduct; 17—abdominal vein; 18—abdominal artery; 19—mantle artery; 20—beginning of oviduct; 21—ovary; 22—cecum; C: 1—oviduct; 2—ovarian mesentery; 3—ovary; 4—oviducal gland; 5—genital opening; D—oviducal gland of *Octopus vulgaris*: 1—central cavity; 2—seminal receptacle; 3, 4—central (3) and peripheral (4) parts of the gland; 5— oviduct; E-G—reproductive system of male *Loligo vulgaris reynaudi* (E,F) and *Octopus dofleini martini* (G); E: 1—genital opening; 2—penis; 3—genital sac opening; 4—lining of visceral mass; 5—genital sac duct; 6—accessory gland (prostate); 7—appendix (cecum) of accessory gland; 8—genital sac; 9-10—glands of outer and middle tunics of spermatophore; 11-12—1st and 2nd parts of the mucilaginous (spermatophoric) gland; 13—appendicular gland; 14—ejaculatory apparatus gland; 15—spermatophoric sac; 16—diverticulum of the genital sac; 17—vas deferens (seminal duct); 18—distal part of spermatophoric sac (fundus); 19—seminal duct ampulla; 20—coelomostome (funnel of seminal duct); 21—testis; 22—genital coelom; 23—ciliated canal (Chun's canal); 24—funnel of ciliated canal; 25—spermatophoric duct; F—scheme of connections of spermatophoric duct, accessory gland and glands of the envelopes of spermatophore; 26—glandular part of spermatophoric duct; 27—dorsal fold; other designations as in E; G; 1—testis; 2—vas deferens (seminal duct); 3—spermatophoric duct; 4, 5—spermatophoric (4) and accessory (5) glands; 6—penis; 7—penial diverticulum; 8—spermatophoric sac; H-J—spermatophore (H-I) and sperm sac (spermatangium) (J) of *Octopus dofleini* (H) and *Dosidicus gigas* (I-J); 1—posterior end of seminal thread; 2—cement body; 3—head; I1, I2, I3—the same, magnified (A,B—from Jaeckel, 1958; C,H—from Ivanov and Strelkov, 1949; D—from Froesch and Marthy, 1975; E,F—from Badenhorst, 1974; G— from Mann et al., 1970; I-J—from Nesis, 1970).

Nautilus pompilius imported from the Philippines and on display at the tropical aquarium of the Zoological Museum at Nancy, France. The mature specimen (167 mm shell diameter) is below. Photo by Dr. D. Terver, Nancy Aquarium, Nancy, France.

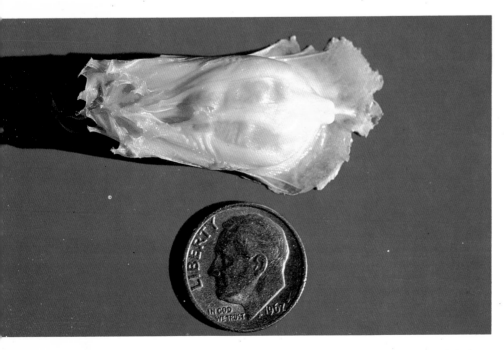

This infertile egg of *Nautilus pompilius* was laid by a secimen in captivity. Photo by Dr. Guido Dingerkus at the New York Aquarium,

Entire head and body of a well preserved *N. pompilius* removed from its shell. Photo by Ken Lucas, Steinhart Aquarium, San Francisco, California.

Frontal view of another *N. pompilius* on display at the Steinhart Aquarium. Note the large opening of the unfused funnel close to the ventral edge of the shell. Photo by Ken Lucas.

the smallest are nearer to the vessels, and the longer the distance from the vessels, the larger are the oocytes. Depending on the phase of development of the main part of the oocytes, there are six distinguishable stages of gonad development: juvenile; unripe; preparatory; ripe; mature gonad; and spent. The necessity of a simultaneous spawning at continuous asynchrony of gonad development has led to the appearance of an accumulating mechanism. In squids such an accumulator is the oviduct (oviducts). The entire process of preparation for reproduction falls into two periods: the first is the development of the gonad, oviducts, and glands; the second is the accumulation of mature eggs in the oviduct (oviducts). Six stages of maturation of the squid's reproductive system are identified (Burukovsky et al., 1977): stages I-III correspond to the unripe gonad; stage IV to the preparatory stage and a ripe gonad; and stage V to a mature gonad. Depending upon the process of accumulation of the ripe eggs, the latter stage is divided into three substages: V_1 – minority of eggs are ripe (up to 5-8% volume of all oocytes); V_2 – ripe eggs in the oviduct amount to 10-60% of the oocytes volume; V_3 – the oviducts are packed with ripe eggs (60-80% of the oocyte volume). Stage VI is the spent condition. This condition is applicable to all squids. (There are also many other schemes of maturation process in squids and other cephalopods).

In all octopuses and cuttlefishes the eggs are accumulated directly in the genital coelom. Therefore, in contrast to squids, the ripest eggs lie in the posterior and not the anterior part of the mantle.

The male genital system consists of a testis, seminal duct (vas deferens), spermatophoric organ, accessory gland (prostate), spermatophoric sac (Needham's organ), and penis (Fig. 10 E,G). In almost all cephalopods (except *Selenoteuthis, Lycoteuthis,* and *Histioteuthis hoylei*) the male genital organs are unpaired. They lie in the left half of the mantle. The testis is spherical in octopuses and elongated-triangular or cigar-shaped in squids and cuttlefishes. It is a white or cream-colored organ of a tubular structure positioned in the posterior part of the mantle in the rear half of the genital coelom. A slender, very long, spirally coiled or curled vas deferens (or a proximal part of the seminal duct) turning into the spermatophoric organ begins at the testis. The seminal duct is not directly connected with the testis, but begins with a funnel that opens into the coelom through a

coelomostome.

The structure of the spermatophoric organ is very complicated. All its parts are tightly packed and are surrounded with a cover forming a genital sac. In squids (Fig. 10 E,F) and cuttlefishes the vas deferens turns into a mucilaginous gland (also known as the spermatophoric gland or the seminal vesicle). It consists of two parts following one another. Then follow a series of glands: the ejaculatory apparatus gland, the glands of the median and outer parts of the spermatophoric tunic, and a voluminous accessory gland (prostate) with an appendix or cecum. A ciliated canal (Chun's canal) goes off from the point of transformation of the median tunic gland into the outer tunic gland, and a slender tubular outgrowth (appendicular gland) runs off from the appendix of the accessory gland. It is followed by a straight spermatophoric duct or the distal part of the vas deferens (already located outside the genital sac). The genital sac has two long outgrowths. One of them runs parallel to the spermatophoric duct but terminates blindly; the other runs in parallel to the penis and terminates (in some species) in an opening into the mantle cavity (it may also terminate blindy in some species).

The spermatophoric duct enters the voluminous spermatophoric sac (Needham's organ), which turns into the penis. In squids and cuttlefishes equipped with a hectocotylus the penis is fairly short and extends only up to the funnel; in squids devoid of the hectocotylus, and particularly in those belonging to families Onychoteuthidae, Gonatidae, Chiroteuthidae, and Mastigoteuthidae, the penis is very long and can be protruded far out of the mantle cavity. It is also very long in *Architeuthis,* having extremely long spermatophores. Usually the penis is a muscular cylindrical tube, but in *Mastigoteuthis* it is curved and hook-like, in Chiroteuthidae it terminates in a spade-like head, and in *Architeuthis* it ends in a complex papillate structure.

In octopuses (Fig. 10 G) the structure of the spermatophoric organ is much simpler. It consists of a long, sinuous spermatophoric gland and a large accessory gland (prostate) with a small blind sac. No ciliated duct is present. The spermatophoric duct is short, but the spermatophoric sac is long (about 1 m in *Octopus dofleini*). It is not continued into the penis, but the penis starts separately near the point where the spermatophoric duct enters the sac. The penis in octopuses is not long, but its structure is more complicated than that of the neritic squids and cuttlefishes: it is T-shaped and consists of the penis proper (a terminal organ) and a blind diverticulum that is often longer than the penis and in some species is coiled and in others, for example, *O. australis* and *O. fontanianus*, is bifurcated.

Spermatogenesis occurs over the entire length of the testicular tubes and their outgrowths. The spermatogonia develop from the terminal epithelium and, passing through the stages of spermatids and spermatocytes, they turn into spermatozoa having a narrow head and an extremely long and slender tail or flagellum. The sperm head is fusiform in squids and cuttlefishes; in some octopuses the head or its anterior part (acrosome) is corkscrew-like, in others it is elongated and conical. The total length of spermatozoa is 0.05 mm in *Loligo pealei*, 0.5 mm in *Octopus dofleini*, and 0.55 in *Eledone cirrosa*. The width of the head is 1-2 microns. The characteristic feature of cephalopod sperm that distinguishes them from the sperm of mammals is a large quantity of glycogen in the head and the ability to use carbohydrates coming from outside. Thanks to this, the spermatozoa can retain their viability during a long period (up to 3½ months) after entering the seminal receptacle of the female. The liquid in which the spermatozoa are immersed in the spermatophore (see below) suppresses their mobility and respiration, while sea water, on the contrary, stimulates their movements. In the seminal receptacle they again lose their activity.

Fully-formed spermatozoa enter the spermatophoric organ, where the spermatophores—extremely characteristic for cephalopods—are formed. Their structure is complicated and their form is peculiar to each species, so they frequently serve as a reliable character for differentiating closely related species, even in such complex genera as *Illex*, *Octopus*, and *Eledone*.

The spermatophore of squids and cuttlefishes is a slightly bent tube that resembles a saber with an elongated blade (Fig. 10 I). The length of a spermatophore is usually a few millimeters or centimeters, but it varies from 2-3 mm to 10-20 cm or even 24 cm. In octopuses the spermatophores resemble a long, thick, gradually narrowing elastic tube (fig. 10 H). Their length usually is also measured in centimeters, but in *O. dofleini* the spermatophores reach 1.0-1.2 m in length. The number of the spermatophores is inversely related to their size (and also somewhat to the mantle

length): in animals with many spermatophores they usually are small, while if the spermatophores are large they are few in number. There are usually about a hundred or several hundreds, rarely above a thousand, but in octopuses with large spermatophores (*O. dofleini*, *Pteroctopus tetracirrhus*) there are only 10-12, *Bathypolypus* has up to 7, and *Benthoctopus* has only one spermatophore whose length is more than 1.5 times the mantle length. Exceptions are Argonautoidea, which have a single spermatophore during the whole life, and Cirrata, which have no spermatophores at all (see below).

The spermatophore gradually narrows starting from the widened posterior end, occupied by the sperm reservoir (seminal thread), toward the head. There is an empty space between the sperm reservoir and the posterior end of the spermatophore. On the opposite side, the sperm reservoir becomes the cement body (absent in octopuses). Between the cement body and the head is located the ejaculatory apparatus, which has the form of a compressed spring. In the widened head, the spring is coiled into a knot. The spermatophore is covered by a double envelope that consists of outer and middle layers (tunic). The sperm reservoir, the cement body, and the ejaculatory apparatus are also surrounded by a third layer, the inner tunic. The double-layered outer tunic mainly consists of mucoproteins. In addition, the reservoir, the cement body, and the spring of the ejaculatory apparatus are covered by a thin membrane separating these parts of the spermatophore from one another. In the anterior part of the head is a "window" closed by a thin membrane. A long filament extends from the head near the membrane. In ommastrephids the sperm reservoir occupies (together with a free distal space) nearly or somewhat more than a half of the spermatophore length; in loliginids it occupies ⅔ to ¾ the length. In the slender and flexible spermatophores of octopuses the sperm reservoir represents a spirally coiled thin thread whose length is usually ⅓ to ½ of the spermatophore length. The ejaculatory apparatus is very long. The spermatophore of *Loligo pealei* contains 7-10 million spermatozoa, and that of *Octopus dofleini*, 0.5-37 billion.

The spermatophore is fully formed in the spermatophoric organ. A mass of sperm is enveloped at first by the membrane, then the cement body and the ejaculatory apparatus are added, after which all are covered by the tunics. In the

Sepia officinalis, the common cuttlefish, on display at Aquarium Berlin, German Democratic Republic. Photo by Hilmar Hansen.

A very young *Sepia* sp. taken from coastal waters of the Philippine Islands. Photo by George Smit.

Sepia latimanus exhibited at the Waikiki Aquarium, Honolulu, Hawaii. Sepias are found in many parts of the world, but none are present in the Hawaiian Islands. Photo by Dr. Bruce Carlson.

Sepiolid eggs, possibly *Euprymna* sp. Photo by Roger Steene.

Right and left: A sepiolid squid, *Rossia moelleri*, from Franz Josef Land (Arctic Ocean), at about 15 m depth (SCUBA), March, 1982. Photo courtesy of Dr. Vladimir G. Averincev, Murmansk Marine Biological Institute, Academy of Sciences, USSR.

course of formation the spermatophore is continuously rotating around its axis, which is why the ejaculatory apparatus and (in octopuses) the seminal thread are coiled into a spiral. The posterior part of the Needham's organ is provided with spiral ridges, due to which the spermatophores are also arranged in a spiral. In the penis they are rearranged parallel to the axis of the body, with their heads forward.

The main function of the spermatophore is to ensure the transmission of the sperm from the male to the female without loss. The space between the outer and inner tunics and in the posterior end of the spermatophore is filled by a solution of high-molecular compounds that cannot escape to the outside, but for sea water the tunic is permeable. One of these compounds is a phosphoglycopeptide. Osmotic pressure inside the spermatophore is higher than that in the sea water despite the spermatophoric plasma being poor in salts, particularly in NaCl. As soon as the spermatophore gets into the water, the sea water begins to penetrate the tunic and to press against the spiral of the ejaculatory apparatus. When a spermatophore gets into the body of the female, the sensitive filament breaks the thin membrane of the "window," and penetration of water into the tunic accelerates. The elastic tunic at first withstands the pressure of the water and of the compressing spring, but finally the strength threshold is reached and the spermatophore "explodes." The spring jumps out through the broken tunic (in loliginids it turns inside out) pulling the cement body and the sperm reservoir behind it. All this process—the spermatophoric reaction—lasts about one second in squids and to 1.2 hours in *O. dofleini*. Once the sperm reservoir is freed from the tunic, it turns into a spermatangium (sperm body or sperm vesicle) (Fig. 10 J). In ommastrephids and loliginids it resembles a cudgel with the "club" smeared with the adhesive contents of the cement body. The cement body of many ommastrephids terminates in a spike similar to that of a World War I German helmet. This spike thrusts through the female's skin near the seminal receptacle and the cement securely glues the sperm body to the receptacle. The empty tunic of the spermatophore drops off together with the uncoiled spring (the females of some squids swallow the tunic).

In octopuses the spermatophoric reaction proceeds inside the mantle cavity of the female and is not so rapid as in squids. Under the pressure of the penetrating water the sperm reservoir gradually moves anteriorly, and as soon as the spring is compressed to the utmost (in *O. dolfeini* this happens when the volume of the content of spermatophore including the water penetrating the tunic increases fivefold) an "explosion" occurs. The sperm body is egg-shaped. The empty tunic of the spermatophore is cast out of the mantle cavity by the flow of the respiratory water.

Sea water stimulates the motility of the spermatozoa, and they fill the seminal receptacles in the vicinity of which the male disposes the sperm bodies. The seminal receptacle of cuttlefishes and loliginids is a horseshoe-shaped depression in the buccal membrane below the mouth. In *Illex* and *Berryteuthis* the spermatophores are located in the mantle cavity, forming a cluster on the inner wall of the mantle. In other ommastrephids and in *Gonatopis* they are circularly arranged on the buccal membrane. In some Enoploteuthidae (*Abralia, Watasenia*, etc.) they are situated on the female's nuchal cartilage; in some Onychoteuthidae they are in special grooves located ventrolaterally in the anterior part of the outer side of female's mantle; in Octopoteuthidae and Cranchiidae the spermatophores are located on the head, at the arm bases, etc. The females of *Vampyroteuthis* have two seminal receptacles on the head in front of the eyes.

There are no spermatophores formed in the Cirrata, and some parts of the spermatophoric complex (in particular the blind sac of the prostate) and the diverticulum (blind appendage) of the penis are absent or reduced, whereas other parts (such as the accessory glands) are highly developed. The role of the spermatophores is played by the sperm reservoirs coiled into a spiral and surrounded by a mucous secretion.

In Argonautoidea a single large spermatophore is formed in the spermatophoric gland. The accessory gland leads into a spacious blind sac that corresponds to the Needham's organ. Here the spermatophore "explodes" and its content fills the Needham's organ. Then the entire blind sac is carried into the hectocotylized arm. At mating the arm breaks off and enters the mantle cavity of the female. It is preserved there during her whole life. Thus, the Needham's organ also carries out the function of the sperm body and the hectocotylized arm functions as a seminal receptacle. In a mature hectocotylus the sperm fills a special cavity (sperm reservoir) at the base or at the tip of the arm. The remnants of the spermatophore tunic are also located inside it. There is a conical, threadlike, sometimes very long, outgrowth on the tip of the hectocotylus. Though it is called a penis, its origin is absolutely different and its function is most likely similar to the function of the calamus of Octopodidae. No true penis is present in Argonautoidea.

In contrast to the continuous synchrony of oocyte maturation, the formation of the spermatophores, at least in some squids, does not proceed continuously. The size of a spermatophore is determined by the dimensions of the parts of the spermatophoric organ, and they grow along with the growth of the mollusc, though in mature specimens they grow slower than the growth of the mantle length. Therefore, in large squids the spermatophores are absolutely longer but proportionately shorter than in small squids. Should the spermatophores be formed continuously and be accumulated in the spermatophoric sac, like the eggs in oviducts, then their dimension would differ noticeably in a single male. But in reality the size range of spermatophores in one male is, as a rule, narrow—the limit of variability is about 10%. It was shown in the squid *Sthenoteuthis pteropus* (Zalygalin et al., 1977) that the distribution curve or spermatophore dimensions is unimodal in recently matured males (stage V_1) and is distinctly bimodal at later substages (V_2-V_3). The males of this species probably produce two different groups of spermatophores, and the rearrangement of the spermatophoric complex occurs between the periods of their formation.

The maturation of genital products in male and female cephalopods is controlled by the optic gland, the endocrine gland that secrets gonadotropin. The maturation process can be regulated by three environmental factors: temperature, light, and nourishment. Under high temperatures cephalopods mature earlier and at smaller dimensions than under low temperatures. In species that spawn in spring or summer in temperate latitudes, a short day period (winter light conditions) stimulates the sexual maturation but suppresses the spawning, whereas the lengthening of the day suppresses the maturation in immature animals but stimulates spawning in the mature ones. On the coasts of western Europe the reproduction of *Sepia officinalis* occurs in spring and summer in shallow waters. The young spend the winter in the depths, where low illumination accelerates

maturation but low temperatures interfere with their maturation and a short day prevents premature oviposition until the spring comes. Spring migration to shallow waters induces early spawning. In this case, the young cuttlefish hatched from the eggs grow during maximal temperatures, which accelerates their growth before they migrate to the depths.

Variations in this scheme are also possible: in the males of the common octopus, *Octopus vulgaris*, a long day may speed up maturation, and as a result the males hatched in spring may have time to mature before the end of the reproductive period. Several weeks before spawning the molluscs stop taking food or drastically reduce their appetite. In accordance with the positive feedback principle, hunger speeds up the ripening of the eggs and sperm. But as a whole, environmental factors serve as a signal rather than as a governing role, and the main factors of maturation are the internal ones. For example, over the entire range from the North Pole to Newfoundland, the squid *Gonatus fabricii* starts spawning approximately at the same time—in March (from January to the middle or to second half of April)—though the light, temperature, and feeding conditions in the high Arctic and in temperate latitudes differ radically at that time. Most cephalopods or tropical regions mature at the age of 6-12 months and reproduce the whole year, without regard to the changes of temperature and illumination. But in temperate latitudes and in the subtropics the spawning of the majority of the shelf and epipelagic species, as well as of many mesopelagic species, is confined to a certain season (usually spring and summer) and the life cycle span is about one year. Thus, their spawning is distinctly correlated with the approach of definite light, temperature, and feeding conditions—the natural signals of the approach of the reproductive time.

Nervous System. The nervous system of the cephalopods (Fig. 11) is more developed than that of any other molluscs. The complexity of its structure and perfection of its organization are not less than those of the nervous system of fishes.

Central nervous system (CNS). The brain of dibranchiate cephalopods is housed in a cartilaginous head capsule. Its relative mass is either equal or exceeds that of the brains of fishes but is less than that of the brains of birds and mammals. The comparatively largest brain are in the fast-swimming epipelagic nektonic squids of the subfamily

Live specimens of *Loligo pealei* at the New York Aquarium. Photo by Dr. Guido Dingerkus.

Eggs of the squid *Sepioteuthis australis* from New South Wales, Australia. Photo by Walter Deas.

Empty egg capsules of *Loligo pealei* at Shark River Inlet, New Jersey. Photo by Aaron Norman.

Sepioteuthis lessoniana from Japanese waters. Photo by Takemura and Susuki.

Sepioteuthis sepioidea is popularly known as the Caribbean reef squid.

Note the chromatophore pattern of this Caribbean reef squid. Photo by Dr. Charles Arneson.

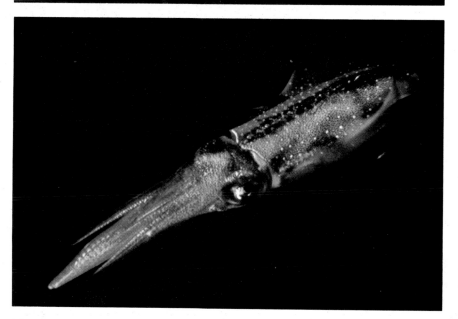

S. sepioidea photographed at night in the Caribbean Sea by Dr. Patrick Colin.

Ommastrephinae and of the family Thysanoteuthidae. The brain of other nektonic but slower squids such as the Illicinae, *Onychoteuthis,* and Gonatidae is somewhat smaller, and it is smaller still in the nektobenthic Loliginidae and Sepiidae. Then comes the brain of the benthic Octopodidae, and, finally, the brain of the planktonic squids Cranchiidae and planktonic octopuses Bolitaenidae (Zuev, 1973, 1975). Thus, the relative size of the brain in cephalopods is related to the speed of their motion, which is primarily conditioned by a necessity to process a large amount of visual information within a shortest period of time.

The CNS of dibranchiate cephalopods (Fig. 11 B-E) is located above and below the esophagus. It consists of four main sections: supraesophageal, subesophageal, optic lobes with optic tracts and adjoining nervous ganglia and glands, and the buccal and brachial ganglia. All sections are connected by numerous commissures. The supra- and subesophageal sections are divided into lobes, numbering 64 in *Octopus.* All sections consist of symmetrical right and left halves joined by nerve connectives. When they are cut apart, each half can function independently. An octopus with isolated halves can, for example, be taught to take a rough object and refuse a smooth object with its right arms and make the opposite decision with its left arms.

The buccal ganglion innervates the buccal mass, beak, radula, and salivary glands. The brachial ganglion innervates the limbs. In octopuses, particularly in the finned ones and in vampyromorphs, these ganglia are close together and are almost fused with the brain. In cuttlefishes and squids they are separate and are connected with the brain by cerebrobuccal and cerebrobrachial connectives and interconnected by a buccal-brachial connective. This is caused by the constancy of the distance between the ganglia and the organs innervated by them, such as the buccal mass, and the points of connection of the arms to the buccal funnel. The squids and cuttlefishes feed on large-size prey and eat it up rapidly, biting it into fairly large pieces. This requires a considerable physical effort, therefore the beak and the buccal funnel are shifted anteriorly to elongate the lever arm of the beak. The buccal and brachial ganglia are correspondingly remote from the main brain. Some octopuses (Cirrata) feed on microplankton, others on large prey, but they eat it slowly in their burrows, biting it into small pieces.

No great muscular efforts are required for this purpose, so the lever arm may be shorter, and the buccal and brachial ganglia are closer to the brain. It is natural that in this case the brain of octopuses is more compact than that of squids and cuttlefishes.

The optic lobes form the largest part of the brain. In octopuses both lobes occupy more than a half the volume, and in squids they comprise up to 80% of the brain volume. In pelagic cephalopods where eyesight plays a major role in life, they are more highly developed than in benthic octopuses. Optic lobes are most developed in fast-swimming nektonic squids. Branching in a definite sequence in the optic lobes are the fibers of the optic nerve, which contact the dendrites of the visual cells. In the optic lobes visual information is coded, classified, and transmitted to the other parts of the brain, mainly to the higher motor centers of the supraesophageal section, the visuostatic center, the center of visual memory, and to the magnocellular lobe. The fibers passing into and out of optic lobes retain distinct and constant topographic relation with one another. The optic lobes also govern the muscle tone of the animal.

The optic lobes are connected to the brain by thick nerves—optic tracts. Usually they are short, but in some genera, particularly in *Eledonella* and *Cirrothauma* (Figs. 74 C, 77 F), they are long and slender. Positioned on the optic tracts on the right and left side of the brain are optic glands, the most important endocrine organs regulating gonadal maturation and the development of secondary sexual characters. Subpedunculate brain lobes (located under the optic tract) control the functions of the optic gland and also are connected with them (see below).

The subesophageal section of the brain contains: the centers that govern the fine movements of the arms; the anterior chromatophore lobe—the center regulating the color of the head and limbs; the lateral pedal lobe—the oculomotor center (regulating eye movements); the posterior lateral pedal lobe—presumably controlling the movements of the arms and tentacles in squids and cuttlefishes; the anterior pedal lobe, which governs the movements of the arms and tentacles; the posterior pedal lobe—governing swimming (regulation of funnel functioning, of head retractors, and of the fins); the magnocellular lobe, which controls the jet swimming and governs the functioning of the stellate ganglion; the pallioviseral lobe innervating the mantle, fins, and ink sac; the posterior chromatophore lobe, which governs the change of color of the mantle, funnel, and fins; the visceral lobe, which innervates the viscera and funnel; the vasomotor lobe governing the musculature of the blood vessel walls; and the fin lobe (absent in the Incirrata).

Concentrated in this section of the brain are motor neurons. Intermediate motor centers actuated by signals from peripheral or from higher motor centers of the supraesophageal section of the brain are also situated here. These are the centers of simple reflexes; the subesophageal lobes are provided only with short-term memory, for example, of pain.

In the ventral part of the magnocellular lobe in squids, cuttlefishes, and vampyromorphs is located a pair of giant cells with a diameter of up to 750 microns (the size of the majority of the nervous cells of the subesophageal and higher motor centers ranges from 5 to 10 microns and that of the centers of sensory integration and memory less than 5 microns) from which the giant nerve fibers originate. These fibers pass the signals to the nerves of the stellate ganglion via the pallioviceral lobe. The magnocellular lobe is connected with the centers of swimming of the subesophageal section. Its function is regulated by signals arriving from the eyes and statocysts and is controlled by the higher motor centers. In *Mastigoteuthis* this lobe also receives the signals coming from the arms and tentacles, but there are no giant cells peculiar to this lobe as *Mastigoteuthis* are poor swimmers.

The lower part of the supraesophageal section of the brain is composed of higher motor centers —anterior, medial, dorsal, and lateral basal lobes as well as the pedunculate and olfactory lobes connected with the optic tract. The pedunclate lobe is the visuostatic center; in conjunction with the anterior and medial basal lobes it forms a structure functionally similar to the cerebellum of the vertebrates. The pedunculate lobe receives the signals from statocysts on the position and movements of the head; it also receives signals from the optic lobes on the position and movements of the eyes and sends the signals to the oculomotor center of the lateral pedal lobe. This center also receives signals immediately from the statocysts and governs the fine movements of the head and eyes that is necessary to aim at prey and to follow it. The anterior basal lobe also governs the arm movement control centers in the anterior pedal lobe. The medial basal lobe governs the control

centers of respiratory and swimming movements of the funnel and fins in the posterior pedal lobe. In addition, the basal lobes govern the functions of the magnocellular and palliovisceral lobes, the lateral basal lobes control the chromatophore centers, and the olfactory lobe controls the olfactory organ.

The upper part of the supraesophageal section of the brain is composed of frontal, subfrontal, and subvertical lobes—the "silent centers," the higher centers of the visual and chemotactile memory and training. In octopuses the buccal ganglion or the buccal brain lobe is added to them. According to the theory proposed by J. Z. Young, each of the systems of visual and tactile memory and training contains two pairs of centers: the lower and the upper. The upper centers of the tactile memory are the medial and lateral inferior frontal lobes; the lower centers are the subfrontal and posterior buccal lobes. The upper centers of the visual memory are the medial superior frontal and vertical lobes, and the lower centers are the lateral superior frontal and subvertical lobes. These two systems (visual and chemotactile) are fully divided at the highest levels of the brain. There are literally "two memories in one brain" in the cephalopods. The above indicated centers contain hypothetical elementary units of memory—mnemons—postulated by J. Z. Young.

Squids and octopuses are at the same time predatory and timid animals; their life passes in the struggle between the desire to attack an unknown but possibly edible object and the fear to suffer a repulse. The base of the mnemon is the classifying cell, which has two axons passing to the motor centers: one of them initiates the attack, the other the retreat. Let us suppose that, meeting an unknown object, the squid or octopus will prefer to attack it. If the object proves edible, the collateral nerve fibers outgoing from the higher motor centers excite one of the numerous minute nerve cells that secrete a mediator substance suppressing the passage of the nerve impulse, exactly the cell that "locks" the axon initiating the retreat. The mnemon will "memorize" that the signal corresponding to this object means that the object is tasty and harmless. But if, on the contrary, the mollusc suffers a repulse, then the attack-initiating axon would be locked, while the axon initiating the retreat will operate, and should the mollusc encounter the same object once again, it will prefer to avoid dangerous contact. The num-

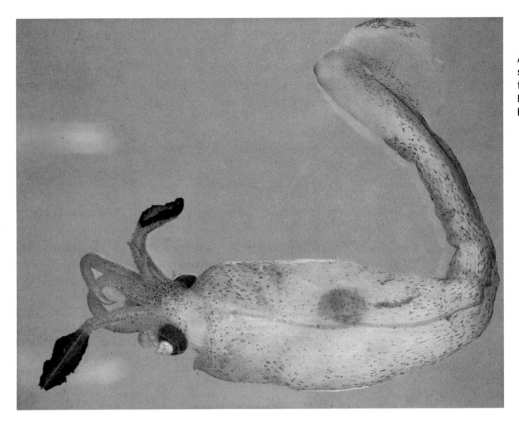

A female cranchiid
squid, *Leachia* sp., from
the Central Pacific.
Photo by Dr. W. E.
Burgess.

Onychoteuthis banksi, an oegopsid squid from Hawaiian waters. Photo by Dr. Warren
E. Burgess.

Grimpoteuthis cf. *umbellata*, a deep-sea cirrate octopod photographed from the manned submersible *Pisces* at Reykjanes Ridge, 58°30′N, 1600 m depth, August 1982. Photo courtesy of Dr. Anatoly Sagalevich, P.P. Shirshov Institute of Oceanology, Academy of Sciences, USSR.

Fig. 11.

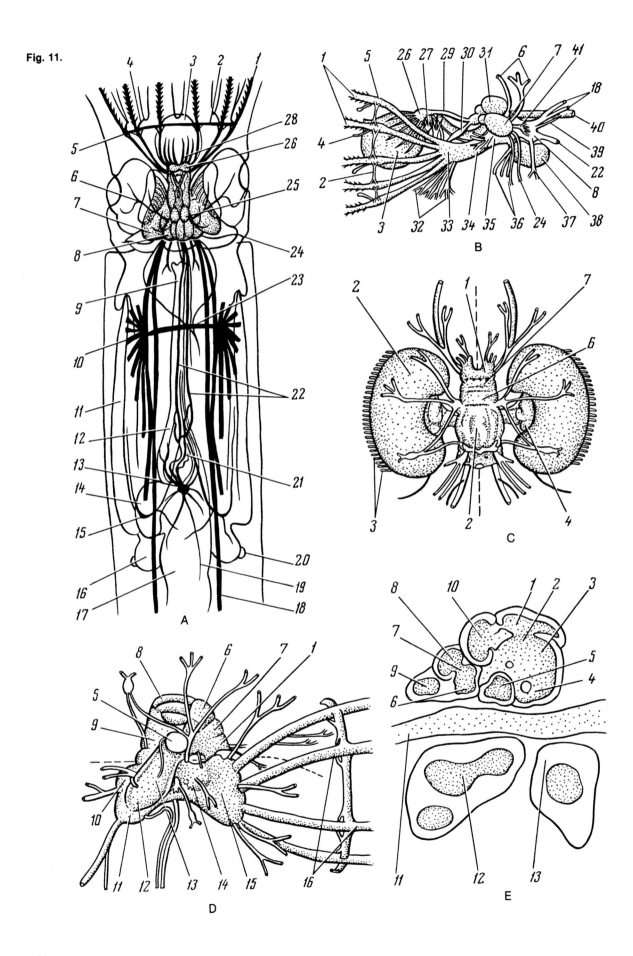

ber of mnemons that have been appropriately altered by experience determine the accuracy of future discrimination of the objects. The function of the upper and lower centers of the visual and tactile memory consists in strengthening the positive ("tasty") and negative ("painful") sustaining signals. The classifying cells of the tactile memory system are located in the posterior buccal and subfrontal lobes, and those of the visual memory are in the optic lobes (J. Young, 1965; Sanders, 1975).

Participation in the system of the short-term memory is not the only function of the vertical lobe (the highest lobe of the cephalopod brain). The lobe also participates in the long-term memory system, playing a role similar to the role of the recording and read-out devices of the memory

Fig. 11. Nervous system of *Todarodes pacificus* (A,B) and *Octopus vulgaris* (C-E); A—general view to nervous system from dorsal side; B—brain from the side; 1—arm nerves; 2—interbrachial comissure; 3—buccal complex; 4—buccal lappet nerve; 5—arm nerve ganglion; 6—optic nerve; 7, 8—optic (7) and palliovisceral (8) lobes; 9—intestine; 10—stellate ganglion; 11—gill, 12—stomach; 13—gastric ganglion; 14—cecum; 15—pallial (mantle) ganglion; 16—branchial heart; 17—gonad; 18—pallial (mantle) nerve; 19—gonadal nerve; 20—branchial heart appendage; 21—gastric nerve; 22—visceral nerve; 23—stellate ganglion connective; 24—olfactory nerve; 25—supraesophageal brain lobes; 26, 27—superior (26) and inferior (27) buccal lobes; 28—buccal nerves; 29, 30—cerebro-buccal (29) and cerebro-brachial (30) connectives; 31—vertical lobe; 32—anterior optic nerves; 33—brachial lobe; 34—brachiopedal connective; 35—pedal lobe; 36—infundibular nerves; 37—posterior infundibular nerve; 38—statocyst; 39—digestive gland (hepatic) nerve; 40—esophagus; 41—nerve of funnel retractor; C,D,—brain from above and from side: 1, 2—buccal (1) and optic (2) lobes; 3—optic nerves; 4—optic gland; 5—optic tract (optic lobe removed); 6-15—superior frontal (6), inferior frontal (7), vertical (8), posterior basal (9), posterior chromatophore (10), vasomotor (11), palliovisceral (12), magnocellular (13), pedal (14), and brachial (15) lobes; 16—brachial nerves; E—longitudinal section through the brain (anterior part at the left) showing position of some lobes: 1-10—supraesophageal lobes: 1—vertical; 2—subvertical; 3-5—dorsal (3), medial (4) and anterior basal (5); 6—posterior buccal; 7—subfrontal; 8—medial inferior frontal; 9—superior buccal; 10—medial superior frontal; 11—esophagus; 12, 13—subesophageal lobes: 12—pedal; 13—palliovisceral. Other lobes not shown (A,B—from Ivanov and Strelkov, 1949; C,D—from Wells, 1966; E—from Sanders, 1975).

storage of modern computers. This is exactly why the vertical lobe grows faster than the other lobes during larval and postlarval stages of cephalopod life, and along with this growth the capabilities in training improve. If the vertical lobe is removed, the octopus' ability for memorizing and training, both visual and tactile, worsens greatly.

The brain of the majority of dibranchiate cephalopods is organized in accordance with a general scheme. The differences between octopuses on the one hand, and squids and cuttlefishes on the other hand, have been partially indicated above. In squids and cuttlefishes the brain is less concentrated, individual lobes are more isolated, the optic lobes are very large, the ventral magnocellular lobe is better developed, there is a system of giant axons, the inferior frontal lobes are less developed, and the suprabrachial commissure is absent. In octopuses the brain is more compact, the optic lobes are not so large, the ventral magnocellular lobe and the system of giant nerve cells and axons are absent, the inferior frontal lobes (the centers of tactile memory) are greatly developed (they are enlarged in abyssal squids also), and the brachial ganglia are connected by the suprabrachial commissure. The basal lobes are better developed in squids, cuttlefishes, and pelagic octopuses than in benthic octopuses. The brain of vampyromorphs combines the characters peculiar to octopuses (compactness and high development of the inferior frontal lobes) with those peculiar to decapod cephalopods (presence of the ventral magnocellular lobe and absence of the suprabrachial commissure). The brain of finned octopuses is extremely compact, the optic lobes are small and underdeveloped, the optic glands are reduced, the entire supraesophageal section of the brain is considerably simplified and is dominated by the centers of the tactile system, yet there are some elements of a system of giant fibers (J. Young, 1977).

The brain of cephalopods grows throughout life, but its relative size decreases with age. During the life of an octopus—from a larva weighing 1 mg to a "giant" with a mass of 10 kg—the number of brain cells increases 1000 times. The main increment of cells falls in the larval and early postlarval periods. The brain of an adult octopus contains about 170 million nerve cells, including 130 million cells in the optic lobe, 30 million in the vertical lobe, and 6 million in the subesophageal lobes (J. Young, 1963; Wells, 1966).

65

Octopus dofleini dofleini, the giant Pacific octopus, Sea of Japan, USSR coast, off Putyatin Island, about 5-10 m (SCUBA). Photo courtesy of the late Mr. Yuri F. Astafyev, author of the book *Eye to Eye with the Octopus*.

Opposite page: Top: *Stauroteuthis* cf. *syrtensis*, another deep-sea cirrate octopod photographed at Reykjanes Ridge, 58°30′N, 1300 m depth, July 1982. Photo courtesy of Dr. Anatoly Sagalevich, P.P. Shirshov Institute of Oceanology, Academy of Sciences, USSR, Moscow. Bottom: *Octopus variabilis* from Peter the Great Gulf, USSR coast of the Sea of Japan. The long and slender first and second arms are characteristic of the species. Photo courtesy of Alexander and Sergej Kochetov, Moscow Zoo, USSR.

Octopuses, cuttlefishes, and at least some squids are well fit for learning. They solve some problems of training and retraining as successfully as rats. They have good memories, including short-term, intermediate, and long-term memories. On the other hand, *Nautilus,* epipelagic octopuses, and, probably (judging by the structure of the supraesophageal lobes of the brain), the deepwater oceanic squids are "stupid" animals with poorly developed ability for learning.

Peripheral nervous system. All organs of the cephalopod body are richly innervated and function under the control of the CNS. The most important parts of the peripheral nervous system (Fig. 11 A) are the following. The nerves of the arms, tentacles, and filaments of vampyromorphs originate from the brachial ganglion. The nerves of the arms are connected in front of the mouth by the circular interbrachial commissure. Each arm nerve passing along the arm axis consists of a pair of nerve cords and of numerous ganglia. In addition, four intramuscular nerve cords pass through the arm. A special nerve ganglion is located at the base of each sucker. The ganglion integrates the signals coming from chemoreceptors and mechanoreceptors (tactile receptors) situated on the sucker rim. On the whole, the number of nerve cells in the arms is enormous: 350 million in octopuses, twice as many as in the CNS. The great number of nerve ganglia gives cephalopod limbs a certain degree of independence. The cut-off arm of an octopus, for example, can transfer a piece of food from one sucker to another in the direction to the mouth, and the hectocotylized arm of Argonautoidea autotomized at mating creeps independently into the female's mantle cavity.

The optic nerve governs the functioning of the muscles moving the eyes. The olfactory nerve innervates the olfactory organ. Besides the nerves passing from the buccal ganglion to the lips, radula, and salivary glands, a pair of sympathetic nerves also originates at the buccal ganglion and runs posteriorly along the esophagus to be connected with a large gastric ganglion. It innervates the main part of the digestive system and governs the processes of digestion and absorption as an integrator of all digestive tract activity. Arising from the visceral ganglion is a pair of large visceral nerves that innervate the organs of the circulatory and excretory systems, gills, genital organs, neurosecretory system of the vena cava, funnel and its retractors, etc. The visceral nerves are,

particularly, connected to the ganglia of the heart and the branchial hearts. A small ganglion is located at the bases of the gills on the branchial (gill) nerve.

The pallial nerve extending from the palliovisceral, magnocellular, and fin lobes innervates the largest of ganglia located outside the brain, the stellate ganglion. A pair of stellate ganglia is situated on the inner surface of the mantle on its anterior part on either side of the dorsal median line. More than a dozen nerves consisting of one giant (up to 0.5-1 mm in diameter) axon originate from each ganglion. The longer is the distance from the ganglion to the section of the mantle innervated by the nerve, the thicker is the axon. The velocity of the nerve impulse conductance is proportional to the square root of the axon diameter. The thickest nerves conduct the impulse five times faster as compared to the thinnest ones. Diameters of the axons are "chosen" so that the impulses initiated by the ganglion in one moment should arrive at the "destination spot" also in one moment. The muscle fibers innervated by the nerves of the stellate ganglion contract on the principle of "all or nothing," i.e., they respond to the first impulse. The system of central control of the giant axons is as follows: the giant cells of the first order in the ventral magnocellular lobe—the giant cells of the second order in the palliovisceral lobe—the giant cells of the third order in the stellate ganglion. Synchronism of the response of the muscles at the right and left sides of the body is ensured by the crossing of the first order giant axons between the pedal and palliovisceral lobes: the right-side lobe governs the left-side ganglion, and vice versa. As a result, the signal coming to the magnocellular lobe from the eyes, statocysts, and skin, and warning about danger, initiates a simultaneous and instant contraction of the entire musculature of the mantle and an immediate flight of the squid (or cuttlefish). A *Loligo vulgaris* with a mantle length of 20 cm jumping with the tail forward is able to reach a speed of 2 meters per second (7.2 km/hr) in only 0.08-0.12 seconds. The system of giant nerve fibers discovered by professor J. Z. Young in the early 1930's plays an outstanding role in the development of neurophysiology: the giant axon of the squid turned out to be an ideal object for investigating the basic mechanism of nerve excitation, conductance of the nerve impulse, structure of membranes, synapses, etc. In those areas of physiological research the giant axon of the squid played the role that had been played by the nerve-muscular preparation of the frog for the neurophysiologists of the second half of the 19th century.

Sense Organs. The sense organs of dibranchiate cephalopods are as follow: eyes, extraocular photoreceptors—the light-sensitive vesicles (parolfactory and epistellar bodies), statocysts, olfactory papillae (pits), chemo- and mechanoreceptors of suckers, lips, etc.

Eyes. The eyes of dibranchiate cephalopods are very large. Their structure is as perfect as that of the vertebrates. They are usually located in the depressions in the cartilaginous capsule of the head and possess a cornea, an iris with a pupil capable of narrowing and widening, a movable crystalline lens, and a retina (Fig. 12 A). The cornea of oegopsid squids is of annular form and is widely open anteriorly, so that the front chamber of the eye freely communicates with sea water. Outside it there is a muscular circular fold of skin, the eyelid. In the lower anterior corner of the eyelid there is a narrow recess, the eye sinus. In some oegopsids, particularly in Onychoteuthidae, the eyelid can shrink, almost completely closing the eye. In myopsid squids the cornea is almost fully closed. Usually there is a small orifice—the "lacrimal pore"—connecting the front chamber of the eye with the environment; neither an eyelid nor a sinus is present. In cuttlefishes and octopuses the fully closed cornea has a circular eyelid but is without a sinus. The eyes of vampyromorphs are of an oegopsid type.

In squids the pupil is round; in octopuses it is usually rectangular, horizontally extended; in cuttlefishes it is W-shaped, with low and widely inclined lateral limbs. In octopuses it contracts into a thin slit in bright light. In cuttlefishes contraction results in a shape that make it seem as if they have two tiny pupils. The pupillary response depends upon the signal of the change of illumination; at an abrupt increase of brightness the squid's pupil contracts within 5 seconds, and at its sudden decrease it widens considerably slower—after 0.5-2 minutes—and then contracts again; this is caused by the redistribution of pigment in retinal cells.

The lens of cephalopods, like that of fishes, is almost spherical and is suspended on the muscles of the ciliary body. Its focal length exceeds the diameter 2.5 times. The refractive properties of the lens probably diminish from the center toward the periphery, due to which a distinct image is obtained in all sections of the retina. As a rule, the lens is transparent for each part of the visible spectrum, but the lenses of *Onychoteuthis banksi* and of the big eye of *Histioteuthis* are yellowish—the yellow pigment cuts off the blue end of the spectrum. It has been supposed that the squids thus are able to "unmask" their prey, the mesopelagic animals with ventral counterillumination bioluminescence.

The lens of cephalopods is capable of accommodation within certain limits. The accommodation is realized by moving the lens anteriorly and posteriorly, as in fishes, but not through the change of its form (which means a change in the focal length of the lens) as in mammals. The lens is retracted posteriorly by the muscles of the ciliary body and moved forward due to the elasticity of the contracted muscles that surround the eyeball. No higher accommodation is necessary for the cephalopods: the vision distance in water is not long and there is no need to see nearer the tips of the arms. In addition, the retinal cells of cephalopods are very long and a certain share of accommodation may be reached by the displacement of the pigment in them.

The retina of cephalopods is not inverted: the light-sensitive elements are directed toward light and the nerve fibers leave in the opposite direction, therefore there is no blind spot in the retina. The light-sensitive cells are rhabdomes arranged horizontally and vertically. Each rhabdome consists of four rhabdomeres. The length of the rhabdomes is 0.15-0.20 mm. The number of retinal light-sensitive cells is extremely great. In cuttlefishes, squids, and shallow-water benthic octopuses it amounts to about 50-100 thousand per 1 mm^2, and in *Bathyteuthis* is 250 thousand per 1 mm^2. Cephalopods, except *Bathyteuthis*, do not have a "yellow spot"—the area of the most distinct vision on the retina, but the squids and octopuses have a "strip of best sight" extending along the eye equator. The length of the rhabdomes and density of their distribution are highest within the limits of this strip. In sepiids the edges of the strip bear two smaller widenings perpendicular to the strip. They are positioned opposite the lateral widenings of the pupil. The retina of some deepwater forms (*Histioteuthis, Bathothauma, Japetella, Cirroteuthis,* and probably *Vampyroteuthis*) is divided into two sections of different structure, and the division of optic lobes corresponds to this. It has been supposed

Octopus briareus, one of the most common octopuses in the western tropical Atlantic. Photo by Dr. Patrick L. Colin taken at night in Discovery Bay, Jamaica, 15 m depth.

Bottom left: A female *Octopus ocellatus* brooding her eggs. The eggs of this species range in size from 10 to 13 mm in diameter. Photo by Takemura and Susuki.
Bottom right: *Octopus vulgaris*, first described almost 200 years ago, is fished commercially in many places of the world. This young individual is from South Africa. Photo by Dr. T.E. Thompson.

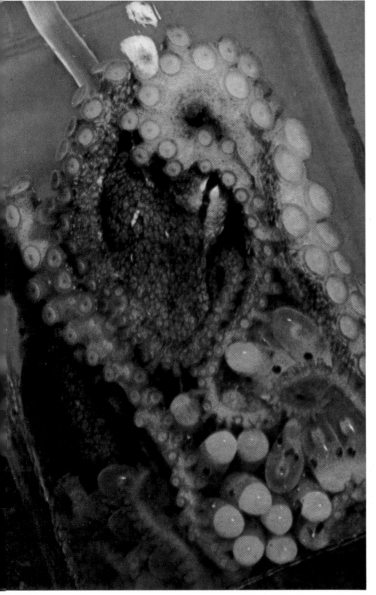

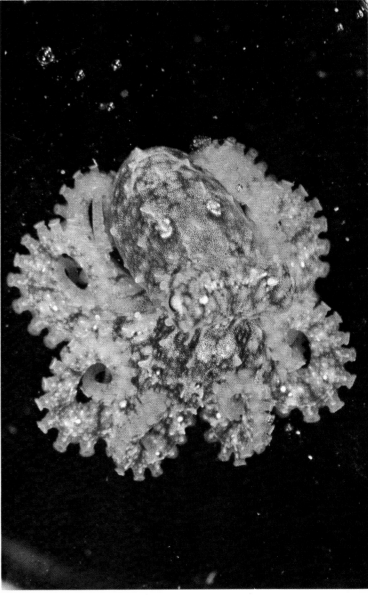

The main defense of octopus against predators is camouflage. This hard-to-see octopus is waiting for an innocent prey to come by. Photo by Michio Goto, *Marine Life Documents.*

Octopus cyaneus, a widely distributed large ocellated octopus found from East Africa to the Hawaiian Islands, is fished extensively for food. Photo by Michio Goto, *Marine Life Documents.*

that some parts of the retina "look" forward and upward, others backward and downward.

Cephalopods have two light-sensitive pigments: rhodopsin and retinochrome. Rhodopsin—the main visual pigment—is contained in rhabdomes. Its maximum absorption differs in various species and is located within 470-500 nm (480 nm in oceanic squids). Retinochrome is contained in the retina outside the rhabdomes. Its maximum absorption is shifted by 15-20 nm toward the long waves. Its function probably consists of supplying an activated retinene (aldehyde of vitamin A_1) that in combination with the protein opsin forms rhodopsin. Light initiates photoisomerization of the retinene without breaking its connection with the opsin, but changing the penetrability for sodium ions of the light-sensitive cell membranes, thus initiating a nerve impulse and registration of the light falling on the cell. The light-sensitive and supporting cells of the retina contain granules of the pigment that migrate to the distal part of the rhabdome at bright light and to the basal part at dim light. Such is the method of adaptation to changes of brightness. Besides that, the length of the rhabdomes increases in animals that stay in semidarkness for a long time.

Vision in most cephalopods is monocular, but their eyes are so large that the vision field of both eyes approaches 360°. During attentive examination of any subject the octopus raises its eyes and moves them together so that the object is looked at by both eyes. Binocular vision is even more typical of cuttlefishes (sepiids and sepiolids). Normally the anterior field of vision of the right and left eyes is overlapped by 10°, but by moving the eyes nearer to one another *Sepia officinalis* obtains an overlapping of the vision field by 75° and follows its prey by both eyes. In this case, the image of the prey gets onto the retina within the strip of best vision of both eyes. Even some squids attacking prey move their eyes together for binocular vision at the very moment of attack.

It has been shown by numerous experiments with the elaboration of conditioned reflexes, with the analysis of the electroretinograms and with other methods, that all cephalopods do not differentiate colors (they are color-blind). But they, like many other animals that have rhabdomes, differentiate the plane of light polarization and are able to orient in the polarized light. Cephalopods have within the retina of one eye two complementary "orthogonally polarized" views of the underwater world. A visual system based on the transformation of these two views into one would lead to enhanced contrast underwater and permit seeing clearly the details of an object obscured by confusing highlights.

The keenness of cephalopod sight is very high, and they are able to perceive images. Their greatly developed eye musculature allows them to follow the movements of the object being scrutinized. The pupils of octopuses and cuttlefishes widen and contract not only at changes of light brightness but also by the will of the animal: a widened pupil is a signal value, particularly in courtship. The sensitivity of the eye is maximal in the bluish green rays penetrating deeper into the sea than other parts of the spectrum.

There is only one blind cephalopod—the abyssopelagic octopod *Cirrothauma*. Its eyes looks like subcutaneous spots and are devoid of lens, ciliary body, and iris, but have a reduced retina and some irregularly located rhabdomes (Fig. 74 C). The optic lobes and centers of the visual memory are also reduced. In the genera *Cirroteuthis* and *Octopus* in addition to the species with normally developed eyes there are some species with the eyes greatly reduced in size. There are species among the deepwater squids and octopuses with unusual eye shapes, with eyes of different sizes and telescopic and stalked eyes.

Eyes of different size are found in the mainly mesopelagic species of *Histioteuthis* (Figs. 53-56). The diameter of the left eye is 1.5-2 times greater than that of the right eye, and they often differ in shape. The sizes of the optic lobes differ also. The sensitivity and keenness of sight of the larger eye are higher than of the smaller one. The larger eye is adapted for vision in the upper layers of water, whereas the smaller one is for vision in the depths. It has been supposed that when the squid is in normal position the larger eye looks upward and perceives the light from above, and the smaller one looks downward and a little forward and perceives bioluminescence (Bityukova & Zuev, 1976; R. Young, 1975).

Stalked eyes are peculiar to larvae and young of cranchiids (Fig. 12 B) and, to a lesser extent, to the larvae of Cycloteuthidae. Structurally the stalked eyes are similar to the telescopic eyes of *Amphitretus*, in which the eyes (like the eyes of another semi-deepwater pelagic octopus, *Dorsopsis*) are close to each other and are located on top of the head (Fig. 77 G-I), and to the elongated eyes of *Bathyteuthis* and the larvae of some Chiro-teuthidae. A stalked eye represents a kind of cylinder cut from the central part of a normal subspherical eye. The optical properties of such an eye are no better than those of an ordinary eye, and its advantages are not very clear. Stalked eyes are mainly peculiar to mesopelagic species and to mesopelagic larvae of bathypelagic species. It has been supposed (R. Young, 1975) that their main function is the camouflage of squid eyes against the sight of a predator waiting for it from below in the daytime. In addition, the spacing of the stalked eyes away from the narrow rod-like (camouflage!) head of the squid makes it easier to measure the exact distance to its prey—the principle of the stereoscopic telescope (J. Young, 1970).

It should be mentioned that though there are species with reduced or smaller eyes among the deepwater cephalopods, species with large and normally developed eyes are met in all depths from the ocean surface down to the abyssal.

The eyes of *Nautilus* differ radically from the eyes of dibranchiate cephalopods. They are deprived of a lens but have a minute pupil (1-2 mm) that communicates between the inner chamber of the eye and the environment (Fig. 14). The pupil narrows in bright light and widens in semidarkness. The eye of a *Nautilus* is a camera obscura with a regulated diaphragm (pupil). In bright light the *Nautilus* is probably able to perceive distinct images, but being strictly nocturnal animals they orient mainly not through the vision but through the senses of touch and smell.

Extraocular Photoreceptors (Fig. 12 C-G). The extraocular photoreceptors or light-sensitive vesicles are one of the most enigmatic organs of cephalopods. The first such organs—the epistellar bodies of octopuses—were discovered by J. Z. Young in 1929. The parolfactory vesicles of squids were noticed by S. Thore in 1939 and described by B. Boycott and J. Z. Young in 1956. They were at first supposed to be neurosecretory organs, and only in the mid- to late 1960's did it become clear that they are photoreceptors closely connected with the nervous system—"eyes in the brain." They are present in all cephalopods except *Nautilus* (Mauro, 1977).

The light-sensitive vesicles of octopuses—the epistellar bodies—are small vesicles disposed singly on the posterior side of the stellate ganglion (Fig. 12 E). They are usually orange or yellow but in *Octopus* are colorless. They lie on the inner mantle-facing side of the ganglion, and light can reach them only through the mantle wall or at inhalation when the mantle bulges and the stellate ganglion is positioned opposite the mantle cavity opening. Among the cells of the epistellar body there are numerous bipolar cells—rhabdome type photoreceptors containing rhodopsin. When the body is illuminated a nerve impulse occurs. The arrangement and main characteristics of their structure are similar in all octopuses, Cirrata included.

The light-sensitive vesicles of squids, cuttle-fishes, and *Spirula* are located in the posterior part of the brain within the area of the olfactory lobe, therefore they are called parolfactory ("near olfactory") vesicles. Their structure is different from the epistellar bodies of octopuses and is extremely variable (Fig. 12 C,D). In *Loligo, Spirula,* and *Sepia* they lie on the optic tract, mainly on its ventral side near the pedunculate lobe, with which they are connected by nerves. The vesicles represent a group of a few (in *Loligo vulgaris* 4 to 15 on each side) small (4-5 times smaller than the epistellar bodies in octopuses) bodies, part of which lies on the surface of the tract and another part sunken in its tissue. Still more different is their structure and arrangement in oegopsid squids. Some squids, such as Onychoteuthidae, Bathyteuthidae, Ctenopterygidae, Brachioteuthidae, Neoteuthidae, Chiroteuthidae, Grimalditeuthidae, Joubiniteuthidae, and Cranchiidae, have only one set of parolfactory bodies located posteriorly below the optic tract, but those bodies may be small and simply structured (in Cranchiidae) or large and complicated (*Bathyteuthis, Ctenopteryx*). Pyroteuthinae, Histioteuthidae, Octopoteuthidae, Cycloteuthidae, and Mastigoteuthidae have two groups of parolfactory bodies, a dorsal and a ventral group. There are three groups of bodies (dorsal, central, and ventral) in Ommastrephidae and Ancistrocheirinae, while Enoploteuthinae has as many as four groups (dorsal, two ventral, and posterior). The structure of the parolfactory bodies is highly specific for families or subfamilies and differs in details in various genera and in species of the same genus. The structure of the parolfactory bodies in semi-deepwater sepiolids of the genus *Heteroteuthis* differs from those of cuttlefishes but resembles the structure in squids: the dorsal group is located above the optic tract, the ventral under the eye and a little behind it.

The position of the light-sensitive vesicles is different in *Vampyroteuthis:* the group of vesicles lies

Octopus ornatus from the Hawaiian Islands. Photo by Scott Johnson, Makua, Oahu, Hawaii.

Octopus macropus, the white-spotted octopus, is of almost world-wide distribution and mainly inhabits coral reefs. Photo by Keith Gillett, Heron Island, Great Barrier Reef, Australia, from *The Australian Great Barrier Reef in Colour.*

This close-up photo shows well the characteristic
rectangular shape of the pupil of the octopus eye.

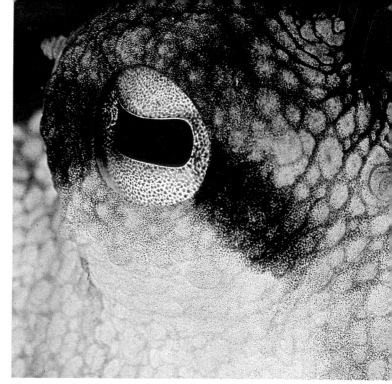

In addition to the W-shaped pupil, the warts or cirri
and the mottled coloration are very evident in this
frontal view of a cuttlefish, *Sepia* sp.

Fig. 12.

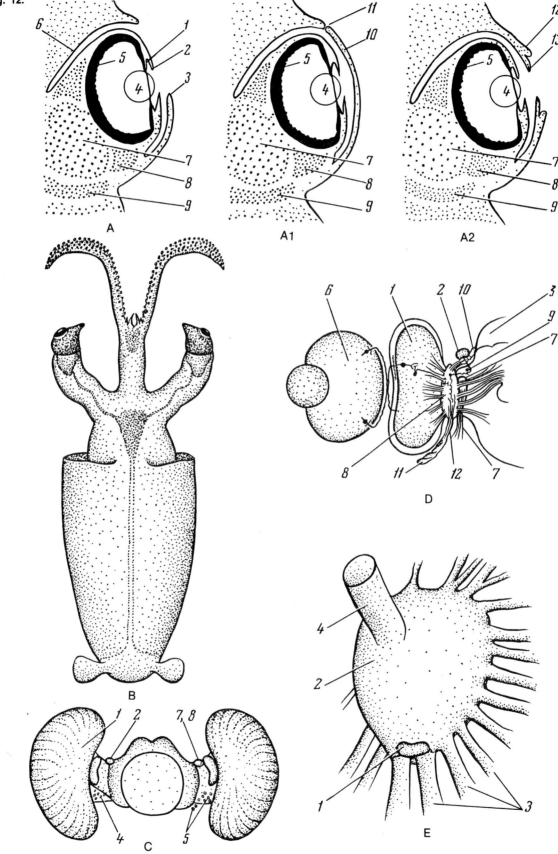

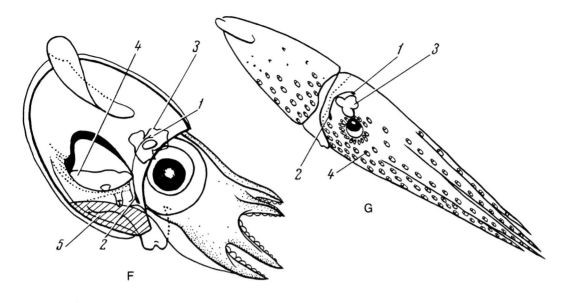

F

G

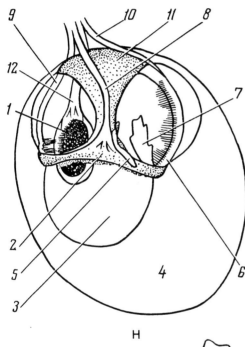

H

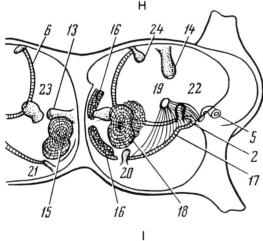

I

Fig. 12. Eyes, extraocular photoreceptors, and statocysts of cephalopods; A-A$_2$, structural scheme of the eyes in Oegopsida (A), Myopsida (A1) and Octopoda (A2): 1—cornea; 2—iris; 3—eyelid; 4—pupil; 5—retina; 6—orbit; 7—optic lobe; 8—white body; 9—cartilage; 10—secondary cornea; 11—pore; 12, 13—secondary (12) and primary (13) eyelid; B—stalked eyes in *Bathothauma lyromma* larva; C, D—parolfactory photosensitive vesicles in *Loligo vulgaris* (C) and *Todarodes sagittatus* (D): 1—optic lobe; 2—optic gland; 3—vertical lobe; 4, 5—deep (4) and superficial (5) photosensitive vesicles; 6—eye; 7, 8—olfactory (7) and pedunculate (8) lobes; 9—optic gland nerve; 10, 11—dorsal (10) and ventral (11) photosensitive vesicles; 12—ventral photosensitive nerve; E—position of epistellar body in *Eledone moschata*: 1—epistellar body; 2—stellate ganglion; 3—stellate nerves; 4—mantle connective; F, G—position of photosensitive vesicles in *Heteroteuthis hawaiiensis* (F) and *Histioteuthis hoylei* (G); animals shown in natural position: 1, 2—dorsal (1) and ventral (2) photosensitive vesicles; 3—brain; 4—photophore; 5—ventral shield; H, I—statocysts of *Octopus* (H) and *Sepiola* (I, open): 1—macula with statolith; 2—longitudinal crista; 3—endolymph; 4—perilymph; 5—Koelliker's canal; 6—vertical crista; 7—anticrista; 8-10—nerves to longitudinal, transverse and vertical cristae; 11—cartilaginous cap; 12—macular nerve; 13, 14—median (13) and dorsal (14) anticristae; 15—macula princeps; 16—dorsal and ventral macula neglecta; 17—anterior transverse crista; 18—statolith; 19—crista nerve; 20-24—hamuli (1-5) (A—from Naef, 1921 after Jaeckel, 1958; B—from N. Voss, 1980; C-E—from Mauro, 1977; F-G—from R. Young, 1977; H-I—from J. Young, 1960, 1977).

Hapalochlaena maculosa, the dreaded highly poisonous blue-ring octopus from Australian waters. Photo by Walter Deas, Camp Cove, Sydney, N.S.W., Australia, from *Beneath Australian Seas.*

Tremoctopus violaceus, young (left) and adult female (right). Both of these individuals belong to the subspecies *T. violaceus gracilis* from the Central Pacific. Photo by Dr. W.E. Burgess.

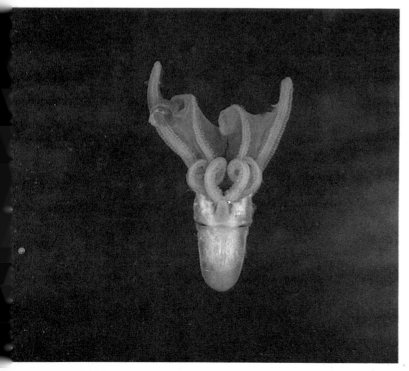

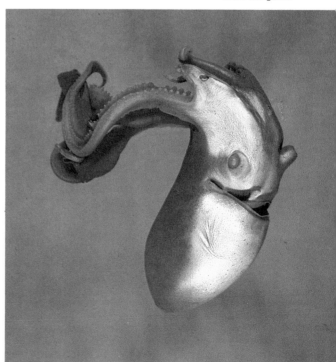

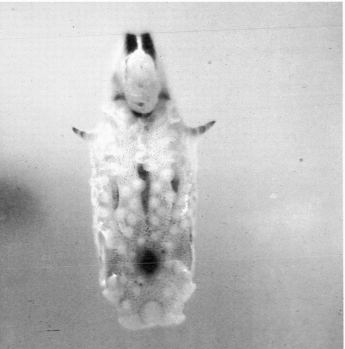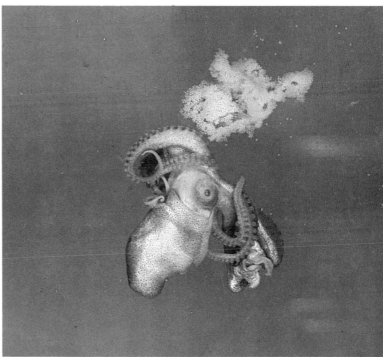

Argonauta hians: (Top left) Underwater in the natural habitat. (Top right) Resting at the bottom of a container immediately after capture. (Bottom left) Frontal view, natural swimming position. Photos courtesy of Everet C. Jones. *Argonauta argo:* (Bottom right) A female from the Central Pacific photographed without the shell or brood case and with the eggs removed from the arms. Photo by Dr. W.E. Burgess.

in the anterior part of the mantle cavity on its dorsal side under the mantle edge and is covered by transparent epidermis. Thus this organ is situated just half way between the position of the parolfactory vesicles of squids and cuttlefishes on one hand and the epistellar bodies of octopuses on the other. Each organ contains about 50 vesicles.

The light-sensitive bodies of decapod cephalopods and vampyromorphs, like those of the octopuses, are usually yellow or orange. They contain light-sensitive cells of a rhabdome type with rhodopsin and generate an impulse when they are illuminated. The dorsal light-sensitive vesicles "look" upward and somewhat rearward, but in animals with normal head-down (*Bathyteuthis*) or oblique positions having the body axis inclined through an angle of 30-45° with the tail higher than the head (*Heteroteuthis, Histioteuthis,* etc.) they "look" directly upward (Fig. 12 F,G). Transparent dermal "windows," particularly visible in Enoploteuthidae, are commonly located above the light-sensitive bodies. Thus these organs can perceive daylight from above. The ventral organs usually "look" at the funnel side adjacent to the head, also through the "windows." In *Heteroteuthis* and Pyroteuthinae they can see the luminescence of the intrapallial photophores. In *Histioteuthis* they see the photophores on the anterior edge of the mantle, and in Enoploteuthinae and Ancistrocheirinae they can see the luminescence of special photophores located on the funnel side adjacent to the head (Fig. 43 S). Cranchiids can adopt almost any position, and their light-sensitive vesicles look both upward and downward. It is, however, unclear what they see, because the light-sensitive vesicles have no dioptric apparatus and are only able to differentiate light from darkness and probably evaluate the intensity of the light. It was suggested by R. Young (1972b, 1973, 1977, 1978; Young, Roper & Walters, 1979) that the main function of the light-sensitive vesicles in mesopelagic squids and sepiolids is to match the intensity of luminescence of their own photophores with the intensity of incident (daylight) radiation that is necessary for successful camouflage. The intensity of luminescence of the photophores changes until the strength of the signal coming to the brain from the ventral light-sensitive vesicles that perceive the animal's own luminescence equalizes with the strength of the signal coming from the dorsal photophores perceiving the incident light. This hypothesis has been proved

by a number of experiments and also by the fact that large differently structured organs are mainly peculiar to species inhabiting in daytime the lower mesopelagic zone at depths from 400 to 800 m, whereas small organs of simple structure are peculiar to the epipelagic and bathypelagic species. But such an explanation does not relate to octopuses, cuttlefishes, loliginids, ommastrephids, *Spirula,* and *Bathyteuthis,* whose light-sensitive bodies are located so that the light of their own photophores does not reach them, or, of course, to *Vampyroteuthis,* whose light-sensitive vescicles are able to look only inside of the mantle (R. Young, 1972). Among the octopuses, the largest epistellar bodies are found not in the mesopelagic *Amphitretus* and the bathypelagic Bolitaenidae and *Vitreledonella,* though theirs are larger than those in the sublittoral *Octopus* and epipelagic *Argonauta,* but in the abyssal *Cirroteuthis* and abyssopelagic *Cirrothauma* (J. Young, 1977), where they reach 1.5 mm in size.

There is no doubt that the functions of the light-sensitive vesicles in cephalopods are diverse and probably differ in different species, but it is most probable that their main function is to give the animal an idea on the general level of illumination in the surrounding water and of long-term changes (seasonal, for example) of illumination. Such information may "start" the process of sexual maturation at corresponding changes of the photoperiod and initiate seasonal migrations of nektonic and nektobenthic species.

Among other possible functions of these organs may be, for example, the perception of bioluminescence of other luminous deepwater animals, but on the whole the functions of these organs are as enigmatic as the functions of their analogues in fishes, amphibians, and reptiles—the pineal or parietal organ called sometime "the third eye."

Statocysts (Fig. 12 H,I). A pair of statocysts is situated in the occipital part of the cartilaginous head capsule. A statocyst is the organ for perceiving the position of the animal relative to gravity (the organ of balance) and angular and linear acceleration. The structure of the statocysts in squids and cuttlefishes is similar although different in details, while the statocysts of octopuses differ greatly.

The statocyst of an octopus (Fig. 12 H) is a round little sac filled with liguid (perilymph) and enclosed in the posterior part of the cartilaginous head capsule. Inside it is another little sac filled with endolymph. On its inner wall there are receptor hair cells. Some of them receive signals on the position of the octopus in the field of gravity (macula cells) and some receive the signals on accelerations at movement (crista cells). The other cells are dispersed in the statocyst wall.

The macula is an oval spot on the wall of a statocyst to which a calcareous (aragonite) statolith is attached. The longitudinal axis of the macula occupies a strictly vertical position. There is only one statolith, and it is comparatively large — in *Octopus vulgaris* its average mass is 0.9 mg. There are three cristae positioned rectangularly to one another: the longitudinal, transverse, and vertical. Each crista is divided into three sections innervated by special nerves. The receptor cells of each section form a functional unit, a cupula (9 cupulae total). The shape of the cupula resembles a segmented sail. A part of the crista is provided with one row of receptor cells, the other part — with two rows; the single-row and double-row sections alternate. The signals on angular and linear acceleration changes are perceived by each cupula separately and also are separately transmitted to the brain, thus reproducing the complete picture of the position and movements of the octopod body. The receptor cells of the macula and crista are fastened by cartilaginous supports that are outgrowths on the statocyst wall. On the side opposite to the macula there is a cartilaginous outgrowth of the statocyst wall — the anticrista — that protects the vertical crista against an abrupt inertial movement of the endolymph that could harm the delicate body when the octopus darts after prey. Near the longitudinal crista there is a Kölliker's canal — a small blind tube opening into the endolymph sac. Its function is enigmatic.

In squids and cuttlefishes (Fig. 12 I) the statocyst grows into the posterior part of the head capsule. The statocyst form is nearly triangular. Its wall is single-layered and filled with endolymph only. There are three maculae and three statoliths: a larger one (in the main macula) and two smaller statoliths. But even the larger statolith is smaller than the statolith of an octopus: in *Todarodes pacificus* its mass is about 0.05 mg. There are the same mutually perpendicular cristae, but the transverse crista is divided into two, instead of one anticrista there are 11-12: four or five cristae hooked at their ends (hamuli) and seven straight rod-like cristae in the middle. They break the fluid flow during the motion of the mollusc, thus accelerating the speed of reaction of the receptors.

It is posible that the anticristae are also receptors. There are four cupulae. Overall, the system of cristae, anticristae, and cupulae is similar to the system of semicircular canals in the inner ear of vertebrates. P. Stephens and J. Z. Young (1978, 1982) have suggested that the horizontal crista that forms an almost closed tunnel registers the angular accelerations at yawing (right and left turns), the longitudinal crista registers the movements in the rolling place ("starboard" and "port" lurchings), and the transverse crista registers the movements in the pitching plane and upward movements of the head and tail as perceived by different sections of this crista. The transverse crista probably also registers linear acceleration both forward and backward.

The structure of the statocyst, and particularly of the anticrista, varies in different species. Rod-like anticristae are well developed in nektonic and nektobenthic species. In *Spirula* the number of anticristae is reduced to nine. In cranchiids there are no rod-like anticristae at all and only three hooked anticristae. In the deepwater species the Kölliker's canal is elongated and widened; it has been supposed that it may perceive vertical displacements during diurnal migrations.

The structure of the statocyst in *Vampyroteuthis*, like the structure of the light-sensitive vesicles, is intermediate between that of octopod and decapod cephalopods. As in octopuses, there are internal and external sacs filled with endolymph and perilymph, but the crista is divided into four parts, the anticristae are numerous, and there are three maculae. The external sac has a spacious posterior projection; a similar projection is found in some deepwater squids (Mastigoteuthidae, Cranchiidae). In Cirroteuthidae the structure of the statocyst is similar in general to its structure in Incirrata, but one or several anticristae may be present.

The statocyst structure reflects, to a certain extent, the mode of life of the molluscs: the slow-moving deepwater species are not able to determine great linear and angular accelerations, which they do not encounter, but they are probably able to determine the depth of their position. The statocyst of *Nautilus* is a thin-walled vesicle filled with endolymph. There is no statolith, but small calcareous grains are present.

The statoliths of dibranchiate cephalopods have a specific shape and, despite their small size (1-2 mm), are fairly rich in characters, allowing identification of at least the family and sometimes even the species. The irregularly elongated statocyst consists of dorsal and lateral domes, a beak, and a wing. The domes and the beak are rigid and semi-transparent; the opaque wing is softer. The stato-lith consists of small calcareous crystals—stato-conia. The statoliths grow along with the growth of the animal, but after a definite size has been gained their growth stops, so the statoliths in adult specimens are but a little larger than those in the young. On the statoliths of cephalopods there are numerous thin "growth rings" from which daily, fortnightly, and monthly have been identified. Thus the mollusc's age may be to some extent read from the statoliths.

Judging from the structure of the statocysts, the cephalopods must be entirely devoid of hearing, experiments on octopuses have proved that they are deaf. The cuttlefishes and squids receive low-frequency sounds corresponding to those received by the human ear. Cuttlefishes react upon a sound with a frequency of 180 Herz. A Pacific squid, *Todarodes pacificus*, positively reacts upon a clear tone of 600 Hz, the sound of a reversing ship (frequencies below 150 Hz were cut off by a filter), of rain falling onto the sea surface, or that produced by a feeding yellowtail. It has been shown experimentally that the transmission of such sounds through a subwater hydrophone arouses the "interest" of squids to the jigs of vertical squid long-lines and the catch increases by 30-60% and may even double. Pacific squids emit sounds when eating (a series of crunches produced by the mandibles stridulating upon one another), during fast swimming, and when reacting to the crunches issued by other squids and played by magneto-phone. It is unclear, however, what organ is used by the squids and cuttlefishes to perceive sounds—such a role might be played by the statolith and macula, which respond to low frequency vibration, or by the mechanoreceptors of the suckers sensing water oscillations. Very intense sounds may injure or even kill squids. It is supposed that sperm whales and other toothed whales can emit short bursts of sound intense enough to kill or debilitate their cephalopod prey.

Chemoreceptors and Mechanoreceptors. The most noticeable but nevertheless enigmatic sense organ is the olfactory organ. In squids, cut-tlefishes, and epipelagic octopuses it is a papilla located on the side of the head between the eye and the mantle aperture; in benthic octopuses it is a depression located in nearly the same place. Ob-viously, the olfactory papilla or pit is located in the path of water entering the mantle cavity. Judg-ing from its position, structure, and innervation it may be supposed that it really perceives some odors, but no distinct experimental proofs are available. In any case, those are not the odors of either food nor enemy, although octopuses perceive the smell of food such as crabs very well. Perhaps it perceives sex pheromones?

The taste receptors are located mainly on the rims of the suckers and on the lip. They are various epithelial ciliary receptor cells, and their number is enormous: up to several hundred per 1 mm² in the sucker rims. The cephalopods have a very delicate tasting ability, their sensitivity to some chemicals being 2-3 order of magnitude higher than that of a man. Also located in the rims and funnels of the suckers are numerous and vari-ous mechanoreceptors, particularly tactile recep-tors that react upon compression, tension, and bending. Up to a quarter of a million receptor cells are located on one arm of a medium-sized oc-topus. The close proximity of the taste and tactile receptors and their unity of representation in the brain allows one to speak about the presence of a special chemotactile ("taste and tactile") sense in cephalopods. It is highly developed in benthic forms, particularly in bottom-dwelling octopuses and in deepwater species. The benthic octopuses have a well-developed chemotactile memory, in-cluding the ability to find their way back home through a "taste and touch" method. By touch they differentiate the kinds of molluscs and dis-tinguish living molluscs from empty shells.

In addition, the cephalopods have numerous in-ternal and external proprioreceptors in the skin, muscles (especially in the stellate ganglion), in the sucker tissue, in the intestine, on the surface of the gills, and on the inner side of the cornea, among other places. The receptors in the skin and muscles allow the animals, even though devoid of a rigid skeleton, to receive information on their own pose, on the relative position of the parts of the body, and on the functioning of the muscles. The func-tion of many receptors has not yet been clarified.

It is interesting that the cephalopods are unable either to determine the mass of an object or to dif-ferentiate heavy objects from light ones.

The olfactory organs in *Nautilus* are the rhino-phores, a pair of small conical tubercles, each with a narrow pore, located under the eyes. The role of tactile and taste organs is played by the tentacles. The structure of the rhinophores is similar to the structure of the olfactory pit in octopuses. Two pairs of short tentacles located in front and behind each eye are equipped with mechanoreceptors. Their task is to protect the eye against mechanical damage by producing a danger signal upon contact with an alien body. The tips of the distal tentacles bear receptor cells similar to the cells of the taste papillae on the tongue. The taste and tactile receptors are particularly numerous on the tips of the long tentacles that drag over the ground behind the chambered nautilus as it swims over the bottom. The chambered nautilus uses them to search for prey (mainly carrion, sleeping fishes, and slow-moving benthic crustaceans). *Nautilus* also has an osphradium—a paired organ inside the mantle cavity that determines the chemical properties of the water entering the mantle cavity.

Endocrine and Neurosecretory Organs. The optic gland (absent in *Nautilus*) is the only organ of internal secretion known at present in cephalopods. The optic glands are small, round, paired bodies of a yellowish color. They lie on the optic tract between the optic lobes and the CNS. The optic gland consists of secretory and supporting cells. The hormone (or hormones) of the optic gland has gonadotropic properties—it stimulates the division of germinal cells; initiates the synthesis of yolk in the follicular cells of the ovary; controls the final stages of the development of oocytes and follicular cells; controls the secretory activity of the accessory nidamental glands; controls the growth and development of the oviducts, the ovidical glands, the spermatophoric complex, and the penis (but not the hectocotylus); governs the formation of spermatophores; and controls the process of mating. In female octopuses it also determines a sudden reduction or complete cessation of feeding before spawning, evokes the reflex of egg brooding, and determines almost imminent post-spawning death. If the optic glands in a female octopus are removed after oviposition, she leaves the eggs immediately, after a few days starts feeding again, may mate, and lives much longer than would an unoperated female (which dies soon after the hatching of the young) though she does not spawn again (Wodinsky, 1977). Probably the function of this hormone is the same in all dibranchiate cephalopods that spawn only once during their life.

The activity of the optic gland is controlled by an inhibiting nerve influence of the subpedunculate lobe of the brain. If an immature octopus is deprived of this part of the brain, a gonadotropic hormone starts to be secreted and the octopus matures much earlier than would occur in nature. The inhibiting effect of the subpedunculate lobe is regulated at least partially by vision and especially through changes of the length of day. Blinding an octopus or cutting its optic nerves leads to precocious maturation. On the whole, this system is similar to the hypothalamic-hypophyseal system of gonad activity control in vertebrates. The cephalopods, like the vertebrates, probably also have a feedback system from the gonad to the optic gland (hormonal), though the secretion of genital hormones by the gonad has not been proved. The gonadotropic hormone of the optic gland is unspecific (similar in different species and genera of octopuses) and is probably a steroid hormone whose chemical structure is still unknown. Its synthesis is not the only function of the optic gland—it also participates in the protection of the organism against alien proteins (antigens).

Neurosecretory cells are found in different places of the central and peripheral nervous system of the cephalopods. The neurohormones are secreted by the cells of the nervous system and are supplied into the blood. The most important neurosecretory organs are located in venous vessels: in the anterior part of the vena cava, in the eye (pharyngo-ophthalmic vein), and in the buccal sinuses. The neurohormone of the vena cava is secreted by the palliovisceral lobe of the brain and exercises a durable exciting effect upon the cephalopod heart; functionally it is similar to the epinephrine of vertebrates. The neurohormone is secreted in stress situations and accelerates the functioning of the heart. The hormone of the subpedunculate lobe of the brain is secreted into the pharyngo-ophthalmic vein. Its effect on the heart is similar (but not identical) to the effect of the neurohormone of the vena cava. Its main function is regulation of the blood pressure in the eye cavity. A strip of tissue—a prolongation of the subpedunculate lobe—passes into the anterior chamber of the eye and probably realizes the feedback in the system of regulation of intraocular pressure. The neurohormone of the buccal sinus is secreted by the lower buccal ganglion. The extremely active neurohormones are of great interest to pharmacology and may be very useful in the future for human medical purposes.

Regeneration and Autotomy

Cephalopods have a highly developed ability for regeneration of damaged or lost parts of the body. Wounds on the body heal rapidly without leaving a trace. This is one of the advantages of using the cephalopods as laboratory animals during the investigation of the CNS function by the removal of some parts of the brain. Lost arms and tentacles (such as those bitten off by a predator) regenerate completely and fairly fast. In young *Sepia officinalis,* for example, 5-14 days after an experimental removal of an arm a subspherical projection appears on the scar. It grows, turns into a cone, elongates, and after 17-25 days rudiments of suckers appear on it. After a month chromatophores appear, and by the second month after amputation the regenerated arm begins functioning. At first it differs from an intact arm by the small size of the suckers. A hectocotylized arm also regenerates. Animals with regenerated limbs are met fairly often. Occasionally the regeneration proceeds abnormally, particularly in octopuses: the regenerated arm starts to branch off or, on the contrary, fuses with the neighboring undamaged arm.

Full regeneration is observed only when the animal is kept under favorable conditions. Under poor conditions the damage site is infected by bacteria and fungi, the weakened animal fails to cope, necrotic dermatitis develops rapidly, and the animal dies. This should be taken into consideration in the breeding of cephalopods in mariculture. The beginning of sexual maturation lowers the regeneration capability; the organism switchs over resources from somatic growth to generative growth.

Autotomy—voluntary breaking off of a limb—is observed in a number of species of oceanic squids and pelagic octopuses. In mature males of the Argonautoidea a hectocotylized arm filled with sperm (Figs. 87 G; 88 B) is cast off at its base in mating and is transferred to the female, whereafter it is preserved in the female's mantle cavity. The tentacles of *Gonatopsis* and probably of *Lepidoteuthis* are autotomized by the end of the larval stage. In the females of *Histioteuthis, Chaunoteuthis, Joubiniteuthis,* and some Cranchiidae the tentacles are autotomized during sexual maturation or during spawning. *Mastigoteuthis* casts off the tentacles when in danger, for example, at the moment of capture; they break off at a definite place near the base. No regeneration of the broken limbs occurs in any of the above-mentioned forms.

The autotomy of parts of the 1st arms in females of *Tremoctopus* is a means for disorienting the enemy. The 1st arms have a wide lateral membrane decorated with longitudinal rows of large colored spots (Fig. 87 H,I). Autotomy occurs along a predetermined line perpendicular to the axis of the arm. The broken-off portion has one sucker and one to three colored spots. Being deprived of nervous control, it instantly widens up to the size of a handkerchief, and the bright spots suddenly blazing before predator's eyes on the transparent membrane distract and probably frighten the enemy, thus allowing the female to flee. Obviously these arms constantly grow lengthwise, but in adult females of *Tremoctopus* their ends are always broken off and they are invariably shorter than the 2nd arms; in the young they are longer.

No autotomy of arms is found in benthic octopuses, except in *Euaxoctopus, O. defilippi,* and a few others, but under poor conditions (such as in small aquaria with stagnant water) autophagy ("self-eating") is frequently observed. Gnawing of its own arms is a frequent prelude to death.

TAXONOMIC SECTION
Keys to Cephalopods of the World

Key to recent subclasses, orders, suborders, and superfamilies of the class Cephalopoda (Fig. 13)

1 (2). Firm outer shell with mother-of-pearl layer secreted by mantle present. Arms multiple (several dozens), slender, suckerless, in two circles. Head and arm bases dorsally covered by a fleshy hood closing aperture when animal retracts into shell. Funnel not fused ventrally. Two pairs of gills. . . . .

. . . .**Subclass Nautiloidea. Order Nautilida.**
One family: Nautilidae; genus: *Nautilus*
(see subhead **1.** and **1.1.**)

2 (1). Shell internal or absent. If external shell present (female *Argonauta*), shell very fragile, without mother-of-pearl layer, and secreted not by the mantle but by tips of dorsal arm pair; animal easily extracted from shell. 8 or 10 appendages, disposed in single circle, always armed with suckers and/or hooks. Head and arms not covered dorsally with hood. Funnel fused into conical tube. One pair of gills. . . . .

. . . .**Subclass Coleoidea. . .3**

3 (10). 10 appendages: 4 pairs of arms and one pair of tentacles (in rare cases tentacles may disappear in adult specimens—always present in larvae—but such specimens have typical squid form). Suckers stalked, with chitinous ring usually having denticulate edge; sometimes ring modified into hook. Arms commonly not connected by webs. Fins always present, variable but not paddle-like. Buccal funnel and buccal attachment present. There are as a rule, nuchal, mantle, and funnel cartilages. In some species mantle is fused with head and (less frequently) with funnel, but if so, mantle cavity communicates with exterior by three openings: one on ventral side of body and two on sides of head. **4**

4 (7). Fins oval or kidney-shaped, situated on sides of body or near posterior end or extend along entire mantle in form of marginal fin, but fins not connected. Tentacular stalks retractile, may be retracted into special pockets at bases of tentacles. Arms and tentacles armed only with suckers. Shell either a calcareous plate, calcareous spiral, thin chitinous pen-like plate, or absent altogether. Funnel cartilages simple; mantle edge near mantle cartilages straight, without protruding "angles." Oviduct unpaired, accessory nidamental glands present. All radular teeth unicuspid or radula absent. . . . .

. . . .**Order Sepiida. . .5**

5 (6). Shell in form of spirally coiled, round cross-sectioned calcareous "horn" in posterior end of body. Large luminous organ lying between fins. Arms short, with broad web, both ventral arms hectocotylized. Radula absent. Mesopelagic animals. . . . .**Suborder Spirulina**
One family: Spirulidae; genus: *Spirula*
(see subhead **2.1.1.**)

6 (5). Shell not coiled spirally and not shifted to posterior part of mantle, sometimes absent. No unpaired posterior photophore. Fins not at posterior end of body. Radula present. Usually benthic animals. . . . .**Suborder Sepiina**
(see subhead **2.1.2.**)

7 (4). Fins located at posterior part of body or along the entire mantle and, as a rule, merge along midline or near posterior end. Tentacular stalks not retractile. Many species with hooks on club and/or arms. Shell never calcified, represented by thin, horny, pen-like or sagittate gladius (very rarely gladius absent). Small projections ("angles") located on anterior edge of mantle near mantle cartilages; ventral mantle edge between these projections slightly excavated. Central radular tooth tricuspid (very rarely unicuspid). . . . .

. . . .**Order Teuthida. . .8**

8 (9). Anterior eye chamber closed (myopsid-type eye). Arm suckers always in two rows, club suckers in four rows, no hooks. Only left oviduct developed. Accessory nidamental glands present. Left or both ventral arms hectocotylized. No external photophores. . . . .**Suborder Myopsida**
(see subhead **2.2.1.**)

9 (8). Anterior eye chamber open (oegopsid-type eye). Armament of arms and tentacles may be different; many species with hooks. As a rule, both oviducts developed. No accessory nidamental glands. Hectocotylization present or absent. Many species with photophores on external surface of body, head, appendages, and/or on ventral surface of eyeball. . . . .**Suborder Oegopsida**
(see subhead **2.2.2.**)

10 (3). Four pairs of arms. Suckers without chitinous rings. Arms commonly connected by more or less deep web. Fins absent or short and paddle-like, situated on mantle sides. No buccal funnel and buccal attachment. Mantle always fused with head in occipital area but, as a rule, not fused with funnel. Mantle and funnel cartilages, if present, simple, in form of tubercle and pit. Mantle cavity connected with exterior in most cases by one opening at ventral side of body, rarely by two, one on each side **11**

11 (12). With special additional appendages – pair of long, thin, thread-like suckerless filaments retractable into pockets – located on outer side of web between 1st and 2nd arms. Only one pair of fins (but larvae may have two pairs, one disappearing by end of larval stage) of elongated oval shape. Great number of small simple photophores and pair of large external photophores of composite structure present. Arm suckers in one row, 2 rows of cirri parallel to sucker row. Proximal parts of arms without suckers. Gladius a wide, very thin plate. Deepwater (bathypelagic) animals . . . .**Order Vampyromorpha**

One family: Vampyroteuthidae; genus: *Vampyroteuthis* (see subhead **2.3.**)

12 (11). No such filaments. Fins either one pair or absent. No external photophores of composite structure; only a few species with simple photophores. Suckers in 1-2 rows, sessile (rarely stalked). Gladius represented by a cartilaginous fin support, reduced to small cartilaginous rods, or absent . . . .
. . . .**Order Octopoda. . .13**

Note: It is possible to identify the octopod families directly by using the key under subhead **2.4.**

13 (14). One pair of paddle-like fins supported by U-, V-, or saddle-like cartilage. Arm suckers in one row flanked on each side by one row of cirri. Mantle opening very narrow, a slit around funnel base, sometimes obliterated. Web usually very deep, reaching tips of arms in some forms. Neither ink sac nor radula present. Only left oviduct developed. Deepwater benthic (rarely pelagic) animals . . . .**Suborder Cirrata**
(see subhead **2.4.1.**)

14 (13). Fins absent. Gladius reduced or absent. Arm suckers in 1-2 rows. No cirri. Mantle opening usually medium size or wide, sometimes reduced to two slits on sides of head. Web commonly not extending to tips of arms. Radula always present; ink sac present or absent. Both oviducts developed . . **Suborder Incirrata. . .15**

15 (16). Radula comb-like; rhachidian (central) tooth and 1st and 2nd lateral teeth multicuspid. Body gelatinous. Suckers in one row. Pelagic deepwater animals . . . .
. . .**Superfamily Bolitaenoidea (Ctenoglossa)** (see subhead **2.4.2.1.**)

16 (15). Radula not comb-like; rhachidian tooth and 1st and 2nd lateral teeth with 1-3 cusps. Body usually firm **17**

17 (18). Only terminal part of 3rd right or left arm hectocotylized. Mature hectocotylus does not break off from body. Males not dwarfs. Arm suckers in one or 2 rows. As a rule, benthic forms (except pelagic family Vitreledonellidae) . . . .
. .**Superfamily Octopodoidea (Heteroglossa)** (see subhead **2.4.2.2.**)

18 (17). Entire 3rd right arm hectocotylized; hectocotylus matures in special sac and is initially inconspicuous from outside, so male appears to have only 7 arms. Hectocotylus breaks off from body at mating. Males dwarfed, considerably smaller than females. Suckers always in 2 rows, at least at distal parts of arms. Pelagic (mainly epipelagic) animals . . . .
. . . .**Superfamily Argonautoidea** (see subhead **2.4.2.3.**)

1. Subclass Nautiloidea

1.1. Order Nautilida

The shells of Recent species of pearly nautilus are large, up to 20-25 cm in diameter, bilaterally symmetrical, and spirally coiled so only the last coil is visible from outside. The umbilicus is open or closed (Fig. 14). The outer surface of the shell is shiny, porcellaneous white, with curved radial reddish stripes. The inner surface is iridescent and pearly. A longitudinal section of the shell shows a spacious last (living) chamber that houses the mollusc body and numerous other (uninhabited) chambers serving as a hydrostatic apparatus. These uninhabited chambers are partly filled with fluid in life. Partitions between these chambers (septae) are perforated in the middle by a continuous tube (siphuncle) passing through all chambers from the very first to the last one. With the aid of the siphuncle the pearly nautilus can pump the fluid out of the chambers, thus compensating for the growth of shell weight with age.

The head of the pearly nautiluses is large, with large eyes of primitive structure, devoid of a lens

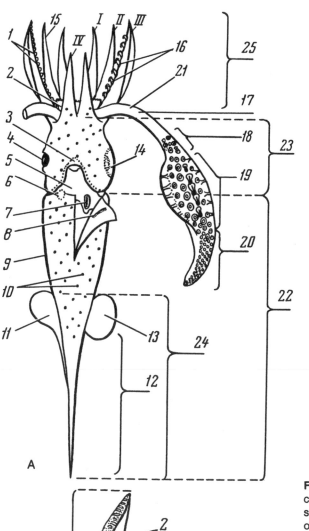

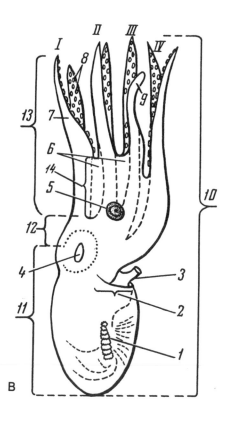

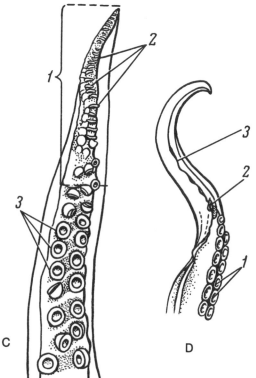

Fig. 13. Some characters used in the identification of cephalopods, and main measurements: A—squids: 1—suckers; 2—buccal membrane; 3—funnel groove; 4—oegopsid (open) eye; 5—funnel; 6—funnel-mantle fusion; 7, 8—funnel (7) and mantle (8) locking cartilages; 9—mantle; 10—photophores; 11—fin, posteriorly concave; 12—tail; 13—fin, posteriorly convex; 14—myopsid (closed) eye; 15—arms (I-IV pairs); 16—hooks; 17—tentacle; 18—carpus with fixing apparatus; 19—manus with suckers and hooks; 20—dactylus; 21—tentacular stalk; main measurements: 22—mantle length; 23—head length; 24—fin length (including tail); 25—arm length; B—octopuses: 1—gill lamellae (in mantle cavity); 2—mantle aperture (entrance to mantle cavity); 3—funnel; 4—eye; 5—ocellus (ocellar spot on web); 6—web; 7—arms (I-IV pairs); 8—suckers; 9—hectocotylus; main measurements: 10—total length; 11—mantle length; 12—head length; 13—arm length; 14—web depth; C—squid hectocotylus: 1—modified portion of hectocotylized arm; 2—lamellae; 3—normal suckers; D—octopus hectocotylus: 1—suckers; 2—calamus; 3—ligula; ligula should be measured from last sucker (A-C—from Roper, 1977; D—from Ivanov and Strelkov, 1949).

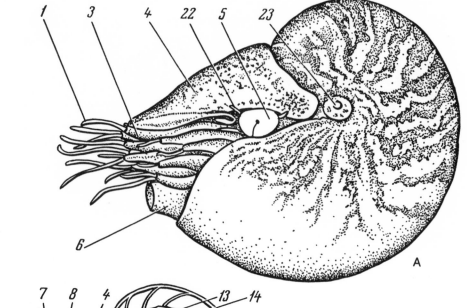

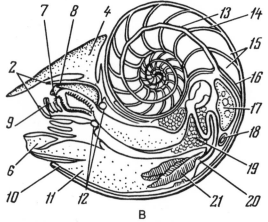

Fig. 14. *Nautilus macromphalus*, female: A—outer appearance; B—sagittal section: 1, 2—outer and inner tentacles; 3—tentacle sheaths; 4—hood; 5—eye; 6—funnel; 7—radula; 8, 9— upper (8) and lower (9) mandible; 10—mantle; 11—mantle cavity; 12—neural ganglia; 13—siphuncle; 14—septum; 15— cameral liquid; 16—posterior mantle end; 17—ovary; 18— heart; 19—digestive gland; 20—anus; 21—gill; 22—ocular tentacle; 23—umbilicus (from Ward et al., 1980).

Fig. 15.

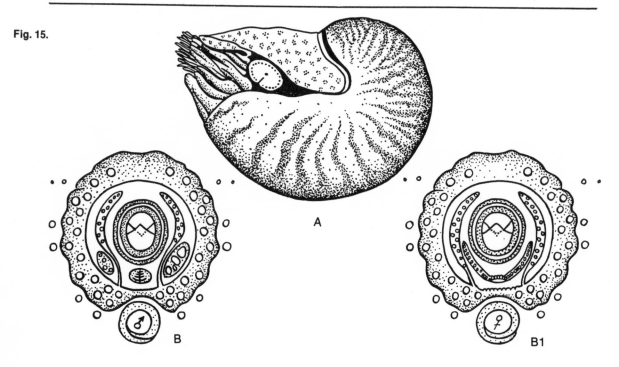

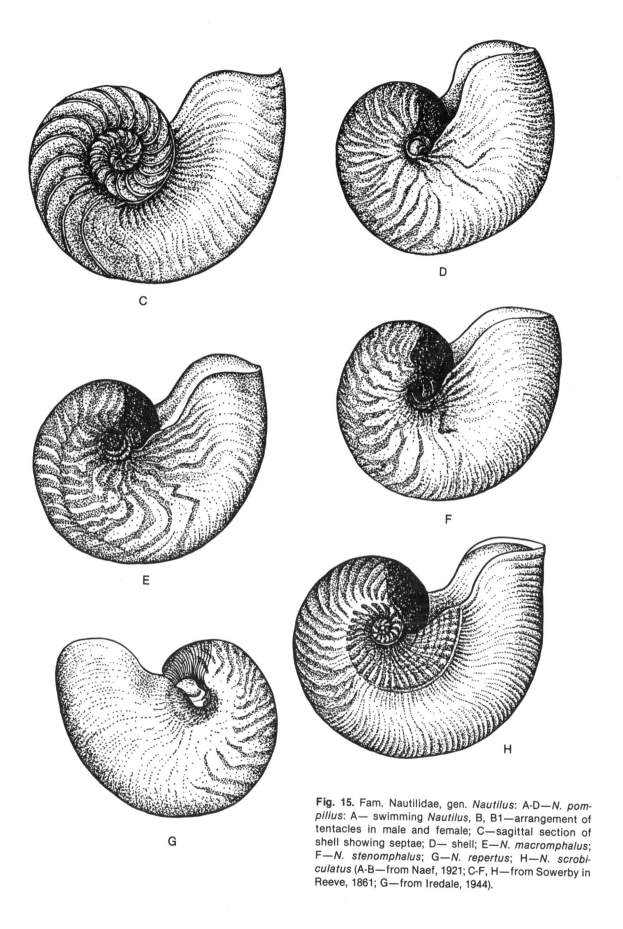

Fig. 15. Fam. Nautilidae, gen. *Nautilus*: A-D—*N. pompilius*: A— swimming *Nautilus*, B, B1—arrangement of tentacles in male and female; C—sagittal section of shell showing septae; D— shell; E—*N. macromphalus*; F—*N. stenomphalus*; G—*N. repertus*; H—*N. scrobiculatus* (A-B—from Naef, 1921; C-F, H—from Sowerby in Reeve, 1861; G—from Iredale, 1944).

and vitreous body and with a small pupil. The mantle conical, coriaceous, slightly muscular, and devoid of chromatophores. The slender, cirrus-like arms are suckerless and arranged in two circles, an outer circle consisting of 38 prehensile arms and an inner circle of 24 (in males) or 48-52 (in females) oral arms. The bases of the dorsal arms merge with a large, thick hood that closes the shell's mouth when the *Nautilus* retracts. There are two ocular (eye) tentacles on each side of head. In the male the lower part of the inner arm circle is modified on the right or (more often) left side into a copulatory organ (spadix). A seminal receptacle is located in a special sac under the buccal cone in females.

The funnel is not fused into a tube — its lower edges are simply coiled one around the other. There is no funnel organ. The beak is strong. The radula consists of 11 longitudinal rows of teeth. There are two pairs of gills, 4 auricles, and 4 renal sacs. An ink sac and luminous organs are absent. The nervous system is of a primitive structure, and the brain consists of 3 pairs of ganglia. No stellate ganglion or giant nerve fibers are present. An osphradium is present. Nidamental and accessory nidamental glands are present. Only one (right) oviduct. Eggs large, benthic. Development direct.

One Recent genus: **Nautilus Linné, 1758.** Type species: *N. pompilius* Linné, 1758. The 3-6 species inhabit the Indo-Malayan zoogeographic subregion of the Indo-West Pacific and also the area from Australia to New Caledonia.

Nautiluses are predatory animals. They live near the bottom not far off the coast at depths from several dozen to 600-700 m but rarely approach the shore (in the cold season only). They are active at night, when they feed on sedentary benthic prey, especially spiny lobsters, prawns, fishes, and carrion. Nautiluses find their prey mainly by smell. Their eggs are very large, up to 40 mm long (with envelope), and are shed singly, supposedly into shallow water at the bottom. A female lays only 10 eggs at intervals of nearly 2 weeks.

Empty shells of pearly nautiluses are lighter than water and may drift a long time on the surface and beach thousands of miles from their original habitats. This explains records from Madagascar, South Africa, Japan, Tasmania, and New Zealand.

Nautiluses are the objects of local fisheries in the Philippines and in Melanesia. They are caught with the aid of fishing baskets and traps with fish or meat as bait. Their meat is edible, but it is the shell that is of main value, as it is used in the production of souvenirs and decorations.

Reviews: Stenzel, 1964; Hamada et al., 1980.

Key to species of the genus *Nautilus*

1 (4). Shell smooth, with closed umbilicus.....2
2 (3). Colored stripes on shell reach umbilicus and pass more or less far onto outer lateral walls of last chamber. Shell diameter to 18 cm...............................**N. pompilius** Linné, 1758
(= *N. alumnus* Iredale, 1944) (Fig. 15 A-D). Nicobar Is., Andaman Is., Sulu Sea, Celebes Sea, South China Sea, Philippines, Moluccas, New Guinea and nearby islands, extreme northern Australia, Melanesia, and western Polynesia to Fiji and Samoa.

A separate species or (more probably) subspecies is **N. (pompilius) belauensis Saunders, 1981,** distinguished by its larger size. The shell has striated growth lines and the coloration is as in *N. pompilius*. Shell length to 18 to 23 cm. It lives in the vicinity of Palau (Belau, southern Micronesia).

3 (2). Color stripes conspicuous only on periphery of shell, not reaching umbilicus nor passing onto outer lateral walls of last chamber. Shell length to 20-25 cm..**N. repertus** Iredale, 1944
(Fig. 15 G). Southern and southwestern Australia. This is probably a subspecies of *N. pompilius*. Specimens with similar coloration are met among samples of typical *N. pompilius*.

4 (1). Shell smooth or wrinkled, with open umbilicus.....................................5
5 (6). Shell smooth, with microscopic growth lines. Umbilicus rather narrow, its edge without a keel. Color lines on shell reach umbilicus and pass onto outer lateral walls of last chamber. Shell length to 18 cm...........................**N. macromphalus** Sowerby, 1849
(Fig. 15 E). New Caledonia and nearby islands.
6 (5). Shell surface wrinkled, with sinusoidal radial folds. Umbilicus wide, its edge with a distinct keel. Color stripes on shell conspicuous only on periphery of last chamber, not passing to its outer lateral walls or reaching umbilicus. Shell length to 19-20 cm.....................**N. scrobiculatus** Solander, 1786
(= *N. umbilicatus* Lamarck, 1822) (Fig. 15 H).

Moluccas, New Guinea, New Britain, New Ireland, Solomons, and Torres Strait.

The key does not include the doubtful species *N. stenomphalus* Sowerby, 1849 (Fig. 15 F), whose taxonomic status needs confirmation. It resembles *N. pompilius* but its umbilicus is very narrow, much narrower than in *N. macromphalus*. The color stripes do not reach the umbilicus. It has been found near New Caledonia, in the Torres Strait, and near the Great Barrier Reef of Australia.

2. Subclass Coleoidea

The shell is internal, chitinous, rarely calcareous, and occasionally absent. The mantle is muscular, but in deepwater forms the musculature degenerates and is replaced by gelatinous connective tissue. Chromatophores are well developed and complicated. Photophores are often present. The eyes are large, complicated, and have a lens, iris, cornea, and vitreous body. Statocysts are also highly developed. Osphradia are absent. These are 4 or 5 pairs of appendages that are muscular and have suckers that are often equipped with chitinous rings. In many (but by far not in all) species one or 2 arms of the male are modified for transferrring spermatophores to the female. The funnel is a muscular conical tube except in deepwater species, and its dorsal side bears a funnel organ. Fast-swimming forms are also equipped with a funnel valve. The mantle is either fused with the head or funnel or is joined to them by a system of cartilages. The beak is strong and well developed. The radula consists of 7 longitudinal rows of teeth (one genus has 5 rows), but in some planktophagous forms, mainly from deepwater, the radula is reduced or absent. There are one pair of gills, 2 auricles, 2 renal sacs, and 2 branchial hearts. An ink sac may be present or absent. The nervous system is highly developed, with a compact brain consisting of several ganglia and lobes. The stellate ganglion is well developed. Some nektonic forms have a system of giant nerve fibers innervating the mantle muscles. The gonad is unpaired; male genital ducts as a rule are unpaired (paired in rare cases) and in females may be paired or unpaired. The eggs are small or large; if small, the development includes larval stages and metamorphosis; if large, development is direct. The subclass includes marine and oceanic predators that may be benthic, nektonic, planktonic, nektobenthic, or benthopelagic. They are found in all seas and oceans with full salinity, from the Arctic to the Antarctic and from the intertidal to abyssal zones.

Locomotion is by different methods: with the aid of water ejection through the funnel accompanied by abrupt contractions of the mantle; with the aid of muscular fins; with the aid of web (umbrella) connecting the arms (pulsating like a jellyfish). Some octopuses can "walk" on arm-tip. The main diet in nektonic species is fishes, macroplankton, and other cephalopods; in benthic species actively moving bottom animals are taken; and in planktonic and semiplanktonic species zooplankton is the major food. Vision or the chemotactile sense are used to find prey. Most are gregarious animals. The majority of species grow rapidly, mature at the age of one or 2 years, and die after their first spawning.

2.1. Order Sepiida
[see couplet 4 (7) in the first key of the taxonomic part]

2.1.1. Suborder Spirulina, Family Spirulidae

Animal small, mantle length to 4.5 cm. Body fusiform, skin smooth, but mantle under skin shagreened. Mantle firm, muscular, not fused with head, dorsal edge with one and ventral edge with 2 tongue-like projections from between which the funnel protrudes. Locking apparatus simple. In young *Spirula* head may be retracted entirely into mantle, but in adults retractile only halfway. Arms short, connected by wide web. Arm suckers small, approximately equal in size, in several rows (up to 6 at arm bases). Tentacles long, slender, partially retractile. Club slightly widened, club suckers small, of similar size, arranged in several rows (up to 12). Eyes large, of oegopsid type, with open anterior chamber. Funnel short, partially covered by anterior edge of mantle. Fins small, round, situated at posterior end of mantle almost perpendicular to longitudinal axis of body, not connected to each other. A large photophore surrounded by annular fold of skin is located between the fins. Body coloration red-brown.

Shell white, calcareous, porcellaneous, multichambered, round in cross-section, resembling a cornucopia, a loosely coiled spiral of approximate-

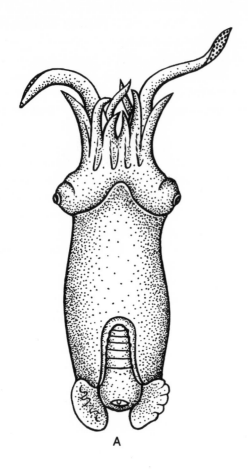

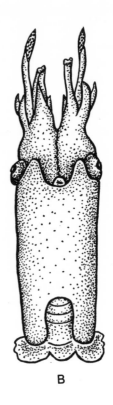

A

B

Fig. 16. Fam. Spirulidae, gen. *Spirula, Spirula spirula*: A—female; B—male (A—from Chun, 1915, after Clarke, 1966; B—from Clarke, 1970).

ly 2.5 whorls, bent ventrally. Shell lies in posterior half of mantle and is visible from both dorsal and ventral sides (in old animals skin sometimes breaks above shell). First chamber spherical, the rest remaining barrel-shaped. Chambers separated by septa perforated at ventral edge by siphuncle. Shell serves as hydrostatic apparatus and can withstand pressures up to 200 atmospheres.

Radula absent. Only left oviduct developed. In males both ventral arms hectocotylized, much longer than the others, not connected by web, devoid of suckers, and greatly modified. Right hectocotylized arm is grooved, concave from outside, with a spoon-like broadening, a sharp tip, and two finger-like outgrowths; left hectocotylized arm round in cross-section, with two spoon-like and one finger-like outgrowths and with a few soft spines at end. Seminal receptacle located on buccal membrane of female. Eggs benthic.

Development long, without metamorphosis.

One genus: **Spirula Lamarck, 1801**; one species: **S. spirula (Linné, 1758)** (Fig. 16). Tropical Atlantic and Indo-West Pacific mesopelagic nerito-oceanic species. *Spirula* lives above slopes and is most often met in the waters of Indonesia, Melanesia, southeastern Africa, between the Canary Islands and northwestern Africa, in the Caribbean Sea, and in the Gulf of Mexico. Empty shells are carried by currents extremely far from the natural habitat. These are gregarious animals. During daytime they inhabit depths of 500-1000 m; at night they are found mainly in 100-300 m. Eggs are deposited at the bottom in the bathyal zone, and the young first live near the bottom. The normal swimming position is head-down. Longevity is 1-1.5 years.

Reviews: Clarke, 1966, 1967; Bruun, 1943, 1955.

2.1.2. Suborder Sepiina — Cuttlefishes

Shell a thick calcareous plate, chitinous "pen," or absent. Shell lies in the layer of muscles on dorsal side of mantle from anterior to posterior end, inconspicuous from outside. Mantle not fused with funnel, but in some cases fused with head at occipital area. Body oval, slightly flattened dorsoventrally. Head not retracted into mantle. Fins located on lateral surface of mantle in form of either a narrow marginal fringe or semicircular or kidney-shaped; fins not united posteriorly. Longitudinal axis of fins subparallel to longitudinal axis of body. No external luminous organs. Sometimes luminous organ present inside mantle on ink sac. Eyes of myopsid type, with closed anterior chamber. Arms commonly short, with weakly developed or no web. Suckers never modified into hooks. Suckers on arms and club often of unequal size. Tentacles retractile, usually short and powerful. One, 2, or several pairs of arms hectocotylized. Radula well developed, teeth unicuspid. Only left oviduct developed. Eggs benthic, developing for a long time. Young develop without metamorphosis, and usually without a pelagic stage. Mainly benthic, but several genera lead pelagic mode of life.

4 families, 19 genera, 150-180 species.

Key to families of the suborder Sepiina

1 (2). Shell in form of thick oval or rhomboidal calcareous plate. Body massive; head somewhat smaller than mantle. Mantle not fused with head at occipital area, its dorsal anterior edge with tongue-like projection. Fins narrow, running laterally along entire length of mantle. . . . .
. . . . **Family Sepiidae**
(see subhead **2.1.2.1.**)
2 (1). Shell rudimentary or absent. Mantle small; head frequently only a bit smaller than mantle. Dorsal anterior edge of mantle without tongue-like projection, sometimes fused with head. Fins semicircular or kidney-shaped, placed in middle of mantle or nearer posterior end. **3**
3 (4). Mantle elongate, slightly narrowed and bluntly pointed posteriorly. Fins positioned in rear half of mantle. Anterior edge of mantle not fused with head. In posterior part of mantle on dorsal side is an oval rough area, an attachment organ that holds the cephalopod to substrate. Both dorsal arms hectocotylized. Very small,

mantle length not over 25 mm. . . . .
. . . .**Family Idiosepiidae**
(see subhead **2.1.2.4.**)
4 (3). Mantle oval, widely rounded posteriorly. Fins located in middle or somewhat posterior from middle of mantle. No attachment organ. One ventral arm or arms of other pairs hectocotylized. **5**
5 (6). Web between 3rd and 4th arms encircles bases of tentacles on outside and inside, forming a type of cutaneous sac. Fins with broad bases and slightly developed "earlets." Mantle fused with head at occipital area; no nuchal cartilage. Left ventral arm hectocotylized. . . . .
. . . .**Family Sepiadariidae**
(see subhead **2.1.2.3.**)
6 (5). Web between 3rd and 4th arms envelops tentacle bases on outside only, without forming sac. Fins with short bases and well developed "earlets." Fin length noticeably greater than length of fin base. Both dorsal arms hectocotylized, sometimes lateral arm pairs also modified. In some species hectocotylization almost inconspicuous. . . . .**Family Sepiolidae**
(see subhead **2.1.2.2.**)

2.1.2.1. Family Sepiidae — True Cuttlefishes

Body dorsoventrally flattened. Mantle elongately oval, much larger than head. Anterior dorsal edge of mantle with tongue-like projection. Fins narrow, extending from anterior to posterior edge of mantle, not connected. Shell (sepion) (Fig. 17 A) lies under skin on dorsal side of mantle from anterior to posterior edge of mantle. Shell a thick oval, lanceolate, or rhomboidal calcareous plate, sometimes with a spine (rostrum) at posterior end. Numerous thin, narrow, oblique septa can be seen from below in posterior part of sepion, making sepion appear as if transversely striated (this part of sepion is known as the phragmocone). Septa supported by thick network of tiny transverse calcareous rods. Periodicity of formation of septa dependent on temperature; under tropical conditions they are formed daily, so age of cuttlefish can be determined by number of transverse striae, the front septa the newest. Undersurface of sepion concave in posterior half and, together with lateral edges of shell, forming a "fork" (inner cone). Shell bordered by lateral ridge that is wide in posterior half and narrow in anterior half of sepion.

Eyes of myopsid type, with closed anterior chamber. Arms with 2-4 rows of suckers. 4th arms considerably broader than the others, with muscular swimming membrane. Left ventral arm hectocotylized. Tentacles retractile, club with 4-6 or more rows of suckers that are sometimes considerably unequal in size. Ink sac well developed. All radular teeth unicuspid.

Benthic, inhabiting continental shelf, sometimes reaching upper bathyal zone. Active at night, but usually sit on bottom during day. Some species cover themselves with sand. 2 genera, 90-110 species.

Reviews: Adam & Rees, 1966; Adam, 1979; Roeleveld, 1972.

Key to genera and subgenera of the family Sepiidae

1 (6). No large subcutaneous gland in posterior part of mantle on dorsal side. Upper side of fins has no bright color spots. Inner cone of shell well developed. Mantle cartilage oval (Fig. 17 B) . . . . **Genus *Sepia* Linné, 1758**. . .2

2 (3). Shell thick, entirely calcareous, tongue-like or lanceolate, anteriorly rounded, sometimes extended posteriorly into spine. Shell almost as long as mantle. Dorsal anterior edge of mantle usually with large tongue-like projection. No cutaneous pores on ventral side of mantle . . . .
. . . . **Subgenus *Sepia* (s. str.)**
(= *Acanthosepion* Rochebrune, 1884; *Ascarosepion* Rochebrune, 1884; *Doratosepion* Rochebrune, 1884; *Lophosepion* Rochebrune, 1884; *Rhombosepion* Rochebrune, 1884; *Spathidosepion* Rochebrune, 1884; *Andreasepia* Grimpe, 1922; *Parasepia* Naef, 1923; *Platysepia* Naef, 1923; *Eusepia* Naef, 1923; *Amplisepia* Iredale, 1926; *Arctosepia* Iredale, 1926; *Crumenasepia* Iredale, 1926; *Decorisepia* Iredale, 1926; *Fiscisepia* Iredale, 1926; *Glyptosepia* Iredale, 1926; *Mesembrisepia* Iredale, 1926; *Ponderisepia* Iredale, 1926; *Solitosepia* Iredale, 1926; *Tenuisepia* Cotton, 1932; *Blandosepia* Iredale, 1940). 80-100 species. Large or medium size, rarely small, cuttlefishes that inhabit the eastern Atlantic from the North Sea to southern Africa and in Indo-West Pacific from the Red Sea to southern Australia and the Japanese Islands, eastward to the Marshall Islands, Guam, and Fiji. Shells of dead cuttlefishes are carried great distances by the currents. On the shores of southern Primorye and the South Kurile Islands (USSR) one may find shells of cuttlefishes carried by currents from Japan, and on the coasts of the Caribbean Sea and Gulf of Mexico rarely are found shells carried from western Africa.

3 (2). Shell slightly narrowed anteriorly and widened or narrowed posteriorly, shorter than mantle. Dorsal anterior edge of mantle straight, without tongue-like projection. Small, mantle length 2-7 cm **4**

4 (5). Shell conspicuously shorter than mantle, usually 75-85% of mantle length, rhomboidal, obtusely acute anteriorly and angular (rarely rounded) laterally. Mantle unusually thick, fins positioned noticeably above midline of sides. Club suckers very unequal in size, disposed in 5-6 longitudinal rows; arm suckers in 4 rows . . . .
. . . .**Subgenus *Metasepia* Hoyle, 1885**
(Fig. 17 D-I). Type species: *S. (M.) pfefferi* Hoyle, 1885. Two species in the Indo-Malayan subregion of Indo-West Pacific.

a (b). Shell obtusely acute at posterior end, without spine or with chitinous (not calcareous) spine. 3-4 median club suckers enormously enlarged, occupying all median part of club. Head and mantle smooth . . . .
. . . .**S. (M.) pfefferi Hoyle, 1885**
(Fig. 17 D-F). Western, northern, and northeastern Australia, in the south to Fremantle and Capricorn Islands. Mantle length to 6 cm.

b (a). Shell extends posteriorly into sharp spine whose dorsal side bears small chitinous plate. 7-9 enlarged suckers on club: 4-5 suckers in second row (from dorsal side) and 3-4 in third row. Head, dorsum, and sides of mantle of live cuttlefish with tubercles, warts, and triangular skin projections . .
. . . .**S. (M.) tullbergi Appellöf, 1886**
(Fig. 17 G-I). From southern Honshu, Japan, to Taiwan and Hong Kong, on the shelf. Mantle length to 7 cm.

5 (4). Shell not considerably shorter than mantle (85-90% mantle length), narrowed anteriorly and much widened and rounded posteriorly, very thin, slightly calcified, without spine. Mantle of normal thickness, fins usually in middle of sides. Club suckers of similar size. Arm suckers in 2 rows . . . .
. . . .**Subgenus *Hemisepius* Steenstrup, 1875**
(= *Hemisepion* Rochebrune, 1884) (fig. 17 J-L). Type species: *S. (H.) typica* (Steenstrup, 1875). 2 species. Southern Africa. Mantle length to 2-3 cm.

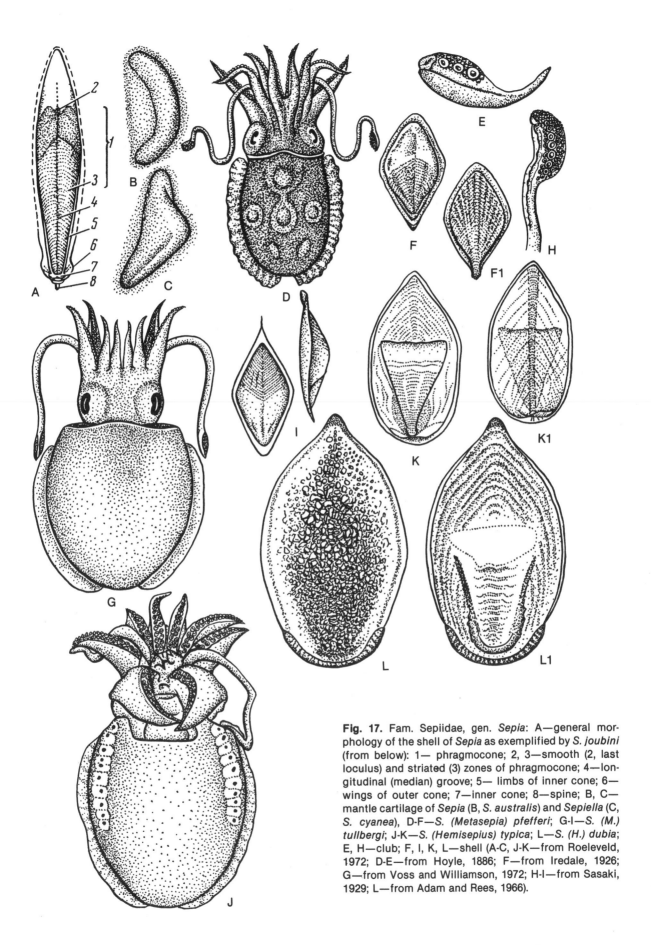

Fig. 17. Fam. Sepiidae, gen. *Sepia*: A—general morphology of the shell of *Sepia* as exemplified by *S. joubini* (from below): 1— phragmocone; 2, 3—smooth (2, last loculus) and striated (3) zones of phragmocone; 4—longitudinal (median) groove; 5— limbs of inner cone; 6—wings of outer cone; 7—inner cone; 8—spine; B, C—mantle cartilage of *Sepia* (B, *S. australis*) and *Sepiella* (C, *S. cyanea*), D-F—*S. (Metasepia) pfefferi*; G-I—*S. (M.) tullbergi*; J-K—*S. (Hemisepius) typica*; L—*S. (H.) dubia*; E, H—club; F, I, K, L—shell (A-C, J-K—from Roeleveld, 1972; D-E—from Hoyle, 1886; F—from Iredale, 1926; G—from Voss and Williamson, 1972; H-I—from Sasaki, 1929; L—from Adam and Rees, 1966).

a (b). A row of approximately 12 cutaneous pores on anterior ventral half of mantle along bases of fins. Shell chitinized dorsally, inner cone slightly developed . . . .
. . . .*S. (H.) typica* **(Steenstrup, 1875)**
(Fig. 17 J, K). South Africa from Saldanha Bay to Durban, on the shelf.

b (a). No cutaneous pores on ventral side of mantle. Shell calcareous on dorsal side, inner cone well developed. . . . .
. . . .*S. (H.) dubia* **Adam & Rees, 1966**
(Fig. 17 L). Cape of Good Hope, South Africa.

6 (1). A large gland whose duct opens between the fins in form of a red spot lies under skin in posterodorsal part of mantle. Row of several large brightly colored spots extending along fin base. Shell narrow tongue-like, without spine, inner cone reduced, outer cone represented by wide chitinized (not calcareous) border around posterior end of shell. Club suckers of equal size, small. Mantle cartilage triangular (Fig. 17 C). . . .
. . . . **Genus *Sepiella* Gray, 1849**
(= *Diphtherosepion* Rochebrune, 1884). Type species: *S. ornata* (Rang, 1837). 6-7 species. Off western and southern Africa and in Indo-West Pacific.

KEYS TO *SEPIA* SPECIES BY GEOGRAPHIC AREA

I. *Eastern Atlantic (North Sea to Angola, including the Mediterranean)*

1 (8). Club suckers conspicuously unequal. Shell with spine. 2

2 (3). Fins starting directly at anterior edge of mantle and extending beyond edge noticeably, reaching anteriorly to level of posterior edge of eyes; fins widen at posterior part of mantle. Arm suckers in 4 rows. 5 longitudinal rows of club suckers, 5-7 suckers of median row conspicuously larger than others, but with no sharp difference between enormous median and small remaining suckers. Shell width in males 30-40% of shell length, in females 33-42% of length. Posterior part of shell widened, edges of outer cone wide, shell outlines sometimes slightly concave on sides. . . . .*S. (S.) officinalis* **Linné, 1758**
(Fig. 18 A-D). From the Shetland Islands, southern Norway (approaches in warm years), and southern part of the North Sea to the Cape of Good Hope and along southeastern coast of Africa to Mozambique. All over the shelf, mainly upper sublittoral. 4 subspecies: *S. o. officinalis* L. (= *S. filliouxi* Lafont, 1868)–from the North Sea to

Cape Verde Islands, mantle length to 27-30 cm; *S. o. mediterranea* Ninni, 1884–the Mediterranean and Adriatic Seas, mantle length to 30 cm; *S. o. hierredda* Rang, 1837–coast of western Africa from Cape Blanc to northern Namibia, mantle length to 50 cm (weight to 9-12 kg); *S. o. vermiculata* Quoy & Gaimard, 1832–southern Africa from the mouth of the Olifants River to Mozambique (Delagoa Bay), drifting shells to the mouth of the Zambezi River, mantle length to 22-24 cm (seldom 29 cm). A most important object of commercial fisheries, caught from the Gulf of Biscay to western Africa and in the Mediterranean.

3 (2). Fins starting a small distance from anterior edge of mantle, not exceeding mantle's front edge and not widening posteriorly. Shell width in males 23-33%, in females 26-35% of shell length. Posterior part of shell not widened. 4

4 (5). 2 rows of suckers on basal parts of arms. In central part of club 3 enormously large suckers occupy all of middle. Shell greatly narrowed posteriorly, spine very small (rather like a small calcareous ridge than a true spine). . . . .
. . . .*S. (S.) elegans* **d'Orbigny, 1826**
(Fig. 18 E-H). From western Scotland and the English Channel (drifting shells may reach the North Sea) to northern Namibia, and entire Mediterranean Sea. Outer shelf and uppermost bathyal. Mantle length to 9 cm.

5 (4). Arm suckers in 4 rows. Shell spine well developed, in preserved specimens often penetrating mantle and protruding outward. . . .6

6 (7). 5 very large suckers in central part of club, middle one largest. Shell gradually narrows anteriorly and posteriorly, shell width in males about 33%, in females about 33-35% of shell length. Dorsally pinkish or pale orange with slightly defined longitudinal groove. . . . .
. . . .*S. (S.) orbignyana* **Férussac, 1826**
(Fig. 18 I-L). From the Irish Sea and English Channel (drifting shells may reach the North Sea) to southern Angola, and entire Mediterranean Sea. Shelf (mostly outer) and uppermost bathyal. Mantle length to 14 cm. An object of a minor fishery.

7 (6). Suckers gradually increasing in size from lateral edges of club to third (from dorsal side) row, no drastically enlarged suckers. Shell gradually narrowing in anterior half, edges of posterior half subparallel. Shell width in males 23-30%, in females 26-33% of shell length. Dorsally white with rounded longitudinal keel. . . . . . .

..........*S. (S.) bertheloti* **d'Orbigny, 1838**

(= *S. mercatoris* Adam, 1937) (Fig. 18 M-O). From the Canary Islands and western Sahara to Angola. Shelf. Mantle length to 18 cm. Fished in negligible quantities.

8 (1). Club suckers small, almost equal in size. Shell without spine, almost rounded posteriorly. Surface of head and mantle rough, tuberculate. 8 oblique rows of club suckers. Shell width 38-46% of shell length. Shell abruptly narrowing anteriorly, sides of posterior half parallel. Wings of outer cone very wide...........................
...............*S. (S.) elobyana* **Adam, 1941**

(Fig. 18 P-R). From Cape Blanc to Gabon. Mantle length to 5 cm. Very rare.

II. *Southern Africa from Namibia to southern Mozambique*

1 (16). Club suckers subequal...............2

2 (9). Anterodorsal portion of mantle protrudes forward as a triangular projection covering posterior part of head. Club suckers in 8 longitudinal (oblique) rows................3

3 (6). 1st and 2nd arms with 2 rows of suckers. Shell without a spine, somewhat narrowed anteriorly 4

4 (5). Anteroventral edge of mantle with incision at funnel base. Shell very pointed anteriorly and angularly rounded posteriorly, limbs of inner cone flattened and lying on surface of phragmocone...........*S. (S.) insignis* **Smith, 1916**

(Fig. 19 A). From the Cape of Good Hope to Natal. Inner shelf. Mantle length to 6 cm.

5 (4). Anteroventral edge of mantle slightly concave. Shell angularly rounded anteriorly and gradually rounded posteriorly, limbs of inner cone swollen and bordering the posterolateral edges of phragmocone..................
.............*S. (S.) hieronis* **(Robson, 1924)**

(Fig. 19 B,C). Western coast of southern Africa from 19°S to the Cape of Good Hope, also Natal and southern Mozambique. Shelf (mainly outer) and upper bathyal, mostly at depths of 200-500 m. Mantle length to 7 cm. Specimens from the southern and eastern coasts of southern Africa differ somewhat in the shape of the shell.

6 (3). Arms with 4 rows of suckers. Shell oval, with spine................................7

7 (8). Buccal membrane with several small suckers. Shell gradually rounded anteriorly and narrowed posteriorly........................

...........*S. (S.) zanzibarica* **Pfeffer, 1884**

[see couplet 32 (33), Geographic Area III]

8 (7). Buccal membrane without suckers. Shell narrowed and bluntly pointed anteriorly, smoothly rounded posteriorly...............
............*S. (S.) acuminata* **Smith, 1916**

Natal, southern Mozambique, Kenya. Outer shelf and uppermost bathyal. Mantle length to 11 cm.

9 (2). Mantle anterodorsally convex without projection. Club suckers not in 8 rows. Shell without spine or with tubercle instead of spine.........
....**10**

10 (11). Club very long, occupying almost half of tentacle. Club suckers in approximately 24 longitudinal rows. Anterior ventral part of mantle without incision, smoothly concave. Arm suckers in 4 rows. Shell perfectly oval, limbs of inner cone very wide posteriorly and abruptly narrowing anteriorly. Obtuse tubercle on posterior end of shell........*S. (S.) simoniana* **Thiele, 1920**

(= *S. natalensis* Massy, 1925). From the Cape of Good Hope to Natal. Shells are found to the region north of the Olifants River mouth. Shelf, mainly inner. A common species. Mantle length to 18.5 cm.

11 (10). Club short, club suckers in 4-6 rows. Anterior side of mantle ventrally with incision at funnel base. Arm suckers in 2 rows. Shell not oval, without a tubercle on posterior end.....**12**

12 (15). Tips of 1st arms attenuated, finger-like, devoid of suckers. Shell chitinous or calcareous..
....**13**

13 (14). None or only a few papillae on mantle and top of head. Shell narrowly acuminate anteriorly, not calcified (?)......................
...............*S. (S.) robsoni* **(Massy, 1927)**

Off the Cape of Good Hope. Upper sublittoral. Mantle length 2 cm.

14 (13). Dorsal side of mantle, head, and arm bases densely beset by small cuticular papillae. Shell very thin, not calcified, widely oval, with slightly narrowed anterior and posterior (?) ends; anterior end of phragmocone convex...........
..............*S. (S.) faurei* **Roeleveld, 1972**

(Fig. 19 D-F). Southern Africa to the east of the Cape of Good Hope. Depth 170 m. Mantle length 2 cm.

15 (12). Ends of 1st arms normal, suckers reaching tips of arms......................
.......**Subgenus** *Hemisepius*, *S. (H.) typica* **(Steenstrup)** and *S. (H.) dubia* **Adam & Rees**

Fig. 18.

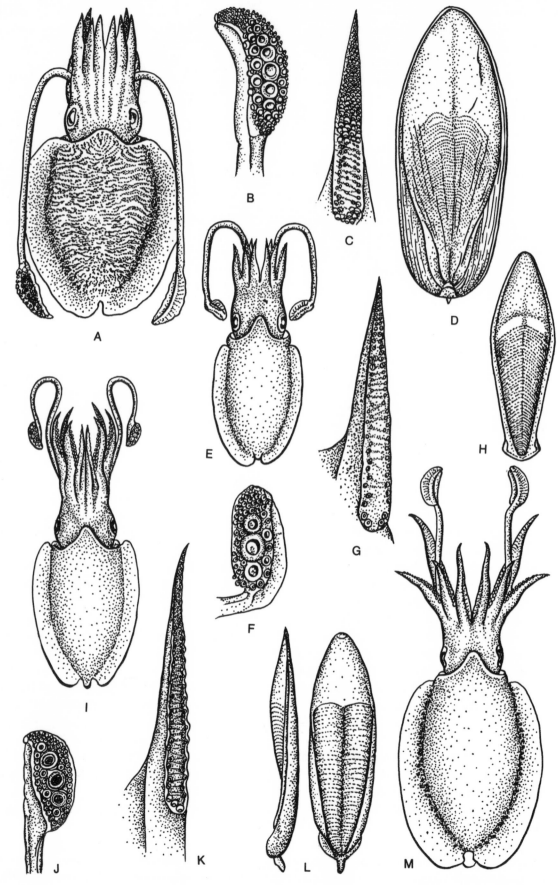

A

B

C

D

E

F

G

H

I

J

K

L

M

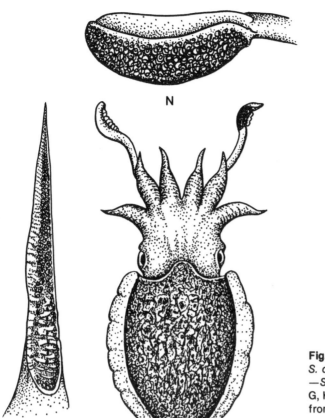

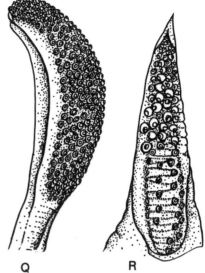

Fig. 18. Gen. *Sepia* s. str. Eastern Alantic species: A-D—
S. officinalis; E-H—*S. elegans*; I-L—*S. orbignyana*; M-O
—*S. bertheloti*; P-R—*S. elobyana*; B, F, J, N, Q—club; C,
G, K, O, R—hectocotylus; D, H, L—shell (A, D, E, H, L—
from Muus, 1959; others from Adam, 1952).

(Fig. 17 J-L) [See couplet 5 (4) of key to genera and subgenera of family Sepiidae]

16 (1). Club suckers differing greatly in size... **17**

17 (20). Dorsal surface of mantle with tubercles and warts (camouflage pattern). 2 large oval spots of rugose skin on ventral side of mantle. 2 stripes of similar rugose skin along ventral side of arms (device for attachment to stones in surf). Shell without spine, sometimes with small obtuse tubercle in posterior part.................**18**

18 (19). 3-4 greatly enlarged suckers occupying entire middle of club. Protective membranes of club not interconnected in carpal part. Ends of 1st-3rd arms not attenuated. Ventral side of shell convex, with longitudinal groove, shell thickness 8-12% of shell length.......................
.....*S. (S.) papillata* **Quoy & Gaimard, 1832**

(Fig. 19 G, H). South Africa: Lüderitz Bay to Natal. Inner shelf. Common species. Mantle length to 13.5 cm.

19 (18). 5 enlarged suckers on club, but size of largest much smaller than club width and suckers do not occupy entire middle of club. Protective membranes of club interconnected in carpal part.

Ends of 1st-3rd arms thin and attenuated. Ventral side of shell flat or concave, without longitudinal groove, shell thickness 4-9% of its length.......
..........*S. (S.) tuberculata* **Lamarck, 1798**

(Fig. 19 I). South Africa from Saldanha Bay to Knysha. Drifting shells may reach Madagascar. Tidal zone and coastal shallows. Mantle length to 8 cm.

20 (17). Mantle surface without tubercles or warts. No spots or rugose skin on ventral side of mantle. Shell with spine...................**21**

21 (24). Shell oval or ovally lanceolate, width 29-46% of length. Wings of outer cone with smooth outlines without protruding "earlets." 5 central club suckers much larger than others..**22**

22 (23). In middle of hectocotylized arm are 9-12 transverse rows of 4 smaller suckers. Shell oval, inner cone well developed and fusing with outer cone, wings of outer cone wide. Shell width 32-46% of shell length.......*S. (S.) officinalis vermiculata* **Quoy & Gaimard, 1832**

[see couplet 2(3), Geographic Area I]

Rather common in shallow waters (littoral, bays, estuaries, and shelf) of southern Africa.

Fig. 19.

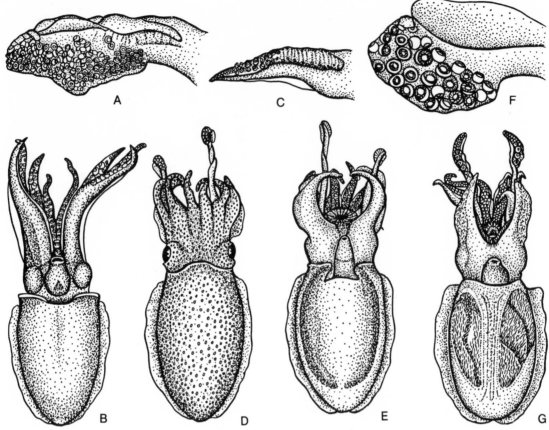

23 (22). In middle part of hectocotylized arm are 6-7 transverse rows of smaller suckers; ventral pairs of suckers rearranged into one longitudinal row. Shell ovally lanceolate, narrowing posteriorly, limbs of inner cone very narrow, wings of outer cone narrow. Unpaired kidney-shaped organ of unkown function (supposedly a photophore) inside mantle cavity on ink sac, unique feature for sepiids . . . .
. . . . . ***S. (S.) australis* Quoy & Gaimard, 1832**
(= *S. capensis* d'Orbigny, 1845) (Fig. 19 J). From northern Namibia southern borders of Natal; Agulhas Bank. Doubtful in the Red Sea. Entire shelf and upper bathyal, mainly in depths less than 250 m. Mantle length to 6 cm. The most common species of South African cuttlefish.

24 (21). Shell lanceolate, greatly narrowed posteriorly, its width 14-26% of its length. Wings of outer cone form "earlets" in posterior part of shell **25**

25 (32). Tips of 2nd and 3rd arms in females attenuated **26**

26 (29). 1st arms in males normal, with 4 rows of suckers. In females distal halves of 2nd and 3rd arms attenuated and bearing 2 rows of suckers **27**

27 (28). Fins in male normal, not extending into a "tail." In females protective membranes of 1st arms greatly widened and twisted around oral surface of arm. Posterior part of inner cone of shell low, its limbs pressed to posterolateral sides of phragmocone . . . . . ***S. (S.) joubini* Massy, 1927**
Natal, shelf. Mantle length to 5 cm.

28 (27). Fins of adult males fused posteriorly and extended into long "tail" (sometimes longer than mantle). Fins of females normal. Protective membranes at tips of 1st arms in females widened. Posterior part of inner cone of shell rounded, elevated, without a longitudinal groove, forming a deep pit over posterior end of phragmocone . . . . ***S. (S.) confusa* Smith, 1916**
(Fig. 19 K). From Zanzibar to Natal. Drifting shells found south to region of Port Elizabeth. Recorded with doubt on Saya-de-Malha Bank and

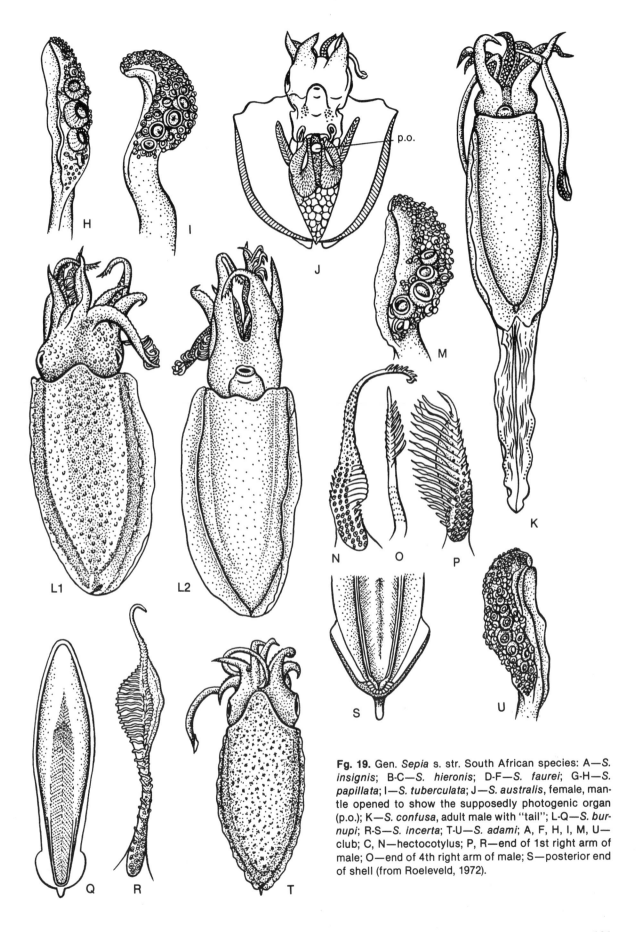

Fg. 19. Gen. *Sepia* s. str. South African species: A—*S. insignis*; B-C—*S. hieronis*; D-F—*S. faurei*; G-H—*S. papillata*; I—*S. tuberculata*; J—*S. australis*, female, mantle opened to show the supposedly photogenic organ (p.o.); K—*S. confusa*, adult male with "tail"; L-Q—*S. burnupi*; R-S—*S. incerta*; T-U—*S. adami*; A, F, H, I, M, U—club; C, N—hectocotylus; P, R—end of 1st right arm of male; O—end of 4th right arm of male; S—posterior end of shell (from Roeleveld, 1972).

Cargados-Carajos Islands. Outer shelf and uppermost bathyal. Mantle length (excluding "tail") to 15 cm.

29 (26). 1st arms of male radically modified. In females 2nd and 3rd arms attenuated only at tips and bearing 4 rows of suckers **30**

30 (31). 1st arms of male widened and bearing 2 rows of processes (long and spear-shaped on inner side and short and conical on outer side). Suckers in distal half of 1st arms in 2 rows. Both ventral arms hectocotylized, the left arm longer than right; both bear row of finger-like processes on tips. In males, fins widened posteriorly and overlapping each other. Posterior part of inner cone of shell low. Striae of striated zone of phragmocone are M-shaped, angular . . . . *S. (S.) burnupi* **Hoyle, 1904**

(= *S. exsignata* Barnard, 1962) (Fig. 19 L-Q). Southern Mozambique to Natal. Inner shelf. Mantle length to 6 cm.

31 (30). 1st arms of male considerably elongated, whip-like at the ends, bearing suckers only on basal part; both protective membranes widened in middle and joined, forming an oval widening. Ventral arms of males not modified. Fins normal. Posterior part of inner cone of shell raised and divided into two parts by deep longitudinal groove. Striae of phragmocone striated zone Λ-shaped, rounded anteriorly . . . .
. . . . *S. (S.) incerta* **Smith, 1916**

(Fig. 19 R,S). Eastern coast of Cape Province and Natal. Inner shelf. Mantle length to 15 cm.

32 (25). In females, tips of the 2nd and 3rd arms not attenuated, bearing 4 rows of suckers. Shell similar to that of *S. joubini*. Males not described
. . . . *S. (S.) adami* **Roeleveld, 1972**

(Fig. 19 T,U). Natal, depth 100 m. Mantle length to 6 cm.

Note: The key does not include *S. (S.) angulata* Roeleveld, 1972, known only from shells of regular oval form, slightly narrowed, angular anteriorly and rounded posteriorly, very wide (50-60% of length), flattened, and without a spine; limbs of the inner cone are flat, wide, and fused with the outer cone, whose wings are very wide. Cape of Good Hope to Cape Agulhas. Shell length to 7.5 cm. *S. S. elegans* can be found off Namibia; [see couplet 4(5), Geographic Area I]

III. *Northern part of Indian Ocean, waters of Indonesia and Indochina Peninsula, Red and Arabian Seas, Persian Gulf, and Eastern Africa to Mozambique*

Note: The key does not include: South African *S. (S.) australis*, recorded with doubt from the Red Sea; *S. (S.) confusa* extending to Zanzibar; Sino-Japanese *S. (S.) lycidas* and *S. (S.) esculenta*, reaching south to the Philippine Islands and Sarawak. These species are included in the keys to the pertinent geographic areas of genus *Sepia*.

1 (40). Shell with spine or at least small tubercle on posterior edge **2**

2 (23). Club suckers of greatly different size **3**

3 (14). Shell oval, wide (30-40% of its length) . . . **4**

4 (13). Club suckers gradually increasing in size to middle row, where 5-7 suckers are considerably larger than others. No striking difference between enormously enlarged middle suckers and small ones **5**

5 (6). Club protective membranes parallel in carpal part and terminating on stalk of tentacle without joining. Inner cone of shell in adults covered with dark callus . . . .
. . . . *S. (S.) pharaonis* **Ehrenberg, 1831**

(= *S. torosa* Ortmann, 1888; *S. rouxii* Férussac & d'Orbigny, 1841; *S. formosana* Berry 1912; *Crumenasepia hulliana* Iredale, 1926; *C. ursulae* Cotton, 1929; *S. tigris* Sasaki, 1929) (Fig. 20 A-C). From the southern part of the Suez Canal and Gulf of Suez to Zanzibar, Madagascar, Kyushu (southern Honshu?), eastern Indonesia, and western and northeastern Australia. Shells reach the Carolines, Lord Howe Island, and New Caledonia. Inner shelf. Mantle length to 42 cm, weight to 5 kg. This species is the most important object of the cuttlefish fishery in the nothern part of the Indian Ocean and southeastern Asia. It is fished from the coast of Arabia to the People's Republic of China, Taiwan, and northern Australia.

6 (5). Club protective membranes fusing in carpal part of club and separating sucker-carrying surface from stalk. Inner cone not covered by a dark callus **7**

7 (8). Spine reduced to tiny obtuse tubercle in posterior part of shell. Shell oval, dorsal side with reticulate sculpture . . . .
. . . . *S. (S.) bandensis* **Adam, 1939**

Java, eastern Indonesia, Philippines, New Guinea, and Marshall Islands. Coastal shallow waters. Mantle length to 7 cm.

8 (7). Shell spine well developed, its length 3-4% of shell length. Dorsal side of shell rugose or granulated, without reticulate sculpture **9**

9 (12). Dorsal side of 1st-3rd arms without

tubercles. No conical "spoon" on ventral side of posterior part of shell. Shell spine round in cross-section **10**

10 (11). Anterior edge of shell gradually rounded. Spine straight . . . .
. . . . *S. (S.) latimanus* **Quoy & Gaimard, 1832**
(= *S. hercules* Pilsbry, 1894; *Ponderisepia eclogaria* Iredale, 1926; *S. harmeri* Robson, 1928) (Fig. 20 D,F). From Malacca Strait to southern Kyushu and northwestern and northeastern Australia, east to Palau (Belau), Guam, New Caledonia, and Fiji (recorded with doubt from Madagascar and southern Australia). Inner shelf, coral reefs. One of the largest species of cuttlefishes, mantle length to 50 cm, weight to 10 kg. Fished in small quantities in the Ryukyus, China, near Taiwan, and in the waters of Indochina.

11 (10). Anterior edge of shell slightly narrowed, roundly triangular. Spine bent upward . . . .
. . . . . . *S. (S). recurvirostris* **Steenstrup, 1875**
(= *S. singaporensis* Pfeffer, 1884) (Fig. 20 G,H). Burma, western Indonesia, Indochina, the South and East China Seas, Philippine Islands. Outer shelf. Mantle length to 17 cm. Fished in small quantities in the South China Sea and in the waters of Indochina.

12 (9). Dorsal part of 1st-3rd arms with scattered tubercles, making longitudinal keels of arms look like denticulated ridges. Shell smoothly rounded anteriorly. Ventral edge of outer cone bent inward, forming a conical "spoon" on posterior end of shell. Spine straight, with longitudinal keel on ventral side . . . . *S. (S.) papuensis* **Hoyle, 1885**
(= *S. galei* Meyer, 1909; *S. prionota* Voss, 1962; *Solitosepia submestus* Iredale, 1926; ?*S. occidua* Cotton, 1929; ?*S. genista* Iredale, 1954; *S. lana* Iredale, 1954) (Fig. 20 I-K). Philippine Islands, Indonesia, western Australia southward to Fremantle, and the Arafura and Coral Seas. Shelf. Mantle length 7-11 cm.

13 (4). All central part of club occupied by 2 enormously large and 2 somewhat smaller suckers. Club protective membranes almost merging in carpal part but not joining. Anterior part of shell narrowed and rounded . . . .
. . . . *S. (S.) prashadi* **Winckworth, 1936**
From the Red Sea and Gulf of Oman to Zanzibar, Madagascar, Mauritius, and eastern India. Outer shelf. Fairly common in the Red and Arabian Seas. Fished locally. Mantle length to 14 cm.

14 (3). Width of shell 15-30% of its length **15**
15 (16). Shell elongate-oval, width 25-28% of

shell length, smoothly rounded toward the anterior and posterior ends, maximum width in middle of shell. Club with 3-5 very large suckers . . . . . *S. (S.) omani* **Adam & Rees, 1966**
(Fig. 20 L-O). Known from the Gulf of Oman, off Pakistan, western India, and the South China Sea near Hong Kong at depths of 50-200 m. Mantle length to 10 cm.

16 (15). Shell narrow, its width is 15-25%, rarely to 29% of its length, lanceolate, acuminate toward anterior and particularly posterior ends; sides slightly angular, the point of maximum width shifted to anterior part of shell. Club suckers gradually increasing in size to the middle row, 5 central suckers usually the largest **17**

17 (18). 1st-3rd arms in males and females with lengthened and attenuated ends, suckers at ends of arms disposed in two rows. Both protective membranes in middle part of 2nd and 3rd arms widened, their trabeculae united by 2/3 their length with membrane of rose-red skin. No apparent hectocotylization. Striae in the anterior area of the striated section of phragmocone M-shaped . . . . *S. (S.) ivanovi* **Khromov, 1982**
Eastern Africa from Kenya to the mouth of Zambezi River. Inner shelf. Mantle length to 7 cm.

18 (17). 1st-3rd arms in males and females not modified. Hectocotylization apparent. Striae in anterior part of striated part of phragmocone slightly arched, with a small concavity in middle, not M-shaped **19**

19 (20). On hectocotylized arm of male are 6-12 proximal transverse rows of normal suckers, then 7-9 transverse rows or pairs of abruptly smaller suckers, then normal gradually smaller suckers on the very tip. No widened lateral membrane in middle part of hectocotylized arm or such a membrane only slightly developed and looking like a smoothly bent arc . . . .
. . . . *S. (S.) kobiensis* **Hoyle, 1885**
(= *S. andreanoides* Hoyle, 1885) (Fig. 20 P-R). Probably a polymorphic species or a complex of related species. Found from southern Hokkaido, Honshu (both coasts) and the Yellow Sea to the Philippine Islands and Gulf of Tonkin and in the nothern part of the Indian Ocean from the Arabian Sea and Persian Gulf to Burma [The cuttlefish described by G.V. Zuev (1971) from the Arabian Sea as "*S. confusa* (?)" probably belongs to this species]. Mainly outer shelf. Mantle length to 7 cm, infrequently reaching 9 cm. Object of

Fig. 20.

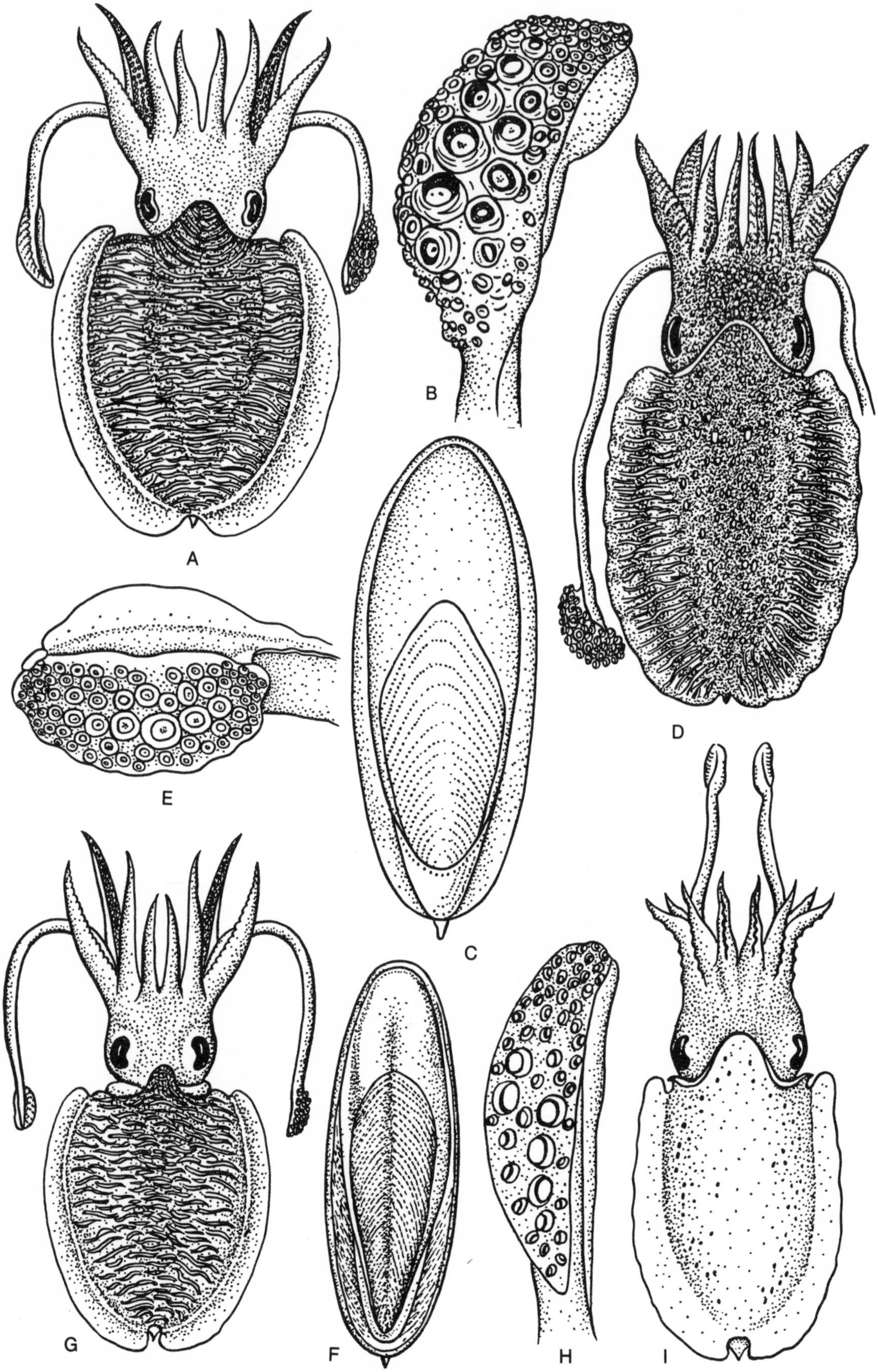

A

B

C

D

E

F

G

H

I

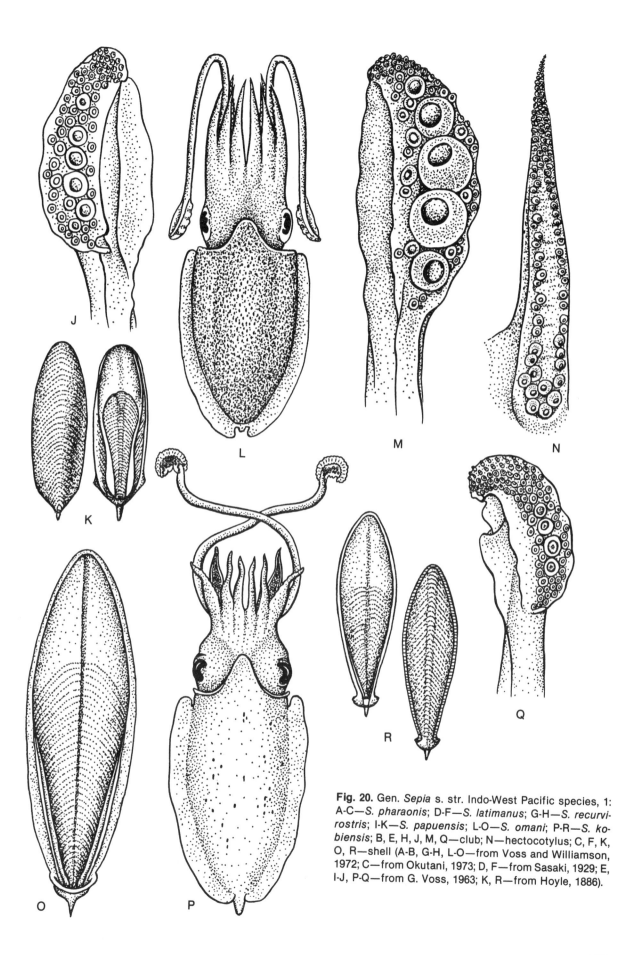

Fig. 20. Gen. *Sepia* s. str. Indo-West Pacific species, 1: A-C—*S. pharaonis*; D-F—*S. latimanus*; G-H—*S. recurvirostris*; I-K—*S. papuensis*; L-O—*S. omani*; P-R—*S. kobiensis*; B, E, H, J, M, Q—club; N—hectocotylus; C, F, K, O, R—shell (A-B, G-H, L-O—from Voss and Williamson, 1972; C—from Okutani, 1973; D, F—from Sasaki, 1929; E, I-J, P-Q—from G. Voss, 1963; K, R—from Hoyle, 1886).

fisheries in southern Japan and China.

Close to this species is *S. (S.) kiensis* Hoyle, 1885, found in the Banda Sea at a depth of 250 m. Its differences from *S. kobiensis* are not clear.

20 (19). 4-6 proximal transverse rows of normal suckers on hectocotylized arm of male, suckers almost or completely absent in middle of hectocotylized arm; a wide scalloped lateral membrane developed; distal third of hectocotylus occupied by small suckers arranged in 4 longitudinal rows **21**

21 (22). Shell greatly swollen on ventral side, its thickness 12% and width-16% of shell length. Arm suckers in 4 rows. . . . .
. . . . *S. (S.) elongata* d'Orbigny, 1845
(Fig. 21 A-D). Red Sea. Mantle length to 10 cm.

22 (21). Shell slightly swollen on ventral side, thickness 7-9% and width 21-25% of shell length. Suckers in distal parts of arms, particularly of 1st and 2nd pairs in males and of 2nd and 3rd pairs in females, disposed in 2 rows . . . .
. . . . *S. (S.) trygonina* (**Rochebrune, 1884**)
(Fig. 21 E). The Red and Arabian Seas, western and southern India. Shelf and upper bathyal. Mantle length to 14 cm.

23 (2). Club suckers small, subequal in size (sometimes central suckers slightly enlarged). . **24**

24 (37). Club suckers disposed in 8-14 oblique rows. Shell width 30-50%, usually 35-45%, of its length **25**

25 (36). Shell oval, smoothly rounded toward anterior and posterior ends, wings of outer cone wide **26**

26 (29). Club suckers in 10-14 oblique rows. . . **27**

27 (28). Club suckers in 10-12 rows in males and 13-14 rows in females. Club long, its protective membranes not reaching carpal part and not joining at base of club. 4-6 transverse rows of very small suckers in middle part of hectocotylus, both dorsal rows inconspicuous or reduced. Width of shell 30-37%, in young up to 40%, of its length . . . . *S. (S.) aculeata* d'Orbigny, 1848
(Fig. 21 F-H). From the eastern coast of the Arabian Sea to eastern Indonesia, China, and the Ryukyu Islands. Inner shelf. Mantle length to 23 cm. An object of fisheries in the waters of India, Sri Lanka, southern China, Taiwan, etc.

28 (27). Club suckers in 10-12 rows in males and females **28a**

28a (28b). Protective membranes fused in carpal part of club. In middle part of hectocotylus 7 transverse rows of decreasing suckers, suckers of

both ventral rows a little smaller than the normal ones, suckers of dorsal rows greatly diminishing but not reduced. Sepion gently rounded anteriorly, with a wide shallow ventral furrow. Spine round in cross-section. Striae of striated zone of phragmocone in its anterior part Λ-like. Shell width 42-48% of its length. No star-like spots on the dorsal side of the mantle. . . . .
. . . .*S. (S.) elliptica* **Hoyle, 1885**
(=*Acanthosepion ellipticum adjacens* Iredale, 1926) (Fig. 21 I-K). From northern coast of the Arabian Sea to South China Sea, northern and eastern Australia, southward to Exmouth Bay and New South Wales. Inner shelf. One specimen was reported captured offshore of Pakistan at 1000 m depth. Mantle length to 13 (16?) cm.

28b (28a). Protective membranes not fused in carp ⌐ part of club. In middle part of hectocotylus 7-9 ⌐ ansverse rows of small subequal suckers. Sepion slightly angular anteriorly, with three deep narrow ventral furrows. Spine with a dorsal and a ventral keel. Striae of striated zone of phragmocone in its anterior part tridentate. Shell width 34-45% of its length. Dorsal mantle side with some 10-50 great (3-5 mm) star-like clear spots
.*S. (S.) stellifera* **Homenko & Khromov, 1984**

The Arabian Sea and west coast of India up to ⁺he Cape Comorin; Saya-de-Malha Bank (?). Man-e length to 16 cm. A common species of western Hindustan at depths of 40 to 200 m. It is commonly confused with *S. (S.) brevimana* (see below), from which it differs in the number of club sucker rows (commonly 10), shell form, stellate spots on the mantle and bigger size.

29 (26). Club suckers in 8 oblique rows. **30**

30 (31). Dorsal protective membrane of club much wider than ventral one, its width in middle of club reaching 50% width of sucker-bearing part. Shell greatly angular anteriorly. Spine length 4-9% of shell length. . . . .
. . . .*S. (S.) brevimana* **Steenstrup, 1875**
(=*S. winckworthi* Adam, 1939). From the Maldive Islands and southern India to western Indonesia and southern China. ?Saya-de-Malha Bank. Shelf. Mantle length to 11 cm.

31 (30). Both protective membranes of club narrow. Shell smoothly rounded or slightly angular anteriorly. Length of spine 1.5-5.5% of shell length **32**

32 (33). Central suckers of club conspicuously larger than lateral suckers. Shell width nearly 33% of its length. Spine base laterally widened

...........S. (S.) zanzibarica Pfeffer, 1884

Off eastern Africa (Kenya, Tanzania, Mozambique). Drifting shells reach Natal and Madagascar. Recorded at Saya-de-Malha Bank. Shelf. Mantle length to 25 cm.

33 (32). Suckers of club of equal or subequal size. Shell width nearly 40% of its length. Spine base not widened laterally.....................**34**

34 (35). Shell width 37-40% of its length. Spine length 3.0-5.5% of shell length.............

........S. (S.) thurstoni Adam & Rees, 1966

Bay of Bengal, southern India, Sri Lanka. Inner shelf. Mantle length to 11 cm.

35 (34). Shell width 40-44% of its length. Spine tiny, its length about 1.5% of shell length ....S. (S.) savignyi Blainville, 1827

The Red Sea, Gulf of Aden, Persian Gulf, and Saya-de-Malha Bank. Shelf. A common species. Mantle length to 19 cm.

36 (25). Shell rounded anteriorly and pointed posteriorly. Wings of outer cone narrow. Structure of protective membranes of club as in *S. brevimana* [see couplet 30 (31)]. Club suckers in 6-8 rows. 2 longitudinal rows of suckers divided by fleshy ridge with lateral grooves on hectocotylized arm....S. (S.) sulcata Hoyle, 1885

(Fig. 21 L-O). Banda Sea, depth 250 m. Mantle length 5 cm.

37 (24). Club suckers arranged in 5-8 longitudinal (oblique) rows. Shell lanceolate, sharply narrowing toward both ends, its width about 25% of its length. Wings of outer cone very narrow.....**38**

38 (39). Mantle wide (over 50% of length). Arm suckers in 4 rows, club suckers in 6-8 rows ....S. (S.) sewelli Adam & Rees, 1966

Eastern Africa from Cape Guardafui (Somalia) to Zanzibar and probably Madagascar. Shelf and edge of slope. Mantle length to 3 cm.

39 (38). Width of mantle about 40% of its length. Suckers in distal parts of arms in 2 rows, club suckers in 5 rows...................

........S. (S.) murrayi Adam & Rees, 1966

Gulf of Oman. Outer shelf. Mantle length to 4 cm.

40 (1). Shell without spine, rounded posteriorly. Club suckers subequal...................**41**

41 (42). 5-6 longitudinal (oblique) rows of suckers on club. Shell narrow, its width 15% of its length, narrowed and slightly bent posteroventrally. Several ridges, calcareous in central part and chitinous in peripheral part, running fan-like from posterior end of inner cone; outer cone encircling inner cone in form of an edging. A small chitinous keel on dorsal posterior end of shell.............S. (S.) arabica Massy, 1916

Red Sea, Persian Gulf, western and southern India, and Laccadive Islands. Outer shelf and edge of slope. Mantle length to 10 cm.

42 (41). 8 longitudinal rows of suckers on club. Shell width 35-50% of its length; shell oval, not acuminate toward posterior end. No ridges or chitinous keel on posterior end of shell......**43**

43 (44). Shell greatly inflated on mid-ventral side, its maximum thickness 21-28% of length. Suckers of only two dorsal rows of middle part of hectocotylus smaller than others................

.............S. (S.) gibba Ehrenberg, 1831

(= S. lefebrei d'Orbigny, 1845). Red Sea. Coral reefs. At night it hides among the spines of venomous long-spined black sea urchins (*Diadema*). Mantle length to 10 cm.

44 (43). Shell not inflated on ventral side, its thickness 14-19% of shell length. All suckers in middle of hectocotylus considerably smaller than others...........S. (S.) dollfusi Adam, 1941

Red Sea and southern part of the Suez Canal. Mantle length to 10.5 cm.

IV. *Japanese waters, the Sea of Japan, and the Yellow, East, and South China Seas*

1 (34). Shell oval or lanceolate, not rhomboidal, its length almost equal to mantle length.......**2**

2 (13). Shell oval, smoothly rounded posteriorly.......................................**3**

3 (6). Club suckers gradually increasing in size toward middle row, 5-7 suckers of middle row conspicuously larger than others............**4**

4 (5). Club protective membranes parallel in carpal part and terminate on tentacular salk without joining. In adult specimens inner cone of shell covered with dark callus...................

..............S. (S.) pharaonis Ehrenberg

[see couplet 5 (6), Geographic Area III]

5 (4). Club protective membranes fused in carpal part and separating the sucker-bearing surface from stalk. Inner cone not covered with dark callus....S. (S.) latimanus Quoy & Gaimard

[see couplet 10 (11), Geographic Area III]

6 (3). Club suckers small, equal, arranged in 8-14 longitudinal (oblique) rows.................**7**

7 (10). Posterior edge of inner cone swollen, bordering posterior half of phragmocone as a wide arc. Anterior part of shell smoothly rounded...**8**

Fig. 21.

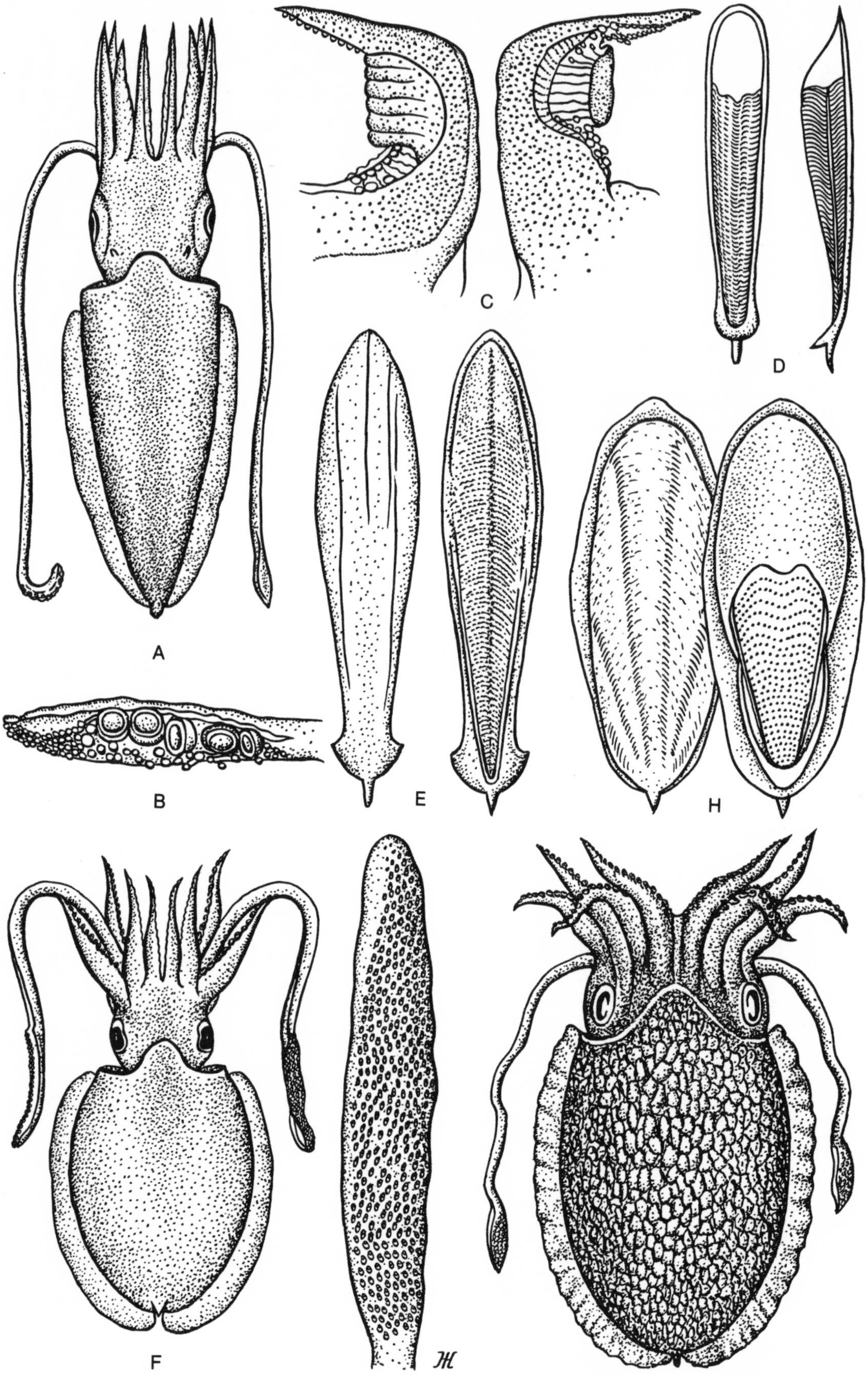

108

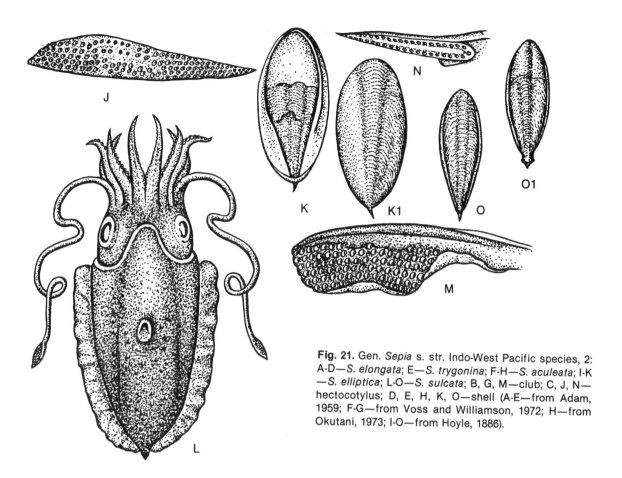

Fig. 21. Gen. *Sepia* s. str. Indo-West Pacific species, 2: A-D—*S. elongata*; E—*S. trygonina*; F-H—*S. aculeata*; I-K —*S. elliptica*; L-O—*S. sulcata*; B, G, M—club; C, J, N— hectocotylus; D, E, H, K, O—shell (A-E—from Adam, 1959; F-G—from Voss and Williamson, 1972; H—from Okutani, 1973; I-O—from Hoyle, 1886).

8 (9). Club suckers 200-250, in 8 rows. Four transverse groups of four smaller suckers in middle part of hectocotylus. Dorsal surface of shell smooth. Striae in anterior part of phragmocone forming anteriorly directed angulate projection. Characteristic color pattern on dorsal side of mantle of adult specimens consists of ocellated spots with light borders and light stripe in middle. . . . .
. . . . **S. (S.) lycidas Gray, 1849**

(= *S. subaculeata* Sasaki, 1914) (Fig. 22 A-C). From southern Honshu (Sea of Japan and Pacific sides) to Vietnam and Sarawak. Inner and (more often) outer shelf. Mantle length to 38 cm, weight to 5 kg. Fished in Japan, South Korea, and China.

9 (8). Club suckers more than 500, in 10-12 rows in males and 13-14 in females. 4-6 pairs of minute suckers in two ventral rows in middle part of hectocotylus (preceded and succeeded by normal suckers). Shell with three rounded ridges on dorsal side diverging radially from posterior end. Striae in anterior part of phragmocone forming an undulate line with two anteriorly directed projec-

tions and a depression between them. Coloration variable, but no ocellated spots present. . . . .
. . . .**S. (S.) aculeata d'Orbigny**
[see couplet 27 (28), Geographic Area III]
10 (7). Posterior edge of inner cone thin and narrow. Anterior part of shell slightly narrowed. Dark transverse stripes on dorsal side of mantle. Row of 6-7 low triangular papillae forming light fringe along bases of fins. 11
11 (12). Posterior edge of inner cone U-shaped, bent outward and forming a semicircular wall edging the posterior part of phragmocone. Club suckers in 10-12 longitudinal rows. 4-6 transverse rows of smaller suckers in middle part of hectocotylized arm. . . . **S. (S.) esculenta Hoyle, 1885**
(= *S. hoylei* Ortmann, 1888) (Fig. 22 D-F). From central Honshu (Sea of Japan and Pacific sides) to Vietnam and the Philippines. Mainly inner shelf. Mantle length to 18 cm. Important object of fisheries in Japan, South Korea, and China.
12 (11). Posterior edge of inner cone V-shaped, fit closely to posterior part of phragmocone. Club suckers in 8-10 longitudinal rows. 8-10 transverse

Fig. 22.

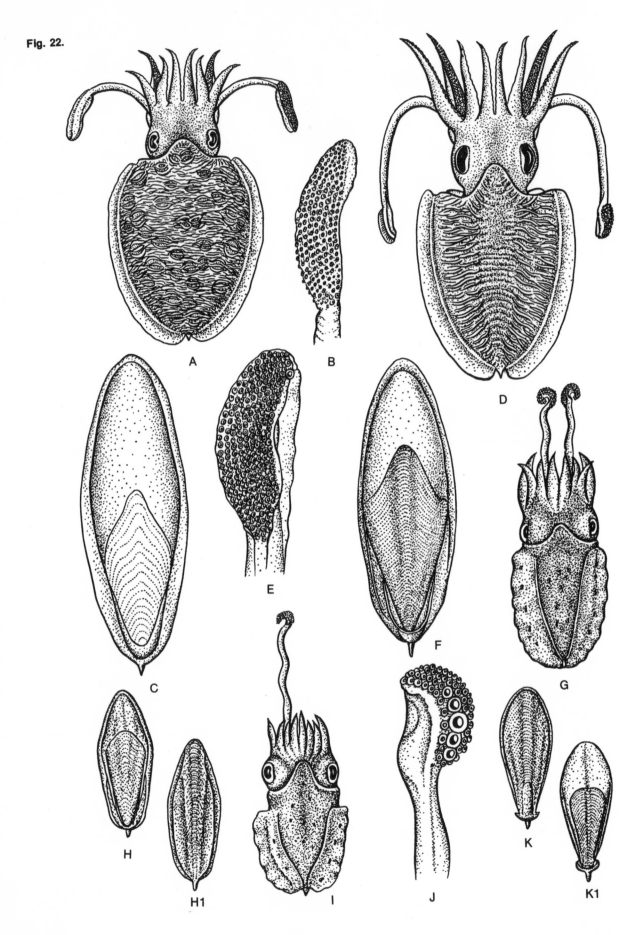

A

B

C

D

E

F

G

H

H1

I

J

K

K1

110

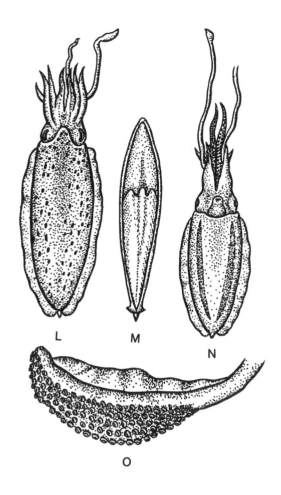

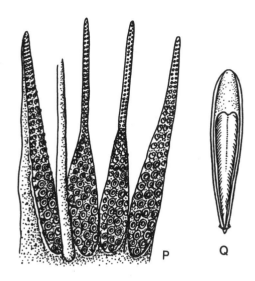

Fig. 22. Gen. *Sepia* s. str. Sino-Japanese species, 1—A-C—*S. lycidas*; D-F—*S. esculenta*; G-H—*S. madokai*; I-K—*S. carinata*; L-M—*S. pardalis*; N-Q—*S. tenuipes*; B, E, J, O—club; P—1st-4th arms of adult female; C, F, H, K, M, Q—shell (A, B, D—from Voss and Williamson, 1972; C, L-N, Q—from Okutani, 1973; E—from G. Voss 1963; F—from Appelloef, 1886; G-K, O-P—from Sasaki, 1929).

rows of smaller suckers on middle part of hecto-cotylized arm....*S. (S.) madokai* Adam, 1939 (= *S. robsoni* Sasaki, 1929, non Massy, 1927) (Fig. 22 G,H). Off Honshu, Shikoku, Kyushu, in the Tsushima Strait, and East and South China Seas. Shelf. Mantle length to 15 cm. Minor object of fisheries in southern Japan and China.

13 (2). Shell lanceolate, narrow toward anterior end and much narrower toward posterior end......**14**

14 (15). Shell width 40% of its length. Suckers at bases and tips of arms in 2 rows, 4 rows medially. 5 middle suckers of club conspicuously larger than others......*S. (S.) carinata* Sasaki, 1920 (Fig. 22 I-K). Sagami Bay, Japan. Lower sublittoral. Mantle length to 3 cm.

15 (14). Shell width 15-30% of its length.....**16**

16 (21). Club suckers of equal size, arranged in 8 longitudinal (oblique) rows...............**17**

17 (20). 1st arms in mature males elongated, whip-like. In distal parts of 1st-3rd arms, suckers arranged in 2 rows. Shell width about 20% of its length...............................**18**

18 (19). Numerous (over 100) longitudinally

elongated dark spots scattered over dorsal side of mantle. Anterior part of phragmocone with two low longitudinal ridges lateral to median line of shell...........*S. (S.) pardalis* Sasaki, 1914 (Fig. 22 L,M). Central and southern Honshu, Shikoku, Kyushu, and South Korea. Mantle length to 23 cm.

19 (18). No dark spots on dorsal side of mantle. 2nd and 3rd arms of male normal; in female these arms attenuated at ends but not longer than remaining arms. Anterior part of phragmocone with one low rounded ridge over median line of shell ....*S. (S.) tenuipes* Sasaki, 1929 (Fig. 22 N-Q). Near central and southern Honshu and Shikoku. Mantle length to 10.5 cm.

20 (17). Arms of mature males of subequal length; ends of 1st and 2nd arms attenuated, whip-like, with 2 rows of suckers; 3rd arms with 4 rows of suckers. Shell width 25-30% of its length.......
.............*S. (S.) appelloefi* Wülker, 1910 (Fig. 23 A-C). Southern Honshu, Shikoku, Kyushu, Tsushima Strait. Outer shelf and upper bathyal. Mantle length to 9 cm.

Fig. 23.

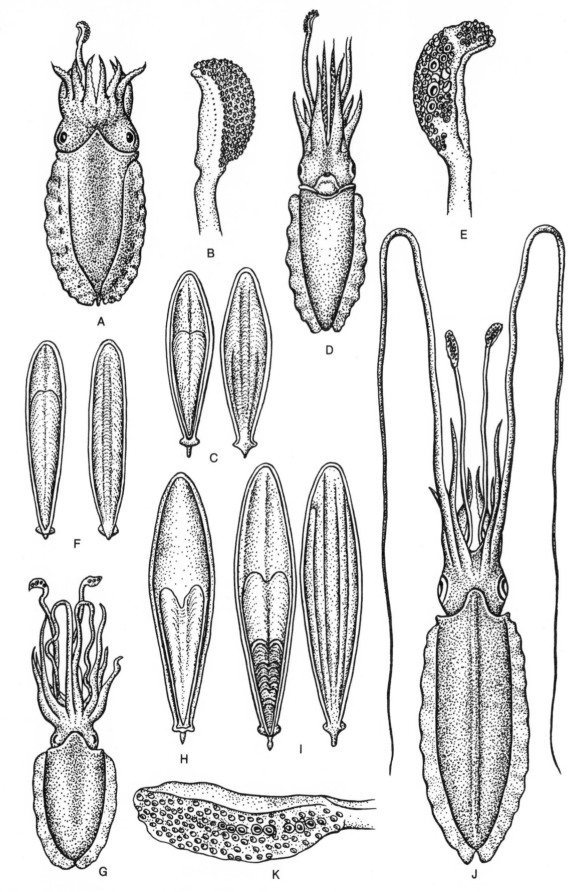

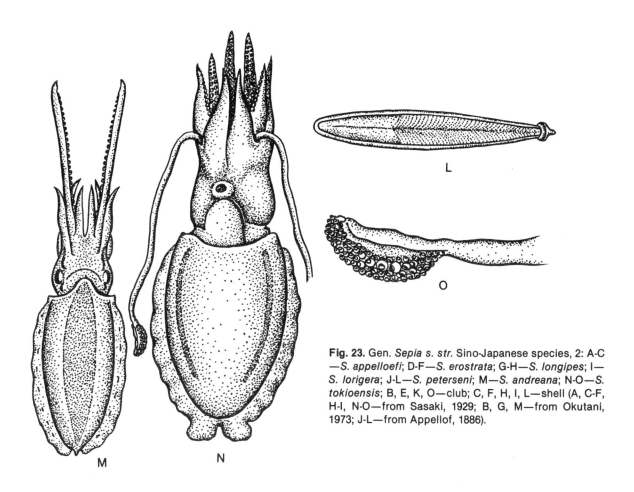

Fig. 23. Gen. *Sepia s. str.* Sino-Japanese species, 2: A-C —*S. appelloefi*; D-F—*S. erostrata*; G-H—*S. longipes*; I— *S. lorigera*; J-L—*S. peterseni*; M—*S. andreana*; N-O—*S. tokioensis*; B, E, K, O—club; C, F, H, I, L—shell (A, C-F, H-I, N-O—from Sasaki, 1929; B, G, M—from Okutani, 1973; J-L—from Appellof, 1886).

21 (16). Club suckers conspicuously unequal in size **22**

22 (23). Shell spine very short, rudimentary. Shell smoothly rounded anteriorly. Male 1st and 4th arms considerably longer than others, their tips attenuated and suckerless (?). Tips of 2nd and 3rd arms of male with 2 rows of suckers . . . . ***S. (S.) erostrata* Sasaki, 1929**
(Fig. 23 D-F). Sagami Bay, Japan. Mantle length 4.5 cm.

23 (22). Shell spine well developed. 4th arms of male not elongated **24**

24 (31). Arms of mature males of greatly unequal size, 1st or 2nd pairs considerably longer than others (females poorly differentiated) **25**

25 (28). In mature males 1st arms elongated, 2-3 times longer than mantle, whip-like, but thickened at ends. Distal suckers of male 1st-2nd arms rudimenatary **26**

26 (27). Both ventral arms of male hectocotylized. Phragmocone with well developed longitudinal keel . . . . ***S. (S.) longipes* Sasaki, 1914**
(Fig. 23 G,H). Pacific and Sea of Japan coasts

of southern Honshu. Shelf. Mantle length to 23.5 cm.

27 (26). Only left ventral arm of male hectocotylized. Phragmocone smoothly arches along median line . . . . . ***S. (S.) lorigera* Wülker, 1910**
(Fig. 23 I). Off southern Honshu, Shikoku, Kyushu, and East China Sea. Outer shelf and upper bathyal. Mantle length to 25 cm. Object of minor fishery.

28 (25). In mature males 2nd arms elongated. Phragmocone with a groove along median line **29**

29 (30). 2nd arms of mature males 3-6 times longer than mantle, gradually attenuated toward tips and becoming filiform . . . . ***S. (S.) peterseni* Appellöf, 1886**
(Fig. 23 J-L). Off central and southern Honshu, Shikoku, Kyushu, and South Korea. Inner shelf. Mantle length to 12 cm.

30 (29). 2nd arms of mature males approximately as long as mantle, almost cylindrical over the entire length, not filiform . . . . ***S. (S.) andreana* Steenstrup, 1875**

113

(= ?*S. sasakii* Wakiya & Ishikawa, 1929) (Fig. 23 M). Pacific coasts of southern Hokkaido, northern and central Honshu, Tsugaru Strait, and northern coast of China (records from near Hong Kong erroneous). Shelf. Mantle length to 12 cm. Object of a minor fishery in northern Japan.

31 (24). Male arms of subequal length or 1st pair slightly longer than others..................**32**

32 (33). Posterior end of each fin expanded and widened into a thickened triangular lobe........

..........*S. (S.) tokioensis* **Ortmann, 1888**
(= *S. misakiensis* Wülker, 1910) (Fig. 23 N,O). From Tsugaru Strait to Kyushu and the Ohsumi Islands. Shelf. Mantle length to 9 cm.

33 (32). Posterior end of fin not extended behind posterior end of mantle and not widening into lobe...........*S. (S.) kobiensis* **Hoyle, 1885**
[see couplet 19 (20), Geographic Area III]

34 (1). Shell rhomboidal, much shorter than mantle, pointed posteriorly....................

.....*S. (Metasepia) tullbergi* **Appellöf, 1886**
[see couplet b (a), subgenus *Metasepia*]

V. Australia

Note: Not included are the following nominal species known only from shells: *Sepia (S.) opipara* (Iredale, 1926); *S. glauerti* (Cotton, 1929) (= ?*Solitosepia mestus* Iredale, non Gray); and *S. whitleyanum* (Iredale, 1926) (= ?*S. elliptica* Hoyle). *S. dannevigi* Berry, 1918, with the shell undescribed, is also not included.

1 (44). Shell with spine or small tubercle on posterior end or pointed posteriorly..........**2**

2 (43). Shell oval, lanceolate, or elongately tongue-shaped, but not rhomboidal..........**3**

3 (42). Shell with a well developed spine (in adult *S. apama* spine covered by callus of posterior edge of inner cone).......................**4**

4 (41). Shell oval with sides bent out or subparallel, oval-lanceolate, or lanceolate, not elongately tongue-shaped....................**5**

5 (28). Shell oval with sides bent out or subparallel. Inner cone well developed, V- or U-shaped or semi-oval. Wings of outer cone wide. Shell width 25-50% of its length............**6**

6 (23). Club suckers greatly unequal..........**7**

7 (22). Club suckers gradually increasing in size to the median row, where 5-7 suckers larger than others; enlarged median suckers not strikingly different from small suckers....................**8**

8 (9). Club protective membranes parallel in carpal part and terminate on tentacular stalk without

joining. In adult specimens, inner cone of shell covered by dark callus......................

...............*S. (S.) pharaonis* **Ehrenberg**
[see couplet 5 (6), Geographic Area III].

9 (8). Club protective membranes converging or fusing in carpal part, isolating sucker-bearing surface from stalk. Inner cone not covered by a dark callus....................**10**

10 (13). Posterior end of outer cone turned under on ventral side of shell, forming wide funnel-shaped "spoon." Shell with fairly wide chitinized fringes on sides of posterior half...........**11**

11 (12). Shell smoothly rounded anteriorly, its width 33-36% (to 39%) of its length. Striae of striated zone of phragmocone smoothly arched. Head and dorsal side of 1st-3rd arms bear scattered tubercles.......*S. (S.) papuensis* **Hoyle**
[see couplet 12 (9), Geographic Area III].

12 (11). Shell bluntly acuminate anteriorly, rounded-triangular, its width 26-30% (in young up to 33%) of its length. Striae of striated zone of phragmocone form narrow triangular projection directed anteriorly and lateral "shoulders," thus resembling a fountain pen nib. No tubercles on head or arms......*S. (S.) plangon* **Gray, 1849**
(Fig. 24 A). Northeastern and eastern Australia (Queensland, New South Wales). Drifting shells are found on Lord Howe Island and the North Island of New Zealand. A common species. Mantle length to 13.5 cm.

13 (10). Posterior edge of outer cone not turned under on ventral side of shell. Shell without wide chitinized fringes........................**14**

14 (17). Limbs of inner cone of shell wide, arched, diverging in posterior part and parallel or slightly converging in anterior part................**15**

15 (16). Ventral side of shell flattened or with a narrow, shallow longitudinal groove. No ridges on dorsal side. Shell width 37-45% (to 50%) of its length............*S. (S.) mestus* **Gray, 1849**
(= *Ascarosepion verreauxi* Rochebrune, 1884; *Solitosepia liliana* Iredale, 1926) (Fig. 24 B). Northeastern and eastern Australia (Queensland, New South Wales). Drifting shells are found at Lord Howe Island. Fished in small quantities. Mantle length to 14 cm.

16 (15). Ventral side of shell with a deep longitudinal groove flanked by wide ridges. Dorsal side with three low longitudinal ridges. Shell width 30-35% (in the young to 40%) of its length. Inner cone of bright pink color..............

..............*S. (S.) rozella* **(Iredale, 1926)**

114

(= *Solitosepia rozella peregrina* Iredale, 1926) (Fig. 24 C). Northeastern and eastern Australia (Queensland, New South Wales) and Shark Bay (?). Shells are found on Lord Howe Island. Mantle length to 15 cm.

17 (14). Shell inner cone narrow, V-shaped, with diverging branches......................**18**

18 (19). Club keel twice as long as sucker-bearing part and continuing on stalk proximal to carpal part. Inner cone of two parts: narrow V-shaped inner part and wide outer part fusing with outer cone and (in adult cuttlefishes) continuing posteriorly as tongue-like projection (callus). In adult specimens, spine completely hidden by callus and inconspicuous. Shell width 35-45% of its length. 2-3 cuticular "earlets" on head above eyes............**S. (S.) apama Gray, 1849**

(= *S. palmata* Owen, 1881; *Amplisepia parysatis* Iredale, 1954) (Fig. 24 D, E). Southwestern, southern, and eastern Australia northward to North-West Cape and southern Queensland, Tasmania, and Lord Howe and Norfolk Islands. Stranded shells are found on the North Island of New Zealand. Mantle length to 48 cm. A common species of the inner shelf. Fished in small quantities in southern and eastern Australia.

19 (18). Club keel but slightly longer than sucker-bearing part, keel extending along the stalk only somewhat farther than carpal part of club. No tongue-like projection of inner cone in posterior part of shell. Spine long, well developed......**20**

20 (21). Shell perfectly oval, sides uniformly convex. Shell width 34-39% of its length..........
.........**S. (S.) latimanus Quoy & Gaimard**
[see couplet 10 (11), Geographic Area III]

21 (20). Sides of shell parallel or slightly bent inward at start of posterior third of shell. Shell width 28-35% of its length. Shell resembles that of *S. chirotrema*, but differs in having slightly developed ridges on dorsal and ventral sides and in that the striae of striated zone of phragmocone have tongue-like projection in anterior part.....
................**S. (S.) irvingi Meyer, 1909**
(Fig. 24 F). Western Australia. Mantle length to 18 cm. Outer shelf.

Along the coasts of southwestern and southern Australia and Tasmania is a related species, *S. (S.) ostanes* (Iredale, 1954) (Fig. 24 G), known only by the shell. In this nominal species striae of the striated zone of the phragmocone are arched anteriorly.

22 (7). Entire central part of club occupied by 3 enormously enlarged suckers. End of hectocotylized left ventral arm attenuated, narrowed and compressed laterally, bearing microscopic suckers. Lateral edges of shell parallel or slightly bent inward. 3 very conspicuous rounded ridges on dorsal side and a deep groove bordered by two ridges on ventral side; striae of striated zone of phragmocone with anteriorly directed angle.....
.............**S. (S.) chirotrema Berry, 1918**

(= *Solitosepia hendryae* Cotton, 1929) (Fig. 24 H-L). Southwestern and southern Australia, Great Australian Bight. Outer shelf and the edge of the slope. Mantle length to 20 cm.

23 (6). Club suckers of subequal size........**24**

24 (27). Club suckers in 8 to 12 (13) longitudinal (oblique) rows..........................**25**

25 (26). Modified suckers in median part of hectocotylus arranged in 3 rows and considerably smaller than normal suckers. Shell width 25-35% of its length; sides parallel; anterior edge narrowly rounded; inner cone V-shaped, its limbs pressed to surface of outer cone.....................
........**S. (S.) novaehollandiae Hoyle, 1909**

(= *S. australis* Férussac, 1835, non Quoy & Gaimard, 1832; *S. hedleyi* Berry, 1918 (in part); *Mesembrisepia macandrewi* Iredale, 1926) (Fig. 24 K-N). Southwestern, southern, and southeastern Australia, Tasmania, northward to the North-West Cape and New South Wales. Over the shelf and the very top of bathyal. Mantle length to 16-18 cm. A common species.

26 (25). Modified suckers in median part of hectocotylus arranged in 4 rows, dorsal suckers much smaller, ventral suckers only a little smaller than normal suckers. Shell width 42-48% of its length; lateral edges convex; anterior edge widely rounded; limbs of inner cone wide, widely diverging (the cone has a semi-oval form), posterior edge of inner cone raised, surrounding the posterior part of phragmocone as an arc-shaped wall.................
...................**S. (S.) elliptica Hoyle, 1885**
[see couplet 28a (28b), Geographic Area III]

27 (24). Club suckers arranged in approximately 20 transverse rows. Shell oval, its width 35-40% of the length; inner cone semi-oval, rounded posterior edge forms an arc-shaped ledge around posterior pit of phragmocone. Spine slightly bent upward..............**S. (S.) smithi Hoyle, 1885**

(= *Acanthosepion pageorum* Iredale, 1954) (Fig. 24 M-P). Northern and northwestern Australia, Timor, Arafura and Coral Seas, and Great Barrier Reef. Mantle length to 17 cm.

Fig. 24.

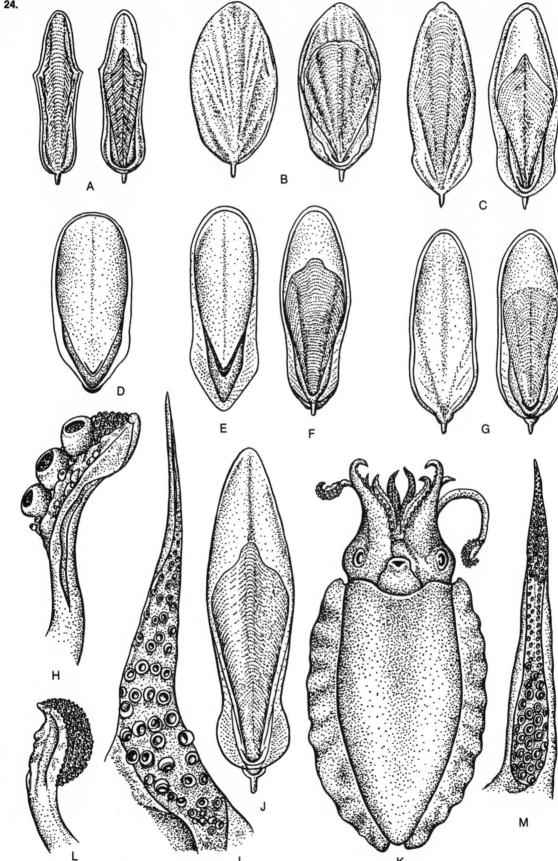

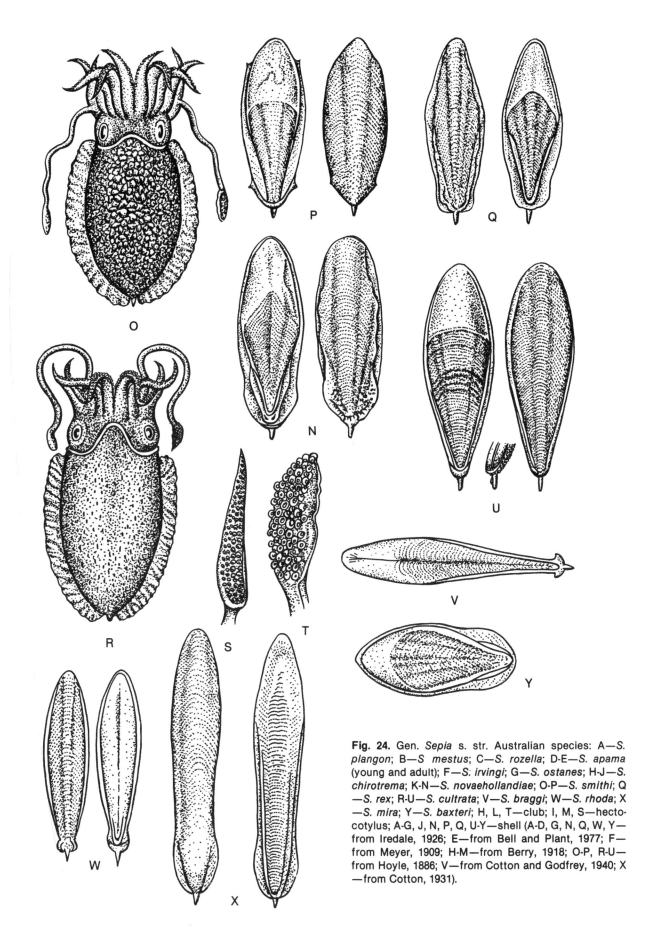

Fig. 24. Gen. *Sepia* s. str. Australian species: A—*S. plangon*; B—*S mestus*; C—*S. rozella*; D-E—*S. apama* (young and adult); F—*S. irvingi*; G—*S. ostanes*; H-J—*S. chirotrema*; K-N—*S. novaehollandiae*; O-P—*S. smithi*; Q —*S. rex*; R-U—*S. cultrata*; V—*S. braggi*; W—*S. rhoda*; X —*S. mira*; Y—*S. baxteri*; H, L, T—club; I, M, S—hectocotylus; A-G, J, N, P, Q, U-Y—shell (A-D, G, N, Q, W, Y— from Iredale, 1926; E—from Bell and Plant, 1977; F— from Meyer, 1909; H-M—from Berry, 1918; O-P, R-U— from Hoyle, 1886; V—from Cotton and Godfrey, 1940; X —from Cotton, 1931).

28 (5). Shell oval-rhomboidal, oval-lanceolate, or lanceolate. Inner cone V-shaped with very narrow limbs **29**

29 (32). Shell width 30-40% of its length. Shell spine with keel on ventral and often also on dorsal sides **30**

30 (31). Shell oval-rhomboidal, smoothly narrowing posteriorly and more narrowed anteriorly. Maximum width approximately in middle of shell. Dorsal side of shell with three low longitudinal ribs, ventral side with a longitudinal groove. 4-5 very large suckers in median part of club. About 10 transverse rows of suckers abruptly diminishing in size in median part of hectocotylized arm . . . .
. . . . *S. (S.) rex* (**Iredale, 1926**)
(= ?*Decorisepia cottesloensis* Cotton, 1929; *D. jaenschi* Cotton, 1931) (Fig. 24 Q). Southwestern, southern and eastern Australia, Tasmania, northward to Exmouth Bay and southern Queensland. Stranded shells were found on the Lord Howe Island. Shelf. Mantle length to 12 (15) cm.

31 (30). Shell oval-lanceolate, triangularly pointed anteriorly, the site of maximum width shifted to anterior part of shell. Dorsal and ventral surfaces of shell flattened, with but slightly developed ridges and without a groove. Club suckers in 5-6 longitudinal rows, central suckers somewhat larger than lateral ones. Dorsal suckers in middle part of hectocotylus microscopically small, ventral suckers but little smaller than normal ones . . . .
. . . . *S. (S.) cultrata* **Hoyle, 1885**
(= *S. hedleyi* Berry, 1918, in part (shell); *Glyptosepia gemellus* Iredale, 1926; *G. macilenta* Iredale, 1926) (Fig. 24 R-U). Southwestern, southern, and eastern Australia, northward to Houtman Abrolhos Rocks on the west and southern Queensland on the east, and Tasmania. Stranded shells found on Lord Howe Island. Outer shelf and upper bathyal, depths 150-650 (820) m. Shell length to 12 cm. A common species.

32 (29). Shell width 16-30% of its length. Spine round in cross-section **33**

33 (34). Shell elongately tongue-like, widely rounded posteriorly. Wings of outer cone without ear-like bend in posterior part of shell. Shell width 25-28% of its length . . . . *S. (S.) reesi* **Adam, 1979**
Rottnest Island near Fremantle. Shell length to 45 mm. The animal not described.

34 (33). Shell narrowly lanceolate, bluntly pointed anteriorly, narrowly pointed posteriorly, rather like a pencil. Maximal width in anterior third of shell. Shell width 16-23% of its length. Wings of outer

cone form bends ("earlets") in posterior part of shell **35**

35 (40). Ventral surface of shell with a narrow longitudinal groove over entire length. Shell thickness 6-9% of its length. Club suckers in 5 longitudinal rows. 5-6 central suckers approximately twice as large as lateral ones **36**

36 (39). Arm tips of male attenuated, bearing 2 rows of suckers. Length of lateral arms in male 33-50%, sometimes 3rd arms up to 67%, of mantle length. Ventral arms of male not hectocotylized. No calcareous keel on posterodorsal side of shell at border with chitinous part **37**

37 (38). 3rd arms of male considerably elongated, up to 50-67% of mantle length, but not otherwise modified. Striae of striated zone of phragmocone in middle of the shell with M-like bend . . . .
. . . . *S. (S.) braggi* **Verco, 1907**
(= ?*Arctosepia limata* Iredale, 1926; *A. versuta* Iredale, 1926; *A. treba* Iredale, 1926) (Fig. 24 V). Southwestern, southern, and eastern Australia, northward at least to Fremantle on the west and southern Queensland on the east, and Tasmania. Mainly outer shelf. A small species, mantle length to 5-6 cm, rarely 8 cm.

38 (37). Length of 3rd arms of male 33-50% mantle length. They are radically modified: in the middle part of arm are thick transverse ridges passing alternately from inner edge of one protective membrane to outer edge of opposite one; each ridge bears 2 suckers, the dorsal one in middle of ridge, the ventral one almost on edge of membrane. Striae of striated zone of phragmocone only slightly bent . . *S. (S.) cottoni* **Adam, 1979**
Western Australia northward to Dampier Land, Great Australian Bight, and Queensland (?). The entire shelf. A common species. Mantle length to 6.5 cm.

39 (36). 2nd and 3rd arms of male short, only 25% of mantle length, considerably shorter than 1st arms; 3rd arms normal. 1st-3rd arms with 4 rows of suckers. Left ventral arm hectocotylized, suckers of median part of arm abruptly smaller. On dorsal side of posterior portion of the shell, calcareous part separated from chitinous part by sharp calcareous keel . . . .
. . . . *S. (S.) vercoi* **Adam, 1979**
Western Australia. Shelf. Mantle length to 5 cm.

40 (35). Ventral surface of shell with a longitudinal ridge along phragmocone, ridge turning into a groove in anterior part of shell. Shell thickness 11-12% of its length . . . .

. . . .*S. (S.) rhoda* **(Iredale, 1954)**

(Fig. 24 W). Western Australia. The animal has not been described.

41 (4). Shell elongately tongue-shaped, narrowed between middle and posterior third and widened near posterior end. Maximum width of shell 20% of length, lying in first third of the length. Dorsal side of shell smooth, cream-colored. Inner cone narrow. Spine straight. . . . .

. . . .*S. (S.) mira* **(Cotton, 1931)**

(Fig. 24 X). Eastern Australia (Queensland, New South Wales). Shell length up to 5.5 cm. The animal is not described.

42 (3). Shell without spine, instead with small obtuse tubercle of pinkish brown color. Shell elongate-oval, roundly pointed anteriorly, its width 41-48% its length. Inner cone narrow, semi-oval. . . . . .*S. (S.) baxteri* **(Iredale, 1940)**

(Fig. 24 Y). Lord Howe Island. Shell length to 9 cm. The animal is not described.

43 (2). Shell rhomboidal, bluntly narrowed anteriorly and angular or rounded-angular laterally, narrowed posteriorly, much shorter than mantle. 3 enormously large suckers occupying entire middle of club. . .*S. (Metasepia) pfefferi* **Hoyle, 1885**

[see couplet 4 (5), family Sepiidae]

44 (1). Shell posteriorly rounded, without spine or tubercle. Shell length up to 48 cm. . . . .

. . . .*Sepia (S.) apama* **Gray, 1849,** adult

[see couplet 18 (19) of this Geographic Area]

Key to species of the genus Sepiella

1 (4). Species distributed in tropical waters of eastern Atlantic and southwestern Indian Oceans. Club suckers in 10-14 rows. 2

2 (3). Shell width 24-30% of its length (in males 24-27%, in females 27-30%. . . . .

. . . .*S. ornata* **(Rang, 1837)**

(Fig. 25 A,B). Tropical western Africa from Mauritania to Angola. Shelf. Mantle length to 10 cm.

3 (2). Shell width 29-36% of its length (29-33% in males, 30-36% in females). . . . .

. . . .*S. cyanea* **Robson, 1924**

(Fig. 17 C). Southeastern Africa from Durban to Port Elizabeth, southern Mozambique, and Madagascar. Inner shelf. Mantle length to 8 cm.

4 (1). Species distributed in northern and eastern Indian and western Pacific Oceans. 5

5 (6). Club suckers in 16-32 rows (usually more than 20 rows). Mantle width about 30% of its length. . . . .*S. japonica* **Sasaki, 1929**

(=*S. maindroni* Hoyle, 1886, non Rochebrune 1884) (Fig. 25 C-E). From central Honshu to Kwang-chow (Canton, People's Republic of China) and the Philippine Islands, rarely found in USSR waters (Possiet Bay in southern Primorye). Inner shelf. Object of an important fishery in Japan, South Korea, and China. Mantle length to 20 cm.

6 (5). Club suckers in 8-24 rows (usually 8-16 rows) **7**

7 (8). Club suckers in 8-10 rows. Shell very narrow, its width 20-25% of its length. . . . .

. . . .*S. ocellata* **Pfeffer, 1884**

(Fig. 25 F,G). Java. Mantle length 5 cm.

8 (7). Club suckers in 10 or more rows. Shell width above 25% of its length. .9

9 (10). Club suckers in 10-12 rows. Shell width about 30% of its length. . . . .*S. weberi* **Adam, 1939**

(Fig. 25 H). Eastern Indonesia (Sumba, Timor).

10 (9). Club suckers in 12-24 rows (usually in 13-20 rows). Shell width 33-43% of its length. . . . .

. . . . . .*S. inermis* **(Férussac & d'Orbigny, 1835)**

(Fig. 25 I-K). From the Persian Gulf and southern part of the Red Sea to the mouth of the Zambezi River, east to eastern Indonesia and the Gulf of Tonkin. Inner shelf. Mantle length to 10-12 cm. This species is the object of several small fisheries and is caught in small quantities in the Arabian Sea, near southern India, and in the waters of Indochina.

Note: The key does not include a doubtful species, *S. melwardi* Iredale, 1954 (Fig. 25 L), from northern Australia, known only by its shell.

2.1.2.2. Family Sepiolidae

Small animals (mantle length 1 to 8, rarely 10 cm). Mantle short, posteriorly rounded, its anterior edge on the back either free or fused with the head; ventral edge of mantle may cover funnel base. Head wide. Fins kidney-shaped, with well developed "ears" anteriorly. Maximum length of fin is conspicuously greater than length of its base. Tentacles retractile, with well defined clubs. Arms fairly short, well developed, without protective membranes. Suckers spherical, usually larger and more different in size in males than in females. Gladius chitinous, rudimentary, or absent. Frequently with luminous organs on the ink sac. A muscular septum is present in the mantle cavity. Cornea locked, with a small pore. One or both dorsal arms hectocotylized. Only left oviduct developed in females. Eggs large, benthic. Development direct, without metamorphosis.

Benthic animals, inhabitants of the shelf, some species live in midwater over the slope or nearby.

3 subfamilies, 14 genera, and 51-56 species. Partial reviews: Joubin, 1902; Naef, 1921-1923; Sasaki, 1929; G. Voss, 1955, 1956, 1963.

Note: Most species of sepiolids can be accurately identified only by mature males. The keys to genera and species of sepiolids thus are based mainly on the characters of mature males.

Key to genera of the family Sepiolidae

1 (18). Anterior edge of mantle not extended forward ventrally, not covering funnel. 1st and 2nd arms not connected or connected only by shallow web. Fins of moderate size, much shorter than mantle. Benthic animals, though some species ascend to surface during reproduction.........................**2**

2 (11). Anterior edge of mantle dorsally fused with head by cutaneous occipital band; no nuchal cartilage. Left dorsal arm hectocotylized. Gladius rudimentary or absent.....................

.................**Subfamily Sepiolinae**...**3**

3 (4). In male, distal suckers on hectocotylized arm greatly modified becoming fleshy papillae with slit-like openings with thickened "lips"; these papillae are closely placed forming a type of "palisade." In the basal part of arm in addition to ordinary suckers there are 1 or 2 small papillae. Arm suckers arranged in 4 rows (in *E. phenax* in 2 rows). 3rd arms in male not bent inward. Club suckers very small, multiple, usually more than 10 rows. Occipital band wide, nearly half head width. A saddle-shaped luminous organ in anterior section of ink sac.............

.........**Genus *Euprymna* Steenstrup, 1887**
(= *Fidenas* Gray, 1849) (Fig. 28 A-T). Type species: *E. morsei* (Verrill, 1881). 7 species in Indo-West Pacific from Hokkaido to Tasmania and from the Persian Gulf and South Africa to the Hawaiian Islands and Polynesia. Shelf and upper bathyal. Some species have value in local fisheries.

4 (3). Entire hectocotylized arm or its basal part modified into special copulatory apparatus with recesses and projections. Arm suckers in 2 rows (sometimes in more than 2 rows on tips of ventral arms). 3rd arms of male usually greatly bent inward toward mouth.........................**5**

5 (8). A luminous organ on ink sac. Occipital band wide, 33-50% of head width.................**6**

6 (7). Luminous organ located on anterior surface of ink sac is either saddle-like or in form of two "ears." Suckers on ends of ventral arms sometimes ar-

ranged in 4-8 rows. Club suckers usually in 4-8 rows.............**Genus *Sepiola* Leach, 1817**
(Fig. 30). Type species: *S. rondeleti* Steenstrup, 1856. 12 or 13 species: 9 or 10 in the waters of western Europe from Norway to the Mediterranean Sea, western Africa, and doubtfully in the Red Sea; 3 in the western Pacific from the Sakhalin and South Kurile Islands to the Philippines. Small benthic animals, inhabiting the sublittoral and upper bathyal but ascending to the surface during the reproductive period. Mantle length 1-3 cm.

7 (6). Luminous organ on ventral side of ink sac, deeply embedded in its tissue. Suckers on all arms in 2 rows. Club suckers in 16 rows.................
.............**Genus *Rondeletiola* Naef, 1921**
One species: *R. minor* (Naef, 1912) (Fig. 29 F,J,K). The Mediterranean Sea and eastern Atlantic off the coasts of Europe and western Africa from Spain to Namibia. Small animals (usual length of mantle to 1.5 cm) that dwell on the bottom mostly in the lower sublittoral and uppermost bathyal, but they may ascend to the surface during the reproductive period.

8 (5). No luminous organs on ink sac. Occipital band narrow, usually less than 33% of head width......**9**

9 (10). Hectocotylized arm with spoon-like widening distal to copulatory apparatus. Both dorsal arms of male fused at bases. Club suckers in more than 10 rows.............**Genus *Sepietta* Naef, 1912**
(= *Sepidium* Lévy, 1912) (Fig. 29 A-E, G-I). Type species: *S. oweniana* (d'Orbigny, 1839). 3 or 4 species off the coasts of Europe from southern Norway to the Mediterranean Sea and near Madeira. At the bottom in the sublittoral, but sometimes in the upper bathyal.

10 (9). Hectocotylized arm widened in basal half in area of copulatory apparatus, distal part of arm normal. Club suckers in 8-10 rows.................
.............**Genus *Inioteuthis* Verrill, 1881**
(Fig. 28 N-T). Type species: *I. japonica* Verrill, 1881 (= *I. inioteuthis* (Naef, 1912)). 3 species in the Indo-West Pacific from Japan to southern Africa. Sublittoral.

11 (2). Anterior edge of mantle not fused with head on the back; nuchal cartilage developed. Left or both dorsal arms hectocotylized. Gladius present.......
.................**Subfamily Rossiinae**...**12**

12 (13). Ink sac reduced and not containing ink. Anal papillae reduced to tiny tubercles. No luminous organ on ink sac. Arm suckers in 2 rows. No suddenly enlarged suckers in middle parts of lateral arms. Both dorsal arms hectocotylized but hectocotylization

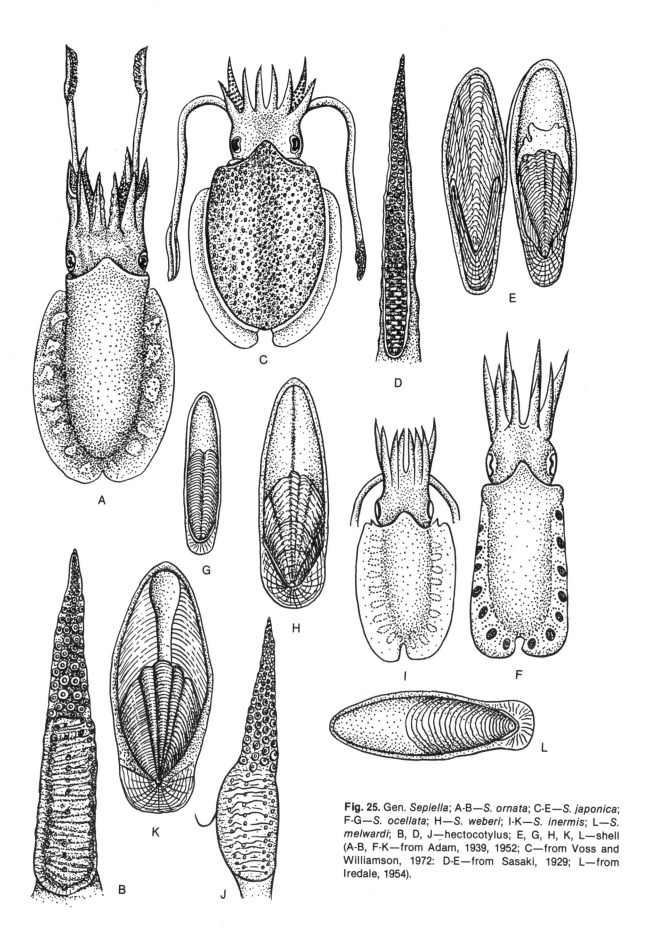

Fig. 25. Gen. *Sepiella*; A-B—*S. ornata*; C-E—*S. japonica*; F-G—*S. ocellata*; H—*S. weberi*; I-K—*S. inermis*; L—*S. melwardi*; B, D, J—hectocotylus; E, G, H, K, L—shell (A-B, F-K—from Adam, 1939, 1952; C—from Voss and Williamson, 1972: D-E—from Sasaki, 1929; L—from Iredale, 1954).

only slightly developed. Club suckers in 6-7 rows...
.... **Genus *Neorossia* Boletzky, 1971**

One species: *N. caroli* (**Joubin, 1902**). Eastern Atlantic from southwestern Iceland and Ireland to Gulf of Guinea and Mediterranean Sea, northwestern Atlantic (southern slope of the Great Newfoundland Bank), and Great Australian Bight. Bathyal (mainly middle bathyal).

13 (12). Ink sac and anal papillae developed normally **14**

14 (17). No luminous organs on ink sac. Arm suckers in 2 or 4 rows. No greatly enlarged suckers in middle part of lateral arms. Both dorsal arms hectocotylized.
.... **15**

15 (16). Tentacular club widened, not bent; club suckers of large or medium size, in 6-12 rows (rarely up to 16 rows, in which case suckers in distal part of arms arranged in 4 rows). Arm suckers in 2 or 4 rows. Suckers on hectocotylized arms smaller (sometimes only slightly). Protective membranes on modified parts of arms developed, separated from sucker stalks by deep groove. No papillar glands on sides of rectum............ **Genus *Rossia* Owen, 1834**

(= *Epistychina* Gistel, 1848; *Allorossia* Grimpe, 1922) (Fig. 26). Type species: *R. palpebrosa* Owen, 1834. 9 or 10 species in the Arctic, boreal Atlantic and Pacific, and tropical western Atlantic. Lower sublittoral and bathyal.

16 (15). Tentacular club narrow, not widened, often twisted and spirally bent, with microscopic suckers in 25-50 rows. Suckers greatly enlarged in middle part of hectocotylized arms. A fleshy cutaneous fold on ventral side of hectocotylized arm. A pair of papillar glands located on both sides of rectum..................................
.... **Genus *Austrorossia* Berry, 1918**

(Fig. 27 H-N). Type species: *A. australis* (Berry, 1918). 3-4 species in lower sublittoral and upper bathyal (from 100-200 to 700-800 m) of tropical and subtropical western and eastern Atlantic and Indo-West Pacific. Species composition of the genus is not determined precisely, and differences between species are doubtful.

17 (14). A paired luminous organ on anterior part of ink sac. Arm suckers in 2 rows, club suckers in 5-8 rows. Size of suckers greatly increasing in middle part of lateral arms. Only left dorsal arm hectocotylized, with a wide outer (ventral) membrane in its middle part and suckers in 4 rows.... **Genus *Semirossia* Steenstrup, 1881**

(Fig. 27 A-G). Type species: *S. tenera* (Verrill, 1880). 3 species off eastern coast of America from

Nova Scotia to Tierra del Fuégo and off southern Chile. Lower sublittoral and upper bathyal.

18 (1). Anterior ventral edge of mantle extended into extensive projecting ventral shield covering funnel from below and sometimes reaching level of eyes or farther forward; in center of ventral shield is an incision for funnel mouth. First 3 pairs of arms joined by deep web. Suckers in 2 rows; in males some suckers on lateral arms greatly enlarged. Club narrow, slightly widened, with very small suckers. Fins large, their length 60-100% of mantle length. A luminous organ on ventral side of ink sac. Usually both dorsal arms hectocotylized. Gladius absent. Benthic (mainly bathyal) or pelagic animals....................
.... **Subfamily Heteroteuthinae...19**

19 (24). Mantle fused with head on dorsal side. Bottom, or near-bottom animals, sometimes ascending to pelagic zone...................**20**

20 (21). Body slightly flattened dorsoventrally. Length of fins 60-80% of mantle length. In males, suckers of 2nd and 3rd arms enlarged. Club suckers in 12 rows. Occipital band narrow......
.... **Genus *Sepiolina* Naef, 1912**

One species: *S. nipponensis* (**Berry, 1911**) (Fig. 31 A-E). Southern Japan, Philippines, Great Australian Bight. Upper bathyal.

21 (20). Body not flattened dorsoventrally, "thick." Fin length usually above 80%, sometimes above 100%, of mantle length. Suckers of 2nd or 3rd arms in males enlarged. Club suckers small, in 8 to approximately 16 rows.............**22**

22 (23). Ventral shield extending only to level of eyes. Site of mantle-to-head fusion lies considerably more dorsally than middle of eye level. Width of occipital band is 40-50% of head width. Fins attach to anterior part of mantle; posterior fin edges do not reach end of body. Eyes small. A pair of abruptly enlarged suckers in middle of male 2nd arms.................................
.... **Genus *Stoloteuthis* Verrill, 1881**

One species: *S. leucoptera* (**Verrill, 1878**). (Fig. 31 F,G). North Atlantic from the Gulf of St. Lawrence to the Straits of Florida and in the Gulf of Biscay. Lower sublittoral and upper bathyal. A related, possibly identical, form was found in the upper bathyal near the Kerguelens, Prince Edward Islands (southern Indian Ocean), and on the Discovery Bank.

23 (22). Ventral shield passes the level of anterior edge of eye and reaches bases of arms. Sites of mantle-to-head fusion located at level of middle of eyes or a little higher; width of occipital band nearly equal to width of head. Fins attached to middle of mantle, their posterior edges almost reaching posterior edge of mantle or surpassing it. Eyes very large. . . . .

. . . . **Genus *Iridoteuthis* Naef, 1912**

(Fig. 31 H-J). Type species: *I. iris* (Berry, 1909). 2 species in the Pacific.

a (b). 3 pairs of enlarged suckers on 3rd arm of male. Posteriorly, fins pass far behind posterior edge of mantle. . . . .***I. iris* (Berry, 1909)**

(Fig. 31 H,I). The Hawaiian Islands (upper bathyal) and (doubtful) Ceram Sea (mesopelagic).

b (a). 3 pairs of enlarged suckers on 2nd arm of male (?). Posteriorly, fins reaching posterior edge of mantle or passing a little beyond it. . . . .

. . . .***I. maoria* Dell, 1959**

(Fig. 31 J). North Island of New Zealand, Cook Strait, and Chatham Rise. Upper bathyal. The record from near the Kerguelen Islands (Nesis, 1974c, p. 82) is erroneous; this was based on *Stoloteuthis* sp.

Note: Structure of the arms of the male *I. maoria* in our disposal differs greatly from that stated in the original description. The tips of the 1st to 3rd arms are widened and laterally flattened. On the 1st pair of arms the suckers of the ventral row are enlarged and those of the dorsal row decrease in size. The distal part of the 2nd arms are occupied by a row of minute suckers with very long stalks. There are several pairs of such rudimentary suckers in the middle part of the 3rd arms; the sucker stalks of the dorsal row are much longer and thicker than those of ventral row; and the distal area of this pair of arms is devoid of suckers. A juvenile specimen caught in the same trawl has the same arm structure as the young specimens of the type series.

24 (19). Mantle not fused with head on dorsal side. Ventral projection reaches level of arm bases. Benthic or pelagic. **25**

25 (26). Suckers in distal parts of arms with long, thick stalks (much thicker than suckers themselves). Fins attached in middle of body and extend beyond anterior edge of mantle. . . . .

. . . . **Genus *Nectoteuthis* Verrill, 1883**

(Fig. 31 K-M). One species: **N. *pourtalesi* Verrill, 1883,** in the bathyal near Florida and the Antilles.

26 (25). Suckers on normal short, thin stalks. Fins attached to posterior half of mantle, not reaching its anterior edge. Pelagic (epi-mesopelagic) nerito-

oceanic; the adults also live on the bottom in the bathyal. . . . . **Genus *Heteroteuthis* Gray, 1849**

(Fig. 31 N-T). Type species: *H. dispar* (Rüppell, 1845). 2 subgenera: *Heteroteuthis* (s. str.) with two species and *Stephanoteuthis* Berry, 1909 (type species: *H. (S.) hawaiiensis* Berry, 1909) with two nominal species. Tropic and subtropic areas of all three oceans.

Note: When identifying the species of *Heteroteuthis* it should be taken into consideration that the structure of arms (the most important taxonomic character) in immature specimens radically differs from that in mature males and (in contrast to other sepiolids) also in mature females.

Key to species of the genus *Rossia*

1 (4). Suckers in middle and distal parts of arms arranged in 4 rows. Club suckers small, similar. Body firm, skin smooth. **2**

2 (3). Club suckers arranged in approximately 10 rows. Anterior edge of fins not reaching anterior edge of mantle. . . . .

. . . . **R. *macrosoma* (delle Chiaje, 1829)**

(Fig. 26 A). From western Norway and the Faeroe Islands to the Mediterranean and Adriatic Seas and northwestern Africa (Senegal, the Azores); also recorded in the Greenland Sea off the coasts of Greenland and Iceland. Mainly upper bathyal.

3 (2). Suckers on club in approximately 16 rows. Anterior edge of fins extending beyond anterior edge of mantle. . . . .**R. *brachyura* Verrill, 1883**

(Fig. 26 B). Greater and Lesser Antilles.

4 (1). Suckers on arms arranged in 2 rows (sometimes in 3-4 rows) in middle part of arms, but never in distal part. **5**

5 (6). Club suckers of very different sizes, considerably larger in proximal part of club than in distal part, the largest suckers located in dorsal rows. In proximal part of club, suckers arranged in 4 rows; in distal part, in 6 rows. Skin smooth, body soft, slightly gelatinous. . . . .

. . . .**R. *moelleri* Steenstrup, 1856**

(Fig. 26 C-E). High Arctic species. From Greenland and Spitsbergen eastward at least to the Laptev Sea, westward to Amundsen Bay, southward to northern Labrador; absent in the Norwegian, White, and southern part of the Barents Seas.

6 (5). Club suckers of approximately similar size, no greatly enlarged suckers present. **7**

Fig. 26.

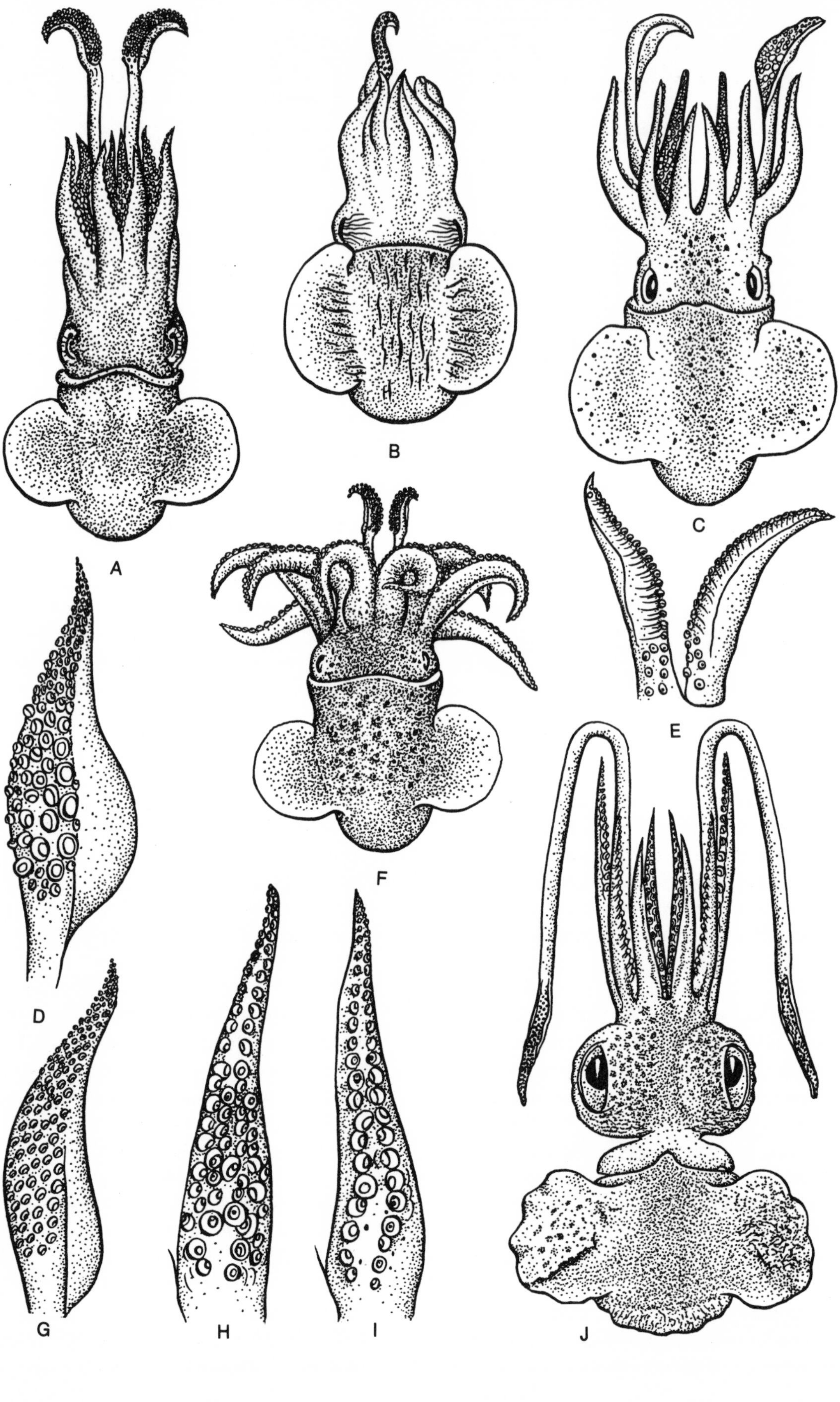

A

B

C

D

E

F

G   H   I   J

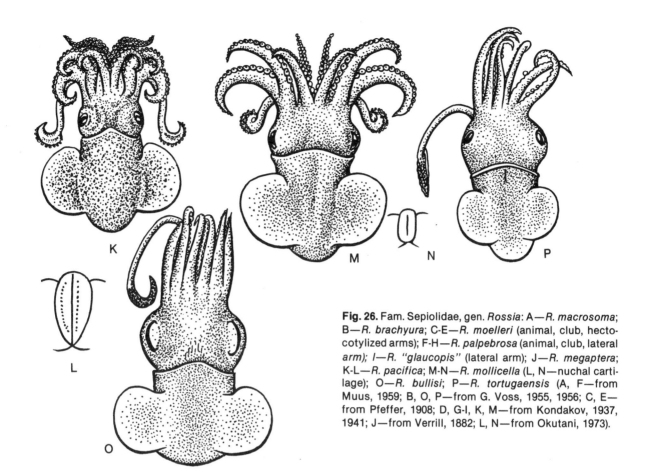

Fig. 26. Fam. Sepiolidae, gen. *Rossia*: A—*R. macrosoma*; B—*R. brachyura*; C-E—*R. moelleri* (animal, club, hecto-cotylized arms); F-H—*R. palpebrosa* (animal, club, lateral arm); I—*R. "glaucopis"* (lateral arm); J—*R. megaptera*; K-L—*R. pacifica*; M-N—*R. mollicella* (L, N—nuchal carti-lage); O—*R. bullisi*; P—*R. tortugaensis* (A, F—from Muus, 1959; B, O, P—from G. Voss, 1955, 1956; C, E—from Pfeffer, 1908; D, G-I, K, M—from Kondakov, 1937, 1941; J—from Verrill, 1882; L, N—from Okutani, 1973).

7 (8). Dorsal side of head and mantle beset by small rounded papillae whose number, size, and distribution vary greatly. In a typical case the papillae are large and sparsely dispersed, but in juveniles and some local forms (for example, in northwestern Atlantic) they are small and poorly visible. Club suckers in 7-10 rows............
................*R. palpebrosa* **Owen, 1834**
(Fig. 26 F-I). Arctic-boreal Atlantic species. From Greenland and Spitsbergen to the Kara Sea and Canadian Arctic Archipelago, southward to South Carolina in the western Atlantic and Scotland and the northern part of the North Sea in the eastern Atlantic. Common in the Barents Sea (except southeastern part) and the Kara Sea; absent in the White Sea
[see note at the end of this key]
8 (7). Surface of body and head smooth, without papillae................................9
9 (10). Anterior edges of fins extend beyond anterior edge of mantle. Club suckers small, in 8 or more rows. Arm suckers globular with wide

openings. Body consistency fairly soft.........
................*R. megaptera* **Verrill, 1881**
(Fig. 26 J). Northwestern Atlantic from the Davis Strait to New England.
10 (9). Anterior edges of fins not reaching anterior edge of mantle....................**11**
11 (16). Club suckers globular..............**12**
12 (15). Arm suckers with narrow, vertically slit-like openings. Club with 7-8 rows of suckers..**13**
13 (14). Body consistency firm. Nuchal cartilage strongly narrowed posteriorly. Suckers on hec-tocotylized arms greatly diminishing in size. Club suckers with wide openings. Suckers in middle parts of arms in adults usually heaped into 3-4 rows..............*R. pacifica* **Berry, 1911**
(Fig. 26 K,L). Pacific boreal species. From the Bering Sea to Tsushima Strait and California. Common in the Sea of Okhotsk and Sea of Japan and off the Kurile Islands. Object of a small fishery in Japan.
14 (13). Body consistency fairly soft. Nuchal cartilage with subparallel edges. Suckers on hec-

tocotylized arms only a little smaller than those on lateral arms. Club suckers with narrow openings. Arm suckers always in 2 rows. . . . .
. . . .*R. mollicella* Sasaki, 1920

(Fig. 26 N,O). Sea of Japan (Peter the Great Bay), Pacific coasts of Hokkaido and Honshu. Outer shelf and upper bathyal.

15 (12). Arm suckers with globose openings. Club suckers with narrow openings, disposed in 10-12 rows. Body consistency fairly soft. . . . .
. . . .*R. bullisi* Voss, 1956

(Fig. 26 M). The Gulf of Mexico and Straits of Florida. Upper bathyal.

16 (11). Arm suckers elongated, barrel-shaped, with narrow vertical slit-like openings. Club suckers with wide openings, arranged in 10 rows. Body consistency fairly soft. . . . .
. . . .*R. tortugaensis* Voss, 1956

(Fig. 26 P). Found off southern Florida and off Surinam.

Note: In the species *R. palpebrosa* Owen, 1834, (= *R. hyatti* Verrill, 1878) is included *R. glaucopis* Lovén, 1846 (= *R. sublaevis* Verrill, 1878). It is yet unknown whether these are two different species or variations of the same species. *R. palpebrosa* differs from *R. glaucopis* in that the suckers in the proximal parts of the arms are arranged in 4 rows (Fig. 26 H, I) and the tubercles on the body are larger and more conspicuous than in *R. glaucopis,* but these characters are very variable. In the Arctic, *R. palpebrosa* is almost as common as *R. glaucopis,* but in the southern parts of the range only specimens similar to *R. glaucopis* are found.

Key to species of genus *Semirossia*

1 (4). Club suckers of subequal size, dorsal suckers only slightly larger than ventral ones. Enlarged suckers in middle parts of male lateral arms gradually becoming smaller toward tips of arms 2
2 (3). Suckers on proximal part (about basal third) of hectocotylized arm arranged in 2 rows, becoming 4 rows in distal part. . . . .
. . . .*S. equalis* (Voss, 1950)

(Fig. 27 A). Western Atlantic from Georgia to Florida and Cuba, Gulf of Mexico, Caribbean Sea, and off Surinam.
3 (2). Suckers on proximal part of hectocotylized arm arranged in 2 rows, becoming closely zigzag (seemingly in 4, but really in 2) rows at middle,

and in 4 rows distally. . . . .
. . . .*S. patagonica* (Smith, 1881)

(Fig. 27 B-D). Southern part of South America from Chiloe Island, Chile, and Anegada Bay, Argentina, to Tierra del Fuégo and the Falkland Islands.
4 (1). Suckers of 2 dorsal rows of club 2-3 times larger than those of 2 ventral rows. Large suckers of middle parts of male lateral arms abruptly replaced by small suckers in distal parts of arms. Suckers on hectocotylized arm at first (in proximal quarter or third of arm) disposed in 2 rows, then in 4, and then again in 2 rows at very end of arm. . . . .*S. tenera* (Verrill, 1880)

(Fig. 27 E-G). Western Atlantic from Nova Scotia to Brazil, including the Gulf of Mexico and Caribbean Sea.

Key to species of the genus *Austrorossia*

1 (2). Diameter of club suckers 0.15-0.25 mm
. . . .*A. antillensis* (Voss, 1955)

(Fig. 27 H,I). Southern Florida, the Gulf of Mexico, Cuba, and Surinam.
2 (1). Diameter of suckers in middle part of club 0.07-0.15 mm, usually not more than 0.1 mm. . .3
3 (4). Club suckers disposed in 24-30 rows. . . . . . .
. . . .*A. bipapillata* (Sasaki, 1920)

(Fig. 27 J-I). From southern Honshu, Japan, to the Philippines.
4 (3). Club suckers arranged in 30-50 irregular rows 5
5 (6). Found in African waters. . . . .
. . . .*A. mastigophora* (Chun, 1915)

[= ?*A. enigmatica* (Robson, 1924] (Fig. 27 M). Western, southern and eastern Africa from Guinea and Somalia to the Cape of Good Hope.
6 (5). Found in Australian waters. . . . .
. . . .*A. australis* (Berry, 1918)

(Fig. 27 N). The Great Australian Bight and Tasman Sea near the Bass Strait. Possibly a synonym of *A. mastigophora.*

Key to species of the genus *Euprymna*

1 (2). Arm suckers in 2 rows. Male without specially enlarged suckers. Modified suckers on hectocotylized arm occupying only very tip of arm. . . . .*E. phenax* Voss, 1962

(Fig. 28 A,B). The Philippines.
2 (1). Arm suckers in 4 rows. Greatly enlarged arm suckers present in male. Modified suckers oc-

cupying approximately half of hectocotylized arm 3

3 (6). Enlarged suckers on 2nd, 3rd, and (if any) 4th arms of male situated only in ventral row . . . 4

4 (5). Enlarged suckers present only on 2nd and 3rd arms of male, 2 in each ventral row . . . . *E. tasmanica* (Pfeffer, 1884)
Eastern and southern Australia and Tasmania.

5 (4). Enlarged suckers present in ventral rows of 2nd, 3rd, and 4th male arms, approximately 10 suckers on each arm . . . . *E. morsei* (Verrill, 1881)
(Fig. 28 C,D). Japan from Hokkaido to the Ryukyus, China, Philippines, Indonesia, India, and Maldive Islands. Object of a minor fishery.

6 (3). Enlarged suckers present at least on 4th arms of male both in dorsal and ventral rows . . . 7

7 (8). Greatly enlarged suckers present in ventral row of 3rd arm (3-4 suckers) and in dorsal and ventral rows of 4th arms of male. No such suckers in dorsal rows of 2nd and 3rd arms of male . . . . *E. stenodactyla* (Grant, 1833)
(Fig. 28 E-G). Indo-West Pacific, from Mascarene Islands to Queensland and Polynesia.

8 (7). Greatly enlarged suckers present in dorsal and ventral rows of 2nd and 4th (sometimes also in 3rd) arms of male 9

9 (10). No greatly enlarged suckers on 3rd arms of male, but present on 1st right arm . . . . *E. albatrossae* Voss, 1962
(Fig. 28 H,I). The Philippines.

10 (9). Greatly enlarged suckers on 3rd arms of male. No greatly enlarged suckers on 1st right arm, but marginal suckers a little larger than suckers of middle rows 11

11 (12). 6-7 pairs of enlarged suckers on 4th arms of male . . . . *E. berryi* Sasaki, 1929
(Fig. 28 J,K). Japan, China, and Gulf of Tonkin. Probably a synonym of *E. morsei*.

12 (11). 3-4 pairs of enlarged suckers on 4th arms of male . . . . *E. scolopes* Berry, 1913
(Fig. 28 L,M). The Hawaiian Islands.

Key to species of the genus *Inioteuthis*

1 (4). Left dorsal arm of male greatly widened in basal half, with deep incision on ventral side . . . 2

2 (3). Left dorsal arm of male much shorter than right arm. Several small suckers present on dorsal side of widened basal part of left dorsal arm. A large ear-like lobe free of papillae in central part of arm copulatory apparatus . . . .

. . . .*I. japonica* Verrill, 1881
[= *I. inioteuthis* (Naef, 1912)] (Fig. 28 N,O). Southern Japan and China.

3 (2). Left dorsal arm of male not shortened. No suckers on dorsal side of widened part of this arm. Two small tongue-like papillae in central part of arm copulatory apparatus . . . .
. . . . *I. maculosa* Goodrich, 1896
(Fig. 28 P,Q). Northern Indian Ocean, the Persian Gulf, Bay of Bengal, Andaman Sea, India, Indonesia, and Philippines.

4 (1). Left dorsal arm of male slightly widened in basal half, without incision on ventral side. Several small papillae on dorsal side of basal part of arm. Two large triangular papillae with a smaller one between them located in central part (ventral side) of arm copulatory apparatus . . . .
. . . . *I. capensis* Voss, 1962
(Fig. 28 R-T). South Africa from Lüderitz Bay to Mossel Bay.

Key to species of the genus *Sepietta*

1 (2). Club suckers large, in approximately 10 rows; suckers in dorsal rows larger than those of ventral rows. Fins rounded, maximum width of fin in middle of its length. Left dorsal arm of male slightly widened distal to copulatory apparatus; in this part of arm, suckers of dorsal row larger than those of ventral row and diminish in size gradually from copulatory appartus toward end of arm. Horn of copulatory apparatus short. Only 3 suckers present proximal to copulatory apparatus . . . . *S. petersi* (Steenstrup, 1887)
(= *S. obscura* Naef, 1916) (Fig. 29 A-G). Mediterranean Sea and (doubtfully) Atlantic coast of Morocco. Upper sublittoral.

2 (1). Club suckers very small, in more than 16 rows, dorsal suckers not larger than ventral suckers. Fins heart-shaped, their outer edges angular, with point of maximum width shifted to posterior edge. Left dorsal arm of male greatly widened distal to copulatory apparatus. 4 suckers present proximal to copulatory apparatus 3

3 (4). 2 large suckers followed by 2-4 small and then again 2 large suckers on left dorsal arm of male in dorsal row distal to copulatory apparatus; suckers then gradually diminishing in size distally. Horn of copulatory apparatus long, over half of arm width, twisted. Fairly large, total length without tentacles to 7-9 cm . . . .
. . . . *S. oweniana* (d'Orbigny, 1839)

Fig. 27.

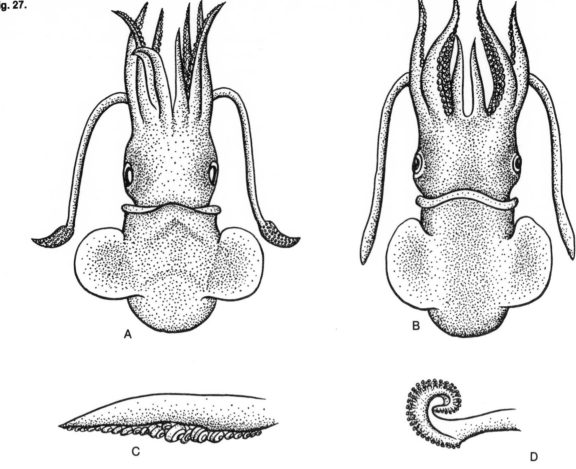

(Fig. 29 B,C,I). From western Norway and the Faeroe Islands to the Mediterranean Sea, Madeira, and Mauritania. Shelf (mainly outer) and upper bathyal.

The systematic position of *S. scandica* (Steenstrup, 1887) remains unclear. Some authors consider it an independent species, but others think that it is only a form of *S. oweniana*. *S. scandica* is recorded in Northern European waters from Iceland and western Norway to the southern part of the North Sea.

4 (3). 4 greatly enlarged suckers on left dorsal arm of male in dorsal row of suckers distal to copulatory apparatus. Horn of copulatory apparatus short, much shorter than half arm width, slightly bent. Small, total length without tentacles to 5 cm. . . . .***S. neglecta* Naef, 1916**

(Fig. 29 D,E,H). From southern Norway and the Orkney Islands to the Mediterranean Sea and the Atlantic coast of Morocco. Upper sublittoral.

Key to species of the genus *Sepiola*

I. Europe, western Africa, and the Red Sea
1 (14). Suckers on 4th arms in 2 rows over entire length of arm. **2**
2 (5). Anterior edge of mantle on ventral side with deep incision opposite funnel and two semicircular projections lateral to edge of incision. Club suckers small, equal in size in both dorsal and ventral rows. **3**
3 (4). Incision in the anteroventral edge of mantle V-shaped, its depth about 33% of ventral length of mantle. Copulatory apparatus developed, as usual, only on left dorsal arm of male. . . . .
. . . .***S. pfefferi* Grimpe, 1921**

(Fig. 30 A-C). Northeastern Atlantic boreal species. From the Faeroe Islands and southern Norway to Brittany, France. Shelf. Probably not a distinct species but a form of *S. aurantiaca*.

4 (3). Incision in anteroventral edge of mantle

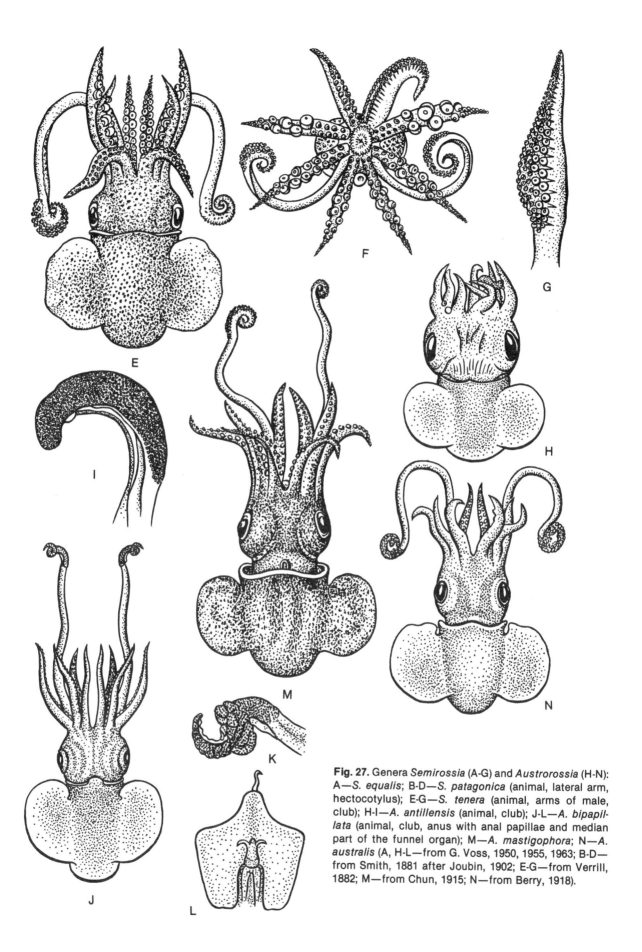

Fig. 27. Genera *Semirossia* (A-G) and *Austrorossia* (H-N):
A—*S. equalis*; B-D—*S. patagonica* (animal, lateral arm,
hectocotylus); E-G—*S. tenera* (animal, arms of male,
club); H-I—*A. antillensis* (animal, club); J-L—*A. bipapillata* (animal, club, anus with anal papillae and median
part of the funnel organ); M—*A. mastigophora*; N—*A.
australis* (A, H-L—from G. Voss, 1950, 1955, 1963; B-D—
from Smith, 1881 after Joubin, 1902; E-G—from Verrill,
1882; M—from Chun, 1915; N—from Berry, 1918).

Fig. 28.

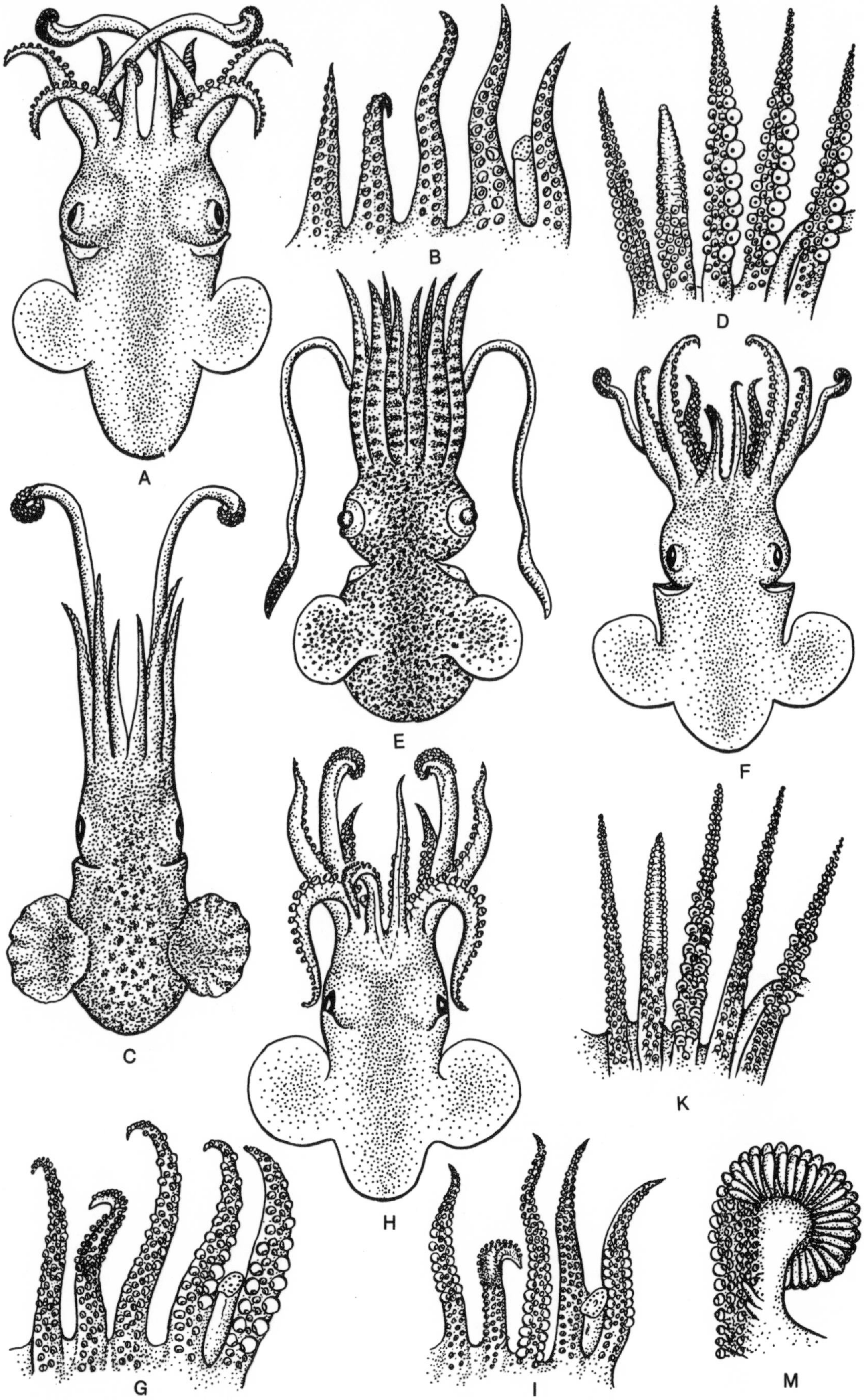

130

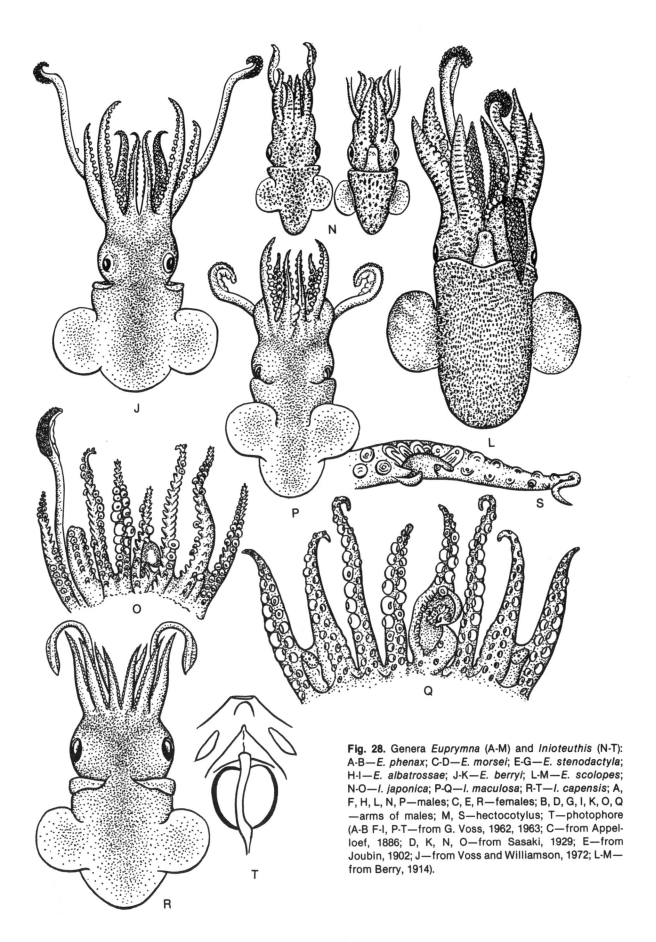

Fig. 28. Genera *Euprymna* (A-M) and *Inioteuthis* (N-T): A-B—*E. phenax*; C-D—*E. morsei*; E-G—*E. stenodactyla*; H-I—*E. albatrossae*; J-K—*E. berryi*; L-M—*E. scolopes*; N-O—*I. japonica*; P-Q—*I. maculosa*; R-T—*I. capensis*; A, F, H, L, N, P—males; C, E, R—females; B, D, G, I, K, O, Q —arms of males; M, S—hectocotylus; T—photophore (A-B F-I, P-T—from G. Voss, 1962, 1963; C—from Appelloef, 1886; D, K, N, O—from Sasaki, 1929; E—from Joubin, 1902; J—from Voss and Williamson, 1972; L-M—from Berry, 1914).

U-shaped, its depth about 25% of ventral length of mantle. Right dorsal arm of male equipped with additional copulatory apparatus comprised of 2 small tongue-like outgrowths in basal part of arm..............**S. aurantiaca Jatta, 1896**
(Fig. 30 D,N). From southern Norway to the Mediterranean Sea. Outer shelf and upper bathyal.

5 (2). Anteroventral edge of mantle undulate, without deep incision......................**6**

6 (7). Left dorsal arm of male suddenly widened, spoon-like, rows of suckers on distal part of arm set far apart. Copulatory apparatus of 2 large tongue-like lobes (one lying in spoon-like widening of arm) and a twisted lateral projection. Anterior edge of mantle on ventral side deeply undulate. Club suckers small, of equal size...................
.....................**S. ligulata Naef, 1912**
(Fig. 30 E,O). The Mediterranean and Adriatic Seas, at depths of 200-250 m. Recorded with doubt in Lusitanian waters.

7 (6). Left dorsal arm of male not or only slightly widened. Copulatory apparatus of one complexly twisted lobe. Anterior ventral edge of mantle only slightly undulate.........................**8**

8 (9). Left dorsal arm of male slightly widened distal to copulatory apparatus and sharply bent at end. Dorsal suckers of club larger than ventral ones.....................................**8a**

8a (8b). Suckers of both rows in distal part of hectocotylized (left dorsal) arm in male of subequal size..................**S. robusta Naef, 1912**
(Fig. 30 F,S). Mediterranean Sea. Outer shelf. Recorded with doubt in Lusitanian waters.

8b (8a). Dorsal row of suckers in distal part of hectocotylized (left dorsal) arm in males with 4 large proximal and some smaller distal suckers; in the ventral row, after the big ventral lobe with three lappets, there are no suckers in proximal 2/3 of the arm and some very small (smaller than dorsal ones) suckers in distal third...............
.....................**S. knudseni Adam, 1984**
Northwest and West Africa, from the Canary Islands to the Gulf of Guinea. Inner shelf.

9 (8). Left dorsal arm of male not widened. Suckers of both distal rows of this arm of greatly unequal size.........................**10**

10 (13). Left dorsal arm of male bent sharply from middle. Dorsal suckers of club somewhat larger than ventral suckers.................**11**

11 (12). All suckers of dorsal row in distal part of left dorsal arm of male much larger than respec-

tive suckers of ventral row...................
..............**S. rondeleti Steenstrup, 1856**
(Fig. 30 G,H,P). The Mediterranean Sea and Lusitanian waters. Shelf and the uppermost bathyal.

12 (11). Only 3-4 suckers in dorsal row in middle of distal part of left dorsal arm of male sharply enlarged...............**S. affinis Naef, 1912**
(Fig. 30 I,R). The Mediterranean Sea. Upper sublittoral.

13 (10). Left dorsal arm of male slightly bent at tip only. 2-3 suckers of dorsal row of this arm directly behind copulatory apparatus suddenly larger. Dorsal and ventral club suckers of equal size...............**S. intermedia Naef, 1912**
(Fig. 30 J,Q). The Mediterranean Sea and possibly the Gulf of Cádiz. Shelf.

14 (1). Suckers on tips of 4th arms in more than 2 rows. Suckers of dorsal rows on club larger than those of ventral rows.....................**15**

15 (16). 3-4 rows of suckers on tips of 4th arms. Left dorsal arm of male not bent and without particularly larger suckers......................
..............**S. steenstrupiana Lévy, 1912**
(= S. tenera Naef, 1912) (Fig. 30 K,M). The Mediterranean Sea. Upper sublittoral. Recorded with doubt from the Red Sea.

16 (15). 4-8 rows of suckers on tips of 4th arms. Left dorsal arm of male strongly bent starting at middle; in middle of its distal area, 3-4 suckers of dorsal row greatly enlarged...................
..............**S. atlantica d'Orbigny, 1839**
(Fig. 30 L,T). Northeastern Atlantic boreal-Lusitanian species found from Iceland, Faeroe Islands and western Norway to Morocco; absent from the Mediterranean Sea. Shelf and edge of the slope.

II. Eastern and southeastern Asia, western Pacific, and nearby seas

1 (4). Copulatory apparatus of left dorsal arm of male consisting of 2-3 large papillae. Not more than one or two enlarged suckers (in dorsal row) between these papillae and modified suckers of distal part of arm.........................**2**

2 (3). Left dorsal arm of male with two horn-like papillae of copulatory apparatus. Suckers of dorsal and ventral rows of right 1st and both 2nd arms of male of equal size. Club suckers small, in 4 rows at base and up to 16 rows in distal part of club.............**S. birostrata Sasaki, 1918**
(Fig. 30 U,V). Southern Sakhalin, South Kurile

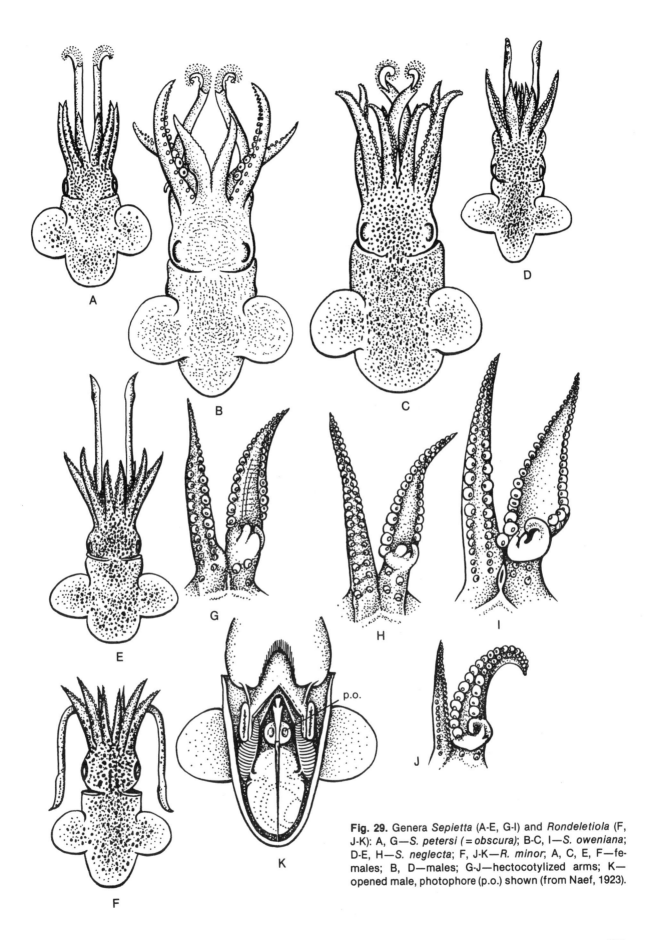

Fig. 29. Genera *Sepietta* (A-E, G-I) and *Rondeletiola* (F, J-K): A, G—*S. petersi (= obscura)*; B-C, I—*S. oweniana*; D-E, H—*S. neglecta*; F, J-K—*R. minor*; A, C, E, F—females; B, D—males; G-J—hectocotylized arms; K—opened male, photophore (p.o.) shown (from Naef, 1923).

Fig. 30.

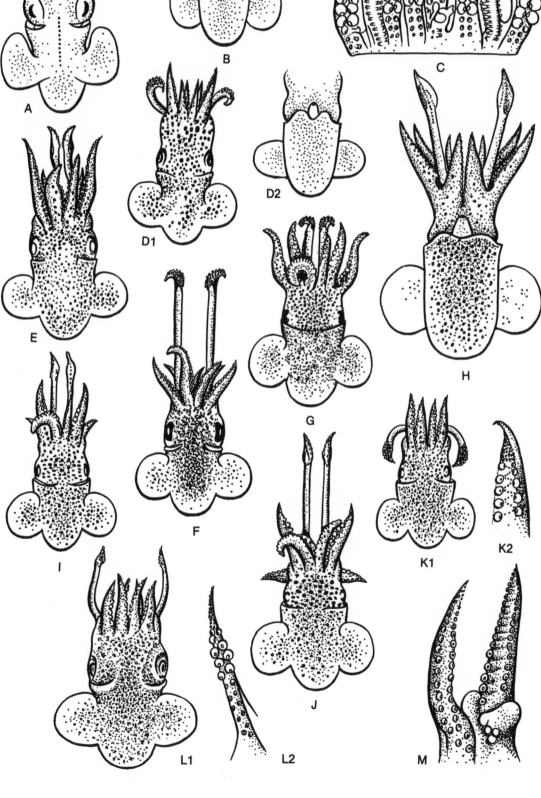

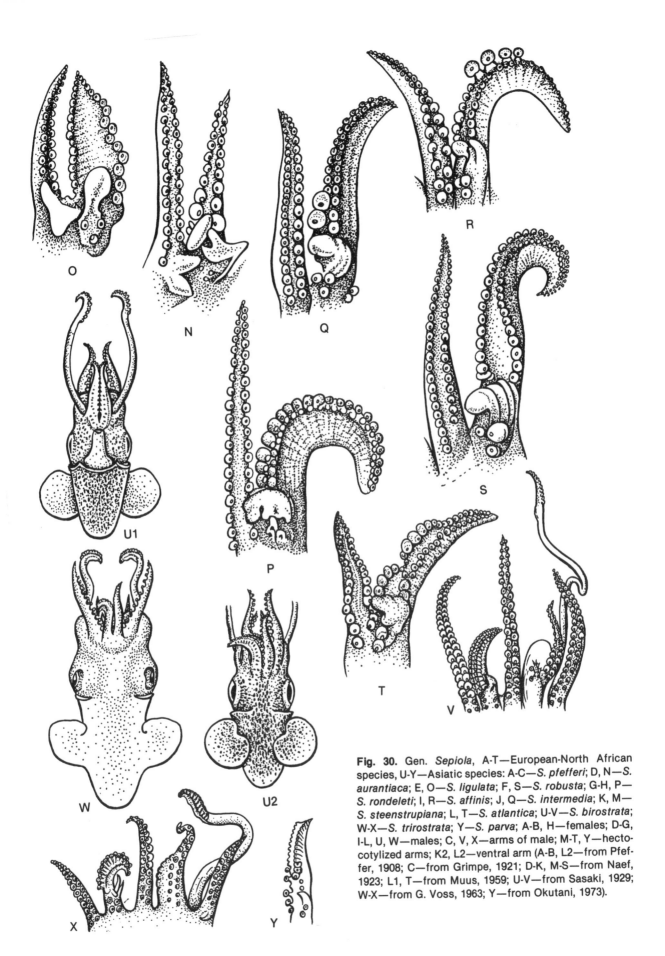

Fig. 30. Gen. *Sepiola*, A-T—European-North African species, U-Y—Asiatic species: A-C—*S. pfefferi*; D, N—*S. aurantiaca*; E, O—*S. ligulata*; F, S—*S. robusta*; G-H, P— *S. rondeleti*; I, R—*S. affinis*; J, Q—*S. intermedia*; K, M— *S. steenstrupiana*; L, T—*S. atlantica*; U-V—*S. birostrata*; W-X—*S. trirostrata*; Y—*S. parva*; A-B, H—females; D-G, I-L, U, W—males; C, V, X—arms of male; M-T, Y—hecto- cotylized arms; K2, L2—ventral arm (A-B, L2—from Pfef- fer, 1908; C—from Grimpe, 1921; D-K, M-S—from Naef, 1923; L1, T—from Muus, 1959; U-V—from Sasaki, 1929; W-X—from G. Voss, 1963; Y—from Okutani, 1973).

135

Islands, Primorye (USSR), Japan, North and South Korea, and China. Shelf.

3 (2). Left dorsal arm of male with two horn-like and one tongue-like papillae forming copulatory apparatus. Suckers of ventral row of right 1st and both 2nd arms of male much larger than suckers of dorsal row. Club suckers large, in 4 rows; dorsal suckers larger than ventral suckers . . . . ***S. trirostrata* Voss, 1962** (Fig. 30 W, X). Philippines, Singapore.

4 (1). Copulatory apparatus of left dorsal arm of male consists of a single nipple-like papilla. Between this papilla and modified suckers of distal part of arm there are several large suckers, 4 in dorsal row and 2-3 in ventral row. Club suckers small, in 8 rows, dorsal suckers not larger than ventral ones . . . . ***S. parva* Sasaki, 1914** (Fig. 30 Y). Southern Japan.

Key to species of the genus *Heteroteuthis*

1 (4). Depth of web between 1st arms in mature males is 33-50% of arm length. 2nd arms not longer than 1st and 4th arms. Suckers reaching to tips of all arms in males . . . . **Subgenus *Heteroteuthis* (s. str.)** . . 2

2 (3). 1st and 2nd arms of mature males equal and considerably shorter than 3rd and 4th arms. Enlarged suckers present on 3rd pair of male arms. 2 enormously large suckers, several times larger than others, attached at angle of 90° to each other followed by 3 smaller suckers distally. Right arms of 1st and 2nd pairs connected from inner side to half their length by muscular band. Tips of 1st and 2nd arms in mature females devoid of suckers, tip of 2nd arm slightly thickened and provided with keel on oral side (triangular in cross-section), not bent outward, not transversely striated. Anterior edge of fins located at level of middle of ventral side of mantle . . . . ***H. (H.) dispar* (Rüppell, 1845)** (= *H. atlantis* Voss, 1955) (Fig. 31 N-Q). Tropical and subtropical Atlantic from the Bermuda Islands to La Plata and from southwestern Ireland to Guinea, the Caribbean Sea, Mediterranean Sea, Madeira, Canaries, Azores. In the Mediterranean it is one of the most common pelagic species, reaching the Aegean Sea. Spawning occurs on the bottom at the slope. The larvae live in the mesopelagic and bathypelagic zones, adult animals in the lower epipelagic and mesopelagic zones. Populations inhabiting the western and eastern Atlantic probably are isolated from each other.

3 (2). Arms in mature male of subequal length. Three enlarged suckers present on 2nd arm, approximately twice as large as normal suckers. Anterior edge of fin located much beyond anterior edge of mantle. Females unknown . . . . ***H. (H.) weberi* Joubin, 1902** (Fig. 31 R). Central Indonesia. Bathyal.

4 (1). Depth of web between 1st arms in mature male about 90% of arm length. No muscular band between 1st and 2nd right arms. 2nd arms equal in length with 3rd arms and considerably longer than 1st and 4th arms. Suckers on 1st and 4th arms tiny; some greatly enlarged suckers on 3rd arms. Tips of 2nd and 3rd arm bare. In mature females, 1st and 2nd arms short, their tips thickened and devoid of suckers; tips of 2nd arms orally flattened, transversely striated, and bent outward . . . . **Subgenus *Stephanoteuthis* Berry, 1909** ***H. (S.) hawaiiensis* (Berry, 1909)** (= ?*H. serventyi* Allan, 1945) (Fig. 31 S,T). Tropical and subtropical western Pacific: Hawaii, Bonin, Ryukyu Islands, Indonesia, Tasman Sea (?), and the Great Australian Bight. Lower epipelagic and mesopelagic zones.

***H. (S.) dagamensis* Robson, 1924.** Western, southern and southeastern Africa. Bathyal. Relationships between these 2 forms are unclear.

2.1.2.3. Family Sepiadariidae

Small animals (mantle length 2-4 cm) with a short body and narrow fins located in the middle or posterior half of body. Fins have wide bases and slightly defined "earlets." Mantle fused with head in occipital area. Arms are joined by a wide web enveloping the tentacular bases on both sides so that each tentacular stalk is inside a cutaneous sac. Proximal part of arms with 2 rows of suckers, distal part with 2 or 4 rows of suckers. The left ventral arm is hectocotylized, its distal part devoid of suckers. Gladius absent. No luminous organs. Eggs large, benthic. Development without metamorphosis. 2 genera, 7 species. Benthic, inhabiting shelf of tropical and subtropical seas.

Key to genera of the family Sepiadariidae

1 (2). Mantle connected with funnel by wide muscular band; mantle and funnel cartilages absent. Anterior edge of mantle smooth. Fins shifted to posterior half of mantle...................

......**Genus *Sepiadarium* Steenstrup, 1881** (Fig. 32 A-C). Type species: *S. kochii* Steenstrup, 1881. 5 species in the Indo-Malayan subregion of the Indo-West Pacific (northward to Japan) and off Australia.

2 (1). Mantle-and-funnel locking apparatus of ordinary type. Anterior edge of mantle smooth or fringed. Fins in middle of body..............

.......**Genus *Sepioloidea* d'Orbigny, 1845** (Fig. 32 D-F). Type species: *S. lineolata* (Quoy & Gaimard, 1832). 2 species off Australia and New Zealand.

Key to species of the genus *Sepiadarium*

1 (2). Length of fins 75-80% of mantle length. Mantle somewhat wider than long. 4th arms not shorter than 2nd arms. Small round red or brown points and black or dark-brown spots on dorsal side of mantle and head...................

................*S. auritum* Robson, 1914. Northwestern Australia.

2 (1). Fin length about half mantle length. 4th pair of arms shorter (infrequently equal) than 2nd pair. Pigment spots light..................3

3 (4). Mantle narrow, its width about 60% of its length. Arm suckers in 2 rows; club suckers in 6 rows...............*S. gracilis* Voss, 1962 (Fig. 32 A,B). The Philippines.

4 (3). Mantle width subequal to its length. Arm suckers, at least on some part of arms, in 4 rows; club suckers in 6-8 rows....................5

5 (6). Club suckers in 6 rows. Hectocotylized arm distally with a series of conical plates, without continuous vertical membrane...............

...............*S. austrinum* Berry, 1921 Southern Australia.

6 (5). Club suckers in 8 rows. Hectocotylized arm distally with a series of transverse paddle-like plates bordered by vertical membrane with serrated edge.............................7

7 (8). 1st arms equal to or longer than 2nd ones. On median parts of female arms distal to middle, suckers attached sparsely, with vacant spaces between. 18-20 low transverse ridges on hectocotylized arm........*S. kochii* Steenstrup, 1881 (Fig. 32 C). Northern part of the Indian Ocean, Indonesia, and South China Sea.

8 (7). 1st arms shorter than 2nd. Arm suckers of male attached densely, without vacant spaces.

About 24 high transverse ridges on hectocotylized arm........*S. nipponianum* Berry, 1932. Japan (southern Honshu, Shikoku, Kyushu). Possibly a subspecies of *S. kochii*.

Key to species of the genus *Sepioloidea*

1 (2). Anterior edges of mantle lateral to the nuchal fold fringed. Sides and ventral surface of head and mantle with numerous tubercles – openings of cuticular pores. Dorsal side of body, head, and arms with longitudinal stripes of light blue, olive-white, or brown......................

.......*S. lineolata* (Quoy & Gaimard, 1832) (Fig. 32 D). Coastal shallows of western, southern, and southeastern Australia.

2 (1). Anterior edges of mantle not fringed. Body surface smooth. Pattern consisting of numerous small dark chromatophores, not color stripes ....*S. pacifica* (Kirk, 1882) (Fig. 32 E,F). New Zealand.

2.1.2.4. Family Idiosepiidae

Very small animals (mantle length of mature males 6-17 mm, of females 8-22 mm) with elongated mantle, slightly pointed posteriorly. Fins small, kidney-shaped, shifted to posterior end of body, attached slightly oblique relative to the body axis. Anterior edge of mantle dorsally straight or slightly concave, not fused with head, but nuchal cartilage is absent. An oval attachment organ with a rough surface (Fig. 33 A) in adult specimens is located on dorsal side of body in posterior half of mantle. Cornea locked. Arms short, a small web only between 3rd and 4th arms. Arm suckers in 2 rows. Tentacles narrow, short, retractile, with non-widened club bearing 2-4 rows of suckers. Both ventral arms hectocotylized. They are usually devoid of suckers on most part of their length. Left arm slender, with two lobes at the top; right arm flattened, wide, fringed by lateral membranes, sometimes with transverse ridges and grooves. Suckers of all arms enlarged in male. No gladius. In females both oviducts developed, but only the left one functioning. Eggs are fairly small, benthic. Development with a pelagic stage, but without metamorphosis.

One genus: ***Idiosepius* Steenstrup, 1881** (= *Idiosepion* Fischer, 1882; *Microteuthis* Ortmann, 1888; *Naefidium* Grimpe, 1920; *Berryidium* Grimpe, 1931). Type species: *I. pygmaeus*

Fig. 31.

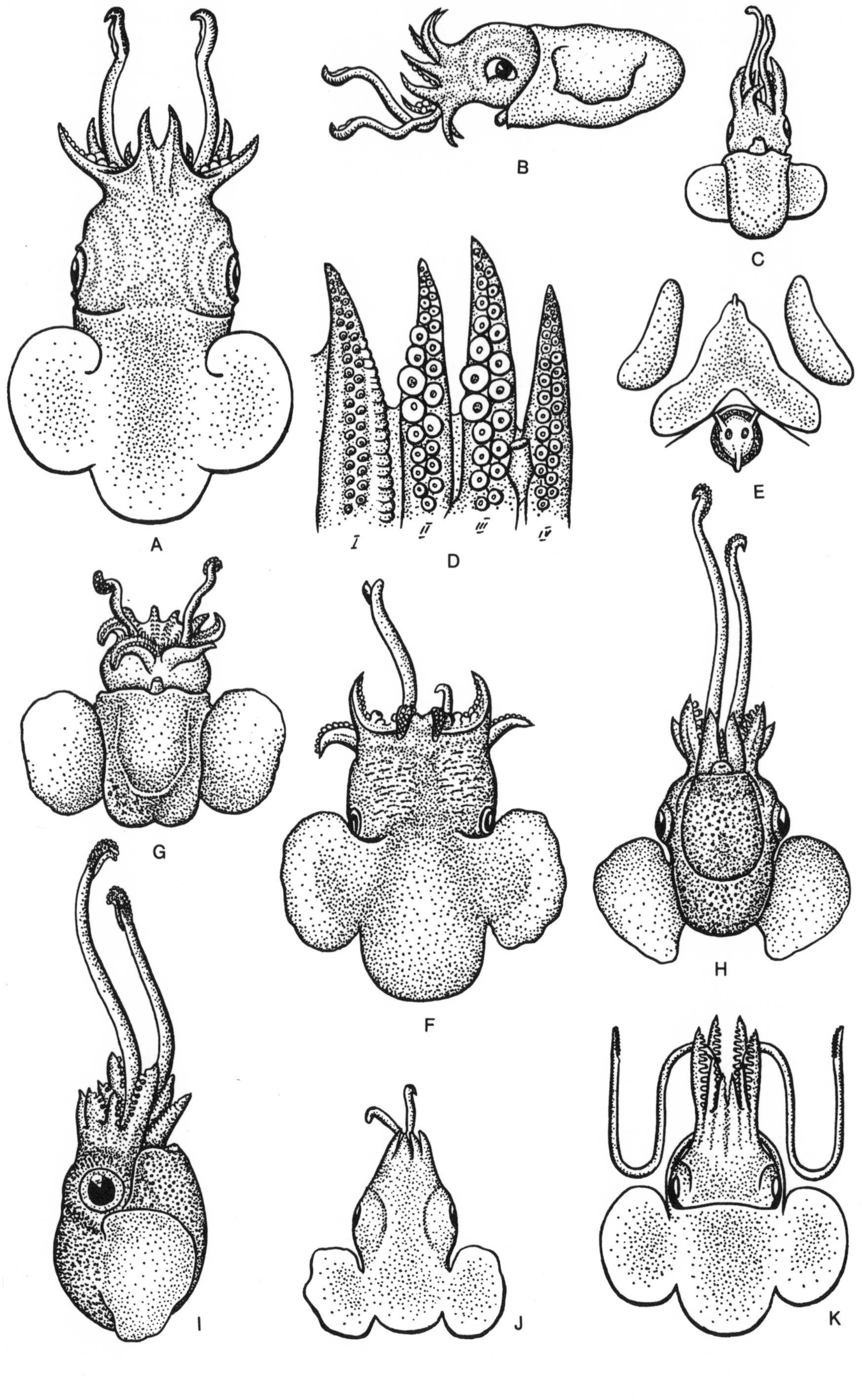

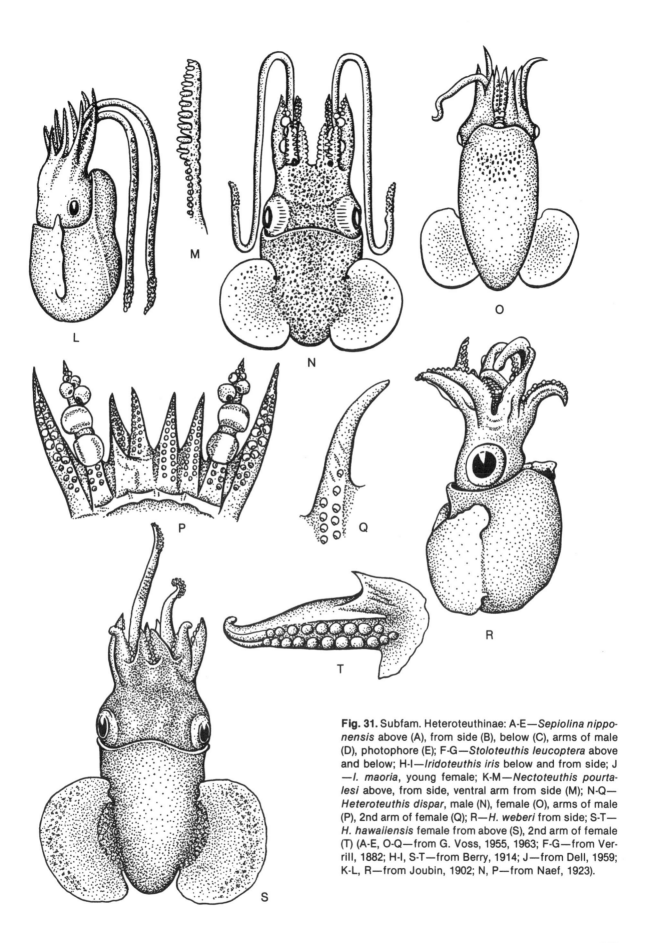

Fig. 31. Subfam. Heteroteuthinae: A-E—*Sepiolina nipponensis* above (A), from side (B), below (C), arms of male (D), photophore (E); F-G—*Stoloteuthis leucoptera* above and below; H-I—*Iridoteuthis iris* below and from side; J—*I. maoria*, young female; K-M—*Nectoteuthis pourtalesi* above, from side, ventral arm from side (M); N-Q—*Heteroteuthis dispar*, male (N), female (O), arms of male (P), 2nd arm of female (Q); R—*H. weberi* from side; S-T—*H. hawaiiensis* female from above (S), 2nd arm of female (T) (A-E, O-Q—from G. Voss, 1955, 1963; F-G—from Verrill, 1882; H-I, S-T—from Berry, 1914; J—from Dell, 1959; K-L, R—from Joubin, 1902; N, P—from Naef, 1923).

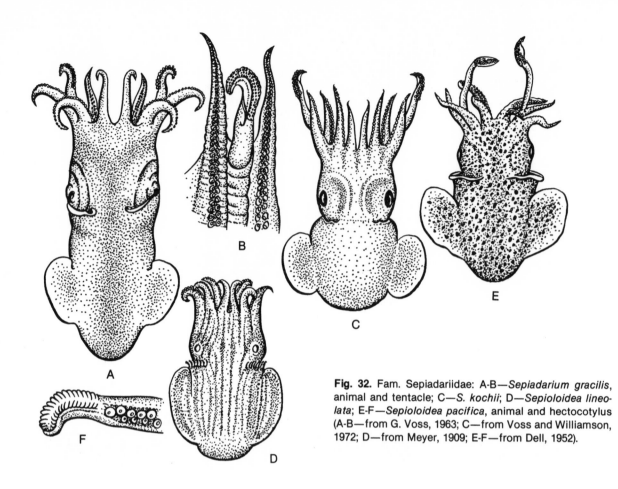

Fig. 32. Fam. Sepiadariidae: A-B—*Sepiadarium gracilis*, animal and tentacle; C—*S. kochii*; D—*Sepioloidea lineolata*; E-F—*Sepioloidea pacifica*, animal and hectocotylus (A-B—from G. Voss, 1963; C—from Voss and Williamson, 1972; D—from Meyer, 1909; E-F—from Dell, 1952).

Steenstrup, 1881. 6 species in the Indo-West Pacific.

These small animals live near the coasts in beds of seaweeds and algae, adhering to the seaweeds by the attachment area on the back. Larvae, juveniles, and "adolescents" often ascend to midwater and to the surface.

Key to species of the genus *Idiosepius*

1 (2). Club very narrow and long, with 2 rows of suckers; sucker diameter 0.25-0.30 mm. Each ventral arm of male with 4 suckers in basal part . . . .***I. biserialis* Voss, 1962** (Fig. 33, F,G). Southern Africa.
2 (1). Club with 4 rows of suckers **3**
3 (4). Club widened; suckers in middle part of club markedly larger than at base, their diameter about 0.33 mm. . . . . .***I. macrocheir* Voss, 1962** (Fig. 33 H-J). Southern Africa.
4 (3). Club not widened; suckers in middle of club not larger than those at base, their diameter about 0.12 mm **5**

5 (6). 7-11 pairs of suckers on ventral arms of male along all its length . . . . .***I. notoides* Berry, 1921** (Fig. 33 L). Southern and eastern Australia.
6 (5). Ventral arms of male with 1-7 suckers only at base. Right ventral arm bears transverse ridges and grooves **7**
7 (8). Right ventral arm of male much shorter and thicker than left, only one sucker at base of each arm . . . .***I. picteti* (Joubin, 1894)** (Fig. 33 K). Eastern Indonesia.
8 (7). Right ventral arm of male not shorter and only slightly thicker than left arm **9**
9 (10). 4-7 suckers at base of ventral arms of male (rarely 3 suckers on right arm) . . . .***I. paradoxus* (Ortmann, 1888)** (Fig. 33 D,E). Southern Hokkaido, Honshu, and Kyushu, Japan, and South Korea.
10 (9). 1-3 suckers at base of ventral arms of male . . . .***I. pygmaeus* Steenstrup, 1881** (= *I. pygmaeus hebereri* Grimpe, 1931) (Fig. 33 A-C). The South China Sea, Philippines, Indonesia, Palau Is., and northern and northeastern Australia.

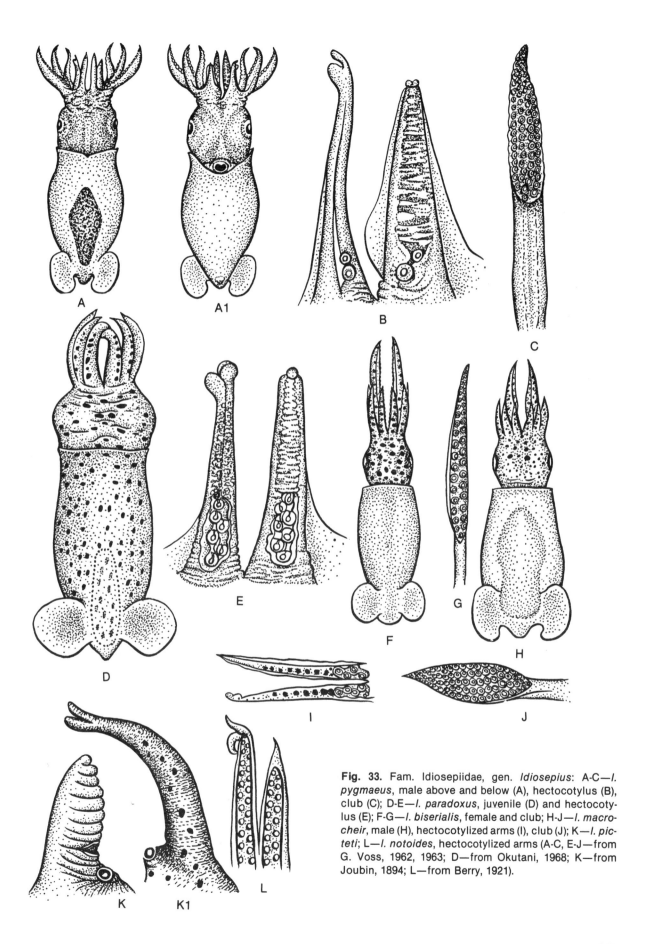

Fig. 33. Fam. Idiosepiidae, gen. *Idiosepius*: A-C—*I. pygmaeus*, male above and below (A), hectocotylus (B), club (C); D-E—*I. paradoxus*, juvenile (D) and hectocotylus (E); F-G—*I. biserialis*, female and club; H-J—*I. macrocheir*, male (H), hectocotylized arms (I), club (J); K—*I. picteti*; L—*I. notoides*, hectocotylized arms (A-C, E-J—from G. Voss, 1962, 1963; D—from Okutani, 1968; K—from Joubin, 1894; L—from Berry, 1921).

2.2. Order Teuthida

[For characteristics see the key to subclasses and orders of class Cephalopoda, couplet 7 (4)]

2.2.1. Suborder Myopsida

Anterior eye chamber entirely covered by a transparent cornea fused with the orbit and communicating with the exterior through a tiny hole, the "lacrimal pore." Mantle muscular. Fins are located in the posterior half of the mantle or extend along most or all its length. Arms and tentacles have suckers only, no hooks. Club without a fixing apparatus. Buccal connective seven-pointed, its formula DDVV. Locking apparatus simple. Gladius pen-like, with a minute narrow rachis without a terminal cone. Photophores either absent or a pair present on the ink sac; luminescence produced by symbiotic bacteria. Only the left oviduct is developed. There are paired nidamental and accessory nidamental glands. One or both ventral arms are hectocotylized. Eggs large, benthic, in gelatinous capsules.

Inhabitants of shelf of tropical and temperate waters; some species also may live in the upper bathyal zone. 2 families, 8 genera, 42-51 species.

Reviews: Zuev & Nesis, 1971; Roper, Young & Voss, 1969.

Key to the families of suborder Myopsida

1 (2). Fins reaching posterior end of mantle, interconnected. Posterior end of mantle conical. Tentacular club with 4 rows of suckers. Mantle length of adults at least 3 cm . . . . . **Family Loliginidae** [see subhead **2.2.1.1.**]

2 (1). Fins kidney-shaped, not reaching posterior end of mantle and not interconnected. Posterior end of mantle rounded. Tentacular club in proximal part with 2, in distal part with 4 rows of suckers. Mantle length in adults 1.5-2 cm (Fig. 40) . . . . **Family Pickfordiateuthidae** [see subhead **2.2.1.2.**]

2.2.1.1. Family Loliginidae

Mantle muscular, elongated, anterior edge on the back with a projection. Fins oval, longitudinally rhomboidal or heart-shaped, situated on the posterior half of mantle and reaching its posterior end. Fin length often exceeding half of mantle length, in some species reaching anterior mantle edge. Cornea closed. Arms with two rows of suckers whose horny rings are provided on distal side with high, obtuse, mostly square teeth, the proximal part of ring as a rule smooth. Tentacles not retractile, but their stalks are contractile. Tentacular club widened, the suckers in 4 rows; central suckers are, as a rule, larger than the marginal ones. Sucker rings usually bearing teeth over the entire edge. Hooks absent. Fixing apparatus not developed. Protective and swimming membranes on arms and club are well defined. Buccal connective seven-pointed, its formula DDVV. Lappets of buccal membrane usually have small suckers. Locking cartilages simple. The gladius resembles a feather with a short quill. Sometimes there are a pair of photophores on the ink sac. Left ventral arm hectocotylized (rarely both ventral arms). Only the left oviduct is developed. The spermatophores are transferred onto the buccal membrane and/or into the mantle cavity of the female. Eggs benthic, in gelatinous capsules. Development with pelagic larval stage.

7 genera, 41-50 species. Inhabitants of the shelf, only a few species sometimes descending to upper bathyal. These squid live near the bottom but are able to ascend into midwater and to the surface. They are active, agile nectobenthic squids. Many species, especially of the genus *Loligo* and to a lesser extent of *Sepioteuthis* and *Alloteuthis,* are very significant species in commercial fisheries.

Partial reviews: Naef, 1921-1923; Sasaki, 1929; Adam, 1939b, 1954; G. Voss, 1963; Cohen, 1976.

Key to the genera of the family Loliginidae

1 (2). Fin oval, forming a lateral fringe reaching almost to anterior edge of mantle. Body oval, broad . . . . **Genus *Sepioteuthis* Blainville, 1824** (= *Chondrosepia* Rüppell & Leuckart, 1828) (Fig. 35 I-M). Type species: *S. sepioidea* (Blainville, 1823). 3-4 species in tropical western Atlantic, Indo-West Pacific, and Australia-New Zealand region. Lives near the coasts on coral reefs and in the meadows of seagrasses on the open shelf. Often rises to the surface. Mantle length to 40 cm. A significant object of fisheries.

2 (1). Fin transversely oval, rhomboidal, or heart-shaped, ending anteriorly far from anterior edge of mantle. Body conical or cylindrical **3**

3 (8). Small squids (mantle length not more than

10-12 cm, usually to 5-6 cm) with relatively short, wide mantle and transversely oval or heart-shaped (rarely rhomboidal) fin whose width equals or exceeds its length..........................**4**

4 (5). Fin transversely oval or elliptical, rounded posteriorly; without an attenuated tail..........
.......**Genus *Lolliguncula* Steenstrup, 1881**
(Fig. 35 A-H). Type species: *L. brevis* (Blainville, 1823). 5-6 species: 5 species in tropical waters of western and eastern Atlantic, the Red Sea, and the eastern Pacific, plus one (doubtful) species on Patagonian shelf. Coastal squids often entering bays and estuaries but sometimes inhabiting open shelf. Mantle length usually up to 5-10 cm. Two species are objects of fisheries.

5 (4). Fin widely heart-shaped or rhomboidal, acuminate posteriorly or attenuated into short tail....................................**6**

6 (7). Body short, broad. Fin length equal or exceeding half mantle length, not as long as wide. Left ventral arm hectocotylized...............
..........**Genus *Loliolus* Steenstrup, 1856**
(Fig. 34 A-J). Type species; *L. typus* Steenstrup, 1856. 2-3 species in northern part of the Indian Ocean and in waters of Indonesia and Australia. Small coastal squids (mantle length to 3-5 cm)

7 (6). Body short but narrow and slender. Fin length in females about 33%, width about 50% of mantle length. Fin widely heart-shaped, not attenuated into tail. Both ventral arms hectocotylized; left arm very long (much longer than right), whip-like, suckerless, with only one row of cirri-like papillae at end; right arm with wide ventral lobe in middle...............................
.............**Genus *Loliolopsis* Berry, 1929**
One species: *L. diomedeae* (Hoyle, 1904) (= *L. chiroctes* Berry, 1929) (Fig. 34 K-N). Tropical eastern Pacific from the Gulf of California to Peru. Mantle length to 11 cm. Coastal squids often living at surface, sometimes above great depths. Object of minor fishery.

8 (3). Squids of medium or large size with narrow, slender mantle and long longitudinally rhomboidal or narrow heart-shaped fin not as wide as long...........................**9**

9 (10). Fin longitudinally rhomboidal, its anterior edges almost straight or slightly concave. No long tail. Arm length equals or more than 25% mantle length........**Genus *Loligo* Lamarck, 1798**
(Figs. 36-38). Type species: *L. vulgaris* Lamarck, 1798. 2 subgenera, 26-32 species in temperate and tropical waters of the Atlantic, Indian, and Pacific

Oceans. In the North Atlantic to Nova Scotia, the Faeroe Islands, and western Norway; in the North Pacific Ocean to the South Kuriles and Dixon Entrance; in the south to Tierra del Fuégo, Berdwood Bank, South Africa, and Tasmania. Live near coasts in open shelf, sometimes in upper bathyal. Usually live near bottom, but some species, especially of subgenus *Doryteuthis*, ascend to the surface and come to lights. Mantle length up to 50 (90) cm. Some are extremely important fishery species.

Note: Y. Natsukari recently subdivided the genus Loligo into 4 genera ["Venus," 42 (4): 313-318, 1983; 43 (3): 229-239, 1984]:

1 (2). Two photophores on the ventral side of the ink sac. *Photololigo* Natsukari, 1984: *P. edulis* (incl. *budo*)—type species, *P. arabica, P. duvauceli, P. chinensis, P. singhalensis, P. sibogae* (to this list it should be added also *L. pickfordae*).

2 (1). No photophores....................3

3 (4). In modified part of the hectocotylus each papilla of the ventral row fusing together with protective membrane to form single long wall-like crest decreasing in height distally. *Nipponololigo* Natsukari, 1983: *N. japonica*—type species, *N. sumatrensis* (= *kobiensis*), *N. uyii, N. beka*.

4 (3). The papillae of the ventral row on hectocotylus not fusing with protective membranes..5

5 (6). In modified part of the hectocotylus a distinct median longitudinal crest present between two rows of papillae with diminishing or rudimentary suckers. *Heterololigo* Natsukari, 1984: *H. bleekeri*—type species, *H. pealei, H. ocula, H. roperi*.

6 (5). No longitudinal crest in modified part of the hectocotylized arm, only inconspicuous ridges. *Loligo* (= *Doryteuthis*): all other species.

This attempt to subdivide this voluminous genus is interesting but new genera are also heterogenous so it is not reasonable to accept this new system prior to full revision of the whole family Loliginidae.

a (b). Sides of gladius arched and not thickened (Fig. 36 C). Mantle length 3-6 times width ....**Subgenus *Loligo* (s. str.)**
17-21 species. Range is the same as for the genus as a whole.

b (a). Sides of gladius straight and thickened (Fig. 38 B). Mantle length 4-9 times (usually 6-8 times) width. . . . . **Subgenus *Doryteuthis* Naef, 1912**

Type species: *D. plei* (Blainville, 1823). 9-11 species in tropical and subtropical western Atlantic and Indo-West Pacific, northward to Hokkaido and South Kurile Islands.

10 (9). Fin heart-shaped or longitudinally rhomboidal, posteriorly attenuated into long (extremely long in males, sometimes more than 50% mantle length), slender tail. Gladius narrow, almost not widened. Mantle length 6-15 times width. Arms usually not more than 25% mantle length. **11**

11 (12). Anterior edge of fin convex. Lappets of buccal membrane without suckers. No longitudinal cutaneous ridge on ventral side of mantle in mature males. No luminous organ on ink sac. . . . .
. . . . **Genus *Alloteuthis* Naef in Wülker, 1920**

(= *Acruroteuthis* Berry, 1920; *Acrololigo* Grimpe, 1921) (Fig. 39 A-J). Type species: *A. media* (Linné, 1758). Three species in eastern Atlantic and the Mediterranean Sea, from southern Norway to Angola. Primarily upper sublittoral squids. Objects of minor fisheries. Mantle length to 20 cm, but more often not above 10-15 cm.

12 (11). Anterior edge of fin straight. Lappets of buccal membrane with several small suckers. In males, longitudinal ridge on ventral side of mantle along median line. Paired luminous organ on ink sac on either side of gut. . . . .
. . . . **Genus *Uroteuthis* Rehder, 1945**

One species: *U. bartschi* Rehder, 1945 (Fig. 39 K-M). Eastern Indonesia, the Philippines, Mozambique. A nearshore species that lives in midwater and near the bottom. Mantle length to 22 cm.

Fig. 34.

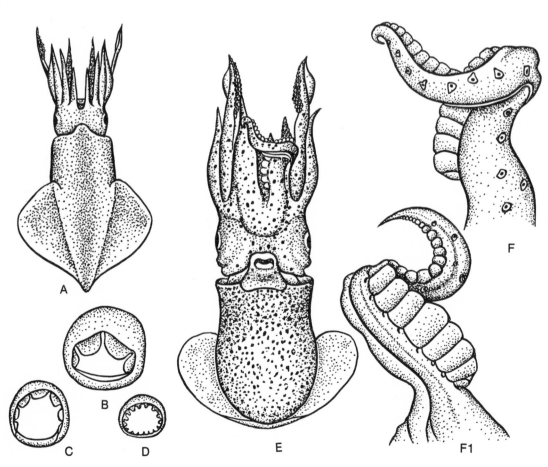

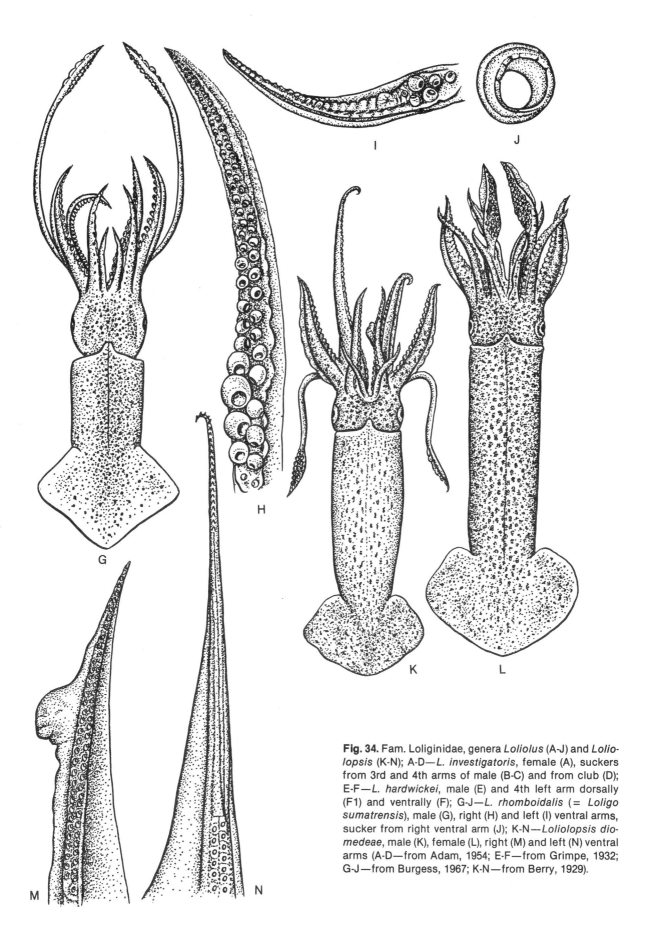

Fig. 34. Fam. Loliginidae, genera *Loliolus* (A-J) and *Loliolopsis* (K-N); A-D—*L. investigatoris*, female (A), suckers from 3rd and 4th arms of male (B-C) and from club (D); E-F—*L. hardwickei*, male (E) and 4th left arm dorsally (F1) and ventrally (F); G-J—*L. rhomboidalis* (= *Loligo sumatrensis*), male (G), right (H) and left (I) ventral arms, sucker from right ventral arm (J); K-N—*Loliolopsis diomedeae*, male (K), female (L), right (M) and left (N) ventral arms (A-D—from Adam, 1954; E-F—from Grimpe, 1932; G-J—from Burgess, 1967; K-N—from Berry, 1929).

145

Key to species of the genus *Loliolus*

1 (2). Club suckers small, central suckers not larger than marginal suckers. On hectocotylus beside high ventral "palisade" are a dorsal protective membrane and a row of stalks of dorsal suckers.....***L. investigatoris* Goodrich, 1896**
(Fig. 34 A-D). India, Bay of Bengal, Indochina, Indonesia. A common species.

2 (1). Central suckers in basal part of club conspicuously larger than marginal ones. No dorsal protective membrane on hectocotylus; there are only a ventral "palisade" and a row of stalks of dorsal suckers, sometimes partially merging with "palisade".......***L. hardwickei* (Gray, 1849)**
(= *L. typus* Steenstrup, 1856, ?*L. affinis* Steenstrup, 1856) (Fig. 34 E, F). India, Indonesia (Java, Madura).

There is also an as yet undescribed species distributed throughout eastern Australia from northern Queensland to southern Victoria in the coastal waters and estuaries.

Key to species of the genus *Lolliguncula*

1 (2). Fin width equals its length and comprising about 40% of mantle length. One sucker on each lappet of buccal membrane. Suckers of male lateral arms considerably larger than those on other arms..........***L. abulati* Adam, 1955**
The Red Sea.

2 (1). Fin width considerably exceeds its length. **3**

3 (6). Fin length 25-30%, fin width about a half of mantle length...........................**4**

4 (5). No suckers on buccal membrane. Fin length 25-30%, fin width 45-53% of mantle length. *Right*(!) ventral arm hectocotylized. In males proximal suckers in both rows on 1st-3rd arms enlarged........................
.......***L. argus* Brakoniecki & Roper, 1985**
Tropical eastern Pacific, Gulf of California to Ecuador, near the surface in coastal waters. Mantle length to 3-4 cm.

5 (4). 2-3 suckers on each lappet of buccal membrane. Fin length 30%, width 42% of mantle length...........***L. ellipsura* (Hoyle, 1885)**
Found on Patagonian Shelf near the Strait of Magellan. A doubtful species.

6 (3). Fin length 40-60%, width more than 50% of mantle length.........................**7**

7 (8). Fin length less than half (on the average 40-45%), fin width on the average 55-65% of man-

tle length. No suckers on buccal membrane. In males suckers of ventral rows on lateral arms enlarged...........***L. mercatoris* Adam, 1941**
(Fig. 35 C,D). Western Africa from Western Sahara to Namibia.

8 (7). Suckers present on lappets of buccal membrane..**9**

9 (12). Fin length about 50% of mantle length. Arm sucker rings bear teeth over distal edge only...**10**

10 (11). Hectocotylized left arm considerably longer (on the average by 25%) than the right ventral arm, its length 45-60% of mantle length.....
...............***L. tydeus* Brakoniecki, 1980**
(Fig. 35 E,F). Tropical eastern Pacific from southern Mexico to the Gulf of Panama, coastal waters, sometimes in very brackish waters.

11 (10). Hectocotylized left arm of approximately the same length as the non-hectocotylized left ventral arm.......***L. brevis* (Blainville, 1823)**
(Fig. 35 G). Tropical western Atlantic from Chesapeake Bay to La Plata, Gulf of Mexico, Caribbean Sea. Of a certain fishery importance.

12 (9). Fin length about 60% of mantle length. Arm sucker rings with teeth over the entire ring, though on proximal edge they are rare and poorly developed. Hectocotylized arm not longer than the right ventral arm.......................
...............***L. panamensis* Berry, 1911**
(Fig. 35 H). Tropical eastern Pacific from the Gulf of California to Ecuador. Mainly at the open shelf. Fished in small quantities.

Key to species of the genus *Sepioteuthis*

1 (6). Fins uniformly narrowing from point of maximum width, which is located in middle or somewhat farther than middle of body, toward the anterior and posterior ends of mantle.........**2**

2 (3). Buccal membrane devoid of suckers. Maximum width of fin in middle of mantle. Maximum distance between opposite edges of fin 60-80%, on average 70-75%, of mantle length............
............***S. sepioidea* (Blainville, 1823)**
(Fig. 35 I,J). Tropical western Atlantic from Bermuda and Florida to southern Brazil. A common species, particularly on coral reefs.

3 (2). Buccal membrane with several small suckers (2-11, usually 5-8 on each lappet)......**4**

4 (5). Maximum distance between opposite edges of fin 50-75%, on the average 60-65%, of mantle length. Point of maximum width of fin shifted toward posterior edge of mantle, distance from it to anterior edge of mantle 55-72%, on the average 60-65%, of mantle length . . . .

. . . . ***S. lessoniana* Lesson, 1830**

(Fig. 35 K,L). Indo-West Pacific from the Red Sea and southern Africa to Hokkaido, Hawaii, and northern and northeastern Australia to the south to Geraldton and Brisbane. An object of fisheries.

5 (4). Maximum distance between opposite edges of fin 65-85%, on average 70-75%, of mantle length. Point of maximum width of fins in middle of mantle . . . .

. . . . ***S. australis* (Quoy & Gaimard 1832)**

(= *S. bilineata* Quoy & Gaimard, 1832) (Fig. 35 M). Western, southern, and southeastern Australia to the north to Dampier and Brisbane, and northern New Zealand, to Tasman Bay. An object of a small fishery in southern Australia.

6 (1). Fin very narrow anteriorly and wide in posterior half of body. Point of maximum width of fins is on border between middle and posterior third of the body. Buccal membrane devoid of suckers . . . .

***S. loliginiformis* (Rüppell & Leuckart, 1828)**

The Red Sea. A doubtful species.

Key to species of the genus *Loligo*

1 (26). Species distributed in Atlantic Ocean and nearby seas 2

2 (17). Species distributed in Western Atlantic . . 3

3 (12). Species distributed in northwestern Atlantic from Nova Scotia to northeastern Brazil 4

4 (11). Small suckers on all lappets of buccal membrane, total number of suckers on all lappets exceeding 15, usually 40-60. More than 26 transverse rows of suckers on club 5

5 (10). Gladius with convex, non-thickened edges. Relation between maximum width of vane and maximum width of stalk (to beginning of vane) 2.4-3.7. Left ventral arm of male not modified to very end, suckers on tip of hectocotylus of equal size in both rows. Squids above 5-6 cm mantle length with fin length not less than 50% of mantle length. Mantle width 20-33% of its length. Usually no long red stripes on ventral side of mantle . . .

. . . . 6

6 (9). Eyes not large, diameter of eyeball 8-18% of mantle length, of lens 2-6% of mantle length . . . 7

7 (8). Suckers on lateral arms of male a little larger than on 1st and 4th arms. Sucker stalks on modified part of hectocotylized arm round or slightly flattened, fairly narrow in some suckers. Sucker rings in middle of hectocotylized arm, equipped with squarish teeth. Teeth rings of large club suckers usually alternate in following order: large-small-medium-small-large. Fin length of adults averages 55-60% of mantle length . . . .

. . . . ***L. (L.) pealei* LeSueur, 1821**

(Fig. 36 A-C). From Nova Scotia (Bay of Fundy, Browns Bank) to Yucatan and along the southern coasts of the Caribbean Sea, and off Surinam. On the shelf and upper part of slope, rarely ascending to surface. Mantle length to 47 cm, usually up to 25-30 cm. Most important object of fisheries in the northwestern Atlantic.

8 (7). Suckers of lateral arms of male greatly enlarged and subequal to largest club suckers. Sucker stalks of modified portion of hectocotylized arm widely triangular, flattened. Sucker rings in middle of hectocotylized arm with sharp teeth. Rings of large club suckers bear teeth of only two sizes, large and small, alternating without a particular order. Fin length in adults on average 50-55% of mantle length . . . .

. . . . ***L. (L.) surinamensis* Voss, 1974**

(Fig. 36 D). From the mouth of the Orinoco River to the mouth of the Amazon River. Inner shelf. Mantle length to 12 cm.

9 (6). Eyes very large, diameter of eyeball 15-21% of mantle length, of lens 6-8% of mantle length. Suckers of male lateral arms not greatly enlarged. Sucker stalks on modified portion of hectocotylized arm very wide, triangular. Fin length about 50% of mantle length . . . .

. . . . ***L. (L.) ocula* Cohen, 1976**

(Fig. 36 E,F). The Caribbean Sea and Greater Antilles. Upper slope (depth 250-400 m). Mantle length to 13 cm.

10 (5). Gladius with straight, thickened edges. Relation between maximum width of vane and maximum width of stalk 1.5-2.4. Hectocotylization reaches to end of arm and occupies 25-50% of arm length. Diameter of suckers of dorsal row at arm tip less than half diameter of ventral row suckers. Fin length in small and medium squids (to 10 cm or sometimes 20 cm) less than 50% of mantle length. Mantle width usually 12.5-20% of mantle length. In adult male, cutaneous ridge present along middle of ventral side of mantle, and 6-8 undulating longitudinal red-brown stripes present on lateroventral surfaces . . . .

. . . . ***L. (D.) plei* (Blainville, 1823)**

Fig. 35.

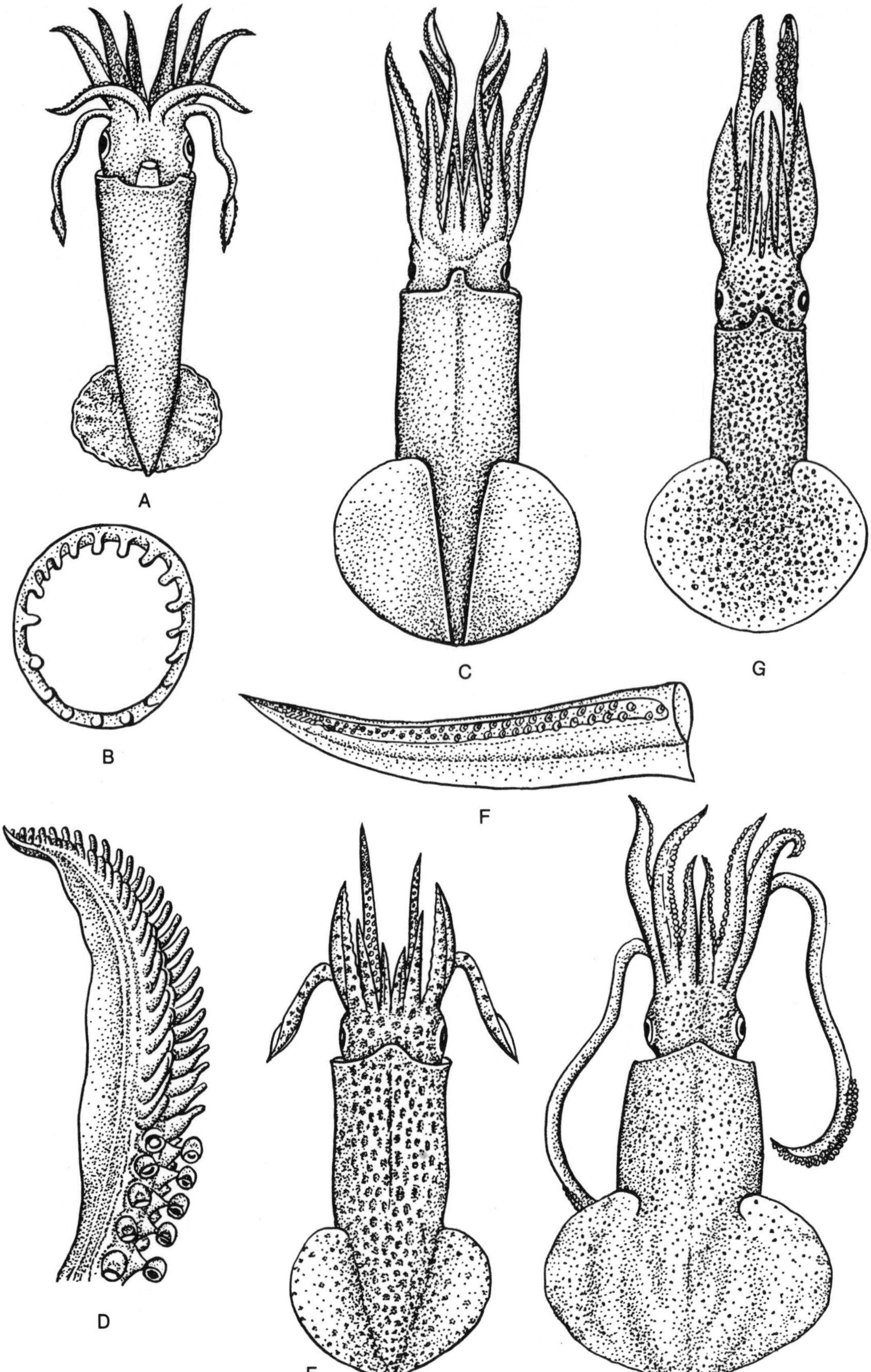

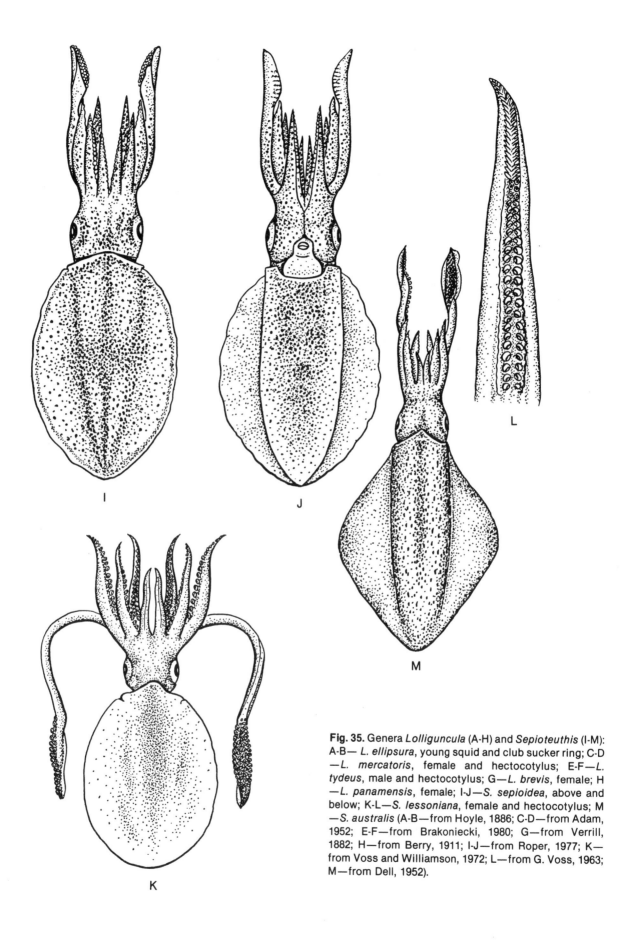

Fig. 35. Genera *Lolliguncula* (A-H) and *Sepioteuthis* (I-M): A-B— *L. ellipsura*, young squid and club sucker ring; C-D —*L. mercatoris*, female and hectocotylus; E-F—*L. tydeus*, male and hectocotylus; G—*L. brevis*, female; H —*L. panamensis*, female; I-J—*S. sepioidea*, above and below; K-L—*S. lessoniana*, female and hectocotylus; M —*S. australis* (A-B—from Hoyle, 1886; C-D—from Adam, 1952; E-F—from Brakoniecki, 1980; G—from Verrill, 1882; H—from Berry, 1911; I-J—from Roper, 1977; K— from Voss and Williamson, 1972; L—from G. Voss, 1963; M—from Dell, 1952).

(Fig. 36 G-I). From Cape Hatteras (rarely reaching Cape Cod) and Bermuda to northeastern Brazil. Common in the Gulf of Mexico, Caribbean Sea, and near the Antilles. Lives both at the surface and at the bottom; will approach lights. Mantle length to 50 cm, usually to 30-35 cm.

11 (4). No small suckers on two ventral lappets of buccal membrane, total number of suckers on other lappets exceeding 6. Gladius with straight, thickened edges. Less than 25 transverse rows of suckers on club. Hectocotylized part of arm reaches to tip and occupies about 60% of length of arm. Suckers of dorsal row at tip of arm minute. Fin length is 33-40% of mantle length, mantle width 16-25% of its length . . . .
. . . . *L. (D.) roperi* **Cohen, 1976**

(Fig. 34 J,K). The Straits of Florida, Antilles, and Caribbean Sea. At the bottom on the shelf, in the upper slope, and at the surface. Mantle length to 7 cm.

12 (3). Species distributed near Brazil, Argentina, and Falkland Islands **13**

13 (14). Fin conspicuously longer than 50% (usually 58-60%) of mantle length; lateral angles of fin rounded. 15-20 (up to 28) teeth of equal size on rings of large club suckers . . . .
. . . . *L. (L.) brasiliensis* **Blainville, 1823**

(= *L. emmakina* Gray, 1849, *L. sanpaulensis* Brakoniecki in Roper et al., 1984). Brazil and northern Argentina, southward to Rawson (records near Cuba are erroneous). Shelf. Mantle length to 20 cm, usually to 15 cm. Object of local fisheries.

14 (13). Fin length not more than 50% of mantle length. In adults, 25 or more teeth on rings of large club suckers **15**

15 (16). No longitudinal cutaneous ridge in middle of ventral side of mantle in mature males . . . .
. . . . *L. (L.) patagonica* **Smith, 1881**

(= *L. gahi* auct., ?non d'Orbigny) (Fig. 36 L). Patagonian-Falkland shelf and the slope from the La Plata to Burdwood Bank. Mainly far from coasts at depths of 80-800 m. Also near southern Chile, to the south from about 50°S. Mantle length to 24 cm. A common species and an important object of fisheries.

16 (15). A longitudinal cutaneous ridge in middle of ventral side of mantle in mature males . . . .
. . . . *L. (L.) gahi* **d'Orbigny, 1835**
[see last couplet of this key]

17 (2). Species distributed in eastern Atlantic and nearby seas **18**

18 (21). Species distributed in northeastern Atlan-

tic, the North and Mediterranean Seas **19**

19 (20). Suckers of middle rows in central part of club 3-4 times larger than suckers of marginal rows. Rings of large club suckers smooth or with irregular small teeth on distal edge. Rings on small suckers on lappets of buccal membrane distally with 7-10 long sharp teeth. Fin length in adults about 67% of mantle length . . . . . . *L. (L.) vulgaris* **Lamarck, 1798**

(Fig. 36 M,N). On the shelves from the Faeroe Is. and southern Norway to Senegal and in the North and Mediterranean Seas; a separate subspecies [see couplet 22 (23) below] near southern Africa. Mantle length to 54 cm. Important object of fisheries.

20 (19). Suckers of middle rows in central part of club somewhat (approximately 1.5 times) larger than those of marginal rows. Large club suckers with teeth over entire ring. Rings of small suckers on buccal membrane lappets distally with 12-15 obtuse teeth. Fin length in adults about 75% of mantle length . . . .
. . . . *L. (L.) forbesi* **Steenstrup, 1856**

(Fig. 36 O,P). On the shelves and the upper slope from central Norway to Cape Blanc, the Canaries, and Mediterranean Sea, but fairly rare to the south from the Gulf of Biscay. Mantle length to 75-90 cm. Object of important fisheries in the North Sea, around the British Islands, at the Canaries, etc.

21 (18). Species distributed in southeastern Atlantic and near southern Africa **22**

22 (23). Suckers of middle rows in central part of club 3-4 times larger than suckers of marginal rows, their rings smooth or with irregular small teeth on distal edge. Arm sucker rings with 20-30 sharp conical teeth over entire ring. Suckers of male lateral arms considerably enlarged. Fin length in adults about 67% of mantle length. No photophores . . . .
. . . *L. (L.) vulgaris reynaudi* **d'Orbigny, 1845**

[see couplet 19 (20) above] Southern Africa from Angola to Durban. Shelf. Mantle length to 45 cm.

23 (22). Suckers of middle rows in central part of club slightly larger than suckers of marginal rows, their rings bearing sharp teeth over entire edge. Arm sucker rings with 5-12 sharp teeth on distal edge **24**

24 (25). Suckers of lateral arms of adult male greatly enlarged (larger than club suckers), sucker rings with 9-12 low obtuse teeth on distal and lateral edges. Rings of non-enlarged arm suckers

with 5-9 low obtuse teeth on distal edge. Club suckers with 15-20 teeth. Fin length in adults about 50% of mantle length. A paired photophore on ink sac. . . . .
. . . .*L. (L.) duvauceli* d'Orbigny, 1839
[see couplet 44 (39) below]

25 (24). Suckers of male lateral arms not enlarged. Arm sucker rings with 10-12 narrow conical teeth on distal edges and a few tiny teeth on proximal edges. Club suckers with 23-24 teeth. Fin length in adults about 67% of mantle length
. . . . . .*L. (Doryteuthis?)* sp. B Robson, 1924
Mantle length 21 cm. Poorly described species of unclear systematic position.

26 (1). Species distributed in Indian and Pacific Oceans **27**

27 (62). Species distributed in Indian and western Pacific Ocean and nearby seas, from Red Sea and southern Africa to Japan, Australia, and Polynesia **28**

28 (29). Club suckers very small, considerably smaller than arm suckers and subequal in size. Distally, club suckers crowded, arranged in more than 4 rows. Arms very short, about 25% of mantle length. Fin much longer than 50% of mantle length. A longitudinal cuticular ridge in middle of ventral side of mantle in adult males. 20-30 small suckers on each lappet of buccal membrane
. . . .*L. (D.) bleekeri* Keferstein, 1866
(Fig. 37 A). Japan from Hokkaido to Kyushu (rare in southern Japan), South Korea, and northern part of China. Shelf and very top of bathyal. During feeding migrations it reaches the South Kurile Strait. Mantle length to 35-40 cm. Fished in Japan in considerable quantities.

29 (28). Club suckers as a rule larger than arm suckers, of distinctly different sizes; central suckers larger than the marginal suckers. Suckers in distal part of club arranged in 4 rows. Arms as a rule longer than 25% (commonly about 50%) of mantle length. Usually not more than 10-13 suckers on each lappet of buccal membrane. . .**30**

30 (49). Sides of gladius arched and not thickened. Mantle usually 3-6 times narrower than long. .**31**

31 (48). Rings of large suckers of arms equipped with teeth. **32**

32 (37). Teeth of large central club suckers very unequal in size: large teeth alternate (particularly on distal edge) with small inconspicuous teeth. Rings of arm suckers distally with 6-15 narrow long teeth, proximally smooth or slightly serrate. Suckers of 3rd arms slightly larger than suckers

on other arms. A paired photophore on ink sac. . .
. . . .**33**

33 (36). Rings of arm suckers distally with 6-12, more often with 6-8, *obtuse* teeth. Maximum width of gladius 14-17% of its length. **34**

34 (35). Club length 25-33% of mantle length. Diameter of largest club suckers about 2% of mantle length. A longitudinal cutaneous ridge along middle of ventral mantle side in mature males. Length of hectocotylized part of arm 50-67% of arm length. . . . .
. . . .*L. (L.) edulis* Hoyle, 1885
(Fig. 37 B-F). Indo-West Pacific from the Red sea and Mozambique to Tsugaru Strait and northern Australia. Shelf. Mantle length to 20-45 cm. An important fishery species. In the northwestern Pacific represented by two forms of unclear taxonomic relationships.

a. 7-8 pairs of normal suckers at base of hectocotylized arm of male. No small suckers on papillae of hectocotylus. Mantle length to 20 cm
. . . .*L. edulis* f. *edulis*
(= *L. edulis* f. *nagasakiensis* Sasaki, 1929) (Fig. 37 B-E). From the Red Sea and Mozambique to Tsugaru Strait.

b. 20-27 pairs of normal suckers at base of hectocotylized arm of male. Papillae of hectocotylus bear rudimentary suckers. Mantle length to 45 cm
. . . .*L. edulis* f. *kensaki*
Wakiya & Ishikawa, 1921
(= *L. edulis* f. *edulis* Sasaki, 1929, non Hoyle, 1885) (Fig. 37 F). From southern Japan to Singapore.

35 (34). Club length 40-50% of mantle length. Diameter of largest club suckers 3-3.5% of mantle length. 13-14 pairs of normal suckers at base of hectocotylized arm; no suckers on papillae of hectocotylus . . . .
. . . . . .*L. (L.) budo* Wakiya & Ishikawa, 1921
(= *L. edulis* f. *grandipes* Sasaki, 1929) (Fig. 37 G,H). Southern Japan (Inner Sea—Seto Naikai, Sea of Japan coast of Honshu, Kyushu). Mantle length to 28 cm. Validity of this species is doubtful; possibly it is a form of *L. edulis*.

36 (33). Arm sucker rings distally with 10-18 long, *sharp*, conical teeth. No cutaneous ridge on ventral side of mantle in males. Hectocotylized part of arm occupies 33-40% of arm length
. . . .*L. (L.) chinensis* Gray, 1849
(= *L. etheridgei* Berry, 1918; *L. formosana* Sasaki, 1929; ?*L. australis* Gray, 1849) (Fig. 37 I,J). Indo-Malayan species: from the Ryukyu

Fig. 36.

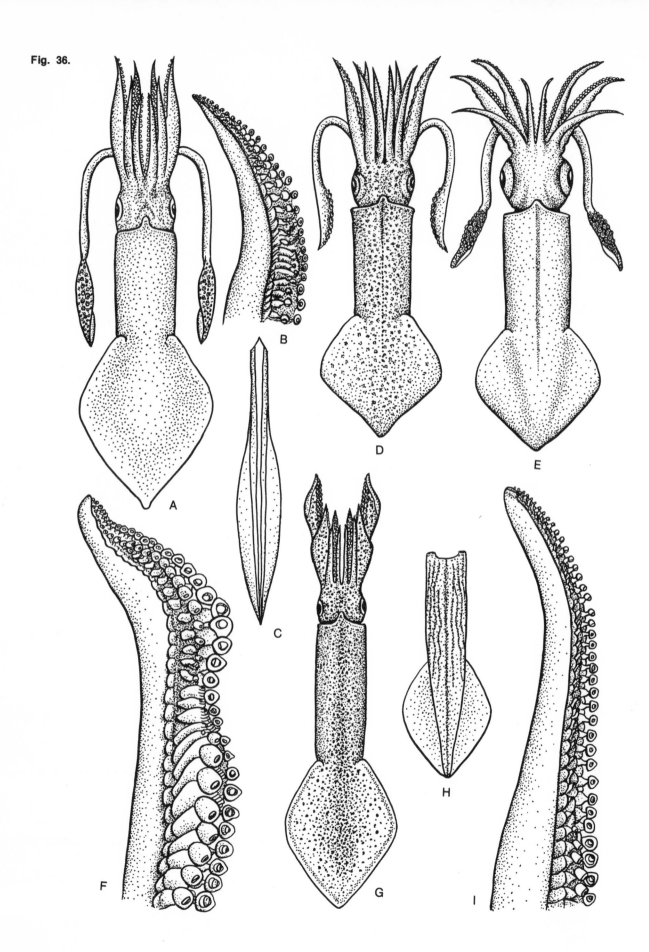

152

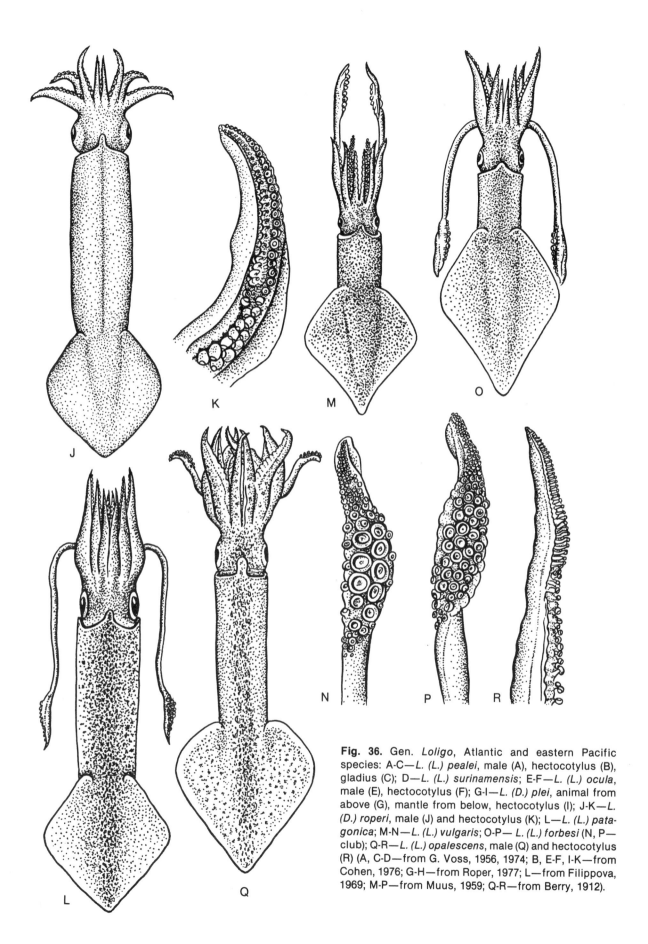

Fig. 36. Gen. *Loligo*, Atlantic and eastern Pacific species: A-C—*L. (L.) pealei*, male (A), hectocotylus (B), gladius (C); D—*L. (L.) surinamensis*; E-F—*L. (L.) ocula*, male (E), hectocotylus (F); G-I—*L. (D.) plei*, animal from above (G), mantle from below, hectocotylus (I); J-K—*L. (D.) roperi*, male (J) and hectocotylus (K); L—*L. (L.) patagonica*; M-N—*L. (L.) vulgaris*; O-P— *L. (L.) forbesi* (N, P—club); Q-R—*L. (L.) opalescens*, male (Q) and hectocotylus (R) (A, C-D—from G. Voss, 1956, 1974; B, E-F, I-K—from Cohen, 1976; G-H—from Roper, 1977; L—from Filippova, 1969; M-P—from Muus, 1959; Q-R—from Berry, 1912).

153

Islands and southern China to northern, western, and eastern Australia and Tasmania. Shelf. Mantle length to 38 cm. An important fisheries species.

37 (32). Teeth of rings of central suckers of club of subequal size, gradually decreasing from distal to proximal edges, or these rings smooth. Rings of arm suckers with obtuse teeth..............**38**

38 (45). Rings of large central suckers of club with teeth.............................**39**

39 (44). Suckers of median rows in central part of club 2-3 times larger than suckers of marginal rows. No photophore on ink sac...........**40**

40 (43). Rings of large arm suckers with 7-13 teeth. Hectocotylized part of arm occupies 50% of arm length...........................**41**

41 (42). Larger club suckers with 20-25 low squarish teeth over entire ring. Rings of arm suckers bear low, wide, rounded teeth over almost entire ring. Suckers of lateral (particularly 3rd) arms of male greatly enlarged, 2-3 times larger than those of 1st and 4th arms and larger than central club suckers. Sucker stalks of ventral row in modified part of hectocotylus fusing together with protective membrane forming single long wall-like crest, the top of which resembles a cutting edge of a bread knife....................
...*L. (L.) japonica* **Steenstrup in Hoyle, 1885**
(Fig. 37 K,L). Japan from Hokkaido to Kyushu, the Yellow Sea, and the northern part of the East China Sea. Coastal shallows. Mantle length up to 13 cm. Object of a fishery.

42 (41). Larger suckers of club with 15-20 triangular teeth, 2-4 teeth on distal edge in Philippine specimens sharp and hook-like, others low; sometimes rings of these suckers with only a few triangular teeth on distal edge. Rings of arm suckers have 7-11 high, narrow, obtuse or squarish teeth on distal edge only. Suckers of lateral arms of male considerably smaller than large club suckers. Sucker stalks in both rows of hectocotylus not fusing together..............
....................*L. (L.) vossi* **Nesis, 1982**
(= *Loligo* sp. A Voss, 1963) (Fig. 37 M-O). The Philippines, Sri Lanka, Arabian Sea, Gulf of Oman, and Mozambique. Shelf. Mantle length to 14 cm.

43 (40). Rings of arm suckers with 3-5 very wide, low, rounded teeth. Club sucker rings with approximately 20 sharp triangular teeth of equal size. Suckers of male lateral arms less than twice as large as suckers of 1st and 4th arms, but larger

than central club suckers. Hectocotylized part of arm occupies 67% of arm length. Structure of hectocotylus as in *L. japonica*...................
.................*L. (L.) beka* **Sasaki, 1929**
(Fig. 37 P). From southern Japan to Hainan Island and the Gulf of Tonkin. Shallow waters. Mantle length to 9 cm. Object of local fishery.

44 (39). Suckers of median rows in central part of club somewhat (maximum 1.5 times) larger than suckers of marginal rows. Suckers of lateral (particularly 3rd) arms of male greatly enlarged (in males from western Indian Ocean and Red Sea larger than central club suckers). Rings of arm suckers bearing 5-9 low obtuse teeth distally. In greatly enlarged suckers of male, up to 9-13 such teeth present over entire ring. A paired photophore on ink sac. A long bolster-like glandular organ on dorsal side of sucker-bearing part of hectocotylized arm.......................
.........*L. (L.) duvauceli* **d'Orbigny, 1839**
(= *L. indica* Pfeffer, 1884; *L. galatheae* Steenstrup in Hoyle, 1885; *L. oshimai* Sasaki, 1929) (Fig. 37 Q-S). Indo-West Pacific, from the Red Sea and southern Africa to southern China, Taiwan, and northern Australia. Inner shelf, on the bottom and in midwater up to surface. Mantle length to 24 (29?) cm, commonly 15-18 cm. Important in local fisheries. In the Gulf of Aden and in the Arabian Sea it is represented by two morphologically distinct forms, small and big (separate species?).

45 (38). 4-5 pairs of largest suckers in the central part of club with smooth rings, rings of other club suckers with teeth. Central club suckers 3-5 times larger than marginal suckers. Suckers of lateral arms of male greatly enlarged. Sucker stalks in modified part of hectocotylus in ventral row fusing together with protective membrane forming long wall-like crest.......................**46**

46 (47). Rings of large suckers on lateral arms with 7-9 wide obtuse teeth, whose width nearly equals its height. Basal part of right (nonhectocotylized) ventral arm in adult males with about 4 pairs of greatly enlarged suckers..............
........*L. (L.) sumatrensis* **d'Orbigny, 1839**
(= *L. kobiensis* Hoyle, 1885; *L. yokoyae* Ishikawa, 1925; *Loliolus rhomboidalis* Burgess, 1967) (Fig. 34 G-I, 37 T-V). Southern Japan, South Korea, China, Thailand, Philippines, Indonesia, Andaman Sea, Bay of Bengal, and Maldive Islands. Shelf. Mantle length to 12 cm. Fished in small quantities.

47 (46). Rings of arm suckers with 3-5 very wide obtuse teeth on distal edge, whose width exceeds its height. No greatly enlarged suckers in basal part of right ventral arm in males.............

.........*L. (L.) uyii* **Wakiya & Ishikawa, 1921**

(= *L. tagoi* Sasaki, 1929; *L. gotoi* Sasaki, 1929) (Fig. 37 W-Y). Southern Japan, China, and Gulf of Tonkin. Inner shelf. Mantle length to 11 cm. Object of minor fisheries.

48 (31). Suckers of 3rd pair of male arms greatly enlarged, their rings smooth.................

..............*L. (L.) aspera* **Ortmann, 1888**

Southern Japan. Mantle length of mature male 5 cm. A doubtful species, probably belonging to *L. uyii.*

49 (30). Gladius narrow, the sides straight or almost straight, thickened. Mantle 4-9, usually 6-8, times longer than wide................**50**

50 (55). Length of fin in adults much more than 50% of mantle length. Club suckers with greatly differing teeth: 10-20 large teeth irregularly alternate with small and almost inconspicuous teeth; total number of teeth 20-40. Mantle length in adults over 10-15 cm....................**51**

51 (54). Fin width in adults 33-50% of mantle length. Hectocotylized part of arm 33-50% of its length. A paired photophore on ink sac.......**52**

52 (53). Arm suckers with 7-11 wide teeth distally. Fin length commonly 50-60% of mantle length...*L. (D.) singhalensis* **Ortmann, 1891**

(Fig. 38 A-D). From South China Sea to the Gulf of Aden, Seychelles Islands, Saya-de-Malha Bank, northern Australia, and the Solomon Sea. Shelf. Lives on the bottom and in midwater to surface. Mantle length to 50 cm, usually to 20-25 cm. Subject of significant fisheries.

53 (52). Arm suckers with 18-24 teeth over entire ring; teeth on distal part of ring higher and wider than on proximal part (but in some specimens only 10 to 13 teeth on the distal part of the ring). Fin length commonly 60-65% of mantle length

.........*L. (D.) arabica* **(Ehrenberg, 1831)**

(Fig. 38 E-G). The Red Sea, Gulf of Aden, Mozambique. Mantle length to 27 cm.

54 (51). Width of fin in adults less than 33% of mantle length. Hectocotylized part of arm occupies 25% of arm length.................

.............*L. (D.) spectrum* **Pfeffer, 1884**

The Marquesas Islands. Mantle length to 28 cm.

55 (50). Fin length in adults not greater than 50% of mantle length. Teeth of club suckers subequal, without alternation of large and small sizes, 10-20

in number. Mantle length 7-16 cm.........**56**

56 (61). Suckers of lateral arms with teeth....**57**

57 (58). Suckers of lateral arms of male greatly enlarged and much larger than the club suckers. Sucker rings of lateral arms of male and female bear wide rough teeth over entire ring. A longitudinal cuticular ridge in middle of ventral mantle side in adult males. Pair of photophores on ink sac

.............*L. (D.) pickfordae* **Adam 1954**

(Fig. 38 H-J). Indonesia (the Flores Island), Seychelles, Saya-de-Malha Bank, Mozambique. Whole shelf. Mantle length to 11 (14?) cm.

58 (57). Suckers of lateral arms of male subequal in size with the club suckers. Sucker rings of lateral arms with 7-9 wide teeth on distal edge. Males with a longitudinal mid-ventral cuticular ridge on mantle........................**59**

59 (60). Rings of large club suckers with 15-20 teeth. Only left ventral arm hectocotylized, bearing 15-20 pairs of normal suckers; modified part occupies 30-45% of arm length and bears papillae to tip. Pair of photophores on ink sac..............

.................*L. (D.) sibogae* **Adam, 1954**

(Fig. 38 K-M). From Taiwan to Singapore, Indonesia, and the western Indian Ocean (Saya-de-Malha Bank and Mozambique). Shelf, on the bottom and in midwater up to surface. Mantle length to 18 cm.

60 (59). Rings of large club suckers with 11-12 teeth. Both ventral arms hectocotylized; left arm bearing 9-10 pairs of normal suckers, modified part occupies more than 50% of arm length; right arm shortened, suckers sharply diminishing in size in its middle part then disappearing, only stalks remaining. Tips of both ventral arms devoid of suckers and papillae...............

....................*L. (D.) reesi* **Voss, 1963**

(Fig. 38 N-Q). The Philippines. At the bottom and at the surface. Mantle length to 7 cm

61 (56). Arm sucker rings indistinctly serrate, with inconspicuous obtuse teeth. Rings of large club suckers with 3-5 narrow long teeth on distal edge, several wide obtuse teeth on the sides, proximally smooth. Fin length somewhat less than 50% of mantle length, its width somewhat over 50% of mantle length......................

..........*L. (D.?) brevipinnis* **Pfeffer, 1884**

(= *L. pfefferi* Hoyle, 1886). The Ellice Islands (Tuvalu, central Pacific). Mantle length 5 cm. Poorly described and doubtful species.

62 (27). Species distributed in eastern Pacific along coasts of North and South America.....**63**

Fig. 37.

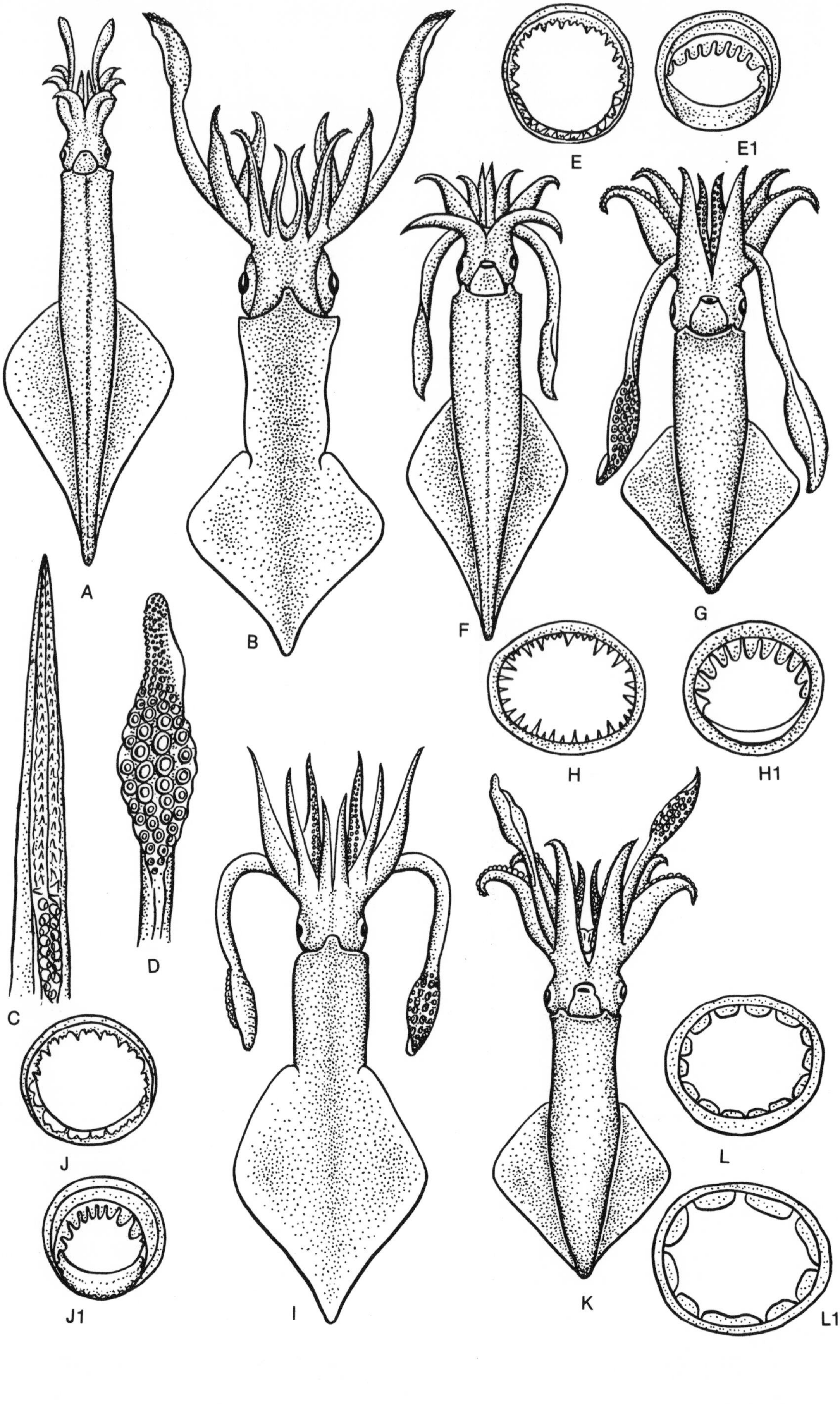

156

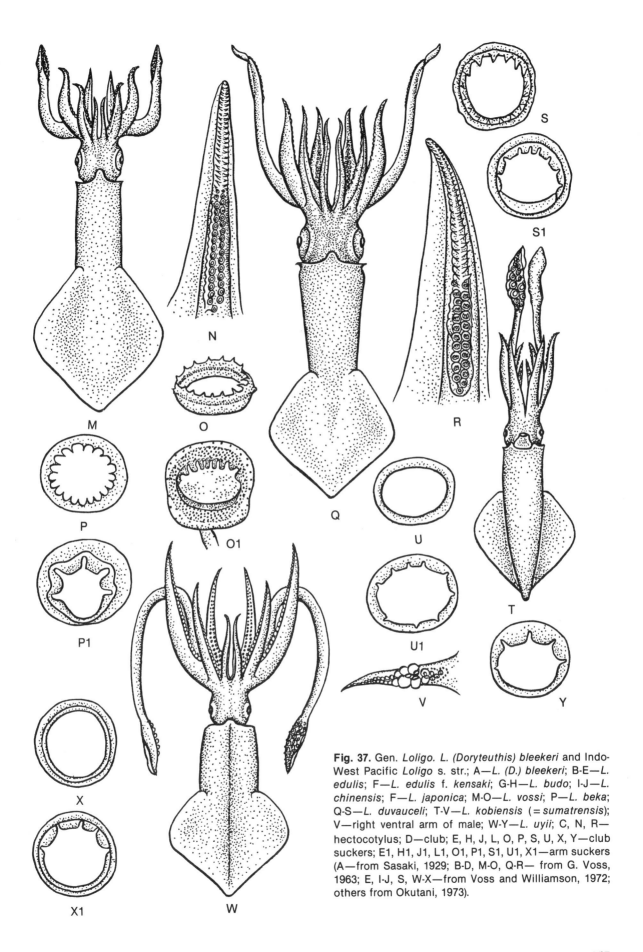

Fig. 37. Gen. *Loligo. L. (Doryteuthis) bleekeri* and Indo-West Pacific *Loligo* s. str.; A—*L. (D.) bleekeri*; B-E—*L. edulis*; F—*L. edulis* f. *kensaki*; G-H—*L. budo*; I-J—*L. chinensis*; F—*L. japonica*; M-O—*L. vossi*; P—*L. beka*; Q-S—*L. duvauceli*; T-V—*L. kobiensis* (= *sumatrensis*); V—right ventral arm of male; W-Y—*L. uyii*; C, N, R—hectocotylus; D—club; E, H, J, L, O, P, S, U, X, Y—club suckers; E1, H1, J1, L1, O1, P1, S1, U1, X1—arm suckers (A—from Sasaki, 1929; B-D, M-O, Q-R— from G. Voss, 1963; E, I-J, S, W-X—from Voss and Williamson, 1972; others from Okutani, 1973).

157

63 (64). Arm suckers with 10-12 obtuse teeth. No longitudinal cutaneous ridge on ventral side of mantle in adult males . . . .
. . . . ***L. (L.) opalescens* Berry, 1911**
(Fig. 36 Q,R). From northern British Columbia to lower Baja California, probably to Peru. At the bottom on inner shelf and in midwater up to surface. Mantle length up to 20 cm. A very important fishery for this species is practiced in California and the Pacific northwest.

64 (63). Arm suckers with 6-7 obtuse teeth. A longitudinal cutaneous ridge in middle of ventral side of mantle in adult males . . . .
. . . . ***L. (L.) gahi* d'Orbigny, 1835**
Along the coasts of Peru and Chile. Shelf. Mantle length up to 28 cm. Object of small local fisheries.

Key to species of the genus *Alloteuthis*

1 (2). Adults with short (less than 1 cm) tail. Fin length (tail included) less than a half of mantle length. Tentacles very long, in living squids considerably longer than the head and mantle together (after preservation tentacular stalks contract). Club wide, diameter of largest club suckers 9-14% of head width. Pairs of central club suckers attached almost perpendicular to club axis . . . .
. . . .***A. media* (Linné, 1758)**
(Fig. 39 A,B). Lusitanian-Mediterranean species, from the southern part of the North Sea to the Mediterranean Sea and Cape Blanc.

2 (1). Adults with long (up to 5-6 cm in males and up to 2 cm in females) tail. Length of fins (tails included) equals or exceeds 50% of mantle length. Tentacles considerably shorter than head and mantle taken together. Club suckers small, diameter of largest 6-8% of head width **3**

3 (4). Fin width in adults above 25% of mantle length. Length of longest arm in adults 20-25% of mantle length. Club narrow, pairs of central suckers attached obliquely to club axis at angle of about 45° . . . . . .***A. subulata* (Lamarck, 1798)**
(Fig. 39 C,D). Boreal-Lusitanian species, from the Shetland Island and southern Norway to Cape Blanc and the Mediterranean Sea, though rare in the latter.

4 (3). Fin width in adults to 20% of mantle length in males and 30% in females. Length of longest arm in adults 15-20% of mantle length. Club broad, pairs of central suckers attached perpendicular to club axis . . .***A. africana* Adam, 1950**

(Fig. 39 G-J). Western Africa from western Sahara to Angola.

2.2.1.2. Family Pickfordiateuthidae

Small squids (mantle length 1.5-2 cm) externally resembling sepiolids, with short posteriorly rounded mantle and separate kidney-shaped fins on sides of mantle above midline at posterior end of body. Arm suckers in two rows. Club widened, without a fixing apparatus, suckers in proximal part of club in 2 rows, in distal part in 4 rows. Cornea closed, pupil slightly U-shaped. Buccal lappets reduced and suckerless, buccal formula DDVV. Locking apparatus simple. Gladius has a short slender stem and very wide oval vane. Photophores absent. The left ventral arm is hectocotylized. Only the left oviduct is developed. Seminal receptacle located on the buccal membrane of female. Eggs large, benthic. The coloration includes large bright red, brown, and yellow chromatophores on the mantle, head, and limbs. Fins colorless, transparent.

One genus: ***Pickfordiateuthis* Voss, 1953**; one species: ***P. pulchella* Voss, 1953** (Fig. 40). The shallows of the tropical western Atlantic — southern Florida and the whole Caribbean Sea, on sand and in the meadows of seagrasses.

Reviews: G. Voss, 1953, 1956.

2.2.2. Suborder Oegopsida

Anterior chamber of the eye widely open and directly communicating with the exterior. Eye opening may be closed only by cuticular eyelid having a circular form with an incision (sinus) in the lower anterior corner. Mantle muscular, semigelatinous, or thin and nearly devoid of musculature. Fins of various forms, located at the posterior end or in front of it, sometimes extending along the entire mantle length. Arms and tentacles bear suckers and/or hooks; occasionally the tentacles are autotomized or reduced at a young age. Club often has a separate fixing apparatus consisting of suckers with smooth cups and corresponding tubercles or knobs, with the aid of which both tentacles can firmly attach to one another (the tubercles or knobs of one club fit into the cups of the opposing one like snap closures). Buccal attachment with 6, 7 or 8 lappets, with formula DDVV or DDVD (rarely DDDD). Locking apparatus simple or modified;

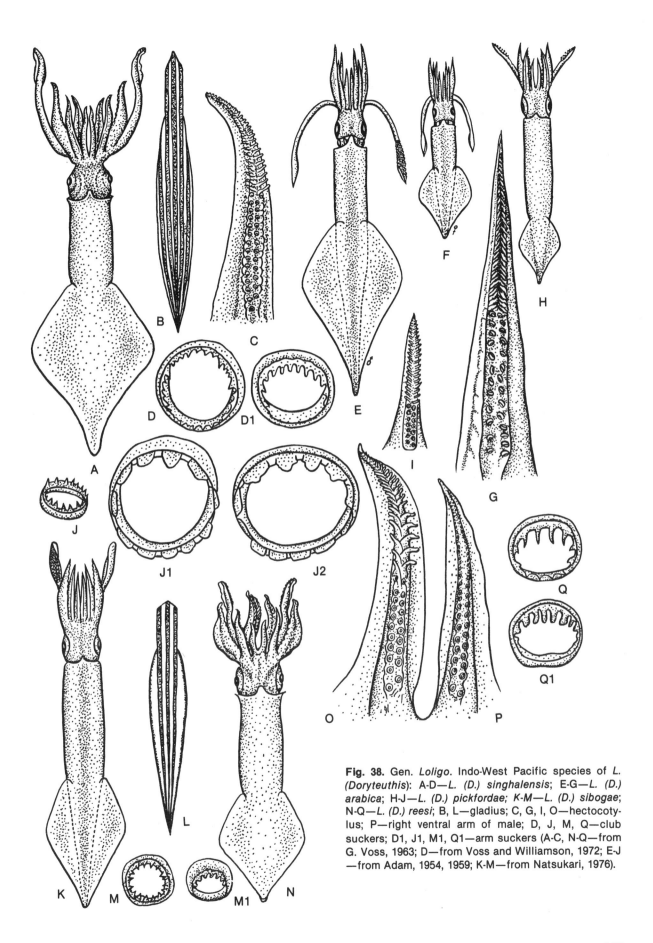

Fig. 38. Gen. *Loligo.* Indo-West Pacific species of *L. (Doryteuthis)*: A-D—*L. (D.) singhalensis*; E-G—*L. (D.) arabica*; H-J—*L. (D.) pickfordae*; K-M—*L. (D.) sibogae*; N-Q—*L. (D.) reesi*; B, L—gladius; C, G, I, O—hectocotylus; P—right ventral arm of male; D, J, M, Q—club suckers; D1, J1, M1, Q1—arm suckers (A-C, N-Q—from G. Voss, 1963; D—from Voss and Williamson, 1972; E-J—from Adam, 1954, 1959; K-M—from Natsukari, 1976).

sometimes mantle fused with funnel or with head in the occipital area; in Cranchiidae mantle fuses with both funnel and head. Photophores are either present or absent; if present, luminescence is biochemical, without symbiotic bacteria. Photophores are often of complicated structure and different on various parts of the body. As a rule, both oviducts are developed. Nidamental glands are present, except in Enoploteuthinae. Accessory nidamental glands are absent (Ctenopterygidae has an unpaired organ of unclear function that is often compared with the accessory nidamental gland but differs in position). Hectocotylus present or absent; if absent, its function is usually carried out by a strongly developed penis. If the hectocotylus is present, it develops on one or both ventral arms, but sometimes the tips of dorsal or other arms are additionally modified. Eggs are comparatively small, enclosed in gelatinous capsules, and laid in the water or onto the bottom. Species devoid of nidamental glands shed the eggs singly into the water.

These are oceanic squids seldom found over the shelf or near coasts. They live in midwater or near the bottom from the surface to the depths. 23 families, 77-81 genera, 200-230 species.

Reviews: Chun, 1910; Pfeffer, 1912; Clarke, 1966; Roper, Young & Voss, 1969; Zuev & Nesis, 1971.

Key to families of the suborder Oegopsida

1 (42). Mantle not fused with head or with funnel [In *Eucleoteuthis luminosa* and *Sthenoteuthis oualaniensis* (family Ommastrephidae) the mantle and funnel cartilages fuse on one or both sides of body, retaining in this case the ⌐ -like form typical for the family.] **2**

2 (31). Mantle-funnel locking apparatus simple, mantle cartilage a long low ridge; funnel cartilage straight or slightly bent, somewhat widened posteriorly **3**

3 (10). Hooks present on arms, at least on first three pairs. If hooks absent, then arm suckers in 4 rows **4**

4 (5). Arm suckers and hooks disposed in 4 rows: on 1st-3rd arms, 2 (median) rows of hooks and 2 (flanking) rows of suckers; on 4th arms, 4 rows of suckers. In some species hooks are absent or poorly developed and armature of all arms consist of 4 rows of suckers. Tentacles either absent or pre-

sent, in the latter case club armed with numerous rows of small suckers, sometimes with one or several large hooks . . . . **Family Gonatidae** (see subhead **2.2.2.5.**)

5 (4). Suckers and hooks on arms always in 2 rows. Armature of tentacles (if any) different . . . **6**

6 (9). Tentacles present. Photophores absent from tips of at least 1st-3rd pairs of arms. Buccal membrane formula DDVD **7**

7 (8). Photophores usually present on surface of mantle, on ventral side of eyeball, sometimes inside mantle, on tentacular stalk, etc. 1-2 rows of hooks on club in addition to suckers, rarely only 4 rows of suckers of subequal size. Tentacles without fixing apparatus . . . .
. . . . **Family Enoploteuthidae** (see subhead **2.2.2.2.**)

8 (7). No photophores. 4 rows of suckers of greatly unequal size on club: the central suckers are much larger than the marginal ones. Tentacles with fixing apparatus . . . .
. . . . **Family Neoteuthidae** part: genus *Alluroteuthis* (adult specimens) (see subhead **2.2.2.11.**)

9 (6). Tentacles present only in larvae and juveniles, bearing cluster of large suckers. In adult tentacles completely reduced. Photophores present on tips of 2nd or all pairs of arms. Buccal membrane formula DDVV . . . .
. . . . **Family Octopoteuthidae** (see subhead **2.2.2.3.**)

10 (3). No hooks on arms; arm suckers in 2 rows **11**

11 (20). Buccal funnel lappets attached to ventral sides of 4th arms; buccal membrane formula DDVV. Arms not connected by deep web **12**

12 (13). Mantle covered with cartilaginous tubercles or scales. Tentacular club with 4 rows of suckers, or no tentacles present. Photophores absent . . . . **Family Lepidoteuthidae** (see subhead **2.2.2.15.**)

13 (12). Skin smooth. Tentacular club of different structure **14**

14 (15). Fins comb-like, consists of many straight or bent cirrus-like muscular "rays" connected by thin membrane; in adults, fins reach anterior edge of mantle. Club an oval plate with numerous rows of small suckers . . . . . **Family Ctenopterygidae** (see subhead **2.2.2.6.**)

15 (14). Fins of normal structure, muscular, their length not above 60% of mantle length. Tentacular club not an oval plate **16**

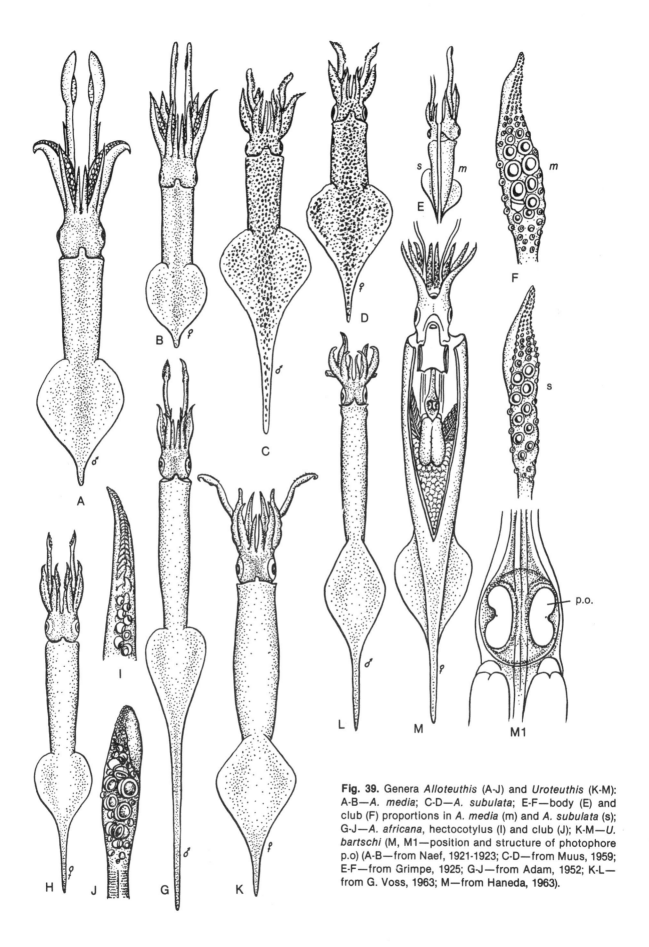

Fig. 39. Genera *Alloteuthis* (A-J) and *Uroteuthis* (K-M): A-B—*A. media*; C-D—*A. subulata*; E-F—body (E) and club (F) proportions in *A. media* (m) and *A. subulata* (s); G-J—*A. africana*, hectocotylus (I) and club (J); K-M—*U. bartschi* (M, M1—position and structure of photophore p.o) (A-B—from Naef, 1921-1923; C-D—from Muus, 1959; E-F—from Grimpe, 1925; G-J—from Adam, 1952; K-L—from G. Voss, 1963; M—from Haneda, 1963).

16 (17). Mantle posteriorly produced into long, slender tail extending far behind fins. Tentacular club narrow, not widened, with 6 rows of similar suckers . . . . **Family Batoteuthidae**
    (see subhead **2.2.2.16.**)

17 (16). Mantle not produced into tail. Fins on posterior end of body rhomboidal, heart-shaped, or transversely oval. Tentacular club widened or tentacles absent **18**

18 (19). Tentacular club bears 2 rows of hooks sometimes flanked by suckers; tentacles rarely absent in adults . . . . **Family Onychoteuthidae**
    (see subhead **2.2.2.4.**)

19 (18). No hooks on club. Suckers in central part of club in many rows, on dactylus in 4 rows . . . . **Family Brachioteuthidae**
    (see subhead **2.2.2.12.**)

20 (11). Buccal funnel lappets attached to dorsal sides of 4th arms, buccal membrane formula DDVD. Arms sometimes connected by wide web (some species of *Histioteuthis*), thus examination of buccal attachment may be difficult **21**

21 (24). Numerous photophores on mantle, head, limbs, or inside mantle cavity **22**

22 (23). Photophores inside mantle cavity, on ventral side of eyeball, or on tentacular stalk. Fins rhomboidal, sometimes produced into tail. Tentacular club with 4 rows of similar suckers. Buccal membrane with 8 lappets . . . .
. . . . **Family Lycoteuthidae**
    (see subhead **2.2.2.1.**)

23 (22). Numerous photophores on mantle, head, around eyelid, and on arms, but photophores absent in the mantle cavity, on eyeball, and on tentacular stalks. Fins kidney-shaped, with posterior incision. Tentacular club with several (4 or more) rows of suckers of different size and structure. Buccal membrane with 6 or 7 lappets . . . .
. . . . **Family Histioteuthidae**
    (see subhead **2.2.2.8.**)

24 (21). Photophores absent or present only at bases or tips of arms **25**

25 (26). Arms short, not longer or slightly longer than head. Arm suckers small and positioned irregularly—in more than 2 rows in middle and at tips of arms. Club not widened, with more than 4 rows of small equal suckers. Fins kidney-shaped, located at end of body and not connected. Photophores conspicuous only in young, located at bases of first 3 pairs of arms. Buccal membrane usually with small suckers . . . .
. . . . **Family Bathyteuthidae**

26 (25). Arms long. Suckers large, always in two rows. Club widened, with suckers of different sizes. Fins not kidney-shaped. No photophores at arm bases. No suckers on buccal membrane . . . **27**

27 (28). Fins wide, rhomboidal or heart-shaped. Tentacular club without group of small suckers in carpal part, with 4 rows of large suckers in central part and 5-7 rows of small suckers in distal part. Large photophore on tip of each 3rd arm in adult females . . . . **Family Psychroteuthidae**
    (see subhead **2.2.2.9.**)

28 (27). Fins narrow, not rhomboidal or heart-shaped. Carpal and occasionally also central parts of club with numerous small suckers, distal part with 4 rows of suckers. No photophores **29**

29 (30). Tentacles not longer or only a little longer than mantle. Fins reaching posterior part of body or extending beyond end of mantle, either inverted heart-shaped with posterior notch or forming lateral fringe. Not more than 4-5 pairs of large suckers in central part of club. Small or medium size . . . . **Family Neoteuthidae**
    (see subhead **2.2.2.11.**)

30 (29). Tentacles several times longer than mantle. Fins lanceolate, inserted on the "tail" and not reaching posterior end of mantle. Over 10 pairs of large suckers in central part of club. May reach giantic size . . . . **Family Architeuthidae**
    (see subhead **2.2.2.10.**)

31 (2). Mantle and funnel locking apparatus specialized. Mantle cartilage not a simple low ridge **32**

32 (35). Mantle cartilage consists of two ridges converging at right angle in form of ⅃ or ⊢ and narrowing at crossing site; funnel cartilage of two similarly converging grooves with tubercles at the crossing site. Always 2 rows of suckers on arms, 4 rows on club. Ventral arms not greatly differing from the other arms in length or in armature **33**

33 (34). Mantle and funnel cartilages ⅃ -shaped. Fins transversely rhomboidal or heart-shaped, fin length about 50% of mantle length . . . .
. . . . **Family Ommastrephidae**
    (see subhead **2.2.2.13.**)

34 (33). Mantle and funnel cartilages ⊢ -shaped. Fins longitudinally rhomboidal, reaching anterior edge of mantle . . . . . **Family Thysanoteuthidae**
    (see subhead **2.2.2.14.**)

35 (32). Funnel cartilage ear-like, oval, triangular, or bottle-shaped; mantle cartilage nose-shaped or

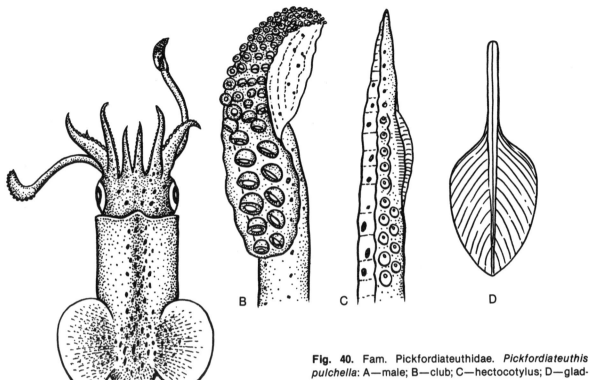

Fig. 40. Fam. Pickfordiateuthidae. *Pickfordiateuthis pulchella*: A—male; B—club; C—hectocotylus; D—gladius (from G. Voss, 1953).

tubercle-like. On 1st-3rd arms 2 or more rows of suckers, 4 or more rows on clubs............**36**

36 (41). 1st-3rd pairs of arms with 2 rows of suckers; 4th arms without suckers or with 1 or 2 rows. Suckers large.......................**37**

37 (38). Tentacular club with numerous (up to 20-40) rows of very small suckers of subequal size and similar structure, without keel or fixing apparatus; tentacles often autotomized at base so only remnants of stalks present. 4th pair of arms longer and thicker than other arms, with 2 rows of suckers. Funnel cartilage oval, with 1 or 2 tubercles, sometimes bottle-shaped. Only small photophores in form of black points on body and arms; large photophores may occur only on eyelid or on ventral side of eyeball; sometimes no photophores present........................
.................**Family Mastigoteuthidae**
(see subhead **2.2.2.19.**)

38 (37). Tentacular club with 4-6 rows of suckers of different sizes. Funnel cartilage ear-like, oval, bottle-shaped, or triangular. Large photophores usually present on the body or on limbs (tentacular club, 4th arms), often also on intestine; some species without photophores.........**39**

39 (40). Funnel cartilage triangular, with deep groove, a deep pit present in middle or at posterior end into which the tubercle-like mantle cartilage enters. 4th pair of arms similar to other arms in length, thickness, or and armature. Fin transversely oval or round, its length above 67% of mantle length, sometimes equal to mantle length. Tentacular club with a keel and fixing apparatus. Photophores always present, but tentacles and 4th arms bear no photophores........
.................**Family Cycloteuthidae**
(see subhead **2.2.2.17.**)

40 (39). Funnel cartilage ear-like or oval with 1 or 2 tubercles, elongate-triangular, or bottle-shaped; mantle cartilage nose-shaped, rarely tubercle-like. 4th arms longer and/or wider than other arms; if only slightly different from other arms in size, then bearing suckers only in 1 row in basal part only. Fin length under 67% of mantle length. Tentacular club has no fixing apparatus and usually no keel. Photophores, if any, disposed along 4th arms and/or in distal part of tentacular club; may also occur on eyeball and intestine
.................**Family Chiroteuthidae**
(see subhead **2.2.2.18.**)

163

41 (36). 6 rows of suckers on 1st-3rd arms, 4 rows on 4th arms. Suckers very small. . . . .
. . . .**Family Joubiniteuthidae**
(see subhead 2.2.2.20.)
42 (1). Mantle fused with funnel and/or with head **43**
43 (44). Mantle fused with both head in the occipital area and with funnel. Gladius present. Club with 4 rows of suckers or 2 rows of hooks . . . .**Family Cranchiidae**
(see subhead 2.2.2.24.)
44 (43). Mantle fused either with head or with funnel **45**
45 (46). Mantle fused with funnel; nuchal cartilage present. Gladius developed. No tentacles in adults. Eyes normal . . . .
. . . .**Family Grimalditeuthidae**
(see subhead 2.2.2.22.)
46 (45). Mantle fused with head in occipital area; nuchal cartilage present or absent. Mantle cartilage oval. Gladius reduced. Tentacles present; club with many rows of small suckers. Eyes reduced in size . . .**Family Promachoteuthidae**
(see subhead 2.2.2.21.)
A new family, genus and species of oegopsid squid to be described elsewhere by K. N. Nesis and I. V. Nikitina based on a specimen from deep water of South Atlantic is not included in the key.

2.2.2.1. Family Lycoteuthidae

Squids of small or (rarely) medium size, strongly built, with muscular, conical mantle. Fins wide, rhomboidal, sometimes extended into a tail. Arms with 2 rows of suckers, tentacles with 4 rows. One or two pairs of arms may be considerably elongated in adults. Buccal membrane with 8 lappets, its formula DDVD. Locking apparatus simple. Gladius narrow, with one or two widenings, spoon-like at the end, sometimes with a rostrum. There are numerous (from 23 or 24 to more than 100) luminous organs of different structure and color located inside mantle cavity, on the ventral side of eyeball, sometimes also on arms, arm tips, mantle surface, and on tail. Male genital organs paired in some genera. Development with larval stage.

Tropical to subtropical, mesopelagic, and benthic-bathyal squids. 2 subfamilies, 4 genera, 5 species.

Reviews: G. Voss, 1962; R. Young, 1964.

Key to genera and species of the family Lycoteuthidae

1 (8) Five luminous organs on ventral side of eyeball, arranged in one row. Tentacular stalk with 2 and mantle cavity with 8-10 luminous organs. Gladius (Fig. 41 P) with constriction at border between middle and posterior third of length, without rostrum. Male genital organs paired (not proved in *Nematolampas*); hectocotylus absent . . . .**Subfamily Lycoteuthinae . . . 2**
2 (3). One large globular photophore on posterior end of body in males and females. Single globular photophore on tip of each 2nd and 3rd arm in mature males (absent in females). Arm tips not attenuate . . . . . .**Genus *Selenoteuthis* Voss, 1958**
One species: *S. scintillans* Voss, 1958 (Fig. 44 A-C). Tropical and subtropical western and eastern Atlantic, Caribbean Sea, and Gulf of Mexico. Mesopelagic, at night also ascending to the epipelagic. Mantle length to 4.5 cm.
3 (2). No large globular photophore on posterior end of body [but see couplet 6 (5)]. Arm tips without globular photophores, attenuate in adults **4**
4 (7). In adult males (mantle length above 8-9 cm) the 2nd arms are elongated and attenuated into a filiform whip (sometimes twice exceeding the mantle length) devoid of suckers and bearing many photophores along the base of the swimming membrane (lateral keel) over the entire arm length; 3rd arms also bear photophores. In adult females arm ends are filiform but not lengthened, in young squids they are normal, without photophores. No photophores on ventral side of mantle near the posterior end . . . .
. . . .**Genus *Lycoteuthis* Pfeffer, 1900**
(= *Thaumatolampas* Chun, 1903, *Asthenoteuthion* Pfeffer, 1912, *Leptodontoteuthis* Robson, 1926, *Oregoniateuthis* Voss, 1956) (Fig. 41 D-L). Type species: *L. diadema* (Chun, 1900). 2 nerito-oceanic species living at and over the bottom on slopes **5**
5 (6). No long tail in males, 3rd arms in adult males are attenuated and filiform but much shorter than the mantle, they bear photophores in the distal half only . . . . . .**L. diadema (Chun, 1900)**
[= ?*Onychoteuthis* (?) *longimanus* Steenstrup, 1857, ?*O. lorigera* Steenstrup, 1875] (Fig. 41 I-L). A circumglobal species of southern subtropical and notalian zones of the World Ocean. Common on Walvis Ridge, over the slope of southwestern

and southern Africa, at the Southwest Indian Ridge, near the North Island of New Zealand, etc. Bathyal and mesopelagic over the slopes and seamounts. Mantle length in males up to 18 cm, females smaller.

6 (5). In adult males posterior end of body extended into a long tail. 8 long slender rod-like photophores deeply buried in dorsal midline of tail terminating in a teardrop-shaped organ at the very end. 11 cuticular photophores are located on dorsal side of mantle and tail and 8 on head. 3rd arms in mature males are normal and bear photophores over the entire length except near the end .... *L. springeri* (Voss, 1956) (Fig. 41 D-H). Subtropical northwestern Atlantic and the Gulf of Mexico, 23 to 32°N. Bathyal and mesopelagic. Mantle length up to 13 cm.

7 (4). 3rd arms filiform, much longer than mantle, distal part of arms suckerless. 2nd arms normal. Several dozen photophores disposed along 3rd pair of arms, 1 photophore on each 1st and 2nd arm pair not far from end of arm. Pair of photophores positioned on ventral side of mantle near posterior end of body at points of attachment of posterior edges of fins to mantle ....
........**Genus *Nematolampas* Berry, 1913** One species: ***N. regalis*** Berry, 1913 (Fig. 41 M). Southwestern Pacific (the Kermadec Islands and presumably the North Island of New Zealand). Mantle length 3 cm.

8 (1). Three photophores on ventral side of eyeball, 1 more behind edge of pupil, all 4 set far apart. One photophore on base of each tentacle and 4 on stalks. Five photophores inside mantle cavity: 2 anal, 2 branchial, and 1 posterior. No photophores on mantle, head, and arms. Gladius (Fig. 41 Q) without constriction, widened in posterior half and bearing well defined very sharp needle-like rostrum above spoon-like end of gladius (unique among squids). Male genital organs unpaired. Right ventral arm hectocotylized........**Subfamily Lampadioteuthinae**
.......**Genus *Lampadioteuthis* Berry, 1916** (Fig. 41 N,O). One species: ***L. megaleia*** **Berry, 1916.** Subtropical North Atlantic in the Gulf Stream and the northern periphery of Sargasso Sea, and southwestern Pacific. Mantle length up to 4 cm.

2.2.2.2. Family Enoploteuthidae

Squids of small or (rarely) medium size with muscular mantle (in some species cartilaginous-gelatinous), usually of conical form, narrowing toward the tail. Fins wide, muscular, rhomboidal or round, located in the posterior half or middle of body. Arms and tentacles firm, with strongly developed keels and protective membranes. Arms bear 2 rows of hooks; suckers present only in basal parts and on the tips of arms; no hooks on 4th arms in some species. Tentacular club in the juveniles with 4 tows of suckers. In adult squids (except *Pterygioteuthis*), 1 or 2 rows of hooks develop on the club, and the marginal suckers in the central part of club may remain or disappear. Locking apparatus simple. Buccal attachment with 8 lappets, its formula DDVD (in *Enigmoteuthis* DDDD). There are numerous photophores whose arrangement and structure are useful specific characters. They may be disposed on the ventral (rarely on dorsal) side of the mantle, head, and arms; on tentacular clubs and ventral side of eyeball; inside the mantle; and even inside the cone of the gladius. Gladius with a short rachis and a widened pen (vane); terminal cone may be well developed or reduced. One of the 4th arms is hectocotylized. Spermatophores are transferred to the inner part of the female's mantle or to special pockets near the nuchal cartilage.

Oceanic pelagic (from epipelagic to bathypelagic), less often nerito-oceanic; some species may live at the bottom in the bathyal. Spawn in midwater. Development with larval stage. Inhabit tropical and temperate waters. Very common but of minor importance in fisheries.

3 subfamilies, 8 genera, 37-40 species and 6 subspecies.

Key to genera of the family Enoploteuthidae

1 (12). Photophores located on surface of mantle, head, and arms, absent in the mantle cavity (one in *Abralia armata*). No photophores or single row on ventral side of eyeball. Posterior end of mantle conical, not produced into acute tail, terminal cone of gladius slightly developed. Posterior end of fins concave or straight. Both oviducts developed **2**
2 (11). Hundreds of small photophores on ventral surface of mantle, head, and arms, differing in structure but only slightly differing in size. Photophores present on ventral side of eyeball. No photophores on tentacular stalk. Nidamental glands absent and replaced by oviducal glands

Fig. 41.

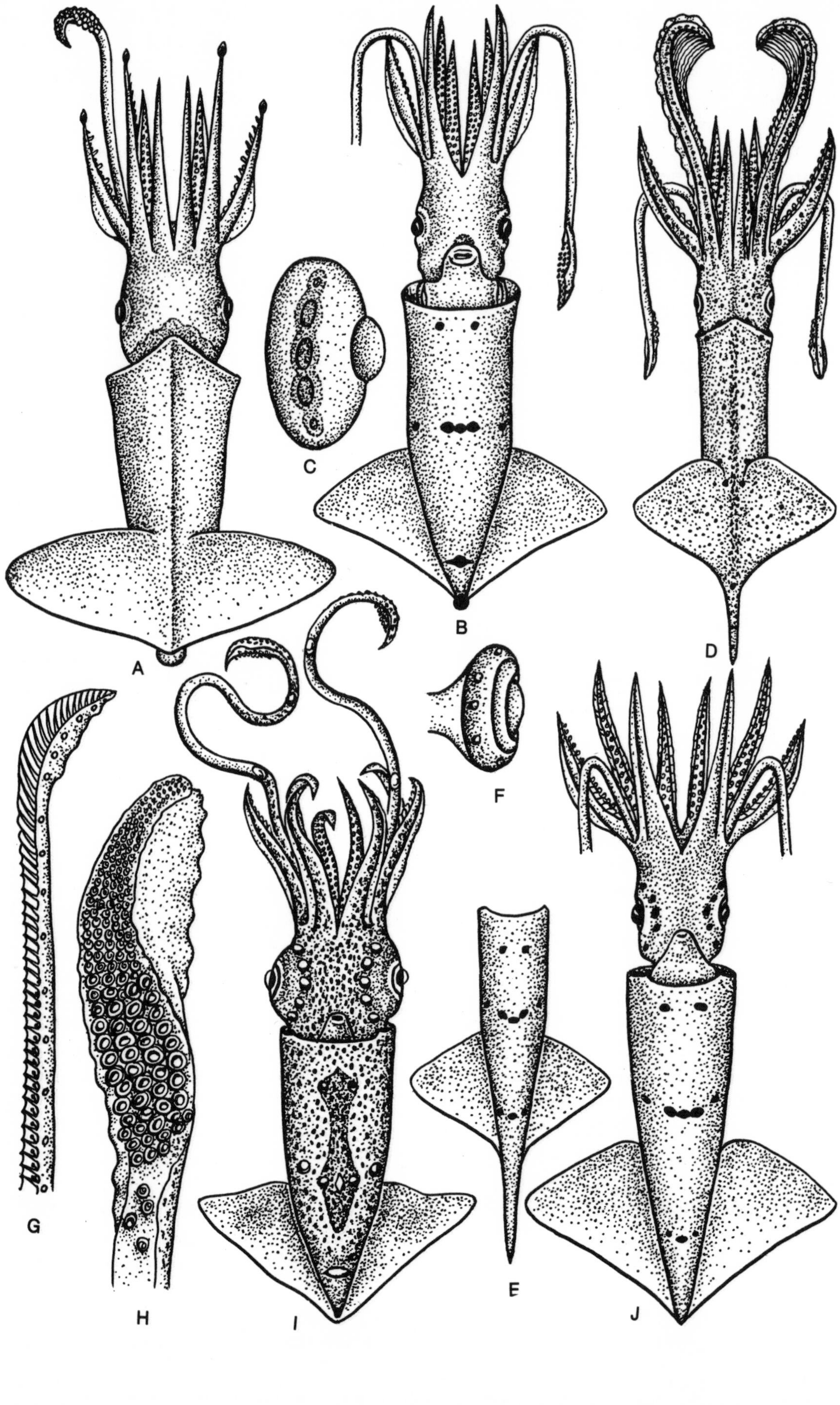

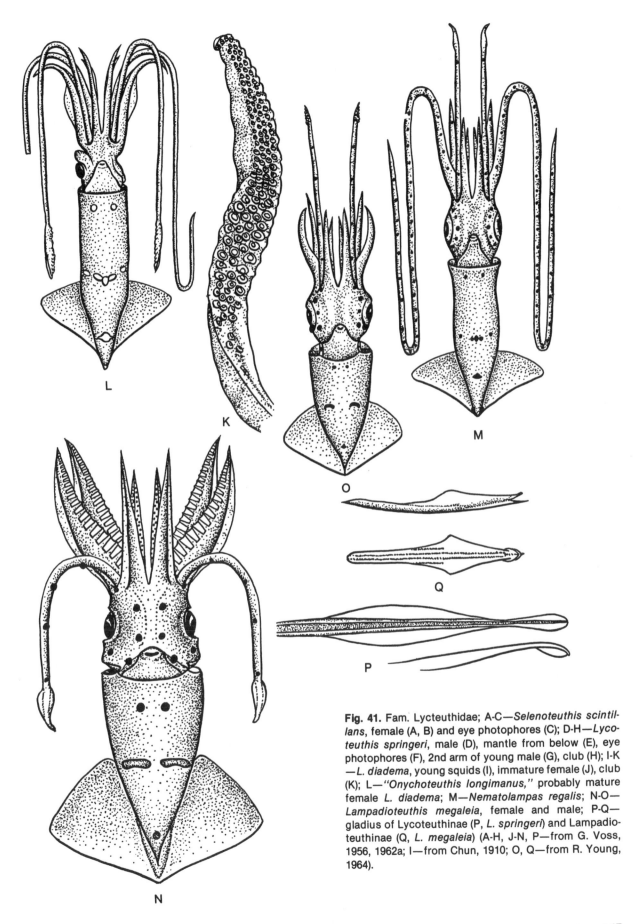

Fig. 41. Fam. Lycteuthidae; A-C—*Selenoteuthis scintillans*, female (A, B) and eye photophores (C); D-H—*Lycoteuthis springeri*, male (D), mantle from below (E), eye photophores (F), 2nd arm of young male (G), club (H); I-K —*L. diadema*, young squids (I), immature female (J), club (K); L—"*Onychoteuthis longimanus*," probably mature female *L. diadema*; M—*Nematolampas regalis*; N-O— *Lampadioteuthis megaleia*, female and male; P-Q— gladius of Lycoteuthinae (P, *L. springeri*) and Lampadioteuthinae (Q, *L. megaleia*) (A-H, J-N, P—from G. Voss, 1956, 1962a; I—from Chun, 1910; O, Q—from R. Young, 1964).

Fig. 42.

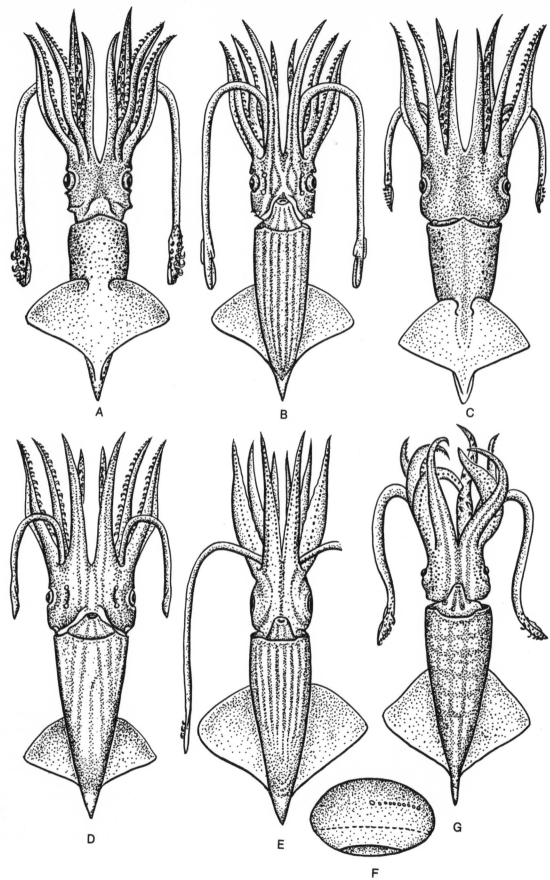

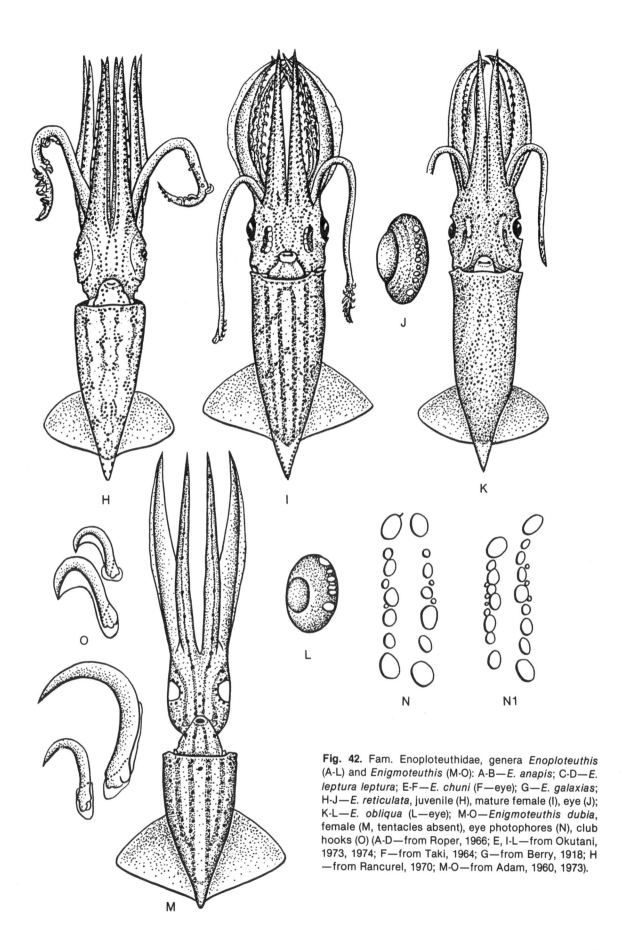

Fig. 42. Fam. Enoploteuthidae, genera *Enoploteuthis* (A-L) and *Enigmoteuthis* (M-O): A-B—*E. anapis*; C-D—*E. leptura leptura*; E-F—*E. chuni* (F—eye); G—*E. galaxias*; H-J—*E. reticulata*, juvenile (H), mature female (I), eye (J); K-L—*E. obliqua* (L—eye); M-O—*Enigmoteuthis dubia*, female (M, tentacles absent), eye photophores (N), club hooks (O) (A-D—from Roper, 1966; E, I-L—from Okutani, 1973, 1974; F—from Taki, 1964; G—from Berry, 1918; H—from Rancurel, 1970; M-O—from Adam, 1960, 1973).

that are greatly enlarged and divided into two halves. Mantle length of adults to 13 cm ....**Subfamily Enoploteuthinae** ... **3**

3 (8). 5-8 photophores of unequal size (one or both marginal photophores usually considerably larger than middle ones) on ventral side of eyeball, separate from one another. Fins reaching posterior end of mantle. In central part of tentacular club are 1 row of hooks and 2 rows of suckers or 2 rows of hooks and several small suckers between them (in larvae and juveniles only suckers are present).....................**4**

4 (5). No large black globular photophores on tips of ventral arms; only silvery photophores smaller than diameter of arms may be present. Hooks on club disposed in one row. 5-8 photophores of different sizes and structure (posterior one usually differing from the others) on ventral side of eyeball. Buccal membrane pink. Left (sometimes right) ventral arm hectocotylized..............
...............**Genus *Abralia* Gray, 1849**
(= *Enoploion* Pfeffer, 1912) (Figs 43, 44). Type species: *A. armata* (Quoy & Gaimard, 1831). 3 subgenera: *Abralia* (s. str.)*; Asteroteuthis* Pfeffer, 1900 (type species: *A. (A.) veranyi* Rüppell, 1844); *Stenabralia* Grimpe, 1931 (type species: *A. (S.) renschi* Grimpe, 1931). 14-15 species in tropical and subtropical Atlantic, Indian, and western Pacific Oceans. Most often in the vicinity of slopes. Small (mantle length to 5-7 cm), active squids.

5 (4). Three large photophores on tip of each ventral arm (in preserved squids they appear like small black balls, but they are green in life). Five round photophores of similar structure on ventral side of eyeball, both marginal photophores larger than middle ones, which are equal. Buccal membrane dark violet. Right ventral arm hectocotylized.............................**6**

6 (7). Hooks on club in 2 rows...............
...........**Genus *Abraliopsis* Joubin, 1896**
(Fig. 45 A-Q). Type species: *A. pfefferi* Joubin, 1896. 2 subgenera: *Abraliopsis* (s. str.) and *Micrabralia* Pfeffer, 1900 [type species: *A. (M.) lineata* (Goodrich, 1896)]. 8-9 species and 2 subspecies in tropical, subtropical, and sometimes temperate Atlantic, Indian, and Pacific Oceans. Small oceanic, mesopelagic, and mesobathypelagic squids, at night ascending into epipelagic zone; common in some areas. Mantle length to 7 cm.

7 (6). Only 2 hooks in 1 row on club...........

.......**Genus *Watasenia* C. Ishikawa, 1913**
One species: *W. scintillans* (Berry, 1911) (Fig. 45 S,T). Northwestern Pacific Ocean from South Kuriles to southern Japan, East China Sea, Sea of Japan, and southern part of the Sea of Okhotsk. Epipelagic to mesopelagic species. Mantle length to 7 cm. Of minor fisheries importance off the coast of southern Honshu (Sea of Japan) during the spawning period.

8 (3). Row of 8-12 (seldom 6-7) photophores on ventral side of eyeball, 2 marginal ones large, the others small and almost adjacent to one another. Posterior end of mantle in adults usually extended into soft conical tail passing beyond edge of fins..
.................................**9**

9 (10). Club with 3 (4) hooks disposed in one row, one hook considerably larger than others, two suckers near each hook. Photophores on ventral side of eyeball unequal (except marginal ones): smaller photophores alternate with larger ones. 6 rows of photophores on ventral side of head. Buccal membrane formula DDDD, all connectives, including those passing to 3rd arms, attached to dorsal side of arms. Fins almost reaching posterior end of mantle.....................
..........**Genus *Enigmoteuthis* Adam, 1973**
One species: *E. dubia* (Adam, 1960) (Fig. 42 M-O). The Red Sea and Gulf of Aden. A nerito-oceanic species lives in mesopelagic zone and at the slope. Mantle length up to 5 cm. (Review: Adam, 1973.)

10 (9). 2 rows of hooks on club, in adults the central part of club suckerless. Photophores on ventral side of eyeball, except marginal ones, small, subequal, often in contact. 6½-10 rows of photophores on ventral side of head. Buccal membrane formula DDVD, the connectives passing to 3rd arms attached to ventral side of arms. Mantle in adults usually passes far beyond posterior end of fins, forming soft tail.......................
......**Genus *Enoploteuthis* d'Orbigny, 1848**
(Fig. 42 A-L). Type species: *E. leptura* (Leach, 1817). 8 species and 4 subspecies in tropical, subtropical, and sometimes temperate Atlantic, Indian, and Pacific Oceans. Epipelagic to mesopelagic and, more rarely, benthic-bathyal oceanic and nerito-oceanic squids. Mantle length to 10-13 cm. (Partial reviews: Roper, 1966; Burgess, 1982.)

11 (2). 22 large semicircular photophores located in strict order on ventral surface of mantle; in addition, large photophores present on head (around eyes, near funnel, at base of 2nd arms) and on tentacular stalk. Numerous minute photophores scattered over body, head, and 4th arms. No photophores inside mantle cavity or on ventral side of eyeball. In adults, posterior end of mantle elongated, forming tail passing over posterior edge of fins. Hooks on club in 2 rows, marginal suckers in the central part of club absent in adults. Nidamental glands developed. Mantle length of adults to 40 cm . . . . **Subfamily Ancistrocheirinae Genus *Ancistrocheirus* Gray, 1849**

(= *Thelidioteuthis* Pfeffer, 1900) (Fig. 46 A-D). Type species: *A. lesueuri* Férussac & d'Orbigny, 1839. 2 species, one of them doubtful. Epi-mesopelagic and benthic-bathyal squids, inhabitants of tropical and subtropical waters. (Review: Nesis, 1978a.)

12 (1). Photophores disposed inside mantle cavity (8-10 photophores of different structure, sizes, and colors), embedded in tentacular stalk tissue, and on ventral side of eyeball (12-15 also of different sizes and structure arranged in several groups). Posterior end of mantle extending into acute tail (needle-like terminal cone of gladius). Fins rounded (kidney-shaped), their posterior edges convex, not reaching end of body. Only one oviduct developed . . . .
. . . . **Subfamily Pyroteuthinae** . . . **13**

13 (14). Hooks present on tentacular club and on 4th arms. Hooks on club disposed in 1 row, on arms in 2 rows over entire length. 12 photophores on ventral side of eyeball, 9 large (of different sizes) and 3 small. 10 photophores in mantle cavity including three disposed transverse to longitudinal axis of body at level of gills. 6-7, sometimes 8, photophores on tentacular stalk of young and adults. Right ventral arm hectocotylized. Only left oviduct developed . . . .
. . . . **Genus *Pyroteuthis* Hoyle, 1904**

(= *Charybditeuthis* Viviani, 1914) (Fig. 46 E-K). Type species: *P. margaritifera* (Rüppell, 1844). 2 species in mesopelagic zones of tropical and subtropical waters. Mantle length to 4-6 cm.

14 (13). No hooks on tentacular club. No hooks or not more than 2 hooks on 4th arms. Hooks few, only in middle of 1st-3rd arms, in one or two rows. 14-15 photophores on ventral side of eyeball, 10 large and 4-5 small. 8 photophores in mantle cavity, including only one at level of gills, on longitudinal axis of body. 4 photophores on tentacular stalk. Left ventral arm hectocotylized. Only right oviduct developed . . . .
. . . . **Genus *Pterygioteuthis* Fischer, 1896**

(Fig. 46 L-S). Type species: *P. giardi* Fischer, 1896. 2 species in epipelagic and mesopelagic zones of tropical and subtropical waters. Mantle length to 2.5-3 cm.

Key to species of the genus *Enoploteuthis*

1 (8). Photophores on ventral side of mantle arranged in straight longitudinal rows, at least in anterior part. No oblique or sinuous rows or "bridges" of isolated clusters of photophores connecting rows **2**

2 (3). 8 ½ rows of photophores on ventral side of head (counting row running along edge of orbit). Unpaired median row of photophores formed by fusion of rows passing along inner (ventral) edges of 4th arms and terminating at level of anterior margin of eyes, rest of head midline devoid of photophores. 1st and 2nd lateral rows (counting from head midline) of photophores united anteriorly (behind 4th arm bases) and posteriorly (at level of funnel opening) on head, forming two short ovals. 4 wide multiserial ill-defined longitudinal bands of photophores on ventral side of mantle. Row of photophores on 3rd arms reaching middle of arm or somewhat farther. Tentacles very long, 1.5-2 times longer than mantle, strong, robust. Many (40-72) suckers in 4 rows on dactylus. Semilunar membrane present on carpal part of club . . . . **E. anapsis Roper, 1964**

(Fig. 42 A-B). Tropical and subtropical Atlantic and Indo-West Pacific. An oceanic species. 2 subspecies.

a (b). Midventral space on mantle, free of photophores, not extending to tail, interrupted near tail by scattered photophores. 1st lateral row of photophores on ventral side of head multiserial. 40-50 club suckers on dactylus . . . .
. . . . ***E. anapsis anapsis* Roper, 1964**

Tropical and subtropical Atlantic, Gulf of Mexico, Caribbean Sea.

b (a). Midventral space on mantle, free of photophores, reaching tail as narrow stripe. 1st lateral row of photophores on ventral side of head a simple chain of photophores. 60-72 club suckers on dactylus . . ***E. anapsis jonesi* Burgess, 1982**

Tropical Indo-West Pacific from eastern Africa to Hawaii and equatorial Pacific eastward to 155-160°W.

3 (2). 7-8 longitudinal rows of photophores on ventral side of head; unpaired median row, if present, complete **4**

4 (5). 7 longitudinal rows of photophores on ventral side of head. Unpaired median row splitting at most anterior and posterior parts of head and passing over 4th arms and to edges of funnel groove. 6-8 longitudinal rows of photophores on ventral side of mantle in anterior part (diffusely distributed in posterior part of mantle). 4 rows of photophores on funnel. Tentacles long, strong, robust, with many (about 90) suckers in 4 rows on dactylus; club with semilunar carpal membrane..
..................*E. chuni* C. Ishikawa, 1914
(= *E. theragrae* Taki, 1964) (Fig. 42 E-F). Pacific and Sea of Japan coasts of central and southern Japan, including Kyushu, Ryukyu, Bonin, and Izu-Oshima Islands, and Kuroshio. A nerito-oceanic species.

5 (4). 8 longitudinal rows of photophores on ventral side of head; midline of head free from photophores. Tentacles weak, slender, club short, with few (10-17) suckers in 2 rows on dactylus; no carpal semilunar membrane on club..........**6**

6 (7). 7 longitudinal rows of photophores on ventral side of mantle, 3 median ones reaching tail. 6 rows of photophores on funnel. 2nd and 3rd lateral rows of photophores on ventral side of head not uniting on 4th arm bases: 2nd row continuing onto median and 3rd row onto dorsal (outer) row on 4th arm.....................
....................*E. leptura* (Leach, 1817)
(Fig. 42 C-D). Tropical Atlantic and Indo-West Pacific nerito-oceanic species. 2 subspecies.

a (b). Unpaired median row of photophores on ventral side of mantle branching off from right or left or both lateral rows far behind anterior mantle margin......*E. leptura leptura* (Leach, 1817)
(Fig. 42 C-D). Tropical Atlantic from Bermuda and Madeira to Brazil and southwestern Africa.

b (a). Unpaired median row of photophores on ventral side of mantle starting in midline but a little behind anterior mantle margin and not branching off from lateral row....................
........*E. leptura magnoceani* Nesis, 1982
(= *E. leptura* d'Orbigny, 1839, part: Atlas (*Onychoteuthis*), pl. 6; pl. 11, fig. 6-14; pl. 12, fig. 10-24). Tropical western and central Pacific Ocean and Australo-Asiatic seas, predominantly in equatorial waters.

7 (6). 8 longitudinal rows of photophores on ventral side of mantle, 4 median ones reaching tail. 4 rows of photophores on funnel. 3rd lateral row of photophores on ventral side of head dividing in front of eye and continuing partly onto median

row on 4th arm, uniting with continuation of 2nd lateral row of head, and partly on dorsal (outer) row on 4th arm. .*E. octolineata* Burgess, 1982
Equatorial waters of central Pacific around and eastward from the Line Islands.

8 (1). Photophores on ventral side of mantle arranged either in sinuous rows connected by "bridges" of isolated bunches of photophores or in oblique diverging rows (besides the longitudinal ones), or photophores diffusely scattered, not forming rows.................................**9**

9 (14). Photophores on ventral side of mantle forming sinuous or oblique and longitudinal rows. Row of photophores on 3rd arms reaching end of arm. Club with carpal semilunar membrane....**10**

10 (13). Photophores on ventral side of mantle forming sinuous longitudinal rows.........**11**

11 (12). 4 sinuous longitudinal rows of photophores on ventral side of mantle, 2 median ones connected by numerous "bridges" of isolated clusters of photophores. 7 longitudinal rows of photophores on ventral side of head, median one complete, 1st and 2nd lateral rows unbranched; these three rows are rather wide bands of numerous adjoining photophores. Three rows of photophores on 4th arms located at equal distances from one another. Tentacles long, strong, robust, club dactylus with about 40 suckers in 4 rows.....*E. galaxias* Berry, 1918
(Fig. 42 G). Western, southern, and southeastern Australia and northern New Zealand. A southern subtropical nerito-oceanic mesopelagic and benthic-bathyal species.

12 (11). 6 sinuous longitudinal rows of photophores on ventral side of mantle, connected by a few "bridges" of isolated clusters of photophores together forming 4 transverse rows in center of ventral side of mantle and oblique on sides; intersection of longitudinal and transverse-to-oblique rows forming reticulated pattern. 8 longitudinal rows of photophores on ventral side of head, each row consisting of one chain of photophores; head midline free from photophores. Median row of photophores on 4th arm shifted somewhat dorsally and at arm base consists of two rather ill-defined rows. Tentacles weak, slender, club dactylus with about 10 suckers in 2 rows........................
..............*E. reticulata* Rancurel, 1970
(Fig. 42 H-J). Indo-West Pacific from western Indian Ocean to Hawaii and area eastward from Marquesas and Tuamotu Archipelagos, in both

equatorial and central waters. Lower epipelagic and mesopelagic zones.

13 (10). Photophores on ventral side of mantle forming 2 longitudinal and 4 oblique diagonal rows branching off from longitudinal ones and diverging posteriorly; in posterior part of mantle photophores are arranged diffusely. 6 ill-defined rows of photophores on ventral side of head with narrow midventral photophore-free stripe; 1st and 2nd lateral rows poorly delineated. Median row of photophores on 4th arm shifted somewhat dorsally. Tentacles weak, slender, shorter than mantle, club dactylus with 10-20 suckers in 2 rows......
.................*E. obliqua* **Burgess, 1982**
(Fig. 42 K-L). Eastern equatorial Pacific from the area to the east of Line Islands up to Central America.

14 (9). Mantle photophores scattered, forming no longitudinal rows or only indistinct longitudinal rows. 8 ½ rows of photophores on ventral side of head, the median row short, but beyond its end in midline of head there are some isolated photophores. 1st lateral row multiserial. 1st and 2nd lateral rows fused near bases of 4th arms and near edge of funnel groove, forming two long ovals.· Row of photophores on 3rd arms reaching only middle of arm. Tentacles very long, on average 2 times longer than mantle, strong, robust, with 60-72 suckers in 4 rows on club dactylus; semilunar carpal membrane present on club.....
..............*E. higginsi* **Burgess, 1982**
Central Pacific: Hawaii and equatorial regions eastward to the area off the Line Islands.

Key to subgenera and species of the genus *Abralia*

1 (14). 5 distinct longitudinal rows of photophores (not counting row passing along edges of eyelid) on ventral side of head; median row splitting into two in posterior half of head........**2**
2 (3). Fin length 50-67%, width above 83% of the mantle length. A luminous organ on ink sac. Photophores on ventral side of mantle distributed diffusely, without a free median longitudinal band. 6 (rarely 5 or 7) photophores on ventral side of eyeball. 6 hooks on tentacular club. Right ventral arm hectocotylized....................
...............**Subgenus *Abralia* (s. str.)**
One species: *A. (A.) armata* **(Quoy & Gaimard, 1832)** (Fig. 43 a-d). Eastern Indonesia and the Philippines.

3 (2). Fin length 20-50% of mantle length, width 33-75% of mantle length. No luminous organ on ink sac. Photophores on ventral side of mantle form 6-8 narrow longitudinal bands, two median bands distinctly isolated from others. Longitudinal median stripe usually (not always) free of photophores. Right ventral arm hectocotylized..
...**Subgenus *Stenabralia* Grimpe, 1931 ... 4**
4 (7). 5 photophores on ventral side of eyeball. 3 longitudinal rows of photophores on 4th arms. A narrow longitudinal stripe free of photophores passing along median line of ventral side of mantle. At ventral posterior end of body on sides of mantle are 2 large photophores. 3-6 isolated photophores larger than normal ones on tips of 4th arms. 4-5 hooks on tentacular club. Suckers on arm tips in 2 rows....................**5**
5 (6). Fin length 50% or a little less of mantle length. Longitudinal stripes of photophores on ventral side of mantle wide, distinctly separated; photophores in stripes close together and differing slightly in size. 3 isolated photophores on tips of 4th arms. .*A. (S.) astrolineata* **Berry, 1914**
Eastern Australia (Queensland) and Kermadec Islands.

6 (5). Fin length about 33% of mantle length. Longitudinal stripes of photophores on ventral side of mantle narrow, slightly separated; photophores in stripes diffuse and differ greatly in size. 4-6 isolated photophores on tips of 4th arms.....
.............*A. (S.) astrosticta* **Berry, 1909**
(Fig. 43 E-G). Philippine Sea, the Kuroshio, the Marshall Islands, and Hawaii. Pelagic and bottom in lower sublittoral and upper bathyal.

7 (4). 6-9 photophores on ventral side of eyeball. 3-4 longitudinal rows of photophores on 4th arms. 6-8 (rarely 5) hooks on tentacular club. No large photophores at end of body and tips of 4th arms. Suckers on arm tips in 3-4 rows.............**8**
8 (11). 6-7 (rarely 8) photophores on ventral side of eyeball, 5 of these large, 1-3 small. Fin length more than 33% of mantle length, width over 50% of mantle length....................**9**
9 (10). 6 photophores on ventral side of eyeball: 2 large terminal, 3 large, and 1 small between them. 3 rows of photophores on 4th arms...........
..............*A. (S.) renschi* **Grimpe, 1931**
(Fig. 43 H-J). The Maldive Islands, Sumatra, and Java.
10 (9). 7-8 photophores on ventral side of eyeball: 2 terminal, 3 large, and 2-3 small between them. 3 rows of photophores on 4th arms, but with a short

incomplete additional row of several photophores between the median and ventral rows near the arm base (in adults only)....................

.........*A. (S.) steindachneri* **Weindl, 1912**

(Fig. 43 K). The Red Sea, Arabian Sea, eastern Africa, Mascarenes Ridge, and Seychelle Islands.

11 (8). 8-9 photophores on ventral side of eyeball: 6 large, 2-3 small (small photophores sometimes absent). Fin length 20-25% of mantle length, width 25-33% of mantle length............**12**

12 (13). 3 longitudinal rows of photophores on 4th arms, 2 isolated additional photophores between them (at arm base). No isolated large photophores in funnel groove.....................

.................*A. (S.) lucens* **Voss, 1962**

(Fig. 43 L-N). The Philippines and Polynesia (Line Islands).

13 (12). 4 longitudinal rows of photophores on 4th arms: 3 ordinary and an additional row of 4-5 photophores between median and ventral rows; 1-2 additional photophores may occur between median and dorsal rows at arm base. One large

isolated white photophore in funnel groove on each side of funnel near base of first nuchal fold.........*A. (S.) spaercki* **Grimpe, 1931**

(Fig. 43 M-S). The Philippines and eastern Indonesia.

14 (1). The photophore pattern on ventral side of head is different.........................**15**

15 (28). Photophores on ventral side of head distributed diffusely or forming 7-13 indistinctly isolated longitudinal rows, not counting row along edge of eyelid. Fin length 50-67%, sometimes 75%, of mantle length; width over 67%, most often 75-95%, of mantle length...........

.**Subgenus** *Asteroteuthis* **Pfeffer, 1900**.....**16**

16 (19). 6-7 photophores on ventral side of eyeball. Suckers on arm tips in 2 rows.........**17**

17 (18). 2 hooks on tentacular club. 3 longitudinal stripes free of photophores on ventral side of mantle. 6-7 ocular photophores..................

.................*A. (A.) grimpei* **Voss, 1958**

(Fig. 44 A-D). Gulf Stream near Florida.

18 (17). 6-7 hooks on tentacular club. Only one

Fig. 43.

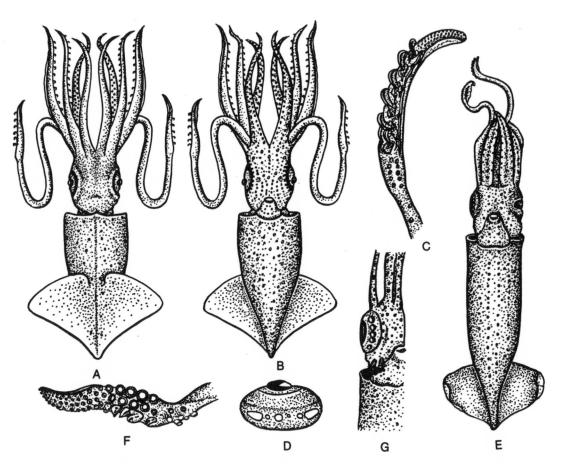

174

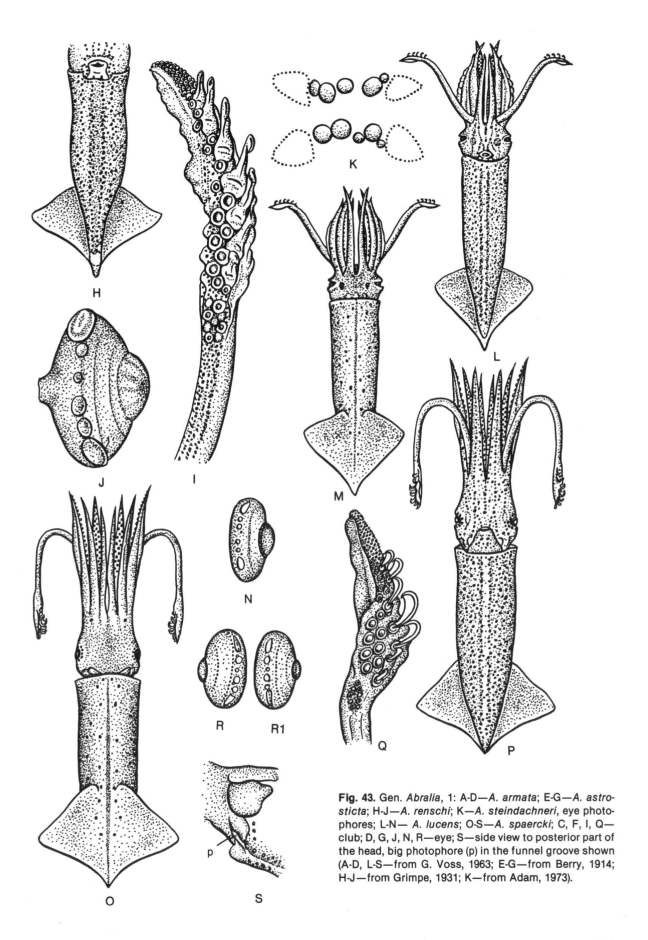

Fig. 43. Gen. *Abralia*, 1: A-D—*A. armata*; E-G—*A. astrosticta*; H-J—*A. renschi*; K—*A. steindachneri*, eye photophores; L-N— *A. lucens*; O-S—*A. spaercki*; C, F, I, Q— club; D, G, J, N, R—eye; S—side view to posterior part of the head, big photophore (p) in the funnel groove shown (A-D, L-S—from G. Voss, 1963; E-G—from Berry, 1914; H-J—from Grimpe, 1931; K—from Adam, 1973).

Fig. 44.

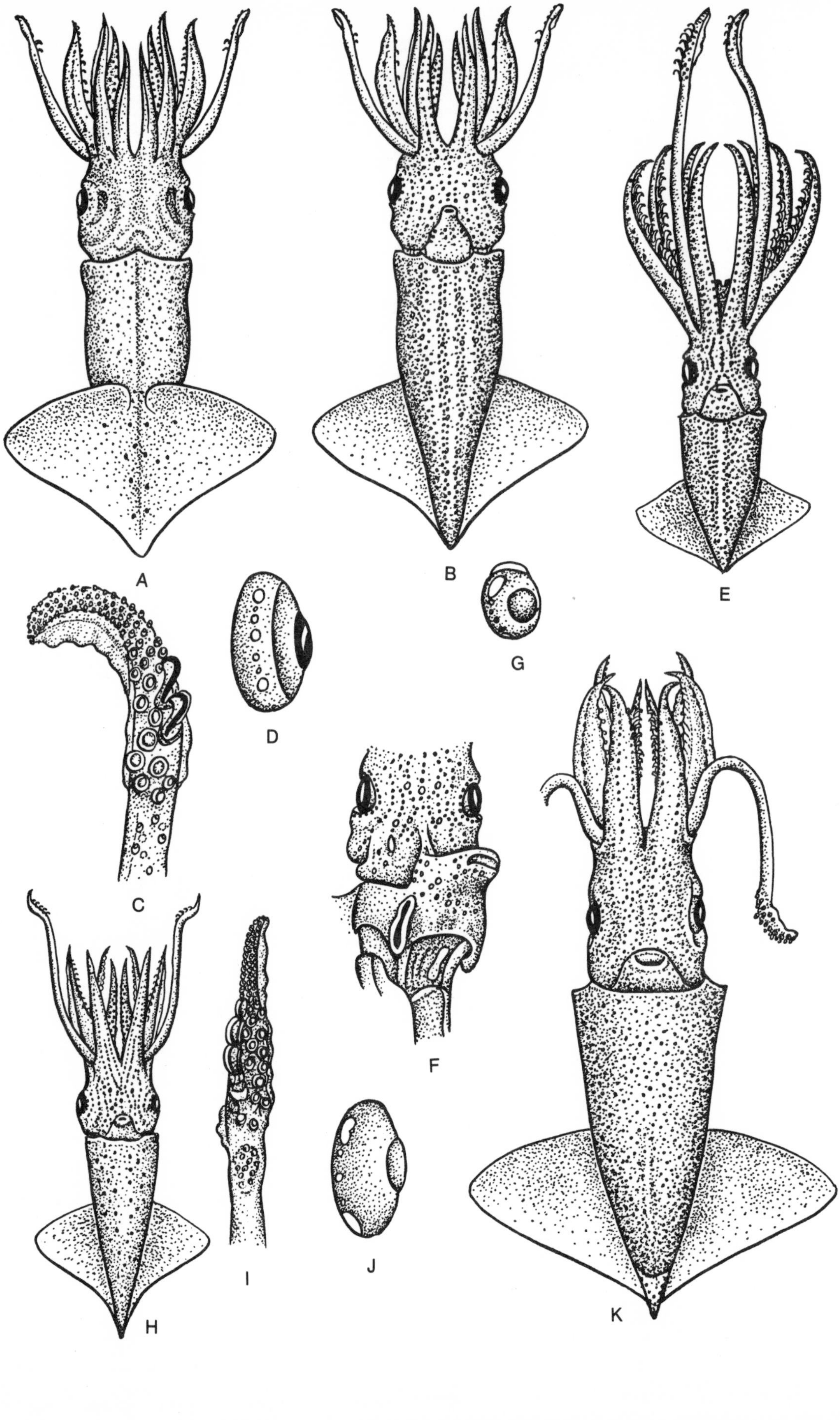

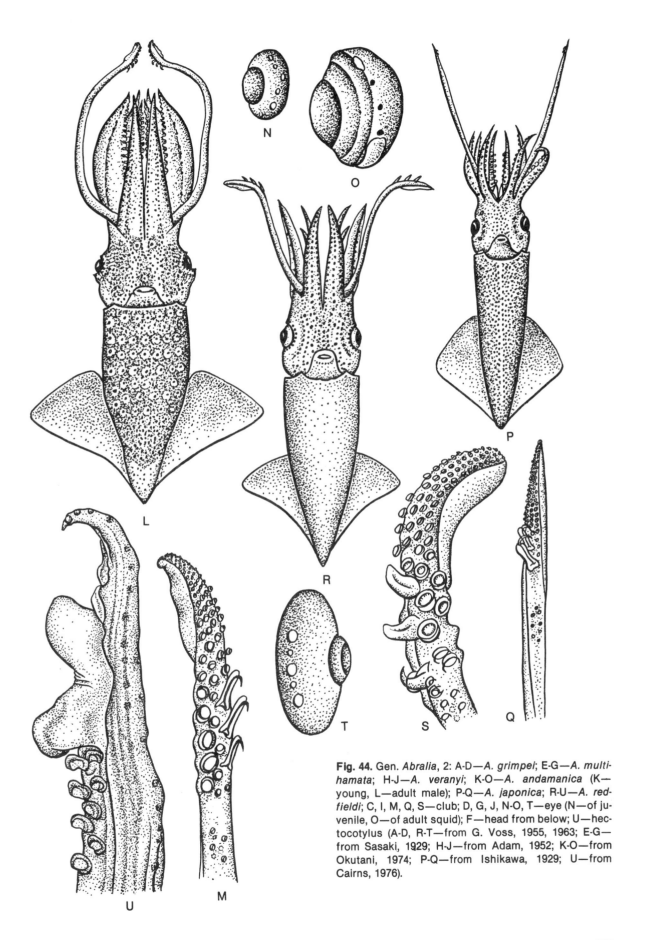

Fig. 44. Gen. *Abralia*, 2: A-D—*A. grimpei*; E-G—*A. multihamata*; H-J—*A. veranyi*; K-O—*A. andamanica* (K—young, L—adult male); P-Q—*A. japonica*; R-U—*A. redfieldi*; C, I, M, Q, S—club; D, G, J, N-O, T—eye (N—of juvenile, O—of adult squid); F—head from below; U—hectocotylus (A-D, R-T—from G. Voss, 1955, 1963; E-G—from Sasaki, 1929; H-J—from Adam, 1952; K-O—from Okutani, 1974; P-Q—from Ishikawa, 1929; U—from Cairns, 1976).

median stripe free of photophores on ventral side of mantle. 6 ocular photophores . . . .
. . . .*A. (A.) multihamata* **Sasaki, 1929**
(Fig. 44 E-J). Taiwan and neighboring coasts of mainland China.

19 (16). 5 photophores on ventral side of eyeball. Photophores on ventral side of mantle not forming longitudinal stripes **20**

20 (25). Posterior photophore on eyeball considerably larger than other 4, oval, egg-shaped, or kidney-shaped; anterior photophore usually oval and larger than 2nd to 4th (except in *A. siedleckyi*); median 3 photophores equal, round (in young squids, 1st, 3rd, and 5th of equal size, round and larger than 2nd and 4th). Fin length about 67% of mantle length. 3-4 (occasionally 5) hooks on tentacular club. Left ventral arm hectocotylized, with 2 lobes on ventral and dorsal sides of arm **21**

21 (24). Club dactylus and manus subequal in length **22**

22 (23). 3-4 rows of tiny suckers on tips of 1st-3rd arms. 1st (anterior) eye photophore in adults oval, much larger than 3rd and only a little smaller than 5th; 5th photophore usually with small incision (sinus). Dorsal flap on hectocotylus about 1.5 times shorter than ventral flap . . . .
. . . .*A. (A.) veranyi* (**Rüppell, 1844**)
(= *Enoploion eustictum* Pfeffer, 1912) (Fig. 43 H-J). Tropical and subtropical western and eastern Atlantic from northern part of the U.S.A. Atlantic coast to the Gulf of Mexico and Surinam, and from Mediterranean Sea and Madeira to Angola. At the bottom in bathyal and in midwater above slopes, sometimes at the surface. Absent in the open ocean far from slopes. A common species.

23 (22). Two rows of tiny suckers on tips of 1st-3rd arms. 1st (anterior) eye photophore in adults round or slightly oval, almost equal to 3rd and 10 times smaller than 5th, the latter (posterior) photophore nearly oval with only inconspicuous incision. Dorsal flap on hectocotylus about 3 times shorter than ventral flap . . . .
. . . .*A. (A.) siedleckyi* **Lipiński, 1983**
Southeastern Atlantic: Schmitt-Ott Seamount to the southwest from the Cape of Good Hope. Mesopelagic. Mantle length 3 cm.

24 (21). Club dactylus considerably longer than manus. Suckers on arm tips in 2 rows. 1st eye photophore in adults much larger than 3rd but smaller than 5th; both elongate-oval. Dorsal flap on hectocotylus longer, equal, or slightly shorter

than ventral flap . . . .
. . . .*A. (A.) andamanica* **Goodrich, 1896**
(Fig. 44 K-O). Tropical Indo-Pacific from the Arabian Sea and the Seychelles to southern Japan, the Hawaiian Islands, and eastern Australia. Probably absent in the westernmost part of the Arabian Sea. In the east almost reaching the shores of Central America. In the midwater (epipelagic and mesopelagic) of the open ocean and near slopes, including the bathyal. A common species split into several indistinctly isolated forms, two of which have been formally described:

a (b). Photophores on ventral side of head arranged in longitudinal rows; longitudinal stripe free of photophores is usually conspicuous in center of ventral side of mantle . . . .
. . . .*A. andamanica* f. *andamanica*
Mainly on the slope and above it.

b (a). Photophores on ventral side of head arranged diffusely, usually no stripe free of photophores in center of ventral side of mantle
. . . . *A. andamanica* f. *robsoni* **Grimpe, 1931**
Mainly in the open ocean.

25 (20). All eyeball photophores round; 1st, 3rd, and 5th larger than 2nd and 4th. Suckers on arm tips in 2 rows. Fin length about 50% of mantle length. 2-3 (occasionally 4) hooks on tentacular club. Right ventral arm hectocotylized, only one dorsal membrane in form of two or three high lobes on common base developed on this arm . .**26**

26 (27). 2 hooks on tentacular club . . . .
. . . .*A. (A.?) japonica* **M. Ishikawa, 1929**
(Fig. 44 P,Q). Southern part of the Sea of Japan, the Kuroshio. A related form (a separate species?) in the eastern equatorial Pacific. Probably an oceanic species. Epipelagic and mesopelagic.

27 (26). 3 (in some adults 4 in one club) hooks on tentacular club in adult squids . . . .
. . . .*A (A.?) redfieldi* **Voss, 1955**
(Fig. 44 C-U). Tropical western Atlantic from off Nova Scotia (43°N) to Argentina (45°S); common near the Bahamas, Bermuda, and the Greater and Lesser Antilles, but rarely at the mainland coasts of America. Also in eastern tropical Atlantic off western Africa. Epipelagic-mesopelagic and bathyal-pelagic nerito-oceanic species.

28 (15). Four distinct longitudinal rows of photophores on ventral side of head and a short midventral row of a small number of photophores not dividing into two in front of funnel. 6 distinct longitudinal rows of photophores on ventral side of the mantle. 5 large and none to 3 small photo-

phores on ventral side of eyeball. Fin short and wide, fin length less than a half, width above 80%, sometimes well above the mantle length. 2-3 club hooks. Right ventral arm is hectocotylized having a big two-humped ventral lobe and a short triangular dorsal lobe. . . . .
. . . . *A.* (n. subgen. ?) *marisarabica* Okutani, 1983

Northern Arabian Sea off Pakistan; ?Seychelles. Mesopelagic above the slope.

Not included in the key is *A. (Asteroteuthis) trigonura* Berry, 1913, described from one heavily damaged specimen. Related to *A. andamanica* but differing in that photophores on ventral side of mantle form 2 distinct and 4 indistinct longitudinal stripes. Distributed near Hawaii in epipelagic and mesopelagic zones but not at the surface.

Key to subgenera and species of the genus *Abraliopsis*

1 (4). Photophores on ventral side of head and mantle disposed diffusely and not forming distinct longitudinal rows. Left ventral arm in male not modified. . . . .
. . . . **Subgenus *Abraliopsis* (s. str.)** . . . 2

2 (3). Isolated carpal membrane on ventral side of tentacle proximal to 1st large hook. Club with well developed keel and 4-5 pairs of long crescentic hooks. About 10 pairs of hooks on 1st-3rd arms reaching almost to tips of arms. Fin length 75-80% of mantle length, width 100% or more of mantle length. Stripe free from photophores (sometimes not conspicuous) in middle of ventral side of mantle starting considerably farther than mantle's anterior edge. On right and left side of this median space wide stripes of photophores limited laterally by poorly defined area more or less free of photophores. Row of photophores along edge of eyelid passing to eye sinus, and extending along the edge of 3rd arms. At least two more rows of small photophores between row of photophores passing along edge of eyelid and row running under ventral edge of eyeball. . . . .
. . . .*A. (A.) hoylei* (Pfeffer, 1884)

(Fig. 45 A-C). 2 subspecies: *A. hoylei pfefferi* **Joubin, 1896**—with 9-10 hooks, occasionally 8 on club—in tropical and subtropical Atlantic, the Gulf of Mexico and Mediterranean Sea; *A. hoylei hoylei*—as a rule 8 hooks on club—in tropical and subtropical Indo-West Pacific from Hokkaido to the Tasman Sea and from eastern

Africa to Hawaii, absent in the Arabian Sea and Bay of Bengal.

3 (2). Tentacular club without carpal membrane but with slightly developed keel in very distal part only. 3 (very seldom 4) pairs of hooks on club, these hooks small (slightly more than width of club) and slightly bent. 7-9 pairs of hooks and 5-10 pairs of suckers with denticulate rings on 1st-3rd arms. Fin length 60-67% of mantle length, width 75-90% (usually 85%) of mantle length. Stripe free from photophores in middle of ventral side of mantle starts on mantle's anterior edge; lateral stripes not isolated. Rows of photophores passing along edge of eyelid and along edge of 3rd arms separated by a free space. Only one row of photophores between row of photophores passing along the edge of eye lid and row under ventral edge of eyeball. . . . .
. . . . .*A. (A.) felis* McGowan & Okutani, 1968

(Fig. 45 D-F). Northeastern Pacific from Washington to Baja California, westward to the area to the east of Japan and the Kuriles.

4 (1). Photophores on ventral side of head arranged in 7-8 clearly defined longitudinal rows; no photophores between rows or they are rare and forming a short additional row. . . . .
. . .**Subgenus *Micrabralia* Pfeffer, 1900** . . . 5

5 (6). Photophores on ventral side of mantle arranged diffusely. 8 longitudinal rows of photophores on ventral side of head; median one consisting of two parallel rows. Club with distinct elongated carpal membrane and longitudinal keel. Hooks very long, 2-3 times longer than width of club. Trabeculae of protective membrane on left ventral arm of male elongated and thickened but not joined by wide membrane. . . . .
. . . .*A. (M.) gilchristi* (Robson, 1924)

(= *Enoploteuthis neozelanica* Dell, 1959) (Fig. 45 G-J). Southern subtropical belt of the Atlantic, Indian, and Pacific Oceans (circumglobal).

6 (5). Photophores on ventral side of mantle arranged in distinctly isolated longitudinal rows. 7 longitudinal rows of photophores on ventral side of head; median row unpaired, sometimes one short additional row between median row and each lateral row. 7

7 (10). Tentacular club with keel and distinct carpal membrane. Stripe free from photophores in middle of ventral side of mantle not reaching posterior end of body. Left ventral arm of male with wide orange protective membrane. No additional rows of photophores between main rows of photophores on ventral part of head.........8

8 (9). Stripe free from photophores in middle of ventral side of mantle terminating in oval widening at level between middle and posterior third of mantle. 4 (occasionally 3) small hooks on tentacular club, length of hooks not more than 1.5 times width of club.......................
..............*A. (M). affinis* **(Pfeffer, 1912)**
(Fig. 45 K-M). Tropical eastern Pacific from southern part of Baja California to northern Chile, westward at least to 126°W.

9 (8). Stripe free from photophores in middle of ventral side of mantle terminating in a cone in posterior third of mantle without widening. 3 (rarely 4) pairs of large (2 times width of club) crescentic hooks on tentacular club...........
.................*A. (M.) chuni* **Nesis, 1982**
(=*A. morisii* of Chun, 1910, part: Taf. V; VII, fig. 3; IX, fig. 3-4) (Fig. 45 N). Tropical Indo-West Pacific, from eastern Africa to the Line Islands. Mainly an equatorial species.

Note: Under the name of *Abraliopsis morisii* there were included more than one species of *Abraliopsis.* It is impossible to determine which is the real *A. morisii* (Vérany, 1837) due to the incomplete description. K. Chun (1910) mentioned under this name three species, one of which is *A. lineata* [see couplet 12 (13) below]; I have described two others under new species names: *A. chuni* and *A. atlantica.*

10 (7). Tentacular club without distinct carpal membrane and keel, only a narrow ventral protective membrane is on club dactylus. A free from photophores stripe in the middle of ventral side of mantle passes gradually narrowing to the posterior end of mantle...................11

11 (14). On ventral side of head between the median (unpaired) and lateral rows of photophores there are separate additional small photophores, sometimes forming a short additional row; between the lateral and the 3rd (from the middle) rows of photophores such photophores are scattered irregularly (in juveniles usually there are no additional photophores). Hooks on club small, not more than 1.5 times exceeding the width of club
....12

12 (13). Left ventral arm of male not modified. Stripe free from photophores in middle of ventral side of mantle usually wide and clearly defined
...........*A. (M.). lineata* **(Goodrich, 1896)**
Tropical Indo-West Pacific from eastern Africa to Polynesia, in the northwestern Pacific reaching

the Kuroshio, in the southwestern Pacific not reaching farther to the south than 15°S.

13 (12). Left ventral arm of male with widened orange ventral protective membrane. Stripe free from photophores in middle of ventral side of mantle usually narrow, sometimes poorly defined, several individual small photophores dispersed in its anterior part.....*A. (M.) falco* **Young, 1972**
(Fig. 45 O-Q). Tropical eastern Pacific, absent in coldest parts of California and Peru Currents. The western boundary of the range is not known, but it is probably considerably farther west than 120°W.

14 (11). No additional small photophores between median (unpaired) and lateral rows of photophores on ventral side of head. Stripe free from photophores in middle of ventral side of mantle wide and clearly defined. Left ventral arm of male with widened orange ventral protective membrane (note: in *A.* sp. cf. *falco* this character was not investigated)......................15

15 (16). Club hooks small, not more than 1.5 times width of club. No additional photophores between lateral and 3rd (from middle) rows of photophores on ventral side of head...........
..............*A. (M.). atlantica* **Nesis, 1982**
(=*A. morisii* of Chun, 1910, part: Taf. VI, fig. 1; Taf. VIII, fig. 1, 5; Taf. X, fig. 1; also *Abraliopsis* sp. of Nesis, 1974a: 53-54; Cairns, 1976: 245; and Roeleveld, 1977: 123) (Fig. 45 R). Tropical and subtropical Atlantic, Caribbean Sea, and the Gulf of Mexico.

See note after *A. (M.) chuni*, couplet 9 (8).

16 (15). Club hooks large, about 2 times width of club. Some separated small photophores may be between lateral and 3rd (from middle) rows of photophores on ventral side of head in front of level of anterior eye margin...................
.........................*A. (M.)* **sp. cf.** *falco*
(=*Abraliopsis* sp. A Shevtsova, 1975; ?*Abraliopsis* n. sp. Young, 1973). North Pacific from northern Japan and southern Kuriles (38-43°N) probably to Hawaii.

Key to species of the genus *Ancistrocheirus*

1 (2). Large photophores on ventral side of mantle arranged in alternating groups of fours and twos, not forming unpaired longitudinal row and not extending to tail. Arrangement formula of photophores is 4 + 2 + 4 + 2 + 4 + 2 + 4.........

.... ***A. alessandrinii*** **(Vérany, 1851)**
(= *A. lesueuri* auct., non Fér. & d'Orb.) Fig. 46
A-D). Tropical to subtropical, reaching notalian
area; a cosmopolitan species. Lower epipelagic
and mesopelagic zones. Adult squids also live near
the bottom in the bathyal.

2 (1). Large photophores on ventral side of mantle forming (in addition to twos and fours) unpaired median longitudinal row and extending to
tail. Arrangement formula: $4 + 2 + 3 + 3 + 2 + 2 + 3 + 1 + 1 + 1$.....................
..... ***A. lesueuri*** **Férussac & d'Orbigny, 1839**
Distribution and habitat unknown; a doubtful
species.

Key to species of the genus *Pyroteuthis*

1 (2). Longitudinal membrane of hectocotylus
long, about 33% of arm length, measured from
first hook; membrane starting after 7th-9th pair of
hooks. Usually no additional small photophore on
tentacular stalk between 1st (basal) and 2nd
photophores (but small photophore present in
specimens from southern and western Australia)
.... ***P. margaritifera*** **(Rüppell, 1844)**
(Fig. 46 E-G). Tropical to subtropical Atlantic
and Indo-West Pacific Oceans. Mesopelagic
(ascends to the lower epipelagic zone). Absent in
eastern Pacific. The eastern boundary of the range
in equatorial waters is in the area of the Line
Islands and in southern central waters it is approximately at 80°W. The species splits into a
series of local forms differing in the arrangement
of photophores on the tentacular stalk: in squids
from equatorial and the western central Pacific
there are 7 (rarely 6 or 8) photophores on the tentacle and no additional photophore; specimens
from the Kuroshio have 6 photophores only, no
additional photophore; in specimens from
southern and southwestern Australia there are
also 6, but including the additional small one.

2 (1). Longitudinal membrane of hectocotylus
short, less than 25% of arm length; membrane
starting after 5th pair of hooks. 7 photophores on
tentacular stalk, including small additional photophore between 1st (basal) and 2nd photophores,
placed nearer to 2nd photophore.............
.... ***P. addolux*** **Young, 1972**
(Fig. 46 H-K). Eastern part of northern central
Pacific from Hawaii to California and in the
California Current. Mesopelagic.

Key to species of the genus *Pterygioteuthis*

1 (2). 2-8 (more often 3-7) hooks on 1st-3rd arms,
present only in middle of ventral sucker row. 4th
arms with 2 rows of very small suckers. Hectocotylized arm bearing 2 non-pigmented glandular areas of subequal length between which is
located a comb-like plate with several conical
teeth. A few very tiny suckers on tip of hectocotylized arm. 14 (rarely 15) photophores on
eyeball............***P. gemmata*** **Chun 1908**
(= *P. microlampas* Berry, 1913. ?*P. schnehageni*
(Pfeffer, 1912) (Fig. 46 P-S). Mainly antiequatorial species. Northern and southern central
and eastern equatorial Atlantic (absent in the
western equatorial Atlantic, Caribbean and
Mediterranean Seas, and the Gulf of Mexico); Indian Ocean – in southern part of central waters;
Pacific Ocean – throughout the northern central
waters and along the southern periphery of
southern central waters. Squids from the California Current differ from Atlantic and western
Pacific individuals in the higher mean number of
hooks on the arms. Mesopelagic species, ascends
to lower epipelagic zone. Mantle length to 36 mm.

2 (1). Hooks on 1st-3rd arms present in middle of
ventral and dorsal rows, 2-5 pairs in all each arm.
4th arms in female devoid of suckers. Hectocotylus with 2 glandular areas of which proximal area is bright orange-red and much longer
than non-pigmented distal area, 2 bent hook-like
teeth between them. 1 or 2 hooks on right (non-
hectocotylized) ventral arm of male. 15
photophores on eyeball.....................
.... ***P. giardi*** **Fischer, 1896**
(Fig. 46 L-M). Tropical-subtropical cosmopolitan mesopelagic (ascends to epipelagic zone)
species with 2 subspecies: ***P. giardi giardi*** (1-2
fairly large hooks on right ventral arm of male)
living in the Atlantic Ocean; and ***P. giardi
hoylei*** (Pfeffer, 1912) (1-2 tiny hooks on right
ventral arm of male) inhabiting the Indian and
Pacific Oceans. Mantle length to 25 mm.

2.2.2.3. Family Octopoteuthidae
(= Octopodoteuthidae, Veranyidae)

Medium and large size squids. Body gelatinous.
Mantle conical, more or less acuminate posteriorly. Fins very large, rhomboidal, extending along
almost the entire length of mantle, fused to the

dorsal side of mantle and with one another along the median line of the back, only small U-shaped area near the anterior edge of mantle remaining unfused. Head broad; arms short and thick, their ends frequently broken off. Two rows of short hooks covered by a hood of soft tissue on the arms. Suckers (if any) present only on the very tips of arms. Tentacles developed only in the larvae, rarely in the juveniles, bearing a cluster of large suckers on a short club. No trace of the tentacles remains in adult squids. Locking apparatus simple. Formula of buccal membrane DDVV. Luminous organs are located on arm tips, sometimes in the tissues of the head, arms, and mantle, and inside the mantle cavity near the anus. Gladius is very thin, with a wide vane starting directly from the anterior end and a small terminal cone. No hectocotylus. Spermatophores are transferred to the female by a long penis. Development includes a larval stage.

Mesopelagic-bathypelagic and benthic-bathyal squids of tropical and temperate waters. 2 genera, 7 to 10 species.

Key to the genera of the family Octopoteuthidae

1 (2). Large composite photophore, whose luminous surface may be covered by lateral cutaneous folds, located on tip of each 2nd arm. Single large round photophore on ink sac. No photophores on other arm tips, on sides of anus, or at posterior end of mantle. Fins in juveniles extremely wide, fin width much greater than mantle length, fin reaching posterior end of body; in adults, fins fall far short of reaching posterior end of mantle. Tentacles reduced at mantle length of 4 to 4.5 cm, rudiments of stalks remaining in adult squids. Mantle length to 170 cm..............
.............**Genus *Taningia* Joubin, 1931** (= *Cucioteuthis* auct.). One species: **T. *danae* Joubin, 1931** (= *Cucioteuthis unguiculata* auct.) (Fig. 47 L-M). Tropical to subtropical (found also in boreal and notalian waters) cosmopolitan species. Mesopelagic and at the bottom in bathyal. Often found in the stomachs of sperm whales.
2 (1). Tips of all arms bearing 1 elongated conical or fusiform photophore without lateral folds of skin. No single photophore on ink sac. Usually with small photophores in tissues of head and posterior end of mantle and inside mantle cavity near anus. Width of fin in juveniles not exceeding

or but a little more than mantle length. Tentacles entirely reduced by end of larval stage (mantle length about 1-1.5 cm). Mantle length to 30-50 cm, usually not exceeding 20 cm.............
........**Genus *Octopoteuthis* Rüppell, 1844** (= *Octopodoteuthis* Krohn, 1845; *Verania* Krohn, 1847; *Veranya* auct.; *Octopodoteuthopsis* Pfeffer, 1912) (Fig. 47 A-K). Type species: *O. sicula* Rüppell, 1844. 6-9 species. Tropical and subtropical waters of all oceans. Mesopelagic, bathypelagic and bathyal.

Key to species of the genus *Octopoteuthis*

1 (10). Paired or single photophore in tissues at posterior end of mantle on ventral side of body (mantle tissue covering photophore transparent). Pair of photophores inside mantle cavity on both sides of ink sac — on dorsal sides of funnel retractor muscles...............................2
2 (5). One large photophore in tissue of posterior end of mantle on ventral side................3
3 (4). Fin extending along tail as thin fringe and reaching posterior end of mantle. Photophores present on bases of 3rd and 4th arms...........
...................**O. *deletron* Young, 1972** (Fig. 47 A,B). Northeastern Pacific from Washington to Baja California; also found off northern Peru and (?) off eastern Honshu. In the specimens from Japanese waters the fin width is about 130% of the mantle length, while it is 70-95% in the adult of typical *O. deletron;* probably the Japanese specimens represent a separate species.
4 (3). Fin terminating just beyond tail photophore, not reaching posterior end of mantle.....
..........**Octopoteuthis sp. A Young, 1972** (Fig. 47 C). Central waters of the northeastern Atlantic.
5 (2). Pair of large photophores in tissue of posterior ventral surface of mantle, one on each side of midline..........................6
6 (9). Tail photophores located on border between middle and posterior third of mantle. No photophores at bases of 3rd and 4th arms...........7
7 (8). Fin reaching posterior end of mantle
....................**O. *danae* Joubin, 1931** (Fig. 47 D-E). Northern subtropical Atlantic (Sargasso Sea, Senegal).
8 (7). Fin not reaching posterior end of mantle, its rear edge located somewhat farther than level of tail photophores. Fin length about 75% of mantle

length. Tail long, acuminate, flattened from above, with narrow lateral fringes . . . .

. . . . ***O. megaptera* (Verrill, 1885)**

(Fig. 47 F,G). Tropical-subtropical cosmopolitan species. Mesopelagic, bathypelagic, and bathyal, at night ascending to epipelagic zone.

9 (6). Tail photophores located at distance of 20-25% of mantle length from posterior end of body. Fin reaches posterior end of mantle. Photophores present at bases of 3rd and 4th arms. Tail short, almost indistinct in juveniles . . . .

. . . . ***O. sicula* (Rüppell, 1844)**

(Fig. 47 H). Tropical-subtropical Atlantic and Indo-West Pacific species, also found in the Mediterranean Sea, and . . . .

. . . . ***O. nielseni* (Robson, 1948)**

(Fig. 47 I), from the tropical eastern Pacific (from Mexico to northern Chile, westward to Hawaii), also keys out here. Differences between these two species are not clear at present. Both species live in the mesopelagic and bathypelagic zones ascending at night to the epipelagic zone.

10 (1). No photophores on tail or head nor in mantle cavity, only elongated photophores on arm tips. In juveniles, fin reaching posterior end of mantle, but adults have a short tail . . . .

. . . . ***Octopoteuthis rugosa* Clarke, 1980**

(= *Octopoteuthis* n. sp. Nesis, 1974a) (Fig. 47 J, K). Atlantic and Indo-West Pacific tropical and subtropical species. Found in the equatorial Atlantic, off Mauritania, southern Africa, southwestern Australia, and the Sulu and Flores Seas (doubtful from South Georgia). Mesopelagic.

Note: The key does not include *O. longiptera* (Akimushkin, 1963) from the southern subtropical Atlantic (eastward from Martin-Vaz Island), described very incompletely.

2.2.2.4. Family Onychoteuthidae

Small to very large squids. Mantle elongately conical, graceful. Body as a rule muscular, rarely semigelatinous. Fin in the posterior part of the mantle, rhomboidal, heart-shaped, or transversely oval. Head rather narrow, may be retracted into mantle in some species. Arms with two rows of suckers, generally with smooth rings. Tentacles firm, strong (in *Chaunoteuthis* present only at preadult stage, then autotomized). Club has 2 rows of hooks and 2 marginal rows of suckers; in adult squids the club suckers generally disappear or re-

main as rudiments only. Fixing apparatus of tentacles is very well developed. Locking cartilages are simple. Buccal membrane formula is DDVV. Luminous organs are present only in *Onychoteuthis* and *Chaunoteuthis* on the ventral side of the eyeballs and on the ink sac. Gladius with a thickened rhachis, narrow vane, and chitinous or cartilaginous terminal cone. No hectocotylus; spermatophores are transferred by a penis to the outer surface of the female's mantle ventrally and located in special cuts probably made by the male's hooks. Development with a larval stage.

Epipelagic, mesopelagic, or benthic-bathyal species. The majority are active nektonic squids. Some are of minor fisheries value. 6 or 7 genera, 13 species.

Partial revision: Clarke, 1980.

Key to genera of the family Onychoteuthidae

1 (12). Body muscular. Tentacles present. Mantle at anterior edge narrower or a little wider than head **2**

2 (7). Posterior end of gladius a short chitinous needle. Skin smooth **3**

3 (4). Photophores present: an elongated photophore on ventral side of eyeball and two on ink sac (anterior photophore small, posterior one large). Intestine bending around posterior photophore on side. Nuchal folds well developed, 7-9. Only hooks in central part of club in juveniles and adults. Mantle slender, conical, fin rhomboidal or slightly heart-shaped, with posteriorly attenuated tail. Gladius visible on dorsal side of mantle and can be felt under skin as sharp, thin rib. In larvae and early juveniles tip of gladius penetrates skin posteriorly and projects outward like a needle . . . .

. . . . **Genus *Onychoteuthis* Lichtenstein, 1818**

(= *Teleonychoteuthis* Pfeffer, 1900) (Fig. 48 A-F). Type species: *O. banksi* (Leach, 1817). One described species with 2 subspecies and one undescribed. All oceans except Arctic, upper boreal Atlantic, subantarctic, and Antarctic. Of some fisheries value in the Kuriles-Hokkaido area.

4 (3). Photophores absent. Nuchal folds absent or scanty (up to 4). 2 rows of hooks and 2 rows of suckers on club in juveniles; in adults some small suckers usually retained in central or proximal part of club. In undamaged specimens gladius not visible or visible only in posterior part of mantle between fins. In larvae and juveniles posterior end

Fig. 45.

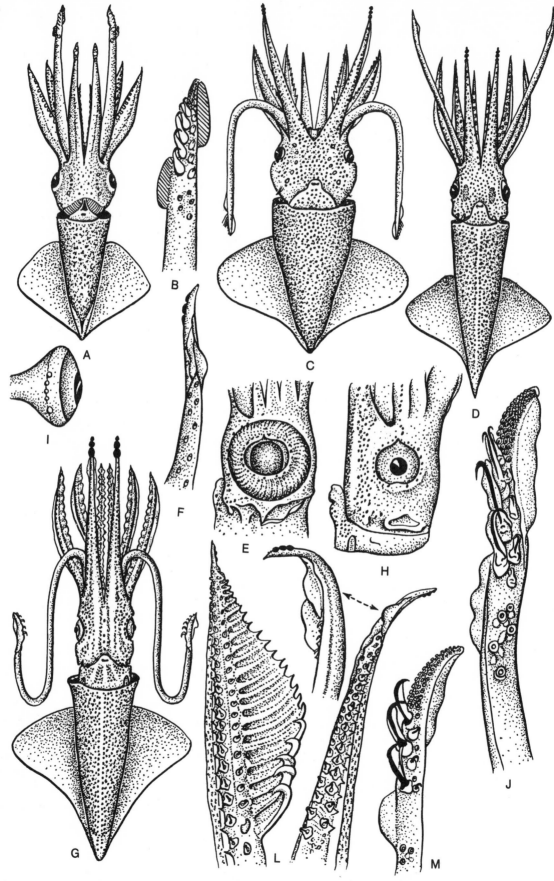

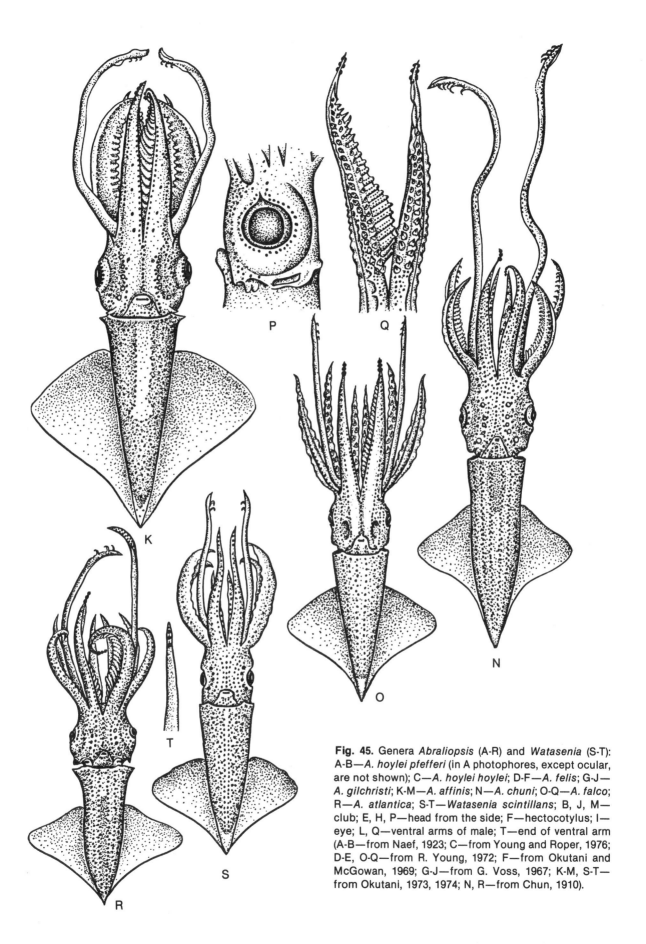

Fig. 45. Genera *Abraliopsis* (A-R) and *Watasenia* (S-T):
A-B—*A. hoylei pfefferi* (in A photophores, except ocular,
are not shown); C—*A. hoylei hoylei*; D-F—*A. felis*; G-J—
A. gilchristi; K-M—*A. affinis*; N—*A. chuni*; O-Q—*A. falco*;
R—*A. atlantica*; S-T—*Watasenia scintillans*; B, J, M—
club; E, H, P—head from the side; F—hectocotylus; I—
eye; L, Q—ventral arms of male; T—end of ventral arm
(A-B—from Naef, 1923; C—from Young and Roper, 1976;
D-E, O-Q—from R. Young, 1972; F—from Okutani and
McGowan, 1969; G-J—from G. Voss, 1967; K-M, S-T—
from Okutani, 1973, 1974; N, R—from Chun, 1910).

Fig. 46.

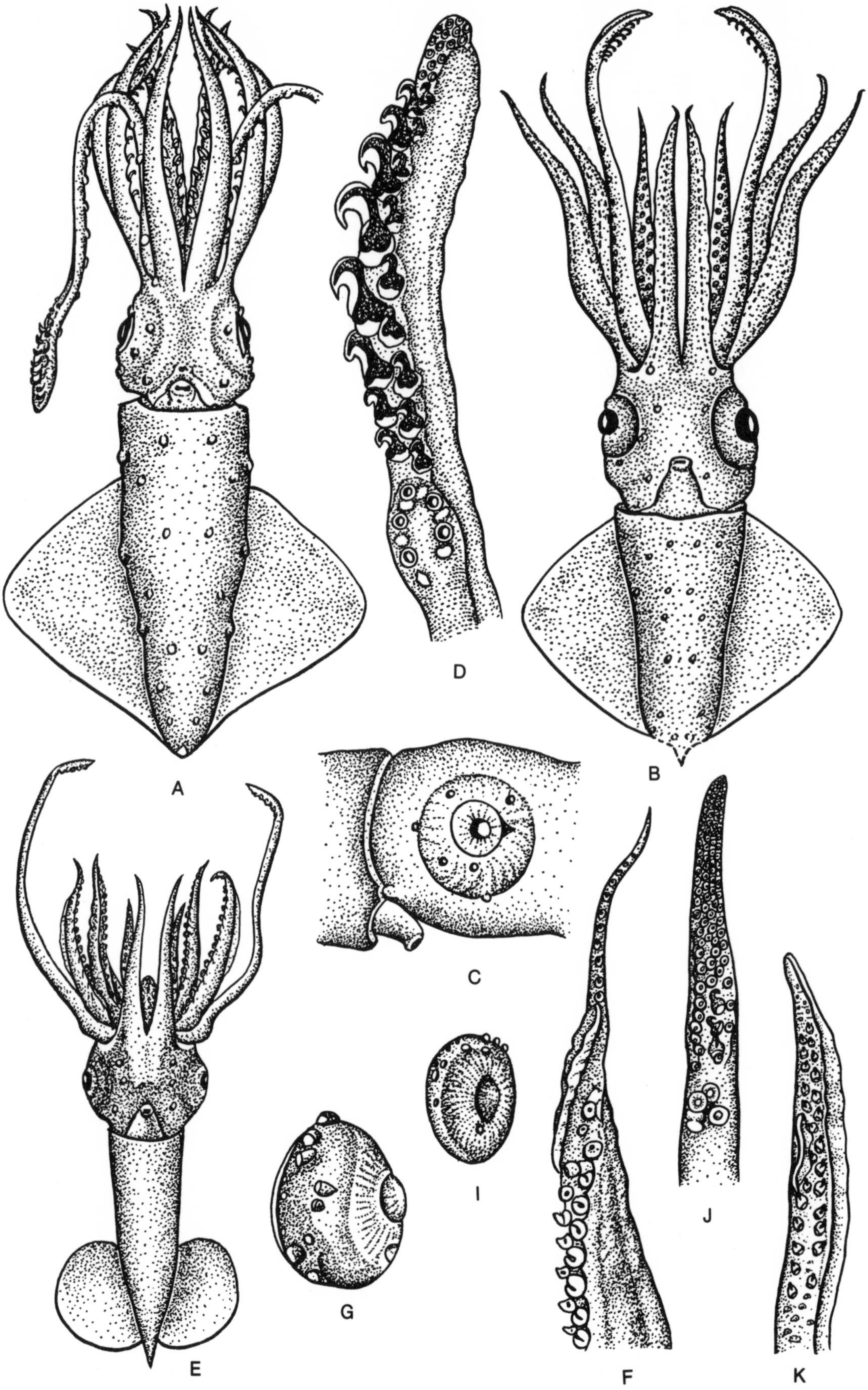

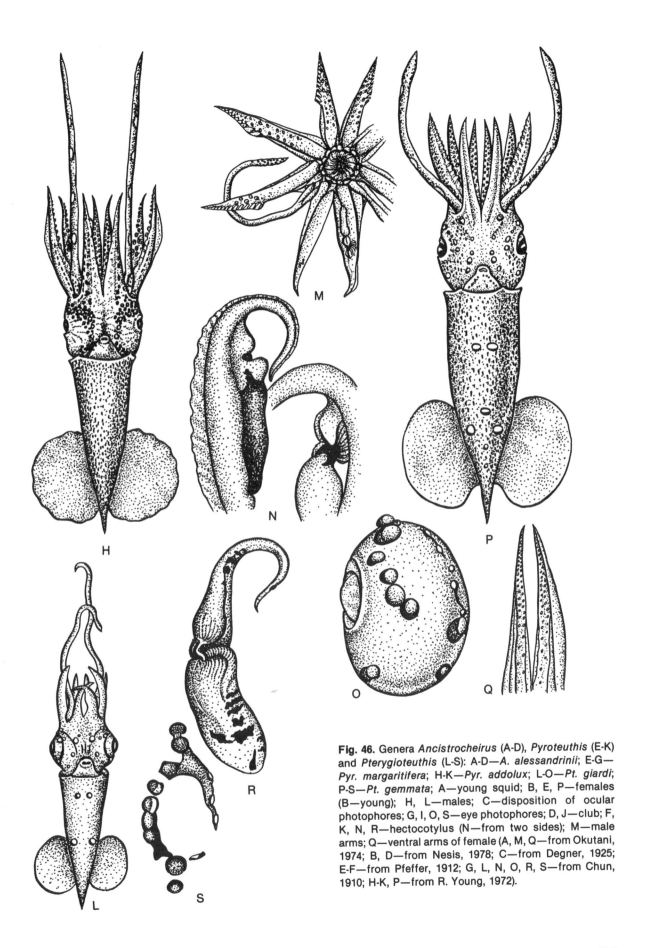

Fig. 46. Genera *Ancistrocheirus* (A-D), *Pyroteuthis* (E-K) and *Pterygioteuthis* (L-S): A-D—*A. alessandrinii*; E-G—*Pyr. margaritifera*; H-K—*Pyr. addolux*; L-O—*Pt. giardi*; P-S—*Pt. gemmata*; A—young squid; B, E, P—females (B—young); H, L—males; C—disposition of ocular photophores; G, I, O, S—eye photophores; D, J—club; F, K, N, R—hectocotylus (N—from two sides); M—male arms; Q—ventral arms of female (A, M, Q—from Okutani, 1974; B, D—from Nesis, 1978; C—from Degner, 1925; E-F—from Pfeffer, 1912; G, L, N, O, R, S—from Chun, 1910; H-K, P—from R. Young, 1972).

of gladius does not penetrate the skin and project outward...............................5

5 (6). Fin transversely oval, its posterior end slightly convex or almost straight. Fin length about 50% of mantle length, fin width in adults nearly equal to mantle length. Gladius with thick obtuse rib, not visible in undamaged specimens. Juveniles dorsally dark, with a bluish shade. No nuchal folds....**Genus *Onykia* LeSueur, 1821**

(= *Onychia* auct.; *Steenstrupiola* Pfeffer, 1884; *Teleoteuthis* Verrill, 1885) (Fig. 48 G,H). Type and the only certain species: **O. carriboea LeSueur, 1821** (= *O. rancureli* Okutani, 1981) (Fig. 48 G,H). Tropical and subtropical cosmopolitan species. The juveniles live near the surface (often in hyponeuston), adults in lower epipelagic and uppermost mesopelagic zones, not ascending to the surface. A common species. Mantle length to 10 cm. Some nominal species were described based on young specimens (see Pfeffer, 1912), and their taxonomic status is unclear.

6 (5). Fin in larvae transversely oval; in adolescents and adults fin rhomboidal, posteriorly angular. Fin length 55-60% of mantle length, width 70-75% of mantle length. Gladius with acute rib posteriorly, visible between fins. Color bright, vivid yellow in living and brown in preserved squids. 3 or 4 short nuchal folds (inconspicuous in juveniles)....................
..........*Onykia* (?) *verrilli* (**Pfeffer, 1900**).

Probably notalian circumpolar species (between 33° and 53°S and possibly southward, in Atlantic, Indian, and Pacific Oceans). Epipelagic-mesopelagic (to bathypelagic?) species, juveniles at night found near the surface. The generic position of this species uncertain, it includes characters of *Onychoteuthis*, *Ancistroteuthis*, and *Onykia*. This is probably a member of a separate genus. Possibly the squid mentioned as "wide" *Moroteuthis* by S. K. Klumov and V. L. Yukhov (1975: 175, fig. 8) is an adult specimen of this species. The "notalian form of *Onychoteuthis*

Fig. 47.

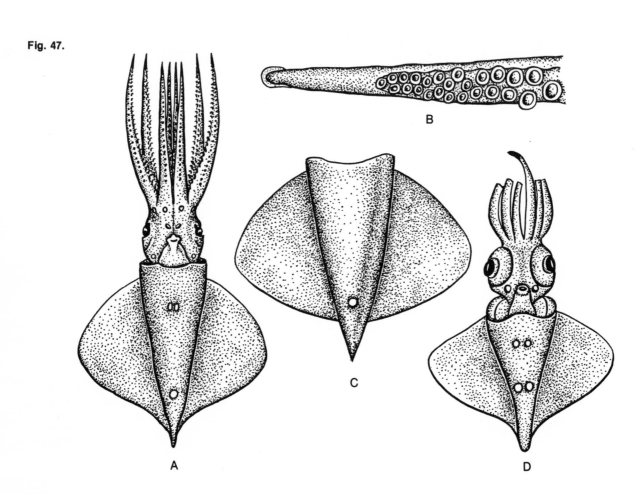

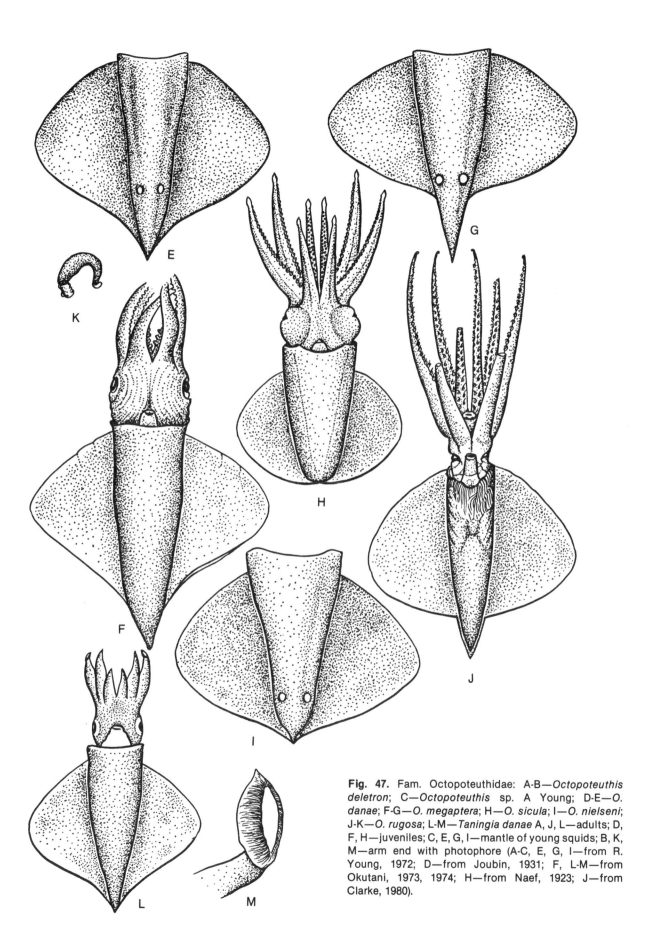

Fig. 47. Fam. Octopoteuthidae: A-B—*Octopoteuthis deletron*; C—*Octopoteuthis* sp. A Young; D-E—*O. danae*; F-G—*O. megaptera*; H—*O. sicula*; I—*O. nielseni*; J-K—*O. rugosa*; L-M—*Taningia danae* A, J, L—adults; D, F, H—juveniles; C, E, G, I—mantle of young squids; B, K, M—arm end with photophore (A-C, E, G, I—from R. Young, 1972; D—from Joubin, 1931; F, L-M—from Okutani, 1973, 1974; H—from Naef, 1923; J—from Clarke, 1980).

Fig. 48.

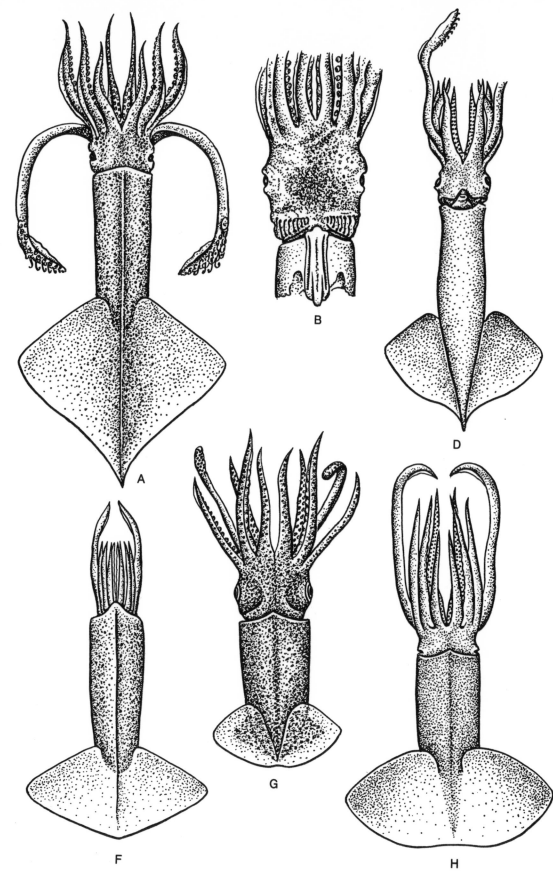

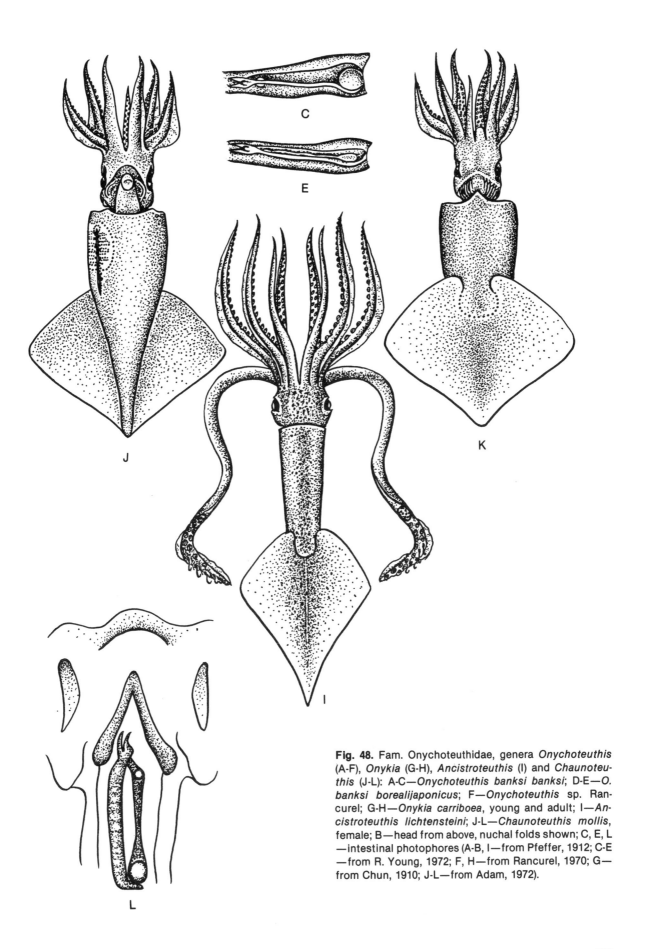

Fig. 48. Fam. Onychoteuthidae, genera *Onychoteuthis* (A-F), *Onykia* (G-H), *Ancistroteuthis* (I) and *Chaunoteuthis* (J-L): A-C—*Onychoteuthis banksi banksi*; D-E—*O. banksi borealijaponicus*; F—*Onychoteuthis* sp. Rancurel; G-H—*Onykia carriboea*, young and adult; I—*Ancistroteuthis lichtensteini*; J-L—*Chaunoteuthis mollis*, female; B—head from above, nuchal folds shown; C, E, L—intestinal photophores (A-B, I—from Pfeffer, 1912; C-E—from R. Young, 1972; F, H—from Rancurel, 1970; G—from Chun, 1910; J-L—from Adam, 1972).

banksi" (Nesis, 1973b: 222) and possibly *Moroteuthis* sp. A Clarke, 1980, also belong here. Mantle length of our young specimens up to 10 cm.

7 (2). Posterior end of gladius a long opaque cartilaginous rostrum in form of a strongly elongated trihedral pyramid with beveled base or (rarely) a round cone. No photophores. Skin smooth or rugose. Gladius not visible on dorsal side of mantle **8**

8 (9). Nuchal folds 6-10, well developed. Gladius very narrow, vane almost not widened in middle. In adult (mantle length exceeding 10-12 cm) fin heart-shaped with attenuated tail. Skin thin, smooth . . . **Genus *Ancistroteuthis* Gray, 1849**

One species: *A. lichtensteini* (Férussac & d'Orbigny, 1839) (Fig. 48 I). Tropical and subtropical Atlantic and Mediterranean Sea. Epipelagic-mesopelagic and benthic-bathyal species. Mantle length to 30 cm. Of minor fisheries value in the Mediterranean Sea.

9 (8). No nuchal folds. Vane of gladius considerably widened in middle. Skin thick, rugose or tuberculate, rarely smooth **10**

10 (11). In adults, tentacular club bears only hooks (usually not more than 30). 10-20 suckers on end of club. Arms not longer than mantle. Fin length equal to or more than 50% of mantle length. Length of rostrum of gladius usually 15 to 25% of mantle length . . . .

. . . . **Genus *Moroteuthis* Verrill, 1881**

(= *Moroteuthopsis* Pfeffer, 1908) (Fig. 49 A-K). Type species: *M. robusta* (Dall in Verrill, 1876). 6 species in boreal, tropical, notalian, and Antarctic waters. Large and giant squids (mantle length up to 2.3 m). At the bottom in bathyal (rarely in lower sublittoral) and in midwater of open ocean, mainly above the slope and submarine rises. The juveniles are pelagic. These squids play an important role in the diet of sperm whales.

11 (10). Tentacular club in adults bears 30-40 hooks and two rows of small marginal suckers. More than 20 suckers on end of club. Arms very long, in adult not less than mantle length. Fin weak, short, widely heart-shaped; fin length about 40% mantle length, its width about 60% of mantle length. Length of rostrum of gladius less than 10% of mantle length . . . .

. . . . **Genus *Kondakovia* Filippova, 1972**

One species: *K. longimana* Filippova, 1972 (Fig. 49 L-O). Antarctic (probably circumantarctic) epipelagic to mesopelagic and benthic-bathyal species, reaching northward to South Georgia.

Mantle length to 85 cm, probably up to 115 cm.

12 (1). Body gelatinous, flabby. Tentacles present only in subadults; in adult females (adult males unknown) only rudiments of stalks remain. Width of mantle at anterior edge greatly exceeding width of head. Fin rhomboidal, its length exceeding half of mantle length; fin width only a little less than mantle length. One elongated photophore on ventral side of eyeball and one on ink sac . . . .

. . . . . . **Genus *Chaunoteuthis* Appellöf, 1890**

One species: *Ch. mollis* Appellöf, 1890 (Fig. 48 J-L). Tropical and subtropical, probably cosmopolitan, mesopelagic species. Mantle length to 17 cm.

Key to species and subspecies of the genus *Onychoteuthis*

1 (4). Fin long, its length exceeding 50% (usually 55%) of mantle length; fin longitudinally rhomboidal or heart-shaped; posterior edges of fin, at least in posterior half, concave and fin attenuated into a small tail; rarely posterior edges straight, in which case width of fin only slightly longer than its length . . . . **O. banksi** (Leach, 1817)

(Fig. 48 A-E). Warm waters of all oceans from the North and Bering Seas to Tasmania. Mainly epipelagic species. Mantle length to 37 cm (such large specimens known only in northern Pacific).

. . . . **2**

2 (3). Posterior photophore on ink sac large, round, not connected with anterior photophore by luminous tissue. 19-24, more often 20-21, hooks on club . . . . . . **O. banksi banksi** (Leach)

(Fig. 48 A-C). Found in all oceans; in the Atlantic northward to the North Sea, in the Pacific to southern Japan, Hawaii, and the southern part of Baja California. The young squids live at the surface (at least at night); the adults are deepwater or benthic. Fin width unusually variable, 55-85% of mantle length. The relative constancy of the fin length produces a great difference in fin shape, which compels us to think that this subspecies consists of two or more different forms. In the tropical and subtropical Atlantic and Pacific the narrow-tailed and wide-tailed forms are found sympatrically.

3 (2). Posterior photophore on ink sac small, very narrow, connected with anterior photophore by thin band of luminous tissue. Usually 25-27 hooks on club. Fin width 70-80% of mantle length . . . . .

. . . . **O. banksi borealijaponicus** Okada, 1927

(Fig. 48 D,E). Northern Pacific from the Aleutian Islands to southern Japan and Baja California (rare in the Sea of Japan and absent in the Sea of Okhotsk). Epipelagic. A commercial species fished in the northwestern Pacific.

4 (1). Fin short and wide (fin length about 40% of mantle length, width 70-85% of mantle length), transversely rhombidal in shape, posterior edges straight or slightly convex, not attenuated into a tail. 8-11 pairs of hooks on club. Ink sac photophores like those of *O. banksi banksi*..........
..........***Onychoteuthis* sp. Rancurel, 1970**
(Fig. 48 F). South central waters of the Indian Ocean and western Pacific, reaching eastward to the Tuamotu Islands. (Not yet formally described).

Key to the species of the genus *Moroteuthis*

1 (8). Skin rugose or covered with tubercles....**2**
2 (3). Fin rhomboidal, not attenuated into tail, fin length equal to or somewhat larger than 50% of mantle length, width exceeds the length. Skin covered with flat, elongated or curved tubercles. Rostrum of gladius triangular in cross-section...
...................***M. ingens* (Smith, 1881)**
(Fig. 49 A-D). Notalian circumpolar species, reaching the Antarctic. Reaches north to northern part of the Patagonian shelf, southern Chile, the Prince Edward, Crozet, and Kerguelen Islands, and the southern islands of New Zealand (Antipodes, Campbell, and others). Lives primarily at the bottom in the lower sublittoral and bathyal. Mantle length to 52 cm.
3 (2). Fin heart-shaped, attenuated posteriorly into tail, its width is usually less than its length...**4**
4 (5). Skin covered with flat, irregular tubercles. Fin in adult specimens very long, with a greatly attenuated tail, fin length about 67% of mantle length, width about 50% of mantle length. Rostrum of gladius triangular in cross-section...
...................***M. robsoni* Adam, 1962**
(Fig. 49 E, F). At the bottom and in the pelagic zone of southern subtropical and notalian areas circumglobally: Southern Atlantic southward to South Georgia, southwestern and southern Africa, southern Australia, New Zealand, Peru, and Chile. Mantle length to 75 cm.
5 (4). Skin is covered with longitudinal and oblique bolsters or flat ridges. Fin length 50-60% of mantle length.........................**6**
6 (7). Cutaneous bolsters long and relatively

wide. Fin width less (often conspicuously) than fin length. Rostrum of gladius round or oval in cross-section. More than 30 hooks on club......
..........***M. robusta* (Dall in Verrill, 1876)**
(= *M. pacifica* Okutani, 1983) (Fig. 49 G). Pacific boreal species, distributed from the Bering Sea and Gulf of Alaska to northeastern Japan and southern California. At the bottom in lower sublittoral and upper bathyal. Juveniles and adolescents also in the midwater up to the surface. A giant squid, mantle length to 2.3 m.
7 (6). Cutaneous bolsters short and narrow, bending and fusing with one another. Fin width approximates fin length or slightly larger. Rostrum of gladius narrowly triangular in cross-section. Not more than 30 hooks on club.............
....***M. loennbergi* Ishikawa & Wakiya, 1914**
(Fig. 49 H). Pacific coast of Honshu in the north to the Tsugaru Strait, the Kuroshio, Indian Ocean (Saya-de-Malha Bank). Epipelagic, mesopelagic, and bathyal. Mantle length to 35 cm.
8 (1). Skin smooth. Fin wide, rhomboidal, not attenuated or but slightly attenuated into tail. Rostrum of gladius triangular in cross-section.....**9**
9 (10). Fin length 60% of mantle length. Length of longest arm slightly exceeding 50% of mantle length. Rostrum of gladius slightly bent at end on ventral side, its length along ventral (shorter) rib not exceeding 10% of mantle length. Radular teeth all unicuspid......................
..........***M. knipovitchi* Filippova, 1972**
(Fig. 49 J). Antarctic (circumantarctic) species, northward to South Georgia and the Kerguelen, Crozet, and Prince Edward Islands. Mesopelagic and bathyal. Mantle length to 45 cm.
10 (9). Fin length about 50% of mantle length. Length of longest arm slightly smaller than mantle length. Rostrum of gladius straight, its length along ventral (shorter) rib 12-14% of mantle length. Rhachidian tooth of radula tricuspid, first lateral teeth bicuspid......................
..............***M. aequatorialis* Thiele, 1920**
(Fig. 49 J, K). The species was described from the equatorial Atlantic. Probably it also includes the squids from Gulf of Mexico and New Caledonian waters erroneously identified as *Ancistroteuthis lichtensteini* (Voss, 1956; Rancurel, 1970); *Onykia japonica* Taki, 1964, from southern Japan; and *Onykia indica* Okutani, 1981 from the central and eastern Indian Ocean. Supposedly a tropical cosmopolitan epipelagic to mesopelagic species. Mantle length to 40 cm.

Fig. 49.

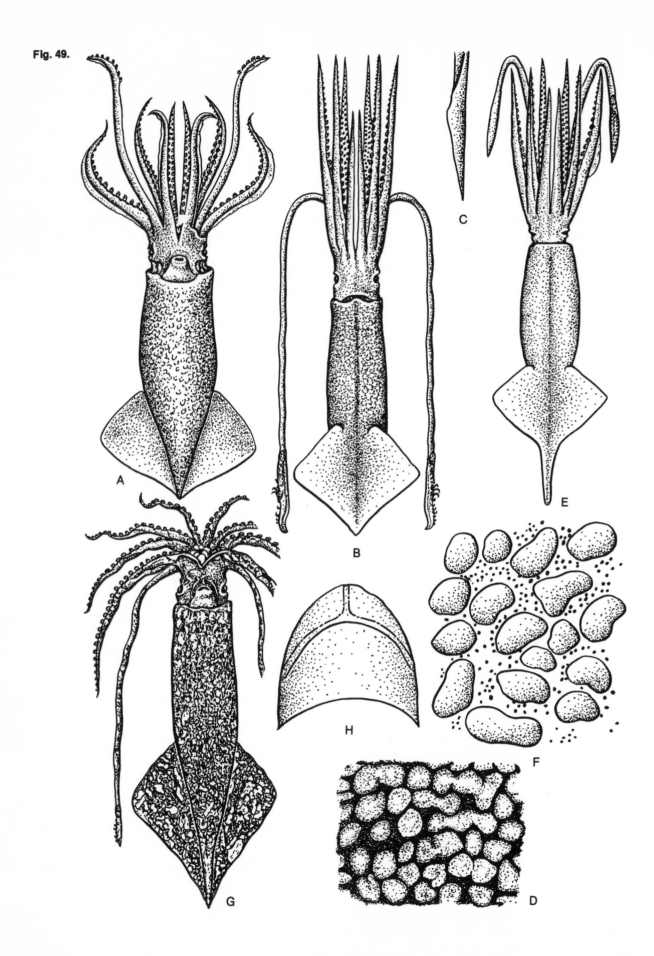

A

B

C

E

G

H

F

D

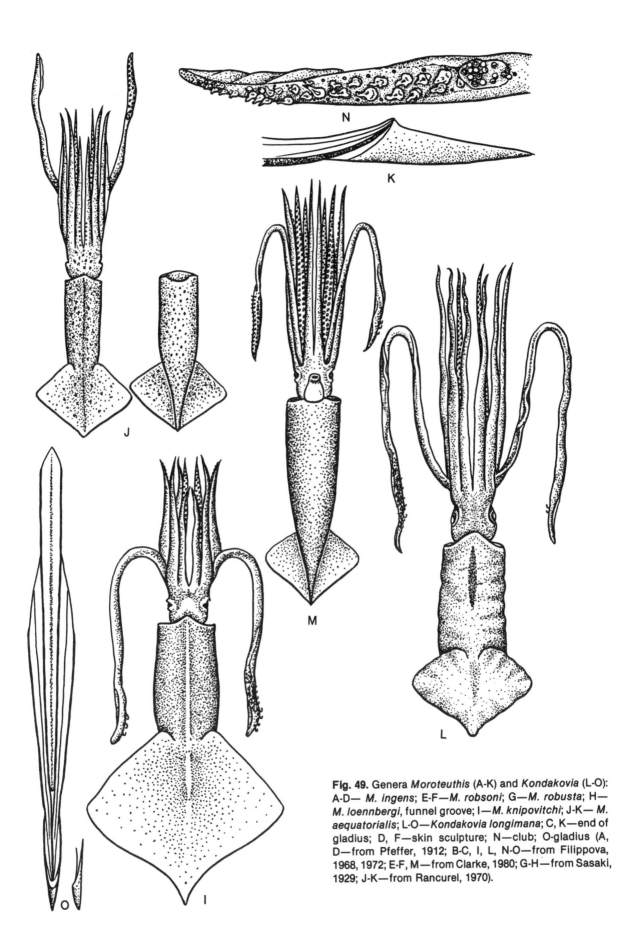

Fig. 49. Genera *Moroteuthis* (A-K) and *Kondakovia* (L-O):
A-D— *M. ingens*; E-F—*M. robsoni*; G—*M. robusta*; H—
M. loennbergi, funnel groove; I—*M. knipovitchi*; J-K— *M.
aequatorialis*; L-O—*Kondakovia longimana*; C, K—end of
gladius; D, F—skin sculpture; N—club; O-gladius (A,
D—from Pfeffer, 1912; B-C, I, L, N-O—from Filippova,
1968, 1972; E-F, M—from Clarke, 1980; G-H—from Sasaki,
1929; J-K—from Rancurel, 1970).

2.2.2.5. Family Gonatidae

Medium size squids with a narrow mantle and a large rhomboidal or heart-shaped fin. Body muscular to semigelatinous. Arms with 4 rows of suckers (in *Gonatopsis* 8-12 rows at arm tips). 1st-3rd arms in adults with 2 median rows of suckers modified into hooks (in *Berryteuthis anonychus* the hooks are present only in small numbers and only in females). Tentacular club long and wide, bearing many rows of suckers that are sometimes strongly differentiated in size, 1 or 2 large and sometimes several small hooks may develop in the central part of club. Fixing apparatus of tentacles is well developed and differentiated. In the genus *Gonatopsis* tentacles are present only in the larvae, and they are completely lost in adults, in *Gonatus* they are lost during reproduction. Hooks are developed on arms and club, and the tentacles are lost rather rapidly at definite body sizes. Locking apparatus is simple. Buccal membrane formula is DDVV. Gladius has a narrow rachis and a terminal cone, vane narrow with one or two widenings. In species with a heart-shaped fin the gladius does not reach the posterior end of the fin. Luminous organs are present (on eyes) only in one species. No hectocotylus. Spermatophores are transferred either into the mantle cavity (*Berryteuthis*) or onto the buccal membrane of female (*Gonatus, Gonatopsis*). Development with larval stage.

These squids live in midwater, mainly mesopelagic and bathypelagic, rarely epipelagic or near the bottom in the bathyal. Found in temperate and cold waters of both hemispheres, most richly represented in the boreal Pacific. They play an important role in the food of marine vertebrates and are of minor fisheries value. 3 genera, 15-20 species.

Reviews: R. Young, 1972; Nesis, 1973a; Kubodera & Okutani, 1977, 1981a,b.

Key to genera of the family Gonatidae

1 (4). Tentacles well developed (except in spawned females)........................2

2 (3). Tentacles armed only with suckers. Fixing apparatus consisting of suckers and knob-like tubercles, without alternating transverse ridges and grooves. In juveniles and sometimes in adults, hooks on arms absent or present in small numbers. Fin rhomboidal or oval, not extending over posterior end of mantle. Radula of 7 longitudinal rows of teeth. Body firm, muscular...........
..............**Genus *Berryteuthis* Naef, 1921**
(Fig. 50 A-E). Type species: *B. magister* (Berry, 1913). 2 species in the Northern Pacific; one is benthic sublittoral-bathyal, the other is pelagic. One of them is an object of fisheries.

3 (2). Tentacles armed either with only suckers or also with one or several hooks (if several, then one larger than others). Fixing apparatus terminating in club manus by series of alternating transverse ridges and deep grooves. Hooks on arms well developed from larval or postlarval stage. Fin heart-shaped, passing beyond posterior end of mantle, attenuated into tail containing cartilaginous rod. Radula of 5 longitudinal rows of teeth. Body and arms often weakly muscular, semigelatinous.... **Genus *Gonatus* Gray, 1849**
(= *Lestoteuthis* Verrill, 1880; *Cheiloteuthis* Verrill, 1881) (Fig. 51). Type species: *G. fabricii* (Lichtenstein, 1818). 2 subgenera: *Gonatus* (s. str.) and *Eogonatus* Nesis, 1972 (type species: *G. (E) tinro* Nesis, 1972). 10-13 species in Arctic, boreal, and notalian areas of the World Ocean, in mesopelagic and bathypelagic. Common squids, but not fished.

4 (1). Tentacles present only in larvae, adult squids completely devoid of tentacles..........
..............**Genus *Gonatopsis* Sasaki, 1920**
(Fig. 50 F-L). Type species: *G. octopedatus* Sasaki, 1920. 2 subgenera: *Gonatopsis* (s. str.) and *Boreoteuthis* Nesis, 1971 (type species: *G. (B.) borealis* Sasaki, 1923). 3-5 species in the northern Pacific. From epipelagic to bathypelagic, bathyal and abyssal zones.

Key to species of the genus *Berryteuthis*

1 (2). Fin large, rhomboidal, fin length at least 50% of mantle length. Hooks on 1st-3rd arms well developed, developing at mantle length of about 75 mm. Club long, suckers in central part conspicuously larger than others.................
..................**B. magister** (Berry, 1913)
(= *Gonatus septemdentatus* Sasaki, 1915) (Fig. 50 A,B). From northern Bering Sea to the Strait of Korea, northeastern Honshu, Oregon, and almost the entire Sea of Okhotsk. Near the bottom at depths from 30 to 1500 m, most often at 100-200 to 600-800 m, the juveniles ascending into midwater and to the surface of the open sea. Mantle length to 38 cm. A common species, in some places (Yamato Bank in the Sea of Japan,

Kurile and Commander Islands, western Bering Sea) serving as an object of fisheries.

2 (1). Fin small, transversely-oval, fin length 25-33% of mantle length. No hooks on arms in males; females with several hooks in basal parts of arms, hooks developing at mantle length between 35 and 60 mm. Club short, compact, with small suckers of equal size. . . . .
. . . . ***B. anonychus* (Pearcy & Voss, 1963)**
(Fig. 50 C-E). Northeastern Pacific from the Gulf of Alaska and Aleutian Islands to southern Baja California, westwardly reaching approximately 170°E. Epipelagic, mainly above the slope and "nearshore abyssal," at night ascending to the surface. Mantle length to 15 cm.

Key to subgenera and species of the genus *Gonatus*

1 (2). No hooks on club. Club suckers small, of equal size. Ridges and grooves of the fixing apparatus on club manus few in number (2-3) and short. Tentacles slender, fairly weak. Arm hooks develop at mantle length of about 20 mm. . . . . . .
. . . . **Subgenus *Eogonatus* Nesis, 1972**
One species: ***G. (E.) tinro* Nesis, 1972** (Fig. 51 A,B). From the northern slope of the Bering Sea to the Sea of Okhotsk, southern Kurile Islands, and British Columbia. Mesopelagic and bathypelagic, also lower epipelagic; adult specimens do not ascend to the surface. Mantle length 12 cm or more.

2 (1). One or several large hooks on tentacular club; central hook very large and sharp, developing simultaneously with arm hooks or somewhat earlier (except in *G. berryi*), distal and small proximal hooks (if any) developing later than central one. Club suckers of different sizes, united into several groups in different positions. Ridges and grooves of manus fixing apparatus numerous (4-6), well developed. Tentacles long and strong . . . . **Subgenus *Gonatus* (s. str.)** . . .3

3 (4). Only one central hook on club (rarely 2 hooks on one club only), developing at mantle length of 15-22 mm. None or not more than 10 small suckers on tentacular stalk between 2 marginal rows of suckers of fixing apparatus. Arm hooks develop at mantle length of 20-26 mm. Mantle width 20-27% of its length; club length 17-22% of the mantle length. 7-8 transverse rows of suckers and hooks in basal half of 3rd arms, 8-9 transverse rows of suckers in basal half of 4th arms. Less than 200 suckers on club. . . . .

. . . . ***G. (G.) onyx* Young, 1972**
(Fig. 51 C,D). From northern slope of the Bering Sea to southern part of the Sea of Okhotsk, northeastern Honshu and northern Baja California. Larvae and juveniles are found farther to the south, to Suruga Bay (Honshu) and southern Baja California. Mesopelagic and lower epipelagic (at night). A very common species. Mantle length to 18 cm.

4 (3). In addition to central hook on club, distal (smaller than central hook) and, usually, some small proximal hooks present. **5**

5 (6). Body and arms very flabby, almost gelatinous. Arms extremely long, almost equal to or even exceeding mantle length. Fin length 40-70% of mantle length. 11-12 transverse rows of suckers and hooks in basal half of 3rd arms, 16 transverse rows of suckers in basal half of 4th arms. Club long (about 20% of mantle length), suckers on club dactylus in juveniles conspicuously larger than those on rest of club. More than 200 suckers on club. Mantle width 23-27% of its length. Arm hooks develop at mantle length of about 25 mm, central club hook develops at mantle length about 40 mm, distal hook at about 45 mm, and proximal hooks at more than 70 mm. . .
. ***G. (G.) madokai* Kubodera & Okutani, 1977**
(= *Gonatus* sp. A Nesis, 1973a; Gonatidae type γ Okutani, 1966; "*Gonatus fabricii* adolescent stage" Sasaki, 1929) (Fig. 51 E-G). From northern Bering Sea to southern Kurile Islands and Gulf of Alaska, very common in the Sea of Okhotsk. Epipelagic, mesopelagic, and bathypelagic. Mantle length to 39 cm.

6 (5). Body and arms not gelatinous. Length of arms 40-75% of mantle length. Fin length 45-55% of mantle length. Number of transverse rows of suckers and hooks in basal half of 3rd and 4th arms, respectively, 6-13 (usually 6-11) and 8-17 (usually 8-15). Suckers on club dactylus in juveniles not larger than rest of club suckers. **7**

7 (8). Biserial row of suckers along ventral edge of tentacular stalk. Large oval whitish photophore on ventral side of eyeball. Width of mantle 25-30% of its length; club length 15-25% of mantle length. Number of transverse rows of suckers and hooks in basal half of 3rd and 4th arms, respectively, 7-9 and 8-10. Less than 200 suckers on club. Hooks develop on arms at mantle length of about 17-22 mm, central club hook at length of 15-19 mm, distal hook at 18-22 mm, and proximal hooks at 22-27 mm. . . . .

Fig. 50.

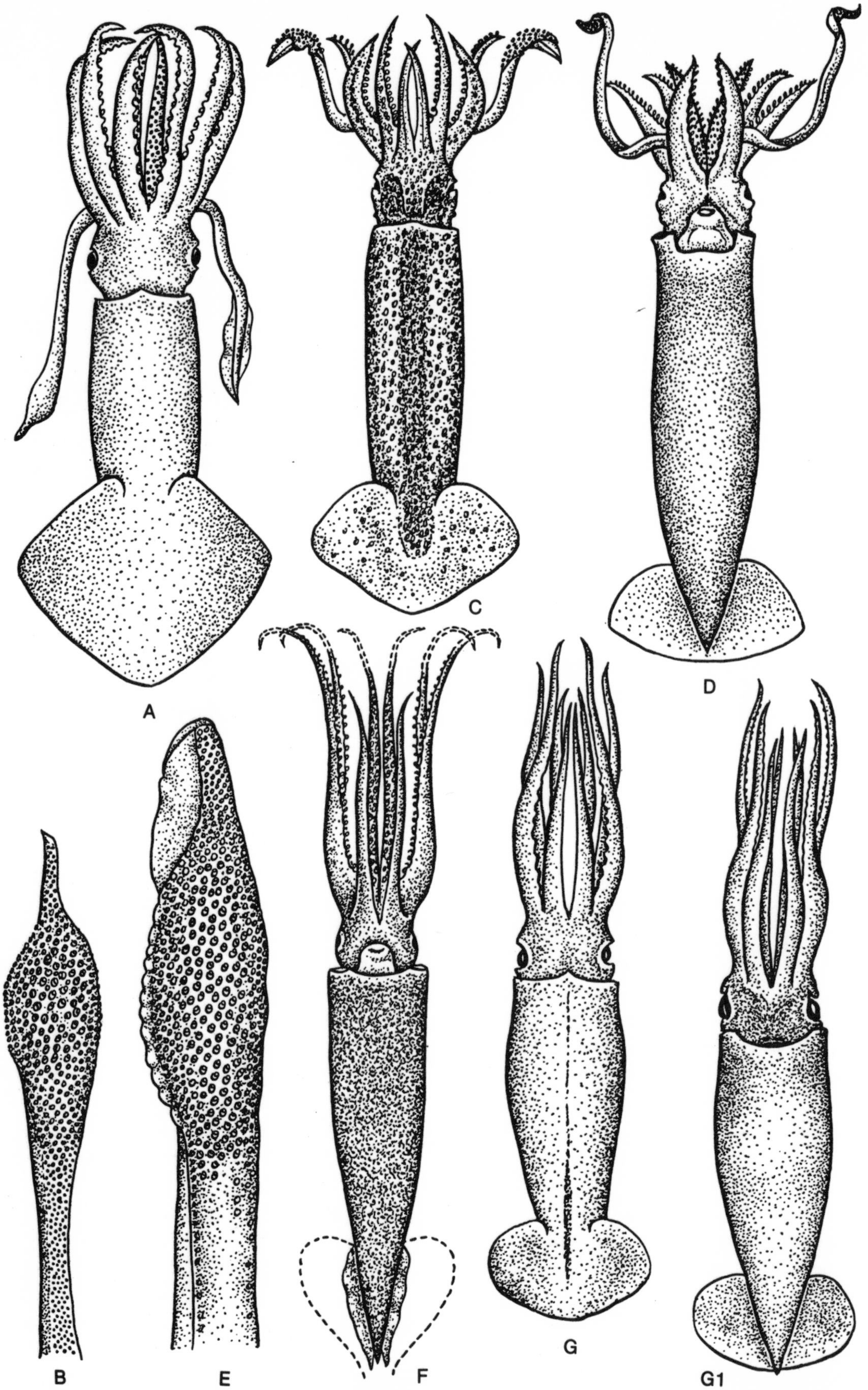

A

B   E   F   G   G1

C

D

198

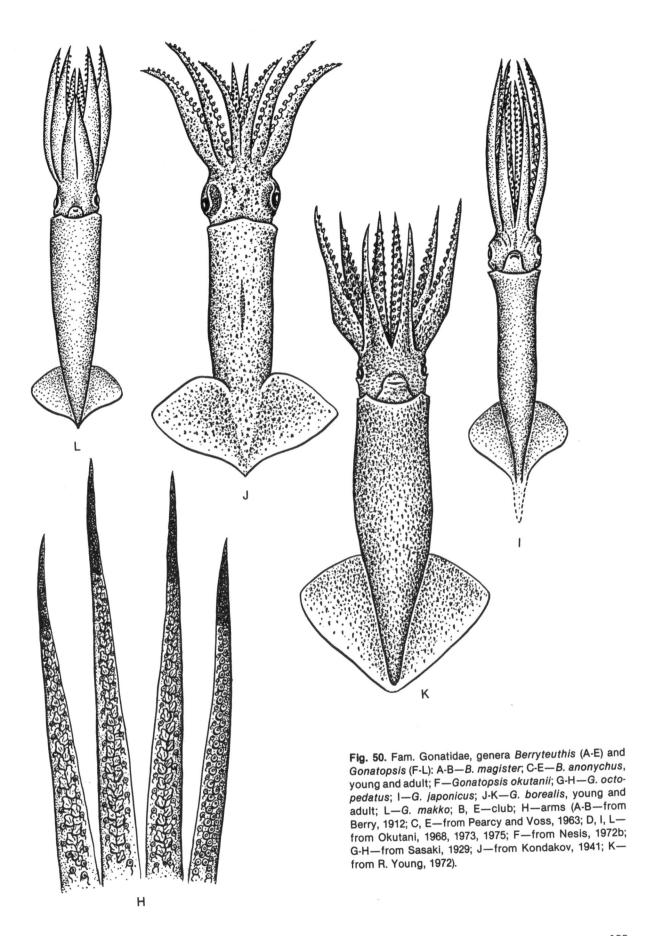

Fig. 50. Fam. Gonatidae, genera *Berryteuthis* (A-E) and *Gonatopsis* (F-L): A-B—*B. magister*; C-E—*B. anonychus*, young and adult; F—*Gonatopsis okutanii*; G-H—*G. octopedatus*; I—*G. japonicus*; J-K—*G. borealis*, young and adult; L—*G. makko*; B, E—club; H—arms (A-B—from Berry, 1912; C, E—from Pearcy and Voss, 1963; D, I, L—from Okutani, 1968, 1973, 1975; F—from Nesis, 1972b; G-H—from Sasaki, 1929; J—from Kondakov, 1941; K—from R. Young, 1972).

.................G. (G.) pyros Young, 1972

(Fig. 51 H-J). From the central Bering Sea to eastern Honshu and northern Baja California. In midwater (mesopelagic and lower epipelagic) and at the bottom in bathyal. Mantle length to 16 cm.

8 (7). One row of suckers along ventral edge of tentacular stalk. No photophores............**9**

9 (10). Club very long and strong, its length 25-37% of mantle length. Mantle width 23-35% of mantle length. On ventral side of club manus between club edge and central hook are 2 rows of large (nearer to edge) and 1-2 rows of very small suckers. Between central and first proximal hook on club are, as a rule, 1 or 2 large suckers. Suckers of ventral row on club dactylus smaller than those of other rows. No small suckers on tentacular stalk between 2 marginal rows of fixing apparatus; ventral row of suckers of fixing apparatus 1.5-3 times shorter than dorsal one. Number of transverse rows of suckers and hooks in basal half of 3rd and 4th arms, respectively, 6-9 and 8-11. Less than 200 suckers on club. Arm hooks develop much earlier than club hooks, at mantle length of 7-9 mm. Central, distal, and proximal club hooks develop at mantle lengths of 14-18, 20-27 and 27-33 mm, respectively............

...................G. (G.) berryi Naef, 1923

(Fig. 51 K,L). From the northern slope of the Bering Sea to the southern Kuriles (and northwestern Honshu?) and northern California. Mesopelagic and bathypelagic. Mantle length to 19 cm.

10 (9). Club short, its length 10-24% of mantle length (but in *G. steenstrupi* to 32-36%). Mantle width 16-25% of its length. On ventral side of club manus between edge of club and central hook are 4 rows of equal suckers or 3 rows of large and 1 row of small suckers. Proximal hooks on club (if any) start immediately after central hook. Suckers on club dactylus more or less equal in size. Small suckers (sometimes very numerous) on tentacular stalk between marginal rows of fixing apparatus suckers. Both rows of suckers of fixing apparatus of subequal length......................**11**

11 (14). Found in northern Pacific. 9-11 transverse rows of suckers and hooks in basal half of 3rd arms, 10-14 transverse rows of suckers in basal half of 4th arms....................**12**

12 (13). Mantle fairly muscular, very narrow, width 16-19% of mantle length. Tentacular club short, 10-13% (17%) of mantle length. Proximal hooks on club usually not developed. Hooks develop on arms at mantle length of 20-25 mm, central hook on club develops at length of about 50 mm, distal hook at about 60 mm............

.G. (G.) kamtschaticus (Middendorff, 1849)

(= *G. middendorffi* Kubodera & Okutani, 1981). Fairly rare nerito-oceanic species. Found in the Bering Sea, eastern Sea of Okhotsk, off the Aleutian, Commander, and Kurile Islands, in the northwestern Pacific, and in the Gulf of Alaska. Mantle length to 30 cm.

13 (12). Mantle width 19-25% of mantle length, mantle rather flabby. Length of tentacular club 17-20% of mantle length. Proximal hooks usually present in adults. Hooks develop on arms at mantle length of 26-29 mm; central, distal, and proximal hooks developing on club at 17-23, 24-30, and 35-40 mm, respectively...................

..........G. (G.) californiensis Young, 1972

(Fig. 51 M,N). Off California and Baja California, probably in the Gulf of Panama. Mesopelagic and, more rarely, bathypelagic. Mantle length to more than 11 cm.

14 (11). Found in the Arctic, northern Atlantic, and Southern Ocean. Mantle width 17-25% of its length. 8-13 transverse rows of suckers and hooks in basal half of 3rd arm....................**15**

15 (18). Found in Northern Hemisphere. 12-17 transverse rows of suckers in basal half of 4th arm......................................**16**

16 (17). Club length 13-17% (20%) of mantle length. 9-13 transverse rows of suckers and hooks in basal half of 3rd arm, 14-17 transverse rows of suckers in basal half of 4th arm. Hooks on arms develop at mantle length of 30-35 mm; central, distal, and proximal hooks develop at 25-30, 30-35, and 35-40 mm, respectively............

........G. (G.) fabricii (Lichtenstein, 1818)

(Fig. 51 O-P). All the deep-sea part of the Polar Basin, Norway, Greenland, western Barents Sea, Baffin Bay, Davis Strait, Labrador Sea, and northwestern Atlantic southward to south of Cape Cod. Lower epipelagic and mesopelagic; at night sometimes (but rarely) ascending to the surface. Also lives at the bottom on the slopes. Larvae and juveniles live in the epipelagic zone. A very common species. Mantle length to 30 (35) cm. Formerly fished in small quantities in Greenland.

17 (16). Club length 20-36%, usually 23-32%, of mantle length. 8-11 transverse rows of suckers and hooks in basal half of 3rd arms, 12-14 transverse rows of suckers in basal half of 4th arms ...

........G. (G.) steenstrupi Kristensen, 1981

Northeastern Atlantic from the Faeroe-Shetland Ridge to the Bay of Biscay, westward to the Reykjanes Ridge and the open part of the Labrador Sea. Mesopelagic. Mantle length to 13 (19?) cm.

18 (15). Found in the Southern Hemisphere. Club length 15-24% of mantle length. 9-10 transverse rows of suckers in basal half of 4th arm. Hooks develop on arms at mantle length about 25 mm, central, distal, and proximal hooks develop on club at mantle lengths of about 20-25, about 25-30, and more than 30 mm, respectively......
........***G. (G.) antarcticus* Lönnberg, 1898**

Notalian circumpolar species, in the south reaching Antarctic (Scotia Arc), north to southern Africa, Cook Strait, and northern Peru. Larvae and juveniles live in epipelagic and mesopelagic zones, the adults in the mesopelagic and bathylpelagic zones. Mantle length to 35 cm.

Note: According to R. E. Young (1972), an undescribed species of *Gonatus* inhabits the Antarctic. This is perhaps the species described by Imber (1978) under the name of *G. phoebetriae* from a single beak from the stomach of a sooty albatross from Marion Island. 2 new species from the northeastern Pacific to be described by K. Jefferts.

Key to species of the genus *Gonatopsis*

1 (2). Rudiments of tentacular stalks remain in adults as short remnants hidden between the bases of 3rd and 4th arms. Arm lengths equal or exceed mantle length. Mantle flabby. Radula with 5 longitudinal rows of teeth...................
.......***G. (Gonatopsis) okutanii* Nesis, 1972**

(Fig. 50 F). From the northern slope of the Bering Sea to the southern Kurile Islands, Gulf of Alaska, Sea of Okhotsk. Mesopelagic, bathypelagic, and abyssal. Mantle length to 25 (45?) cm. A doubtful species, probably synonym of *Gonatus madokai*.

2 (1). No tentacular rudiments.............3

3 (4). Terminal third of 1st-3rd arms beset by very small suckers arranged in 6-12 longitudinal rows. Arm lengths 80-85% of mantle length, their tips are attenuated and bent. Fin small, kidney-shaped, fin length 20-30% of mantle length. Mantle flabby. Radula with 5 longitudinal rows of teeth. Tentacles disappear and arm hooks develop at mantle length between 30 and 60 mm........
...***G. (Gonatopsis) octopedatus* Sasaki, 1920**

(Fig. 50 G-H). From northern slope of the Ber-

ing Sea to the Sea OF Okhotsk, Sea of Japan, northeastern Honshu, and the Gulf of Alaska. Mesopelagic, bathypelagic, and lower bathyal. Mantle length to 24 cm.

4 (3). Hooks run almost to tips of arms. Suckers on arm tips arranged in 4 longtudinal rows. Arm length under or equals 75% of mantle length, fin length 30-55% of mantle length.............**5**

5 (6). Fin heart-shaped, posteriorly attenuated into tail; fin length 30-45%, width 35-55% of mantle length. Mantle narrow, its width 20-23% of its length. Radula width 5 longitudinal rows of teeth
..***G. (Gonatopsis) japonicus* Okiyama, 1969**

(Fig. 50 I). Southern part of the Sea of Okhotsk and central part of the Sea of Japan. Mesopelagic and bathypelagic, juveniles also near surface. Mantle length to 27 cm, probably up to 75 cm.

6 (5). Fin rhomboidal, wider than long, posteriorly not attenuated into tail.................**7**

7 (8). Fin large, its length 37-45% of mantle length, its width 60-80% of mantle length. Mantle width about 25% of its length, firm, muscular. Arms short, their length about 50% of mantle length. Radula with 7 longitudinal rows of teeth. Tentacles disappear at mantle length of 12-15 (sometimes 10) mm. Hooks develop on arms at mantle length 35-45 (30) mm.................
.....***G. (Boreoteuthis) borealis* Sasaki, 1923**

(Fig. 50 J,K). From the northern slope of the Bering Sea to the northern part of the Sea of Japan, northeastern Honshu, and the area to the south of Baja California; also the Sea of Okhotsk and Subarctic North Pacific. From epipelagic to bathypelagic and at the bottom in bathyal and abyssal zones. Juveniles and adult squids are often fished with a light at the surface in the open ocean. Mantle length to 33 cm. A common species, fished in small quantities as a side product of squid jiggering and salmon gillnetting.

8 (7). Fin small, its length about 30% of mantle length, fin width less than 50% of mantle length. Mantle narrow (width about 20% of length), soft, flabby. Arms fairly long, about 67% of mantle length.............***G. (Gonatopsis) makko*
Okutani & Nemoto, 1964**

(Fig. 50 L). From Bering Sea to the Sea of Japan, northeastern coast of Honshu, and the Gulf of Alaska. Mesopelagic and at the bottom, 650-1200 m. A doubtful species. Most specimens reported as *G. makko* are probably adult *G. japonicus*.

Note: In the Bering Sea (off the Aleutian

Fig. 51.

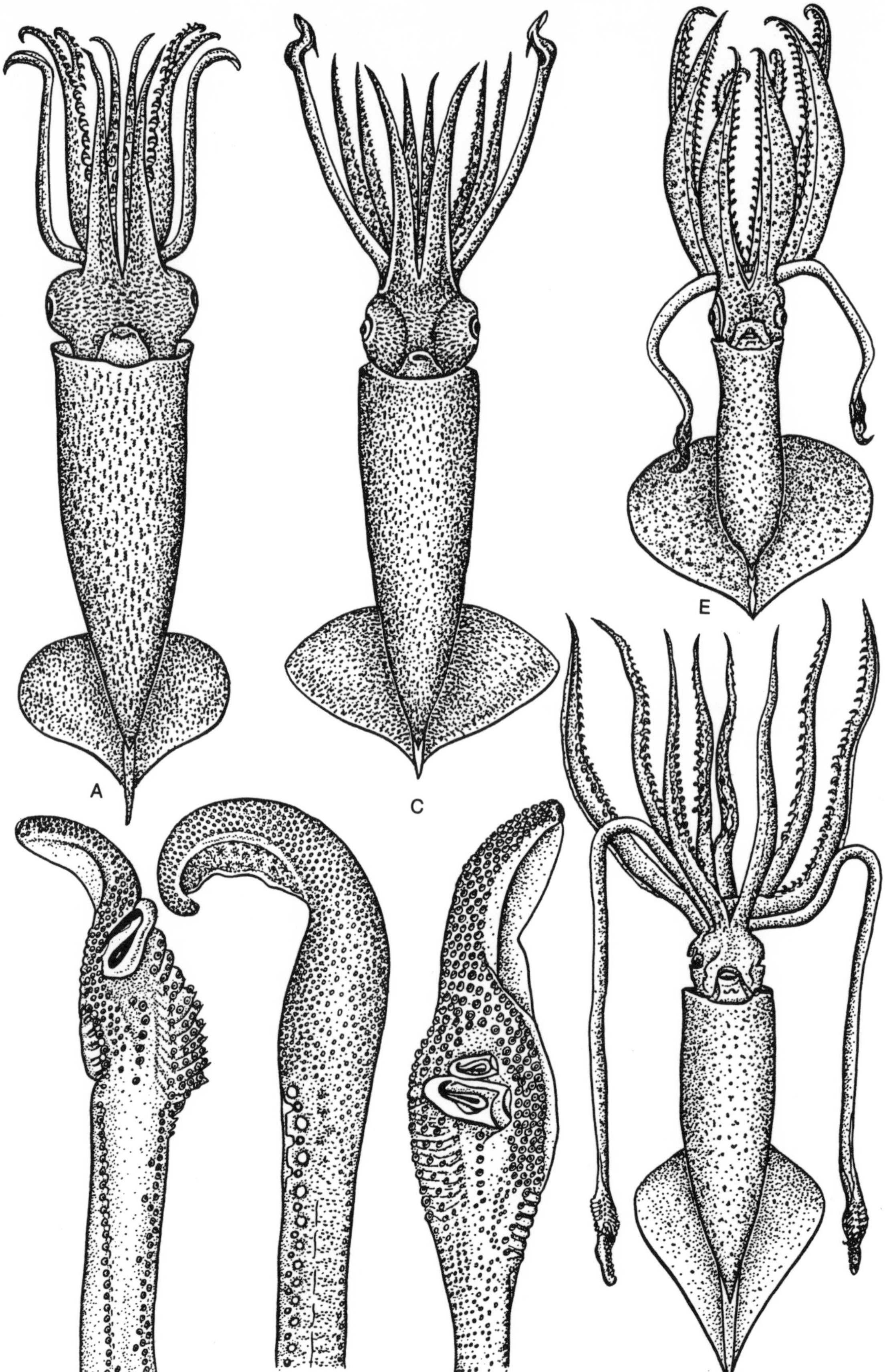

202

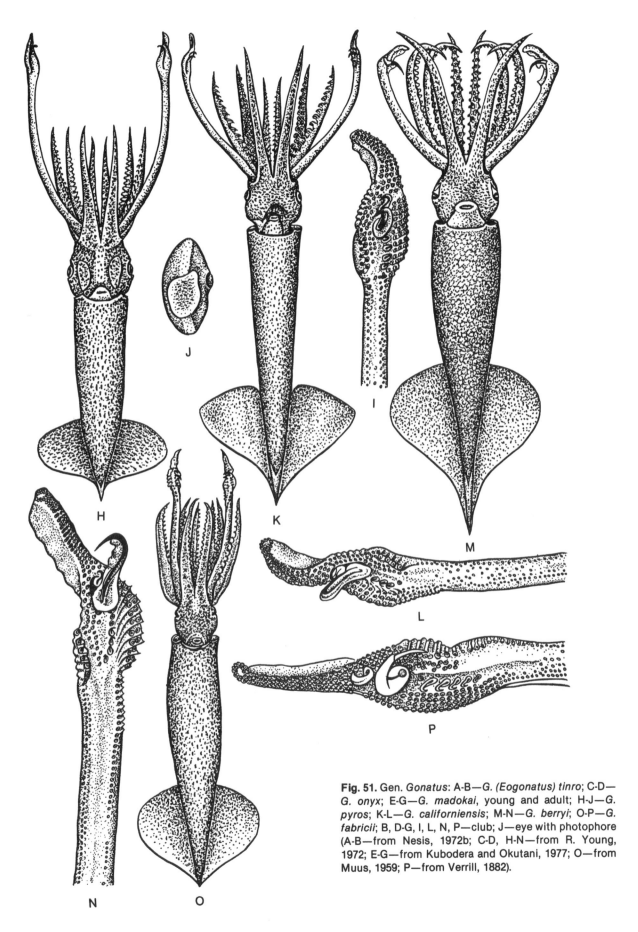

Fig. 51. Gen. *Gonatus*: A-B—*G. (Eogonatus) tinro*; C-D—*G. onyx*; E-G—*G. madokai*, young and adult; H-J—*G. pyros*; K-L—*G. californiensis*; M-N—*G. berryi*; O-P—*G. fabricii*; B, D-G, I, L, N, P—club; J—eye with photophore (A-B—from Nesis, 1972b; C-D, H-N—from R. Young, 1972; E-G—from Kubodera and Okutani, 1977; O—from Muus, 1959; P—from Verrill, 1882).

Islands, in the Gulf of Alaska, and off the southern Kuriles) were caught larvae of a *Gonatopsis (Boreoteuthis)* species that do not belong to any of the gonatid species known from adult specimens.

2.2.2.6. Family Ctenopterygidae

Small squids having wide mantle flattened from above and an unusual "ribbed" fin. Fin short in the young and almost equal to the mantle length in adults. The fin is composed of a series of soft "rays," especially long at the posterior end of the mantle, joined in most of their length by a thin membrane. Head wide but not wider than the mantle. Arms fairly short; the 1st-3rd arms of the suckers are arranged in 4-6 rows distally. 4th arm strongly widened at the base. Arm sucker rings smooth. Tentacles narrow, club not widened, club looks like an oval platform and bears numerous tiny suckers arranged in many rows. No fixing apparatus. Buccal membrane formula is DDVV. Tiny suckers arranged in 2 rows on lappets of buccal membrane. Locking apparatus simple. One elongated photophore is on the ventral side of the eyeball. A large photophore is situated on ventral side of the ink sac under the intestine; it looks like a small yellowish ball lying on the concave surface of the ink sac (like a fried egg on a black frying pan) and covered with a light-reflecting layer. A light organ supposely present in posterior part of the body in mature males. Gladius with a long rhachis and a wide vane bent toward the ventral side at the end, without a terminal cone. No hectocotylus. Between the intestinal photophore and nidamental glands in females there is a large single gland of unknown function that is considered to be homologous with the accessory nidamental gland of myopsid squids but differs in position. Development with larval stage. Tropical to subtropical mesopelagic to bathypelagic squids; the juveniles live in the epipelagic zone. Mantle length to 9 cm.

One genus: ***Ctenopteryx* Appellöf, 1880.** Type species: *C. sicula* (Vérany, 1851). 2 species.

Fig. 52.

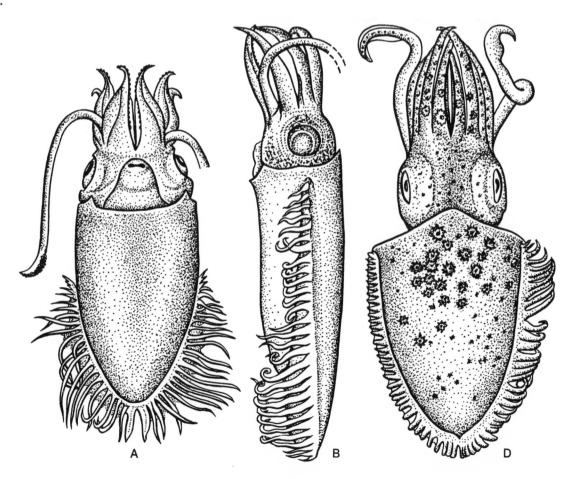

A   B   D

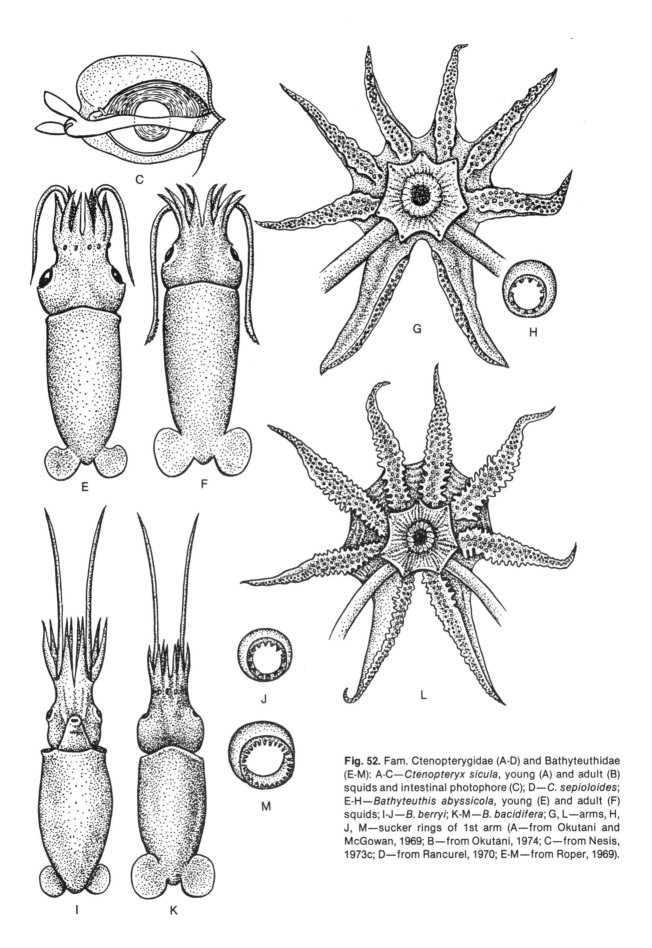

Fig. 52. Fam. Ctenopterygidae (A-D) and Bathyteuthidae (E-M): A-C—*Ctenopteryx sicula*, young (A) and adult (B) squids and intestinal photophore (C); D—*C. sepioloides*; E-H—*Bathyteuthis abyssicola*, young (E) and adult (F) squids; I-J—*B. berryi*; K-M—*B. bacidifera*; G, L—arms, H, J, M—sucker rings of 1st arm (A—from Okutani and McGowan, 1969; B—from Okutani, 1974; C—from Nesis, 1973c; D—from Rancurel, 1970; E-M—from Roper, 1969).

Key to species of the genus *Ctenopteryx*

1 (2). Mantle width about half (40-60%) of mantle length . . . . **C. sicula (Vérany, 1851)**
(Fig. 52 A-C). Tropical to subtropical cosmopolitan species.
2 (1). Mantle width 67-75% of mantle length . . . .
. . . . **C. sepioloides Rancurel, 1970**
(Fig. 52 D). Central Pacific (Hawaiian and Tuamotu Islands).

2.2.2.7. Family Bathyteuthidae

Small squids with a short and wide posteriorly rounded cartilaginous-gelatinous mantle and short kidney-shaped fins not joined at end of body. Head very wide, eyes projecting, directed somewhat forward. At natural posture of squid (head down), eyes directed downward and somewhat to the side. Arms short, wide at bases, their basal parts are joined by a thick web. 1st-3rd arms with 2-4 rows or irregularly positioned suckers, 4th arms with 2 rows. Tentacles long, slender, club not distinct, club suckers are disposed in 8-10 rows. Fixing apparatus absent. Suckers of arms and club are very small. Buccal membrane lappets with a few minute suckers (not present in all specimens). Buccal membrane formula is DDVD. Locking apparatus simple. Gladius with a long narrow rachis and oval vane, without terminal cone. One photophore on the base of each 1st-3rd arm, conspicuous only in young, in the subcuticular tissues. Liver with large inclusions of fat. Development without larval stage. Body coloration is deep red-brown. Mantle length to 7.5 cm.

Bathypelagic and meso-bathypelagic squids that do not perform conspicuous vertical migrations.

One genus: **Bathyteuthis Hoyle, 1885** (= *Benthoteuthis* Verrill, 1885; ?*Chunoteuthis* Robson, 1921; ?*Indoteuthis* Grimpe, 1922) (Fig. 52 E-M). 3 species.

Review: Roper, 1969.

Key to species of the genus *Bathyteuthis*

1 (4). Protective membranes of arms well developed, fleshy, their outer borders straight or slightly wavy, without projecting free trabeculae .
. . . . **2**
2 (3). Arms short, blunt. Arm suckers not numer-

ous, about 100 on 1st-3rd arms in adults. Arm sucker rings with 8-18 truncated teeth. Gills short, narrow . . . . . . **B. abyssicola Hoyle, 1885**
(= *Benthoteuthis megalops* Verrill, 1885) (Fig. 52 E-H). Cosmopolitan species, living in the eutrophic zones of the World Ocean: in the Atlantic north to Ireland, mainly in the northern and eastern Atlantic (absent in the Caribbean Sea and Gulf of Mexico); in the Indian Ocean mainly off eastern Africa; in the Pacific mainly in equatorial (to Hawaii) and southeastern part and in the Solomon Sea. This species is relatively rare in the tropics but is fairly common and distributed circumglobally in notalian and Antarctic zones. Lives at depths of 500 to 3000 m (usually 1000 to 2250 m), the juveniles sometimes found in lower epipelagic zone.
3 (2). Arms long, with attenuated, thin tips. Arm suckers fairly numerous, 250-300 on 1st-3rd arms in adults. Arm sucker rings with 10-14 triangular teeth. Gills long, wide . . . .
. . . . **B. berryi Roper, 1968**
(Fig. 52 I,J). California Current; bathypelagic.
4 (1). Protective membranes of arms poorly developed, supporting trabeculae free and projecting outward as finger-like outgrowths at arm bases. Arms short, blunt. Arm suckers numerous, about 150 on 1st-3rd arms in adults. Arm sucker rings with 18-34 truncated teeth. Gills long, wide
. . . . **B. bacidifera Roper, 1968**
(Fig. 52 K-M). Tropical Indo-Pacific (mainly equatorial); mesopelagic to bathypelagic species.

2.2.2.8. Family Histioteuthidae

Medium and large squids with a small, usually conical, mantle and large head. The tissues are gelatinous-cartilaginous. Fins small, round, joined posteriorly, situated on posterior end of body and sometimes extending beyond the end of the mantle. Eyes large, asymmetrical, the left eye usually much larger than the right one. Arms long, thick at the bases, with 2 rows of suckers. The tentacles are very long, with a small club bearing 4-8 rows of suckers usually differing greatly in size. Tentacles are often autotomized in mature females. The fixing apparatus extends along the tentacular stalk for a distance 2-3 times greater than the club length. Buccal membrane with 6 or 7 lappets (Fig. 53 A,B), the formula DDVD. Inner umbrella (a web joining the arms and leaving the tentacles outside) is often well developed. Locking apparatus is simple, funnel cartilages are slightly bent posteriorly and widened. Entire ventral surface of mantle, head, and arms beset by numerous composite photophores of one or two types; their light is directed forward. There are few photophores on the dorsal side of the body and none on the fins and tentacles. The photophores are arranged on the mantle in oblique rows and on the arms in longitudinal rows. A ring of photophores around each eyelid. They are disposed in strictly specific order. Specially modified photophores are present on the arm tips in some species. Gladius thin, with a short rachis and wide vane, without terminal cone. Both dorsal arms are hectotoctylized. Male genital organs are single or (in *H. hoylei*) paired. Development without larval stage.

Bathypelagic or meso-bathypelagic, also benthic-bathyal squids. Sometimes found in the lower sublittoral. Found throughout the World Ocean except the Arctic and Antarctic. Numerous in some areas, serving as food for sperm whales and other predators.

One genus: **Histioteuthis** d'Orbigny, 1841 (= *Lolidona* Risso, 1854; *Calliteuthis* Verrill, 1880; *Histiopsis* Hoyle, 1885; *Stigmatoteuthis* Pfeffer, 1900; *Meleagroteuthis* Pfeffer, 1900; *Histiothauma Robson,* 1948*)* (Figs. 53-56). Type species: *H. bonnellii* (Férussac, 1835). 13 species and 8-11 subspecies.

Reviews: N. Voss, 1969; Nesis, 1971.

Key to species of the genus *Histioteuthis*

1 (4). Arms joined by an inner web to half length or more. One large long photophore on end of each 1st-3rd arm. 2
2 (3). Buccal membrane with six lappets: connective to 4th arm not split. Segments of inner web passing to 3rd and 4th arms joined at midline. 17 photophores around right eye. Limbs of dorsal member of funnel organ smooth. . . . .
. . . .**H. bonnellii (Férussac, 1835)**
(= *H. bonelliana* auct.; *H. ruppelli* Vérany, 1846) (Fig. 53 A, C-H). Atlantic tropical-subtropical (reaching the boreal zone) species living also in southwestern Indian Ocean. In the Atlantic from the Newfoundland Banks, West Greenland, Iceland and (rarely) northern Norway to the southern subtropical convergence; found in the Mediterranean Sea, but absent in the Caribbean Sea and Gulf of Mexico. Mainly (but not exclusively)

nerito-oceanic species. Lower epipelagic and mesopelagic (sometimes bathypelagic) and at the bottom in bathyal (rarely in lower sublittoral) zones. 2 subspecies:
a. No large photophores behind and ventrally to left eye. . . . . . **H. b. bonnellii (Férussac, 1835)**
(Fig. 53 C-G). Northern Atlantic. Mantle length up to 33 cm.
b. 2-3 large round photophores posterior and ventral to left eye. . **H. b. corpuscula Clarke, 1980**
(Fig. 53 H). Southern Atlantic and southwestern Indian Ocean. Mantle length to 9 cm.
3 (2). Buccal membrane with seven lappets; connectives to 4th arms completely separated. Segments of inner umbrella (web) passing from 3rd to 4th right and left arms joined by a narrow common web between 4th arms. 16 photophores around right eye. Limbs of dorsal member of funnel organ with longitudinal ridge. . . . .
. . . .**H. macrohista N. Voss, 1969**
(Fig. 53 B, I-L). Southern subtropical and notalian circumglobal species. Mesopelagic and bathypelagic. Mantle length to more than 7 cm.
4 (1). Depth of inner umbrella not exceeding 30% of length of longest arm. Photophores on arm tips numerous, not elongated. 5
5 (6). Depth of inner umbrella 17-30% of length of longest arm. Tips of 3rd arms bear series of several oval black photophores, largest of which is 2-3 times larger than ordinary photophores. 4 rows of photophores (not counting small ones) on 4th arms. . . . .**H. atlantica (Hoyle, 1885)**
(Fig. 53 M-P). Southern subtropical and notalian circumglobal species. Mesopelagic and bathypelagic, also descends to the abyssopelagic zone. Mantle length to 20 cm.
6 (5). Inner umbrella not deeper than 15% of length of longest arm. Photophores on arm tips of ordinary structure. 7
7 (14). Photophores on ventral sides of mantle, head, and arms densely distributed; more than 4 longitudinal rows of photophores in basal parts of 4th arms. 8
8 (9). Buccal membrane asymmetrical, with 6 lappets. Longitudinal row of cartilaginous tubercles on back along median line of anterior part of mantle and along 1st-3rd arms in basal parts dorsally. About 20 photophores around right eye. . . . .
. . . .**H. bruuni N. Voss, 1969**
(Fig. 53 Q, R). Southeastern Atlantic: Walvis Ridge, Namibia. Bathypelagic. Mantle length to 8 cm.

Fig. 53.

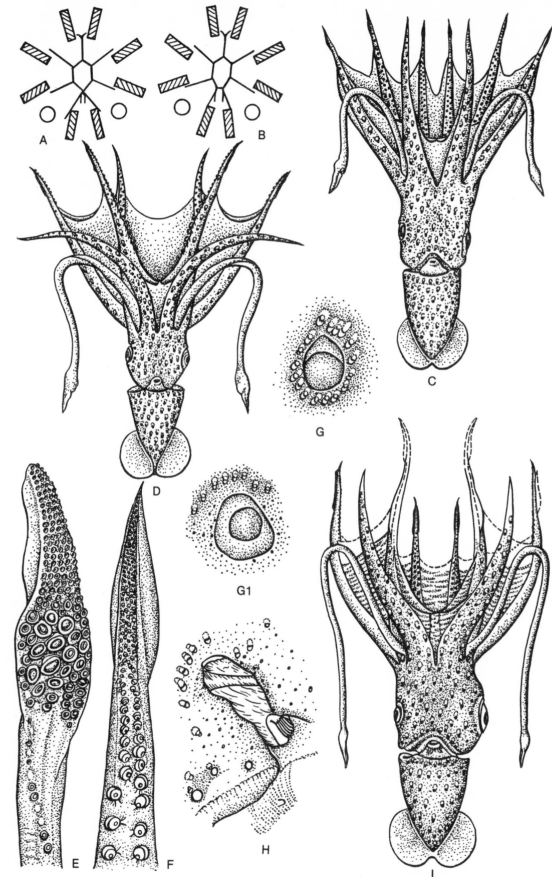

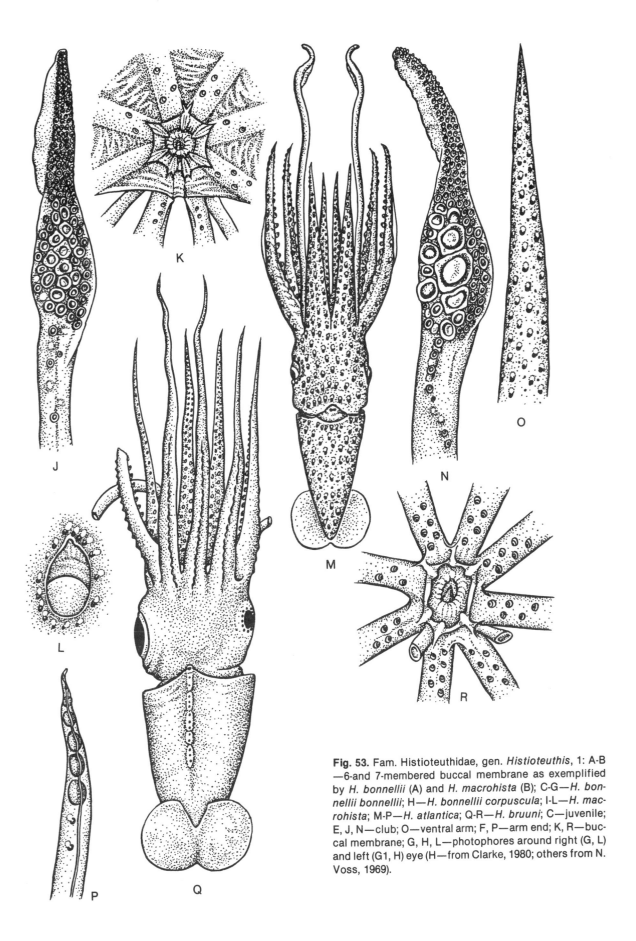

Fig. 53. Fam. Histioteuthidae, gen. *Histioteuthis*, 1: A-B —6-and 7-membered buccal membrane as exemplified by *H. bonnellii* (A) and *H. macrohista* (B); C-G—*H. bonnellii bonnellii*; H—*H. bonnellii corpuscula*; I-L—*H. macrohista*; M-P—*H. atlantica*; Q-R—*H. bruuni*; C—juvenile; E, J, N—club; O—ventral arm; F, P—arm end; K, R—buccal membrane; G, H, L—photophores around right (G, L) and left (G1, H) eye (H—from Clarke, 1980; others from N. Voss, 1969).

Fig. 54.

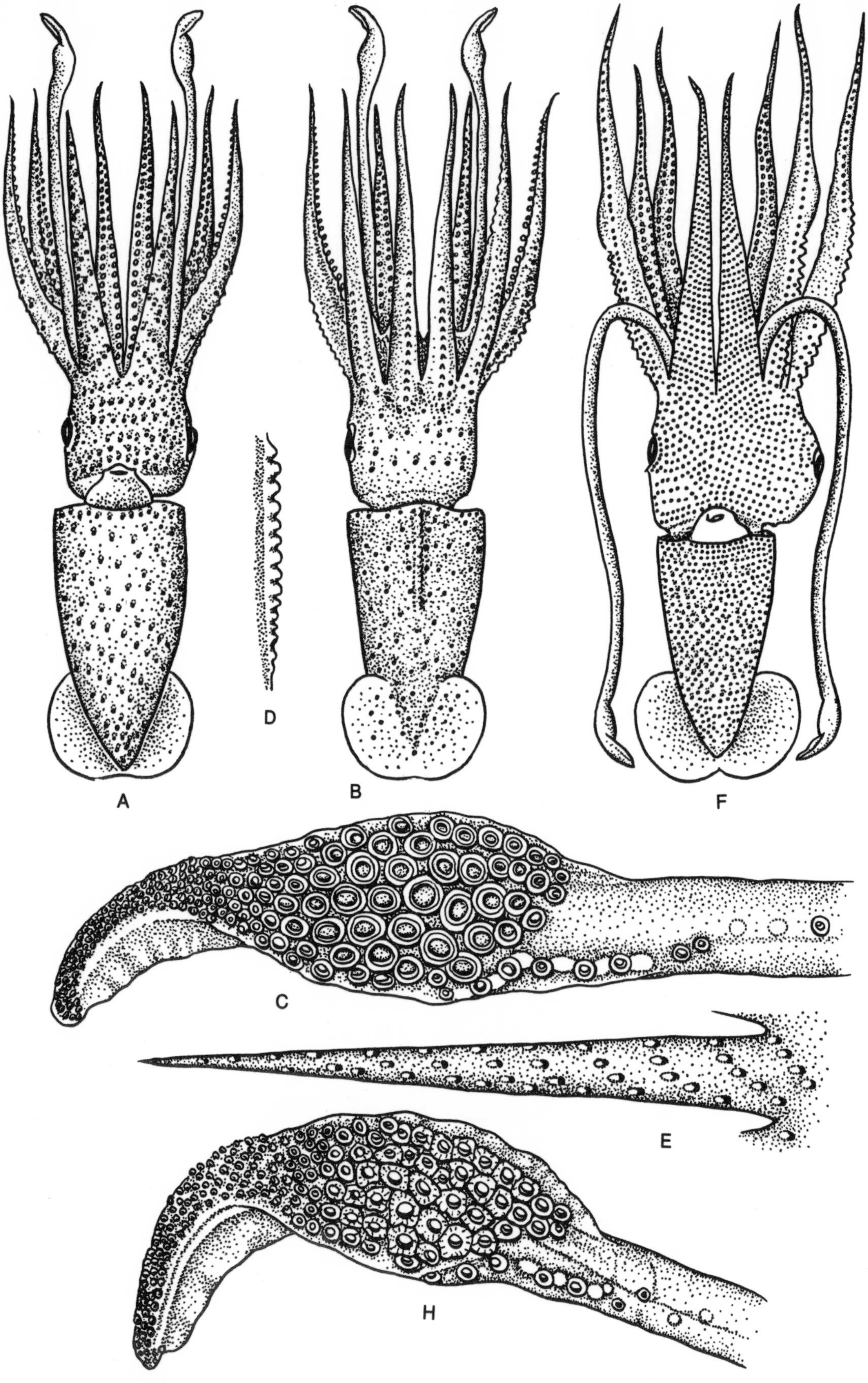

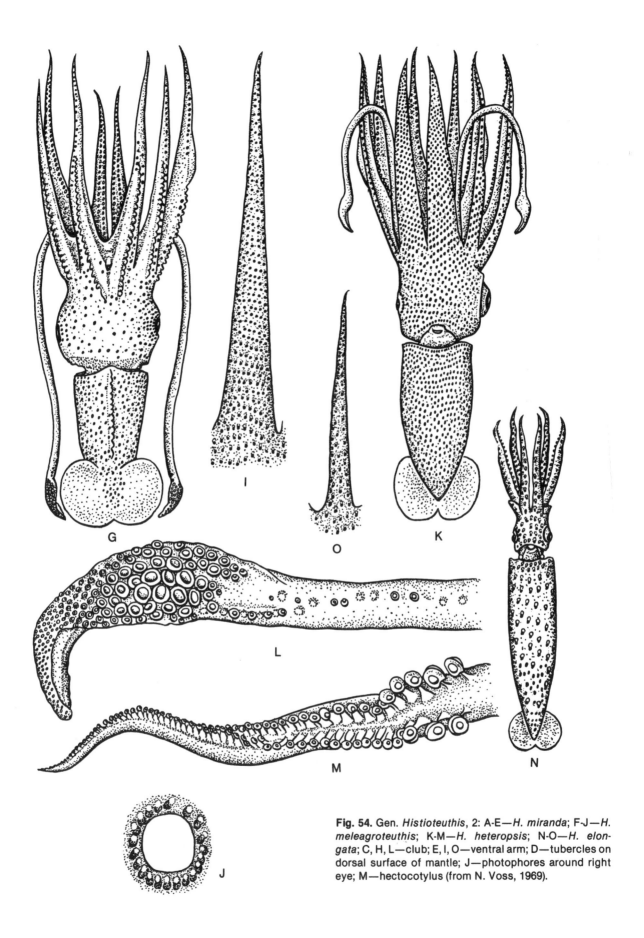

Fig. 54. Gen. *Histioteuthis*, 2: A-E—*H. miranda*; F-J—*H. meleagroteuthis*; K-M—*H. heteropsis*; N-O—*H. elongata*; C, H, L—club; E, I, O—ventral arm; D—tubercles on dorsal surface of mantle; J—photophores around right eye; M—hectocotylus (from N. Voss, 1969).

211

A

B

C

D

D1

E

F

G

H

I

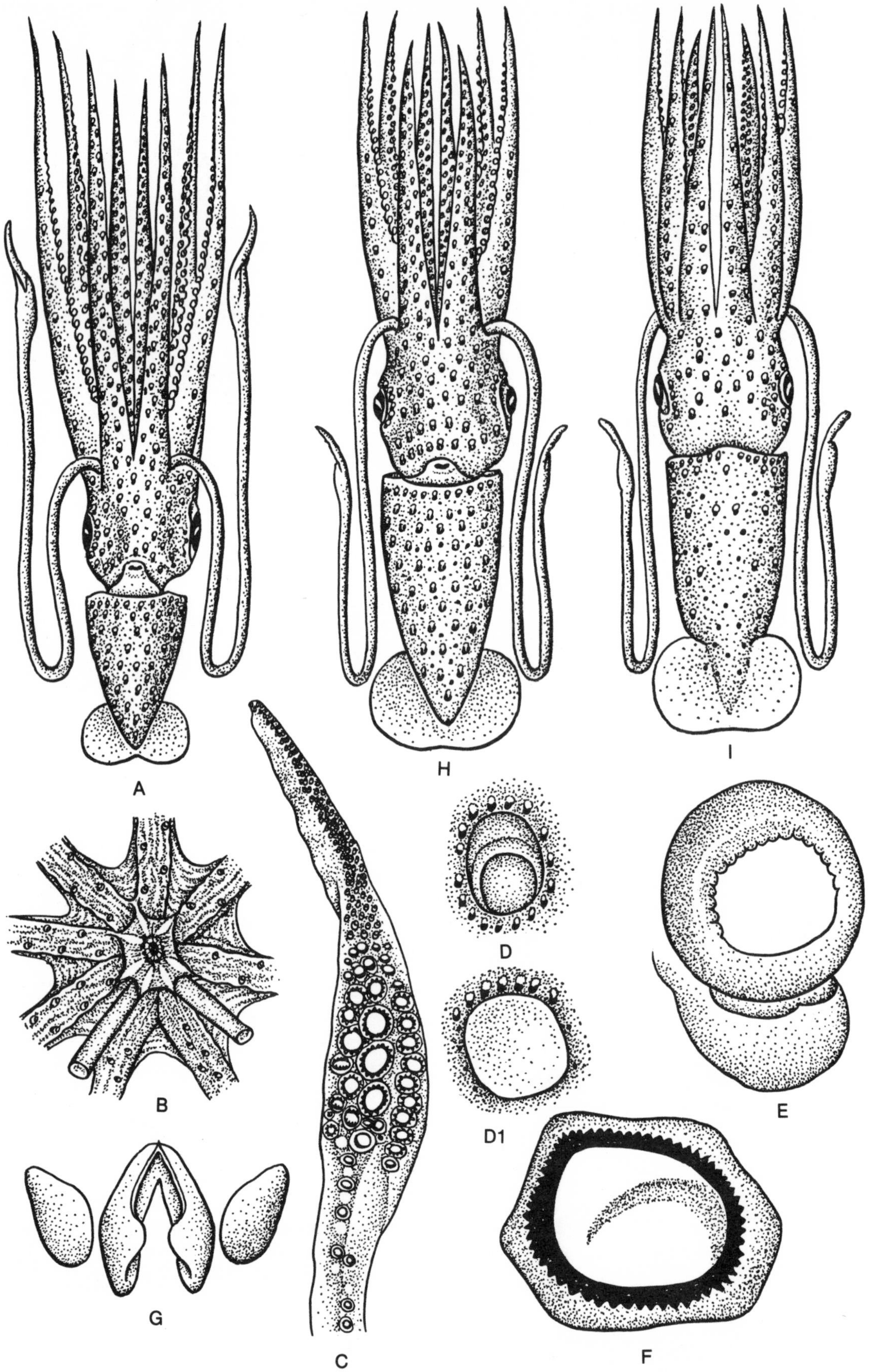

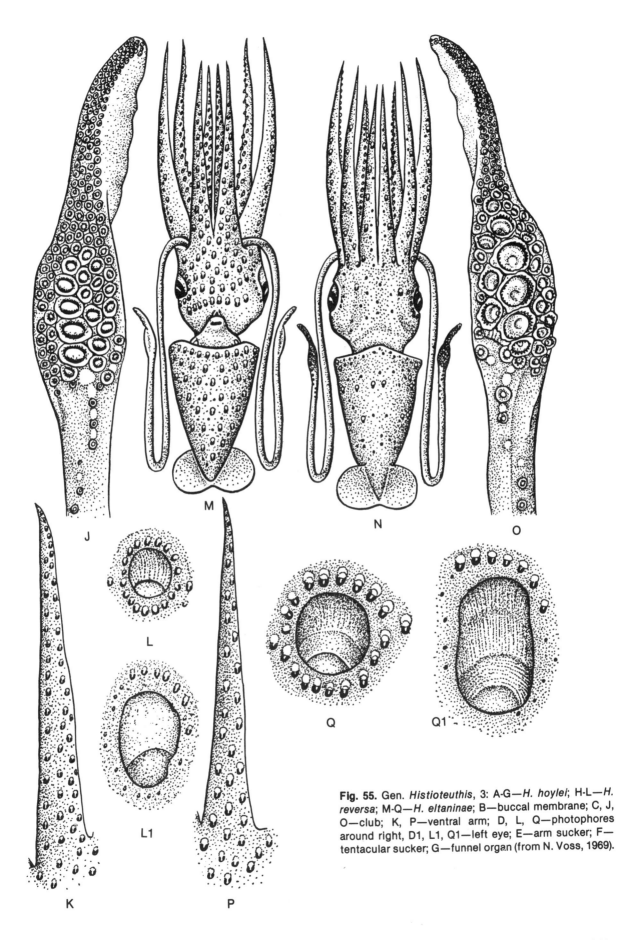

Fig. 55. Gen. *Histioteuthis*, 3: A-G—*H. hoylei*; H-L—*H. reversa*; M-Q—*H. eltaninae*; B—buccal membrane; C, J, O—club; K, P—ventral arm; D, L, Q—photophores around right, D1, L1, Q1—left eye; E—arm sucker; F—tentacular sucker; G—funnel organ (from N. Voss, 1969).

213

Fig. 56.

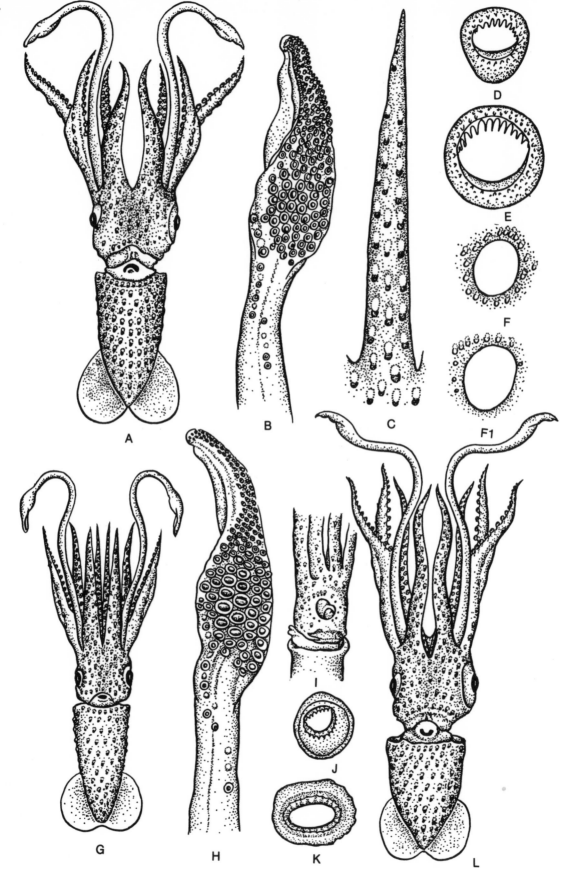

214

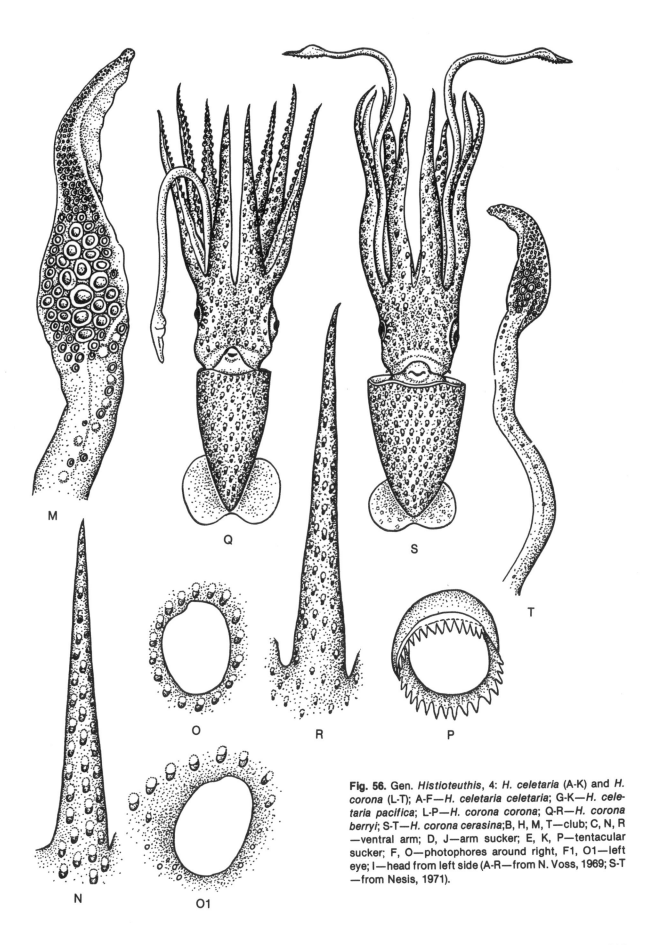

Fig. 56. Gen. *Histioteuthis*, 4: *H. celetaria* (A-K) and *H. corona* (L-T); A-F—*H. celetaria celetaria*; G-K—*H. celetaria pacifica*; L-P—*H. corona corona*; Q-R—*H. corona berryi*; S-T—*H. corona cerasina*;B, H, M, T—club; C, N, R —ventral arm; D, J—arm sucker; E, K, P—tentacular sucker; F, O—photophores around right, F1, O1—left eye; I—head from left side (A-R—from N. Voss, 1969; S-T —from Nesis, 1971).

9 (8). Buccal membrane symmetrical, with 7 lappets. Cartilaginous tubercles on mantle and arms present or absent....................**10**

10 (11). 5 longitudinal rows of photophores in basal parts of 4th arms. 9-10 oblique (diagonal) rows of photophores on ventral side of mantle, 10 photophores (starting from side) in one oblique row. 16 photophores around right eye. Cartilaginous tubercles on dorsal side of mantle and in basal parts of 1st-3rd arms dorsally.....................
.....................**H. miranda (Berry, 1918)**
(= ?*Histiothauma oceani* Robson, 1948) (Fig. 54 A-E). Tropical and subtropical Pacific from the Philippines to New Guinea, the Tasman Sea, southern Australia, and New Zealand; eastward to Hawaii, the Galapagos Islands, and the Nazca Ridge; Gulf of Aden, southern Africa and the southern Indian Ocean. Probably a nerito-oceanic species. Lives mainly in the mesopelagic zone and at the bottom in the bathyal. Mantle length to 26 cm.

11 (10). 8-9 longitudinal rows of photophores in basal parts of 4th arms. More than 20 oblique (diagonal) rows of photophores on ventral side of mantle, a single oblique row containing 19-27 photophores. 19-21 photophores around right eye
.....................**12**

12 (13). Longitudinal rows of cartilaginous tubercles on anterior dorsal side of mantle and in basal parts of 1st-3rd arms. About 30 transverse rows of photophores, 24-27 photophores in one oblique (diagonal) row, counting from side......
.....................**H. meleagroteuthis (Chun, 1910)**
(= *Meleagroteuthis hoylei* Pfeffer, 1908; *M. separata* Sasaki, 1915) (Fig. 54 F-J). Tropical to subtropical cosmopolitan species: in the Atlantic from 45°N to the Cape of Good Hope; in the Pacific from the Kurile Islands and Oregon (possibly from the Bering Sea) to New Zealand. Mainly nerito-oceanic species. Lower epipelagic and mesopelagic zones (sometimes in bathypelagic) and at the bottom in bathyal. Mantle length to 11 cm.

13 (12). Cartilaginous tubercles absent from mantle and arms. About 20-25 rows of photophores on ventral side of mantle, 19-22 photophores in one oblique row......**H. heteropsis (Berry, 1913)**
(Fig. 54 K-M). Eastern Pacific tropical-subtropical nerito-oceanic species: from California to central Chile. Mesopelagic. Mantle length to 13 cm.

14 (7). Photophores on ventral side of mantle, head and arms scarce, 3-4 rows in basal parts of 4th arms, 9-10 photophores on ventral side of mantle in oblique (diagonal) row counting from side....................**15**

15 (16). Mantle very elongated and narrow, mantle width 25-33% of its length. Head markedly narrower than mantle. Peculiar large oval black photophores without lenses present in posterior part of mantle on ventral side and in distal parts of arms, in addition to ordinary photophores. Left eye slightly larger than right one..............
......**H. elongata (N. Voss & G. Voss, 1962)**
(Fig. 54 N,O). Subtropical northern Atlantic from Newfoundland to Cape Hatteras and Madeira; Mediterranean Sea. Mesopelagic. Mantle length to 18 cm.

16 (15). Mantle conical, its width 40-67% of its length. Head not narrower or but little narrower than mantle. No black photophores without lenses. Left eye greatly larger than right one...**17**

17 (22). Rings of large arm suckers with denticulate or serrate edges (in adult *H. reversa* this character not always distinct). Suckers on club manus differ greatly in size: central suckers 3 or 4 times larger than marginal suckers. Limbs of dorsal member of funnel organ with longitudinal ridge or flap.....................**18**

18 (19). Arms very long, in adults 2-2.5 times longer than mantle. Outer umbrella shallow (to 14% of longest arm length) at arm bases. All photophores on ventral side of mantle of similar type, their size gradually diminishing from anterior to posterior end of body. 17 photophores around right eye. Limbs of dorsal member of funnel organ with triangular flap hanging freely into the funnel aperture. Head very large, head length 50-75% (usually about 67%) of mantle length. Skin often beset (especially in adults) by small fleshy papillae. Double set of genital organs in males............**H. hoylei (Goodrich, 1896)**
(= *H. dofleini* (Pfeffer, 1912); *Stigmatoteuthis chuni* Pfeffer, 1912; *S. arcturi* Robson, 1948) (Fig. 55 A-G). Widely distributed tropical to subtropical cosmopolitan species reaching the boreal and notalian areas: in the Atlantic from the Gulf Stream and Gibraltar to the submarine Rio Grande Rise (and South Georgia?), the Gulf of Mexico, and Caribbean Sea (seldom); absent in the Mediterranean Sea; in the Indian Ocean southward to the Mozambique Channel; in the Pacific from the Aleutian Islands to 40-45°S. From the lower epipelagic to bathypelagic, mainly in the mesopelagic and at the bottom in the

bathyal zones. Mantle length to 21 cm. According to N. Voss (1969), the species includes two or more subspecies and it is possible that *H. hoylei* (type locality: Andaman Sea) and *H. dofleini* (type locality: southern Japan) are subspecies and not synonyms.

19 (18). Arm length 100-150% of mantle length. Outer umbrella absent. Large photophores on ventral side of mantle alternating with small ones. 17 large and one small photophore around right eye. Limbs of dorsal member of funnel organ with longitudinal ridge but without flap. Head length 33-50% of the mantle length. Skin smooth. Genital organs of male normal **20**

20 (21). 4 rows of photophores in basal parts of 4th arms: 3 rows of large and 1 row of small photophores. Outer (dorsal) row of large photophores consisting of 5-8 organs . . . .
. . . . ***H. reversa*** **(Verrill, 1880)**
(= *Calliteuthis meneghinii* Pfeffer, 1912) (Fig. 53 H-L). Tropical to subtropical Atlantic species reaching the boreal and notalian areas; northward reaches the Great Newfoundland Bank and the area southward of Iceland, southward approximately to 45°S; Mediterranean Sea; not found in the Gulf of Mexico, and very rare in the Caribbean Sea. Lives in the mesopelagic, lower epipelagic, and at the bottom in the bathyal zones. Mantle length to 13.5 cm.

21 (20). Only 3 rows of large photophores in basal parts of 4th arms. Outer (dorsal) row consisting of 2-3 photophores . . . ***H. eltaninae*** **N. Voss, 1969**
(Fig. 55 M-Q). Notalian circumglobal meso-bathypelagic species only rarely found to the south of the Antarctic convergence. Mantle length to 11 cm.

22 (17). Rings of large arm suckers smooth (only rings of smallest suckers in distal parts of arms may be serrate). Suckers of club manus differ in size but largest not more than 3 times size of smaller. Limbs of dorsal member of funnel organ smooth **23**

23 (24). Suckers in middle part of club differ slightly in size: central ones not more than 1.5 times larger than marginal suckers. Rings of suckers of marginal ventral row on club manus considerably widened. On arm tips most distal group of photophores of outer (dorsal) row separated from preceding photophores by free space, as if 1 or 2 photophores were "dropped out." Mantle elongated, cylindrical, its anterior part with subparallel sides . . . .

. . . . ***H. celetaria*** **(G. Voss, 1960)**
(Fig. 56 A-K). Tropical mesopelagic (or meso-bathypelagic) and benthic-bathyal species. Mantle length to 28 cm. 2 subspecies:
a. Two areas free of photophores ("windows") between eye and funnel on ventral side of head. Rings of large suckers on club manus with teeth only on distal edge . . . .
. . . . ***H. c. celetaria*** **(G. Voss, 1960)**
(Fig. 56 A-F). Atlantic from Bermuda Islands and Madeira to 30°S.
b. No areas free of photophores on ventral side of head. Rings of large suckers on club manus with teeth over entire ring . . . .
. . . . ***H. c. pacifica*** **(G. Voss, 1962)**
(= *Calliteuthis japonica* Massy, 1916, ?non Pfeffer, 1912) (Fig. 56 G-K). Indo-West Pacific from southern Japanese Islands to the area south of Madagascar, northern Australia, and Hawaii.

24 (23). Central suckers in middle part of club 2 or 3 times larger than marginal suckers. Rings of suckers of marginal ventral row on club manus not widened. On arms outer (dorsal) row of photophores runs to tips without interruption. Mantle conical or goblet-like . . . .
. . . . ***H. corona*** **(N. Voss & G. Voss, 1962)**
(Fig. 56 L-T). Tropical and subtropical meso-bathypelagic (ascending up to lower epipelagic) and benthic-bathyal species reaching notalian area. Mantle length to 16 cm. 4 subspecies:
a. 4 rows of photophores in basal part of 4th arms. Rings of large suckers on club manus with about 30 teeth. Ring length 40% of the mantle length . . . . ***H. c. berryi*** **N. Voss, 1969**
(Fig. 56 Q-R). California Current, Hawaii.
b. 3 rows of photophores in basal parts of 4th arms. Rings of large suckers on club manus with 20-25 teeth. Fin length 45-55% of mantle length . . . .
. . . . ***H. c. inermis*** **(Taki, 1964)**
Southern Japan (Pacific coast).
c. 3 rows of photophores in basal parts of 4 arms. Rings of large suckers on club manus with 33-35 teeth. Fin length 35-50% of mantle length . . . . . .
. . . . . . ***H. c. corona*** **(N. Voss & G. Voss, 1962)**
(Fig. 56 L-P). Atlantic Ocean from Cape Hatteras and Gibraltar to the Tropic of Capricorn; Indian Ocean off eastern Africa.
d. 3 rows of photophores in basal part of 4th arms. Rings of large suckers on club manus with 50-60 teeth. Fin length 30-40% of mantle length . . . .
. . . . ***H. c. cerasina*** **Nesis, 1971**
(Fig. 56 S,T). Eastern equatorial Pacific from

the Equator to the Tropic of Capricorn, westward to the Line Islands.

Note: Squids with characters intermediate between the two latter subspecies (a separate subspecies or a variation of *H. c. cerasina*), were found in the Tasman Sea and over the slope of the New Zealand Plateau between the Bounty and Antipodes Islands.

2.2.2.9. Family Psychroteuthidae

Medium and large squids. Mantle cylindrical anteriorly and conical posteriorly, muscular. Fin rhomboidal, with attenuated end. Head small. Arms with two rows of suckers. Tentacular club widened, with 4 rows of very unequal suckers in proximal part and 5-7 rows of small suckers in distal part. Fixing apparatus extends along the stalk. Locking cartilages simple, the funnel cartilage slightly bent, not widened. Buccal membrane formula DDVD. Gladius pen-like, with a short rachis and long vane, abruptly widening at first and then gradually narrowing, spoon-like at the end, not reaching the end of the tail. A large composite photophore on the tips of the 3rd arms in mature females consists of transverse light plates arranged in a zigzag manner and covered by black vanes (screens). Mantle length to 44 cm.

One genus: *Psychroteuthis* **Thiele, 1920** (Fig. 57 A-D). Type and the only described species: *P. glacialis* **Thiele, 1920** (with fin length 55-60% of mantle length), distributed in Antarctic. There are 2 undescribed species: one in Antarctic (Roper, Young & Voss, 1969), the other (with fin length 48-50% of mantle length) found off Bonin Islands in the stomach of a sperm whale (Iwai, 1956). Squids of this genus live in the mesopelagic zone but mainly at the bottom in the bathyal.

2.2.2.10. Family Architeuthidae

Giant squids, the largest of molluscs. Mantle narrow, posteriorly acuminate and attenuated into a short tail. Muscular layer is rather weakly developed. Fins small, semiround or semioval, together forming a longitudinal oval, not reaching posterior end of mantle. Head not wide. Arms very long, with two rows of suckers. Tentacles extremely long, several times longer than the man-

tle; club not very widened, the proximal (carpal) part with many small suckers; in the central part are 4 rows of large suckers, the middle suckers much larger than the marginal suckers. Distally the suckers abruptly become smaller and slightly different in size. Central club suckers bear similar conical teeth over entire ring. Fixing apparatus runs along the tentacular stalk over almost its entire length and ends in the carpal area by a group of small toothless suckers and knobs. Locking cartilages simple. Buccal membrane formula is DDVD. Gladius feather-like, with a short and wide rachis, posteriorly acuminate, with a small terminal cone, not reaching the end of the tail. No photophores. Both ventral arms are hectocotylized. There is very long penis in males. Mantle length up to 5 m, more often 1-2 m.

One genus: *Architeuthis* **Steenstrup, 1856** (=*Architeuthus* auct.; *Megaloteuthis* Kent, 1874; *Dinoteuthis* More, 1875; *Mouchezis* Vélain, 1877; *Megateuthis* Hilgendorf, 1880; *Plectoteuthis* Owen, 1881; *Steenstrupia* Kirk, 1882; *Dubioteuthis* Joubin, 1899) (Fig. 57 E-K). Type species: *A. dux* Steenstrup, 1857. 15 nominal species have been described, but their differences have not been established, and the number of existing true species is unknown. Most probably there are three very similar species: *A. dux* **Steenstrup, 1857,** in the North Atlantic; *A. martensi* **(Hilgendorf, 1880),** in the North Pacific; and *A. sanctipauli* **(Vélain, 1877),** in the Southern Ocean. Another possibility is that there is only one species with three geographic subspecies, *A. dux dux*, *A. dux martensi*, and *A. dux sanctipauli* (for synonymies see Clarke, 1966).

The genus *Architeuthis* is antitropical, found in the northern Atlantic and nearby seas from southern Labrador to the Gulf of Mexico and from northern Norway to the Azores (absent in the Mediterranean Sea); in the northern Pacific it ranges from the Bering Sea to the Sea of Japan, southern Japan (Bonin Islands), Hawaii, and California; in the notalian and southern subtropical areas of the Southern Ocean it is circumglobal. Rarely is it found in the tropical southern Atlantic and doubtfully in the Antarctic. The young squids inhabit midwater (epipelagic and probably uppermost mesopelagic), adults live in the epipelagic and mesopelagic zones and over the bottom in the bathyal and above submarine rises. The majority of presently known giant squids specimens were found either dying or dead

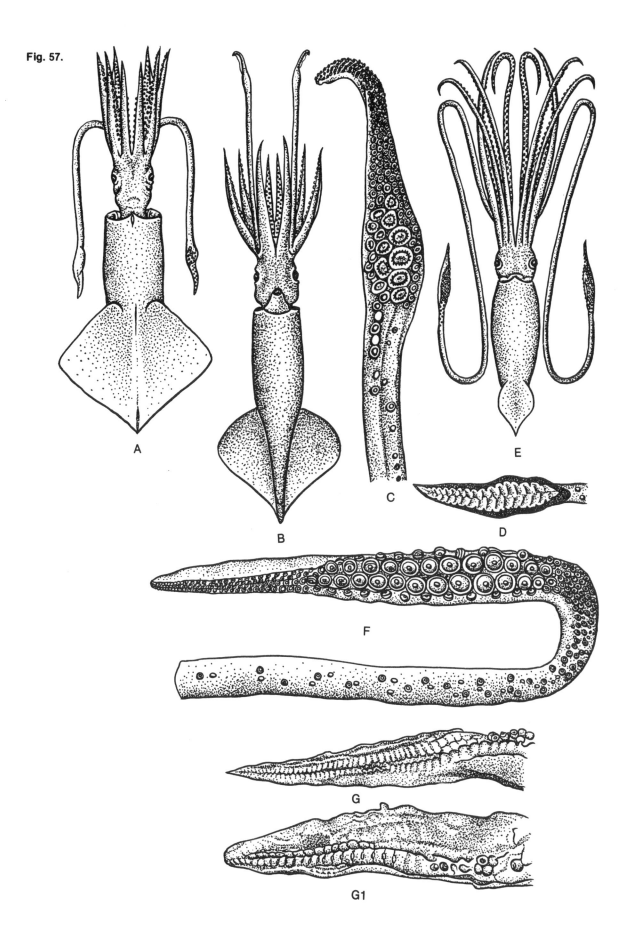

Fig. 57.

219

Fig. 57.

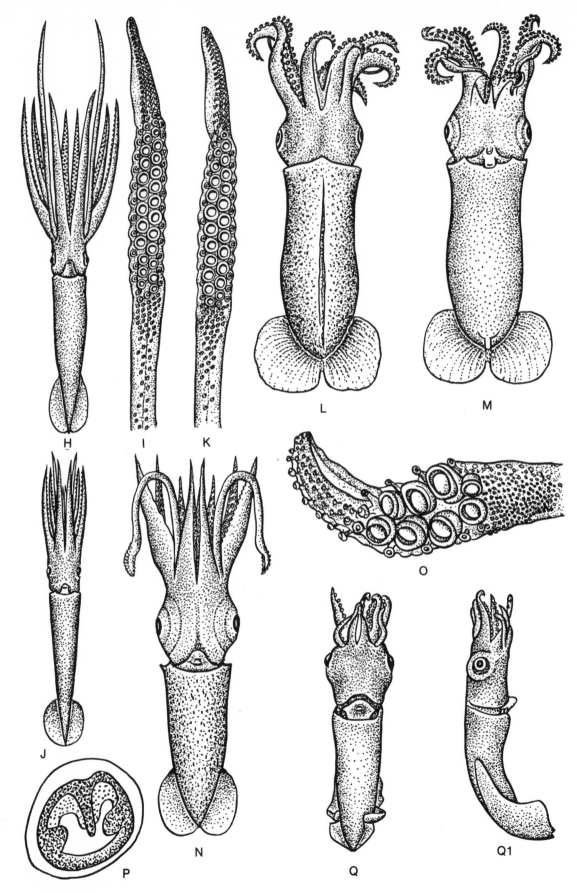

H   I   K   L   M

J   N   O   P   Q   Q1

220

on shores and on the sea surface or extracted from the stomachs of sperm whales. Only recently have some been caught by large fishing trawls.

Recently R. B. Toll and S. C. Hess (1981) have found the remains of a mature male *Architeuthis* with the mantle length of only 18 cm in the stomach of a swordfish caught in the Straits of Florida. This "pigmy giant squid" may be an undescribed species.

Reviews: Nesis, 1974d; Roper & Boss, 1982.

2.2.2.11. Family Neoteuthidae
(= Alluroteuthidae)

Medium and small squids with conical mantle and large head. Fins without anterior "earlets," kidney-shaped, inversely heart-shaped (narrow anteriorly and wide posteriorly, with incision on posterior edge) or in the form of a lateral fringe. Arms with 2 rows of suckers. In adult *Alluroteuthis* the suckers on the 1st-3rd arms are modified into hooks. Suckers on the 4th arms are much smaller than on the 1st-3rd arms. Tentacular club bears in its proximal part a large number of small suckers arranged in more than 10 rows; in the central part of the club are 4 rows of large suckers of equal or different size, while on the distal end are 3-4 rows of gradually smaller suckers. Tentacular fixing apparatus present. Locking cartilages simple. Buccal membrane formula is DDVD. No photophores. Gladius with a short rachis and wide vane. Development with larval stage. 3 genera, 3-4 species.

Key to genera and species of the family Neoteuthidae

1 (2). Fins kidney-like, extending a little behind posterior end of mantle, their length and width about 40% of mantle length. Tentacles slender, weak, in juveniles shorter than arms, in subadults somewhat longer. In central part of club, 4 pairs of suckers of two median rows strongly enlarged, many times larger than marginal suckers. Zone of

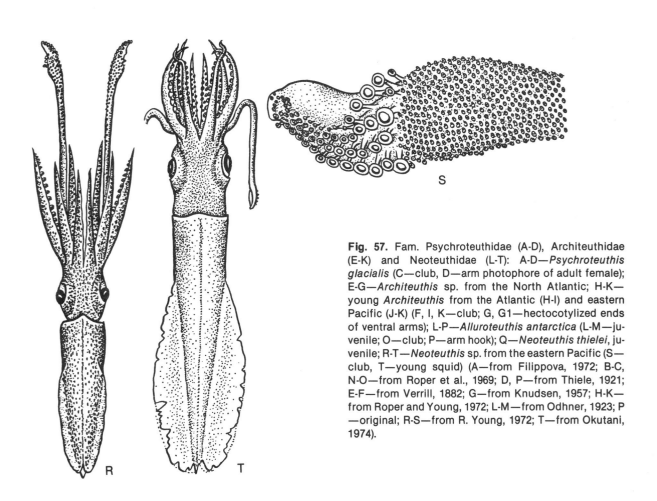

Fig. 57. Fam. Psychroteuthidae (A-D), Architeuthidae (E-K) and Neoteuthidae (L-T): A-D—*Psychroteuthis glacialis* (C—club, D—arm photophore of adult female); E-G—*Architeuthis* sp. from the North Atlantic; H-K—young *Architeuthis* from the Atlantic (H-I) and eastern Pacific (J-K) (F, I, K—club; G, G1—hectocotylized ends of ventral arms); L-P—*Alluroteuthis antarctica* (L-M—juvenile; O—club; P—arm hook); Q—*Neoteuthis thielei*, juvenile; R-T—*Neoteuthis* sp. from the eastern Pacific (S—club, T—young squid) (A—from Filippova, 1972; B-C, N-O—from Roper et al., 1969; D, P—from Thiele, 1921; E-F—from Verrill, 1882; G—from Knudsen, 1957; H-K—from Roper and Young, 1972; L-M—from Odhner, 1923; P—original; R-S—from R. Young, 1972; T—from Okutani, 1974).

small suckers in proximal part of club occupying less than 50% of club length. Fixing apparatus consists of suckers and tubercle-like knobs and located in carpal part of club and along stalk. Suckers in middle parts of the 1st-3rd arms in adolescent and adult specimens modified into hooks due to extensive growth of middle tooth in distal part of ring..........................
........**Genus *Alluroteuthis* Odhner, 1923**

One species: ***A. antarctica* Odhner, 1923** (Fig. 57 L-P). Antarctic circumpolar meso-bathypelagic species. Mantle length to 27 cm. Review: Filippova & Yukhov, 1982.

2 (1). Fins in the form of a narrow lateral fringe; fin length is much more than half of mantle length, fin width much smaller than its length. Tentacles long, strong, with widened carpal part. No arm hooks, arm sucker rings with high turret-like teeth.............................**3**

3 (4). Carpal part of the club occupies less than 50% of its length. Two enormous big suckers occupies whole central part of club, with also some smaller suckers along the margin of this part and on the dactylus. Fixing apparatus consist of suckers and tubercles-knobs and located in carpal part and on distal part of stalk................
...............**n. gen. & sp. Nesis & Nikitina**

Found in the southeastern Pacific (Subantarctic).

4 (3). Carpal part of club occupies 67-80% of its length. Four rows of suckers in central part of club, median ones not bigger than lateral. Fixing apparatus located along the margin of carpal part of club, not reaching stalk, and consists of modified suckers only.........................
.............**Genus *Neoteuthis* Naef, 1921**

(Fig. 57 Q-T). Type and only described species: *N. thielei* Naef, 1921. 2 species, one undescribed.
....**5**

5 (6). Fin gradually widening to posterior end and extending beyond rear end of mantle; maximum width of fin at posterior margin...............
......................***N. thielei* Naef, 1921**

(Fig. 57 Q). Tropical and subtropical Atlantic, Caribbean Sea. Meso-bathypelagic species. Mantle length to 17 cm.

6 (5). Fin in form of narrow lateral fringe, not passing beyond posterior end of mantle; maximum width of fin at middle of mantle.........
...............***Neoteuthis* sp. Young, 1972**

(Fig. 57 R-T). Eastern Pacific from Baja California to northern Chile and off Hawaii; western tropical Indian Ocean (?). Mesopelagic

and bathypelagic. Squids of this species were also collected in the notalian zone of the Pacific to the east of New Zealand (Young, 1972).

Note: C. F. E. Roper, R. E. Young, G. L. Voss (1969) include the Antarctic species *Parateuthis tunicata* Thiele, 1920, in the family Neoteuthidae, supposing that it is a larva of *A. antarctica*. According to our data, *P. tunicata* is a separate species not related to the family Neoteuthidae (see subhead 2.2.2.23.).

2.2.2.12. Family Brachioteuthidae

Small nektonic squids with a thin, narrow, weakly muscular mantle, acuminate posteriorly. Head small, narrow; larvae have a long neck. Fin rhomboidal or heart-shaped. Arms with two rows of suckers. Many rows of small suckers in proximal part of tentacular club, the distal part with 4-6 rows of initially large and then gradually smaller suckers. Fixing apparatus along tentacular stalk. Locking cartilages simple. Buccal membrane formula is DDVV. Gladius with a very thin rachis, widening only in the posterior third, and a well developed narrow cone. Photophores absent or present on ventral side of eyeball. Development with larval stage. Mantle length to 10-17 cm.

Young squids are epi-mesopelagic, and adults live mainly in the mesopelagic and bathypelagic zones, but sometimes ascend to the epipelagic.

One genus: ***Brachioteuthis* Verrill, 1881** (= *Tracheloteuthis* Steenstrup, 1882; *Verrilliola* Pfeffer, 1884; *Entomopsis* Rochebrune, 1884) (Fig. 58). Type species: *B. beani* Verrill, 1881. 4 species, one of them not described and two others doubtful.

Key to species of the genus *Brachioteuthis*

1 (2). Mantle very narrow, slightly widening anteriorly and then abruptly narrowing in front of the fin. Fin irregularly longitudinally rhomboidal; fin width and length comprising about 50% of the mantle length; width-to-length ratio approximately 0.9-1.1. Single sausage-like photophore on ventral side of eyeball. Color light purple-brown or chocolate. Skin of reticular-fibrous structure....
......................***B. picta* Chun, 1910**

(Fig. 58 A). Tropical and subtropical Atlantic, including southern peripheral zone, and tropical parts of the Indian and Pacific Oceans, southward to 40-45°S. Mesopelagic and bathypelagic, the juveniles epipelagic. Mantle length to 8 cm.

2 (1). Mantle cylindrical, without abrupt narrowing in front of fin. Fin transversely rhomboidal or widely heart-shaped, not attenuated or only slightly attenuated posteriorly; fin width-to-length ratio usually 1.2-1.4 . . . .**3**

3 (4). Fin length 35-50% of mantle length, width 45-60% of mantle length. Mantle nearly colorless, with scarce small chromatophores. Eye photophores present or absent . . . .
. . . .**B. riisei (Steenstrup, 1882)**

(Fig. 58 B-J). According to existing data this is a cosmopolitan species (except boreal Pacific). In the Atlantic found from southern part of the Norwegian Sea and Iceland to the extreme southern Atlantic, present in the Mediterranean Sea but absent in the tropical western Atlantic, Gulf of Mexico, and Caribbean Sea; in the Indian Ocean it lives almost everywhere except the Arabian Sea and northern part of the Bay of Bengal; in the Pacific, to the south of northern border of central waters; in Southern Ocean circumglobally. Common in the northern Atlantic, subantarctic, and Antarctic, rare in the tropics. Found in the epipelagic and mesopelagic zones, the adults also in the bathypelagic. Mantle length normally to 8 cm (in the Antarctic to 17 cm). A composite species. 2 types distinguishable among larvae and juveniles:

a. Neck of moderate length. Eyes directed forward and laterally at an acute angle to longitudinal axis of body . . . .
. . . .**B. riisei (Steenstrup, 1882)**
[= *B. nympha* (Pfeffer, 1884); *B. velaini* (Rochebrune, 1884)] (Fig. 58 B-F). Northern Atlantic, Mediterranean Sea, temperate waters of southern Atlantic, Indian and Pacific Oceans, and tropical eastern Pacific. Adult squids of this form have eye photophore.

b. Extremely long neck in larvae. Eyes directed laterally, perpendicular to longitudinal axis of body. No photophores . . . .
. . . .**B. behni (Steenstrup, 1882)**
(= *B. gracilis* (Pfeffer, 1884); ?*B. clouei* (Rochebrune, 1884)) (Fig. 58 G,H). Equatorial Atlantic, equatorial and central waters of the Indo-Pacific.

The notalian-Antarctic "*B. riisei*" probably also represents a separate species (Fig. 58 I-J). It has no photophores, and the skin of adult specimens

(mantle length exceeding 6 cm) under the epidermis is of reticular-fibrous structure formed by a network of connective tissue fibers (conspicuous only in well preserved specimens).

4 (3). Fin length 50-55% of mantle length, width 60-67% of mantle length. Coloration intensively purple-brown. No photophores (?) . . . .
. . . .**B. beani Verrill, 1881**
(Fig. 58 K,L) Northwestern Atlantic off the eastern coast of the U.S.A. **B. bowmani Russell, 1909** (Fig. 58 M) also will key here. Northeastern Atlantic near Faeroe-Iceland Ridge. Mantle length in both to 6 cm. Both these species were found at the bottom in the bathyal. Their taxonomic status is unclear.

2.2.2.13. Family Ommastrephidae

Swift and strong nektonic squids mainly of medium and large size. Mantle is cylindrical or conical, muscular. Fin terminal, transversely rhomboidal or heart-shaped. Head large. Arms strong, with well developed protective membranes and swimming keels; they bear two rows of suckers with denticulate rings. Tentacles with widened club bearing 4 rows of suckers (in *Illex* 8 rows at the end of the club); suckers of middle rows in central part of club are greatly enlarged. Fixing apparatus short. Funnel groove (Fig. 59 A) triangular; in many species the anterior part of the funnel is separated by an arched transverse fold of skin (foveola) and sometimes bears longitudinal cutaneous ridges; foveola may be followed by a few more small arched cutaneous pockets on both sides of the funnel groove nearer to the tail. Funnel cartilages with two deep grooves joined to each other in the form of inverted T (⊥). Mantle cartilages consist of two ridges (horizontal and vertical) corresponding to the form of funnel cartilage. Buccal membrane formula is DDVD.

Many species have luminous organs, thousands of tiny yellow grains of irregular form scattered in the mantle muscles and in the tissues of the head and arms, sometimes grouped into round or oval spots or longitudinal stripes; some species have photophores on the eyeball and inside the mantle.

Gladius narrow, without vane, narrowing posteriorly and widening slightly at the rear end, with a small terminal cone. One or both ventral arms are hectocotylized. Spermatophores are transferred to the buccal membrane, rarely into

Fig. 58.

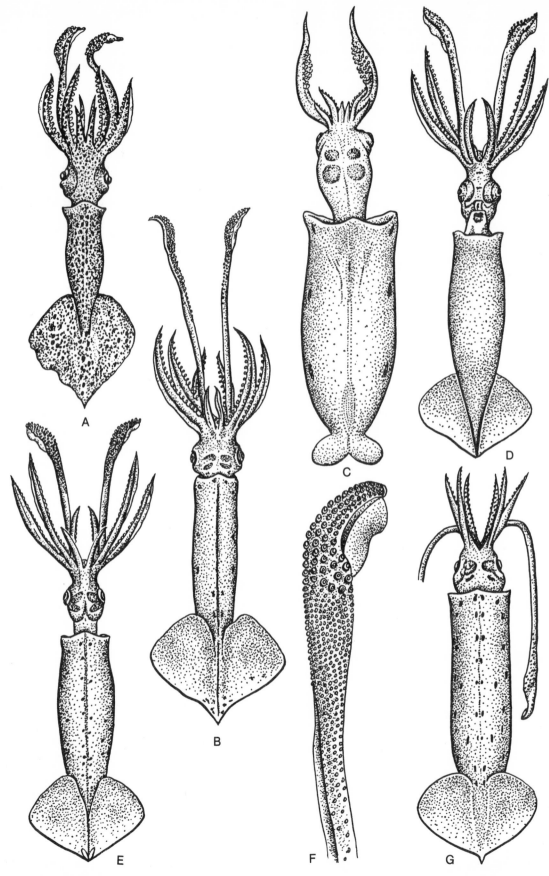

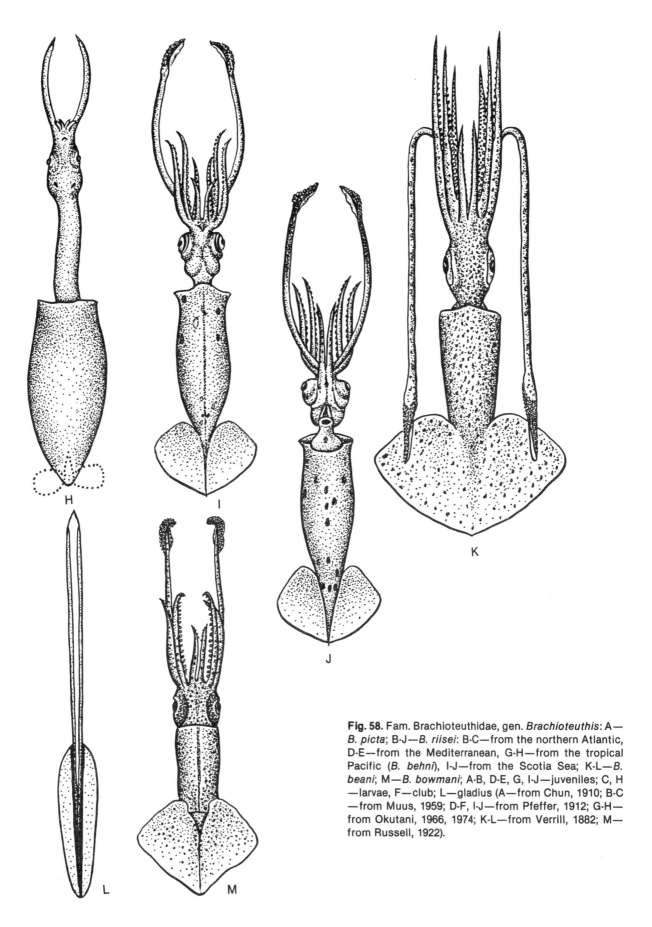

Fig. 58. Fam. Brachioteuthidae, gen. *Brachioteuthis*: A—
B. picta; B-J—*B. riisei*: B-C—from the northern Atlantic,
D-E—from the Mediterranean, G-H—from the tropical
Pacific (*B. behni*), I-J—from the Scotia Sea; K-L—*B.
beani*; M—*B. bowmani*; A-B, D-E, G, I-J—juveniles; C, H
—larvae, F—club; L—gladius (A—from Chun, 1910; B-C
—from Muus, 1959; D-F, I-J—from Pfeffer, 1912; G-H—
from Okutani, 1966, 1974; K-L—from Verrill, 1882; M—
from Russell, 1922).

225

the mantle cavity, of the female. Eggs are rather small and are deposited on the bottom or in midwater. The larva—a rhynchoteuthis—has a proboscis composed of the fused tentacles. At the end of the larval stage the proboscis splits, starting from the base, and thus the tentacles are separated.

Ommastrephids live at the surface, in midwater, at the bottom in the middle or lower sublittoral, and in the bathyal. Most species are widely eurybathic and perform diel vertical migrations, ascending to the surface at night. They are found from the upper boreal (sometimes even Arctic) to notalian areas. Most species migrate over a long distance (to several thousand miles) for feeding and spawning. They are predators feeding on small fishes, macroplanktonic crustaceans, and small squids.

This is the most important family of all cephalopods for fisheries usages. In temperate latitudes ommastrephids dominate in world catches of squids, and ommastrephid fishing is promising in some tropical areas, too. 4 subfamilies, 11 genera, 17-18 species and 7-8 subspecies.

Reviews: Zuev et al., 1975; Wormuth, 1976; Nigmatullin, 1979.

Key to subfamilies and genera of the family Ommastrephidae

1 (12). Funnel groove (Fig. 59 A1) without foveola or with a foreola but without lateral pockets. Funnel cartilage short, with almost straight longitudinal groove. Tentacular fixing apparatus weakly developed, without tubercle-like knobs. Rings of large suckers in middle part of club without enlarged teeth **2**
2 (5). Funnel groove simple, without foveola. Carpal group of club suckers short. Luminous organs absent . . . .**Subfamily Illicinae** . . . **3**
3 (4). 8 transverse rows of small suckers at end of club. Mantle width 17-25% of mantle length. Fin heart-shaped or narrowly rhomboidal, fin width 45-60% of mantle length. One ventral arm hectocotylized . . . .
. . . .**Genus *Illex* Steenstrup, 1880**
(Fig. 59 B-I). Type species: *I. illecebrosus* (LeSueur, 1821). 2 species and 3 subspecies in the Atlantic Ocean from southern Greenland and Iceland to the Falkland Islands and Namibia, and in the Caribbean and Mediterranean Seas. They live at the bottom in the middle and lower sublittoral and upper bathyal, in temperate latitudes

during feeding migrations sometimes ascending to the surface and approaching shores. Spawning takes place at or over the bottom. The young squids live in pelagic zone sometimes far from the coasts. The genus is of a high fisheries value, mainly in the northwestern, southwestern, and eastern central Atlantic and Mediterranean. Review: Roper, Lu & Mangold, 1969.

4 (3). 4 transverse rows of suckers at end of club. Mantle width 33% of mantle length. Fin widely rhomboidal, its width 75-85% of mantle length. Both ventral arms hectocotylized . . . .
. . . .**Genus *Todaropsis* Girard, 1890**
One species: ***T. eblanae* (Ball, 1841)** (Fig. 59 J-L). Eastern Atlantic from Shetland Islands to the Cape of Good Hope, and the Indian Ocean from the Agulhas Bank, Mascarenes Ridge, and Timor Sea, and along the western and southeastern Australia. At the bottom in lower sublittoral and upper bathyal, not ascending to the surface or approaching the shore. Mantle length to 27 cm. An object of minor fisheries in the northeastern Atlantic.

5 (2). Funnel groove (Fig. 59 A2) with foveola and as a rule with longitudinal cutaneous ridges (not always conspicuous in *Ornithoteuthis*), but without lateral pockets. No small subcutaneous photophores **6**
6 (11). Mantle cylindrical. Fin rhomboidal or slightly attenuated posteriorly, fin length less than or equal to 50% of mantle length. No photophores. Carpal group of suckers on club extended, occupying considerable part of stalk . . . .
. . . .**Subfamily Todarodinae** . . . **7**
7 (10). No finger-like projections on tentacular stalk proximal to first suckers. No cirri-like projections beyond edge of protective membranes along arms and club **8**
8 (9). One ventral arm (usually right, rarely left) hectocotylized. Species inhabiting temperate and cold waters and absent from tropical waters . . . . .
. . . .**Genus *Todarodes* Steenstrup, 1880**
(= *Ommastrephes* or *Ommatostrephes* auct., non d'Orbigny; *Sagittatus* Risso, 1854) (Fig. 59 M-Q). Type species: *T. sagittatus* (Lamarck, 1799). 3 species living both at the bottom and in the pelagic zone. Of a high fisheries value.
9 (8). Both ventral arms hectocotylized, one arm in proximal and distal parts, other only in proximal part. Species inhabiting tropical and subtropical Indo-West Pacific and Australia-New Zealand area . . . .

.... **Genus *Nototodarus* Pfeffer, 1912**

(Fig. 60 A-E). Type species: *N. sloani* (Gray, 1849). 2-3 species, one of them with 4-5 subspecies, or 5-6 separate species. At the bottom in the lower sublittoral and upper bathyal, sometimes ascending to the surface, but seldom approaching shores. Mantle length to 42 cm. Object of major fisheries around New Zealand and off Victoria and Tasmania, also fished in some other areas.

10 (7). Biserial row of finger-like projections extending from first suckers almost to base of tentacular stalk in proximal part of club. Protective membranes of arms and tentacles short, their trabeculae longer than membranes and projecting along edges of arms and clubs like cirri; suckers situated at bases of projections. One ventral arm hectocotylized............. **Genus *Martialia* Rochebrune & Mabille, 1887**

One species: **M. hyadesi Rochebrune & Mabille, 1887** (Fig. 60 F-H). Patagonian shelf and slope and Tierra del Fuégo from off La Plata to Cape Horn; South Georgia; southern Pacific (Eltanin fracture zone); Maquazie Is.). Near the bottom in the lower sublittoral and upper bathyal and in midwater. Mantle length to 45 cm.

11 (6). Mantle narrow, conical, attenuate posteriorly into thin tail. Fin narrow heart-shaped, strongly attenuate posteriorly, its length exceeding 50% of mantle length. 2 photophores on viscera: large round one near anus and small oval one at posterior end of intestine; in adult squids narrow band of luminous tissue passes from small photophore with two gaps (to pass arteries) to posterior end of body. One photophore on eyeball. Carpal group of club suckers short......... **Subfamily Ornithoteuthinae** .... **Genus *Ornithoteuthis* Okada, 1927**

(Fig. 60 I-P). Type species: *O. volatilis* (Sasaki, 1915). 2 very similar nerito-oceanic species in tropical Atlantic and Indo-West Pacific. The juveniles live in midwater, the adults in the lower epipelagic and mesopelagic zones and at the bottom in the bathyal.

12 (1). Funnel groove (Fig. 59 A3) with foveola, longitudinal cutaneous ridges, and lateral pockets (the latter sometimes absent in *Eucleoteuthis* and *Hyaloteuthis*). Funnel cartilage elongated, its longitudinal groove slightly bent anteriorly; anterior part of mantle cartilage also slightly bent correspondingly. Fixing apparatus with one or several knobs alternating with suckers with smooth rings. Rings of large club suckers with either one large tooth in distal part of ring or with 4 large teeth, one at each quadrant. Small cutaneous photophores on head, mantle, fins, and arms; ocular, intestinal, and large superficial photophores may also be present.............. .... **Subfamily Ommastrephinae ... 13**

13 (16). No large photophores on eyeball and surface of body. Mantle cylindrical; fin rhomboidal, not attenuate or slightly attenuate posteriorly. Rings of large suckers of club with 4 large teeth, one at each quadrant.....................**14**

14 (15). Tips of all arms in adults thin and whip-like, attenuate, bearing a number (100-200 pairs) of small suckers. Ends of trabeculae of protective membranes project beyond membrane's edge in form of narrow triangular or cirri-like projections. Ventral protective membrane of 3rd arms narrow, not exceeding width of arm. No suckers with denticulate rings in carpal part of club proximal to first knob. Fin rhomboidal, not attenuate posteriorly. One intestinal photophore, conspicuous only in juveniles (absent in larvae and obsolete in subadults and adults)...................... .... **Genus *Dosidicus* Steenstrup, 1857**

(Fig. 61 A-D). One species: **D. gigas (d'Orbigny, 1835).** The giant squid of Peru and Chile. Eastern Pacific from Baja California and the Gulf of California to central Chile (in some years reaching Cape Monterey, California), southward to Chiloé Island, Chile. To the west in equatorial area it reaches 125-140°W. Lives at the surface and in midwater (epipelagic and mesopelagic) on the open ocean, during feeding migrations sometimes approaching shores. Mantle length to 120 cm. As yet of secondary fisheries value, but highly promising for future fisheries exploitation near western Mexico, Peru, and Chile.

15 (14). Tips of arms not attenuate; about 35 pairs of suckers on arms. Ends of trabeculae of protective membranes not projecting beyond edge of membranes. Ventral protective membranes of 3rd arms very wide, in adult females extending into large triangular lobe. 4-7 suckers with denticulate rings in carpal part of club proximal to the first knob. End of fin slightly attenuate posteriorly. Wide silvery longitudinal stripe extending along ventral side of mantle almost from anterior edge to level of beginning of fin. No intestinal photophores...................... ..... **Genus *Ommastrephes* d'Orbigny, 1839**

(= *Cycria* Leach in Gray, 1849; *Lolimnites*

Fig. 59.

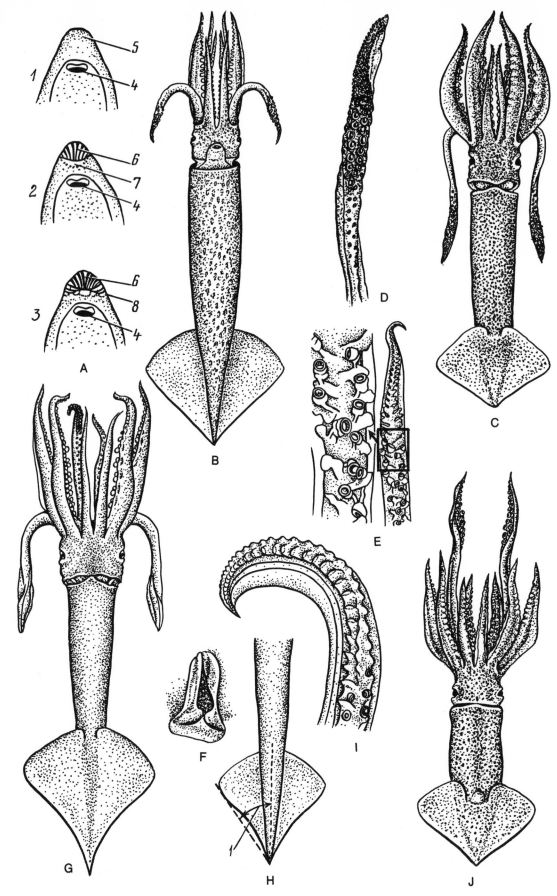

228

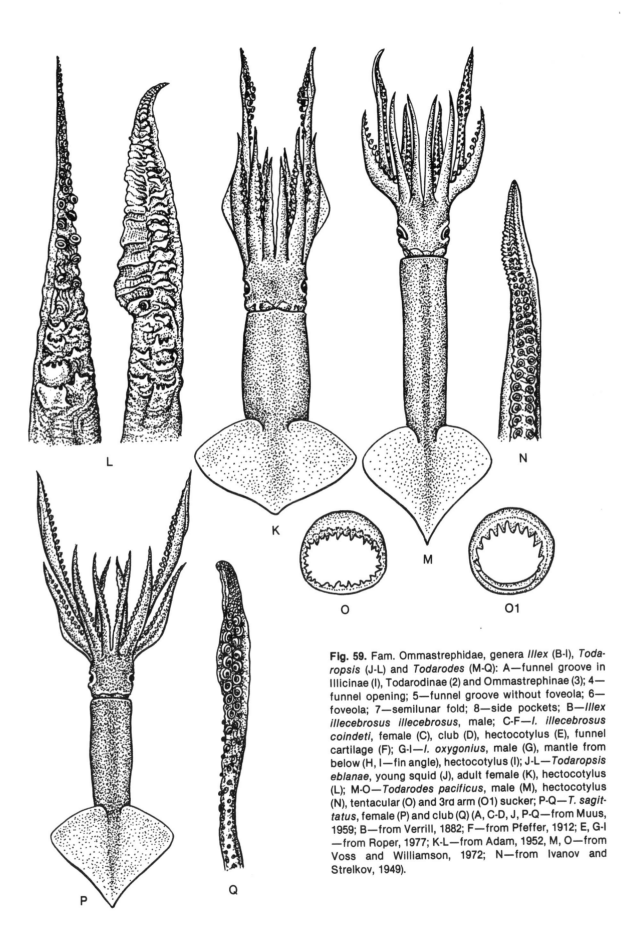

Fig. 59. Fam. Ommastrephidae, genera *Illex* (B-I), *Todaropsis* (J-L) and *Todarodes* (M-Q): A—funnel groove in Illicinae (I), Todarodinae (2) and Ommastrephinae (3); 4—funnel opening; 5—funnel groove without foveola; 6—foveola; 7—semilunar fold; 8—side pockets; B—*Illex illecebrosus illecebrosus*, male; C-F—*I. illecebrosus coindeti*, female (C), club (D), hectocotylus (E), funnel cartilage (F); G-I—*I. oxygonius*, male (G), mantle from below (H, I—fin angle), hectocotylus (I); J-L—*Todaropsis eblanae*, young squid (J), adult female (K), hectocotylus (L); M-O—*Todarodes pacificus*, male (M), hectocotylus (N), tentacular (O) and 3rd arm (O1) sucker; P-Q—*T. sagittatus*, female (P) and club (Q) (A, C-D, J, P-Q—from Muus, 1959; B—from Verrill, 1882; F—from Pfeffer, 1912; E, G-I —from Roper, 1977; K-L—from Adam, 1952, M, O—from Voss and Williamson, 1972; N—from Ivanov and Strelkov, 1949).

Fig. 60.

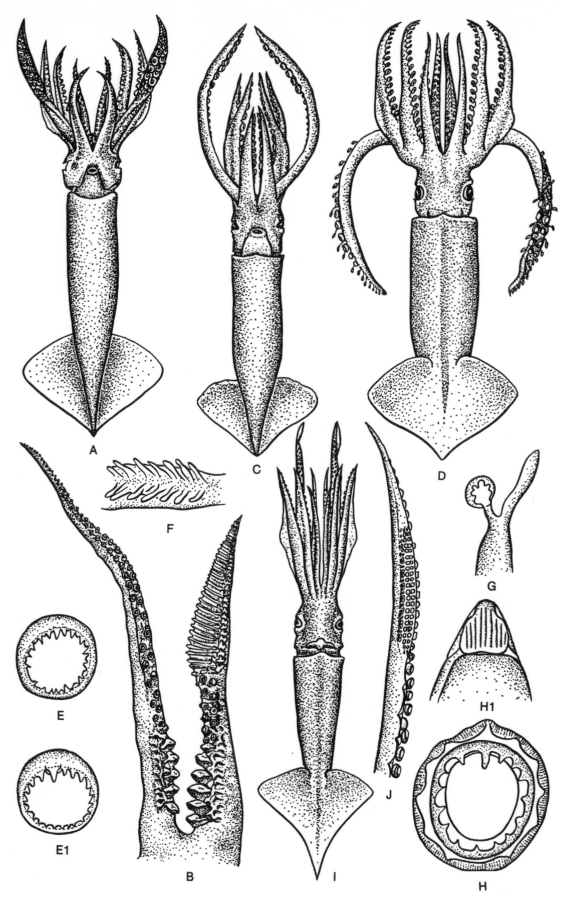

Risso, 1854). One species: **O. bartrami** **(LeSueur, 1821)** (= *O. caroli* Furtado, 1887) (Fig. 61 E-G) with three formally undescribed subspecies. Bi-subtropical (antiequatorial) species: a North Atlantic subspecies— from the Great Newfoundland Bank and North Sea to Florida, the southern part of the Sargasso Sea, and Mauritania; a North Pacific subspecies— from the southern Kuriles (in rare cases to the Commander and western Aleutian Islands) and southern British Columbia, to Taiwan, the Bonin Islands, and western Mexico, rarely in the Sea of Japan; a southern subspecies—from Brazil and the area off the Falkland Islands to Angola and southern Africa and further eastward between 20-25° and 35-40°S to the Great Australian Bight (135°E), then in the southern Pacific from southern Queensland, New Caledonia, and Tasmania to at least 150°W, perhaps much farther to the east. Mantle length in the North Atlantic subspecies to 86 cm; in the North Pacific to 53 cm; in the southern subspecies to 65 cm. A common

epipelagic to mesopelagic species fished in large quantities in the Kuriles-Hokkaido area and eastward in the North Pacific. Also fished in other parts of the range.

16 (13). One photophore on ventral side of eyeball, one or two on intestine, usually also large superficial photophores present on ventral or dorsal side of mantle. Not more than 2 suckers with denticulate rings in carpal part of club proximal to first knob. No silvery stripe on ventral side of mantle **17**

17 (18). Two photophores on intestine; one near anus, another at posterior end (obsolete in adults but very visible in juveniles and adolescents). No luminous spots or stripes on ventral side of mantle, head, or 4th arms. Adults usually with single large oval photophores on back in anterior part of mantle. Rings of large club suckers with 4 large teeth, one at each quadrant. Mantle cylindrical; fin rhomboidal, not attenuated posteriorly. Ventral protective membranes on 3rd arms subequal to arm width . . . .

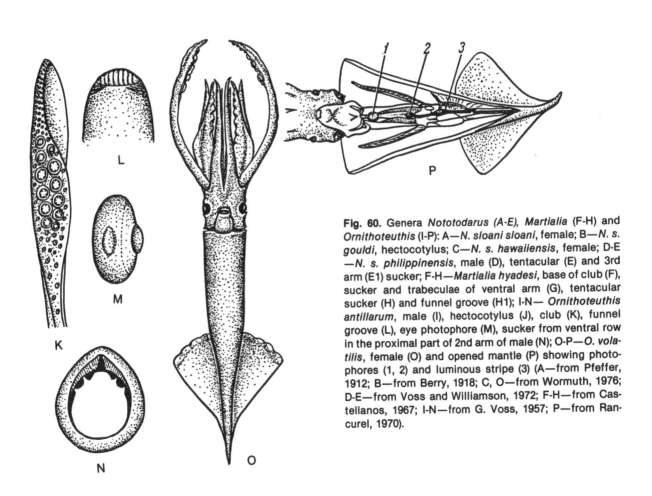

Fig. 60. Genera *Nototodarus (A-E)*, *Martialia (F-H)* and *Ornithoteuthis (I-P)*: A—*N. sloani sloani*, female; B—*N. s. gouldi*, hectocotylus; C—*N. s. hawaiiensis*, female; D-E —*N. s. philippinensis*, male (D), tentacular (E) and 3rd arm (E1) sucker; F-H—*Martialia hyadesi*, base of club (F), sucker and trabeculae of ventral arm (G), tentacular sucker (H) and funnel groove (H1); I-N— *Ornithoteuthis antillarum*, male (I), hectocotylus (J), club (K), funnel groove (L), eye photophore (M), sucker from ventral row in the proximal part of 2nd arm of male (N); O-P—*O. volatilis*, female (O) and opened mantle (P) showing photophores (1, 2) and luminous stripe (3) (A—from Pfeffer, 1912; B—from Berry, 1918; C, O—from Wormuth, 1976; D-E—from Voss and Williamson, 1972; F-H—from Castellanos, 1967; I-N—from G. Voss, 1957; P—from Rancurel, 1970).

Fig. 61.

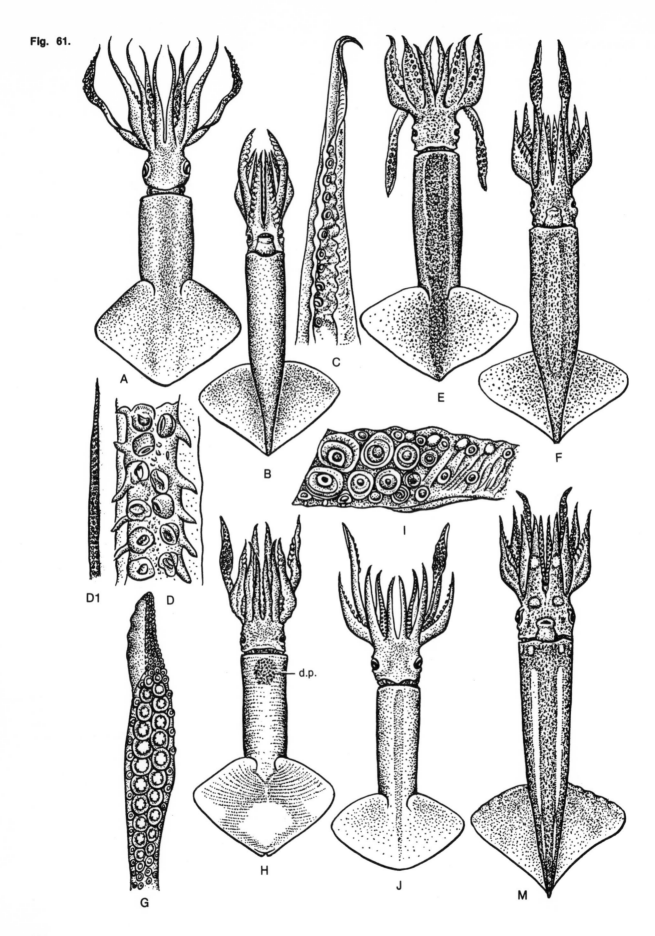

d.p.

232

.........**Genus _Sthenoteuthis_ Verrill, 1880**
(= _Symplectoteuthis_ Pfeffer, 1900) (Fig. 61 H-L). Type species: _S. pteropus_ (Steenstrup, 1855). 2 species in the epipelagic zone of the tropical Atlantic and Indo-Pacific.

18 (17). One photophore on intestine at border of middle and posterior thirds. Luminous spots and/or stripes on ventral side of mantle, head, and ventral arms; no dorsal photophore. Rings of large club suckers with one large tooth on distal edge. Protective membranes of 3rd arms narrow.
.... **19**

19 (20). Pair of long strips of luminous tissue extending along ventral side of mantle, one on each side of midline, each stripe broken posteriorly by gap at level of maximum width of fin; 2 oval luminous spots near anterior margin of mantle in front of each stripe, 2 more at the base and in middle of each ventral arm. Mantle conical, narrowing posteriorly, fin heart-shaped, with attenuate end. Mantle and funnel cartilages fused in juveniles and adults at one or both sides........
.........**Genus _Eucleoteuthis_ Berry, 1916**

One species: _E. luminosa_ **(Sasaki, 1915)** (Fig. 61 M,N). Distributed in the northern Pacific in a strip from the southern Kuriles and Japan (25°-45°N) to California and western Mexico (15-40°N), and in the southern Atlantic, Indian, and southwestern Pacific Oceans (in the Atlantic Ocean found between 10 and 35°S, in the Indian and Pacific Oceans between 15 and 35°S, to the east up to 80°W). Epipelagic. Mantle length to 22 cm.

20 (19). 19 round luminous spots arranged in strict order on ventral side of mantle. They form pairs converging or set apart; luminous spot at base, in middle, and near end of each ventral arm. Mantle cylindrical; fin rhomboidal, with straight posterior edges. Mantle and funnel cartilages are not fused.... **Genus _Hyaloteuthis_ Gray, 1849**

One species: _H. pelagica_ **(Bosc, 1802)** (Fig. 61 O). Atlantic, Pacific, and probably Indian Oceans, in northern and southern central waters; in the eastern Pacific also found in equatorial area. Oceanic species. Epipelagic and uppermost mesopelagic, sometimes bathypelagic. Mantle length to 9 cm.

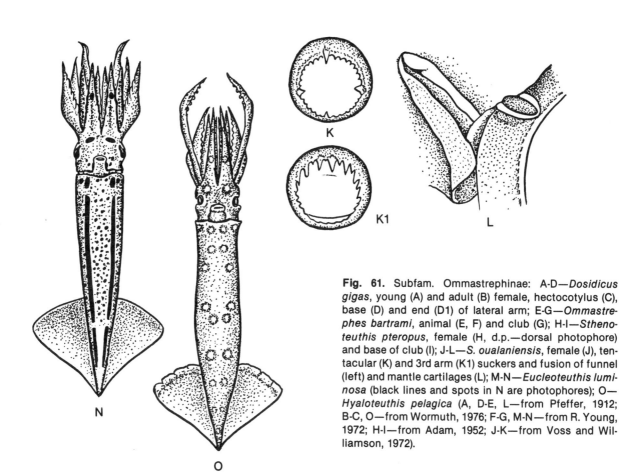

Fig. 61. Subfam. Ommastrephinae: A-D—_Dosidicus gigas_, young (A) and adult (B) female, hectocotylus (C), base (D) and end (D1) of lateral arm; E-G—_Ommastrephes bartrami_, animal (E, F) and club (G); H-I—_Sthenoteuthis pteropus_, female (H, d.p.—dorsal photophore) and base of club (I); J-L—_S. oualaniensis_, female (J), tentacular (K) and 3rd arm (K1) suckers and fusion of funnel (left) and mantle cartilages (L); M-N—_Eucleoteuthis luminosa_ (black lines and spots in N are photophores); O—_Hyaloteuthis pelagica_ (A, D-E, L—from Pfeffer, 1912; B-C, O—from Wormuth, 1976; F-G, M-N—from R. Young, 1972; H-I—from Adam, 1952; J-K—from Voss and Williamson, 1972).

Key to species of the genus *Illex*

1 (6). Fin wide, with more or less obtuse tail, fin width-to-length ratio 1.3-1.5, fin angle (angle formed by posterior edges of fin) 80-100° and more. Head not wider than mantle at anterior border. Length of longest arm in males 50-90%, in females 45-60% of mantle length............
............*I. illecebrosus* (LeSueur, 1821)
(Fig. 59 B-F). Three allopatric subspecies, with intermediate forms in the areas where ranges come into contact....................2
2 (3). Fin heart-shaped, width-to-length ratio 1.3-1.4; fin angle 80-100°. Relative length of arms equal in males and females, largest arm 45-55% of mantle length. Suckers on lateral arms of males not enlarged, their diameter 1.5-1.8% of mantle length. Hectocotylus length 15-25% of hectocotylized arm length.....................
..........*I. i. illecebrosus* (LeSueur, 1821)
(Fig. 59 B). Northwestern Atlantic. The northern limit of the range during feeding migrations is Labrador, during spawning Nova Scotia; the southern limit is near southeastern Florida, the eastern limit at the Middle Atlantic Ridge. Rarely found off southern Greenland, Iceland, on Porcupine Bank, and in the North Sea. During feeding migrations in the northern part of the range it inhabits the surface waters and often approaches the coasts; in other areas it lives at the bottom at depths to 700 m (usually 100-500 m). Mantle length to 34 cm. Fished in large quantities in Newfoundland, Nova Scotia, on Georges Bank, and off New England.
3 (2). Fin rhomboidal, width-to-length ratio 1.4-1.5; fin angle usually obtuse (90-100° and more). Length of longest arm in males 55-90%, in females 48-57% of mantle length. Suckers of lateral arms in males conspicuously enlarged, their diameter 3-3.5% of mantle length. Hectocotylus length at least 30% of hectocotylized arm length.....................4
4 (5). Hectocotylus length 50-67% of hectocotylized arm length.....................
.... *I. i. argentinus* (Castellanos, 1960)
Southwestern Atlantic from Rio de Janeiro (rarely) to Falkland Islands and Burdwood Bank. At the bottom in the lower sublittoral and bathyal (up to 1350 m), sometimes at the surface, the juveniles living nearer the coasts. Mantle length to 40 cm. Fished in large quantities off Uruguay and Argentina.

5 (4). Hectocotylus length about 33% of hectocotylized arm length.....................
.................*I. i. coindeti* (Vérany, 1837)
(Fig. 59 C-F). Eastern Atlantic from southern England to Namibia; Mediterranean Sea; tropical western Atlantic in the Gulf of Mexico and Caribbean Sea from Cape Canaveral to Venezuela and Surinam; recorded with doubt in the Red Sea. Lives at the bottom at depths from 40-50 to 500-600 m and in midwater. Mantle length to 29 cm. Fished in small quantities in the Mediterranean Sea and off northwestern Africa.
6 (1). Fin narrow, attenuated into long, sharp tail, fin width-to-length ratio about 1.1; fin angle acute (50-70°, rarely up to 80°). Head wider than mantle at anterior edge. Arms short, length of longest arm in males 45-55%, in females 35-45% of mantle length. Hectocotylus length about 33% of hectocotylized arm length.....................
....*I. oxygonius* Roper, Lu & Mangold, 1969
(Fig. 59 G-I). Tropical and subtropical western Atlantic from Delaware Bay to Cuba, also recorded in the Gulf of Guinea. Near the bottom at depths of 50 to 600 m. Mantle length to 24 cm.

Key to species of the genus *Todarodes*

1 (2). Fin rhomboidal, not attenuate into tail; fin length about 40% of the mantle length. Club short and narrow with 10-12 small suckers in proximal part and 8-9 pairs of large suckers in middle rows of central part.....................
.............*T. pacificus* Steenstrup, 1880
(Earlier used name *Ommastrephes sloani pacificus* is erroneous) (Fig. 59 M-O). Northwestern Pacific, Sea of Okhotsk, Sea of Japan, Yellow (southern part) and East China Seas, and northern part of South China Sea. Northern limit during the feeding migrations is off eastern Kamchatka (probably near Commander Islands), in the central part of the Sea of Okhotsk, and in the northern part of the Tatar Strait; southern limit is off Hong Kong. Epipelagic above shelf and slope, in productive waters also over great depths. Sometimes descending to the bottom (for feeding and laying eggs). Mantle length to 30-35 cm. The most important object of fisheries in Japan, the USSR, North and South Korea, and northern China.
2 (1). Fin heart-shaped, extended posteriorly into small tail; fin length about half mantle length. Club long and wide, 10-12 pairs of large suckers

in middle rows of central part of club........**3**

3 (4). Sucker-bearing part of club comprises 75-83% of total length of tentacle. Proximal part of club with 10-12 pairs of small suckers, central part with 14-15 pairs of large suckers.........
...............***T. sagittatus* (Lamarck, 1799)**
(Fig. 59 P,Q). Northeastern Atlantic and adjacent areas. In the north during feeding migrations it approaches the Barents Sea (in very rare cases even the Kara and White Seas) and Iceland. The southern limit is off Guinea and off the Canary Islands, with the western limit off Bermuda and in the area southward from Nova Scotia (Kelvin Seamounts); common in the Mediterranean Sea. In the open ocean and near the coasts, at the surface and near the bottom at depths down to 2,500 m, but usually above the slope and at the bottom near the slope. Mantle length to 60-65 (75) cm, usually 30-40 cm. Fished in considerable quantities in the Mediterranean Sea and off southwestern Europe, in some years also in Norway, Iceland, and the Barents Sea.

4 (3). Sucker-bearing part of club comprises 67-75% of total length of tentacle. Proximal part of club with 2-5 pairs of small suckers, central part with 12-14 pairs of large suckers.........
.................***T. angolensis* Adam, 1962**
(= *T. filippovae* Adam, 1975). Notalian circumglobal species; in areas of cold currents it reaches to the north: off southern Africa to Angola, off New Zealand to Kaipara Bay, and off South America to southern Peru. To the south it reaches South Georgia. The juveniles live in the epipelagic and probably also in the mesopelagic zones, the adults at the bottom on slopes both near the coasts and in the open ocean. Mantle length to 56 cm.

Key to species of the genus *Nototodarus*

1 (10). Body surface smooth. Mantle rather narrow, average mantle width 20-25% of mantle length. Fin comparatively narrow, fin width less than 70% of mantle length. Fin angle about a right angle (90 -110°). .***N. sloani* (Gray, 1849)**
(Fig. 60 A-E). Four subspecies were recognized until recently: *N. sloani hawaiiensis* (Berry, 1912), off Hawaii; *N. sloani philippinensis* Voss, 1962, off the Philippines; *N. sloani gouldi* (McCoy, 1888), off Australia; and *N. sloani sloani* (Gray, 1849), around New Zealand. Recently it was found that a separate, as yet unnamed form is widely

distributed throughout the Indian Ocean and may overlap with at least one of the described forms. It was also shown (Smith et al., 1981; Kawakami & Okutani, 1981) that there are two distinct forms around New Zealand with partially overlapping ranges but very distinct morphological, genetic, and parasitological characters; one of these is almost indistinguishable from the Australian form, while the other is distinct and represented by two different subtypes. Unfortunately, the range of variability of most of these forms is still unknown and their taxonomic status remains unclear. The following key is therefore only provisional **2**

2 (7). Head not wider than mantle, head width 15-25%, usually 17-20%, of mantle length.....**3**

3 (6). 4th right arm of adult male with 4-6 high, wide triangular papillae in the basal part of the arm, then 2-10 pairs of suckers and two rows of long, narrow, finger-like papillae in distal part up to arm tip **4**

4 (5). Usually 5-10 pairs of suckers in middle part of 4th right arm in adult male. 35-40 pairs of suckers on each 1st arm in both sexes. Fin length more than 40%, usually about 45%, of mantle length.........***N. sloani sloani* (Gray, 1849)**
(Fig. 60 A). Northern and western New Zealand to the north from the southern subtropical convergence. Mantle length to 42 cm. Also keying here is ***N. sloani gouldi* (McCoy, 1888)** (Fig. 60 B). Southwestern, southern, and eastern Australia northward to Queensland, Tasmania, and the Bass Strait. Mantle length to 41 cm.

5 (4). 2-5 pairs of suckers in middle part of 4th right arm in adult male. 25-27 pairs of suckers on each 1st arm in both sexes. Fin length 35-40% of mantle length. . . . .
. . . .***N. (sloani) hawaiiensis* (Berry, 1912)**
(Fig. 60 C). Hawaiian and Midway Islands. Mantle length to 16 cm.

6 (3). 4th right arm of adult male with first 4-6 low, then about 5 high, wide, triangular papillae, followed by from 3 to 45-50 pairs of suckers and then a row of high, narrow finger-like papillae on the dorsal (outer) side and a row of short conical tubercles on the ventral (inner) side reaching arm tip. 70-100 pairs of suckers on each 1st arm in both sexes. Fin length usually about 45% of mantle length. . . . .***Nototodarus* sp.**
Eastern and southern New Zealand, Chatham, Steward, Campbell, and Auckland Islands, and New Zealand Plateau, mostly to the south from

the southern subtropical convergence but also in Cook Strait, Tasman Bay and off the western coast of South Island, N.Z. (in latter areas overlapping with *N. s. sloani*). Mantle length to 40 cm. According to Kawakami & Okutani (1981), this form is represented by two almost sympatric subtypes: form "a" with 3-7 pairs of suckers in the middle part of the 4th right arm in the adult male and the club longer than half of the mantle length; and form "b" with 25 to 45-50 pairs of suckers and a club shorter than half of the mantle length. I think that form "a" is represented by late-maturing males and form "b" by early-maturing males.

7 (2). Head wider than mantle, head width 20-33%, usually 25-30%, of mantle length. Two rows of long, narrow, finger-like papillae in distal part of 4th right arm in adult males..........**8**

8 (9). 1st arm length about 33-50% of mantle length .. *N. (sloani) philippinensis* **Voss, 1962**

(Fig. 60 D-E). South China Sea, southern part of East China Sea, and the Philippines. Mantle length to 18 cm.

9 (8). 1st arm length about 50-67% of mantle length ....*N. (sloani)* **n. ssp. or n. sp.**

Western and northern Indian Ocean; off Somalia, Madagascar, Mascarene Ridge, Saya-de-Malha Bank, southwestern India, Sri Lanka, and the Andaman Sea, and probably also off northwestern Australia. Mantle length to 29 cm.

10 (1). Mantle and head rough, skin covered by mosaic of minute soft tubercles and scales. Mantle width about 33% of its length. Fin width 70-90% of mantle length. Fin angle obtuse (120-130°). Length of longest arm 50-75% of mantle length ....

....*N. nipponicus* **Okutani & Uemura, 1973**

Off southwestern Honshu and in the East China Sea, at the bottom at depths of 100-250 m. Mantle length to 27 cm. Fished in small quantities as a bycatch to *Todarodes pacificus*.

Note: The key does not include a poorly described *N. insignis* (Gould, 1846) from the Fiji Islands (mantle length to 25 cm). Obviously it is a form of *N. sloani*. Unidentified *Nototodarus* specimens were found in the Bismarck and Coral Seas and offshore areas of the Eastern Pacific.

Key to species of the genus *Ornithoteuthis*

1 (2). Middle part of ventral side of hectocotylized arm with honeycombed cutaneous sculpture of

4-5 longitudinal rows of depressions, about 20-25 in each row; 2 rows nearer to oral (sucker-bearing) surface of arm with depressions considerably larger than others; depressions in 1 or 2 rows located nearer to aboral (opposite) surface smaller. Atlantic..........*O. antillarum* **Adam, 1957**

(Fig. 60 I-N). Amphi-Atlantic tropical to subtropical species. Western Atlantic from the area off Georges Bank to Uruguay, Gulf of Mexico, and the Caribbean Sea; eastern Atlantic from Cape Verde Islands to Angola. At the bottom in the bathyal and in midwater (lower epipelagic and mesopelagic) above slope, juveniles also found in equatorial zone in midwater above great depths. Mantle length in the tropics to 12-13 cm, on the periphery of the range up to 25 cm.

2 (1). Middle part of ventral side of hectocotylized arm with ridged-and-honeycombed cutaneous sculpture of 2-2.5 longitudinal rows of small depressions, about 10-15 in each row. Transverse cutaneous ridges depart from nearest to oral arm side row (2 ridges from each depression) to the oral surface, they either merge or branch off. Lives in Indo-West-Pacific....................

..................*O. volatilis* **(Sasaki, 1915)**

(Fig. 60 O,P). Indo-West-Pacific tropical species, from the Arabian Sea to southeastern Africa and to the area southward from Madagascar, and from southern Honshu to the Coral Sea, eastward reaches the Line Islands. Mode of life as in preceding species. Mantle length to 22 cm.

Key to species of the genus *Sthenoteuthis*

1 (2). Mantle and funnel cartilages fused on one or both sides at postlarval stage. 6-8 pairs of suckers on hectocotylized arm. Lives in the Indian and Pacific Oceans....................

............*S. oualaniensis* **(Lesson, 1830)**

(Fig. 61 J-L). Strictly tropical Indo-Pacific species: from the Red Sea to Mozambique Channel and Natal (in warm years up to Agulhas Bank), from southern Japan to southern Queensland and from the south of Baja California to northern Chile. Mantle length to 39 cm. Common, potentially commercial epipelagic species. Fished off the Ryukyu Islands and Taiwan.

2 (1). Mantle and funnel cartilages not fused (except in extremely rare cases). 11-13 pairs of suckers on hectocotylized arm. Lives in the Atlantic Ocean.....*S. pteropus* **(Steenstrup, 1855)**

(Fig. 61 H,I). Strictly tropical Atlantic species: from Florida (some specimens reach in summer Georges Bank) and the Gulf of Mexico to Uruguay and from Madeira and Canary Islands to Namibia; never found in the Mediterranean Sea. Mantle length to 60-65 cm. Very common, especially in productive zones, potentially commercial epipelagic species.

2.2.2.14. Family Thysanoteuthidae

Large nektonic squids with a strong muscular mantle and very long longitudinal rhomboidal fin extending along the entire body. Arms short, with 2 rows of suckers and highly developed protective membranes dilated on long cirri-like trabeculae. Tentacles with 4 rows of suckers. Fixing apparatus present. Funnel cartilage with a ⊢-shape groove, the mantle cartilage with ridges of corresponding form. Nuchal cartilage with two projections entering the grooves on anterior edge of mantle. Buccal membrane formula is DDVV. No photophores (except one supposedly at the ink sac). Gladius resembles a long spearhead on a short shaft. Left ventral arm hectocotylized. Pelagic egg mass looks like a long (up to 1-2 m) cylinder or "stocking" of transparent gelatinous mucus; pink-violet eggs are disposed in one layer (in a double spiral) at the surface on the "stocking" over its entire length. Development with larval stage.

One genus: *Thysanoteuthis* Troschel, 1857, one species: *T. rhombus* Troschel, 1857 (Fig. 62 A-C). Tropical to subtropical cosmopolitan epipelagic species. Lives in open ocean, rarely approaches the coasts. Minor object of fisheries in Japan. Mantle length to 100 cm.

The larval genus *"Cirrobrachium"* Hoyle, 1904 with 2 species known only by juveniles also belongs to the family Thysanoteuthidae. Type species of the genus is *C. filiferum* Hoyle, 1904 – it is the larva of *T. rhombus*. The taxonomic status of the second species, *C. danae* Joubin, 1933 (the only known specimen with a mantle length 1.5 cm was taken in the central Atlantic) is unclear; it can be differentiated from juvenile *T. rhombus* by the following characters:

a. Protective membranes on 1st arms very weakly developed, width of protective membranes on 2nd-3rd arms enlarged at the arm ends reaching the maximum in the distal third of arms. *C. danae* Joubin, 1933 (Fig. 62 D).

b. Protective membranes on 1st arms wide. Width of protective membranes on 1st-3rd arms is maximal in the middle of arm and gradually diminishes toward the end. *T. rhombus* Troschel (= *C. filiferum* Hoyle).

2.2.2.15. Family Lepidoteuthidae
(= Pholidoteuthidae)

Scaled squids. Large animals with narrow cylindrical mantle whose surface (except the sector between the fins) is covered on the dorsal and ventral sides by flat cartilaginous plates of connective tissue resembling the ganoid scales of primitive fishes (*Polypterus, Lepisosteus*) and in juveniles by denticulate warts resembling papillae of sea stars. Fin round, longitudinally-oval, rhombic or heart-shaped, posteriorly extended into a short or long tail. Arms long, with two rows of suckers. Tentacles long, slender, with 4 rows of suckers; absent in adult *Lepidoteuthis*. Locking cartilages simple. Buccal membrane formula is DDVV. Gladius with a narrow vane, usually with a constriction in posterior third of its length, and with a more or less long terminal cone. Photophores are not described (may be present on eyes of some species). Development with larval stage. Benthic-bathyal and meso-bathypelagic squids. Fairly active deep-water predators. Play a certain role in the food of sperm whales, dolphins and sharks. 3 genera, 4 species.

Key to genera and species of the family *Lepidoteuthidae*

1 (2). Scales large, round or irregularly rectangular, slightly overlapping one another in anterior part of mantle like fish scales. Tentacles are present only in larvae and juveniles, they are completely reduced in adults. Fin round in the young and elongatedly-oval in adult squids, not reaching the posterior end of mantle which is attenuated into a long tail. . . . . **Genus *Lepidoteuthis* Joubin, 1895**
One species: *L. grimaldii* Joubin, 1895 (Fig. 62 E,F). Tropical and subtropical Atlantic (reaches the notalian zone), southern Indian Ocean and western Pacific (from Honshu to New Caledonia, eastward to Hawaii). Mantle length to 1 m.

2 (1). Scales small, polygonal, round or serrate, in adults contacting but not overlapping each other, in juveniles not contacting. Tentacles well developed. Fin rhomboidal or heart-shaped, reaching the posterior end of mantle..........3

3 (4). Scales arranged in regular oblique rows, close but not contacting, in juveniles they resemble stellate cartilaginous warts with 6-9 points, in adults they are round. Fin kidney-shaped in juveniles and rhomboidal in adults, not attenuated or almost not attenuated into a tail. Club suckers small, round.................................

.....**Genus *Tetronychoteuthis* Pfeffer, 1900**

One species: ***T. dussumieri*** (d'Orbigny, **1839**) (= *T. massyae* Pfeffer, 1912) (Fig. 62 G-I). Tropical, subtropical, and notalian areas of Atlantic, Indian and Pacific Oceans, boreal Atlantic. Mantle length up to 72 cm.

4 (3). Scales arranged in irregular rows, they are tetra-, penta- or hexagonal, flat, not serrate, with raised edges, and closely contacting. Fin rhomboidal, extended into a tail. Club suckers elongately oval, as if flattened from sides. Mantle length up to 78 cm........................

.........**Genus *Pholidoteuthis* Adam, 1950**

(Fig. 62 J-N). Type species: *P. boschmai* Adam, 1950. 2 species.........................5

5 (6). Length and width of fin in adults about 50% of mantle length. Gladius with constriction in posterior third....***P. boschmai* Adam, 1950**

(Fig. 62 M,N). Described from the Flores Sea (Indonesia). Recorded also (with some doubt) off Australia and southern Africa and on Nazca Ridge (eastern Pacific). Bathyal.

6 (5). Fin length in adults 70-75%, width 60-70% of mantle length. Gladius has a slightly widened vane, without constriction...................

.......................***P. adami* Voss, 1956**

(Fig. 62 J-L). Tropical and subtropical Atlantic, reaches boreal and notalian regions. At the bottom in bathyal. Most often at depths of 500-2000 m.

2.2.2.16. Family Batoteuthidae

Small squids with a long narrow mantle and small transversely oval fin posteriorly extended into a long slender acuminate tail. Head is very small. Arms with two rows of suckers. Tentacles

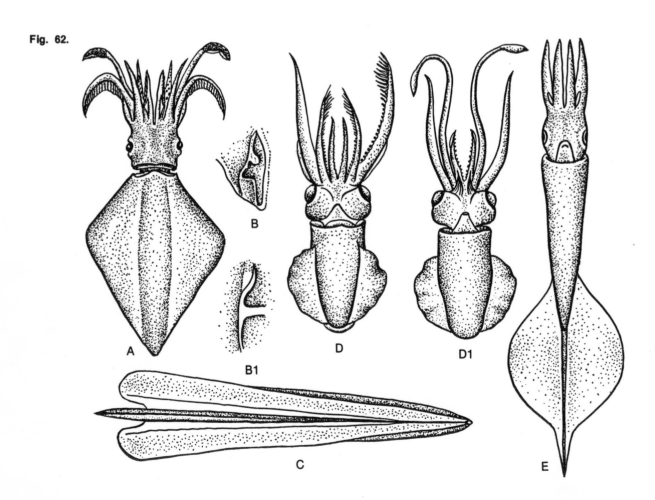

Fig. 62.

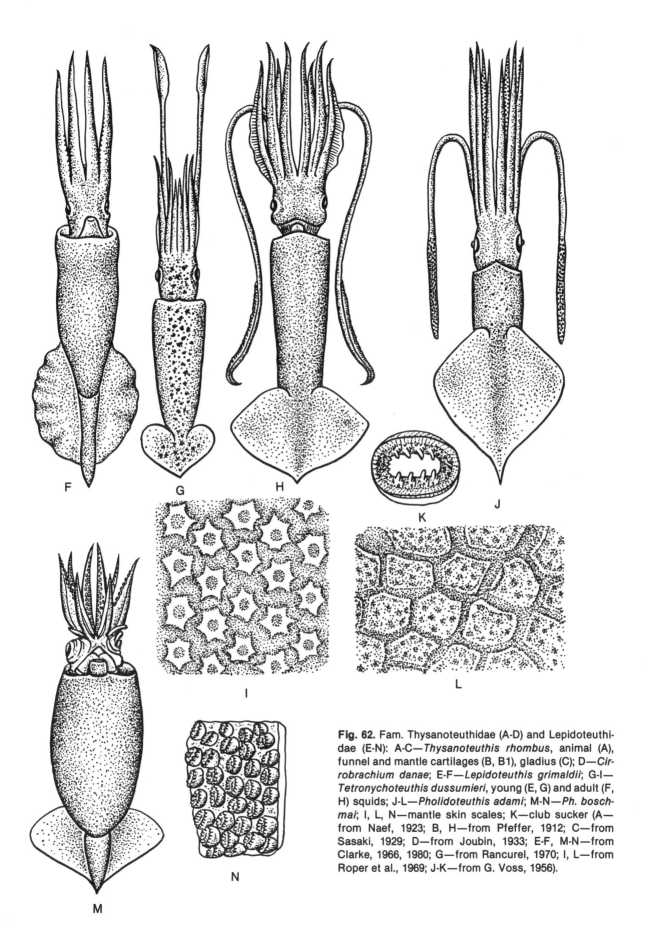

Fig. 62. Fam. Thysanoteuthidae (A-D) and Lepidoteuthidae (E-N): A-C—*Thysanoteuthis rhombus*, animal (A), funnel and mantle cartilages (B, B1), gladius (C); D—*Cirrobrachium danae*; E-F—*Lepidoteuthis grimaldii*; G-I—*Tetronychoteuthis dussumieri*, young (E, G) and adult (F, H) squids; J-L—*Pholidoteuthis adami*; M-N—*Ph. boschmai*; I, L, N—mantle skin scales; K—club sucker (A—from Naef, 1923; B, H—from Pfeffer, 1912; C—from Sasaki, 1929; D—from Joubin, 1933; E-F, M-N—from Clarke, 1966, 1980; G—from Rancurel, 1970; I, L—from Roper et al., 1969; J-K—from G. Voss, 1956).

without distinctly defined club, bearing 6 rows of sucker almost along the entire length. Locking apparatus simple. Buccal membrane formula is DDVV. Gladius rod-like, without vane, with a long cone. The viscera are located in the most forward part of the mantle cavity, only the gonad is shifted to the posterior end. Development with larval stage. Probably sluggish bathypelagic squids.

One genus *Batoteuthis* Young & Roper, **1968**. One species: *B. skolops* Young & Roper, **1968** (Fig. 63 A-C). Found in the southern Pacific, Scotia Sea, and off Falkland Islands. Supposedly notalian meso-bathypelagic species, reaching the Antarctic. Mantle length to 27 cm.

Description: Young and Roper, 1968.

2.2.2.17. Family Cycloteuthidae

Medium size squids with a widely conical semigelatinous mantle and a large round fin, whose length exceeds 67% of mantle length. Arms with 2 rows of suckers. Tentacles long, club compact, widened, with 4 rows of suckers and slightly developed fixing apparatus. Funnel cartilage triangular or irregularly oval, with a deep groove receiving a nose-like or tubercle-like mantle cartilage. Buccal membrane formula is DDVV. Photophores are present, may be situated on eyes, surface of mantle and head, ink sac, etc. Gladius with a short or long stem and widened vane, posteriorly rounded or extended into a more or less narrow cone. Hectocotylus absent. Development with larval stage. Mantle length to 60 cm. They live in lower epipelagic and mesopelagic zones, sometimes at the bottom in the bathyal. Inhabit tropical and subtropical waters of all oceans.

2 genera, 4-5 species. A larva described from the Sargasso Sea as a separate genus and species *Enoptroteuthis spinicauda* Berry, 1920 (Fig. 63 S), probably belongs to this family, but it is unclear to what genus.

Reviews: Young and Roper, 1969a; Filippova, 1968.

Key to genera and species of the family *Cycloteuthidae*

1 (4). Mantle posteriorly extended into a tail. Fin length 60-80% of the mantle length. Suckers of middle and marginal rows in central part of club are of subequal size. Photophores situated on ink sac and a series of 15-30 small photophores of different size and shape on eye iris around the pupil. No photophores on body surface. Gladius thin, narrow, with long terminal cone. . . . .
. . . .**Genus *Cycloteuthis* Joubin, 1919**
(Fig. 63 D-L). Type species: *C. sirventi* Joubin, 1919 . . . . **2**

2 (3). Mantle cylindrical-conical, gradually narrowing from beginning of fin towards tail, head wider than mantle. Fin transversely oval or rhomboidal, considerably wider than long. In adults the fin length is about 80%, fin width about 90% of the mantle length. No longitudinal muscular ridge on dorsal side of mantle. . . . .
. . . .***C. sirventi* Joubin, 1919**
(Fig. 63 D-H). Tropical and subtropical waters of the Atlantic and (?)Indo-West Pacific.

3 (2). Mantle funnel-like, abruptly narrowing before the beginning of fin. Head narrower than mantle and may be retracted into it. Mantle cartilages located at a considerable distance from anterior edge of mantle. Fin round, its width nearly equal the length and comprises about 50% of mantle length. A double muscular ridge runs along the dorsal side of the mantle. . . . .
. . . . *C. akimushkini* Filippova, 1968**
(Fig. 63 I-L). Tropical and subtropical Indian and Western Pacific Oceans, subtropical southern Atlantic.

4 (1). Mantle not extended into a tail. Fin in adults very large, fin length almost equal or even somewhat larger than mantle length. In central part of club 4 pairs of suckers in middle rows greatly enlarged, suckers of marginal rows very small. No photophores on ink sac. One or several photophores on body surface. Gladius vane wide, heavily thickened, terminal cone short or absent
. . .**Genus *Discoteuthis* Young & Roper, 1969**
(Fig. 63 M-R). Type species: *D. discus* Young & Roper, 1969 . . . . **5**

5 (6). A single photophore on ventral mantle side near posterior end of body. Several photophores around pupil. No photophore near anterior edge of mantle or on head. Club suckers large and globose. Anterior mantle edge even. Funnel cartilage with one groove extending forward from a deep pit. Gladius rounded posteriorly. . . . .
. . . .***D. discus* Young & Roper, 1969**
(Fig. 63 M-O). Tropical and subtropical Atlantic, probably Indian and Pacific Oceans.

6 (5). Two photophores at anterior edge of mantle on ventral side near the mantle cartilages, two

more on web connecting the bases of 3rd and 4th arms. No single photophore near posterior end of body, no ocular photophores (?). Large club suckers flattened, not globose. Anterior mantle edge on ventral and lateral sides with some (4 or more) short finger-like projections directed forward (are developed only in juveniles). Funnel cartilage with two grooves diverging at an obtuse angle from the central pit. Gladius with a short terminal cone. . . . . ***D. laciniosa* Young & Roper, 1969**
(Fig. 63 P-R). Tropical and subtropical Atlantic, Indian and Pacific Oceans.

A larva not belonging to any of these two species was captured in the Sargasso Sea. It is like *D. laciniosa* but differs from the larvae of this species of the same size in that the fin has no anterior and posterior "earlets" and that the eyes are very large.

2.2.2.18. Family Chiroteuthidae
(= Valbyteuthidae)

Medium-size and small squids (mantle length 20-40 cm) with gelatinous tissues. Mantle conical or sac-like, attenuated posteriorly into a thin and long tail which is preserved only in larvae and juveniles. Fin small, round, longitudinally or transversely-oval. Head long, usually narrow. Structure and armature of 4th arms usually greatly different from those in the other arms. The 4th arms are either much wider and (particularly in juveniles) longer than the other, or bear very small suckers which are often arranged in one row or present in the basal part only. Tentacles, as a rule, very long with a slender stalk, and usually with a widened club bearing 4 (rarely 6) rows of suckers. Club structure in larvae and adult squids in some genera substantially different, definitive suckers develop in proximal part of club and thereafter the larval club is reduced. Club with well developed protective membranes, sometimes with a keel. Funnel cartilage ear-like, oval, elongatedly triangular or bottle-shaped, more often with two tubercles on ventral side (tragus) and posterior side (antitragus), sometimes only with antitragus or without tubercles. Mantle cartilage nose-shaped. Buccal membrane formula DDVV. Photophores may be situated on eyeball, ink sac, 4th arms, and on the club end. In some forms photophores are absent. Gladius very thin, rod-like, with a long terminal cone, passes far behind posterior end of fin. A second additional fin or several small "fins" may be present on the cone in the larvae and juveniles of some species. In the adults gladius breaks off approximately at the level of posterior end of fin or somewhat farther. Hectocotylus absent. Penis long, with spear-like head. Spermatophores are transferred into the mantle cavity of female, sometimes into the ovary. Development is usually with complicated metamorphosis: in addition to the above-mentioned accessory fin the larvae often have a very long neck and extended snout (between mouth and eyes), so that the body length in the larval squid (from the mouth to the end of gladius) may exceed the body length of older squids.

Bathypelagic or meso-bathypelagic squids; sometimes found at the bottom in the bathyal. 7-9 genera, 6-18 species, 2 subspecies. Only the larvae of some genera and species are described and their taxonomic status is doubtful.

Review: Nesis, 1980a.

Key to genera of the family *Chiroteuthidae*

1 (4). 4th arms much wider and, as a rule, also longer than other arms. Photophores on club end and on eyeballs. Funnel cartilage ear-shaped, with tragus and antitragus. Tentacular club with 4 rows of suckers and 4th arms with 2 rows. Larvae with a long neck and usually with well developed snout. **2**
2 (3). Tentacular club long, with several dozens of transverse rows of suckers in manus. A row of photophores along entire length of 4th arms. One photophore at club end. 4th arms much longer than other arms. None or 2 photophores on ink sac. . . . . **Genus *Chiroteuthis* d'Orbigny, 1839**
(= *Chirothauma* Chun, 1910, *Bigelowia* Macdonald & Clench, 1934) (Fig. 65). Type species: *Ch. veranyi* (Férussac, 1835). Larvae are known under the "generic" name *Doratopsis* Rochebrune, 1884 (= *Leptoteuthis* Verrill, 1884, *Chiridioteuthis* Pfeffer, 1912, *Toroteuthis* Tomlin, 1931, *Diaphanoteuthis* Tomlin, 1931). 5 species and 2 subspecies in all oceans from the Sub-Arctic to Sub-Antarctic. Lives in mesopelagic and bathypelagic zones and at the bottom in bathyal.
3 (2). Tentacular club short, with not more than 10 transverse rows of suckers on manus. 4th arms much wider but not longer than the others and devoid of photophores (?). A pair of small

Fig. 63.

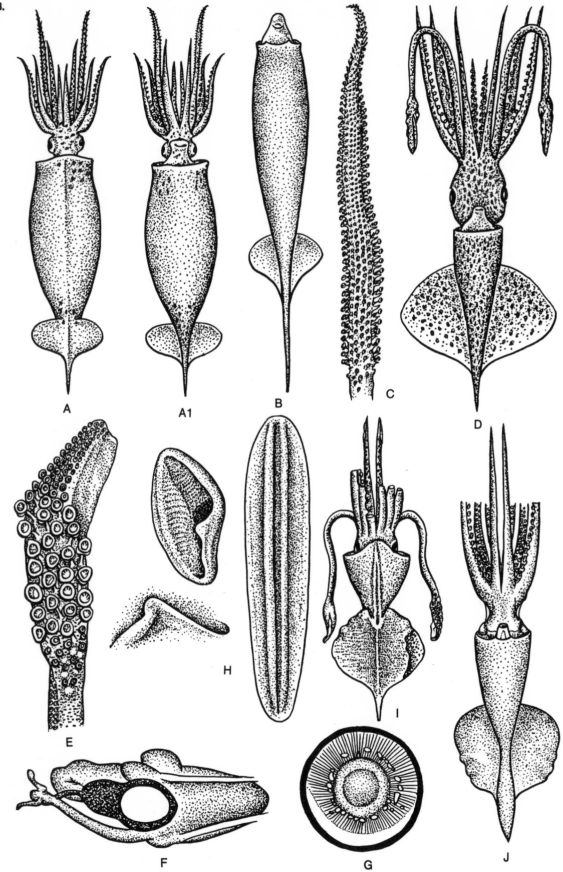

A
A1
B
C
D
E
H
I
J
F
G

242

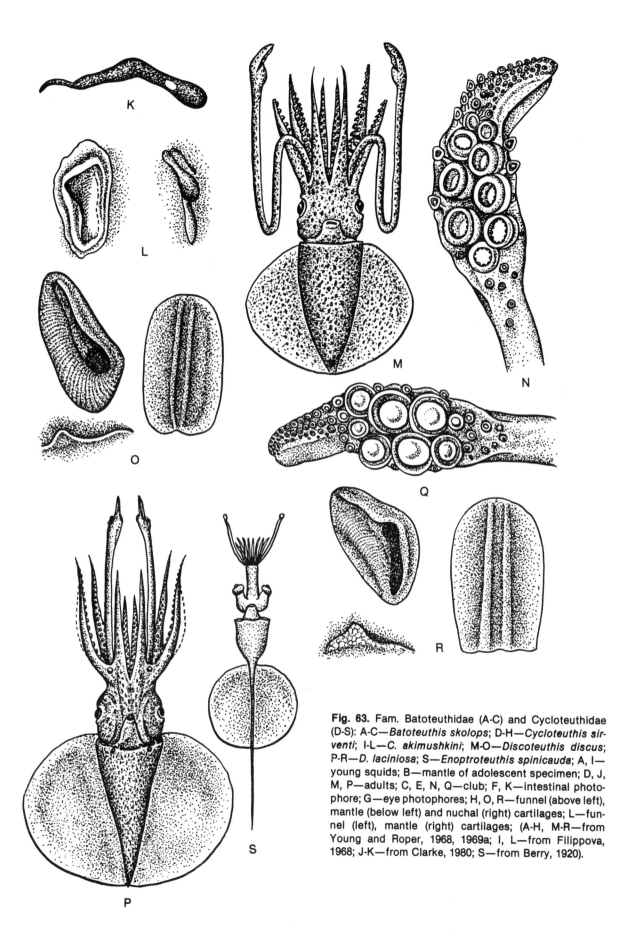

Fig. 63. Fam. Batoteuthidae (A-C) and Cycloteuthidae (D-S): A-C—*Batoteuthis skolops*; D-H—*Cycloteuthis sirventi*; I-L—*C. akimushkini*; M-O—*Discoteuthis discus*; P-R—*D. laciniosa*; S—*Enoptroteuthis spinicauda*; A, I—young squids; B—mantle of adolescent specimen; D, J, M, P—adults; C, E, N, Q—club; F, K—intestinal photophore; G—eye photophores; H, O, R—funnel (above left), mantle (below left) and nuchal (right) cartilages; L—funnel (left), mantle (right) cartilages; (A-H, M-R—from Young and Roper, 1968, 1969a; I, L—from Filippova, 1968; J-K—from Clarke, 1980; S—from Berry, 1920).

243

photophores located side by side on the club end. One photophore on ink sac..................

.............**Genus *Chiropsis* Joubin, 1933**

One species: ***Ch. mega* Joubin, 1933** (Fig. 64 A-C), lives in the Sargasso Sea in bathypelagic zone.

4 (1). 4th arms not wider than others and bear no photophores. Funnel cartilage without tragus, often also without antitragus, elongated, skittle- or bottle-shaped or oval but not ear-shaped. Tentacular club with 4-6 or more rows of suckers, 4 arms without suckers or with 1-2 rows of suckers **5**

5 (8). One photophore on club end and one (?) on eyeball. Proximal part of club in adults with a widened basal membrane, suckers start distal to the beginning of basal membrane. On 4th arms the suckers extend to arm tips.............. **6**

6 (7). Skin covered by tiny conical cartilaginous tubercles. Funnel cartilage with a narrow deep groove bent like a boomerang and forkedly split at posterior (caudal) end, no true tragus nor atitragus. Rectal photophore absent. Club suckers in 4 rows, sucker rings with 3-5 low conical teeth without an enlarged tooth. Arm suckers with 3-4 low rounded teeth. Fin longitudinally oval. Larvae with a short neck and snout and short 3rd arms...... **Genus *Asperoteuthis* Nesis, 1980**

Type and the only species: ***A. famelica* (Berry, 1909)** (= *Chiroteuthis famelica* Berry, 1909, *Ch. acanthoderma* Lu, 1977) (Fig. 64 D-K). Central waters of the North Pacific. Meso-bathypelagic species.

7 (6). Skin smooth. Funnel cartilage oval, with tooth-like antitragus. Rectal photophore present (on ink sac). Club suckers in larvae in 4 rows, in adults in 6 rows. Arm sucker rings with 8-9 long obtuse teeth. Larvae with very long neck and snout...................... **n. gen. B Nesis**

(Fig. 64 L-N). One undescribed species: "*Chiroteuthis* n. sp." Nesis, 1974a (= *Mastigoteuthis?* A Clarke, 1980). Probably an Atlantic southern subtropical-notalian (southward to South Georgia) meso-bathypelagic species.

8 (5). No photophores. Basal membrane of club not widened........................... **9**

9 (14). Suckers on 4th arms extends to the ends of arms in 2 rows, or at first in 2 and then in 1 zigzag row. Funnel cartilage without tragus and antitragus **10**

10 (11). Club suckers in 4 rows. Funnel cartilage bottle-shaped. Fin transversely oval followed by a large second lanceolate fin situated on the gladius, but often broken off. Olfactory papilla shifted posteriorly, to the area of funnel. Larval mantle smooth, 3rd arms normally developed.........

.... ***"Doratopsis" sagitta* Chun, 1908**

(Fig. 64 O,P). Only the larvae known, found in tropical Atlantic, Indian and Pacific Oceans. Taxonomic status of the species is uncertain, probably it belongs to a separate genus.

11 (10). Club suckers in 6 or more rows. Funnel cartilage simple (skittle-shaped), oval or triangularly-oval. 3rd arms in larvae underdeveloped, much shorter than the other arms. Fin transversely oval........................ **12**

12 (13). Funnel cartilage simple, slightly widened posteriorly (skittle-shaped). Larvae with a short neck.... **Genus *Chiroteuthoides* Berry, 1920**

Type species: *Ch. hastula* Berry, 1920. 2 species, one of them not described and known only by the larvae.

a (b). Larval fin oval, in a form of ∞, 4th arms are long........... ***Ch. hastula* Berry, 1920**

(Fig. 64 Q). Tropical Atlantic, Caribbean Sea. Mesopelagic and bathypelagic.

b (a). Larval fin heart-shaped, 4th arms short...

.... ***Chiroteuthoides* sp. Nesis.**

Equatorial western Pacific. Only the larvae known.

13 (12). Funnel cartilage oval or triangular oval. Larvae with a long neck....................

.... **Genus *Tankaia* Sasaki, 1929**

Only the larvae are known: *T. borealis* Sasaki, 1929 (Fig. 64 R) from boreal Pacific off Hokkaido and *Tankaia* sp. Nesis from Flores Sea, Indonesia.

14 (9). Suckers on 4th arms arranged in one row only in basal part of arms, distal part without suckers. Funnel cartilage usually (except *Valbyteuthis levimana* and *V.* sp.) with an antitragus . **15**

15 (16). Fin present and attached wholly on the extended cylindrical posterior part of mantle. Anterior part of mantle narrow-conical. Funnel cartilage elongated triangular, antitragus represented by a transverse fold with a small anterior projection. Funnel valve present. Only one sucker on the base of each 4th arm. Tentacles autotomized .... **n. gen. A Nesis, 1975a**

One undescribed species, Caribbean Sea, bathypelagic.

16 (15). Mantle abruptly narrowing at the level of anterior part or middle of fin, so that at least a part of mantle is located on the narrow conus of

gladius. Fin transversely oval. Anterior part of mantle goblet-shaped or sac-like. Funnel cartilage oval with well developed tooth-like antitragus, or elongate triangle with a deep bent depression and without antitragus. Funnel valve absent. More than one sucker on 4th arms. Tentacles not autotomized. Larvae with a long neck.........
..........**Genus *Valbyteuthis* Joubin, 1931**
(Fig. 64 S-X). Type species: *V. danae* Joubin, 1913. 4-5 species in bathypelagic (rarely in mesopelagic to bathypelagic zones) of tropical and temperate waters. At least some of the larvae attributed to the "genus" *Planktoteuthis* Pfeffer, 1912 belong to *Valbyteuthis*.

Supplemental key to Chiroteuthidae, mainly of juveniles or damaged specimens

1 (10). Funnel cartilage without tragus or antitragus **2**
2 (7). Funnel cartilage simple, elongated or slightly widened posteriorly (skittle- or bottle-shaped) or split at the end. Suckers on 4th arms running to the end of arms.............................**3**
3 (4). Funnel cartilage with a narrow deep groove bent like a boomerang and forkedly split at posterior end. Fin longitudinally oval. Skin beset by tiny conical cartilaginous tubercles. Larvae with a short neck, 3rd arms short. Adults with one photophore at the end of club...............
.................*Asperoteuthis famelica*
(Fig. 64 D-K).
4 (3). Funnel cartilage skittle- or bottle-shaped, not split. Fin transversely oval or heart-shaped. Skin smooth. Photophores not known........**5**
5 (6). Suckers on 4th arms running in two rows to the end of arms. Larvae with a long neck and well developed 3rd arms. Funnel cartilage straight, conspicuously widened posteriorly (bottle-shaped) ....*"Doratopsis" sagitta*
(Fig. 64 O,P).
6 (5). Suckers on ventral arms arranged in two rows in basal part and in one row in distal part. Larvae with a short neck and underdeveloped 3rd arms. Funnel cartilage is slightly widened (skittle-shaped) posteriorly and slightly bent..........
.....................*Chiroteuthoides* **spp.**
(Fig. 64 Q).
7 (2). Funnel cartilage oval, triangular-oval or elongately triangular.....................**8**
8 (9). Suckers on ventral arms in two rows, running to the end of arms. 6 or more rows of club

suckers. Larvae with a very long neck and almost without a snout..............*Tankaia* **spp.**
(Fig. 64 R).
9 (8). Suckers on ventral arms in one row, not farther than the middle of arm. 4 rows of club suckers. Larvae with a short neck and a snout of approximately the same length as neck........
.....................*Valbyteuthis*
A part of species: *V. levimana ("Doratopsis" lippula), V.* sp. (see key to the species of *Valbyteuthis*).
10 (1). Funnel cartilage with tragus and antitragus or only with antitragus.............**11**
11 (16). Funnel cartilage without tragus, elongately triangular or oval................**12**
12 (15). Suckers present only in basal part or at the base of 4th arms, arranged in one row. No rectal photophore.........................**13**
13 (14). Funnel cartilage oval. Funnel valve absent ....*Valbyteuthis*
The majority of species: *V. oligobessa, V. danae, "Doratopsis" exophthalmica* (Fig. 64 S-X). (see key to the species of *Valbyteuthis*).
14 (13). Funnel cartilage elongately triangular, with a deep bent groove. Funnel valve present ....**n. gen. A**
15 (12). Suckers in two rows along the entire length of 4th arms. One rectal photophore on ink sac.....................**n. gen. B**
(Fig. 64 L-N).
16 (11). Funnel cartilage ear-shaped, with tragus and antitragus.........................**17**
17 (18). Two or no photophores on ink sac. Photophores on 4th arms present............
.....................*Chiroteuthis* **spp.**
(Fig. 65).
18 (17). One photophore on ink sac. No (?) photophores on 4th arms........*Chiropsis mega*
(Fig. 64 A-C).

Key to species of the genus *Valbyteuthis*

1 (8). Funnel cartilage oval. Tentacular club not widened or slightly widened, with weakly developed protective membrane, without noticeable keel.................................**2**
2 (7). Funnel cartilage with a more or less developed antitragus. Fin width considerably larger than its length. Tentacular club without keel.................................**3**
3 (4). Only 2-3 (4) suckers on 4th arm. In adults 4th arms very slightly longer than others (much

Fig. 64.

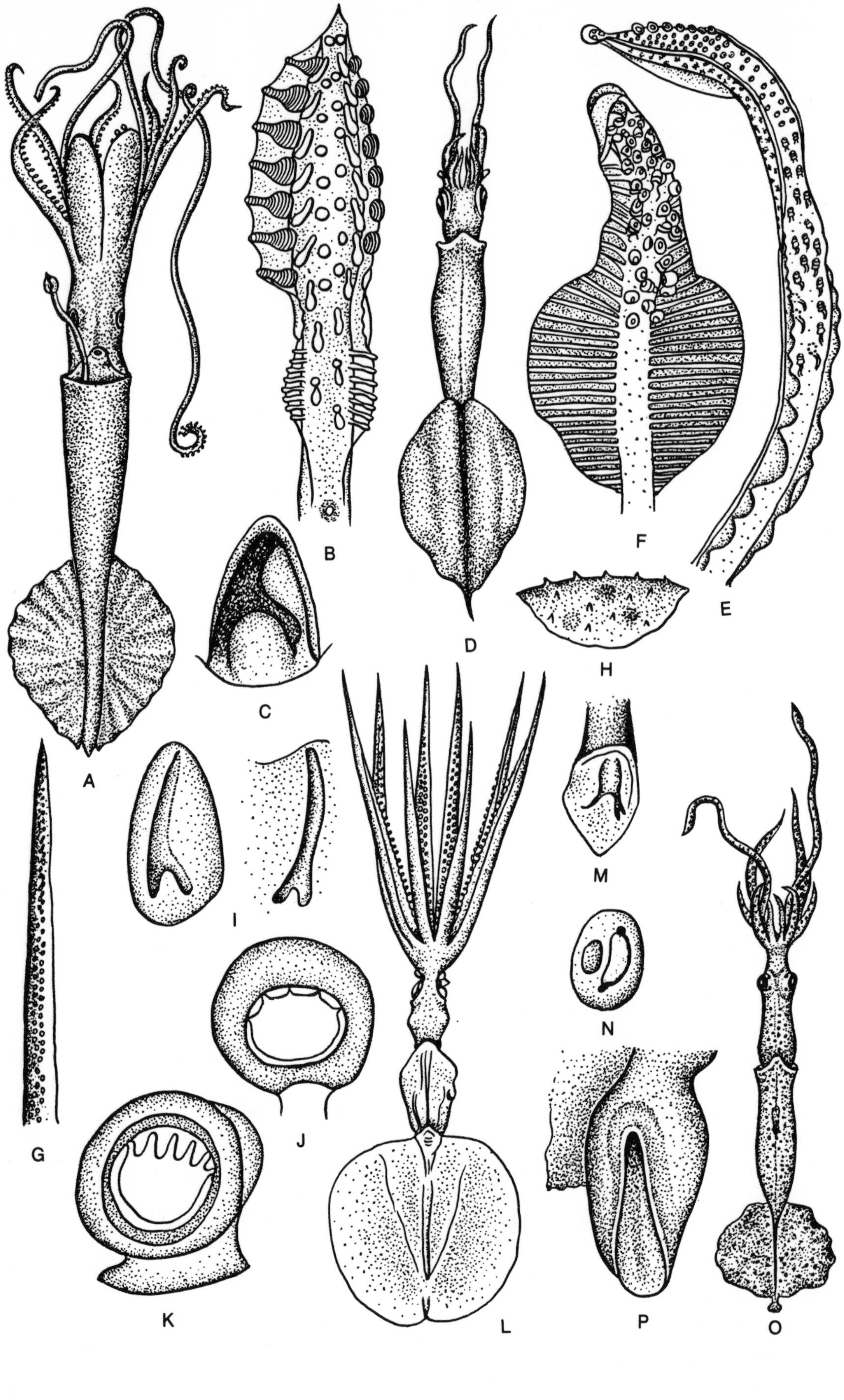

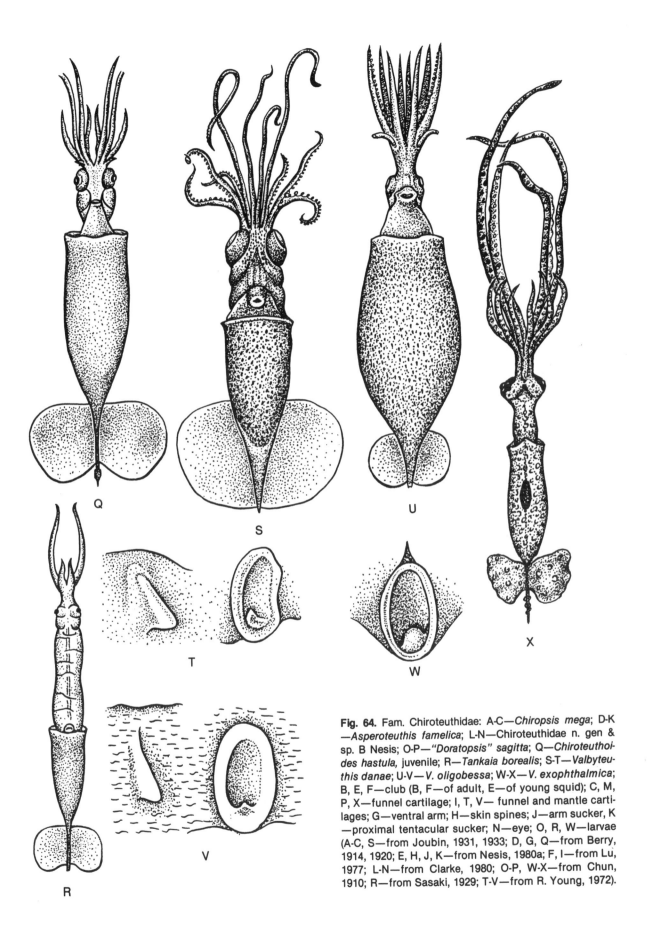

Fig. 64. Fam. Chiroteuthidae: A-C—*Chiropsis mega*; D-K —*Asperoteuthis famelica*; L-N—Chiroteuthidae n. gen & sp. B Nesis; O-P—*"Doratopsis" sagitta*; Q—*Chiroteuthoides hastula,* juvenile; R—*Tankaia borealis*; S-T—*Valbyteuthis danae*; U-V—*V. oligobessa*; W-X—*V. exophthalmica*; B, E, F—club (B, F—of adult, E—of young squid); C, M, P, X—funnel cartilage; I, T, V—funnel and mantle cartilages; G—ventral arm; H—skin spines; J—arm sucker, K —proximal tentacular sucker; N—eye; O, R, W—larvae (A-C, S—from Joubin, 1931, 1933; D, G, Q—from Berry, 1914, 1920; E, H, J, K—from Nesis, 1980a; F, I—from Lu, 1977; L-N—from Clarke, 1980; O-P, W-X—from Chun, 1910; R—from Sasaki, 1929; T-V—from R. Young, 1972).

longer and thicker in the juveniles). Antitragus of funnel cartilage is but slightly developed, being a small tubercle. Fin length 17-25% of mantle length. Club slightly widened. Arm suckers with 25-30 narrow high obtuse teeth . . . .
. . . . ***V. oligobessa* Young, 1972**
(Fig. 64 U-V). Equatorial Pacific from Indonesia to southern California and Baja California. Bathypelagic.

4 (3). Ten or more suckers on 4th arms. These arms distinctly the longest. Funnel cartilage with a well developed tooth-like antitragus 5

5 (6). Tentacular club compact, slightly widened. 12-15 suckers running almost to the middle of 4th arms. Arm suckers with 7-10 low wide teeth on distal edge. Fin length equals or exceeds half of mantle length . . . . ***V. danae* Joubin, 1931**
(Fig. 64 S,T). Bathypelagic zone of the tropical eastern Pacific from California to Central Chile, westwards to the eastern Polynesian Islands.

6 (5). Tentacular club long, as if stretched, not widened . . . . . . **"*Doratopsis (Planktoteuthis)*"** ***exophthalmica* Chun, 1908**
(Fig. 64 W,X). Only larvae are known, found in subtropical Northern Atlantic and in the Gulf of Mexico.

7 (2). Funnel cartilage without antitragus. Fin round, fin length and width about 33% of mantle length. Tentacular club with a low keel . . . .
. . . . ***Valbyteuthis* sp.**
(= *Chiroteuthis* sp. Rancurel, 1970). An undescribed species, probably widely distributed in the subtropical southern Atlantic, in the Indian and Pacific Oceans (see Roper and Young, 1967).

8 (1). Funnel cartilage elongated, with a deep depression but without antitragus. Tentacular club compact, widened, with well defined protective membranes and keel. 4th arms much longer than the others, with 6-11 suckers. Arm suckers with low wide teeth. Fin length is about 40% of mantle length . . . .
. . . . ***V. levimana* (Lönnberg, 1896)**
Atlantic tropical-subtropical meso-bathypelagic species. "*Doratopsis (Planktoteuthis)*" *lippula* Chun, 1908 is probably a larva of this species. Larvae resembling "*D*". *lippula* were in some cases found also in the Pacific Ocean off Hawaii and New Guinea.

Key to species of the genus *Chiroteuthis*

1 (2). No photophores on ink sac. Photophores on ventral side of eyeball in the form of two parallel bands. Club very long and narrow, not widened, of equal width along its entire length. Stalks of club suckers with a wing-like lateral fringe. Mantle narrow conical in anterior and cylindrical in posterior part, passes beyond posterior edge of round fin . . . . ***Ch. capensis* Voss, 1967**
(= ?*Bigelowia atlantica* Macdonald & Clench, 1934) (Fig. 65 A-E). Atlantic tropical meso-bathypelagic species.

2 (1). Two photophores on ink sac. Club widened in the middle and sometimes also in basal part. Mantle wide 3

3 (6). Photophores on ventral side of eyeball in two parallel bands, with one round photophore at the anterior and two at the posterior end between the ends of bands. Mantle conical, extending in adults somewhat farther than posterior edge of fin. 4th arms very wide. Stalks of club suckers with a big intermediate swelling in a form of dark-color cup with ribbed wall, thin cylindrical sucker stalk proper arise from the center of cup. Club protective membranes divided into a proximal part with branched trabeculae and a more narrow and longer distal part with unbranched trabeculae 4

4 (5). Arm sucker rings with long sharp teeth on distal edge. Diameter of suckers in the middle of 3rd arm exceeding not more than twice the diameter of suckers of 4th arms . . . .
. . . . ***Ch. veranyi* (Férussac, 1835)**
(Fig. 65 F-I). 2 subspecies.

a (b). Fin round. Photophores on ink sac round or egg-shape. Club protective membranes with a small constriction in the middle or on the border between basal and middle third of club . . . .
. . . . ***Ch. veranyi veranyi* (Férussac, 1835)**
(Fig. 65 F,G). Eastern Atlantic from the Reykjanes Ridge and Bay of Biscay to Namibia, Mediterranean Sea, the Azores, Canary, Madeira Islands, notalian and southern subtropical areas of Atlantic, Indian and Pacific Oceans from off southern Africa to Peru and Chile; in eastern Pacific in the north reaches equatorial area. Absent in northern Pacific. At the bottom in the bathyal and in the mesopelagic and upper bathypelagic zones above the slope. Larva is *Doratopsis vermicularis* (Rüppell, 1844).

b (a). Fin longitudinally oval. Photophores on ink sac longitudinally oval, truncated at both ends. Club protective membranes without constriction
. . . . ***Ch. veranyi lacertosa* Verrill, 1881**

(Fig. 65 H, I). Northwestern Atlantic from Nova Scotia to Delaware Bay, Gulf of Mexico, Lesser Antilles. Larvae is supposedly *Doratopsis diaphana* (Verrill, 1884).

5 (4). Arm suckers with obtuse truncated teeth on distal side or smooth with only slightly conspicuous notches. Suckers in the middle of 3rd arms large, their diameter exceeds more than three times the diameter of suckers on 4th arms . . . . **Ch. calyx Young, 1972**

(Fig. 65 J-O). Northern Pacific boreal species; from southern part of Bering sea and Gulf of Alaska to Sea of Okhotsk, northeastern Honshu and Baja California, mainly in mesopelagic zone in the vicinity of slope. Larva is *Doratopsis* cf. *vermicularis* Berry, 1963.

6 (3). Photophores on ventral side of eyeball round, numerous, arranged in two or three arched longitudinal rows. Trabeculae of club protective membranes unbranched. 4th arm not very wide **7**

7 (8). Photophores on ventral side of eyeball (on the average 20-25) arranged in three arched longitudinal rows, close together (except the marginal ones). Stalks of club suckers elongately conical, sometimes with a wing-like lateral fringe. Rings of club suckers with a big acute central tooth. Club protective membranes without widening in basal part. Mantle cylindrical anteriorly, continues behind posterior edge of fin and forms at posterior end a fusiform widening fringed by a narrow membrane. Arm sucker rings with obtuse teeth distally and smooth proximally. Funnel cartilage with wide low rounded tragus . . . .
. . . . **Ch. picteti Joubin, 1894**

(= *Ch. macrosoma* Goodrich, 1896, *Ch. imperator* Chun, 1908) (Fig. 65 P-R). Tropical Indo-West-Pacific from the Gulf of Aden to southern Honshu, Indonesia and Hawaii. Mesopelagic and bathyal. Larva is *Doratopsis pellucida* (Goodrich, 1896).

8 (7). Photophores on ventral side of eyeball (10-14) of unequal size (large and small), arranged in two arcs at unequal distances from one another. Stalks of club suckers with small intermediate widening in a form of a dark-color cup or film. Club sucker rings with six acute teeth without a big central tooth. Club protective membranes sharply widened in basal third; here they are coriaceous, trabeculae inconspicuous, so that it seems as if an oval "fin" is present on the club. In the remaining basalmost and distal part of club the

membranes are ordinary, filmy, with conspicuous trabeculae. Mantle without fusiform widening behind posterior edge of fin. Rings of basal arm suckers with low obtuse teeth on distal parts, proximally smooth; rings of distal arm suckers with high acute teeth. Funnel cartilage with high narow subacute tragus . . . .
. . . . **Ch. joubini Voss, 1967**

(= *Ch. lacertosa* Joubin, 1933, non Verrill) (Fig. 65 S,T). Northern subtropical and tropical Atlantic, Sargasso Sea; western and southern Indian Ocean (equator to 45°S) (our data); southeastern Africa, southwestern Australia, Banda Sea. Mantle length to 25 cm, may be up to 50 cm.

2.2.2.19. Family Mastigoteuthidae

Squids of medium size (mantle length 15-30 cm) with cartilaginous-gelatinous tissue. Anterior part of mantle cylindrical, posterior conical. Fin long, round, rhomboidal or heart-shaped, fin length usually not less than a half of the mantle length. 4th arms are as a rule considerably longer than the other arms. Club suckers in 2 rows. Tentacles long, may be several times longer than mantle, with a thin stalk and not widened or almost not widened club bearing very numerous tiny suckers arranged in many rows. Club without keel and fixing apparatus, suckers occupying 50-75% of its length. Tentacles are often autotomized at capture. Buccal membrane formula is DDVV. Funnel cartilage is ear-like or oval, with one or two tubercles (tragus and antitragus), rarely with three tubercles or without them; mantle cartilage is nose-shaped or in the form of a right angle. Many species have photophores, usually they are scattered over the surface of mantle, ventral side of head and ventral arms, sometimes on the fin and on lower eyelid near the eye sinus. Gladius is narrow, with a long terminal cone, usually passes beyond the posterior end of fin in the form of a thin needle-like tail. Hectocotylus absent. Development without larval stage. Bathypelagic and meso-bathypelagic squids, some species are benthic. 2 genera, 14-18 species.

Review: Nesis, 1977c.

Key to genera of the family Mastigoteuthidae

1 (2). Suckers on 4th arms extending to the end of arms. Tentacular club not widened, round in

Fig. 65.

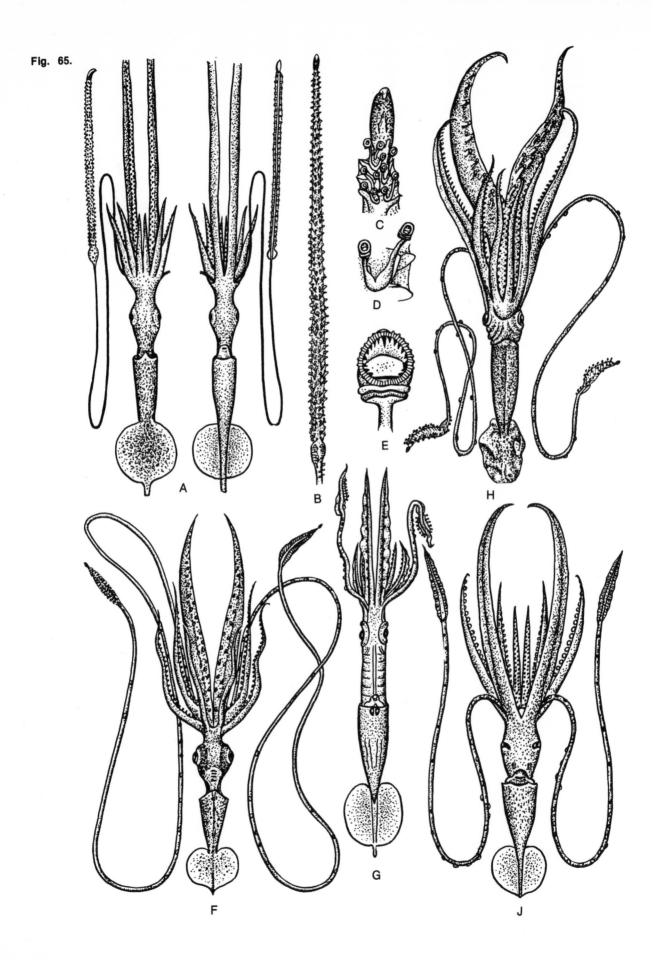

A

B

C

D

E

F

G

H

J

250

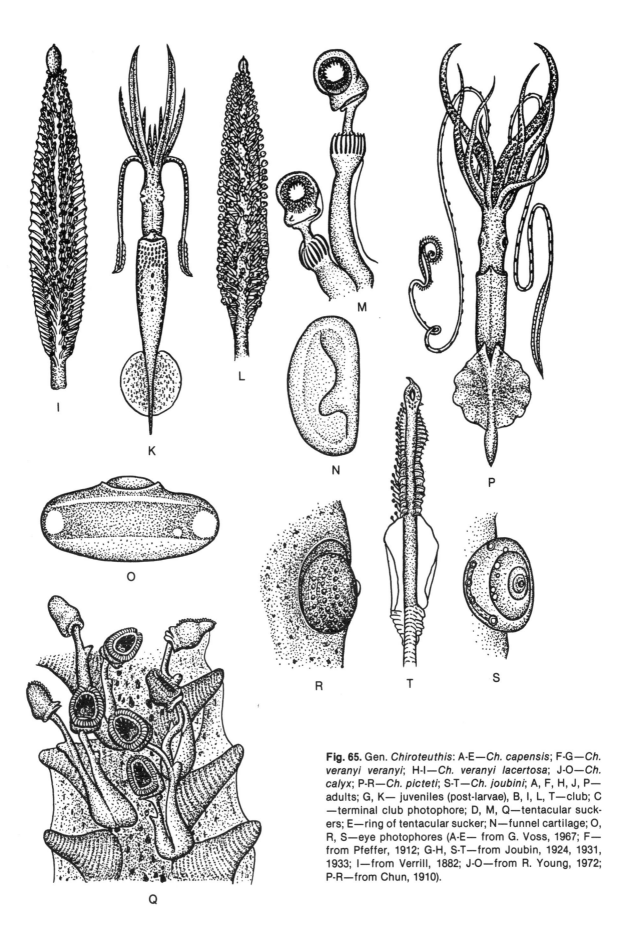

Fig. 65. Gen. *Chiroteuthis*: A-E—*Ch. capensis*; F-G—*Ch. veranyi veranyi*; H-I—*Ch. veranyi lacertosa*; J-O—*Ch. calyx*; P-R—*Ch. picteti*; S-T—*Ch. joubini*; A, F, H, J, P—adults; G, K— juveniles (post-larvae), B, I, L, T—club; C—terminal club photophore; D, M, Q—tentacular suckers; E—ring of tentacular sucker; N—funnel cartilage; O, R, S—eye photophores (A-E— from G. Voss, 1967; F—from Pfeffer, 1912; G-H, S-T—from Joubin, 1924, 1931, 1933; I—from Verrill, 1882; J-O—from R. Young, 1972; P-R—from Chun, 1910).

cross-section, suckers located almost along its entire perimeter (except *M. latipinna*). No stellate warts on skin. Fin rhomboidal, round or heart-shaped, needle-like tail absent or very short. Fin length usually considerably exceeds 50% of mantle length (except adult females of some species). Anterior edge of the mantle on dorsal side straight or with a slightly defined angular projection . . . . .
. . . . **Genus *Mastigoteuthis* Verrill, 1881**
(= *Chiroteuthopsis* Pfeffer, 1900, *Idioteuthis* Sasaki, 1929) (Figs 66, 67 A-C). Type species: *M. agassizi* Verrill, 1881. 2 subgenera, 12-16 species in all oceans, except the Arctic.

2 (1). Suckers on 4th arms only in basal part of arms not crossing middle of arm. Tentacular club slightly widened, manus flattened, suckers only on this flattened surface. Skin of head, mantle and partly of fin beset by tiny tubercles or stellate warts. Fin longitudinally-oval or widely heart-shaped, fin length exceeds a little half of mantle length, posteriorly extended into a long needle-like tail (sometimes longer than the fin itself). Anterior edge of the mantle on the back with large tongue-like projection. Funnel cartilage with tragus and small antitragus. No eye photophores .
. . . . **Genus *Echinoteuthis* Joubin, 1933**
(Fig. 67 D-G). Type species: *E. danae* Joubin, 1933. Probably 2 species, one of them not described.

Key to subgenera and species of the genus *Mastigoteuthis*

1 (22). No photophores on ventral side of eyeball. Fin not reaching anterior edge of mantle, fin width considerably less than mantle length. Photophores scattered over surface of body or absent . . **Subgenus *Mastigoteuthis*(s. str.)** . . **2**
(Fig. 66)
2 (11). Numerous small black photophores surrounded by a light ring scattered over surface of body, especially on ventral side. A small (less than 1 mm) photophore on eyelid inside near eye sinus (not described in *M. talismani*). Funnel cartilage with tragus (slightly defined in *M. agassizi*), antitragus present or absent **3**
3 (6). Arm sucker rings on distal side with 10-20 sharp teeth, proximally with low flattened teeth or smooth. Fin heart-shaped or rhombic, posteriorly extended into a small tail needle, fin length in young squids about 67%, in adult males 55-60%, in adult females 40-50% of mantle length. Eyes

large, protruding **4**
4 (5). Antitragus absent or very slightly developed, funnel cartilage as if undercut posteriorly . . . .***M. grimaldii* Group**
(Fig. 66 A-F). 4 nominal bathypelagic species distributed in tropical and subtropical waters of all oceans. Differing only in structure and position of club suckers (it should be taken into consideration that the tentacles are as a rule autotomized at capture). Status of species is uncertain.
a (f). Club sucker rings smooth on inner side . . .**b**
b (e). Club suckers arranged in 30-40 rows . . . . .**c**
c (d). Club occupies 67-75% of tentacle length. Diameter of club suckers is 0.2 - 0.4 mm . . . .
. . . .***M. grimaldii* (Joubin, 1895)**
(Fig. 66 A,B). Tropical and subtropical Atlantic, Gulf of Mexico.
d (c). Club occupying about 50% of tentacle length. Diameter of club suckers 0.15-0.25 mm
. . . .***M. dentata* Hoyle, 1904**
(Fig. 66 C,D). Tropical and subtropical Indo-Pacific (except California Current). Northward reaches the Kurile Islands and southward to southern Africa, southern Australia, New Zealand, and central Chile.
e (b). Suckers on tentacular club in 20-30 rows, their diameter is about 0.1 mm. Club occupies 67% of tentacle length . . . .
. . . .***M. schmidti* Degner, 1925**
Northern Atlantic from Iceland to Canary Islands and Madeira. Probably a synonym of *M. grimaldii*.
f (a). Club sucker rings on inner side with 3 distal teeth. Club suckers arranged in about 20 rows, diameter about 0.3 mm. Club occupying 50% of tentacle length . . . . . .***M. pyrodes* Young, 1972**
(Fig. 66 E,F). California Current.
5 (4). Funnel cartilage with well developed antitragus. About 20 rows of club suckers, diameter about 0.15 mm. Sucker rings smooth on inner side . . . . ***M. psychrophila* Nesis, 1977**
(Fig. 66 G). Notalian-Antarctic circumglobal meso-bathypelagic species.
6 (3). Arm sucker rings smooth or with a few slightly obtuse teeth. Fin is round or rhomboidal
. . . .**7**
7 (10). Fin length 50-67% of the mantle length. A small photophore inside on eyelid near eye sinus
. . . .**8**
8 (9). Fin transversely oval or slightly rhomboidal, extended posteriorly into a short tail, its

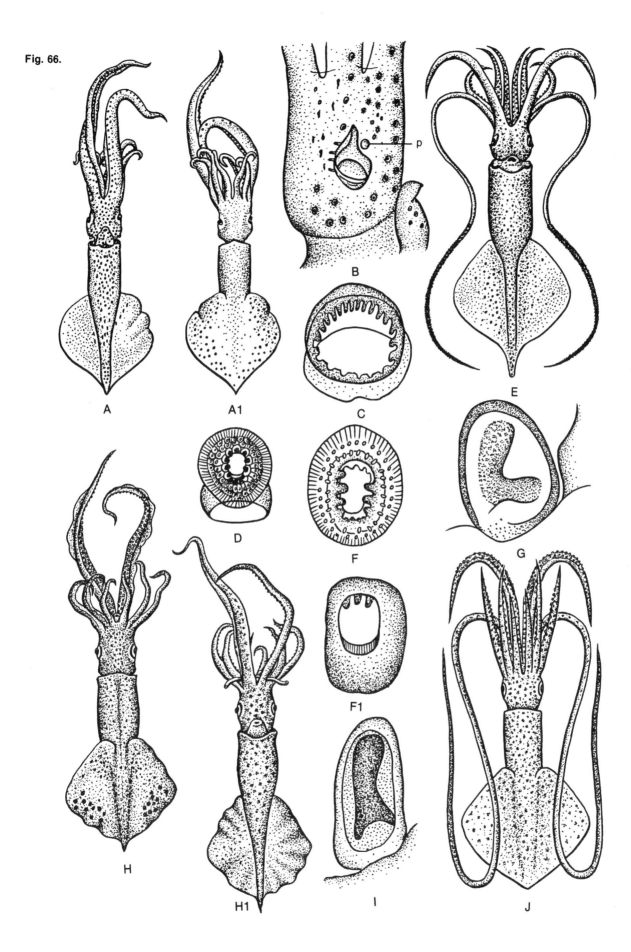

Fig. 66.

A

A1

B

C

D

E

F

F1

G

H

H1

I

J

p

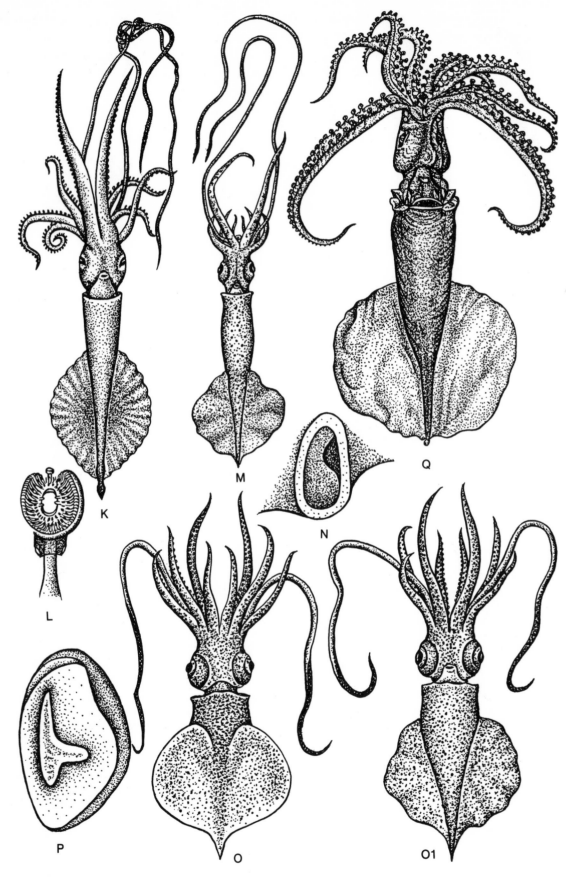

Fig. 66.

K

L

M

N

O

O1

P

Q

254

length in the young 50-60% of mantle length. Tragus and antitragus well developed. Eyes small, not protruding. Arm sucker rings smooth or with 3-5 small teeth distally . . . .
. . . .**M. flammea Chun, 1908**
(Fig. 66 H,I). Gulf of Guinea and ?northern subtropical Atlantic; Great Australian Bight. Bathypelagic.

9 (8). Fin rhomboidal, not extended into a tail. Fin length is about 67% of mantle length. Tragus and antitragus are but slightly developed. Eyes big. Arm sucker rings smooth . . . .
. . . .**M. agassizi Verrill, 1881**
(Fig. 66 J). Boreal and northern subtropical Atlantic, northward reaches the area southward of Iceland.

10 (7). Fin length about 90% of mantle length. Tragus well developed, antitragus absent. Arm sucker rings smooth . . . .
. . . . . .**M. talismani (Fischer & Joubin, 1906)**
Tropical and northern subtropical Atlantic—area off the Azores and Cape Verde Islands.

11 (2). Body surface devoid of photophores, sometimes with a photophore inside eyelid near eye sinus **12**

12 (17). Arm sucker rings with teeth. Funnel cartilage with tragus (in adult *M. glaukopis* poorly developed) **13**

13 (16). A large (1-4 mm) distinct white photophore inside eyelid near eye sinus. Skin smooth **14**

14 (15). Arm suckers with 10-15 teeth on distal edge, proximal edge smooth. Club suckers large (0.3-0.5 mm), rings with 2-3 long obtuse teeth on lateral sides. Tragus well defined, antitragus almost inconspicuous . . . .
. . . .**M. atlantica Joubin, 1933**
(= *?M. iselini* Macdonald & Clench, 1934) (Fig. 66 K,L). Tropical and northern subtropical Atlantic (northward to the Bay of Biscay) and Indo-West Pacific. Bathypelagic.

15 (14). Arm suckers with 5-10 low obtuse teeth on distal edge, proximally with flattened teeth or smooth. Club suckers small (0.06-0.1 mm), with

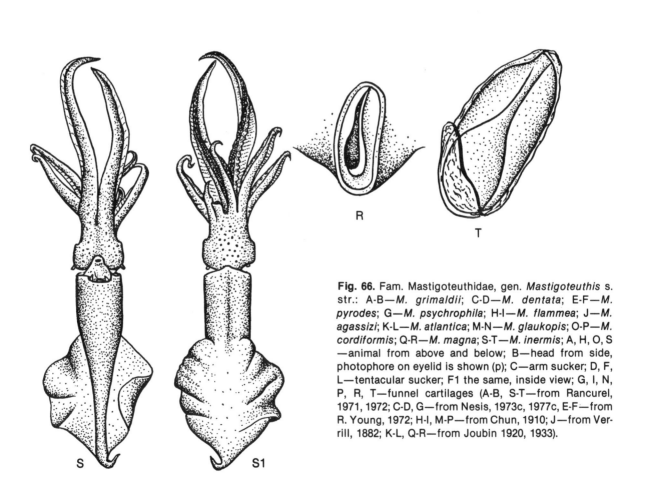

R

T

S

S1

Fig. 66. Fam. Mastigoteuthidae, gen. *Mastigoteuthis* s. str.: A-B—*M. grimaldii*; C-D—*M. dentata*; E-F—*M. pyrodes*; G—*M. psychrophila*; H-I—*M. flammea*; J—*M. agassizi*; K-L—*M. atlantica*; M-N—*M. glaukopis*; O-P—*M. cordiformis*; Q-R—*M. magna*; S-T—*M. inermis*; A, H, O, S —animal from above and below; B—head from side, photophore on eyelid is shown (p); C—arm sucker; D, F, L—tentacular sucker; F1 the same, inside view; G, I, N, P, R, T—funnel cartilages (A-B, S-T—from Rancurel, 1971, 1972; C-D, G—from Nesis, 1973c, 1977c, E-F—from R. Young, 1972; H-I, M-P—from Chun, 1910; J—from Verrill, 1882; K-L, Q-R—from Joubin 1920, 1933).

Fig. 67.

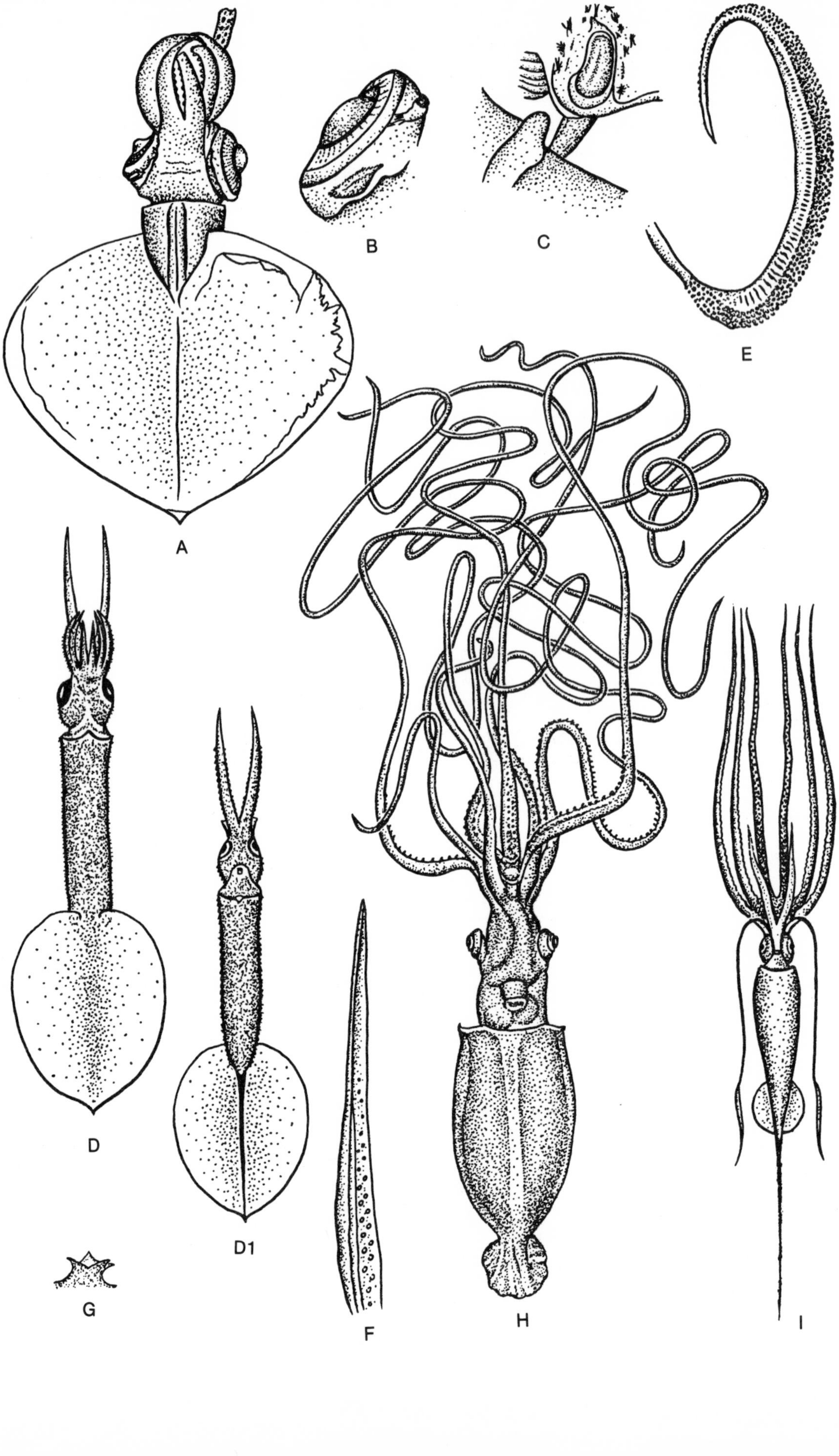

smooth rings. Tragus poorly developed or absent, no antitragus . . . .
. . . . ***M. glaukopis* Chun, 1908**
(Fig. 66 M,N). Western Indian Ocean and Flores Sea. Bathypelagic.

16 (13). Photophores absent. The skin of head, mantle and arm bases beset by small soft cuticular tubercles. Arm suckers with low rounded or slightly pointed teeth. Club suckers with sharp teeth along entire ring. Funnel cartilage with tragus and slightly developed antitragus. Fin length 70-80% of the mantle length . . . .
. . . . ***M. cordiformis* Chun, 1908**
(Fig. 66 O,P). Southern Japan, Philippines, Indonesia. Lives mainly at the bottom in bathyal.

17 (12). Arm sucker rings smooth. Photophores absent. Funnel cartilage without tragus and antitragus **18**

18 (21). Funnel cartilage bottle- or skittle-shaped, narrowed anteriorly, widened and rounded posteriorly. Tentacular club round in cross-section, with rudimentary protective membranes. Suckers microscopically small, their rings smooth. Fin length about 67% of mantle length **19**

19 (20). Fin width exceeds or equals fin length and comprises 70-80% of the mantle length . . . . .
. . . . ***M. magna* Joubin, 1913**
(Fig. Q,R). Tropical and northern subtropical Atlantic, Indian Ocean and Tasman Sea. Bathypelagic and bathyal, at night ascends to the mesopelagic zone.

20 (19). Fin width less than fin length and comprises about 50% of the mantle length . . . .
. . . . ***M. inermis* Rancurel, 1972**
(Fig. 66 S-T). Equatorial Atlantic, Gulf of Guinea. Bathypelagic.

21 (18). Funnel cartilage oval or egg-shaped. Proximal part of club slightly widened and flattened, with well developed protective membranes. Suckers in proximal part of club not smaller than arm suckers, their rings distally with teeth. Fin length about 83% of mantle length . . . .
. . . . ***M. latipinna* (Sasaki, 1916)**
From southern Japan to northwestern Australia, at the bottom in bathyal.

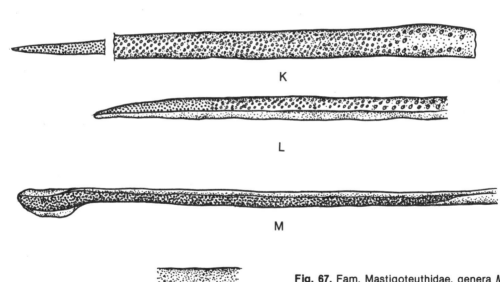

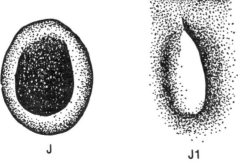

Fig. 67. Fam. Mastigoteuthidae, genera *Mastigoteuthis (Mastigopsis)* (A-C) and *Echinoteuthis* (D-G); fam. Joubiniteuthidae (H-M): A-C—*Mastigoteuthis hjorti*, animal (A), eye (B), funnel and mantle cartilages (C); D-G—*Echinoteuthis danae*, young squid (D), club (E), ventral arm (F) and skin tubercle (G); H-M— *Joubiniteuthis portieri*, young (H) and adult (I) squids, funnel and mantle cartilages (J), 3rd (K) and 4th (L) arm, club (M) (A-C— from Rancurel, 1973; D-H—from Joubin, 1924, 1933; I-M—from Young and Roper, 1969b).

22 (1). Two big oval white photophores on ventral side of eyeball: one in anterior part at the level of bases of 2nd and 3rd arms, the second in postero-median part at the level of funnel opening. No photophores on eyelid nor on body surface. Fin very big, reaching almost the anterior edge of mantle, fin width fairly exeeds mantle length. Funnel cartilage oval, slightly widened posteriorly, without tragus and antitragus. Arm sucker rings with 10-15 long obtuse teeth distally. Club suckers microscopically small. . . . .
. . . .**Subgenus *Mastigopsis* Grimpe, 1922**

One species: ***M. (M.) hjorti* Chun, 1913** (Fig. 67 A-C). Tropical and northern subtropical Atlantic, Indian Ocean, Tasman Sea, (?) eastern equatorial Pacific. Mesopelagic and bathypelagic.

Young squids belonging to this subgenus (separate species?) were caught in the Sulu Sea and in equatorial western Indian Ocean.

Key to species of the genus *Echinoteuthis*

1 (2). Anterior part of mantle to the beginning of fin narrow, cylindrical. Cartilaginous skin tubercles stellate. . . . . . . ***E. danae* Joubin, 1933** (Fig. 67 E-G). Tropical and subtropical Atlantic, supposedly mesopelagic and bathypelagic.

2 (1). Anterior part of mantle to the beginning of fin conical (goblet-shaped). Cartilaginous skin tubercles are round. . . ***Echinoteuthis* sp. Nesis** (= *Mastigoteuthis grimaldii* of Allan, 1945, non Joubin). Southern part of Tasman Sea and Great Australian Bight. Mesopelagic and bathypelagic. The differences between these species may be only site-related.

2.2.2.20. Family Joubiniteuthidae

Medium-size squids with a narrow cylindrical cartilaginous-gelatinous mantle, extended posteriorly into a very long (longer than mantle) slender needle-like tail which is usually broken off in adults. Fin small, oval or round. Head narrow, on a long neck. Eyes small. The first three pairs of arms are extremely long, slender, particularly at the ends. They are flexible and bear very small suckers arranged in 6 rows. 4th arms are much shorter than the others and bear 4 rows of suckers. Tentacles in the juveniles are very thin and weak, shorter than 1st-3rd arms, with a filiform stalk and a long club compressed laterally and bearing 8-12 rows of tiny suckers. Club protective membranes are developed only at its distal end. No fixing apparatus. In adults tentacles are completely reduced. Funnel cartilage oval, without tragus and antitragus, mantle cartilage – an elongated tubercle. Buccal membrane formula DDVV. Photophores absent. The gladius is needle-like, not widened in the middle, with a long cone. Hectocotylus absent. Color brown-violet.

One genus: ***Joubiniteuthis* Berry, 1920** (= *Valdemaria* Joubin, 1931). Only one species: ***J. portieri* (Joubin, 1912)** (= *Valdemaria danae* Joubin, 1931) (Fig. 67 H-M). Mesopelagic and bathypelagic zones of the tropical and subtropical Atlantic, including the Caribbean Sea, and the Northern Pacific (Japan, Hawaii).

Review of the family: Young and Roper, 1969b.

2.2.2.21. Family Promachoteuthidae

Mantle wide, thick, semigelatinous, fused with the head in occipital area, nuchal cartilage present or absent. Head small. Eyes very small, greatly reduced in size, nearly covered by transparent tissue. Arms with 2 rows of suckers. Tentacles long and robust, club not widened, without protective membranes and fixing apparatus, with numerous (6-20 rows) very small suckers. Fin wide heart-shaped or transversely oval. Funnel cartilage oval, without tragus and antitragus, mantle cartilage tubercle-like. Buccal membrane formula is DDVV. Photophores absent. Gladius either absent or reduced. No ink sac.

One genus: ***Promachoteuthis* Hoyle, 1885** (Fig. 68 A-D) with two species (one of them is not described), known only from young specimens captured in bathypelagic and abyssopelagic zones. The young squids differ in the following characters:

1 (2). Arms length 40-50% of mantle length. Fin length about 75% of mantle length, width exceeding it 1.5 times. Arm suckers rings smooth . . . .***P. megaptera* Hoyle, 1885**
Northwest Pacific to the southeast of Honshu. Abyssopelagic.

2 (1). Arm length about 25% of mantle length. Fin length less than 50%, width about 67% of mantle length. Arm sucker rings dentate. . . . .
. . . .***P.* sp. Roper & Young, 1968**
Southeastern Pacific westward of central Chile and southwestward of the Strait of Magellan, ?Southern Atlantic. Bathypelagic.

Review of the family: Roper and Young, 1968.

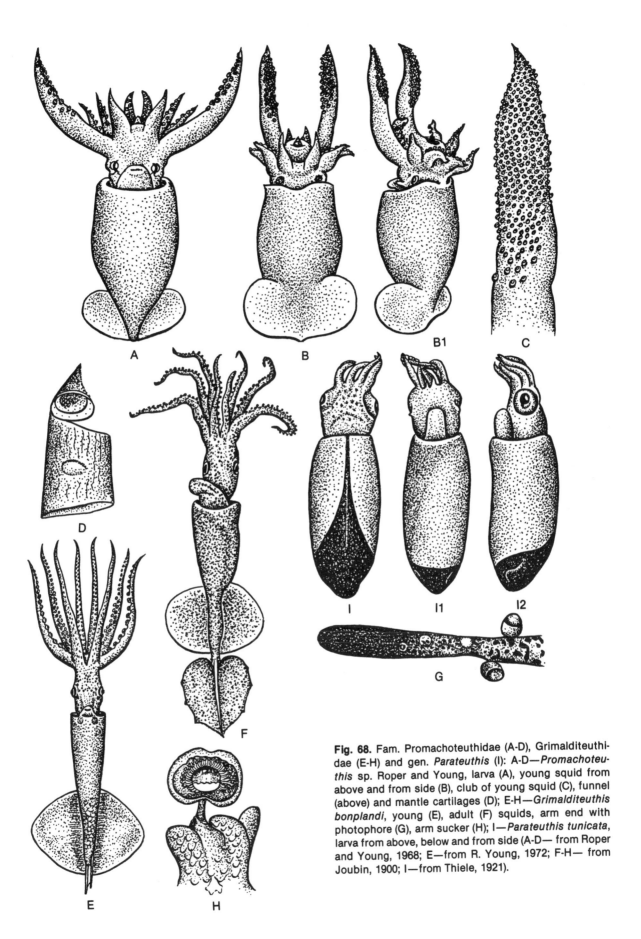

Fig. 68. Fam. Promachoteuthidae (A-D), Grimalditeuthidae (E-H) and gen. *Parateuthis* (I): A-D—*Promachoteuthis* sp. Roper and Young, larva (A), young squid from above and from side (B), club of young squid (C), funnel (above) and mantle cartilages (D); E-H—*Grimalditeuthis bonplandi*, young (E), adult (F) squids, arm end with photophore (G), arm sucker (H); I—*Parateuthis tunicata*, larva from above, below and from side (A-D— from Roper and Young, 1968; E—from R. Young, 1972; F-H— from Joubin, 1900; I—from Thiele, 1921).

2.2.2.22. Family Grimalditeuthidae

Medium size squids with gelatinous narrow conical mantle posteriorly extended into a long tail. Fin transversely oval or round, fin length is about 50% of the mantle length measured to the fin end. It is followed by a second fin (on a long needle-like tail) of approximately the same size, but heart-shaped. Usually the gladius end with the second fin is broken off. Head narrow, fused with funnel but not fused with head in occipital area. Arms long, slender, with 2 rows of suckers whose stalks rise out of the centres of thick tubercles with three obtuse tops. One elongated dark photophore on arm ends in adult squids. Tentacles are lost completely, even in the juveniles only short rudiments of stalks remain. Buccal membrane formula is DDVV. Gladius very narrow, with a long terminal cone. Hectocotylus absent.

One genus: *Grimalditeuthis* Joubin, 1898 with one species: *G. bonplandi* (Vérany, 1837) (Fig. 68 E-H). Lives in mesopelagic and bathypelagic zones of tropical and subtropical Atlantic and northern Pacific (Hawaii, California).

Review: R. Young, 1972.

2.2.2.23. Family incertae sedis

Genus *Parateuthis* Thiele, 1921. One species: *P. tunicata* Thiele, 1921 (Fig. 68 I). Only the larvae are known with mantle length of 5-8 mm, captured in the Antarctic at depths of 2000-3425 m. Mantle fusiform, muscular in anterior part and thin, filmy, semitransparent in posterior part where the inner yolk sac is visible through it. Fins tiny, petaloid. Mantle not fused with head or funnel, but the locking cartilages are poorly developed (the mantle and funnel cartilages are almost not developed). Head narrow, with big eyes. Arms short, with 2 rows of suckers. Gladius absent or greatly reduced. Structure of club and buccal membrane is unknown. These larvae do not belong to any of the known families of Oegopsida.

2.2.2.24. Family Cranchiidae

Sluggish planktonic and semiplantonic-seminektonic squids, ranging from small to giant ones. Mantle fused with funnel and head in the occipital area, it is thin, coriaceous or semigelatinous. Mantle surface is smooth or bearing small cartilaginous tubercles usually disposed in definite places, rarely over the entire body (*Cranchia*). Fins of very different shapes: paddle-, kidney-, egg-shaped, round, or lanceolate, from small to very long but the fin length does not exceed 60% of the mantle length. Head short and narrow. Eyes very big, in adults they are as a rule ball-like and sessile, while in the young they are usually stalked and flattened or tubular. Arms with 2 rows of suckers (several rows on arm ends in males of certain species). In *Mesonychoteuthis* some suckers in the middle part of the arms are modified into hooks. Protective membranes present, arm keels are weakly developed. Tentacles long, with slightly widened club bearing 4 rows of suckers with denticulate rings. Suckers of middle rows are sometimes modified into hooks. Fixing apparatus well developed, isolated or running along the stalk. In adult squids the tentacles are sometimes autotomized. Buccal membrane with six lappets, formula is DDVV. Gladius thin, rod-like, with a posterior rhombic widening—the lanceola, whose posterior end may be extended into a long acute cone. In the latter case mantle is extended into a tail. Posterior end of mantle may not reach the posterior end of gladius. Fins are either entirely or by the posterior part attached to posterolateral side of the lanceola. In *Bathothauma* the lanceola is reduced and the fins are attached directly to the mantle. Photophores (several round or 1-2 elongated ones) are always present on eyeball, sometimes there are photophores on arm ends (in adult females) and on the liver. In juveniles the body is usually transparent or semitransparent, slightly pigmented, coloration of adult specimens is usually purple, brown or yellow.

Characteristic to the family is a spacious closed body cavity (coelom) containing a considerable quantity of NH_4Cl solution. Density of this solution is lower than sea water, so the coelom serves as a float that maintains the squid in the state of neutral buoyancy ("bathyscaphoid squids"). A horizontal membrane divides the mantle cavity into an upper (containing the coelom) and lower part communicating by two round openings—the spiracles, located above the gills; the respiratory flow of water passes posteriorly along the upper chamber on both sides of coelom, then through the spiracles passing by the gills forward to the head and goes out through the funnel. Nidamental glands are paired (each gland is subdivided into two) or single. Hectocotylus present in the Cranchiinae (one of 4th arms are hectocotylized), ends of one or several arms are additionally modified in the males of all genera. Spermatophores are transfered to the surface of body, head or arms or into the mantle cavity of females (to genital openings or directly into the oviduct). Development with larval stage. Larvae have very short arms and long tentacles, minute fins, often stalked elongated eyes pointed downward (with a rostrum), suckers running along the entire or almost entire tentacular stalk.

Mainly mesopelagic or meso-bathypelagic squids. The larvae and young of some species live in the epipelagic zone. 2 subfamilies, 15 genera, 31-37 species.

Reviews N. Voss, 1980; N. and R. Voss, 1983.

Synonymies of the family is very confused since many genera and species are described by larvae, while others by adult specimens. Due to this, different growth age stages of the same species were sometimes attributed to different genera and similar stages of different squids were united under one specific name. The keys are based upon the characters of adult and semi-adult specimens.

Key to subfamilies and genera of the family Cranchiidae

1 (8). 2 or 4 hyaline stripes present on ventral side of mantle start from the sites of mantle-funnel fusion and bearing cartilaginous tubercles with one or several acute tops. Ocular photophores numerous, round, encircling the eyeball as a ring or two arcs. Fins round or semicircular, not extending into a long tail. Lateral sides of funnel in adults fused with ventral side of head. One ventral arm in male hectocotylized . . . .
. . . .**Subfamily Cranchiinae. . .2**
2 (3). Entire surface of mantle and dorsal surface of fins is beset by cartilaginous tubercles, whose tops bear 3-5 sharp spines. Fins small, round, together resembling symbol of infinity (∞). Mantle ball- or barrel-shaped. 14 photophores on eyeball: 6 around the pupil, 7 arched along ventral side of eyeball and 1 between them. A large photophore on ends of all arms in adult females. Larvae with sessile eyes. Funnel valve present
. . . .**Genus *Cranchia* Leach, 1817**
One species: *C. scabra* Leach, 1817 (Fig. 69

A-C). Tropical-subtropical cosmopolitan mesopelagic to bathypelagic species. Juveniles live in epipelagic and mesopelagic zones. Mantle length up to 15 (20?) cm.

3 (2). Cartilaginous tubercles and small separate spines present only on hyaline stripes and sometimes along dorsal midline. **4**
4 (5). A pair of hyaline stripes present on anteroventral side of mantle diverging like an inverted V from each mantle-funnel fusion site. In *L. reinhardti* a stripe of small cartilaginous spines runs also along dorsal midline. 4-14 photophores on eyeball. Larvae with sessile eyes. Mantle in larvae and juveniles ball- or barrel-shaped, in adults widely fusiform. Fins in juveniles resemble together symbol of infinity (∞), in adults a regular circle or an oval. Funnel valve present
. . . .**Genus *Liocranchia* Pfeffer, 1884**
(= *Fusocranchia* Joubin, 1920) (Fig. 69 D-G). Type species: *L. reinhardti* (Steenstrup, 1856).

2-3 species in mesopelagic and bathypelagic zones (juveniles in epipelagic and mesopelagic) of tropical and subtropical waters of all oceans. Mantle length to 20-25 cm.

5 (4). 2 hyaline stripes parallel to the longitudinal body axis in anteroventral side of mantle. No cartilaginous spines on the back. The number of eye photophores ranging from 5 to 21, arranged in outer and inner arcs or rings around the pupil. Mantle elongated, cylindrical or narrowly fusiform. Larvae with stalked eyes. Fins round or transversely oval. Funnel valve absent. **6**
6 (7). Fin length 20-30% of the mantle length. Arms end not attenuated, 3rd arms having less than a hundred suckers. Arm sucker rings with several teeth on distal edge. A large photophore may be present only on the ends of 3rd arms in adult females. . . . .
. . . .**Genus *Leachia* LeSueur, 1821**
(= *Perothis* Rathke, 1835, *Dyctidiopsis* Rochebrune, 1884) (Fig. 69 H-R). Type species: *L. cyclura* LeSueur, 1821. 2 subgenera: *Leachia* s. str. with 2-3 species and *Pyrgopsis* Rochebrune, 1884 (type species: *P. rynchophorus* Rochebrune, 1884) with 4-5 species in mesopelagic and bathypelagic zones (juveniles in epipelagic) mainly of tropical and subtropical waters. Mantle length to 15-20 cm.

7 (6). Fin length 33-40% of mantle length. Arm ends attenuated, 3rd arms in adults with more than two hundred suckers. Sucker rings in middle part of 3rd arms with three large hook-like teeth

Fig. 69.

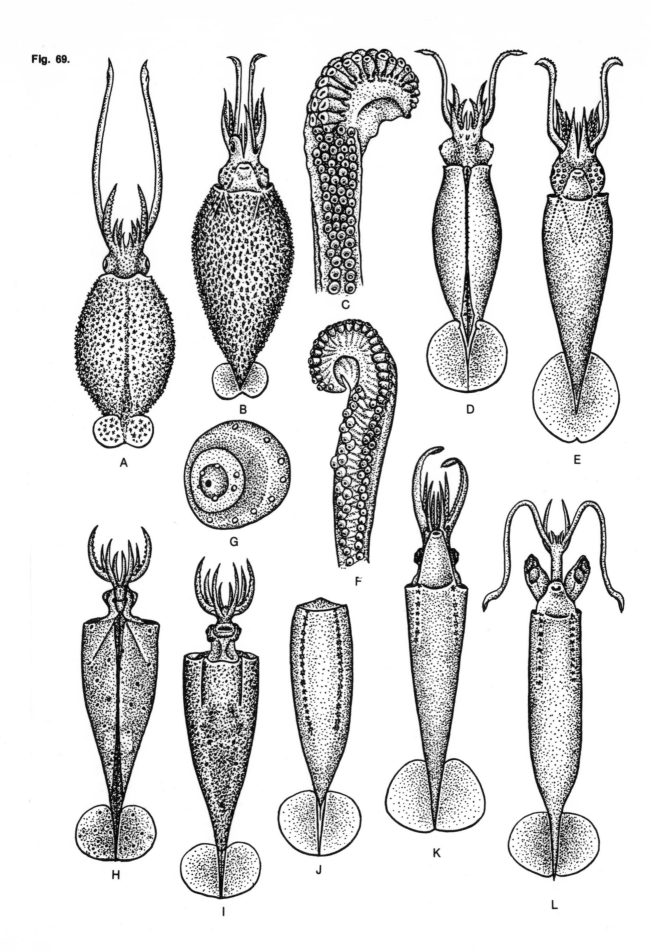

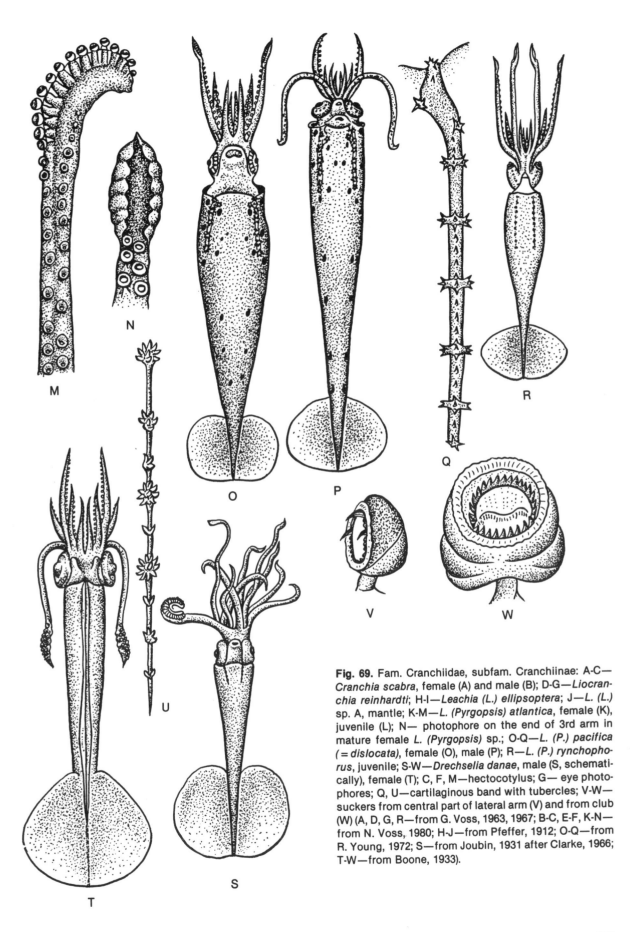

Fig. 69. Fam. Cranchiidae, subfam. Cranchiinae: A-C—
Cranchia scabra, female (A) and male (B); D-G—*Liocranchia reinhardti*; H-I—*Leachia (L.) ellipsoptera*; J—*L. (L.)*
sp. A, mantle; K-M—*L. (Pyrgopsis) atlantica*, female (K),
juvenile (L); N— photophore on the end of 3rd arm in
mature female *L. (Pyrgopsis)* sp.; O-Q—*L. (P.) pacifica*
(=*dislocata*), female (O), male (P); R—*L. (P.) rynchophorus*, juvenile; S-W—*Drechselia danae*, male (S, schematically), female (T); C, F, M—hectocotylus; G— eye photophores; Q, U—cartilaginous band with tubercles; V-W—
suckers from central part of lateral arm (V) and from club
(W) (A, D, G, R—from G. Voss, 1963, 1967; B-C, E-F, K-N—
from N. Voss, 1980; H-J—from Pfeffer, 1912; O-Q—from
R. Young, 1972; S—from Joubin, 1931 after Clarke, 1966;
T-W—from Boone, 1933).

on distal edge, teeth are of equal size or the middle tooth is largest. A large photophore on ends of all arms in adult females. . . . .
. . . . **Genus *Drechselia* Joubin, 1931**

One species: *D. danae* Joubin, 1931 (Fig. 69 S-W). In mesopelagic-bathypelagic zone of tropical eastern Pacific (Gulf of Panama). Mantle length up to 17 cm.

8 (1). No hyaline stripes with cartilaginous tubercles. Separate cartilaginous tubercles may be present only at the mantle-funnel fusion sites and rarely at mantle-head fusion site. 1-2 photophores on ventral side of eyeball, usually of crescent or semilunar form around the eyeball; rarely 3 photophores (2 long and one round). Fins of different shape, short or long but not round, sometimes mantle attenuated into a long tail. Lateral sides of funnel not fused with head. Larvae with stalked eyes. Ends of 1st and/or 2nd, sometimes 3rd or first three arms modified in males but there is no true hectocotylus. . . . .
. . . . **Subfamily Taoniinae. . .9**

9 (22). Mantle of adults attenuated posteriorly into a long acuminate tail, gladius end needle-like or narrowly conical. Fin long, lanceolate, egg-shaped or longituindally oval. Funnel valve present or absent **10**

10 (15). Several suckers of middle rows on tentacular club modified into hooks. Tail long, needle-like, fin lanceolate or leaf-shaped. No photophores on arm ends. Funnel valve absent **11**

11 (14). No hooks on arms. Fin lanceolate, not so wide as long. **12**

12 (13). Club hooks with one tooth, with widened base and an aperture reduced to a small slit; hooks covered by a hood. Marginal suckers of central part of club reduced or absent. Arm sucker rings smooth or (rarely) with low round teeth. Usually (but not always) cartilaginous tubercles present at mantle-funnel fusion site. Dorsal (middle) component of funnel organ with three finger-like papillae. . . . . . **Genus *Galiteuthis* Joubin, 1898**

(= *Taonidium* Pfeffer, 1900, *Crystalloteuthis* Chun, 1906, ?*Zygaenopsis* Rochebrune, 1884, ?*Zygocranchia* Hoyle, 1909, ?*Euzygaena* Chun, 1910, ?*Phasmatoteuthion* Pfeffer, 1912) (Fig. 71 M-T). Type species: *G. armata* Joubin, 1895. 5 species in bathypelagic and bathyal zones (juveniles in epipelagic and mesopelagic) of all oceans, except the Arctic Ocean. Mantle length to 66 cm, but probably to 2.7 m.

13 (12). Club hooks develop as a result of intensive growth of one or two teeth of sucker ring; hook base not widened, ring aperture not reduced and the hook not covered by a hood. Besides one or two main hook-like teeth on the ring there are often additional small lateral teeth. Marginal suckers of central part of club well developed. Arm sucker rings with low teeth (on distal edge in juveniles and over the entire ring in adults). No cartilaginous tubercles at mantle-funnel fusion sites. Dorsal (middle) component of funnel organ with a median finger-like papilla and two short conical tubercles. . . . .
. . . . **Genus *Belonella* Lane, 1957**

(= *Toxeuma* Chun, 1906, *Taonius* auct., non LeSueur) (Fig. 71 F-I). (Type species: *B. belone* (Chun, 1906). 3 species in bathpelagic and bathyal zones (juveniles in epipelagic and mesopelagic) of all oceans, except the Arctic Ocean. Mantle length up to 54 (60?) cm.

14 (11). Several pairs of hooks in middle parts of arms. Club hooks with one tooth, without aperture, covered by a hood (as in *Galiteuthis*). One tubercle with 4-6 spines in each mantle-funnel fusion site; one conical tubercle on anterior edge of mantle in the middle of dorsal side (in adults all these tubercles are almost inconspicuous). Fin oval in juveniles and widely lanceolate in adults. Dorsal (middle) component of funnel organ with three finger-like papillae. Adult squids of giant size, mantle length to 200-225 cm. . . . .
. . . . . **Genus *Mesonychoteuthis* Robson, 1925**

One species: *M. hamiltoni* Robson, 1925 (Fig. 71 U-W). Antarctic (the young are found also in the notalian zone to the southern subtropical convergence) circumpolar bathypelagic species. Usual component of sperm whale food in the Antarctic. Leading member of the Antarctic teuthofauna by biomass.

15 (10). No hooks on club. Tail needle-like or narrowly conical. Fin lanceolate, longitudinally oval or egg-shaped. Adult females usually have photophores on arm ends. **16**

16 (19). Funnel valve present. Dorsal (middle) component of funnel organ with two triangular flaps, without median papilla. Large photophores on ends of 1st, 2nd or 3rd arms of adult females. Rings of large suckers in middle parts of arms with low rounded teeth. **17**

17 (18). 2 large dumb-bell-like photophores, each with a pair of round lenses, on the liver. Fin lanceolate (egg-shaped in juveniles), its anterior

edge do not pass beyond lateral sides of mantle, attached at the place of maximal width of lanceola or a little ahead of it. In adult specimens large arm suckers with small round teeth are suddenly replaced near the arm ends by small suckers with several sharp fang-like teeth on distal edge. Some greatly enlarged suckers in distal part of 3rd arm (to lesser degree in 2nd arms). A large elongated photophore on the ends of 3rd or first three arms in adult females. . . . .
. . . . . . **Genus *Megalocranchia* Pfeffer, 1912**

(= *Corynomma* Chun, 1906, *Ascoteuthis* Berry, 1920, *Carynoteuthis* G. Voss, 1960, *Phasmatopsis* auct., non Rochebrune) (Fig. 72 J-T). 2-3 mesobathypelagic species in tropical and subtropical waters of all oceans. Type species: *M. maxima* (Pfeffer, 1884). Mantle length up to 81 cm.

18 (17). No photophores on liver. Fin elongately lanceolate, in adults its anterior edges pass onto the lateral sides of mantle beyond site of maximal width of lanceola. No suckers with fang-like teeth on arm ends. No sharply enlarged suckers on arms. Large elongated photophore on ends of all arms in adult females. . . . .
. . . . **Genus *Egea* Joubin, 1933**

One species: **E. inermis Joubin, 1933** (= *Phasmatopsis lucifer* G. Voss, 1963, ?*Teuthowenia elongata* Sasaki, 1929) (Fig. 72 F-I). Tropical and subtropical Atlantic and Indo-West-Pacific. From epipelagic to bathypelagic zones. Mantle length to 42 cm.

19 (16). Funnel valve absent. Dorsal (middle) component of funnel organ with a median papilla. No photophores on arms nor on liver. Rings of large arm suckers smooth or indistinctly denticulate **20**

20 (21). Mantle in adults gelatinous (jelly-like). Tentacles autotomized. Arms short, weak, without conspicuously enlarged suckers in distal parts. Eyes directed somewhat forward. Funnel enormously large, covering entire underside of head. No cartilaginous tubercles on mantle-funnel fusion sites. Dorsal (middle) component of funnel organ with conical median papilla and two low triangular papillae on lateral limbs. Anterior edges of fins attached dorsally, not to sides of mantle. Posterior end of mantle is needle-like. . . .
. . . . **Genus *Taonius* Steenstrup, 1861**

(= *Desmoteuthis* Verrill, 1881, ?*Phasmatopsis* Rochebrune, 1884) (Fig. 71 A-E). One species: **T. pavo (LeSueur, 1821).** Widely distributed, but rare tropical-subtropical species, reaches boreal and notalian waters. Supposedly mesopelagic squid. Mantle length to 40-45 cm. Taxonomic status somewhat uncertain.

21 (20). Mantle coriaceous, firm. Arms strong, several considerably enlarged suckers in distal parts of lateral arms. Tentacles not autotomized. Eyes look aside. Funnel of normal size. One or several cartilaginous tubercles on mantle-funnel fusion sites. Dorsal (middle) component of funnel organ with three conical or finger-like papillae. In juveniles and adults, anterior edges of fins are attached to lateral sides of mantle far ahead of the site of maximal width of lanceola. Posterior end of gladius narrowly conical, but not needle-like. A large photophore on ends of all arms in adult females. . . . . . **Genus *Teuthowenia* Chun, 1906**

(= *Desmoteuthis* Verrill, 1881, part, *Verrilliteuthis* Berry, 1916, *Anomalocranchia* Robson, 1924) (Fig. 70 J-R). Type species: *T. megalops* (Prosch, 1849). Two species. Boreal and northern subtropical Atlantic, southern subtropical and notalian areas of the Atlantic, Indian Ocean and southwestern Pacific. Mesopelagic and bathypelagic zones, juveniles in epipelagic. Mantle length to 38 cm.

22 (9). Mantle not attenuated into a long tail, end of gladius either widely conical or lanceola reduced and does not define the form of posterior end of body. Fins short, semicircular, kidney-, paddle- or tongue-shaped, attached to postero-lateral sides of lanceola or directly to the mantle. No photophores on arm ends in mature females. Funnel valve absent. **23**

23 (28). Lanceola present. Fins attached to postero-lateral sides of lanceola. Mantle obtusely rounded or acuminated posteriorly. Snout and eye stalks in larvae short or of moderate length. . . . **24**

24 (27). Fins semicircular or kidney-shaped, each fin not so wide as long. Posterior end of gladius passes beyond end of mantle. Lanceola big, rhomboidal. 2 eye photophores. Funnel reaches base of 4th arms. **25**

25 (26). Fins semicircular or semi-elliptical, together forming an almost regular circle. Fins pass beyond posterior end of gladius and divided by a narrow slit or connected with each other. Arms of moderate length. Several enlarged suckers on distal parts of lateral arms. Rings of large arm suckers with low conical or turret-shaped teeth. Dorsal (middle) component of funnel organ with three conical or finger-like papillae. Tentacles not autotomized. Sometimes there are small tubercles on mantle-funnel fusion sites. Eyes of larvae on long stalks . . . .

. . . . **Genus *Ligurialla* Issel, 1908** (= *Vossoteuthis* Nesis, 1974) (fig. 70 F-I). Type species: *L. podophtalma* Issel, 1908. 1-3 mesopelagic species in tropical, subtropical and notalian regions of the Atlantic, Indian Ocean, and western Pacific. Mantle length to 24 cm.

26 (25). Fins kidney-shaped, not passing beyond the posterior end of gladius and not close to one another. Arms very short, without enlarged suckers. Arm sucker rings smooth or slightly denticulate. Dorsal (middle) component of funnel organ with a small median papilla and two wide triangular flaps on lateral limbs. Tentacles often autotomized in adults. No tubercles on mantle-funnel fusion sites. Eyes of larvae on short stalks . . . . **Genus *Sandalops* Chun, 1906** (= *Uranoteuthis* Lu & Clarke, 1974). One species: ***S. melancholicus* Chun, 1906** (= *Uranoteuthis bilucifer* Lu & Clarke, 1974) (Fig. 72 A-E). Tropical and subtropical Atlantic (mainly in cen-

tral waters) and Indo-West-Pacific. Mesopelagic and bathypelagic, larvae and juveniles sometimes found in lower epipelagic zone. Mantle length to 11 cm.

27 (24). Fins paddle- or tongue-shaped, each fin much wider than long. Posterior end of mantle bent down and may slightly pass beyond posterior end of gladius or not reaching it. Lanceola small, short and narrow. Dorsal (middle) component of funnel organ with three conical papillae. One large oval or triangular photophore on ventral side of eyeball. Funnel enormously large, covering entire under side of head and passing beyond the bases of 4th arms . . . .

. . . . **Genus *Helicocranchia* Massy, 1907** (= *Hensenioteuthis* Pfeffer, 1900, *Ascocranchia* G. Voss, 1962) (Fig. 70 A-E). Type species: *H. pfefferi* Massy, 1907. 3 species in epipelagic (juveniles) and mesopelagic zones of tropical and subtropical waters. Mantle length to 8 cm.

28 (23). Lanceola reduced. Posterior end of mantle widely rounded. Paddle-shaped fins directly at-

Fig. 70.

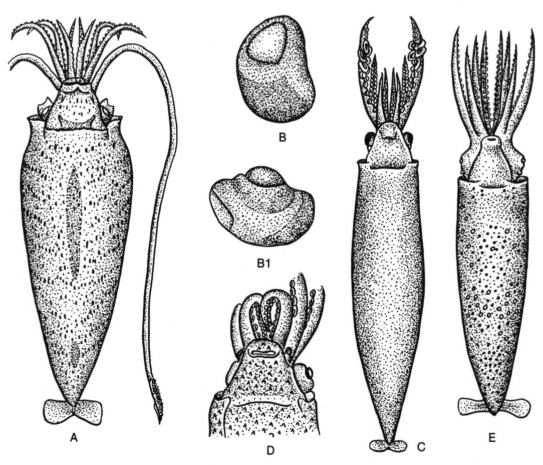

266

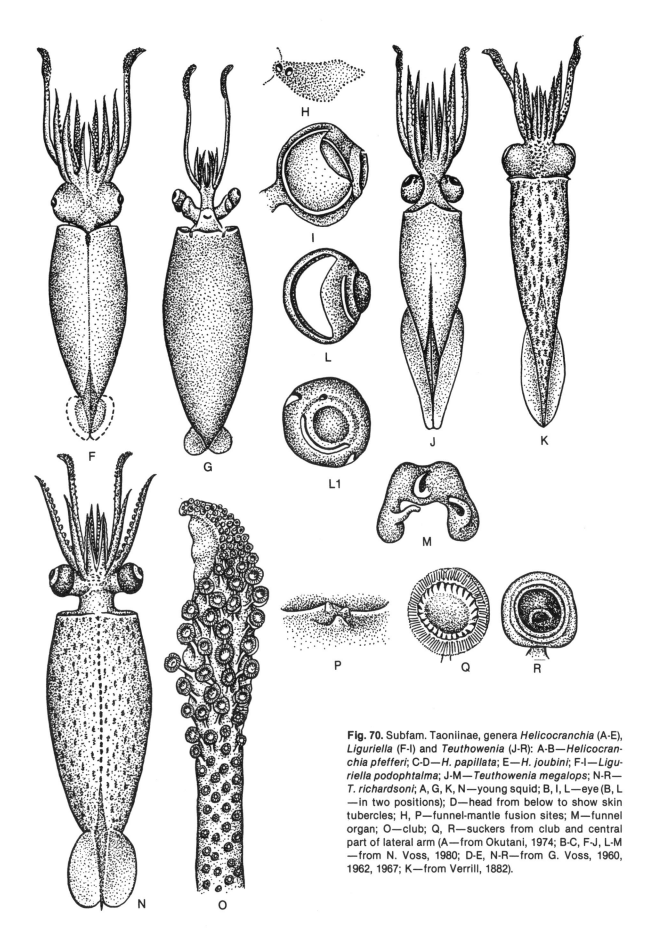

Fig. 70. Subfam. Taoniinae, genera *Helicocranchia* (A-E), *Liguriella* (F-I) and *Teuthowenia* (J-R): A-B—*Helicocranchia pfefferi*; C-D—*H. papillata*; E—*H. joubini*; F-I—*Liguriella podophtalma*; J-M—*Teuthowenia megalops*; N-R— *T. richardsoni*; A, G, K, N—young squid; B, I, L—eye (B, L —in two positions); D—head from below to show skin tubercles; H, P—funnel-mantle fusion sites; M—funnel organ; O—club; Q, R—suckers from club and central part of lateral arm (A—from Okutani, 1974; B-C, F-J, L-M —from N. Voss, 1980; D-E, N-R—from G. Voss, 1960, 1962, 1967; K—from Verrill, 1882).

Fig. 71.

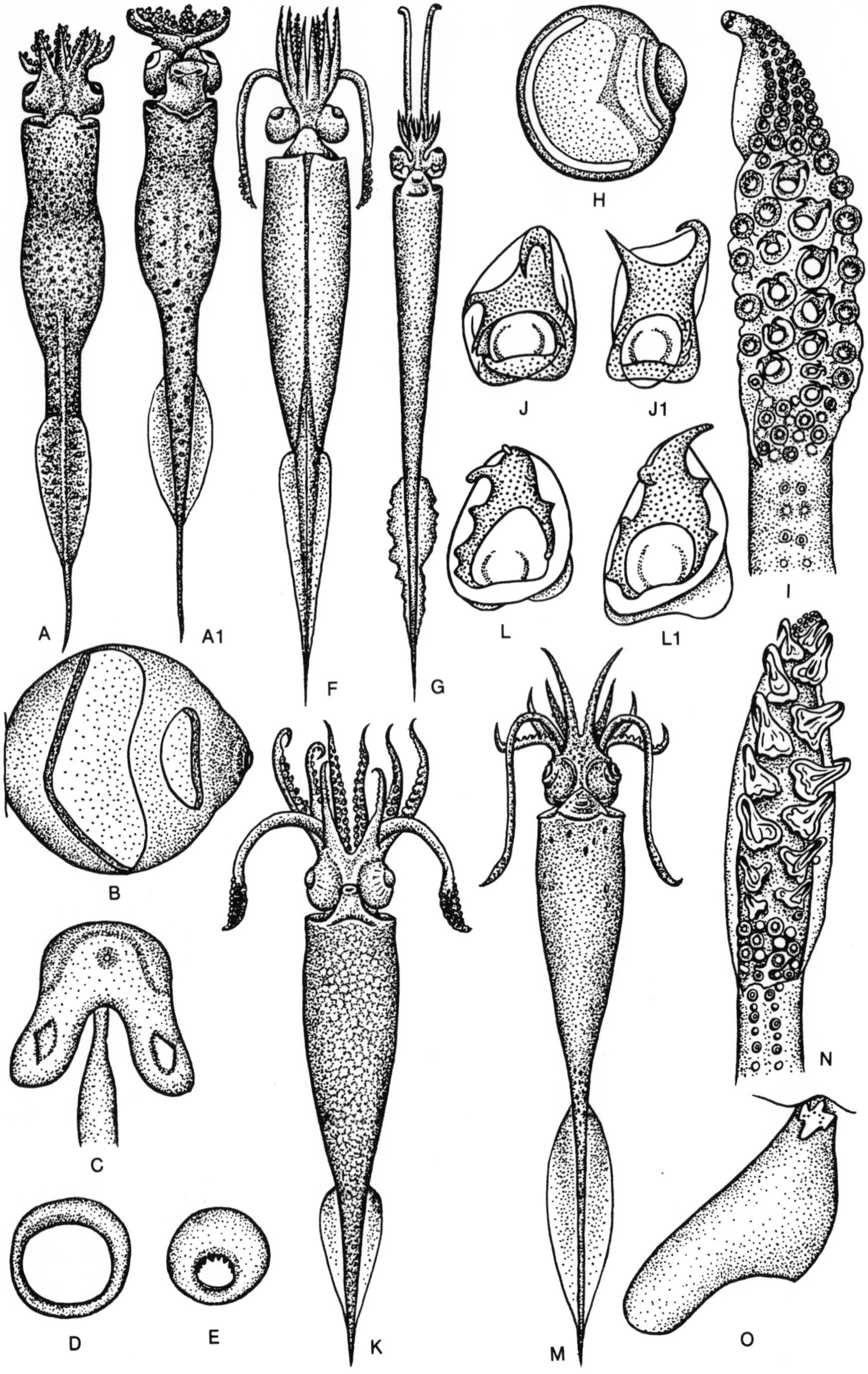

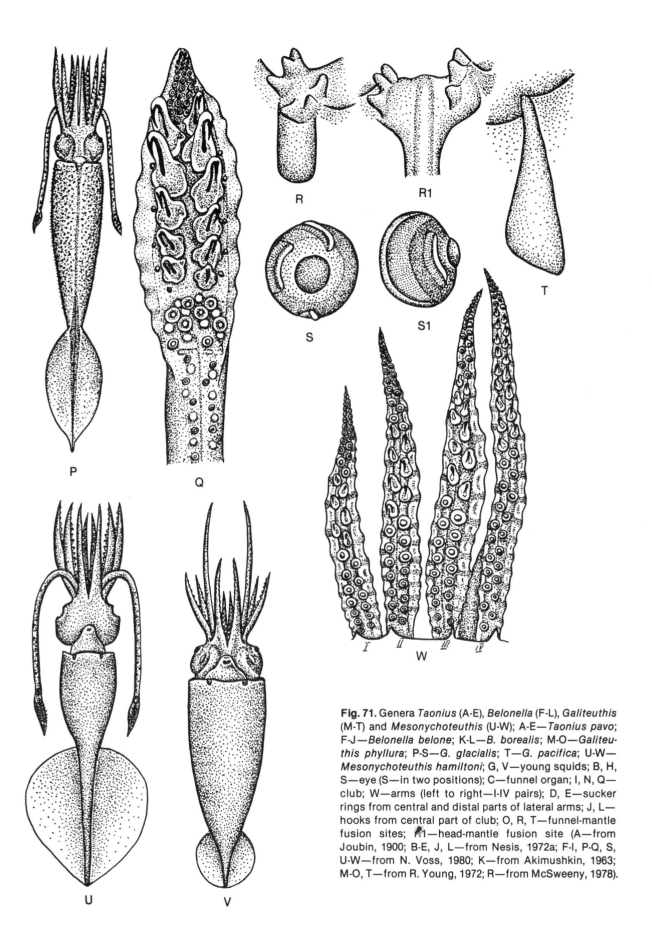

Fig. 71. Genera *Taonius* (A-E), *Belonella* (F-L), *Galiteuthis* (M-T) and *Mesonychoteuthis* (U-W); A-E—*Taonius pavo*; F-J—*Belonella belone*; K-L—*B. borealis*; M-O—*Galiteuthis phyllura*; P-S—*G. glacialis*; T—*G. pacifica*; U-W—*Mesonychoteuthis hamiltoni*; G, V—young squids; B, H, S—eye (S—in two positions); C—funnel organ; I, N, Q—club; W—arms (left to right—I-IV pairs); D, E—sucker rings from central and distal parts of lateral arms; J, L—hooks from central part of club; O, R, T—funnel-mantle fusion sites; M1—head-mantle fusion site (A—from Joubin, 1900; B-E, J, L—from Nesis, 1972a; F-I, P-Q, S, U-W—from N. Voss, 1980; K—from Akimushkin, 1963; M-O, T—from R. Young, 1972; R—from McSweeny, 1978).

269

tached to the mantle ahead of its posterior end and fairly separated from one another. Mantle cylindrical, translucent. One large semilunar photophore on ventral side of eyeball. Dorsal (middle) component of funnel organ without a median papilla, but with two conical papillae on lateral limbs. Larvae with extremely long eye stalks and long slender muzzle, adults with sessile eyes . . . . .
. . . . **Genus *Bathothauma* Chun, 1906**
(= *Leucocranchia* Joubin, 1912). One species: ***B. lyromma* Chun, 1906** (= *Leucocranchia pfefferi* Joubin, 1912) (Fig. 72 U-W). Tropical-subtropical cosmopolitan meso-bathy-pelagic species (adults live in bathypelagic). Mantle length to 20 cm.

Key to species of the genus *Liocranchia*

1 (2). A row of cartilaginous tubercles reaching the beginning of fin running along the dorsal median line above gladius. 14 photophores on eyeball: 6 encircling the pupil, 7 in an arc on ventral side of eyeball and 1 between them. A large photophore on ends of 3rd arms in mature females. Ends of 3rd arms of mature males are attenuated and bear 4-8 rows of very small suckers
. . . .***L. reinhardti* (Steenstrup, 1856)**
(= *L. intermedia* Robson, 1924, *Fusocranchia alpha* Joubin, 1920) (Fig. 69 D-G). Tropical-subtropical cosmopolitan meso-bathypelagic species. Common and numerous.
2 (1). No cartilaginous tubercles along dorsal median line. 4 photophores in an arc on eyeball. Mature specimens not described . . . .
. . . .***L. valdiviae* Chun, 1906**
Indo-Pacific tropical bathypelagic species, larvae and juveniles in epipelagic and mesopelagic zones.
Note: The key does not include *L. gardineri* Robson, 1921, described from a larva from the western Indian Ocean.

Key to species of the genus *Leachia*

This key is preliminary, since the complete cycle of development is described as yet only for one species — *L. pacifica*.
1 (6). No photophores on ends of 3rd arms in mature females. Eyes sessile at a mantle length up to more than 4 cm . . . .

. . . .**Subgenus *Leachia* (s. str.). . .2**
2 (5). Length of ventral hyaline stripes with cartilaginous tubercles comprises 20-33% of mantle length **3**
3 (4). 6 eye photophores at a mantle length 7-9 cm: 5 in outer row (at a mantle length 4-6 cm there are 4 of them), 1 near pupil . . . .
. . .***L. (L.) ellipsoptera* Adams & Reeve, 1845**
(= *L. cyclura* auct., part) (Fig. 69 H,I). Tropical and Northern subtropical Atlantic.
4 (3). 8 eye photophores at a mantle length 6-7 cm: 5 in outer row and 3 near the pupil . . . .
. . . .***L. (L.) cyclura* LeSueur, 1821**
[= *L. eschscholtzi* (Rathke, 1835), *L. guttata* (Grant, 1835)]. Tropical and southern subtropical Indo-West-Pacific.
5 (2). Length of ventral hyaline stripes with cartilaginous tubercles comprises 40-60% of the mantle length. 8 eye photophores at a mantle length 8.5-10 cm . . . .***L. (L.)* sp. A Nesis**
(= *L. eschscholtzi* of Pfeffer, 1912: p. 655-656, Taf. 47, fig. 12-14, non Rathke) (Fig. 69 J). Southwestern Atlantic (eastward of Argentina) and (?) New Zealand area. Probably a southern peripheral species.
6 (1). A large elongated photophore on ends of 3rd arms in mature females (Fig. 69 N). Eyes in larvae and juveniles are stalked at a mantle length up to 5-10 cm . . . .
.**Subgenus *Pyrgopsis* Rochebrune, 1884. . .7**
7 (14). Photophores on 3rd arms of female develop at a mantle length of 4-12 cm or more . .**8**
8 (13). Length of ventral hyaline stripes with cartilaginous tubercles up to 20% of mantle length. Fin width-to-length ratio of 1.2-1.6 . . . .**9**
9 (10). Fin with convex anterior end almost straight posterior edge, the site of maximal width of fin situated conspicuously farther of the middle of its length. Hyaline stripes with cartilaginous tubercles straight, length is about 14% of mantle length . . . . . .***L. (P.) atlantica* (Degner, 1925)**
(= ?*Pyrgopsis* sp. Adam, 1960, ?*P. lemur* Mercer, 1966, non Berry) (Fig. 69 K-M). Tropical and subtropical Atlantic, northward reaches the area to the south of Great Newfoundland Bank and Bay of Biscay.
10 (9). Fin round or transversely oval, maximal width of fin approximately in the middle of its length **11**
11 (12). Fin transversely oval, its width-to-length ratio is 1.3-1.6, usually 1.35-1.5. Hyaline stripes with cartilaginous tubercles in large specimens

distinctly bent in anterior part: the second (counting from the edge of mantle) tubercle shifted ventrally to the others (it is conspicuous at a mantle length 6-7 cm, but in specimens from California Current sometimes as early as at 2 cm). Length of stripes 12-17% of mantle length. . . . .*L. (P.) pacifica* (Issel, 1908)

(= *L. dislocata* Young, 1972, ?*Pyrgopsis schnehageni* Pfeffer, 1884, ?*P. lemur* Berry, 1920) (Fig. 69 O-Q). Tropical-subtropical cosmopolitan species.

12 (11). Fin almost round, its width-to-length ratio is 1.2-1.3. Hyaline stripes with cartilaginous tubercles straight, length about 20% of mantle length. . . . .*L. (P.) sp. B Nesis*

(= ?*P. lemur* of Voss, 1958, non Berry). Tropical Atlantic.

13 (8). Length of ventral hyaline stripes with cartilaginous tubercles 25-50% of mantle length. Fin widely oval, fin width-to-length ratio of 1.6-1.9. The site of maximal width of fin somewhat farther from the middle of its length. . . . .
. . .*L. (P.) rynchophorus* (Rochebrune, 1884)

(= *P. pacifica* Massy, 1916, Robson, 1924, Allan, 1945, G. Voss, 1967, non Issel) (Fig. 69 R). Southern subtropical species found from southern Africa to New Zealand.

14 (7). Photophores on ends of 3rd arms developed at a mantle length of 3.5-4 cm. . . . .
. . . .*L. (P). sp. C Nesis*
Tropical Indian Ocean.

Key to species of the genus *Helicocranchia*

1 (2). Fin paddle-shaped with narrow base and widened distally. Bases of fins connected by a narrow membrane distally to the end of gladius. Mantle surface smooth. Suckers in middle part of 3rd arms in females not enlarged. Arm sucker rings with a few low rounded teeth distally, proximal edge smooth. Color light with scarce large oval, orange or dark-brown chromatophores forming transverse rows on sides and ventral part of mantle. No small black chromatophores. . . . .
. . . .*H. pfefferi* Massy, 1907

(= *H. beebei* Robson, 1948) (Fig. 70 A,B). Tropical-subtropical cosmopolitan mesopelagic species (juveniles live in the epipelagic zone and even at the surface, the adults in mesopelagic and bathypelagic).

2 (1). Fins tongue-like, of subequal width at the base and in the middle, set on lanceola of gladius,

posterior edges of both fins fused. Suckers in middle part of 3rd arms in females considerably larger than on other arms, with smooth rings. Sucker rings of other arms with small denticles. Color reddish-brown **3**

3 (4). Mantle thick, coriaceous, muscular. Surface of mantle (particularly in anterior part) and funnel beset by numerous small, sharp cuticular papillae . . . .*H. papillata* (Voss, 1960)

(= ?*Hensenioteuthis* Pfeffer, 1912, *Teuthowenia megalops* Joubin, 1933, non Prosch) (Fig. 70 C,D). Central waters of northern Atlantic. Mesopelagic and bathypelagic.

4 (3). Mantle thin, semigelatinous, smooth or almost smooth. Color reddish-brown or brick-red with a few light oval spots and numerous very small almost black points scattered over entire surface of mantle. . . . . . .*H. joubini* (Voss, 1962)

(Fig. 70 E). Tropical and subtropical Atlantic, southwestern Pacific. Mesopelagic and bathypelagic.

Key to species of the genus *Teuthowenia*

1 (2). One tiny cartilaginous tubercle in each mantle-funnel fusion site. . . . .
. . . .*T. megalops* (Prosch, 1849)

[= *Desmoteuthis hyperborea* (Steenstrup, 1856), *D. tenera* Verrill, 1881, *D. thori* Degner, 1925, *Verrilliteuthis megalops* auct. part, *Megalocranchia megalops* auct., *Desmoteuthis megalops* auct.] (Fig. 70 J-M). A North Atlantic boreal-subtropical species; from southwestern Greenland, Denmark Strait, Faeroe-Iceland and Faeroe-Shetland Ridges to the Sargasso Sea and Canary Islands. Rarely found in the Caribbean Sea (sterile zone of expatriation), absent in Norwegian, North and Mediterranean Seas. Common and numerous squid species.

2 (1). 2-5 conical cartilaginous tubercles (one in juveniles) in the mantle-funnel fusion sites. . . . . . .
. . . .*T. richardsoni* (Dell, 1959)

(= ?*Desmoteuthis pellucida* Chun, 1910, ?*Anomalocranchia impennis* Robson, 1924, *Megalocranchia megalops australis* G. Voss, 1967) (Fig. 70 N-R). A notalian-southern subtropical species: Southern Atlantic, southern Indian Ocean and southwestern Pacific eastward at least to New Zealand and Kermadec Islands. Probably the proper name for this species should be *T. pellucida* Chun.

Fig. 72.

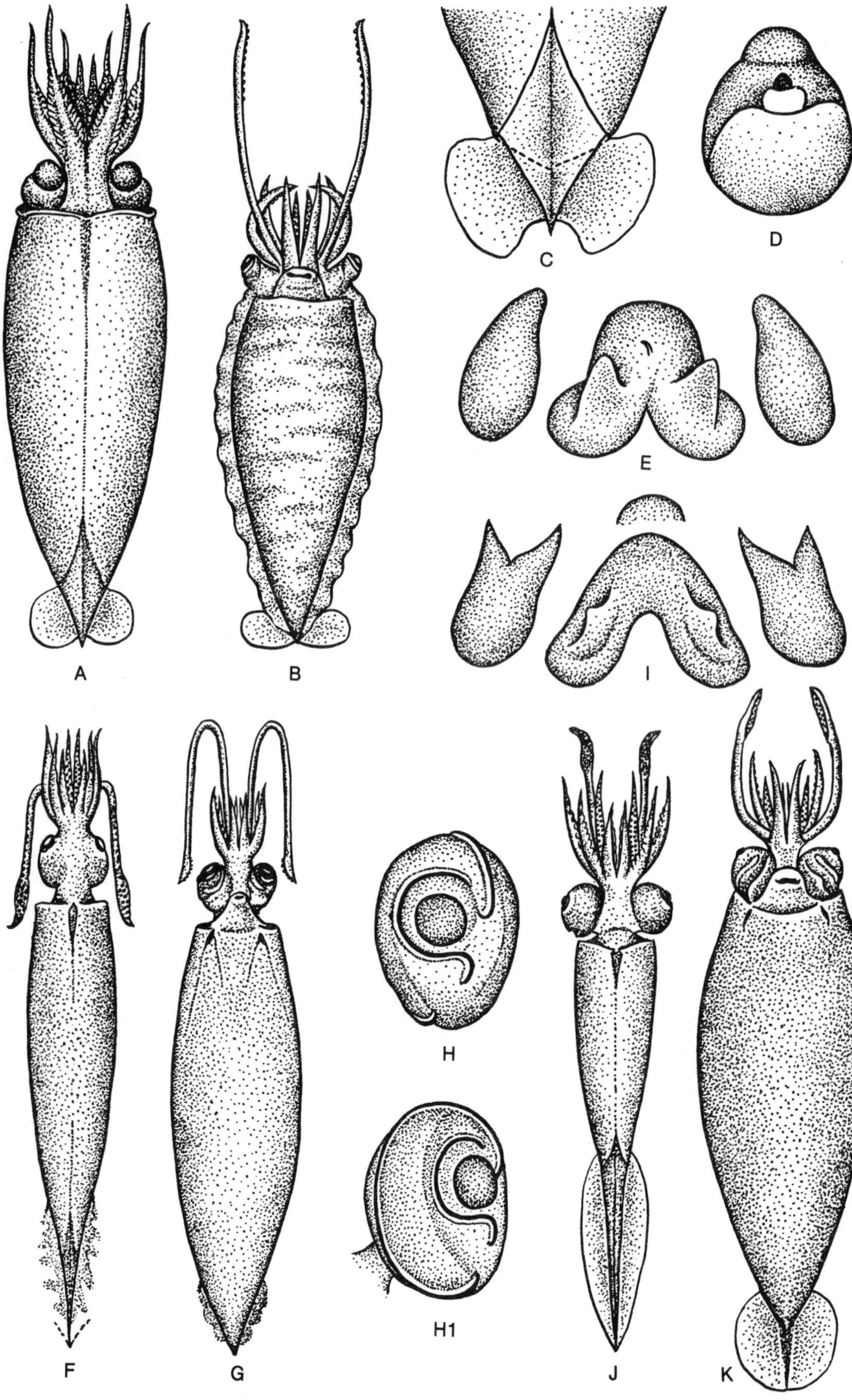

A

B

C

D

E

I

F

G

H

H1

J

K

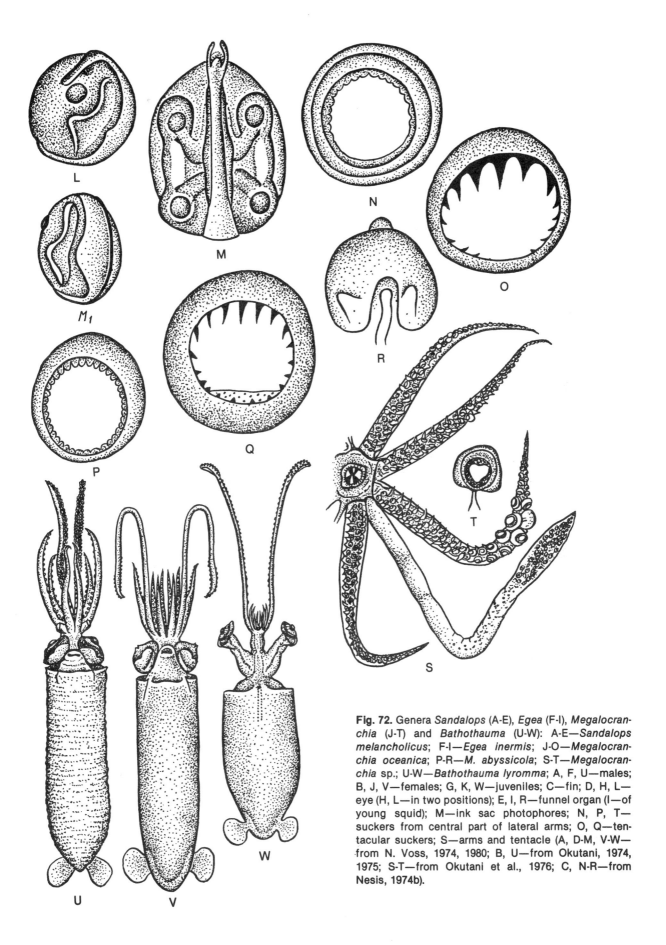

Fig. 72. Genera *Sandalops* (A-E), *Egea* (F-I), *Megalocranchia* (J-T) and *Bathothauma* (U-W): A-E—*Sandalops melancholicus*; F-I—*Egea inermis*; J-O—*Megalocranchia oceanica*; P-R—*M. abyssicola*; S-T—*Megalocranchia* sp.; U-W—*Bathothauma lyromma*; A, F, U—males; B, J, V—females; G, K, W—juveniles; C—fin; D, H, L—eye (H, L—in two positions); E, I, R—funnel organ (I—of young squid); M—ink sac photophores; N, P, T—suckers from central part of lateral arms; O, Q—tentacular suckers; S—arms and tentacle (A, D-M, V-W—from N. Voss, 1974, 1980; B, U—from Okutani, 1974, 1975; S-T—from Okutani et al., 1976; C, N-R—from Nesis, 1974b).

Key to species of the genus *Liguriella*

1 (2). Rings of large club suckers distally with 5-7 long sharp teeth. One or two small conical tubercles on each mantle-funnel fusion site......
..................***L. podophtalma* Issel, 1908**
(= *Vossoteuthis pellucida* Nesis 1974, non Chun 1910, "*Bathothauma lyromma*" Allan, 1940, non Chun, 1906) (Fig. 70 F-I). Southern subtropical-notalian mesopelagic species, distributed in the southern Atlantic and Pacific, in the Tasman Sea and off New Zealand.

2 (1). Rings of large club suckers with about 15-25 sharp conical teeth over the entire ring (higher on distal ridge).....................**3**

3 (4). About 25 low conical teeth on large club suckers............***L. pardus* (Berry, 1916)**
Southern subtropical probably mesopelagic species found off Kermadec Islands and in the Bismarck Sea. Taxonomic position is uncertain.

4 (3). About 15 high sharp teeth on large club suckers. No tubercles in the mantle-funnel fusion sites..................***Liguriella* sp. Nesis**
(= "*Teuthowenia megalops*" of Morales & Guerra, 1977, non Prosch). Northwestern Africa seawards of Cape Verde (Dakar), Cape Blanc and Cape Timiris. Mesopelagic. Status of this species is unclear, may be it belongs to *Teuthowenia*.

Larvae of unidentified species of *Liguriella* were found in the northern central water of the western Pacific and in the Philippine Sea (Nesis, 1974b).

Key to species of the genus *Belonella*

1 (4). Protective membranes of arms narrow, their width is subequal to arm sucker diameter..**2**

2 (3). Two, rarely one, hook-like teeth on the largest central club suckers, no small teeth on their sides..........***B. belone* (Chun, 1906)**
(= *B. pacifica pacifica* Nesis, 1972, *Galiteuthis triluminosa* Lu & Clarke, 1974, *Taonius pavo* auct., non LeSueur) (Fig. 71 F-J). Tropical and subtropical Atlantic, tropical Indian and Pacific Ocean; in the latter from Kyushu to Tonga. Bathypelagic and bathyal, the young usually live in the mesopelagic zone.

3 (2). One or two hook-like teeth on the largest central club suckers, 2-3 small teeth lateral on each side of ring......***B. borealis* Nesis, 1972**
(= *Taonius pavo* Akimushkin, 1963, non LeSueur, *B. pacifica borealis* Nesis, 1972a) (Fig. 71 K,L). A Pacific boreal species: from the Bering Sea to eastern Honshu and southern California, also in the Sea of Okhotsk. Mesopelagic and bathypelagic, bathyal and abyssal.

4 (1). Protective membranes of arms wide, subequal to arm width. On the largest central club suckers one tooth is much larger than the others, laterally there are 1-5 small teeth.............
..................***Belonella* sp. Nesis, 1974a**
Notalian-Antarctic circumglobal bathypelagic and bathyal species, found in the Scotia Sea, Indian Ocean sector of the Antarctic, off the Antipodes Islands and westward of southern Chile.

Key to species of the genus *Galiteuthis*

1 (6). Cartilaginous tubercles present on mantle-funnel and sometimes also on mantle-head fusion sites......................................**2**

2 (3). 2-4 small conical tubercles on the mantle-funnel fusion sites (difficult to see in adults, but easily felt by touch). No tubercles on dorsal side of mantle near the mantle-head fusion. Arm suckers with smooth rings. Mantle surface smooth. Anterior eye photophore narrow, rod-like................***G. armata* Joubin, 1898**
[= ?*Zygocranchia zygaena* (Vérany, 1851), *Taonidium pfefferi* Russell, 1909, *G. suhmi* Chun, 1910, non Hoyle, 1885]. Tropical and northern subtropical Atlantic, from the Bay of Biscay to the Gulf of Guinea and Straits of Florida, Mediterranean Sea. Meso-bathypelagic and benthic-bathyal species.

***G. phyllura* Berry, 1911** (= *Crystalloteuthis beringiana* Sasaki, 1920) (Fig. 71 M-O). A boreal Pacific meso-bathypelagic and benthic-bathyal species, distributed from Bering Sea to northern Japan and Baja California and in the Sea of Okhotsk. Probably reaching gigantic size, mantle length to about 2.7 m.

Difference between the Atlantic and Pacific species is very small and needs confirmation based on larger material.

3 (2). Tubercles on mantle-funnel fusion sites are large, multipointed........................**4**

4 (5). One tubercle with several (5-6 in adults) points on mantle-funnel fusion sites. No tubercles on dorsal side of mantle at the mantle-head fusion site. Arm suckers with smooth rings. Mantle surface smooth.........***G. suhmi* (Hoyle, 1885)**
(= *Taonidium suhmi* Hoyle, 1885, non 1912). Southern subtropical-notalian circumglobal meso-bathypelagic species.

5 (4). Two three-pointed cartilaginous tubercles on mantle-funnel fusion sites, these tubercles close to each other and form a short ridge. On mantle-head fusion site two small three-pointed tubercles on both sides of anterior end of gladius. Arm sucker rings distally with low rounded teeth. Mantle surface, especially in anterior part, rough to touch, "shagreen" due to numerous microscopic cuticular spines . . . . **G. glacialis (Chun, 1906)**

(= *Teuthowenia antarctica* Chun, 1910, *Crystalloteuthis glacialis* Chun, 1906, *G. aspera* Filippova, 1972, ?*Taonidium suhmi* Hoyle, 1912, non 1885) (Fig. 71 P-S). Antarctic circumpolar meso-bathypelagic species, ascending to lower epipelagic. One of the most common squids in the Antarctic. Northward of the Antarctic convergence *G. glacialis* found only in places where great masses of Antarctic intermediate waters flow out and drift to the north.

6 (1). No cartilaginous tubercles on mantle-funnel and mantle-head fusion sites. Arm sucker rings smooth. Mantle surface smooth. Anterior eye photophore round or oval . . . . **G. pacifica (Robson, 1948)**

(= *Taonidium pacificum* Robson, 1948) (Fig. 71 T). Tropical Indo-Pacific species, distributed from western Indian Ocean to New Caledonia, southern California and northern Chile. Meso-bathypelagic species, recorded also in the abyssopelagic zone.

Key to species of the genus *Megalocranchia*

1 (4). Rings of large club suckers with 6-12 close together large teeth on distal edge of ring, proximal edge with small teeth 2

2 (3). Rings of large club suckers with 10-12 large teeth on distal edge, proximally with small teeth. Large suckers of 3rd arms with close together regular turret-shaped teeth . . . . **M. abyssicola (Goodrich, 1896)**

(= ?*Megalocranchia maxima* Pfeffer, 1884, *Corynomma speculator* Chun, 1910, part, ?*Helicocranchia fisheri* Berry, 1909, *M. maxima* Sasaki, 1929) (Fig. 72 P-R). Indo-Pacific tropical-subtropical meso-bathypelagic species (often ascending to lower epipelagic zone).

3 (2). Rings of large club suckers with 6-8 large teeth on distal edge, proximally with small teeth. Large suckers of 3rd arm with irregular low rounded teeth . . . . **M. oceanica (Voss, 1960)**

(= *Corynomma speculator* Chun, 1910, part, ?*Teuthowenia (Ascoteuthis) corona* Berry, 1920, *M. abyssicola* Joubin, 1924, non Goodrich, 1896, *Carynoteuthis oceanica* G. Voss, 1960, ?*Phasmatopsis cymoctypus* Clarke, 1962, non Rochebrune, 1884) (Fig. 72 J-O). Atlantic tropical-subtropical (mainly bi-central) meso-bathypelagic species (larvae and juveniles live also in epipelagic zone).

4 (1). Rings of large club suckers with 15-18 teeth over the entire perimeter, of which 2-3 distal teeth very wide and set far apart, the rest narrower and closer together. Large suckers of 3rd arms with about 10 turret-shaped teeth . . . . **Megalocranchia sp. Nesis** (Fig. 72 S,T). Pacific Ocean off northeastern Honshu and in the Kuroshio Current. Status of this species is unclear.

2.3. Order Vampyromorpha

Medium size animals (total length up to 37.5 cm, mantle length up to 11-13 cm). Tissues gelatinous. Widely conical mantle is fused with the wide head in occipital area without nuchal constriction. Two tongue-shaped fins are present in posterior part of mantle. Mantle aperture wide, reaching the level of the center of eye. Eyes large, of oegopsid type, without sinus. Arms short, connected by a deep web, with one row of suckers, starting far from arm base. Suckers without chitinous rings, sessile in the middle and stalked in distal part of arms. Two rows of short cirri (a pair between each two suckers) on both sides of suckers. Arm ends slender, attenuated, devoid of suckers; the cirri begin proximal to the first sucker and reaching to arm ends, at the very end they fuse into a membrane. A pair of very long, thin, filiform sensitive filaments are present on dorsal side of body between bases of 1st and 2nd arms, may be completely retracted into special pockets. These are tactile sense organs, but they are homologous to the squid tentacles. Statocysts, olfactory papillae and parolfactory vesicles are present. Two large composite photophores of facet structure are located dorsally in posterior part of mantle on sides of midline behind the fins. Numerous microscopic small photophore are scattered on the surface (mainly ventral) of the mantle, head and on fins. On the dorsal side of head behind the eyes photophores form two oval spots.

No buccal membrane. Funnel is almost entirely embedded in the tissue of ventral side of head. Funnel valve present. Funnel organ looks like two small bolsters. There is a primitive mantle-and-funnel locking apparatus. Gladius slender, transparent, very wide, gradually narrowing posteriorly. No median septa in the mantle cavity. Radula well developed, teeth are all unicuspid. Ink sac absent. Crop and salivary glands are small. Blind sac of the stomach (cecum) is not coiled spirally. Gills well developed. Renal sacs are fully separated. Stellate ganglion is rudimentary, no giant fibers.

Males and females are of subequal size. No hectocotylization. Penis is separated from the Needham sac. Both oviducts are developed, their efferent openings are widened and resembles the big suckers. No nidamental or accessory nidamental glands. Two seminal receptacles present on the head of female anterior to the eyes. Eggs are large, 3-4 mm in diameter, shed singly into the water. The larvae resemble adult specimens, but they pass a long development with a change of fins: larval fins are positioned at the very end of body, behind the composite photophores, during growth the larval fins shorten and definitive fins appear ahead of these photophores, so that at a certain stage of development a juvenile has two pairs of fins. Then the larval fins are reduced and the definitive fins reach the final size.

Chromatophores are primitive, not able to extend or contract. Color of the body, head, and outer side of arms is dark-violet or dark-purple, inner side of arms is velvet black.

One family **Vampyroteuthidae**, one genus: *Vampyroteuthis* Chun, 1903 (= *Melanoteuthis* Joubin, 1912, *Hymenoteuthis* Berry, 1916, *Watasella* Sasaki, 1920, *Retroteuthis* Joubin, 1929, *Hansenoteuthis* Joubin, 1929, *Danateuthis* Joubin, 1929). One species: *V. infernalis* **Chun, 1903** (Fig. 73). Tropical-subtropical bathypelagic species, descending also to the abyssopelagic zone. Lives mainly at depths of 700-1500 m, but where the thermocline is rather shallow the juveniles sometimes may be found at depths 300-500 m. Not gregarious animals, not performing noticeable vertical migrations. Probably swim with their head down.

Reviews: Pickford, 1946, 1949, 1959.

2.4. Order Octopoda—Octopuses.

Animals from small to very large (*Octopus dofleini*—total length to 3-5 m). Body may be firm, muscular in coastal species or soft, gelatinous, even jelly-like in deep-water species. Mantle usually sac-like, widely fused with the head at occipital area. Mantle aperture wide, narrow or reduced. Mantle-funnel locking apparatus poorly developed or absent, in some species mantle fused with funnel. Mantle surface is smooth or with various tubercles, warts, cirri (often above the eyes). Fins may be present (one pair) or absent. Eyes are usually large, with closed cornea, with or without eyelids, sometimes reduced in size, or telescopic. Always with eight arms. Suckers in one or two rows, usually flattened, rarely spherical or fusiform, always without chitinous rings. Cirri on the sides of suckers (probably tactile organs) may be present or absent. Arms are often connected by a web (umbrella). The web plays a locomotory role (medusoid locomotion). in those forms with deep web. In many forms the web is poorly developed or absent. No sensitive filaments. Statocysts are well developed. No olfactory papilla, only an olfactory pit (rarely ridge). Luminous organs are present only in a few species and are simple concentrations of photogenic tissue. Chromatophores are of composite structure, they are able to extend and contract, but in some mostly deep-sea forms they are simple. Funnel is free or fused with head. Funnel valve present. Funnel organ is well developed, either a simple piece or divided into 2-4 parts. Buccal membrane absent. Visceral sac is not connected with the mantle on dorsal side, but is usually connected to the ventral side by a median mantle septum and muscle—the mantle adductor. Gladius is represented either by cartilaginous support of fins or is reduced to a pair of tiny rods or absent.

Radula, crop, posterior salivary glands and ink sac are usually well developed, of different structure but sometimes may be absent. Stomach is usually muscular, the blind sac of stomach (cecum) is well developed, usually not coiled spirally. Liver is large, as a rule positioned in front of stomach. Two halves of each gill are parallel and fused on both sides or resemble the segments of an orange. The circulatory system is not closed. Pericardial cavity is reduced. Renal sacs are separated. Brain is highly developed, concentrated, with distinct lobes. Optic lobes are usually small. Stellate ganglion is present, with an epistellar body—additional organ of photoreception. No giant nerve fibers.

Hectocotylus usually present, one of 3rd arms is usually modified. Either the end of arm or the whole arm is hectocotylized, in latter case it is developed in a special subcutaneous sac and breaks off from the male body at mating. Hectocotylus, as a rule, consists of an elongated spoon-shaped ligula and a finger-like calamus. Sometimes large suckers are present on some arms in males. Females have no seminal receptacles around the mouth, nor nidamental or accessory nidamental glands. Oviducts are paired or single (the left only). The spermatophores are inserted into the mantle cavity of female, the sperm penetrate the oviducts or even the ovary. The eggs range from very small to very large, elongated and provided with stalks. In benthic forms they are laid onto the bottom, females of many octopuses guard the eggs and care for them until all are hatched. The eggs of pelagic octopuses either develop inside the female's body (ovovivipary) or she carries them. Incubation period is usually long, in some forms up to a year. Development is either direct or with pelagic larval stage. The larvae resemble the adults. Two suborders, 11 families, about 40 genera, approximately 200 species.

Benthopelagic, benthic or pelagic animals, living from littoral and epipelagic to ultra-abyssal and abyssopelagic zones. Found from Arctic to Antarctic. They are, as a rule, solitary animals active during dusk and dawn or at night. Planktophagous, benthophagous or predators. Growth rate is high, most species reach sexual maturity at the age of one year or several months. Females of most species die after the first spawning. Some species of the family Octopodidae are of a high fishery importance.

Review: Robson, 1929, 1932.

Key to the families of the order Octopoda

1 (4). Fins present. Arms with cirri. Mantle aperture very narrow or reduced . . . .**Suborder Cirrata. . .2**

2 (3). Bell-like animals, mantle elongated, well developed. Umbrella thin, much thinner than arms, rarely (*Froekenia*) absent. Fins in the middle or at the posterior end of mantle. Funnel directed forward. Bentho-pelagic or pelagic animals . . . . . .

. . . .**Family Cirroteuthidae** (see subhead **2.4.1.1.**)

3 (2). Animals have the form of a thick flapjack, mantle very shortened and represents a "hump" above the extended arms. Umbrella thick, arms are incorporated in the it and project upward only like bolsters. Funnel directed rearward. Fins sitting "on top" behind the eyes. Benthic (suprabenthic) animals . . . . . . **Family Opisthoteuthidae**

One genus: *Opisthoteuthis* Verrill, 1883 (see subhead **2.4.1.2.**)

4 (1). No fins, no cirri on arms. Suckers in one or two rows. Mantle aperture narrow or (more often) wide . . . .**Suborder Incirrata. . .5**

5 (14). Body gelatinous or semigelatinous. Arm suckers in one row (or in one row within umbrella and in two rows in distal parts of arms). Mesopelagic and bathypelagic or benthic animals **6**

6 (11). Mantle aperture wide. Funnel not fused with mantle **7**

7 (10). Arm suckers in one row. Eye diameter not exceeding 25% of mantle length. Head width usually 1.5-2.5 times less than the mantle length. No hectocotylization or only tip of an arm in male modified, hectocotylus not broken off from the body at mating. Rhachidian (central) radula tooth multicuspid. Body usually semitransparent. Oceanic pelagic animals **8**

8 (9). Arms not longer than the mantle. Diameter of suckers 3-7% of mantle length. Eyes round or oval. Normal position of liver in front of stomach. Liver oval. Radula comb-like. Mantle semitranspatent, pigmented. with circumoral ring-like luminous organ in adult females . . . .

. . . .**Family Bolitaenidae** (see subhead **2.4.2.1.1.**)

9 (8). Arms in adults 2-3 times longer than mantle. Proximal suckers small, set widely apart, distal suckers very large and set close to one another, in adult specimens the suckers diameter 10-17% of mantle length. Eyes narrow, almost rectangular. Liver long, thin, acuminate posteriorly, positioned behind the stomach. Radula not comb-like. 1st and 2nd lateral radular teeth unicuspid. Mantle almost transparent and colorless. No luminous organs . . . .

. . . .**Family Vitreledonellidae**

One genus and species: *Vitreledonella richardi* Joubin, 1918 (see subhead **2.4.2.2.2.**)

10 (7). Arm suckers in one row within umbrella, then in two rows outside it and again in one row on the very tips. Eyes enormously large, eye diameter 33-40% of mantle length. Head width equals or exceeds mantle length. 3rd right arm in male completely hectocotylized, develops in a special sac under the eye and breaks off from the body at mating. Radula not comb-like, rhachidian tooth with three cusps. Tissues gelatinous but not transparent. Nerito-oceanic animals living at the bottom in the bathyal and in midwater mostly above slopes (juveniles may be also found far away from slopes)...........**Family Alloposidae**

One genus and species: *Alloposus mollis* **Verrill, 1880** (see subhead **2.4.2.3.1.**)

11 (6). Mantle fused with funnel, mantle aperture reduced to two slits on sides of head. Arms 1.5-3 times longer than the mantle. Funnel very long. Liver behind stomach. Radula comb-like. 3rd right arm hectocotylized, ligula very long, thin, calamus short.........................**12**

12 (13). Eyes telescopic, set close together on the "head crown" and directed upwards. Umbrella well developed. Funnel not fused ventrally with head. Body transparent, almost colorless, with gelatinous covering....**Family Amphitretidae**

One genus and species: *Amphitretus pelagicus* **Hoyle, 1885.** (see subhead **2.4.2.1.2.**)

13 (12). Eyes normal. Web short, thin. Funnel ventrally fused with head, only anterior funnel end free. Body semitransparent but with numerous chromatophores. Gelatinous covering absent..............**Family Idioctopodidae**

One genus and species: *Idioctopus gracilipes* **Taki, 1962** (see subhead **2.4.2.1.3.**)

14 (5). Body muscular, firm or soft to the touch but not gelatinous nor transparent. Suckers either in one or in two rows over the entire arm length. Benthic or epipelagic species..............**15**

15 (16). Benthic animals. Males and females are but slightly different in size. Only the end of 3rd arm hectocotylized in male, this arm develops normally and does not break off at mating. Eggs usually laid at the bottom. Mantle-funnel locking apparatus absent. Suckers in 1 or 2 rows........
.......................**Family Octopodidae**
(see subhead **2.4.2.2.1.**)

16 (15). Epipelagic (very rarely mesopelagic) animals. Males dwarf, many times smaller than females. Entire 3rd arm hectocotylized in male, hectocotylus develops in a special sac, so that immature male seems to have only 7 arms (conspicuous even in larvae). At mating hectocotylus breaks off from body and penetrates the mantle cavity of female. Females viviparous or carry the eggs on arms or in the shell. Mantle-funnel locking apparatus present. Suckers in 2 rows.....**17**

17 (18). Female secretes a thin ribbed calcareous shell wherein it sits and lays eggs. Tips of 1st arms of female with a wide, thin, very elastic lappet that secret shell. In a living octopus it may cover the whole shell from outside. Web very weakly developed. 3rd arms somewhat shorter than other arms. Posterior end of female's mantle slightly bent upwards. Skin smooth. No cephalic water pores. 3rd left arm in male hectocotylized, other arms are of subequal length.............
....................**Family Argonautidae**

One genus: *Argonauta* **Linné, 1758** (see subhead **2.4.2.3.4.**)

18 (17). Shell absent. Tips of 1st arms without lappet. Posterior end of mantle in female not bent upwards. 3rd right arm hectocotylized.......**19**

19 (20). 1st and 2nd arm connected by a wide web. Tips of 1st arms in adult females autotomized, so these arms are often considerably shorter than 2nd arms; they bear one row of suckers. 1st and 2nd arms in males and females are much longer than 3rd and 4th arms. Mantle ventrally smooth. 2 pairs of cephalic water pores at the bases of 1st and 4th arms. Eggs are incubated on 1st arms..........**Family Tremoctopodidae**

One genus: *Tremoctopus* **delle Chiaje, 1830** (see subhead **2.4.2.3.3.**)

20 (19). Web absent. 1st and 4th arms in males and females much longer than 2nd and 3rd arms. Arm tips not autotomized. Suckers in 2 rows up to the tips. Mantle of adult females ventrally with transverse ridges forming a reticular structure. One pair of cephalic water pores at the base of 4th arms. Females viviparous. .**Family Ocythoidae**

One genus and species: *Ocythoe tuberculata* **Rafinesque, 1814.** (see subhead **2.4.2.3.2.**)

2.4.1. Suborder Cirrata

Small or medium size, rarely large animals. Tissues gelatinous, jelly-like. Mantle sac-like, widely oval. In the middle or at posterior end of body is a pair of paddle- or tongue-shaped fins supported by saddle-, U- or V-shaped cartilage (modified gladius). Arms with one row of flat or spherical, rarely fusiform, sessile or stalked suckers. Web, as a rule, very deep, often reaches the ends of arms and together with fins is the main locomotory organ. Web sectors are either usually connected directly with arms or are fused to one another and attached to arms by an intermediate thin web—a secondary umbrella. Funnel aperture very narrow, reduced to a circular slit around the funnel base, sometimes fully closed. Mantle-funnel propulsion is used only for flight from danger. Mantle-funnel locking apparatus absent. Funnel not fused with head. Eyes as a rule well developed but sometimes reduced. Chromatophores of primitive structure. Violet, purple, brown, chocolate tones dominate in coloration, some species are transparent.

Median mantle septum usually present. Radula, crop, ink sac are absent. Posterior salivary gland unpaired, shifted forward. Stomach muscular, blind sac (cecum) not coiled spirally. Gills small, with a few filaments.

Hectocotylus either absent or the ends of 1st arms are hecocotylized. In males of some species some suckers on all the arms are greatly enlarged. Only left oviduct developed. Eggs are large, in a coriaceous envelope, laid singly at the bottom. Fecundity is low. Development direct, without pelagic stage.

Deep-water benthic or benthopelagic animals. Only some species live always or from time to time in the pelagic zone. Planktophagous animals. 7-8 genera, 28-33 species.

Taxonomy of the suborder is in chaotic state. Most investigators distinguish 3 families: Cirroteuthidae, Stauroteuthidae and Opisthoteuthidae. Validity of the last family is doubtless, but as far as the first two are concerned, the same genera are attributed by different investigators to one and sometimes to another family. I attribute all Cirrata, except *Opisthoteuthis*, to the family Cirroteuthidae.

Most species of Cirrata are described by single, as a rule heavily damaged specimens, and sometimes only by fragments. Many species were identified doubtfully. The span of individual, age and sexual variations are unknown for majority of species. Therefore the keys to Cirrata should be used rather cautiously, taking into consideration that some characters used to differentiate the species may in fact turn out to be of no real taxonomic value.

2.4.1.1. Family Cirroteuthidae
(= Stauroteuthidae)

Medium size or large animals (overall length up to 1.3-1.5 m). Tissues gelatinous, jelly-like. Mantle conical or sac-like, usually poorly defined from head. The animal looks like a bell. Mantle aperture resembles a circular slit or closed. Funnel is directed forward. Fin cartilage saddle-shaped (like a butterfly with open wings) without anteriorly directed "horns," U- or V-shaped, buckle-shaped or semicircular (with "horns" directed forward). Web, as a rule, present, reaching or almost reaching the arm ends on one or both sides of each arm. It is thin, filmy, much thinner than arms. Neighboring sectors of umbrella sometimes fused with one another and attached to the arms by an intermediate web (secondary umbrella). Eyes well developed or reduced.

Longitudinal axis of the gill may be parallel or perpendicular to the body axis; in the first case the branchial filaments are positioned as usually one after another, in the second case they lie in the longitudinal body axis, so the gill resembles a half of an orange cut into two. No crop, but sometimes there is a particular outgrowth of esophagus ("third stomach"). Hectocotyus absent or (rarely) ends of 1st arms are modified.

Benthopelagic and benthic-bathyal (mainly lower bathyal) and abyssal (up to ultra-abyssal) animals; one genus is primarily abyssopelagic. 6-7 genera, 20-25 species.

Key to genera of the family Cirroteuthidae

1 (2). Eyes reduced, without lens and iris, embedded within gelatinous tissue and look like small dark balls. Arms are 3-4 times longer than body. Secondary web present in distal part of arms. Suckers in median and distal parts of arms modified, barrel-like, without openings, only with a small cup-like funnel. Fins large, exceeding the mantle width, located in the middle of body. Funnel long and thin. Fin cartilage saddle-shaped. Longitudinal gill axis parallel to longitudinal body axis...**Genus *Cirrothauma* Chun, 1911**

One species: *C. murrayi* Chun, 1911 (Fig. 74 A-C). Lives in bathypelagic and abyssopelagic zones or close to the bottom in the abyssal zone (1500-4500 m) in tropical and northern subtropical Atlantic and Caribbean Sea (Cayman Trench). Octopuses of this genus (species not identified) were captured in the abyssopelagic zone (2900-4100 m) of Scotia Sea and Southeastern Pacific off Southern Chile, in Japan Trench eastward and southward of Honshu

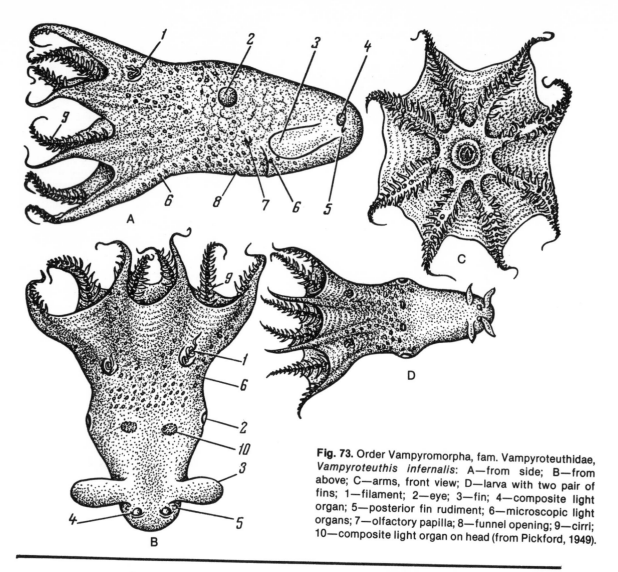

Fig. 73. Order Vampyromorpha, fam. Vampyroteuthidae, *Vampyroteuthis infernalis*: A—from side; B—from above; C—arms, front view; D—larva with two pair of fins; 1—filament; 2—eye; 3—fin; 4—composite light organ; 5—posterior fin rudiment; 6—microscopic light organs; 7—olfactory papilla; 8—funnel opening; 9—cirri; 10—composite light organ on head (from Pickford, 1949).

Fig. 74.

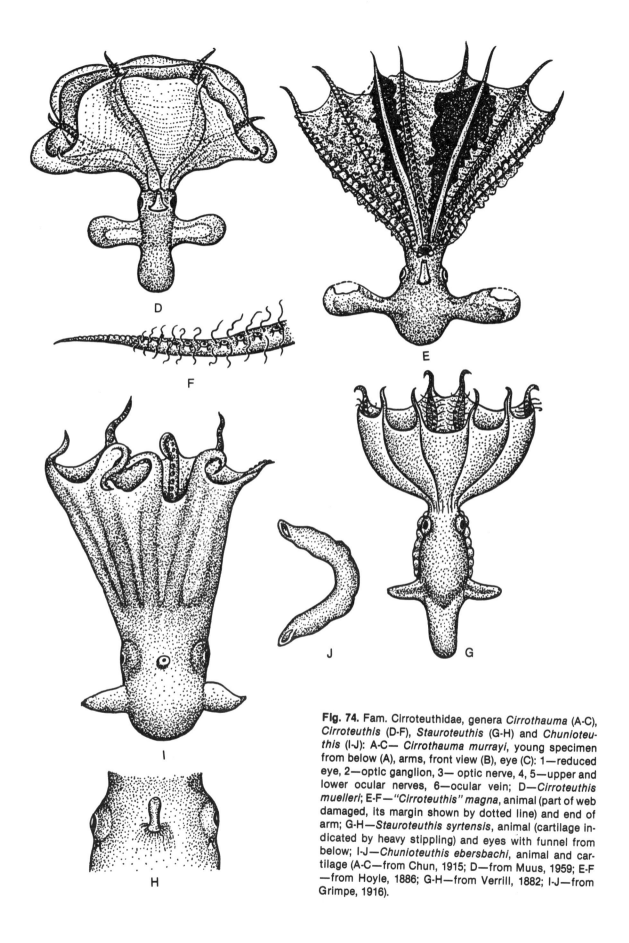

Fig. 74. Fam. Cirroteuthidae, genera *Cirrothauma* (A-C), *Cirroteuthis* (D-F), *Stauroteuthis* (G-H) and *Chunioteuthis* (I-J): A-C— *Cirrothauma murrayi*, young specimen from below (A), arms, front view (B), eye (C): 1—reduced eye, 2—optic ganglion, 3— optic nerve, 4, 5—upper and lower ocular nerves, 6—ocular vein; D—*Cirroteuthis muelleri*; E-F—"*Cirroteuthis*" *magna*, animal (part of web damaged, its margin shown by dotted line) and end of arm; G-H—*Stauroteuthis syrtensis*, animal (cartilage indicated by heavy stippling) and eyes with funnel from below; I-J—*Chunioteuthis ebersbachi*, animal and cartilage (A-C—from Chun, 1915; D—from Muus, 1959; E-F —from Hoyle, 1886; G-H—from Verrill, 1882; I-J—from Grimpe, 1916).

(4000-6200 m) and (?) near the surface in Central Polar Basin. Mantle length up to 22 cm, total length up to 1 m.

2 (1). Eyes well developed, with lens and iris...**3**

3 (4). Umbrella absent. Arms 5-6 times longer than body. Fin cartilage semicircular or buckle-shaped. First suckers at arm bases are conical, with tiny opening, other suckers of ordinary type. Tissues extremely gelatinous..............
...............**Genus *Froekenia* Hoyle, 1904**

Type species: *F. clara* Hoyle, 1904. Two species. Mantle length up to 11 cm, total length to about 60 cm.

a. Fin cartilage semicircular................
....................***F. clara* Hoyle, 1904**

Tropical Eastern Pacific (Gulf of Panama) at the slope, depth 1000 m.

b. Fin cartilage buckle-shaped with "horns" directed forward.......***Froekenia* n. sp. Nesis**

Seamounts of tropical Western Indian Ocean, depths 500-800 m.

4 (3). Web well developed.................**5**

5 (12). Mantle aperture a narrow circular slit around funnel base........................**6**

6 (9). Sectors of main umbrella fused outside of arms and connected with dorsal arm side by secondary umbrella. Umbrella symmetrical: web length along dorsal and ventral sides of arms equal....................................**7**

7 (8). Web reaches the very or almost very ends of arms. Cirri reach the arm ends. Fin cartilage saddle-shaped. Longitudinal gill axis parallel to longitudinal body axis....................
.........**Genus *Cirroteuthis* Eschricht, 1838**

(Fig. 74 D-F). Type species: *C. muelleri* Eschricht, 1838. 3 species and 3 more of unclear taxonomic position, provisionally attributed to this genus (see below). Live at the bottom in the abyssal, in the Arctic ascend to bathyal and (rarely) to epi-mesopelagic zones. This genus includes the largest of finned octopuses and abyssal invertebrates: total length up to 1.2-1.5 m.

8 (7). Web not reaching the ends of arms by approximately 33% of their length. Cirri terminate before the edge of web. Fin cartilage V-shaped with "horns" directed forward. Longitudinal gill axis perpendicular to longitudinal body axis.....
.........**Genus *Stauroteuthis* Verrill, 1879**

One species: ***S. syrtensis* Verrill, 1879** (Fig. 74 G,H). Found in the northwestern Atlantic, recorded also (with some doubt) at the Reykjanes Ridge and the Bay of Biscay. Middle and lower bathyal zones. Total length to 22 cm.

9 (6). No secondary umbrella. Main umbrella assymetrical: on dorsal side of arms umbrella attached to the back (aboral) side of arm, and reaches, gradually thinning, almost the end, on ventral side umbrella attached to lateral side of arm by far not reaching arm end (often only up to arm middle). Usually a round or oval hollow inflation with firm walls located ventrally at the place of umbrella attachment to lateral arm side....**10**

10 (11). Fin cartilage saddle-shaped. Cirri reach only the place of web attachment to latero-ventral side of arms.

3 species of unclear generic position, each described only by a single specimen. They are provisionally attributed to genus *Cirroteuthis* (see key to species).

11 (10). Fin cartilage semicircular, horseshoe-shaped, U-shaped or buckle-shaped, with "horns" directed forward (see Fig. 75 K). Cirri usually reach the arm ends. Longitudinal gill axis perpendicular to longitudinal body axis..............
........**Genus *Grimpoteuthis* Robson, 1932**

(Fig. 75). Type species: *G. umbellata* (Fischer, 1883). 11-13 species in the bathyal (usually middle and lower) and abyssal zones of all oceans, except Arctic Ocean. Total length to 60 cm (possibly up to 1-1.2 m).

12 (5). Mantle apperture completely closed— mantle edge fused with base of funnel. Secondary umbrfella present in proximal parts of arms. Umbrella symmetrical, not reaching the arm ends, cirri reaching only the edge of umbrella. No inflations at places of umbrella attachment to lateral side of arms ventrally. Fin cartilage widely V- or U-shaped ....
........**Genus *Chunioteuthis* Grimpe, 1916**

(Fig. 74 I,J). Type species: *Ch. ebersbachi* Grimpe, 1916. 2 species. Total length to 40 cm.

a. A small acuminate tubercle in the middle of each sector of umbrella. Arms 3.5-4 times longer than mantle. Fin cartilage widely V-shaped.....
..............***Ch. ebersbachi* Grimpe, 1916**

(Fig. 74 I,J). Lower bathyal at southern slope of Great Newfoundland Bank and (?) off northeastern coast of the USA.

b. No tubercles on umbrella. Arms 5 times longer than mantle. Fin cartilage widely U-shaped, slightly bent............................
..............***Ch. gilchristi* (Robson, 1924)**

Abyssal off southern Africa.

Key to species belonging to and provisionally attributed to the genus *Cirroteuthis*

1 (6). Umbrella symmetrical. Secondary umbrella present 2
2 (5). Eyes small, their diameter about 10% of the mantle length. Arm length 50-67% of total length. Animals of modest size, total length about 20-30 cm 3
3 (4). Arm length about 67% of total length. Suckers conical. . . . .
. . . .*C. muelleri* **Eschricht, 1838**
(Fig. 74 D). Central Polar Basin, Scandic Basin, Baffin Bay. At the bottom in the bathyal and abyssal and in midwater (mesopelagic and bathypelagic zones), was caught once at the surface (?).
4 (3). Arm length a little more than 50% of total length. Suckers in median parts of arms high, barrel-like, with tiny openings, in most proximal and distal parts suckers conical. . . . .
. . . .*Cirroteuthis* **n. sp. A Nesis**
Naturaliste Plateau off Southwestern Australia, uppermost abyssal.
5 (2). Eyes large, eye diameter up to 40% of the mantle length. Arm length 67-80% of total length. Total length to 1.3-1.5 m . . . .*Cirroteuthis*
n. sp. B Roper & Brundage, 1972
North Atlantic from Canary Islands to Dakar and the Caribbean Sea. Abyssal, depths of 2500-5200 m, in upwelling off Cape Blanc ascending to depths of 1300-2000 m (Golovan & Nesis, 1975).
6 (1). Umbrella assymetrical. Secondary umbrella absent 7
7 (8). 1st arms twice as thick as the others. Cirri present laterally to each sucker, and not between suckers, length of cirri not exceeding diameter of largest sucker. A few enlarged suckers, with a diameter 8-9% of the mantle length on basal parts of arms. A hollow inflation present ventrally at places of web-to-arm attachment. . . . .
. . . .*"C." massyae* **(Grimpe, 1920)**
Bay of Biscay off Southwestern Ireland, lower bathyal. The subgenus *Cirroteuthopsis* Grimpe, 1920 was proposed for this species.
8 (7). All arms of subequal length and thickness. Cirri situated, as usual, between neighboring suckers, length of cirri 10-15 times greater than sucker diameter. No particularly enlarged suckers. No inflations at places of web-to-arm

attachment 9
9 (10). Diameter of suckers about 2-2.5% of mantle length . . . .*"C." hoylei* **Robson, 1932**
Eastern Pacific westward of Central Chile, abyssal.
10 (9). Diameter of suckers about 4.5% of mantle length . . . .*"C." magna* **Hoyle, 1885**
(Fig. 74 E,F). Southern Ocean between Prince Edward and Crozet Islands and to northeast from Bouvet Island. Lower bathyal and abyssal. Total length to 115 cm.

Key to species of the genus *Grimpoteuthis*

1 (6). Fin width (measured along longer axis, perpendicular to body axis) considerably exceeds body width. Fin cartilage horseshoe-shaped, rounded 2
2 (3). Fin width is 2-3 times as large as the body width and subequal to the body length. Mantle 6-7 times shorter than arms. Eyes small. . . . .
. . . .*G. megaptera* **(Verrill, 1885)**
Abyssal of tropical and northern subtropical Atlantic.
3 (2). Fin width not more than 1.5-2 times exceeding the body width. Mantle 2.5-4 shorter than arms. Diameter of suckers 3-4% of mantle length
. 4
4 (5). Cirri on arms start after the 3rd-7th sucker. Eyes rather small. . . . .*G. pacifica* **(Hoyle, 1885)**
Abyssal of Coral Sea and Southern Ocean southward of Tasmania.
5 (4). Cirri on arms start after 2nd sucker. Eyes large. . . . .*G. wuelkeri* **(Grimpe, 1920)**
(Fig. 75 A). Subtropical northeastern Atlantic. Abyssal.
6 (1). Fin width equal or less than body width
. 7
7 (14). Fin width subequal to body width. 8
8 (13). Body 2-3 times as short as arms. Maximal body width is at the level of eyes. 9
9 (12). Suckers small, diameter 1.5-6% of mantle length 10
10 (11). Fin cartilage buckle-shaped, its straight or slightly rounded posterior part turned into forward-directed "horns" not gradually but with an acute angle. Eye diameter about 40% of mantle length. . . . .*G. meangensis* **(Hoyle, 1885)**
(Fig. 75 B). Indian Ocean, Indonesia, Kermadec Islands, (?) Cuba. Bathyal.
11 (10). Fin cartilage posteriorly rounded or

Fig. 75.

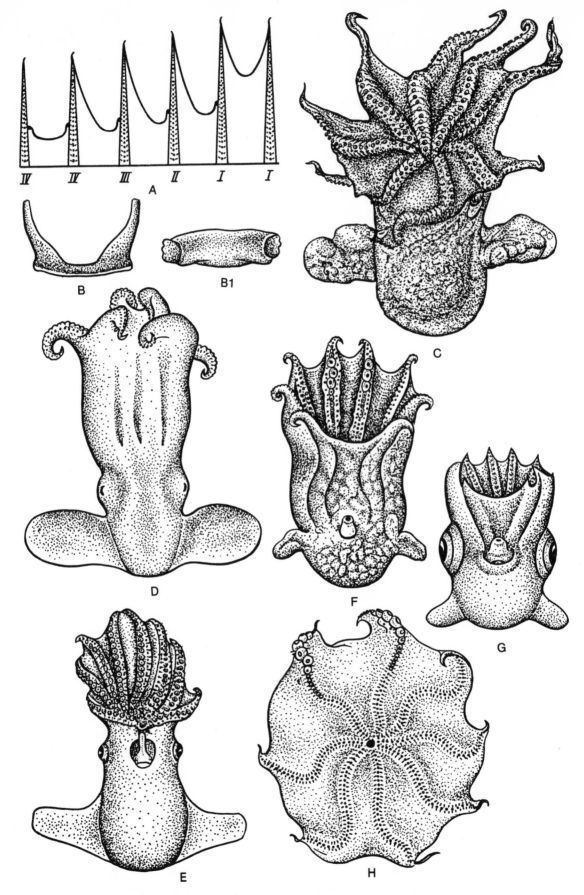

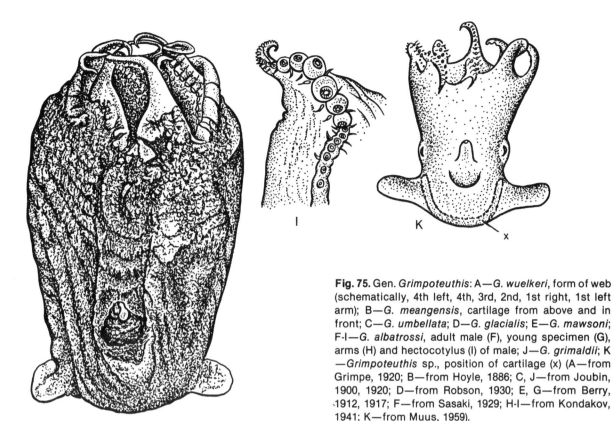

Fig. 75. Gen. *Grimpoteuthis*: A—*G. wuelkeri*, form of web (schematically, 4th left, 4th, 3rd, 2nd, 1st right, 1st left arm); B—*G. meangensis*, cartilage from above and in front; C—*G. umbellata*; D—*G. glacialis*; E—*G. mawsoni*; F-I—*G. albatrossi*, adult male (F), young specimen (G), arms (H) and hectocotylus (I) of male; J—*G. grimaldii*; K—*Grimpoteuthis* sp., position of cartilage (x) (A—from Grimpe, 1920; B—from Hoyle, 1886; C, J—from Joubin, 1900, 1920; D—from Robson, 1930; E, G—from Berry, 1912, 1917; F—from Sasaki, 1929; H-I—from Kondakov, 1941; K—from Muus, 1959).

almost straight, no angles at places of transition of posterior part of cartilage into "horns." Eyes small, eye diameter 17-20% of mantle length. . . .
. . . .***G. umbellata* (Fischer, 1883)**
(Fig. 75 C). Tropical, northern subtropical and boreal Atlantic (Reykjanes Ridge to northwestern Africa), Nova Scotia, Caribbean Sea. Lower bathyal and abyssal (1100 to 5400 m). Total length to 55-60 cm.
12 (9). Diameter of largest sucker (ca. the 19th) 8-9% of mantle length. . . . .
. . . .***G. glacialis* (Robson, 1930)**
(Fig. 75 D). Antarctic Peninsula, upper bathyal.
13 (8). Body 1.5 times shorter than arms. Eyes rather small. Maximal width of body behind eyes. Suckers small. . . . . . .***G. mawsoni* (Berry, 1917)**
(Fig, 75 E). Antarctic (Adelie Land), upper bathyal.
14 (7). Fins considerably narrower than body
. . . . **15**
15 (18). Body short, 4-6 times shorter than arms, widely rounded posteriorly, much wider than long. Fin width 3-4 times smaller than interocular distance. Fin cartilage arc-shaped. Eyes large. . . . **16**
16 (17). Diameter of largest suckers (6th or 7th) in

young animals 8-9% of mantle length, much smaller in adults. Cirri extending to ends of arms, cirri length exceeds diameter of largest suckers. Several suckers near ends of dorsal arms in male also greatly enlarged, spherical. . . . .
. . . .***G. albatrossi* (Sasaki, 1920)**
(Fig. 75 F-I). Northern Pacific boreal species, from the Bering Sea to the Sea of Okhotsk and southern California. Depths 136-3400 m, as a rule more than 700-800 m. Total length to 54 cm. Taxonomic position is doubtful, probably belonging to *Opisthoteuthis*.
17 (16). Diameter of largest suckers (4th-7th) about 15-20% of mantle length. Cirri not reaching arm ends, cirri length less than diameter of suckers in middle parts of arms (not the largest)
. . . .***G. grimaldii* (Joubin, 1903)**
[= ?*G. caudani* (Joubin, 1896)] (Fig. 75 J). Northeastern Atlantic (off the Azores, Bay of Biscay), lower bathyal.
18 (15). Body 1.5-2 times shorter than arms. . . **19**
19 (22). Body width equal or less than body length. Fin width 50% of interocular distance or more. Fin cartilage horseshoe-shaped (not described in *G. plena*). Eyes small. **20**

285

20 (21). Body width subequal to body length. Diameter of suckers 4-4.5% of mantle length .... *G. plena* **(Verrill, 1885)**

Northwestern Atlantic, to the east of Chesapeake Bay. Depth about 2000 m.

21 (20). Body width approximately 67% of body length. Diameter of suckers about 3% of mantle length....... *G. hippocrepium* **(Hoyle, 1904)**

Tropical Eastern Pacific, abyssal.

22 (19). Body a little wider than long. Fin width 33% of interocular distance or less. Fin cartilage wide U-shaped. Eyes large. In males 3 suckers in proximal part and 3-4 in distal part (near web edge) on all arms enlarged, the proximal ones are the biggest, 5-8% of mantle length. Consistency medusoid, gelatinous .... *G. bruuni* **G. Voss, 1982**

Southeastern Pacific off northern Chile, depth 250-360 m. Mantle length to 3 cm.

Grimpoteuthis not identified to species were found in Antarctic and Subantarctic, off southern Africa, in northern Indian Ocean, off Indonesia, in tropical eastern Pacific, in Caribbean Sea and tropical western Atlantic, in the bathyal, abyssal and ultra-abyssal zones. Among them were specimens as big as 1-1.2 m in total length.

2.4.1.2. Family Opisthoteuthidae

Small and medium-size animals. Body flattened, mantle reduced to a hump lying on extended arms, connected by thick web. Animal resembles a thick flapjack. Tissues semigelatinous. Umbrella reaching almost to arm ends. No secondary umbrella. Fins short, sitting on the "crown" of body. Fin cartilage is arc-shaped or almost straight. Funnel very short, directed posteriorly. Mantle aperture is a narrow circular slit. Eyes well developed. Longitudinal gill axis is perpendicular to the body axis. Mature males of some species have enlarged suckers in basal parts of arms, in others particularly enlarged suckers are positioned also (or only) on the ends of some or all arms. Sometimes the basal enlarged suckers are barrel-like while the distal ones are spherical.

One genus: *Opisthoteuthis* **Verrill, 1883.** Type species: *O. agassizi* Verrill, 1883. 8-9 species. Live in bathyal (125-2250 m) of tropical and temperate waters, on the bottom and above it but rarely ascend to midwater. Diameter of body with arms up to 80 cm. Reliable identification of species is possible only by mature males, but for a half of the species they are not described.

Fig. 76.

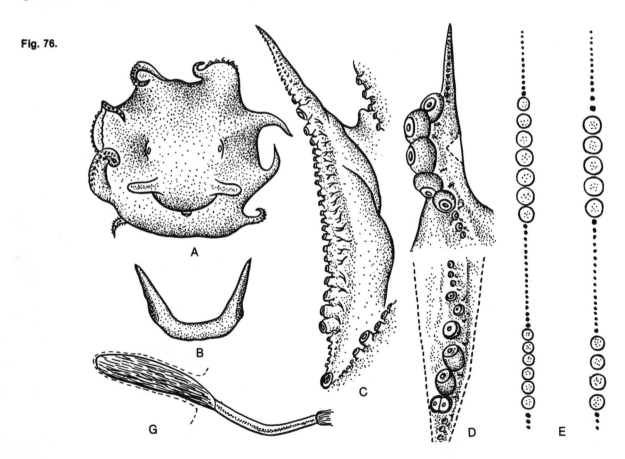

A   B   C   D   E   G

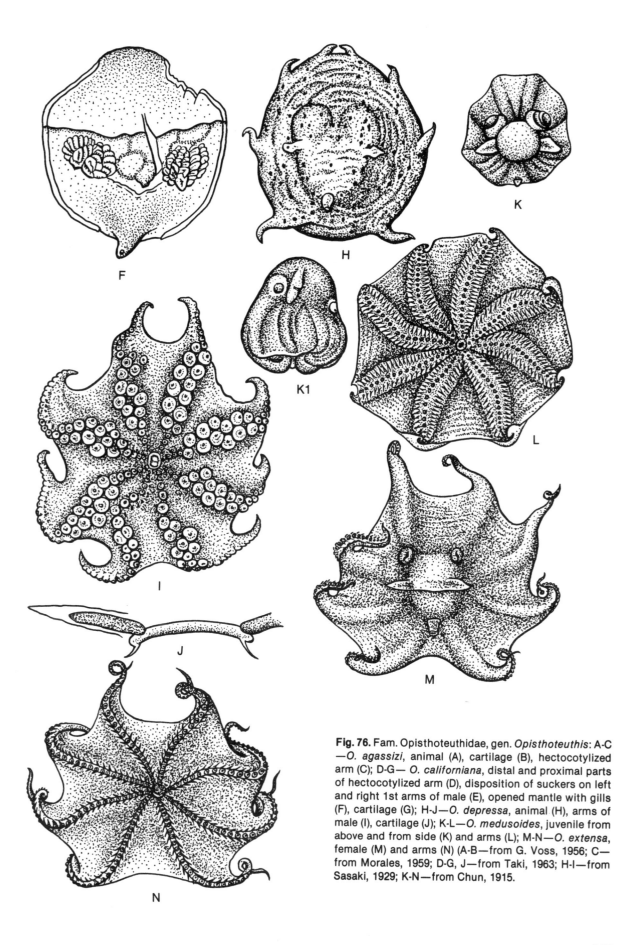

Fig. 76. Fam. Opisthoteuthidae, gen. *Opisthoteuthis*: A-C
—*O. agassizi*, animal (A), cartilage (B), hectocotylized
arm (C); D-G— *O. californiana*, distal and proximal parts
of hectocotylized arm (D), disposition of suckers on left
and right 1st arms of male (E), opened mantle with gills
(F), cartilage (G); H-J—*O. depressa*, animal (H), arms of
male (I), cartilage (J); K-L—*O. medusoides*, juvenile from
above and from side (K) and arms (L); M-N—*O. extensa*,
female (M) and arms (N) (A-B—from G. Voss, 1956; C—
from Morales, 1959; D-G, J—from Taki, 1963; H-I—from
Sasaki, 1929; K-N—from Chun, 1915.

287

Key to species of the genus *Opisthoteuthis*

1 (8). Species distributed in Atlantic and northern Pacific. **2**

2 (3). In mature males 4-5 basal suckers (usually from 6th-7th to 9th-11th) and 2-3 distal suckers (usually from 23rd-24th to 25th-26th) enlarged on all arms. Fin width exceeds half of interocular distance, fins tongue-shaped, with rounded ends. Species distributed in the Atlantic. . . . .***O. agassizi* Verrill, 1883**
(Fig. 76 A-C). From Georges Bank to the Caribbean Sea and from Faeroe Bank to Namibia; western Mediterranean. Depths 500-2250 m.

3 (2). Mature males do not have enlarged distal suckers or have them only on the ends of 1st arms. Fin width less than half of the interocular distance. Species distributed in the Pacific. **4**

4 (5). Some basal suckers (usually from 3rd-4th to 11th-12th) enlarged on all arms and 5-8 (usually 6-7) distal suckers on 1st arms. Fins conical with acuminate ends, 1.5-2 times wider than long. . . . .
. . . .***O. californiana* Berry, 1949**
(Fig. 76 D-G). Northern Pacific boreal species: from the Bering Sea to Sea of Okhotsk, central Honshu and southern California. Depths 125-1100 m, usually more than 300-400 m.

5 (4). Only basal suckers (10-15) enlarged in males. These suckers are so large that they seem to be arranged in 2 or 3 rows instead of one. **6**

6 (7). Fins short and wide, 1.5-2 times wider than long, ends of fins rounded or obtuse. Dorsal side of body spotted, spots arranged in longitudinal rows along upper side of body and arms. About 15 enlarged suckers on each arm of male. . . . .
. . . .***O. depressa* Ijima & Ikeda, 1895**
(Fig. 76 H-J). Pacific coast of central and southern Honshu. Depths 130-1100 m.

7 (6). Fins tongue-shaped, 5 times wider than long, ends of fins acuminate. Color purple-violet or lilac, without spots. About 10 enlarged suckers on each arm of male. . . . .
. . . .***O. japonica* Taki, 1962**
Pacific coast of southern Honshu. Depth 150 m.

8 (1). Species distributed in Indian Ocean and off southern Australia. **9**

9 (10). Body semitransparent, slightly pigmented. Arms connected by web almost to the very ends. 19th-20th sucker on 4th arms slightly enlarged
. . . .***O. medusoides* Thiele, 1915**
(Fig. 76 K,L). Eastern Africa, depth 400 m. Taxonomic position somewhat doubtful.

10 (9). Body intensely colored. Arm ends free from web. **11**

11 (12). No ocellar spots on upper side of body. Depth of umbrella at center of sectors between arms about 50% of arm length. . . . .
. . . .***O. extensa* Thiele, 1915**
(Fig. 76 M-N). Off the southern coast of Sumatra, depth 770 m.

12 (11). Small ocellar spots scattered over upper side of body Depth of umbrella at center of sectors between arms about 67% of arm length. **13**

13 (14). Suckers of proximal parts of arms (5th-7th) larger than remaining ones. Fins located near posterior edge of eyes. Brown tones dominate in coloration. Males have 3-4 enlarged suckers in distal parts of 3rd-4th arms near web edge. . . . . . .
. . . .***O. pluto* Berry, 1918**
Great Australian Bight, depths 275-1100 m.

14 (13). All suckers equally small. Fins situated in middle of body. Gray tones dominate in coloration. . . . .***O. persephone* Berry, 1918**
Great Australian Bight and Bass Strait, depths 275-550 m.

Unidentified (new?) species of *Opistoteuthis* were found in the abyssal zone near Peru, in the bathyal off Kerguelen and Crozet Islands, and in the Gulf of California.

2.4.2. Suborder Incirrata

Typical octopuses. No fins or cirri on arms. Web not reaching the arm ends. Secondary umbrella always absent. Suckers always sessile, flattened, rarely spherical or barrel-like. Eyes well developed. Funnel aperture is of different sizes but never closed. Gladius is greatly reduced or absent. Radula always present, though reduced in some deep-water species. Longitudinal gill axis parallel to the body axis. Posterior salivary gland paired. Hectocotylus, as a rule, present—one of 3rd arms is modified. Both oviducts are developed.

3 superfamilies, 9 families, 33-35 genera, 165-180 species. Distributed in all fully saline seas and oceans, at all depths except ultra-abyssal and abyssopelagic zones.

2.4.2.1. Superfamily Bolitaenoidea (Ctenoglossa)

Deep-sea octopuses with gelatinous, usually semitransparent body. Suckers in one row.

Radula comb-like, rhachidian and both lateral teeth are multicuspid.

3 families, 6 genera, 6-7 species. Live in tropical and subtropical (rarely boreal) regions.

Reviews: Thore, 1949; Taki, 1963.

2.4.2.1.1. Family Bolitaenidae

Body gelatinous, pigmented. Arms short, shorter than mantle, 3rd arms are longer than the others. Umbrella of modest size. Suckers in one row. Mantle aperture wide. A luminous organ—a thick ring under the integument around the mouth in adult females. Stomach behind liver. Radula comb-like. Ink sac present, but small. 4 genera, 4-5 species. Mesopelagic and bathypelagic.

Key to genera and species of the family Bolitaenidae

1 (6). Eyes of normal size, located on sides of head **2**

2 (5). Suckers close to one another, distance between neighboring suckers not more than twice sucker diameter **3**

3 (4). Eyes large, diameter exceeds 18% of mantle length. Optic nerves short, optic ganglia in close proximity to brain (this easily seen through semitransparent tissue). Suckers large, diameter on the average 6% of mantle length, distance between neighboring suckers shorter than sucker diameter. Maximum depth of umbrella 25-33% of longest arm length. No hectocotylus, only some enlarged suckers in middle part of right 3rd arm in male. Brown tones dominate coloration . . . . **Genus *Japetella* Hoyle, 1885** (= *Chunella* Sasaki, 1920, *Bolitaenella* Grimpe, 1922). One species: ***J. diaphana* Hoyle, 1885** (= ?*Octopus brevipes* d'Orbigny, 1838) (Fig. 77 A-C). Tropical-subtropical cosmopolitan bathypelagic species, juveniles also found in epipelagic and mesopelagic zones. In the northern Pacific reaches the boreal waters—in the north up to the Gulf of Alaska, forming a special form, known as *J. diaphana heathi* (Berry, 1911) (Fig. 77 B). Found in the waters of USSR in the southern Sea of Okhotsk and eastward of the Kurile Islands. *J. diaphana* is one of the most common pelagic oc-

topuses. Not performing noticeable diel vertical migrations. Eggs small, connected by stalks. Larvae covered by sticky gelatinous envelope facilitating buoyancy in water. Mantle length to 10-15 cm.

In the waters of California was found a separate form (a different species?) *Japetella* sp. Young, 1972 differing from *J. diaphana* by the absence of brilliant iridescent silvery layer enveloping the eyes from inside and the liver.

4 (3). Eyes small, eye diameter in adult specimens (mantle length above 6 cm) is 9-12%, in juveniles less than 17% of the mantle length. Optic nerves long, optic ganglia situated at a considerable distance from brain. Suckers small (on the average 4% of the mantle length), distance between neighboring suckers equal or exceeding sucker diameter. Maximal depth of web 33-50% of longest arm length. 3rd left arm hectocotylized, and 2-3 greatly enlarged urn-shaped suckers are on 3rd right arm of male distally to the middle. Red tones dominate in coloration . . . . **Genus *Eledonella* Verrill, 1884** One species: ***E. pygmaea* Verrill, 1884** (Fig. 77 D). Tropical-subtropical (not reaching the boreal waters) bathypelagic species. The juveniles are also found in epipelagic and mesopelagic zones. More rare than *J. diaphana*. Eggs small, connected by stalks. Mantle length to 20 cm.

5 (2). Suckers set wide apart within web and close to each other outside web, in distal part of arms. Eyes large. Optic nerves long, optic ganglia remote from brain. Maximum depth of umbrella 50-67% of longest arm length. Body coloration light purple, umbrella inside dark purple . . . . **Genus *Bolitaena* Steenstrup, 1859** One species: ***B. microcotyla* Steenstrup in Hoyle, 1886** (Fig. 77 E,F). Rare tropical-subtropical (or, possibly, bi-central) cosmopolitan meso-bathypelagic species. Eggs large, carried by female on the arms until larvae hatch. She does not feed during incubation. Mantle length to 4 cm.

6 (1). Eyes very large, about 25% of mantle length, situated on dorsal side close together and directed upward. Optic nerves short. Suckers very closely together. Umbrella depth about 33% of longest arm length . . . . **Genus *Dorsopsis* Thore, 1949** One species: ***D. taningi* Thore, 1949** (Fig. 77 G). Caught off Dakar in the bathypelagic zone.

Fig. 77.

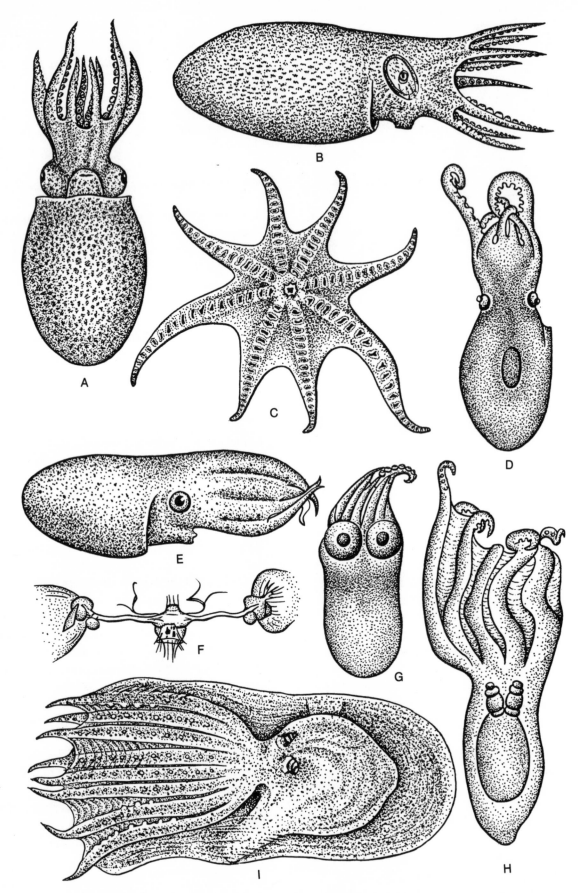

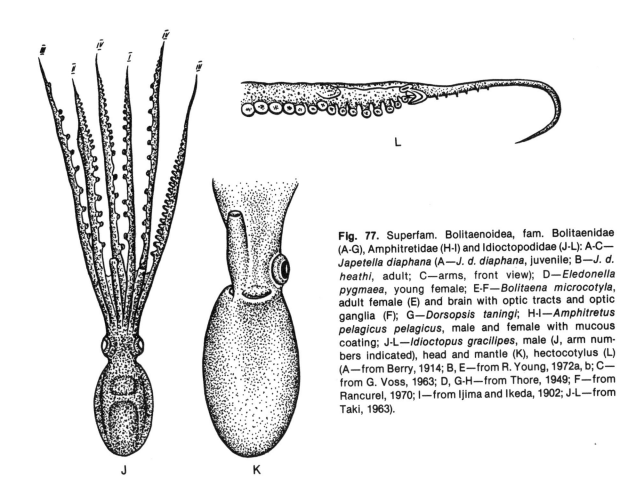

2.4.2.1.2. Family Amphitretidae

Body gelatinous, semitransparent, almost colorless, enveloped in a layer of gelatinous tissue. Arms long, with one row or suckers. Umbrella very deep. Mantle fused with funnel. The mantle aperture is represented by two openings on the sides of head. Funnel is very long. Eyes on dorsal side of head, telescopic, directed upward, their bases in contact. Radula comb-like. Stomach in front of liver, ovary is above liver. Ink sac present. 3rd right arm is hectocotylized, ligula long, narrow and naked, calamus very short and located on ventral side of arm. Eggs large. Mantle length to 9 cm.

One genus: *Amphitretus* Hoyle, 1885. One species: *A. pelagicus* Hoyle, 1885 with 2 subspecies: *A. pelagicus pelagicus* Hoyle (Fig. 77 H,I) in the tropical Indo-Pacific and *A. pelagicus thielei* Robson, 1930 in the southern subtropical and notalian Atlantic. The Atlantic subspecies differing from Indo-Pacific one by a narrow elongate mantle (in *A. p. pelagicus* mantle is rounded or widely oval). Meso-bathypelagic species, juveniles are found also in the epipelagic zone.

2.4.2.1.3. Family Idioctopodidae

Body elongately oval with distinct nuchal constriction. Tissues gelatinous, semitransparent. Arms slender, long, compressed laterally, suckers in one row. Umbrella is rather short. Funnel fused with mantle and with ventral surface of head over most part of its length. The mantle aperture is represented by two narrow slits on the sides of head, reaching the level of lower edge of eye. Radula comb-like. Crop and salivary glands present. Ink sac rudimentary. Stomach in front of liver. 3rd right arm is hectocotylized, ligula long, narrow, round, suckerless; calamus shifted to ventral side of arm and looks like a short triangular projection.

One genus: *Idioctopus* Taki, 1962. One species: *I. gracilipes* Taki, 1962 (Fig. 77 J-L). Found off the Pacific coast of southern Japan at the bottom in upper bathyal. Mantle length is 5 cm, total length is 20 cm.

Review: Taki, 1963.

2.4.2.2. Superfamily Octopodoidea (Heteroglossa)

Benthic or pelagic octopuses. Sucker on arms in one or two rows. Radula not comb-like, rhachidian tooth multicuspid, the median cusp is the largest, the first and second marginal teeth with one or two cusps. Shape of rhachidian teeth differs in neighboring rows but it is repeated in each 3rd or 4th rows (seriation of radula). Hectocotylus always present – 3rd right, or rarely left arm, is modified. Hectocotylization affects only the end of arm, which is not developed inside a special sac and does not break off from body at mating. Hectocotylus as a rule with ligula and calamus. Males are not dwarfed. 2 families, 23-25 genera, more than 150 species.

2.4.2.2.1. Family Octopodidae

Body either firm, muscular, or flabby, weakly-muscular, but not gelatinous or semitransparent. Arms muscular, usually several times longer than body, with 1 or 2 rows of suckers. Umbrella short or of modest size, usually not exceeding a half of the longest arm length. Mantle aperture not reduced. Radula not comb-like, seriation of rhachidian tooth is typical. Liver in front of stomach and gonad. 3rd right (rarely left) arm is hectocotylized, in addition males often have enlarged suckers in the middle of some arms, sometimes ends of all arms are modified. Eggs benthic, guarded by female, rarely she incubates them on her arms. Development is direct or with a pelagic larval stage.

Benthic animals, found from the Arctic to Antarctic and from the littoral to abyssal. Some species are of commercial value.

3 subfamilies, 22-24 genera, 150-160 species. The taxonomy of the family both at the generic and species level is poorly elaborated, many genera considered to be valid are in fact poorly differentiated from the others. Most species of the family (about 90) are attributed to the genus *Octopus* which is extremely heterogenous and particularly in need of revision.

The key to genera does not contain poorly described and doubtful genera *Laetmoteuthis* Berry, 1913 and *Haptochlaena* Grimpe, 1922; the doubtful genus *Pinnoctopus* d'Orbigny, 1845 is provisionally included in the genus *Octopus*. Due to poor elaboration of systematics of the genus *Oc-topus* it was impossible to compile a key to all species, but keys are included to all Atlantic and non-tropical North Pacific species.

Key to subfamilies and genera of the family Octopodidae

1 (32). Ink sac present, sometimes small and deeply buried in liver but ink always secreted **2**
2 (21). Arms with two rows of suckers . . . . **Subfamily Octopodinae**. . .**3**
3 (16). 3rd right arm hectocotylized **4**
4 (13). Body firm, more or less muscular. Funnel organ W- or VV-shaped. Mantle aperture not narrow or slightly narrow **5**
5 (10). Hectocotylus well developed, with more or less long differentiated ligula and calamus. Mantle aperture wide **6**
6 (7). No bright color rings scattered over body and arms, no ocellar spots on mantle, only round ocellar spots may be present on web in front of eyes as well as different stripes, spots, patterns, etc., rarely coloration uniform . . . . **Genus *Octopus* Lamarck, 1798**
(= *Polypus* Schneider, 1784, ?*Eledonenta* Rochebrune, 1884 *Macrotritopus* Grimpe, 1922) (Figs. 81-82). Type species: *O. vulgaris* Lamarck, 1798. Into the genus *Octopus* we include: *Pinnoctopus* d'Orbigny, 1845, *Tritaxeopus* Owen, 1881, *Amphioctopus* Fischer, 1882, *Enteroctopus* Rochebrune & Mabille, 1887, *Paroctopus* Naef, 1923 (= *Pseudoctopus* Grimpe, 1923), *Macroctopus* Robson, 1929, *Robsonella* Adam, 1938 (= *Joubinia* Robson, 1929, preoccupied), and *Callistoctopus* Taki, 1964. These "genera" do not have unequivocal characteristics that would allow the differentiation of all their species from other species of *Octopus*. In a broad sense the genus *Octopus* includes about 90 species distributed in the sublittoral and upper bathyal of all oceans, except the Arctic and Antarctic. Northern border of the range passes through Long Island Sound, in the southern part of the North Sea and near Bering Strait, southern border – near Cape Horn, Falkland, Crozet, Kerguelen, Auckland and Campbell Islands. Octopuses from very small to very large sizes. Total length of the largest species – *O. dofleini* is up to 3-5 m. In some species the eggs are small and the development with pelagic larval stage, in others the eggs are large and development is direct. Many species (*O. vulgaris, O. dofleini, O. maya* and others) are of

high commercial value. Artificial cultivation of octopuses is developed in Japan. About 10 species live in the USSR Far East (Kondakov, 1941; Akimushkin, 1963).

7 (6). Bright blue rings on mantle and arms or ocellar spots on dorsal side of mantle **8**

8 (9). A pair of large ocellar spots on dorsal side of mantle between head and posterior end of body on both sides of midline. Ocellar spots surrounded from outside by incomplete (C-shaped) colorless ridge. Arms very long and slender, arm length about 90% of total length, arm ends often break off. Funnel organ W-shaped (?). 11-13 filaments in demibranch. Web very short, web depth 5-6% of longest arm length . . . .
. . . . . **Genus *Euaxoctopus* Voss, 1971** (in part)
Only the species *E. pillsburyae* Voss, 1975 (Fig. 78 O-Q) keys out here. See couplet 17 (18).

9 (8). Numerous bright blue ringed spots or also meandering stripes, iridescent when octopus is excited, present on mantle, head and arms. No ocellar spots on mantle. Arms short (about 67% of total length), subequal but not attenuated, not breaking off. 6-7 filaments in demibranch. Web

deep, 25-45% of the longest arm length . . . .
. . . . **Genus *Hapalochlaena* Robson, 1929**
(Fig. 78 Q-D). Type species: *H. lunulata* (Quoy & Gaimard, 1832). 2 poorly differentiated species in the Indo-West Pacific. Sublittoral, mostly upper, sometimes littoral. Mantle length to 3-6 cm.

a (b). Only blue rings on head and mantle. Ink sac conspicuously reduced in size. Females lay eggs at bottom. Egg length 3.5 mm . . . .
. . . . ***H. lunulata* (Quoy & Gaimard, 1832)**
Philippines, Indonesia, Melanesia, northern and western Australia.

b (a). Besides (rarely instead of) rings there are usually meandering blue stripes on head, mantle and arms. Ink sac well developed. Females carry eggs on the arms. Egg length 7-8 mm . . . .
. . . . ***H. maculosa* (Hoyle, 1883)**
(= *Octopus pictus* Brock, 1882, non Blainville, *O. fasciata* Hoyle, 1886) (Fig. 78 A,B,D). Indo-West Pacific from southern Honshu to Tasmania, westward to the Gulf of Aden. The most dangerous species of cephalopods. The secretion of posterior salivary glands contains 2 potent toxins: maculotoxin (similar to tetrodotoxin) and

Fig. 78.

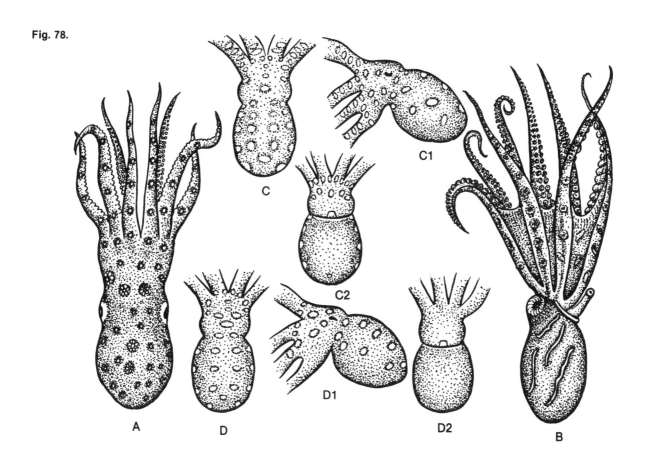

A   D   D1   C   C1   C2   D2   B

Fig. 78.

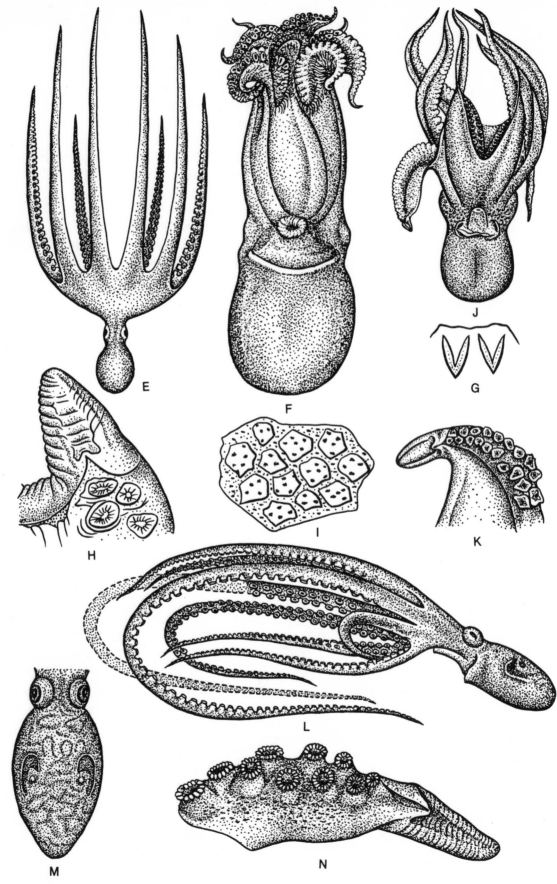

E

F

G

J

H

I

K

L

M

N

294

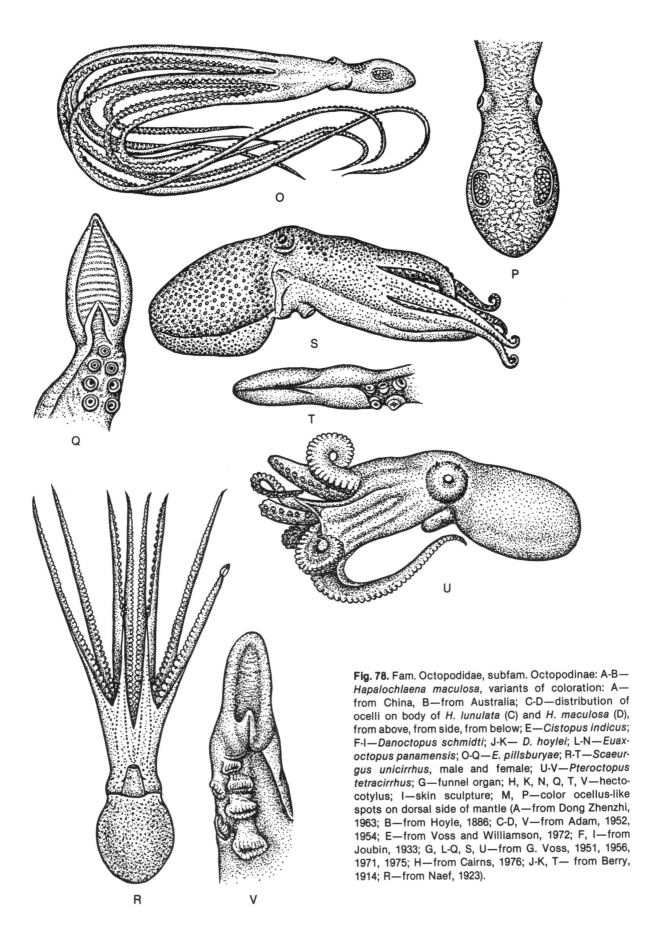

Fig. 78. Fam. Octopodidae, subfam. Octopodinae: A-B—*Hapalochlaena maculosa*, variants of coloration: A—from China, B—from Australia; C-D—distribution of ocelli on body of *H. lunulata* (C) and *H. maculosa* (D), from above, from side, from below; E—*Cistopus indicus*; F-I—*Danoctopus schmidti*; J-K— *D. hoylei*; L-N—*Euaxoctopus panamensis*; O-Q—*E. pillsburyae*; R-T—*Scaeurgus unicirrhus*, male and female; U-V—*Pteroctopus tetracirrhus*; G—funnel organ; H, K, N, Q, T, V—hectocotylus; I—skin sculpture; M, P—color ocellus-like spots on dorsal side of mantle (A—from Dong Zhenzhi, 1963; B—from Hoyle, 1886; C-D, V—from Adam, 1952, 1954; E—from Voss and Williamson, 1972; F, I—from Joubin, 1933; G, L-Q, S, U—from G. Voss, 1951, 1956, 1971, 1975; H—from Cairns, 1976; J-K, T— from Berry, 1914; R—from Naef, 1923).

hapalotoxin. The bite of adult female may be fatal to man. Some cases of death occurred in Australia. A person dies of paralysis of respiratory muscles. First aid is by a long continuous artificial respiration.

10 (5). Hectocotylus very short, with a small undifferentiated ligula, without calamus **11**

11 (12). Web between base of each arm with a water pore opening on inner surface of web at the level of the 3rd pair of suckers. Water pores poorly visible in fixed specimens. Arms with attenuated ends, 1st arms the longest, 5-7 times longer than body. Suckers on 1st and 2nd arms in male greatly enlarged. Web depth 13-17% of longest arm length. Head noticeably narrower than mantle. Mantle aperture wide. Funnel long, funnel organ W-shaped . . . .
. . . . **Genus *Cistopus* Gray, 1840**

One species: ***C. indicus*** (d'Orbigny, 1840) (Fig. 78 E). Coastal tropical Indo-Malayan species, found from Western India to southern China and Indonesia. Mantle length to 11 cm. Minor object of fisheries.

12 (11). No water pore on oral surface of web. Arms very short, subequal to mantle length. Head not narrower than mantle; mantle narrow, elongated, body form squid-like. Suckers in males not enlarged. Web depth 33% of the longest arm length. Mantle aperture fairly narrow. Funnel short, almost entirely buried in head tissue; funnel organ VV-shaped . . . .
. . . . **Genus *Macrochlaena* Robson, 1929**

One species: ***M. winckworthi*** (Robson, 1929). In shallow waters of Southern India.

13 (4). Body slightly muscular, soft to the touch, with subcuticular layer of semigelatinous tissue. Head and mantle wide. Arms short, 1.5-3 times longer than mantle. Funnel organ VV-shaped . . . **14**

14 (15). Mantle aperture narrow. Funnel almost entirely buried in head tissue. Arms 1.5-2.5 time longer than mantle. Web depth 33-50% of the longest arm length. Eyes of ordinary size. Under magnification, skin nearly completely beset by low wide tubercles, as if shagreened (very conspicuous on sides and posterior surface of mantle). Ink sac conspicuously reduced in size . . . .
. . . . **Genus *Danoctopus* Joubin, 1933**

(= *Berrya* Hoyle, 1939, *Hapaloctopus* Taki, 1962) (Fig. 78 F-K). Type species: *D. schmidti* Joubin, 1933. 2-3 species in upper bathyal (rarely in the lower sublittoral zone) in tropical western Atlantic and Indo-West Pacific. Their differences

are minor and insufficiently defined.

a (b). Hectocotylus length 4-8% of hectocotylized arm length . . . . ***D. schmidti*** Joubin, 1933
(Fig. 78 F-I). Caribbean Sea, Straits of Florida, Bahama Islands. Depths 300-1200 m.

b (a). Hectocotylus length usually 10-13% of hectocotylized arm length . . . . **c**

c (d). Web width 33-40% of longest arm length
. . . . ***D. hoylei*** (Berry, 1909)
Fig. 78 J-K). Indo-West Pacific from the Gulf of Aden and Persian Gulf to southern Japan and Hawaii. Depths 50-850 m, usually more than 200 m.

d (c). Web width 40-50% of longest arm length
. . . . ***D. keralensis*** (Oommen, 1966)
[= ?*D. annae* (Oommen, 1980)]. Arabian Sea and off southwestern India. Depths 200-400 m. Possibly synonym of preceding species.

15 (14). Mantle aperture wide. Funnel free by 33% of its length. Web depth about 33% of longest arm length. Eyes very large, almost contacting on "top" of the head. Skin smooth, not shagreened. Ink sac well developed . . . .
. . . . **Genus *Sasakinella* Taki, 1964**

One species: ***S. eurycephala*** Taki, 1964. Pacific coast of Southern Honshu.

[Males of *Sasakinella* are not described. The supposition that 3rd right arm is hectocotylized—couplet 3 (16) was made on the basis of general similarity of this genus with *Danoctopus* for which this is characteristic.]

16 (3). 3rd left arm hectocotylized **17**

17 (18). Body elongated, egg-shaped. Arms very long and slender, arm length 80-85% of total length, arm ends break off easily. Web depth only about 9% of longest arm length. No supraocular cirri. A pair of bright hook-shaped spots surrounded by a light stripe on dorsal side of mantle in the middle between head and posterior end of body on both sides of midline. Funnel organ VV-shaped. Hectocotylized arm 3-6 times shorter than opposite one. Mantle length to 3 cm . . . .
. . . . **Genus *Euaxoctopus* Voss, 1971**

Type species: *E. panamensis* Voss, 1971 (Fig. 78 L-Q).

Genus *Euaxoctopus* includes 2 species in which different arms of the 3rd pair are hectocotylized: the only case of this kind in octopuses.

a (b). 3rd left arm hectocotylized. Funnel organ VV-shaped. 11-13 filaments in demibranch. Hook-like shaped ocellar spots on dorsal side of mantle . . . . ***E. panamensis*** Voss, 1971

= ?*Tremoctopus scalenus* Hoyle, 1904) (Fig. 78 L-N). Gulf of Panama (Pacific Ocean). Upper sublittoral.

b (a). 3rd right arm hectocotylized. Funnel organ W-shaped (?). 7 filaments in demibranch. C-shaped ocellar spots on mantle. . . . .
. . . . ***E. pillsburyae*** **Voss, 1975**
(Fig. 78 O-Q). Southern part of the Caribbean Sea and coasts of Guianas. Upper sublittoral. See couplet 8 (9).

18 (17). Body of common octopus form, widely oval. Arms of moderate length and thickness. Web deep. Supraocular cirri present. No ocellar spots on mantle. Hectocotylized arm not shortened. Mantle length up to 12-16 cm. **19**

19 (20). Body firm to the touch. Skin densely covered with small round flat-topped papillae. One cirrus above each eye. A low longitudinal skin ridge or fold usually passing on the sides of mantle. Web depth 20-30%, rarely up to 40% of the longest arm length. Arm ends not broken off. Funnel organ W-shaped, rarely VV-shaped. Ligula of hectocotylus long (8-10% of arm length), with edges twisted inward, calamus also long. . . . . . . **Genus *Scaeurgus* Troschel, 1857**
One species: **S. unicirrhus (delle Chiaje, 1830)** (= *S. patagiatus* Berry, 1913) (Fig. 78 R-T). Tropical-subtropical Atlantic-Indo-West Pacific (eastward to Nazca Ridge) lower sublittoral-upper bathyal species, very characteristic component of the fauna of seamounts and slopes of oceanic banks.

20 (19). Body soft to the touch, flabby. To the naked eye skin almost smooth or with scarce solitary warts. Two cirri or tubercles above each eye. Web depth 30-40% of longest arm length. No lateral skin fold. Arm ends often broken off. Funnel organ VV- or W-shaped. Ligula and calamus short, hectocotylus length 3-7% of the hectocotylized arm length. . . . .
. . . . **Genus *Pteroctopus* Fischer, 1882**
(Fig. 78 U,V). Type species: *P. tetracirrhus* (delle Chiaje, 1830). Two species found in Atlantic Ocean and Sea of Okhotsk.

a (b). Arms 3-4 times longer than mantle. Funnel organ VV-shaped. Diameter of suckers 4-6% of mantle length. Egg length 7 mm. . . . .
. . . . ***P. tetracirrhus*** **(delle Chiaje, 1830)**
(Fig. 78 U,V). Atlantic tropical-subtropical lower sublittoral-upper bathyal species: from southern Florida, Gulf of Mexico and Caribbean Sea to Uruguay and from Mediterranean Sea to Gabon. Usually at depths from 150-200 to 500 m.

b (a). Arms 2.3 times longer than mantle. Funnel organ W-shaped. Diameter of suckers 11% of mantle length. . . . .
. . . . ***P. witjazi*** **Akimushkin, 1963**
Off Southwestern Kamchatka at a depth of 100 m. A doubtful species.

21 (2). Arms with one row of suckers. . . . .
. . . .**Subfamily Eledoninae. . .22**

22 (29). Body usually without tubercles with stellate bases (ordinary tubercles often present). Funnel organ W- or VV-shaped. **23**

23 (24). Hectocotylus very short, with almost undeveloped ligula and calamus. Ends of all other arms in male with modified suckers converted into papillae or narrow plates. Distributed in boreal, tropical, and subtropical waters. . . . .
. . . .**Genus *Eledone* Leach, 1817**
(= *Moschites* Schneider, 1785, *Ozoena* Rafinesque, 1814, *Epistrophea* Gistel, 1848, *Hoylea* Rochebrune, 1886, *Acantheledone* Fort, 1941) (Fig. 80 A-K). Type species: *E. moschata* (Lamarck, 1798). 6 species in the Atlantic Ocean and nearby seas from northern Brazil to central Argentina and from Lofoten Islands to southern Africa, and (?) in Red Sea. Common animals of sublittoral (mainly lower) and upper bathyal zones. *E. moschata* and *E. cirrosa* are important commercial species in southern Europe.

24 (23). Hectocotylus with a well developed ligula and calamus (no calamus in *Pareledone*). Ends of other arms in male not modified. Live in Antarctic and temperate waters of southern hemisphere. **25**

25 (28). Small and medium-size animals (mantle length up to 10 cm, total length up to 35 cm, usually less). Head wider, equal or somewhat narrower than mantle. Crop present. Ink sac well developed. Skin smooth or tuberculate. **26**

26 (27). Radula degenerated: 1st lateral tooth very poorly developed, 2nd tooth cuspless, 3rd absent. Funnel organ VV-shaped. Skin beset by conical tubercles. 2 cirri above each eye. . . . .
. . . .**Genus *Vosseledone* Palacio, 1978**
One species: **V. charrua Palacio, 1978** (Fig. 79 A,B). From southern Brazil to northern Argentina, mainly at depths of 100-800 m.

27 (26). Radula normal. Funnel organ VV- or W-shaped. . . . .
. . . .**Genus *Pareledone* Robson, 1932**
(Fig. 80 L-Q). Type species: *P. charcoti* (Joubin, 1905). 7-8 species: 6-7 in Antarctic and Scotia Arc

in sublittoral and bathyal zones (2 species reach northward along the Patagonia shelf to the region of Rio de Janeiro), 1 species off southern Africa. In the Antarctic these octopuses are common and numerous.

28 (25). Large animals, mantle length up to 20-25 cm, total length up to 70-85 cm. Head much narrower than mantle. Ink sac poorly developed. Skin devoid of tubercles . . . .
. . . .**Genus *Megaleledone* Taki, 1961**

One species: ***M. senoi* Taki, 1961.** Antarctic circumpolar sublittoral and bathyal species. The largest Antarctic octopus. Eggs of this species are among the largest of dibranchiate cephalopods: egg length without stalk is 34 mm.

29 (22). Body beset by tubercles with stellate bases. Funnel organ is (VV) or fourfold (IIII). Supraocular cirri present **30**

30 (31). Funnel organ VV-shaped. The arms outside web with wide fringes on ventral side. One cirrus above each eye. Ligula and calamus well developed . . . . . .**Genus *Velodona* Chun, 1915**

One species: ***V. togata* Chun, 1915** (Fig. 79 C,D). Found off Kenya at a depth of 750 m. Near Natal at depths of 400-450 m *V. togata* var. *capensis* Robson, 1924 was caught differing by more dense arrangement of tubercles and presence of cirri on body.

31 (30). Funnel organ IIII-shaped. Arms without wide fringes. Two cirri above each eye. Ligula short, slightly developed . . . .
. . . .**Genus *Tetracheledone* Voss, 1955**

One species: ***T. spinicirris* Voss, 1955** (Fig. 79 E-G). Upper bathyal of tropical western Atlantic and nearby seas, from North Carolina to the Caribbean Sea.

32 (1). Ink sac absent. Mainly deep-sea (bathyal, abyssal) but in high latitudes inhabiting also the shelf . . . . .**Subfamily Bathypolypodinae**. . .**33**

33 (40). Arm suckers in 2 rows **34**

34 (39). Funnel organ W- or VV-shaped. Posterior salivary glands not reduced **35**

35 (38). Arm suckers small, not more than 15%, as a rule 3-8% of the mantle length (except the high Arctic *Benthoctopus sibiricus*: see Fig. 84 A,B). Calamus short, slender **36**

36 (37). Ligula short, narrow, its length 4-15%, usually 5-7% of hectocotylized arm length. Arms usually 2.5-6 times longer than mantle. Skin smooth, no supraocular cirri. Crop present
. . . .**Genus *Benthoctopus* Grimpe, 1921**
(= *Atlantoctopus* Grimpe, 1921) (Fig. 84). Type

species: *B. piscatorum* (Verrill, 1879). 15-23 species (including several undescribed ones) in the bathyal and at the foot of the continental slope in all oceans from the Arctic to the Subantarctic. In high latitudes they live also on shelves but in the tropics usually at depths exceeding 500 m. Mantle length up to 10-17 cm. Egg length up to 28-35 mm.

37 (36). Ligula long, conical, spoon-like or round, frequently with sharp transverse ridges, ligula length usually 13-35%, sometimes up to 40% of hectocotylized arm length. Arms usually 1.5-3 times longer than mantle. Skin as a rule beset by tubercles and warts either over entire body or over head and arm bases. Conical cirri ("horns") often present over eyes. Funnel organ as a rule VV-shaped. Crop reduced or absent . . . .
. . . .**Genus *Bathypolypus* Grimpe, 1921**

(Fig. 83). Type species: *B. arcticus* (Prosch, 1849). 4-5 species in lower sublittoral and bathyal of Arctic, boreal Atlantic, Mediterranean Sea and off southern Africa. Mantle length up to 10 cm, usually to 4-5 cm. Egg length up to 10-20 mm.

38 (35). Suckers very large, sucker diameter in male up to 22% of mantle length. Calamus very long and thick, almost subequal to ligula length, ligula bent outward at a right angle to arm axis. Hectocotylized arm twice as short as opposite 3rd left arm. Arms 4-5 times longer than mantle. Skin with small tubercles. Funnel organ VV-shaped
. . . .**Genus *Grimpella* Robson, 1928**

One species: ***G. thaumastocheir* Robson, 1928** (Fig. 79 H). In shallow waters off southern Australia.

39 (34). Funnel organ consists of 4 parts, IIII-shaped. Arms 2-3 times as long as mantle. Skin smooth. Crop present. Posterior salivary glands reduced . . . .
. . . .**Genus *Teretoctopus* Robson, 1929**

Type species: *T. indicus* Robson, 1929. 2 species in the bathyal of the northern Indian Ocean and nearby seas.

a (b). Arm length about 70% of total length. Diameter of suckers 4% of the mantle length. Web depth 35-40% of the longest arm length. Length of ligula about 6% of the hectocotylized arm length . . . .***T. indicus* Robson, 1929**
Bathyal of Arabian Sea.

b (a). Arm length 75-80% of total length. Diameter of suckers 5-7% of the mantle length. Web depth 30-35% of the longest arm length. Length of ligula 12-16% of the hectocotylized arm

length............*T. alcocki* **Robson, 1932**
Arabian Sea, Bay of Bengal, Andaman Sea. Upper and lower bathyal.

40 (33). Arm suckers in one row...........**41**
41 (44). Arms 2-5 times longer than mantle. Web depth less than 50% of the longest arm length. Crop poorly developed or absent. Lateral teeth of radula present (sometimes 1st lateral tooth absent in *Graneledone antarctica*)................**42**
42 (43). Dorsal side of mantle, head and often of 1st-3rd arms beset by conical or composite stellate papillae or warts. Funnel organ VV-shaped. 5-8 filaments in demibranch.....................
..........**Genus *Graneledone* Joubin, 1918**
(Fig. 85). Type species: *G. verrucosa* (Verrill, 1881). 5-6 species in lower bathyal and abyssal of northern Atlantic, northern Pacific, Antarctic and in the tropical Pacific Ocean.
43 (42). Body smooth. Funnel organ V-shaped (?). 4-6 filaments in demibranch. Eyes small........
.........**Genus *Bentheledone* Robson, 1932**
Type species: *B. rotunda* (Hoyle, 1885). 2 species in the southern Ocean (Indian Ocean sector), forms not defined to species are found in abyssal of the eastern Pacific.

a (b). Arms twice as long as mantle. Diameter of suckers 5% of the mantle length. Color dark-purple............**B. rotunda (Hoyle, 1885)**
(Fig. 79 I). Found in the abyssal of Australo-Antarctic Basin.
b (a). Arms three times as long as mantle. Diameter of suckers 8% of the mantle length. Color grayish-white......**B. albida (Berry, 1917)**
Found in abyssal zone to the north of Wilkes Land, Antarctic.
44 (41). Arms 1.3-1.7 times longer than mantle. Web depth 60-67% of longest arm length. Body covered by small tubercles or granules. Funnel organ consists of two or four parts. 4-6 filaments in demibranch. 1st and 2nd lateral teeth of radula greatly reduced or absent. Eyes very large.......
........**Genus *Thaumeledone* Robson, 1930**
(Fig. 79 J,K). Type species: *T. brevis* (Hoyle, 1885). 2 species in the bathyal of southern Atlantic.

a (b). Funnel organ is IIII-shaped. Three supraocular cirri......*T. brevis* **(Hoyle, 1885)**
(Fig. 79 J). Southwestern Atlantic off Montevideo. Lower bathyal.
b (a). Funnel organ VV-shaped. No supraocular cirri..............*T. gunteri* **Robson, 1930**
(Fig. 79 K). Off South Georgia. Upper bathyal.

Key to species of the genus *Eledone*

1 (6). Whole body densely beset by minute papillae with larger ones scattered between them. Supraocular cirri or tubercles present. Arms of subequal length. No large dark spots on dorsal side of body, only dark patterns may be present. Octopuses not having musk odor............**2**
2 (5). Low peripheral skin fold or ridge passing on the sides of body. Suckers in males not enlarged, sucker diamter 9-13% of the mantle length. Two rows of short papillae on ends of all arms in males, except hectocotylized arm (Fig. 80 D)...**3**
3 (4). Funnel organ W-shaped. One cirrus-like papilla above each eye. Color yellow-brown or bright red. Inner wall of anterior part of spermatophore with numerous very small spines. Egg length about 7 mm........................
.................*E. cirrosa* **(Lamarck, 1798)**
(Fig. 80 A-D). Boreal-Lusitanian-Mediterranean species: from Iceland and Lofoten Islands (Norway) to Casablanca (Morocco) and Mediterranean Sea, eastward to Marmara Sea. Sublittoral and upper bathyal to depths of 500-800 m, usually at 50-200 m. Of high commercial value.
4 (3). Funnel organ VV-shaped. 3-4 cirri-like papillae above each eye. Color purple-red with dark patterns. Spermatophores rather undifferentiated, without spines ..*E. massyae* **Voss, 1964**
Tropical and subtropical southwestern Atlantic, near the coasts of Brazil, Uruguay and Argentina from Trinidade Island to (Brazil) to Rawson (Argentina). Upper sublittoral.
5 (2). No peripheral skin fold. Proximal arm suckers in males greatly enlarged, sucker diameter exceeds 20% of mantle length. A brush of cirri-like papillae in 3-4 rows on the very tips of all arms in male, except hectocotylized arm (Fig. 80 F). Spermatophores with spines, like those in *E. cirrosa*........*E. thysanophora* **Voss, 1962**
(Fig. 80 E,F). Coastal waters of southern Africa.
6 (1). Body smooth or with scarce small papillae on dorsal side. No peripheral skin fold. Suckers in basal parts of 1st and 2nd arms in male greatly enlarged, their diameter 11-22% of the mantle length....................................**7**
7 (10). Arms of subequal length............**8**
8 (9). Skin smooth, with only traces of wrinkles. Color dark-brown, almost black..............
....................*E. nigra* **(Hoyle, 1910)**
Namibia (Lüderitz Bay) to Capetown. Littoral and upper sublittoral.

9 (8). Dorsal surface of mantle, head and web with scarce small papillae, large "horns" above eyes. Body yellowish, gray-brown or gray-yellow with large distinct dark spots. Ink with strong musk odor, even body of preserved octopuses smells musky. Two rows of short flattened papillae on ends of all arms in male, except the hectocotylized arm (Fig 80 I). Spermatophores without spines. Egg length about 15 mm.......
...........*E. moschata* (**Lamarck, 1798**)
(Fig. 80 G-I). Mediterranean Sea, Gulf of Cadiz. Sublittoral and uppermost bathyal, usually upper sublittoral. Of minor commercial value.

10 (7). 1st arms are by 33-50% longer than the 2nd ones, 2nd arms considerably longer than 3rd and 4th arms. Body smooth, no supraocular cirri. Color gray-lilac or reddish brown, without large dark spots. 2 rows of flattened plates on ends of all arms of male, except hectocotylized arm (Fig. 80 K). Spermatophores without spines. Egg length 8-9 mm............*E. caparti* **Adam, 1950**
(Fig. 80 J-K). Tropical western Africa from Mauritania (?) and Sierra Leone to Angola. Sublittoral.

Key to species of the genus *Pareledone*

1 (2). Dorsal side of body, head and arms beset by close or isolated tubercles and small warts, usually 1-2 larger tubercles above each eye. Funnel organ VV-shaped........*P. charcoti* (**Joubin, 1905**)
[= *P. aurorae* (Berry, 1917)] (Fig. 80 L,M). Antarctic (circumpolar), Scotia Arc, Falkland Islands, Patagonian shelf, northward reaches the area of Rio de Janeiro. In the Antarctic from littoral to bathyal, possibly to abyssal, off the Falkland Islands and Patagonia in the lower sublittoral and upper bathyal. The most common octopus in Antarctic.

2 (1). Dorsal side of body, head and arms smooth or with small scattered tubercles.............**3**

3 (6). Skin smooth. Funnel organ W-shaped. Peripheral skin fold on mantle sides usually absent.................................**4**

4 (5). Diameter of suckers 7-11% of mantle length. Arm length about 70% of total length. 6-7 filaments in demibranch....................
................*P. adelieana* (**Berry, 1917**)
Eastern Antarctic, sublittoral and upper bathyal.

5 (4). Diameter of suckers 4-6% of the mantle length. Arm length about 60% of total length. 8

filaments in demibranch....................
.................*P. umitakae* **Taki, 1961**
(Fig. 80 N). Cosmonauts Sea (Antarctic), bathyal.

6 (3). Skin beset by tubercles and warts.......**7**

7 (8). Diameter of suckers 14-15% of the mantle length. Arm length about 75% of total length. Funnel organ VV-shaped. Peripheral skin fold absent. Skin with small granules set close together..
.................*P. carlgreni* **Thore, 1945**
Off Cape of Good Hope.

8 (7). Diameter of suckers 5-11% of the mantle length. Arm length about 67% of total length. Skin with scarce granules or papillae. Species distributed in the Antarctic and on Patagonian shelf.................................**9**

9 (12). Funnel organ VV-shaped............**10**

10 (11). Skin with scarce small granules, almost smooth. Peripheral skin fold absent. 9-11 filaments in demibranch....................
................*P. turqueti* (**Joubin, 1905**)
(Fig. 80 O). Antarctic (circumpolar), Scotia Arc, South Georgia, Patagonian shelf, northward to the region off Rio de Janeiro; from upper sublittoral to upper bathyal.

11 (10). Skin with scattered but distinct papillae. Peripheral skin fold on mantle sides developed. 8-10 filaments in demibranch................
................*P. harrisoni* (**Berry, 1917**)
Antarctic circumpolar species. From upper sublittoral to upper bathyal.

12 (9). Funnel organ W-shaped. Peripheral skin fold present. Skin with scarce distinct papillae. 7-9 (10) filaments in demibranch..............
............*P. polymorpha* (**Robson, 1930**)
(Fig. 80 P,Q). South Georgia, South Shetland and South Sandwich Islands. Sublittoral and uppermost bathyal.

Note. The key does not include *P. antarctica* (Thiele, 1920), described (very incompletely) from the Davis Sea. Probably it is a synonym of *P. harrisoni*.

Key to species of the subfamily Octopodinae of the Atlantic Ocean

1 (34). 3rd right arm hectocotylized.........**2**

2 (33). Body firm, more or less muscular. Mantle aperture not narrow....................**3**

3 (4). One large semiround or C-shaped ocellar spot on dorsal side of mantle on each side of midline. Arms very long (80-84% of total length),

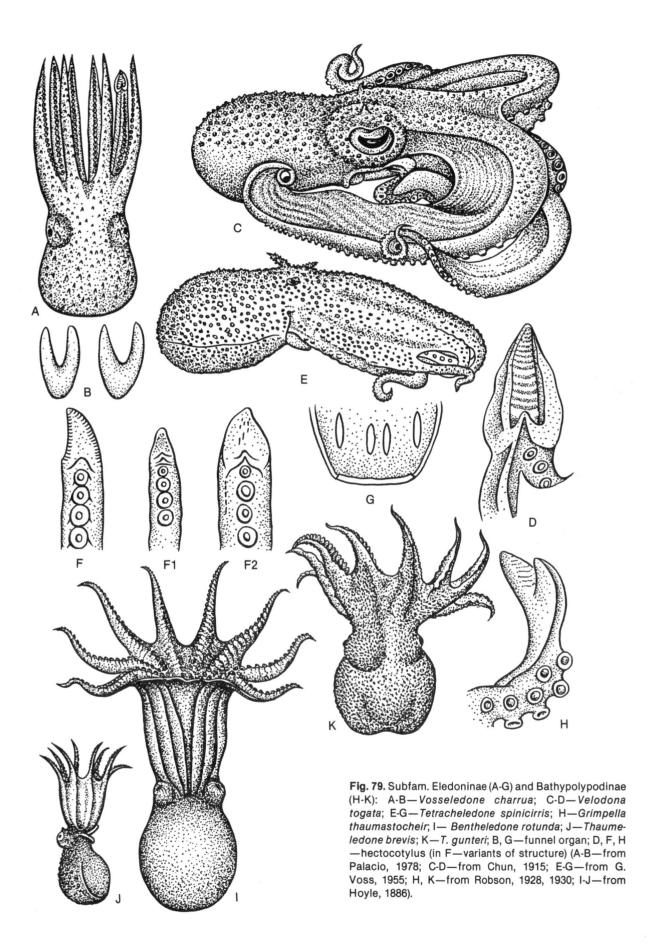

Fig. 79. Subfam. Eledoninae (A-G) and Bathypolypodinae (H-K): A-B—*Vosseledone charrua*; C-D—*Velodona togata*; E-G—*Tetracheledone spinicirris*; H—*Grimpella thaumastocheir*; I— *Bentheledone rotunda*; J—*Thaumeledone brevis*; K—*T. gunteri*; B, G—funnel organ; D, F, H —hectocotylus (in F—variants of structure) (A-B—from Palacio, 1978; C-D—from Chun, 1915; E-G—from G. Voss, 1955; H, K—from Robson, 1928, 1930; I-J—from Hoyle, 1886).

Fig. 80.

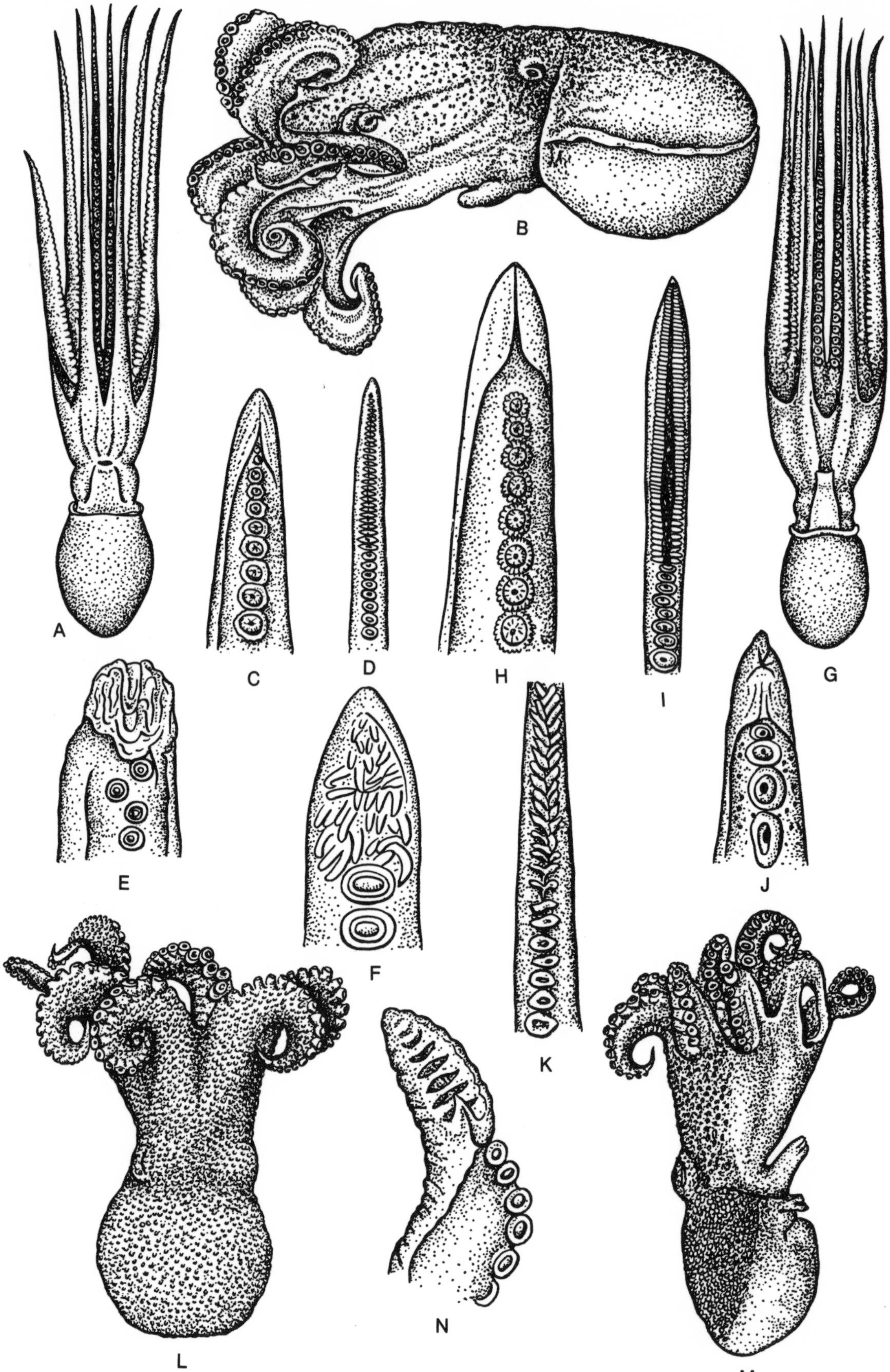

302

often broken off at ends. 7 filaments in demibranch. Ligula length 7-10% of hectocotylized arm length. Funnel organ W-shaped (?). Mantle length up to 2.5 cm.....................

........***Euaxoctopus pillsburyae* Voss, 1975**

[see couplet 17 (18) in the key to subfamilies and genera of Octopodidae]

4 (3). No ocellar spots on dorsal side of mantle (genus *Octopus*)..........................**5**

5 (26). Species found tropical and subtropical Atlantic, southward to Southern Brazil and Cape of Good Hope [O. *fontanianus* may be found off southern Africa, see couplet 29 (30)].........**6**

6 (9). One round ocellar spot in front of each eye on outer side of web between 2nd and 3rd arms **7**

7 (8). Center of ocellar spot is surrounded by a blue ring. Small animals, mantle length up to 7 cm, more often to 3-4 cm. 6-7 filaments in demibranch. Ligula length 3-5% of hectocotylized arm length. Egg length 1.6-1.8 mm............

.............***O. hummelincki* Adam, 1936**

(Fig. 81 A,B). Tropical Western Atlantic from the Bahamas and southern Florida to Baia (Brazil); Caribbean Sea. Mainly near islands, on coral reefs in upper sublittoral.

8 (7). No blue ring around the center of ocellar spot. Large animals, mantle length up to 20 cm. 9-10 filaments in demibranch. Ligula length 1.4-1.9% of hectocotylized arm length. Egg length about 17 mm.....***O. maya* Voss & Solis, 1966**

(Fig. 81 C,D). Shallow waters of the Gulf of Campeche and Yucatan Peninsula. Important fishery species.

9 (6). No ocellar spot on web...............**10**

10 (11). Wide transverse dark brown or yellowish brown stripes on light yellowish background on mantle, head and arms. Small animals, mantle length to 3 cm. 6-7 filaments in demibranch. Ligula length 6-9% of hectocotylized arm length. Egg length about 6 mm....................

.....................***O. zonatus* Voss, 1968**

(Fig. 81 E,F). Southern part of the Caribbean Sea, inner shelf.

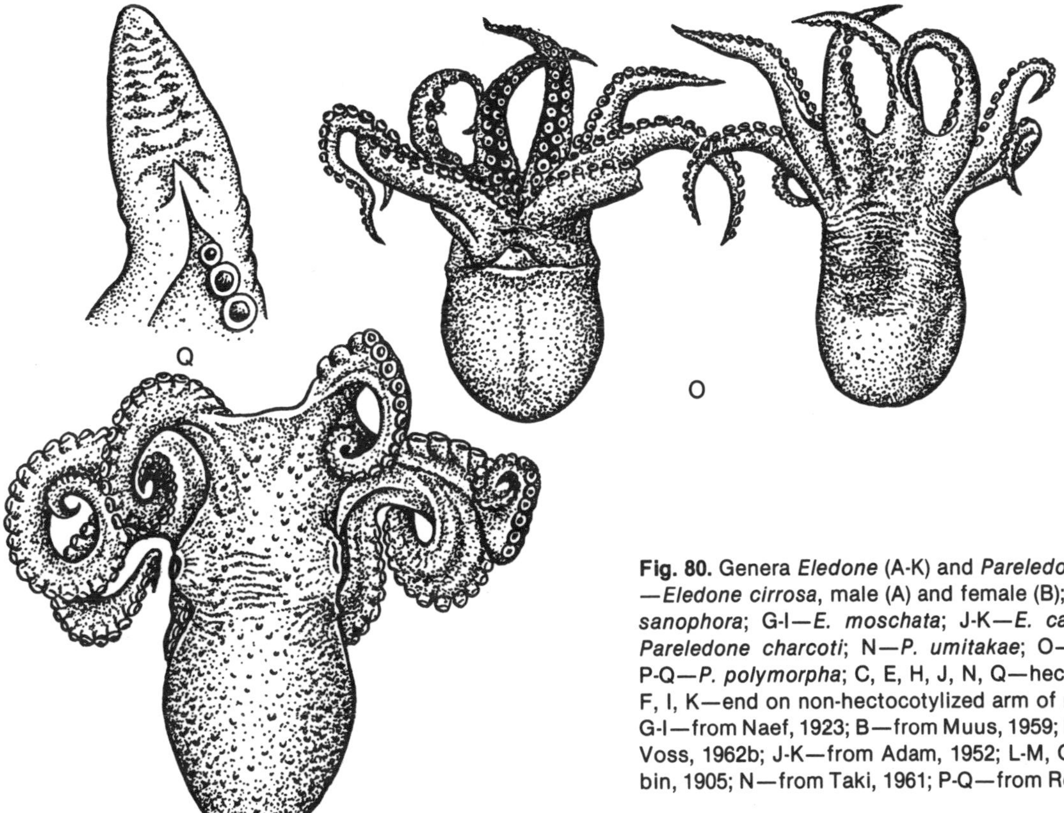

Fig. 80. Genera *Eledone* (A-K) and *Pareledone* (L-Q): A-D —*Eledone cirrosa*, male (A) and female (B); E-F—*E. thysanophora*; G-I—*E. moschata*; J-K—*E. caparti*; L-M—*Pareledone charcoti*; N—*P. umitakae*; O—*P. turqueti*; P-Q—*P. polymorpha*; C, E, H, J, N, Q—hectocotylus; D, F, I, K—end on non-hectocotylized arm of male (A, C-D, G-I—from Naef, 1923; B—from Muus, 1959; E-F—from G. Voss, 1962b; J-K—from Adam, 1952; L-M, O—from Joubin, 1905; N—from Taki, 1961; P-Q—from Robson, 1930).

11 (10). No brown transverse stripes on mantle and head **12**

12 (13). Mantle, head, and arms densely covered by small distinct rounded papillae set close together. A dark purple or brown stripe passes along dorsal side of entire length of each arm. Web inside with white reticulated stripes on tomato red background. Mantle length up to 11 cm. 8-10 filaments in demibranch. Ligula length 4-6% of hectocotylized arm length. Egg length 2-2.5 mm . . . . **O. burryi Voss, 1950**
(= *O. vincenti* Pickford, 1955) (Fig. 81 G-I). Tropical western and eastern Atlantic: from Georgia to the Gulf of Mexico, Caribbean Sea and northern Brazil, western Africa from the Canary Islands, Senegal and Cape Verde Islands to Angola and St. Helena. Inner (rarely outer) shelf, on sandy and muddly bottom.

13 (12). Mantle, head and arms smooth or with separate scattered papillae (mainly between eyes). No dark longitudinal stripes on arms **14**

14 (15). 1st arms conspicuously thicker and longer than others (2nd arms sometimes similarly thick, but shorter). Arm length 80-90% of total length. Mantle narrow, longitudinal-oval. Large animals, mantle length up to 18 cm. 9-13 filaments in demibranch. Ligula large, 5-14% (on the average 10%) of hectocotylized arm length. Egg length 1.8-2.5 mm. Bright white spots on body in live octopuses . . . .
. . . . **O. macropus Risso, 1826**
(= *O. bermudensis* Hoyle, 1885) (Fig. 81 J,K). Tropical Atlantic Indo-West Pacific species, in the western Atlantic mainly near islands: Bermuda, Bahama Islands, southern Florida to Brazil, Caribbean Sea, Mediterranean Sea, western Africa to the Gulf of Guinea, Ascension and St. Helena Islands. Near the coast on coral reefs and rocks.

15 (14). 2nd and 3rd arms longest or all arms are subequal in length and thickness **16**

16 (17). 2nd and 3rd arms noticeably longer ànd thicker than 1st and 4th, their length 80-90% of total length. Medium size animals, mantle length up to 10-12 cm. 6-8 filaments in demibranch. Ligula length 3-4% of hectocotylized arm length. Ligula oval with a dozen transverse ridges. Egg length 10-14 mm . . **O. briareus Robson, 1929**
(Fig. 81 L). Tropical Atlantic from southern Florida to northern Brazil, Caribbean Sea, and eastern Gulf of Mexico. Coastal shallows, coral reefs.

17 (16). All arms of subequal thickness, 2nd and 3rd arms usually somewhat longer than others **18**

18 (19). Arms very long, 85-90% of total length, slender, often conspicuously asymmetrical—one arm may be much longer than opposite arm of same pair. Small or medium-size animal, mantle length to 5 cm. 11 filaments in demibranch. Ligula short, 1.9-2.5% of hectocotylized arm length. Egg length 2 mm . . . .
. . . . **O. defilippi Vérany, 1851**
(Fig. 81 M,N). Tropical and subtropical western and eastern Atlantic: from Florida and Bahama Islands to Rio de Janeiro and from the Mediterranean Sea to Angola, probably also in the Indian Ocean and southwestern Pacific. The whole shelf and upper slope. Larva called "macrotritopus" (*Macrotritopus* spp.): 3rd arms very much longer than other arms.

19 (18). Arm length not exceeding 85% of total length. Arms symmetrical, arm ends not attentuate **20**

20 (25). Arm length 70-85% of total length. Mantle length in adult animals more than 3 cm. 7-11, usually 8-10 filaments in demibranch **21**

21 (24). Ligula short, 2.5-3% of hectocotylized arm length **22**

22 (23). Ligula with well developed calamus (50% of ligula length) and longitudinal groove. Web depth 20-25% of the longest arm length. Diameter of largest arm suckers in males on the average 15-16% of the mantle length. Skin beset by small tubercles and warts, several "horns" situated on head and median part of dorsal side of mantle where they often form a diamond figure. Mantle length up to 20 (30) cm. Egg length 1.8-2.5 mm
. . . . **O. vulgaris Lamarck, 1798**
[= *O. rugosus* (Bosc, 1792)] (Fig. 81 O-S). Tropical-subtropical cosmopolitan species. In the Atlantic from Long Island to southern Brazil and from southern part of the North Sea to the Cape of Good Hope; common in Gulf of Mexico, Caribbean and Mediterranean Seas, found also near oceanic islands. Whole shelf, sometimes upper part of slope but usually in coastal shallows. Most important octopus of commercial fishery.

23 (22). Ligula very short, without calamus, with transverse groove. Web depth 33% of the longest arm length. Diameter of largest arm suckers in male 22% of the mantle length. Skin smooth. Mantle length 5 cm . . . .
. . . . **O. schultzei (Hoyle, 1910)**

Namibia (Lüderitz-Bay).

24 (21). Ligula very long, 12-16% of hectocotyliz-ed arm length. Web extending far along ventral edges of arms, web depth on the average 25% of longest arm length. Skin smooth, with small tubercles, one "horn" above each eye. Mantle length up to 12 cm. Egg length 5 mm.........
.................***O. salutii*** Vérany, 1851
(Fig. 81 S,T). Bay of Biscay to the Gulf of Cádiz, Mediterranean Sea. Upper bathyal and lower sublittoral.

25 (20). Arm length 65-70% of total length. Small animals, mantle length up to 5 cm, usually to 2-3 cm. 5-6 (rarely 7) filaments in demibranch. Ligula length 4-7% of the hectocotylized arm length. Egg length 6-8 mm.......***O. joubini*** Robson, 1929
(= *O. mercatoris* Adam, 1937) (Fig. 81 U,V). Tropical western Atlantic, Gulf of Mexico, Caribbean Sea; from Georgia to Venezuela and Guianas. Coastal shallows and inner shelf. Often in empty shells. A popular species kept in home aquariums.

26 (5). Species found off Uruguay, Argentina.

Falkland Islands and Tierra del Fuego.......**27**

Note: The key does not include *O. hyadesi* Rochebrune & Mabille, 1887, *O. pentherinus* Rochebrune & Mabille, 1887, and *O. membranaceus* (Rochebrune & Mabille, 1887, non Quoy & Gaimard, 1832), described from the area of Cape Horn from young specimens (mantle length 12-20 mm) and very incompletely.

27 (28). Suckers in middle parts of all arms in males and females enlarged, their diameter 16-20% of the mantle length. Large animals, mantle length up to 8-19 cm. Arm length 72-83% of total length. Ligula length 5-9% of the hectocotylized arm length. Web extending far along ventral side of arms. Skin smooth............
............***O. megalocyathus*** Gould, 1846
[= *O. patagonicus* Lönnberg, 1898, *O. brucei* (Hoyle, 1912)]. Strait of Magellan, Tierra del Fuégo, Burdwood Bank, and Falkland Islands.

28 (27). Enlarged suckers present only in middle parts of 2nd and 3rd arms. Diameter of suckers in females 7-12% of the mantle length. Small animals, mantle length 2-4 cm. Arm length

Fig. 81.

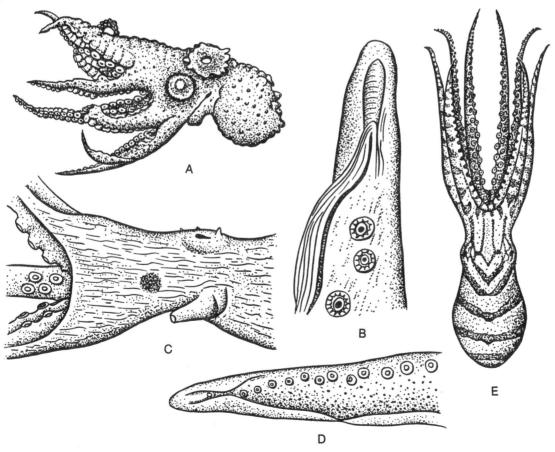

305

Fig. 81.

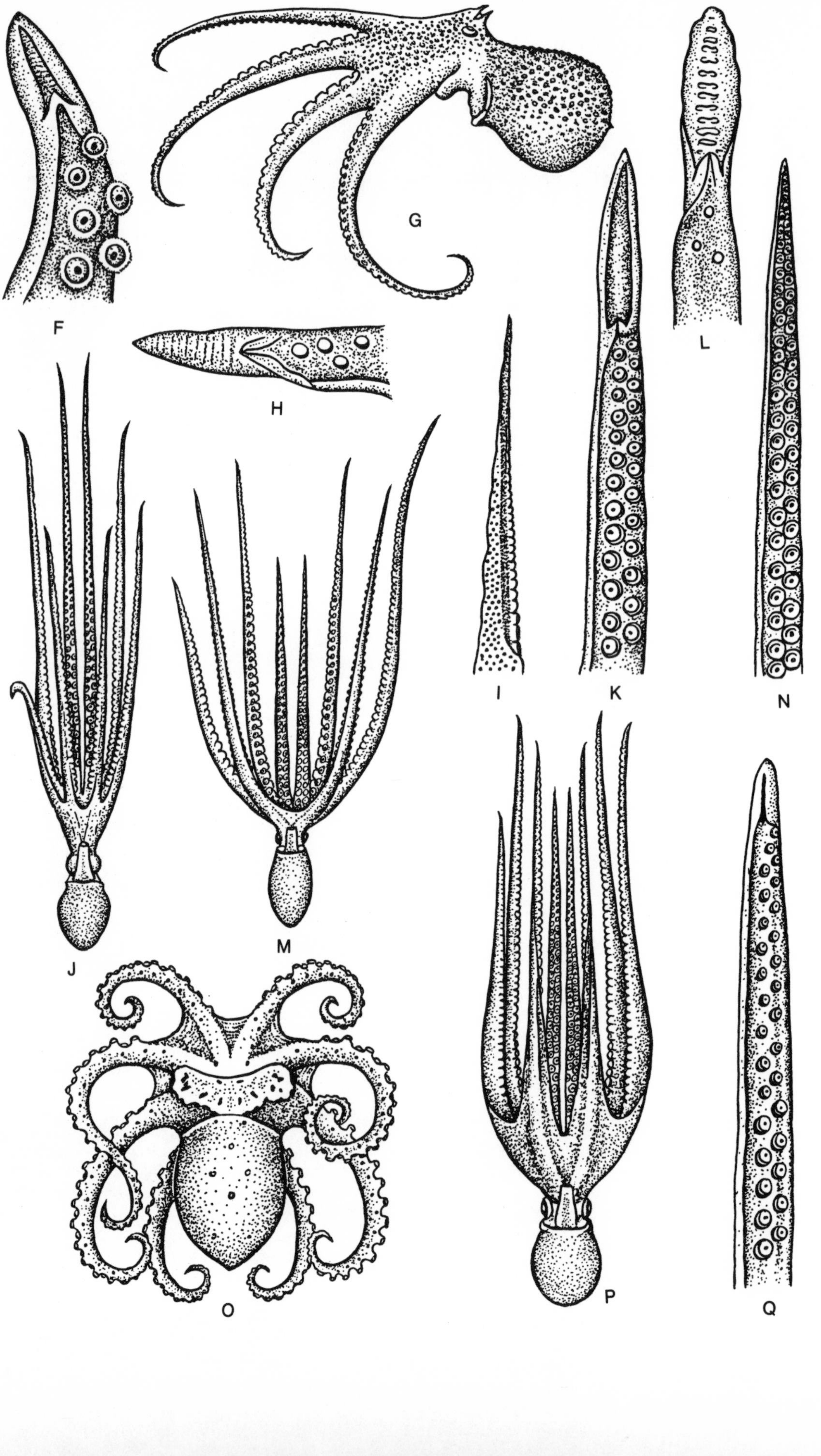

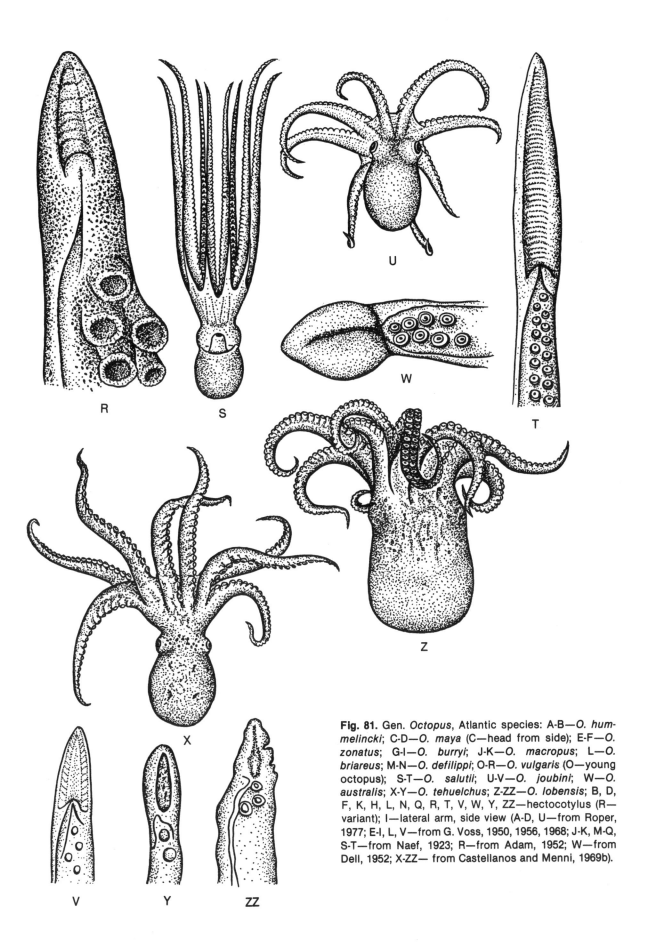

Fig. 81. Gen. *Octopus*, Atlantic species: A-B—*O. hummelincki*; C-D—*O. maya* (C—head from side); E-F—*O. zonatus*; G-I—*O. burryi*; J-K—*O. macropus*; L—*O. briareus*; M-N—*O. defilippi*; O-R—*O. vulgaris* (O—young octopus); S-T—*O. salutii*; U-V—*O. joubini*; W—*O. australis*; X-Y—*O. tehuelchus*; Z-ZZ—*O. lobensis*; B, D, F, K, H, L, N, Q, R, T, V, W, Y, ZZ—hectocotylus (R— variant); I—lateral arm, side view (A-D, U—from Roper, 1977; E-I, L, V—from G. Voss, 1950, 1956, 1968; J-K, M-Q, S-T—from Naef, 1923; R—from Adam, 1952; W—from Dell, 1952; X-ZZ— from Castellanos and Menni, 1969b).

60-80% of total length. Web of ordinary structure **29**

29 (30). Skin rough, many small tubercles and warts on dorsal side of mantle, head and arms, one "horn" above each eye. Ligula with inflated lateral sides and very narrow, deep, almost closed groove. Ligula length 5-9% of the hectocotylized arm length. 1-2 pairs of greatly enlarged suckers in middle part of male's lateral arms, diameter of suckers 13-17% of mantle length. Arm length 70-80% of total length. 8-11 filaments in demibranch. Egg length 3-5 mm . . . .
. . . . ***O. fontanianus*** d'Orbigny, 1835
(= *Robsonella fontaniana*, *Joubinia fontaniana* auct.). Southern part of South America from northern Peru and Golfo Nuevo (Argentina) to Cape Horn. Closely related forms are found near Natal [*O. fontanianus* var. *africanus* (Robson, 1929)] and off southern and southwestern Australia, New Zealand, Norfolk, Steward, Campbell, Auckland, Antipodes, Chatham Islands (*O. australis* Hoyle, 1885) (Fig. 81 W). Probably these are local forms of one circumglobal notalian-southern subtropical species. The species is distributed from the littoral to upper bathyal zones.

30 (29). Skin smooth, scarce tiny tubercles on head, anterior part of mantle and at arm bases. No supraocular cirri. No greatly enlarged suckers. Arm length on the average 65-70% of total length. Sides of ligula not inflated, groove not sharply narrowed **31**

31 (32). Body oval, head narrow, nuchal constriction usually distinct. Skin smooth, shining. 6th-7th pairs of suckers on lateral arms in male and female somewhat enlarged. Ligula with a deep and fairly narrow groove. Egg length 10-15 mm . . . . ***O. tehuelchus*** d'Orbigny, 1835
(Fig. 81 X,Y). From southern Brazil to Golfo Nuevo (Argentina). Recorded with doubt at Cape Horn. Littoral and coastal shallows.

32 (31). Body round, head wide, nuchal constriction inconspicuous. Skin rough, opaque. Enlarged suckers absent. Ligula with wide shallow groove . . . . . . ***O. lobensis*** Castellanos & Menni, 1969
(Fig. 81 Z,ZZ). Golfo San Matías and Golfo Nuevo (Argentina), coastal shallows.

33 (2). Body slightly muscular, soft to the touch, with subcuticular layer of semigelatinous tissue. Mantle aperture narrow. Funnel almost entirely buried in head tissue. Head and mantle wide, arms short, 60-65% of total length. Web depth 50% of the longest arm length. Funnel organ VV-shaped. Skin beset by low wide tubercles, as if shagreened, a small light spot in the center of each tubercle, a pair of "horns" above each eye. Color orange. 9-10 filaments in demibranch. Mantle length up to 4 cm . . . .
. . . . ***Danoctopus schmidti*** Joubin, 1933
[see couplet 14 (15) in the key to subfamilies and genera of Octopodidae].

34 (1). 3rd left arm hectocotylized **35**

35 (36). Dorsal side of mantle, head and arm bases densely beset by large round papillae, sometimes arranged in longitudinal rows. One long "horn" above each eye. In fixed specimens there is usually a skin fold on the sides of mantle between dorsal and ventral sides. Body firm to the touch, arm ends not breaken off. Web 20-33%, sometimes up to 40% of longest arm length. Diameter of suckers 6-10% of hectocotylized arm length. Funnel organ as a rule W-shaped. 12-14 filaments in demibranch. Color orange or orange-red. Egg length 2 mm. Mantle length to 12 cm . . . ***Scaeurgus unicirrhus*** (delle Chiaje, 1830)
[see couplet 19 (20) in the key to subfamilies and genera of Octopodidae]. In the Atlantic Ocean from Georgia to Brazil and from Bay of Biscay to Namibia, in the Gulf of Mexico, Caribbean, and Mediterranean seas, on many submarine banks and tops of seamounts. Mainly at depths of 100-400 m.

36 (35). Skin of dorsal side covered with microscopic closely set tubercles, almost smooth. A pair of "horns" above each eye. No lateral skin fold. Arm ends often broken off. Skin soft to the touch, gelatinous (particularly in living specimens). Umbrella depth 33-40% of longest arm length. Diameter of suckers 4-6% of mantle length. Ligula length 3-7% of hectocotylized arm length. Funnel organ VV-shaped. 8-10 filaments in demibranch. Color yellowish brown or red-brown. Egg length 7-8 mm. Mantle length up to 16 cm . . . .
Pteroctopus tetracirrhus (delle Chiaje, 1890)
[see couplet 20 (19) in the key to subfamilies and genera of Octopodidae].

Key to species of the subfamily Octopodinae of the Northern Pacific (from the Bering Strait to Korea, Central Honshu, and Baja California)

1 (32). Species distributed in the northwestern Pacific, Bering Sea, the Sea of Okhotsk and Sea of

Japan, southward to Korea, Noto and Boso Peninsulas **2**

2 (3). Arms of greatly unequal length: 1st arms much longer and thicker than the others (twice as long as 3rd-4th arms), its length about 80% of total length. Web very short, 6-10% of the longest arm length. Funnel organ VV-shaped. Hectocotylus large, 11-23% of the hectocotylized arm length. Egg length 8 mm . . . .

. . . . ***Octopus variabilis*** **(Sasaki, 1929)**

[*O. macropus* var. *minor* (Sasaki, 1920), *O. variabilis* var. *minor* (Sasaki, 1929), *O. macropus* auct., non Risso] (Fig. 82 a,b). Japan from Hokkaido to the Ryukyus, Peter the Great Bay (USSR), Korea, northern and eastern China, Taiwan. Shelf, usually on mud. Mantle length to 10 cm.

3 (2). Arms slightly differing in length and thickness, sometimes 1st arm longer but not thicker than others. Longest arm length usually less than 80% of total length. Web depth 13-33%, usually 20-25% of longest arm length **4**

4 (7). Large ocellar spots (up to 7 mm) on web in front of eyes on each side between 2nd and 3rd arms. Brick red transverse stripe on head. Body beset by granules, usually row of several elongated tubercles on sides and a pair of large papillae above eye. Hectocotylus short, ligula length 4-7% of the hectocotylized arm length . . . **5**

5 (6). Diameter of largest sucker in males 9-30% of the mantle length. 7-8 filaments in demibranch. Egg length 10-13 mm . . . .

. . . . ***O. ocellatus*** **Gray, 1849**

(= *O. fangsiao* d'Orbigny, 1840, *O. areolatus* de Haan in Férussac & d'Orbigny, 1840). Japan (northwards to Southern Hokkaido), Southern Korea, China. Coastal shallows. Mantle length up to 5-6 cm. Of secondary fishery importance. Differences between this and the next species are not well established, many specialists consider it as a synonym of *O. membranaceus*.

6 (5). Diameter of largest sucker in males 6-10% of the mantle length. 8-9 filaments in demibranch. Egg length 3 mm . . . .

..***O. membranaceus*** **Quoy & Gaimard, 1832**

[*O. pulcher* Broch, 1887, *O. brocki* Ortmann, 1888, *O. ovulum* (Sasaki, 1917)] (Fig. 82 C). Indo-West Pacific tropical-subtropical species, from Central Honshu to the Red Sea, eastern Africa and northern Australia. Coastal shallows. Mantle length to 8 cm. A common species, of minor fishery importance in southeastern Asia.

7 (4). No ocellar spots on web, no red transverse stripe on head nor elongated tubercles on sides. . **8**

8 (29). Body smooth or covered with papillae, granules, tubercles, cirri, but not with stellate warts **9**

9 (14). Body smooth, sometimes only with poorly visible wrinkles or tiny warts on head. Supraocular cirri present **10**

10 (11). Funnel organ VV-shaped. Body firm, fleshy. No peripheral skin fold on mantle sides. Web deep, 30-40% of longest arm length. Hectocotylus long, 13-21% of hectocotylized arm length, open. Diameter of largest sucker 8-15% of mantle length. Egg length 22-28 mm . . . .

. . . . ***O. conispadiceus*** **(Sasaki, 1917)**

(Fig. 82 D,E). Lower boreal northwestern Pacific species, distributed from the Tatar Strait and southern Kuriles to the Korean Strait and Inner Sea (Seto-Naikai). Sublittoral, mainly sandy grounds of upper sublittoral. Mantle length up to 25 cm, total length up to 1.5 m. Of fishery importance in northern Japan, North and South Korea, caught in very small quantities in the Far East of the USSR.

11 (10). Funnel organ W-shaped. Body flabby, not muscular. Peripheral skin fold usually present. Diameter of largest suckers 7-9% of the mantle length **12**

12 (13). 1st arms the longest. Web depth about 33% of the longest arm length. Hectocotylus long (7-15% of hectocotylized arm length). One conical tubercle above each eye . . . .

. . . . ***O. leioderma*** **(Berry, 1911)**

(Fig. 82 F,G). Upper boreal North Pacific species: from the Bering Strait to Sea of Okhotsk, Kurile Islands and northern California, not found in the Sea of Japan. Sublittoral and bathyal (off Washington, Oregon, and California only in the lower sublittoral and bathyal). Mantle length to 10 cm. Egg length 17-18 mm.

13 (12). Arms of subequal length. Web depth 25% of the longest arm length. Hectocotylus short, about 4% of the hectocotylized arm length. 3 small tubercles above each eye, the central one is the largest and flattened laterally. Egg length 9 mm . . . . ***O. ochotensis*** **(Sasaki, 1920)**

Sea of Okhotsk, lower sublittoral. Mantle length up to 5 cm.

14 (9). Warts (not stellate, papillae or cirri present on body **15**

15 (24). Supraocular cirri present, like conical "horns" or laterally flattened "ears" **16**

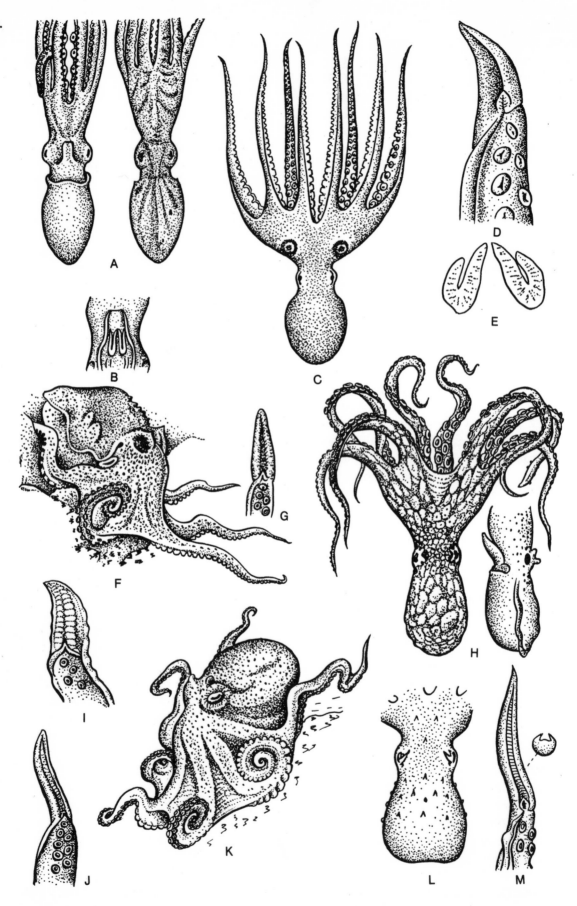

Fig. 82.

A

B

C

D

E

F

G

H

I

J

K

L

M

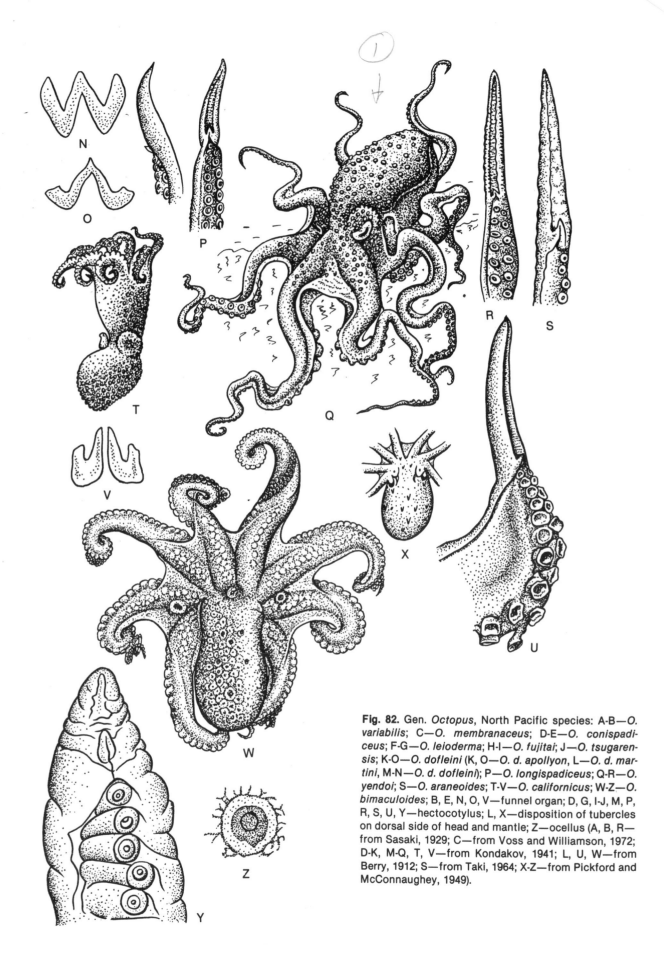

Fig. 82. Gen. *Octopus*, North Pacific species: A-B—*O. variabilis*; C—*O. membranaceus*; D-E—*O. conispadiceus*; F-G—*O. leioderma*; H-I—*O. fujitai*; J—*O. tsugarensis*; K-O—*O. dofleini* (K, O—*O. d. apollyon*, L—*O. d. martini*, M-N—*O. d. dofleini*); P—*O. longispadiceus*; Q-R—*O. yendoi*; S—*O. araneoides*; T-V—*O. californicus*; W-Z—*O. bimaculoides*; B, E, N, O, V—funnel organ; D, G, I-J, M, P, R, S, U, Y—hectocotylus; L, X—disposition of tubercles on dorsal side of head and mantle; Z—ocellus (A, B, R—from Sasaki, 1929; C—from Voss and Williamson, 1972; D-K, M-Q, T, V—from Kondakov, 1941; L, U, W—from Berry, 1912; S—from Taki, 1964; X-Z—from Pickford and McConnaughey, 1949).

16 (19). A few separate warts scattered on head and dorsal side of mantle. No papillae or cirr **17**

17 (18). Coloration of body dorsal side marbled (dark stains against pink-brown background). Arm length about 80% of total length. Diameter of largest suckers 9-12% of mantle length. Ligula length 14% of hectocotylized arm length . . . .
. . . . ***O. fujitai* (Sasaki, 1929)**

(Fig. 83 H,I). Southern coast of the Sea of Japan. According to N.N. Kondakov (1941) and I.I. Akimushkin (1963), also in Olyutorsky Bay and the Sea of Okhotsk. Lower sublittoral. Mantle length up to 5 cm.

18 (17). Coloration of mantle dorsal side uniform red-brown, several dark transverse stripes or spots between eyes. Arm length about 70% of total length. Several greatly enlarged suckers near web edge on 1st arms of males, their diameter 15-16% of the mantle length. Ligula length 9% of the hectocotylized arm length . . . .
. . . . ***O. tsugarensis* (Sasaki, 1920)**

(Fig. 82 J). Tsugaru Strait (depth 356 m), Sea of Okhotsk. Mantle length up to 4 cm.

19 (16). Head and dorsal side of mantle covered with numerous low granules and warts, among which are some larger cirri or "horns" **20**

20 (21). One flattened rounded "ear" above each eye, and a conical papilla ("horn") may be present. Hectocotylus very long (8-25%, usually 10-20% of hectocotylized arm length), ligula narrow, in fresh specimens almost closed (tubular). Diameter of largest suckers 10-16% of the mantle length. A few conical "horns" on head and mantle. Egg length 6-8 mm. Very large animals . . . .
. . . . ***O. dofleini* (Wülker, 1910)**

[.= *O. gilbertianus* (Berry, 1912), *O. apollyon* (Berry, 1913), *Paroctopus asper* Akimushkin, 1963, *O. punctatus* auct., non Blainville, *O. hongkongensis* auct., non Hoyle, ?*O. madokai* (Berry, 1921)] (Fig. 81 K-O). North Pacific boreal species, lives in the sublittoral and upper bathyal. The largest of recent octopuses: mantle length up to 60 cm and more, total length up to 3-5 m. Common species, commercially important in northern Japan, North and South Korea, in the Far East of the USSR, on the Aleutian Islands, off British Columbia, Washington, and Oregon. Object of interest to skin divers. Lives mainly in rocks and among stones. 3 subspecies: *O. dofleini dofleini* (Wülker) [=?*O. madokai* (Berry)] (Fig. 82 M,N)—Southern Kurile Islands, Southern

Sakhalin, Primorye Territory, Korea, northern coasts of Yellow Sea, Hokkaido, Honshu, Shikoku; *O. d. apollyon* (Berry) [= *O. gilbertianus* (Berry), *P. asper* Akimushkin, *O. punctatus* auct., non Blainville] (Fig. 82 K,O)—from the Bering Sea to the Kurile Islands, northern part of the Sea of Japan and Gulf of Alaska; *O. d. martini* Pickford, 1964 (Fig. 82 L)—from British Columbia to southern California. Probably there is a 4th, undescribed subspecies in the bathyal off the Channel Islands, California.

21 (20). Supraocular cirri not flattened (conical or cylindrical). Ligula length up to 10% of the hectocotylized arm length **22**

22 (23). 1st arms the longest. A few greatly enlarged suckers on 1st-2nd arms of male, their diameter 15-24% of the mantle length. Ligula long, about 10% of the hectocotylized arm length. No conical papillae ("horns") on dorsal side of mantle . . . . . . ***O. longispadiceus* (Sasaki, 1917)**

(Fig. 82 P). Sea of Okhotsk, Sea of Japan, Pacific coast of Kurile Islands, Hokkaido, Honshu. Depths about 100-800 m. Mantle length to 8 cm.

23 (22). 1st arm usually the shortest. Diameter of the largest suckers on 1st-2nd arms in male 12-16% of mantle length. Ligula short, 2-5% of hectocotylized arm length. A few large conical papillae on dorsal side of mantle. Eggs small (1.8-2.5 mm) . . . . . . ***O. vulgaris* Lamarck, 1798**

[= *O. rugosus* (Bosc, 1792)] (see couplet 22 (23) key to *Octopodinae* in Atlantic Ocean). In northwestern Pacific distributed northwards up to Tsugaru Strait but usually not found to the north of Noto and Boso Peninsula. Commonest octopus of central and southern Japan. Most important commercial species, object of mariculture. Mantle length of Japanese specimens up to 12 cm.

24 (15). Supraocular cirri absent. Head and dorsal side of mantle beset by scarce small warts and pustules **25**

25 (28). 3rd right arm hectocotylized. Ligula length 6-12% of hectocotylized arm length **26**

26 (27). Funnel almost entirely embedded in tissue of ventral side of head. Arm length 70-82%, usually 75% of total length. Diameter of the largest suckers in female 9-12%, in male 13-16% of the mantle length. Ligula length 6-7% of hectocotylized arm length. Egg length 17 mm . . . . ***O. yendoi* (Sasaki, 1920)**

(Fig. 82 Q,R). Sea of Okhotsk, Sea of Japan, Pacific coast of northern Japan. Lower sublittoral and uppermost bathyal. Mantle length to 6 cm.

27 (26). Funnel half-free. Arm length 65-70% of total length. Diameter of largest suckers in female 5-8%, in male 9-10% of mantle length. Ligula length 9-12% of hectocotylized arm length. Egg length 13 mm..... ***O. araneoides* (Taki, 1964)**

(Fig. 82 S). Northeastern Honshu, shelf and uppermost bathyal. Secondary species of commercial fishery. Mantle length up to 9-10 cm.

28 (25). 3rd left arm hectocotylized. Ligula length 5% of the hectocotylized arm length..........

...... ***Pteroctopus witjazi* Akimushkin, 1963**

[see couplet 20 (19), in the key to subfamilies and genera of Octopodidae]

29 (8). Head, mantle and arm bases are densely beset by large stellate or lobate warts........**30**

30 (31). Funnel organ W-shaped. Arm length 60-65% of total length. Umbrella deep, 30-33% of longest arm length. Dorsal side gray-brown.....

.... ***O. spinosus* (Sasaki, 1920)**

Tsugaru Strait, Hokkaido. Lower sublittoral and upper bathyal. Mantle length up to 2.5 cm.

31 (30). Funnel organ VV-shaped. Arm length 70-75% of total length. Web depth 22-30% of the longest arm length. Dorsal side of body dark orange to brick red or pink..................

.... ***O. californicus* (Berry, 1911)**

(Fig. 82 T-V). See couplet 39 (40) of this key.

32 (1). Species distributed in the northeastern Pacific from the Gulf of Alaska to Baja California.................................**33**

33 (60). Arm length 67-88% of total length. Web depth 15-20% of the longest arm length. Suckers in 2 rows along the entire arm starting from the 3rd sucker.............................**34**

34 (37). Large (up to 20 mm) ocellar spot on web in front of each eye between 2nd and 3rd arms (Fig. 82 Z). Hectocotylus very short, ligula length 2-3% of the hectocotylized arm length. Head and mantle covered with small granules and conical papillae.................................**35**

35 (36). Diameter of the largest suckers in male 16-26%, on the average 19%, in female 9-18%, on the average 13% of the mantle length. Arm length 75-80% of total length. Egg length 2-4 mm......

.... ***O. bimaculatus* Verrill, 1883**

Southern California, Baja California, Gulf of California. Lower littoral and upper sublittoral, mainly in rocks. Mantle length up to 10-18 cm. Minor species of commercial fishery.

36 (35). Diameter of largest suckers in male 10-15%, on the average 13%, in female 7-15%, on

the average 10% of the mantle length. Arm length usually 80-90% of total length. Eggs large, 10-17 mm long..................***O. bimaculoides*** **Pickford & McConnaughey, 1949**

(Fig. 82 W-Z). Central and southern California, northern Baja California. Littoral, mainly on intertidal mudflats. A common species. Mantle length up to 7-20 cm.

37 (34). No ocellar spots on web............**38**

38 (57). Ends of arms normal, suckers on the ends not modified...........................**39**

39 (40). Surface of head, mantle and arm bases densely covered with large stellate warts. Coloration pink, red or orange [see entry 31 (30)]. Funnel organ VV-shaped. Hectocotylus large, ligula length 14-17% of the hectocotylized arm length. Egg length 12-15 mm.......................

.... ***O. californicus* (Berry, 1911)**

(Fig. 82 T-V). California, lower sublittoral and upper bathyal. Japan Sea (Peter the Great Bay and Tatar Strait), upper sublittoral. Mantle length up to 12 cm.

40 (39). Body surface smooth or beset by granules, papillae, cirri, but not by stellate warts. Funnel organ not VV-shaped...............**41**

41 (42). Arms extremely long (about 85% of total length), very delicate, snakelike, their ends often break off. Web short, 14-22% of longest arm length. Hectocotylus very short, 2-2.5% of hectocotylized arm length. Separate papillae of three sizes scattered over the body, largest ones composite; papillae extend onto inner side of web. 6-7 filaments in demibranch....................

.... ***O. alecto* (Berry, 1953)**

Upper Gulf of California. Small animals, mantle length to 2-3 cm.

42 (41). Arm length 67-80% of total length. Web depth 20-33% of longest arm length........**43**

43 (44). 1st arms longest (about 70% of total length). Hectocotylus long, ligula length 7-15% of hectocotylized arm length. Skin smooth, sometimes with separate poorly visible wrinkles and tubercles on head. One conical tubercle above each eye. Peripheral skin fold usually present. No greatly enlarged suckers......................

.... ***O. leioderma* (Berry, 1911)**

[see couplet 12 (13) of this key].

44 (43). Arms are of subequal length or 1st arms are shorter than others. Peripheral skin fold absent...............................**45**

45 (46). Arm length 67% of total length. Funnel organ I Λ I-shaped. Web extends along ventral sides of 1st-3rd arms up to ends as a wide sail-like membrane. Head, mantle, arm bases and inner side of web beset by closely set papillae. Ligula length 5% of the hectocotylized arm length. Gills very large: 15-17 filaments in demibranch......

.............*O. veligero* **Berry, 1953**

Baja California, depths of up to 200 m. Mantle length up to 5-7 cm.

46 (45). Arm length 70-80% of total length. Funnel organ W-shaped. No wide web along ventral sides of arms. Gills of normal size..........**47**

47 (48). Giant octopuses. Hectocotylus very long, narrow, almost tubular, ligula length 8-25%, usually 10-20% of the hectocotylized arm length. Diameter of largest suckers 10-16% of the mantle length. One laterally flattened rounded "ear" above each eye, conical "horns" may be present also. Body beset by wrinkles, folds and papillae. A few conical papillae on head and mantle. Egg length 6-8 mm....*O. dofleini* **(Wülker, 1910)**

[For subspecies *O.d. apollyon* (Berry, 1913) and *O.d. martini* Pickford, 1964 see couplet 20 (21) of this key].

48 (47). Small or medium-size octopuses, total length up to 30 cm. Ligula length up to 10-12% of hectocotylized arm length. Flattened supraocular "ears" never present, only with conical "horns" **49**

49 (52). Very small animals (mantle length 2-3 cm). Skin smooth, sometimes only with poorly visible papillae or warts on head. 5-6 filaments in demibranch......................**50**

50 (51). One sucker of 4th pair on 1st-3rd arms of male greatly enlarged (in females 5th-6th pair of suckers somewhat enlarged). Ligula open, conical, its length 6-7% of hectocotylized arm length. Calamus very long, 50% of ligula length. Color bright red dorsally, much lighter ventrally. Egg length 10-12 mm.......................

.............*O. micropyrsus* **Berry, 1953**

Southern California. Lower littoral and upper sublittoral, often in holdfasts of giant kelp. One of the smallest octopuses: mantle length of mature male is 10 mm, maximal mantle length 25 mm.

51 (50). One sucker of 5th or 6th pair of suckers on 2nd-3rd arms of male and female greatly enlarged. Ligula narrow, elongated, its length 10-12% of hectocotylized arm length. Calamus small. Color reddish or brown dorsally, lighter ventrally. Egg size 5 mm.....................

.............*O. fitchi* **Berry, 1953**

Upper Gulf of California. Common on rocky littoral and in upper sublittoral under stones. Mantle length up to 2-3 cm. Bite painful but not dangerous.

52 (49). Mantle length up to 5-10 cm. Body covered with a network of small low warts connected by narrow ridges-wrinkles, or granulated (low papillae separated by narrow grooves); small "horns" may be present on head (including those above eyes) and on back....................**53**

53 (56). One or two suckers on 1st-3rd arms (as a rule, 6th pair) greatly enlarged. Hectocotylus long, 7-11% of hectocotylized arm length. Inner side of web smooth....................**54**

54 (55). Eyes large, projecting. 2nd arm usually longer than others. 20-24 transverse folds on ligula. 11-13 filaments in demibranch. Eggs small, 3-4 mm..........*O. rubescens* **Berry, 1953**

From southern Alaska to Baja California and Gulf of California. Throughout the sublittoral from lowest littoral up to 200 m. Mantle length up to 5-10 cm. A common Californian octopus. Is known to bite.

55 (54). Eyes very small. Arms of equal length. About 10 transverse folds on ligula. 7-8 filaments in demibranch. Eggs large (9-10 mm long)......

.....*O. digueti* **Perrier & Rochebrune, 1894**

Gulf of California, southward reaching Mazatlán. Littoral and upper sublittoral, often in empty bivalve and gastropod shells. Mantle length to 6 cm.

56 (53). No greatly enlarged suckers, though on the average suckers of lateral arms larger than those on 1st and 4th arms. Hectocotylus small, ligula length 1.5% of hectocotylized arm length. Inner surface of umbrella and arm bases beset by papillae........*O. hubbsorum* **Berry, 1953**

Gulf of California. Littoral and upper sublittoral. Mantle length to 5-7 cm.

57 (38). Suckers on male arm ends (except hectocotylized arm) replaced by a brush of small finger-like papillae arranged in 4 rows. No greatly enlarged suckers. Body smooth............**58**

58 (59). Head and mantle above with very conspicuous dark bands outlined by a fine greenish-yellow line on a light background; bands longitudinal on head and transverse on mantle. Pale round or oval spots on arms. No cirri over eyes. Ligula length 8% of hectocotylized arm length. 8-9 filaments in demibranch. Egg length 3.5-4 mm

.............*O. chierchiae* **Jatta, 1889**

Pacific coast of Central America (El Salvador to Panamá), recorded in the lower Gulf of California. Coastal shallows. Mantle length to 2-4 cm.

59 (58). No dark bands or pale spots. Color: conspicuous dark spots over body, dark spots and stripes on arms on reddish-brown background. A few papillae over eyes. Ligula length 10-11% of the hectocotylized arm length. . . . .

. . . . ***O. penicillifer* Berry, 1954**
Extreme south Baja California. Upper sublittoral. Mantle length up to 3-4 cm. A related species ***O. stictochrus* Voss, 1971** is described from the Gulf of Panama.

60 (33). Arm length 62% of total length. Web depth 13% of longest arm length. First 5 or 6 suckers on arms are arranged in one row. . . . .

. . . . ***Octopus* (?)*pricei* (Berry, 1913)**
Central California. Taxonomic status is unclear. Mantle length 2 cm.

Note: The key does not include the species *O. oshimai* (**Sasaki, 1929**) described from the waters of Taiwan. N.N. Kondakov (1941) and I.I. Akimushkin (1963) recorded it from southern Primorye Territory and southwestern Sea of Okhotsk; this identification needs confirmation.

Key to species of the genus *Bathypolypus*

1 (2). Hectocotylus narrow, conical, its length about 14% of hectocotylized arm length. Ligula with numerous indistinct transverse grooves, calamus short. Entire body beset by closely set tubercles. No supraocular cirri. Suckers large, 8-12% of the mantle length. 9-10 filaments in demibranch. . . . . ***B. salebrosus* (Sasaki, 1920)**
(Fig. 83 I). Northwestern Pacific boreal species: Bering Sea, Sea of Okhotsk, Pacific coasts of Kurile Islands, Hokkaido and northeastern Honshu, bathyal. Mantle length up to 9-10 cm.

2 (1). Hectocotylus much wider than arm, spoonlike or round, sometimes with lateral lobes. Ligula with several (4-16) sharp transverse ridges. Skin sculpture variable, from heavily tuberculate to almost smooth. Supraocular cirri usually present, often they are high conical "horns." Suckers small, from 2.5 to 7-8% of mantle length. 6-9 filaments in demibranch. 3

3 (4). Hectocotylus with parallel edges or widening distally, without lateral lobes. Ligula with 8-16 transverse ridges. Calamus short. In young males ligula develops into a cone distally, in adults top of ligula has a median tubercle with two projections on the sides. Body more or less densely covered with stellate tubercles, sometimes

slightly visible, in rare cases almost smooth. Conical supraocular "horns" almost always well defined. . . . . ***B. arcticus* (Prosch, 1849)**
[= *B. bairdii* (Verrill, 1873), *B. lentus* (Verrill, 1880), *B. obesus* (Verrill, 1880), *B. faeroensis* (Russel, 1909)] (Fig. 83 B-E). Atlantic-Arctic arctic-boreal species. Western Arctic eastward to Vilkitsky Strait, westward to Franklin Strait, probably circumpolar; Norway, Greenland, Baffin Seas; Northern Atlantic, southward to the Straits of Florida, southwestern Spain (Gulf of Cádiz), northern part of North Sea and Kattegat. Common in Barents and Kara Seas, absent on White and Pechora Seas. Mantle length up to 7 cm. Sublittoral (mainly lower) and bathyal, in the southern part of range only in bathyal. A very variable species, represented by two forms whose status is unclear, may be different species.

a (b). Head narrower than body, its width is 60-80% of mantle length. Ligula length not more than 20% of hectocotylized arm length. 8-10 filaments in demibranch. . . . .

. . . . ***B. arcticus* f. *arcticus* (Prosch)**
Mainly Arctic regions.

b (a). Head equal or wider than body, not narrower than the mantle length. Ligula length 20-33%, sometimes up to 40% of hectocotylized arm length. 6-7 filaments in demibranch. . . . .

. . . . ***B. arcticus* f. *proschi* Muus, 1962**
Mainly boreal regions.

4 (3). Hectocotylus round or with parallel edges in basal half and converging into a cone in distal half. Side lobes usually distinct and may entirely conceal inner surface of ligula. Ligula with 4-7 transverse ridges. Calamus long, 33-40% of ligula length, which is 12-18% of the hectocotylized arm length. 6-7 filaments in demibranch. 5

5 (6). Hectocotylus globose, almost spherical, with distinct lateral lobes in adults. Supraocular cirri sharp, conical. Skin on head with a few tubercles. Web depth 33-40% of longest arm length. Ligula with 4-5 transverse ridges. . . . . . .

. . . . ***B. valdiviae* (Chun & Thiele, 1915)**
(= *B. grimpei* Robson, 1924) (Fig. 83 F-H). Southern, southwestern (Namibia) and southeastern Africa, Agulhas Bank and nearby regions. Bathyal. Mantle length to 45 cm.

6 (5). Hectocotylus with parallel or slightly convex edges in basal part and converging into a cone in distal part. Skin on head around eyes with numerous small round tubercles having 1-4 low tops. Supraocular cirri absent or but slightly visi-

ble. Web depth 17-33% of longest arm length. Ligula with 6-7 transverse ridges. . . . .
. . . . ***B. sponsalis* (P. & H. Fischer, 1892)**
(Fig. 83 A). Western Mediterranean Sea and northeastern Atlantic from the Bay of Biscay to Cape Blanc and Cape Verde (Dakar). Bathyal, mainly middle and lower. Mantle length to 10 cm.

Key to species of the genus *Benthoctopus*

Species of the genus *Benthoctopus* are poorly studied, therefore it is impossible to compile a general key. Only keys for identification of arcto-boreal and notalian species and a list of tropical species are given.

I. Arctic and boreal regions
1 (4). In adult males some suckers in middle part of arms greatly enlarged, the diameter considerably exceeds 10% of mantle length. In females suckers not enlarged, the diameter 8-9% of mantle length. Funnel organ W-shaped. 2
2 (3). Diameter of largest suckers in male (8th-12th pairs) about 25% of mantle length, diameter of non-enlarged suckers about 17% of the mantle length. Ligula length about 12% of the hectocotylized arm length. Depth of largest sector of web about 30% of the longest arm length. . . . . . .
. . . . ***B. sibiricus* Löyning, 1930**
(Fig. 84 A,B). Eastern Arctic: Laptev, East Siberian, Chukchi Seas, and probably Beaufort Sea. Middle and lower sublittoral and probably upper bathyal. Most shallow-water and cold-water species of the genus.
3 (2). Diameter of the largest suckers in male (14th-17th pair) about 15% of the mantle length. Ligula length 7.5% of the length of hectocotylized arm. Web depth 25% of the longest arm length
. . . . ***B. abruptus* (Sasaki, 1929)**
(Fig. 84 C). Pacific coast of southern Honshu. Upper bathyal.
4 (1). No greatly enlarged suckers. Diameter of suckers in males and females not exceeding 10% of mantle length. 5
5 (8). Funnel organ VV-shaped. Diameter of suckers about 6% of mantle length. 6
6 (7). Ligula without transverse ridges, its length 5% of hectocotylized arm length. Umbrella depth about 20% of longest arm length. . . . .
. . . . ***B. fuscus* Taki, 1964**
(Fig. 84 D). Eastern coast of Honshu, bathyal.
7 (6). Ligula with 8-10 distinct transverse ridges,

its length 7% of hectocotylized arm length. Web depth about 25% of longest arm length. . . . .
. . . . . . ***B. ergasticus* (P. & H. Fischer, 1892)**
(Fig. 84 E,F). Northeastern Atlantic from southwestern Ireland to Senegal. Middle and lower bathyal, depths of 450-1400 m.
8 (5). Funnel organ W-shaped. 9
9 (12). 6-10 filaments (rarely more) in demibranch. Web depth 25-33% of the longest arm length 10
10 (11). Ligula with about ten transverse ridges. . . . . ***B. piscatorum* (Verrill, 1879)**
(Fig. 84 G,H). Northern Atlantic and western Arctic from Newfoundland, Danmark Strait and western Spitsbergen to the area off Delaware Bay and Southwestern Ireland. Depths 80-2500 m, in the northern part of range usually less than 750 m, in the southern as a rule more than 900 m.
11 (10). Ligula without transverse ridges of with indistinct ridges. . . . .
. . . . ***B. profundorum* Robson, 1932**
[= *B. januarii* (Sasaki, 1929), non Hoyle]. From the Bering Sea to Kyushu and to the Gulf of Alaska, probably also off western coasts of Canada and USA to California; Sea of Okhotsk. Depths 150-3400 m. A common and numerous octopus. Probably a mixture of some closely related species.
12 (9). 11-12 filaments in demibranch. 13
13 (14). Web depth 20% of longest arm length. Mantle aperture very wide. . . . .
. . . . ***B. violescens* Taki, 1964**
Eastern coast of Honshu.
14 (13). Web depth 25% of the longest arm length. Mantle aperture fairly narrow. . . . .
. . . . ***B. hokkaidensis* (Berry, 1921)**
(= *Polypus glaber* Sasaki, 1929, non Wülker) (Fig. 84 I,J). From Cape Navarin (Bering Sea) to southern Honshu and Oregon; Sea of Okhotsk. Upper bathyal, depths of 130-1000 m.

Unidentified species of *Benthoctopus* was recorded in Bukhta Provideniya (Providence Bay, Chukotka Peninsula).

II. Notalian region
1 (6). Funnel organ W-shaped. Skin smooth. . . .2
2 (5). Diameter of suckers 7-12% of the mantle length. Southwestern Atlantic. 3
3 (4). Diameter of suckers 12% of mantle length. Web sector between dorsal arms shortest or one of the shortest. . . . . ***B. eureka* (Robson, 1929)**

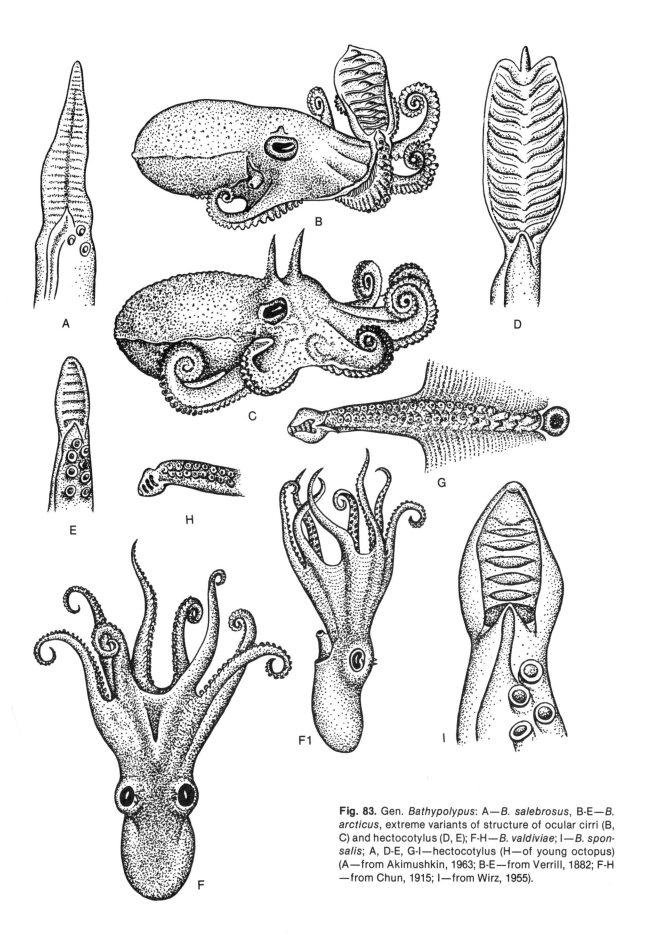

Fig. 83. Gen. *Bathypolypus*: A—*B. salebrosus*, B-E—*B. arcticus*, extreme variants of structure of ocular cirri (B, C) and hectocotylus (D, E); F-H—*B. valdiviae*; I—*B. sponsalis*; A, D-E, G-I—hectocotylus (H—of young octopus) (A—from Akimushkin, 1963; B-E—from Verrill, 1882; F-H —from Chun, 1915; I—from Wirz, 1955).

Fig. 84.

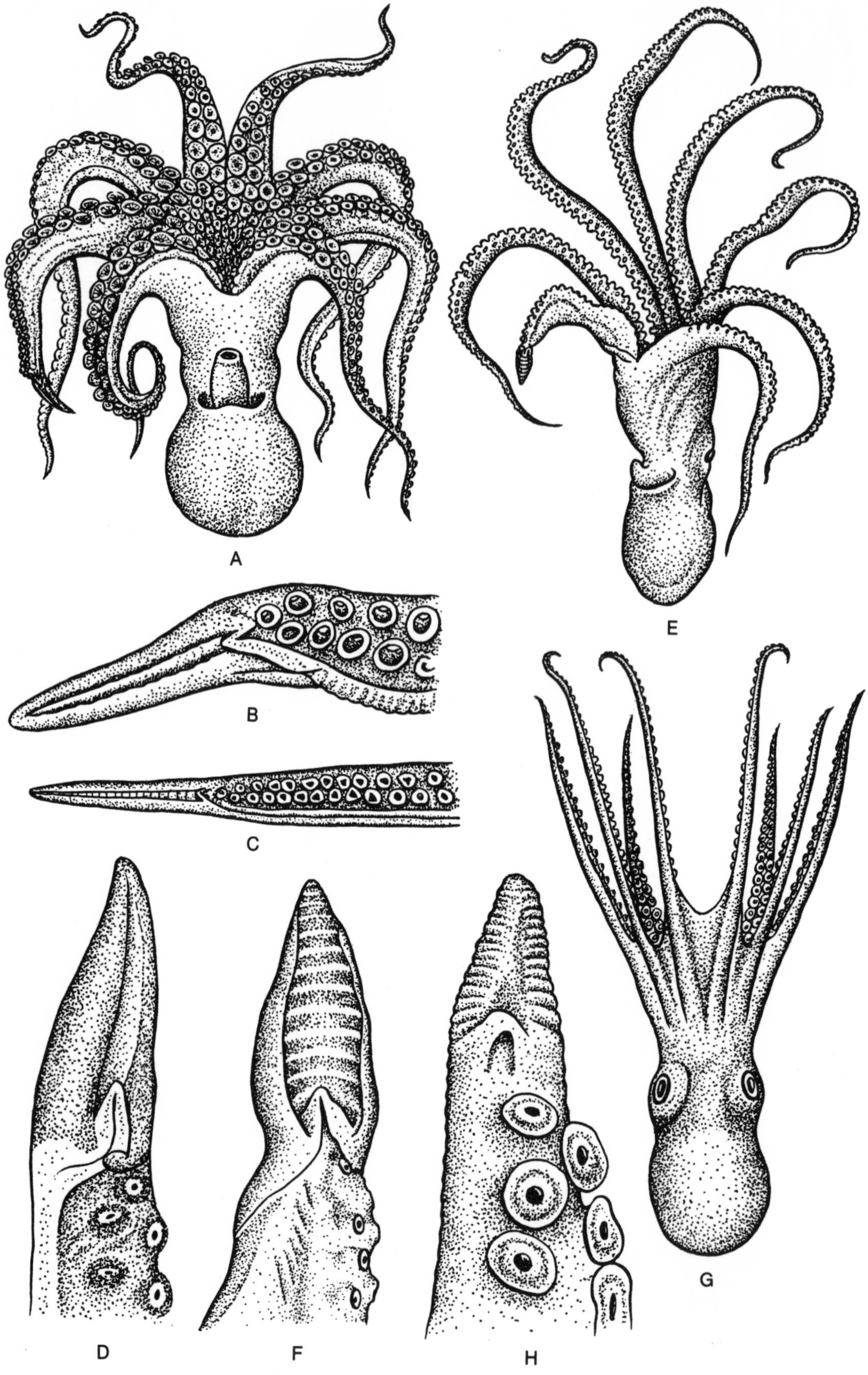

318

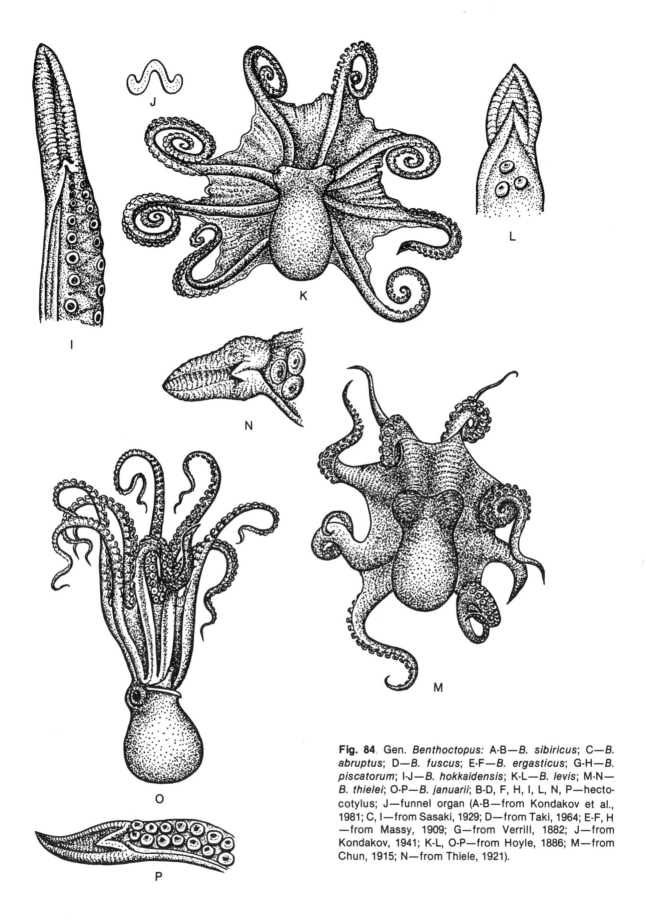

Fig. 84. Gen. *Benthoctopus*: A-B—*B. sibiricus*; C—*B. abruptus*; D—*B. fuscus*; E-F—*B. ergasticus*; G-H—*B. piscatorum*; I-J—*B. hokkaidensis*; K-L—*B. levis*; M-N—*B. thielei*; O-P—*B. januarii*; B-D, F, H, I, L, N, P—hectocotylus; J—funnel organ (A-B—from Kondakov et al., 1981; C, I—from Sasaki, 1929; D—from Taki, 1964; E-F, H—from Massy, 1909; G—from Verrill, 1882; J—from Kondakov, 1941; K-L, O-P—from Hoyle, 1886; M—from Chun, 1915; N—from Thiele, 1921).

From Northern Argentina to Falkland Islands, sublittoral.

4 (3). Diameter of suckers 7-8% of mantle length.

A species or several species close to *B. januarii*. Falkland Islands, Burdwood Bank and nearby areas. Depths of 80-450 m.

5 (2). Diameter of suckers 3-4% of mantle length. All web sectors of subequal depth . . . .

. . . . ***B. berryi*** **Robson, 1924**

To the southwest from Capetown, depth of 2200 m.

6 (1). Funnel organ VV-shaped 7

7 (8). Diameter of suckers 9-13% of mantle length. Web depth about 33% of longest arm length. Web sector between dorsal arms is deepest or one of the deepest. Skin rough. Southwestern Atlantic . . . . . . ***B. magellanicus*** **Robson, 1930**

Patagonia, Falkland Islands, Tierra del Fuégo. Lower sublittoral.

8 (7). Diameter of suckers 6-9% of mantle length. Web sector between dorsal arms short. Skin smooth. Southern Indian Ocean 9

9 (10). Web depth 33-40% of longest arm length. Ligula length 7-9% of hectocotylized arm length. Diameter of suckers 6-8% of mantle length . . . . . .

. . . . ***B. levis*** **(Hoyle, 1885)**

(Fig. 84 K,L). Heard Island. Lower sublittoral and upper bathyal.

10 (9). Web depth 25% of longest arm length. Ligula length 13% of hectocotylized arm length. Diameter of suckers 9% of mantle length . . . .

. . . . ***B. thielei*** **Robson, 1932**

(Fig. 84 M,N). Kerguelen Island. Lower sublittoral and (rarely) upper bathyal. Common and numerous on Kerguelen Plateau.

III. Tropical Zone of the World Ocean

1. Western Atlantic

a (b). Funnel organ VV-shaped. Arms 4-6 times longer than mantle. Hectocotylized arm almost twice shorter than opposite (3rd left) arm, ligula length 6-9% of hectocotylized arm length . . . .

. . . . ***B. januarii*** **(Hoyle, 1885)**

Fig. 84 O,P). From the Gulf of Mexico to southeastern Brazil. Upper bathyal.

b (a). Funnel organ W-shaped. Arms 2.5-4 times longer than mantle. Hectocotylized arm 33-25% shorter than opposite arm, ligula length 3-5% of hectocotylized arm length . . . .

. . . . ***B. oregonae*** **Toll, 1981**

Southern Caribbean Sea, bathyal.

2. Eastern Atlantic

B. ergasticus **(P. & H. Fischer, 1892)** [see couplet 7 (6) Arctic and boreal regions of this key]. From Southwestern Ireland to Senegal. Depths 450-1400 m. Absent in Mediterranean Sea. Differs from look-alike *Bathypolypus sponsalis* [see couplet 6 (5) in the key to genus *Bathypolypus*] by the structure of hectocotylus.

B. cf. januarii **(Hoyle, 1885).** Off Namibia at a depth of 1580 m.

3. Indo-West Pacific.

A complex of 3-4 undescribed species, related to *B. januarii* and *B. profundorum*. Found in the Andaman Sea and Indonesian Seas. Depths 500-1900 m.

4. Eastern Pacific.

B. sp. aff. januarii **Nesis, 1973.** From the Cocos Island to northern Peru. Depths 570-1850 m.

Doubtful species: ***B. lothei*** **(Chun, 1913)** (= ?*B. ergasticus*) — off the Canary Islands at a depth of 1365 m; ***B. pseudonymus*** **Grimpe, 1922** — off the Azores Islands at a depth of 1600 m. Generic designation unclear.

Key to species of the genus *Graneledone*

1 (2). Upper side of mantle and head with a few very large warts, consisting of several small conical tubercles on a common base, separate simple conical tubercles scattered among the warts. Dorsal side of arms smooth. One very large composite tubercle above each eye. Funnel organ VV-shaped. 7 filaments in demibranch. 1st lateral (admedian) tooth of radula small, with two little cusps on wide base . . ***G. macrotyla*** **Voss, 1976**

(Fig. 85 A-C). Scotia Sea, depth of 1650-2050 m.

2 (1). Mantle, head and often dorsal side of arms covered with numerous small papillae consisting of several small acute spines 3

3 (4). Papillae scattered over dorsal side of mantle and head almost not reaching dorsal side of web and arms. Papillae scarce: 13-15 papillae along the line crossing dorsal mantle surface from one to the other side in the middle of back. The papillae stellate, 7-8 small spines in one papillae. 3-5 enlarged papillae above each eye. Ligula length 3.5-7% of hectocotylized arm length. 7-8 filaments in demibranch . . . .

. . . . ***G. verrucosa*** **(Verrill, 1881)**

(= ?*G. verrucosa* var. *media* Joubin, 1918) (Fig.

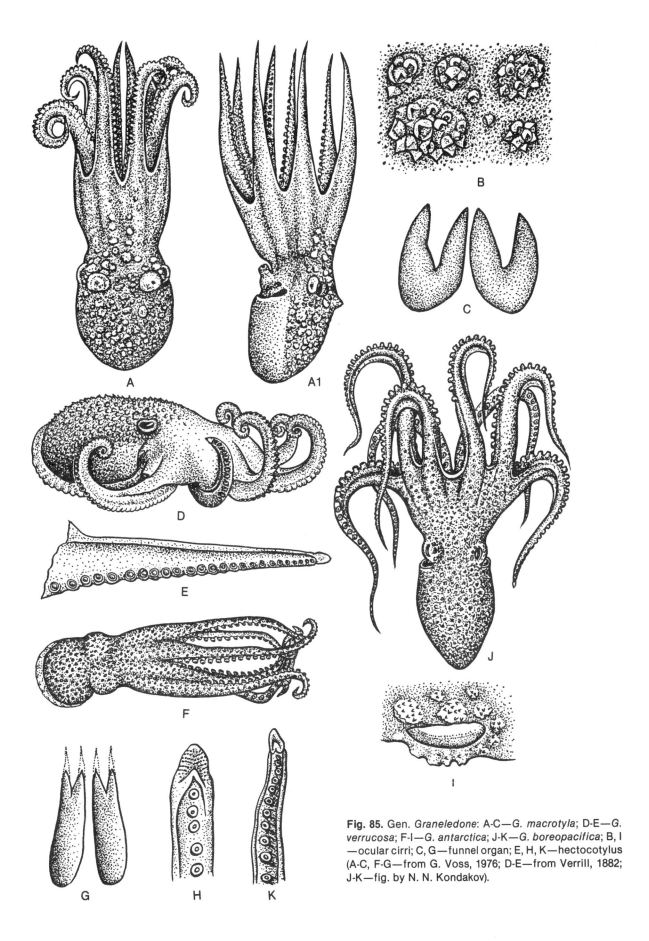

Fig. 85. Gen. *Graneledone*: A-C—*G. macrotyla*; D-E—*G. verrucosa*; F-I—*G. antarctica*; J-K—*G. boreopacifica*; B, I —ocular cirri; C, G—funnel organ; E, H, K—hectocotylus (A-C, F-G—from G. Voss, 1976; D-E—from Verrill, 1882; J-K—fig. by N. N. Kondakov).

321

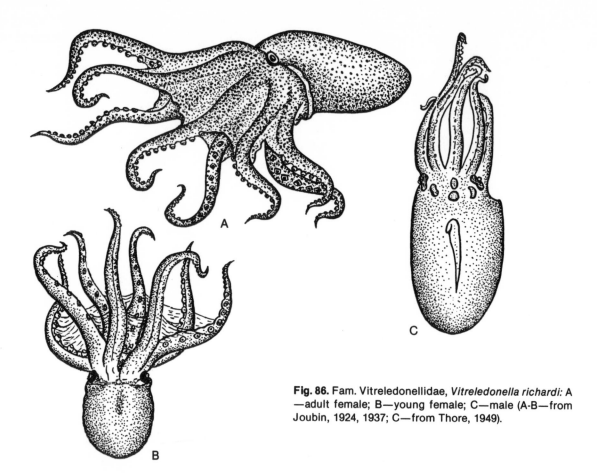

Fig. 86. Fam. Vitreledonellidae, *Vitreledonella richardi:* A—adult female; B—young female; C—male (A-B—from Joubin, 1924, 1937; C—from Thore, 1949).

85 D,E). Northwestern Atlantic from the area southward of Iceland to the area northeastward of Cape Hatteras. Depths of 850-2300 m.

4 (3). Papillae scattered on dorsal side of mantle, head, umbrella and at least basal parts of 1st-3rd arms. Papillae dense: 25-30 papillae along the line crossing dorsal mantle surface in middle of back. The papillae not stellate, up to 12-14 small spines in one papilla. 1st lateral (admedian) tooth of radula large, unicuspid, with a narrow base **5**

5 (6). Funnel organ consists of two elongate oval pads slightly split at anterior ends. Ligula with small calamus and shallow longitudinal groove with 12-13 transverse folds. Ligula length about 3% of hectocotylized arm length, calamus length 40-50% of ligula length. 6 filaments in demibranch. Diameter of suckers 6-8% of mantle length. 2-3 enlarged papillae above each eye. Rhachidian tooth of radula unicuspid, symmetrical . . . . **G. antarctica Voss, 1976**

(Fig. 85 F-I). Ross Sea, abyssal. Similar form lives near Kerguelen and Heard Islands in upper bathyal.

6 (5). Funnel organ VV-shaped. Ligula with a large calamus and deep longitudinal groove

without conspicuous transverse folds. No greatly enlarged papillae above eyes. Rhachidian tooth of radula with three cusps, slightly assymmetrical **7**

7 (8). Papillae on head and dorsal side of web closely set, almost connecting, their diameter 1-2 mm. Ligula length 3.3% of hectocotylized arm length, calamus length 55% of ligula length. Diameter of suckers 7% of mantle length. 5-6 filaments in demibranch . . . . **G. challengeri (Berry, 1916).**

Off Kermadec Islands, depth of 1150 m.

8 (7). Papillae on head and dorsal side of web scarce, as on dorsal side of mantle, their diameter 2-4 mm. Ligula length 4-5% of hectocotylized arm length, calamus length 70% of the ligula length. Diameter of suckers 5-6% of mantle length. 7-8 filaments in demibranch . . . . **G. boreopacifica Nesis, 1982**

(Fig. 85 J,K). Sea of Okhotsk and Pacific Ocean off northeastern Honshu (Sanriku coast), probably also Oregon and California. Mantle length to 13 cm. Depths of 1000-2000 m.

Unidentified species of *Graneledone* is found in the tropical Eastern Pacific, depths of 1865-2500 m.

2.4.2.2.2. Family Vitreledonellidae

Deep-sea pelagic octopuses with transparent as glass and almost colorless gelatinous body. Arms of medium length, in adults 2-3 times longer than mantle. Suckers in one row, widely apart within the web, closely set and greatly enlarged outside the web: diameter of large distal suckers in adults up to 10-17% of the mantle length. Web depth in adults 40-60% of the longest arm length. Eyes small, narrow, almost rectangular, the diameter is about 20% of the mantle length. Eyes directed to the side. Optic nerves are very long, optic ganglia at a distance from brain. Mantle aperture very wide. Radula with multicuspid rhachidian and unicuspid 1st and 2nd lateral teeth. Liver is very long, equal or exceeding the head width, narrow, acuminate posteriorly. Stomach in front of liver, ovary above it. Posterior salivary gland unpaired. Ink sac developed. 3rd left arm is hectocotylized, smaller than the right arm, ligula short. Supposedly viviparous forms brooding the eggs up to the hatching of larvae.

One genus: *Vitreledonella* **Joubin, 1918,** one species: *V. richardi* **Joubin, 1918** (Fig. 86). Tropical-subtropical cosmopolitan bathypelagic species, juveniles living in epipelagic and mesopelagic zones. Mantle length to 11 cm, total length to 45 cm.

Review: Thore, 1949.

2.4.2.3. Superfamily Argonautoidea

Pelagic or benthic-pelagic octopuses with muscular, rarely semigelatinous tissue. Eyes very well developed. Suckers in two rows over the entire arm length, or only in distal parts. The hectocotylized arm is wholly modified, of a very complicated structure, consisting of several parts. It is developed in a special sac, so that it seems as if an immature male has only 7 arms — this character is visible even in larvae. A mature hectocotylus is filled with sperm out of the only spermatophore, breaks off from the male body at mating and creeps in, wriggling snake-like, through the funnel into the mantle cavity of female. Males often (but not always) are much smaller than females, dwarf. Female lays the eggs at the bottom, or carries the egg herself, or the eggs develop in her body. There is a pelagic larval stage.

Radula not comb-like, the rhachidian tooth is either uni- or tricuspid, without seriation. Mantle aperture wide. Mantle-funnel locking apparatus and ink sac are present. Stomach and liver are in "normal" position.

4 families, 4 genera, 8-11 species.

2.4.2.3.1. Family Alloposidae

Body gelatinous, mantle short, head wide, not narrower than mantle. Arms relatively short, with a very deep web. Arm length order is 1.2.3.4. Suckers small, in one row within the web, in two rows outside web, and again in one row on the very tips of arms. No enlarged suckers. Eyes very big, about 33% of the mantle length. The funnel is entirely embedded in head tissue, it opens in front of eyes. Funnel organ is W-shaped. Mantle aperture wide. Mantle-funnel apparatus is of hook-like type, slightly developed. Central tooth of radula is tricuspid. The mantle is connected with the intestinal mass by a ventral median septum, with the head by two pairs of lateral septa one of which bears the stellate ganglion. 3rd right arm is hectocotylized. The hectocotylus is developed in a sac in front of the right eye, it breaks off at mating. Males are not dwarfed. Eggs of medium size, supposedly benthic.

One genus: *Alloposus* **Verrill, 1880** (= ?*Haliphron* Steenstrup, 1859, *Alloposina* Grimpe, 1922, *Heptapus* Joubin, 1929). One species: *A. mollis* **Verrill, 1880** (Fig. 87 A-D). A very widely distributed (from tropics to boreal and notalian regions) cosmopolitan species. Larvae and juveniles live in pelagic (from epipelagic to bathypelagic) zone, mainly (but not exclusively) above slopes and submarine rises, the adults at the bottom in bathyal. Found in the USSR waters in the northwestern Pacific. Mantle length to 40 cm, total length up to 2 m.

Review: Thore, 1949.

2.4.2.3.2. Family Ocythoidae

Females large, with a firm body. Arms long, 1st and 4th much longer than 2nd and 3rd arms. Suckers small, in 2 rows. No web, no arm fringe. One pair of cephalic water pores on ventral part of head at the base of 4th arms. Funnel very long, funnel organ I Λ I-shaped, locking cartilages composite, knob-like. Ventral side of mantle in adult females with reticular sculpture of crossing skin ridges and tubercles at crossing points. A hydrostatic organ is reported to be located inside

Fig. 87.

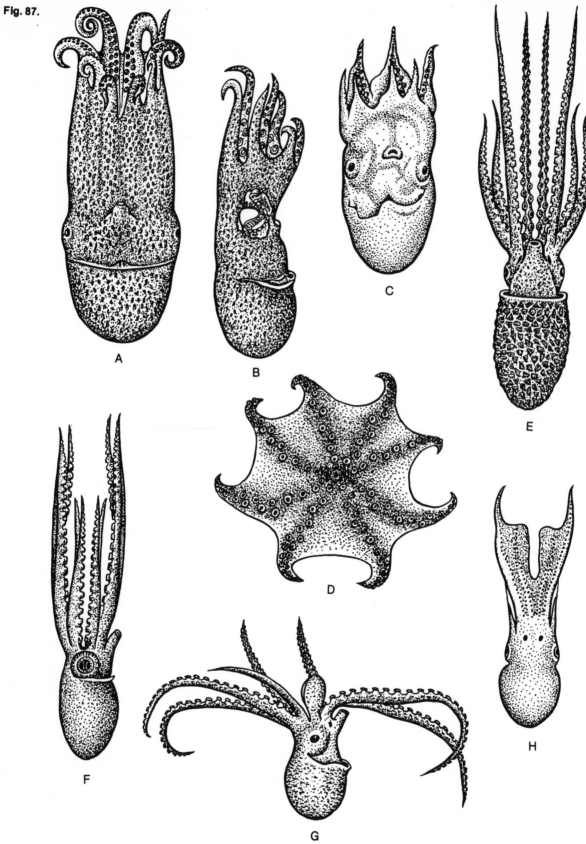

A

B

C

D

E

F

G

H

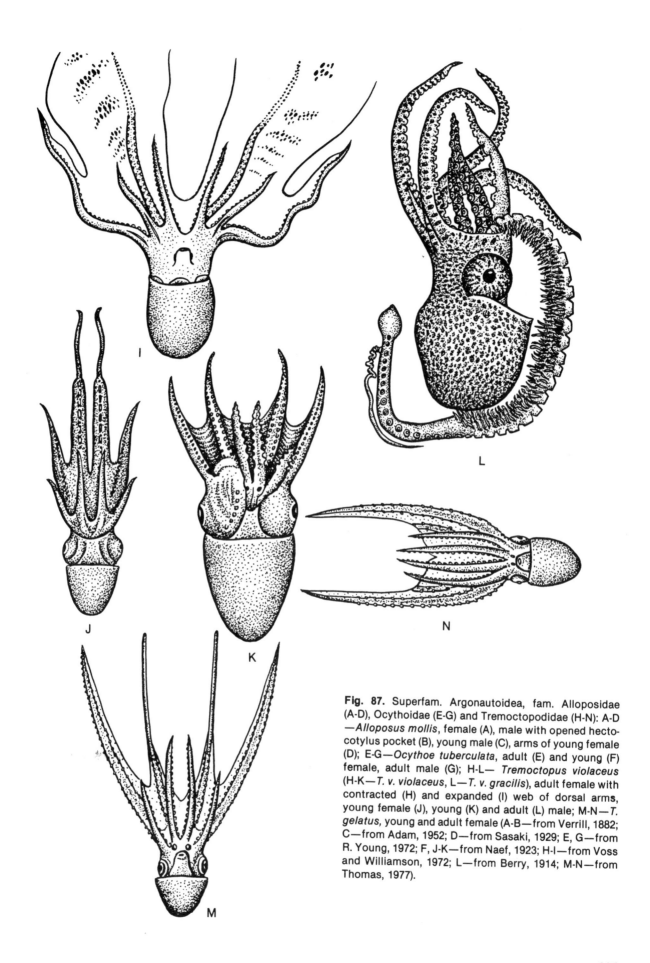

Fig. 87. Superfam. Argonautoidea, fam. Alloposidae (A-D), Ocythoidae (E-G) and Tremoctopodidae (H-N): A-D —*Alloposus mollis*, female (A), male with opened hectocotylus pocket (B), young male (C), arms of young female (D); E-G—*Ocythoe tuberculata*, adult (E) and young (F) female, adult male (G); H-L— *Tremoctopus violaceus* (H-K—*T. v. violaceus*, L—*T. v. gracilis*), adult female with contracted (H) and expanded (I) web of dorsal arms, young female (J), young (K) and adult (L) male; M-N—*T. gelatus*, young and adult female (A-B—from Verrill, 1882; C—from Adam, 1952; D—from Sasaki, 1929; E, G—from R. Young, 1972; F, J-K—from Naef, 1923; H-I—from Voss and Williamson, 1972; L—from Berry, 1914; M-N—from Thomas, 1977).

the mantle cavity on dorsal side. Males small. 3rd right arm is hectocotylized. Hectocotylus with a very long slender "penis" and with suckers in two rows. Eggs developing in oviducts of female, hatched larvae extruded.

One genus: **Ocythoe Rafinesque, 1814** (Fig. 87 E-G) (= *Parasira* Steenstrup, 1861). One species: **O. tuberculata Rafinesque, 1814** (Fig. 87 E-G). Bi-central (bi-subtropical) cosmopolitan surface-living species. Mantle length up to 30 cm in females and up to 3 cm in males. Males often sit in empty tests of doliolids and salps.

Review: Roper and Sweeny, 1976.

2.4.2.3.3. Family Tremoctopodidae

Females large, total length up to 2 m. Body usually firm. Suckers small, in two rows. Arms of first two pairs are connected by web continuing into a wide fringe on both sides of 1st arms and on dorsal side of 2nd arms. Large ocellar spots are located along the fringes in longitudinal rows. No fringe on 3rd and 4th arms, web between them is poorly developed. 1st and 2nd arms are much longer than 3rd and 4th ones. In young females the 1st arms are very long, suckers on their ends are arranged in one row and set widely apart, shallow grooves pass across the arms. At an attack of a predator a piece of this arm bearing one sucker, 1-3 ocellar spots and (sometimes) a part of luminous gland breaks off along the groove widens suddenly thus disorienting and frightening the attacker. Due to this, the ends of 1st arms are always broken off in adult females.

Skin smooth. 2 pairs of cephalic water pores on the head at the bases of 1st and 4th arms. Funnel of medium size. Funnel organ IIII-shaped. Locking apparatus round or triangular. Luminous organs are sometimes located along edge of the fringe on 1st arms.

Eggs small, carried by female on basal part of 1st arms. Males and young females usually carry by the suckers of 1st arms small pieces of stinging tentacles of *Physalia* (Portuguese man-of-war) — an additional means of defence against enemies. Males are very small — mantle length up to 15 mm, total length up to 4 cm. 3rd right arm is hectocotylized. Two rows of small suckers in basal and middle part of hectocotylus, besides that there is a border of small cirri-like papillae in the basal part. Distal part of hectocotylus is modified into a seminal sac with a "penis." In immature males the hectocotylus develops in a sac between funnel and eye.

One genus: **Tremoctopus delle Chiaje, 1830** (= *Philonexis* d'Orbigny, 1835) (Fig. 87 H-N). Type species: *T. violaceus* delle Chiaje, 1830. Two species and 2 subspecies in the tropics and subtropics of all oceans.

Review: Thomas, 1977.

Key to species of the genus *Tremoctopus*

1 (2). Body firm, muscular. Adult females dark blue-purple dorsally and light golden ventrally, males and juveniles bright with small dark points. 13-16 filaments in demibranch of female and 9-11 in male . . . . **T. violaceus delle Chiaje, 1830** (Fig. 87 H-L). Tropical and subtropical waters of all oceans from the Gulf Stream, Bay of Biscay, southern Kurile Islands and California to Uruguay, southern Africa, New Zealand and Chile. Epipelagic, at night ascending to the surface. Mantle length of females to 0.3-0.5 m. 2 subspecies.

a (b). In adult females ocellar spots arranged in one row only on outer side of fringe of 1st arms. 15-19 pairs of suckers in middle part and 22-23 pairs in proximal part of hectocotylus . . . . **T. violaceus violaceus delle Chiaje** (Fig. 87 H-K). Atlantic Ocean, Caribbean and Mediterranean Seas.

b (a). In adult females ocellar spots are arranged in two rows or in a double row on outer and in one row on inner side of fringe of 1st arms. 19-22 pairs of suckers in middle part and 27-29 pairs in proximal part of hectocotylus . . . . **T. violaceus gracilis (Souleyet, 1852)** (Fig. 87 L). Indian and Pacific Oceans.

2 (1). Body gelatinous, so transparent that a newspaper can be read through the body of a living female. Adult females are pale orange-red. Eyes very large. Ink sac reduced in size. 8-11 filaments in female's demibranch and 7-8 of male's one . . . . **T. gelatus Thomas, 1977** (Fig. 87 M,N). Atlantic Ocean off southern Florida, Indian Ocean to the south of Madagascar, Pacific to the north and northeast of Hawaii. Probably bi-subtropical species. Supposedly mesopelagic or bathypelagic species, only females washed ashore or found in *Alepisaurus* (lancetfish) stomachs are known, a male was caught on the surface. Mantle length of females up to 33 cm.

2.4.2.3.4. Family Argonautidae

Females secrete a thin, laterally compressed calcareous shell with one chamber and a flat keel fringed by two rows of tubercles; lateral sides of shell with radial ribs; shell center is pressed in or bent outward into a sharp "horn." 1st arms are the longest, their ends bearing a wide sail-like lobe that secretes and forms the shell. Female is positioned in the shell with its head forward, 1st arms are usually pushed outward, their lobes are widened and cover the entire shell from outside, the remaining arms are kept inside the shell, keeping the shell on the body of female. Web a very weakly developed. Suckers small, in two rows. No cephalic water pores. Funnel long. Funnel organ I Λ I-shaped. Locking cartilages knob-like. Skin smooth. Posterior end of mantle usually bent slightly upward.

Males are tiny, dwarf. 3rd left arm is hectocotylized. Hectocotylus with a long slender "penis" and numerous suckers in 2 rows (Fig. 88 B). It is kept for fairly long time in the mantle cavity of a female. Eggs are very small, female broods them in the shell until larvae are hatched. Spawning is intermittent.

One genus: *Argonauta* Linné, **1758** (= *Argonautina* Steinmann, 1925, *Argonautella* Steinmann, 1925) (Fig. 88). Type species: *A. argo* Linné, 1758. 4 real and 2-3 doubtful species in epipelagic zone (but not only at the surface) of tropical and subtropical areas. Total length of females up to 45 cm and more, of males to 2 cm; mantle length in females to 10 cm, of males to 1.1 cm.

Key to species of the genus *Argonauta* on the characters of the shell

1 (4). Shell large (diameter up to 25-30 cm), laterally flattened, with narrow keel (width up to 15% of shell diameter). Ribs numerous, close together, often split into two. Animals living mainly near coasts **2**
2 (3). Keel very narrow, its width equals, rarely exceeds 6% of shell diameter. Ribs smooth, more than 50 in large shells. Each rib terminating on the keel in an acute tubercle . . . .
. . . .*A. argo* Linné, **1758**
(Fig. 88 A-C). Tropical-subtropical cosmopolitan species, in the north reaching Cape Cod, Portugal, Mediterranean Sea, southern Hokkaido

and California, in the south—southern Africa, New Zealand and Peru. Young females of this species very similar to those of *A. hians.*
3 (2). Width of keel 10-15% of shell diameter. Ribs representing chains of separate tubercles or nodules. 30-40 ribs on large shells . . . .
. . . .*A. nodosa* Solander, **1786**
(Fig. 88 D). Tropical Indo-West Pacific from Red Sea and southern Japan to southern Africa, Tasmania and New Zealand, eastward to Polynesia and (?)Chile. Most common in Australia—New Zealand region.
4 (1). Shell small (diameter up to 10 cm), laterally not flattened. Keel wide (10-15% of shell diameter). Ribs not numerous. Oceanic species
. . . .**5**
5 (6). Shell surface usually smooth. Center of spiral not pressed in, "horn" in center of shell either present or absent. Not more than 35 ribs, set apart. Tubercles on keel brown, usually 15-20. Shell diameter to 10 cm. . . . .
. . . .*A. hians* Solander, **1786**
(Fig. 88 E). Tropical cosmopolitan species. Not found in the Mediterranean Sea, rest of range similar to that of *A. argo.*
6 (5). Shell surface usually finely granulated, *i.e.* beset by very small tubercles. Center of spiral slightly depressed, "horns" absent. Ribs numerous, close together, usually 40-45. Tubercles on keel white, their number 20-33. Shell diameter to 7 cm. . . . .
. . . .*A. boettgeri* Maltzan, **1881**
(Fig. 88 F,G). Tropical Indo-West Pacific species distributed from the Western Indian Ocean to Hawaii and from southern Honshu to New Zealand.

Doubtful species of *Argonauta:*

A. cornuta Conrad, 1854 (Fig. 88 H)—close to *A. hians,* but the keel is narrower, ribs thinner (45 in all), up to 30 large tubercles, keel convex, bearing small tubercles between the large ones along the sides of keel, surface granulated, "horns" strongly developed (the last character differentiating *A. cornuta* from *A. boettgeri*). Eastern Pacific Ocean from the Gulf of California to Peru.

A. nouryi Lorois, 1852 (Fig. 88 I)—shell elongated, attenuated, oval in outline, edge of mouth seen from the side almost straight, no "horns", ribs low, numerous, keel narrow, concave, tubercles almost invisible, and shell surface finely granulated. Eastern Pacific Ocean from

Fig. 88.

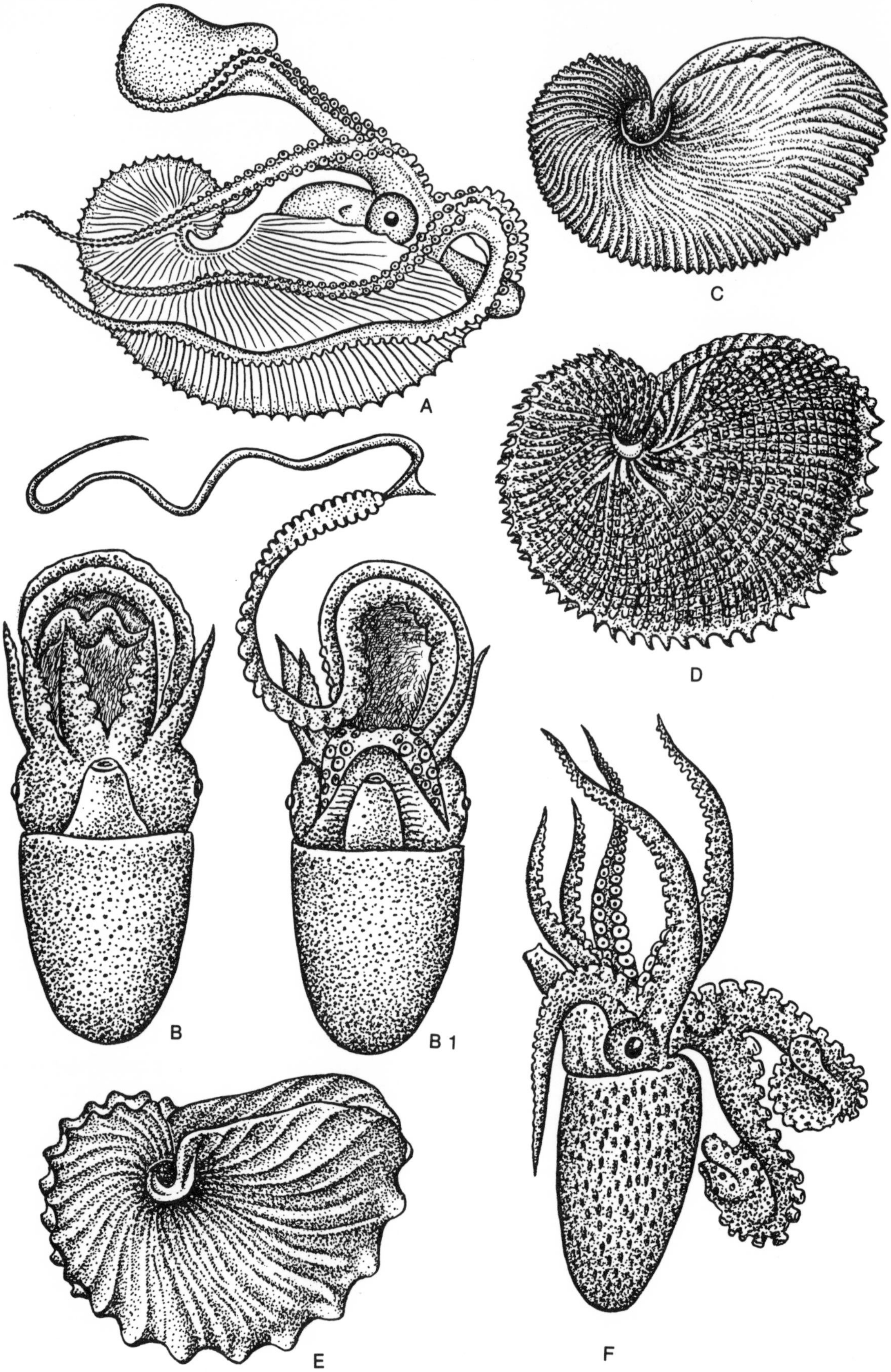

A

C

B

B 1

D

E

F

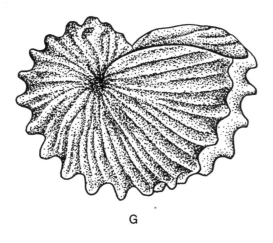

G

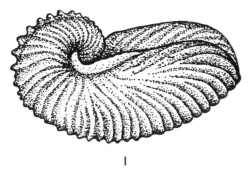

I

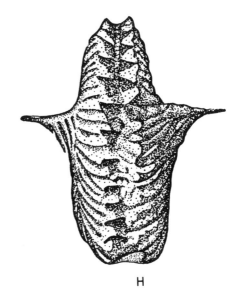

H

Fig. 88. Fam. Argonautidae, gen. *Argonauta*: A-C—*A. argo*, female in the shell (A), male with coiled (B) and extended (B1) hectocotylus, shell (C); D-E—shells of *A. nodosa* (D) and *A. hians* (E); F-G—*A. boettgeri*, female and shell; H-I—shells of *A. cornuta* (rear view) and *A. nouryi* (A—from Voss and Williamson, 1972; B—from Naef, 1923; C-E—from Sowerby in Reeve, 1861; F-G—from Berry, 1914; H-I—from Keen, 1968).

Gulf of California to Peru, westward to Marquesas Islands, a doubtful record for Japan (Kii Peninsula, Honshu).

In addition, eastern Pacific *A. argo* are often called as a separate species ***A. pacifica* Dall, 1869,** though the difference from typical *A. argo* are not clarified.

Key to species of *Argonauta* using characters of adult females

1 (2). 4th arms much (1.5-2 times) longer than the 3rd arms and 10-20% longer than 2nd arms

.............................*A. argo* **Linné** (Fig. 88 A).
2 (1). 4th arms shorter than 2nd ones and not longer than 3rd arms.....................3
3 (4). Length of 4th arms about 70-90% of the length of 2nd arms and subequal to 3rd arms....
....................*A. nodosa* **Solander**
4 (3). 4th arms much shorter than 2nd and 3rd, their length in large females usually about 60% of the 2nd arms length (in small females the 4th arms relatively longer).....................
..*A. hians* **Solander** and *A. boettgeri* **Maltzan** (Fig. 88 F).

329

Bibliography

An asterisk (*) indicates an important review, a monograph of general importance, a systematic revision of families and genera, or a faunistic review of a wide area.

Literature to General Section

* Akimushkin, I. I. 1963. *Cephalopods of the seas of the USSR*. Moscow: Nauka. 236 pp.(in Russ. Eng. translation: Jerusalem: IPST, 223 pp.)

Aldrich, M. M., V. C. Barber., and C. J. Emerson. 1971. Scanning electron microscópical studies of some cephalopod radulae. *Can. J. Zool.*, 49(12):1589-1594.

Altman, J. S. and M. Nixon. 1970. Use of the beak and radula of *Octopus vulgaris* in feeding. *J. Zool.*, 161(1):25-38.

Andrews, P. L. R. and E. M. Tansey. 1983. The digestive tract of *Octopus vulgaris*: the anatomy, physiology and pharmacology of the upper tract. *J. Mar. Biol. Assoc., U. K.* 63(1):109-134.

* Appellöf, A. 1893. Die Schalen von *Sepia, Spirula* und *Nautilus*. *Kgl. Svenska VetAkad. Handl.*, 25(7):1-106.

Arnold, J. M., R. E. Young, and M. V. King. 1974. Ultrastructure of a cephalopod photophore, I-II. *Biol. Bull.*, 147(4):507-534.

Atkinson, B. G. 1973. Squid nidamental gland extract: isolation of a factor inhibiting ciliary activity. *J. Exp. Zool.*, 184(3):335-340.

* Badenhorst , J. H. 1974. The morphology and histology of the male genital tract of the squid *Loligo reynaudi* (d'Orbigny). *Ann. Univ. Stellenbosch*, 49A(1):36 pp.

Bandel, K. and S. v. Boletzky. 1979. A comparative study of the structure, development and morphological relationships of chambered cephalopod shells. *Veliger*, 21(3):313-354.

Barber, V. C. 1967. A neurosecretory tissue in octopus. *Nature*, 213(5080):1042-1043.

Barber, V. C. 1968. The structure of mollusc statocysts, with particular reference to cephalopods. *Symp. Zool. Soc. Lond.*, No. 23:37-62.

Baumann, F., A. Mauro, R. Milecchia et al. 1970. The extra-ocular receptors of the squid *Todarodes* and *Illex*. *Brain Res.*, 21(2):275-279.

* Best, E.M.H. and M.J. Wells. 1983, 1984. The control of digestion in Octopus, I-II. *Vie Milieu*, 33(3-4): 135-142; 34(1): 1-7

* Bidder, A. M. 1950. The digestive mechanism of the European squids *Loligo vulgaris, Alloteuthis media*, and *Alloteuthis subulata*. *Quart. J. Microsc. Sci.*, ser. 3, 91(1):1-43.

* Bidder, A. M. 1966. Feeding and digestion in cephalopods. In: *Physiology of Mollusca*, NY-Lond., 2:97-124.

Bidder, A. M. 1976. New names for old: the cephalopod "mid-gut gland." *J. Zool.*, 180:441-443.

Bityukova, Yu. E. and G. V. Zuev. 1976. Eye asymmetry in squids, family Histioteuthidae, in relation to its ecology. *Biol. Morya (Kiev)*, No. 38:63-67(in Russ.).

Blank, R. 1978. Neurosekretorische Komplexe bei *Loligo*. *Zool. Jahrb., Anat.*,99(4):505-526.

Bloodgood, R. 1977. The squid accessory nidamental gland: ultrastructure and association with bacteria. *Tissue & Cell*, 9(2):197-208.

* Boletzky, S. v. 1976. The larvae of Cephalopoda: a review. *Thalassia Jugosl.*, 10:45-76.

Borer, K. T. and C. E. Lane. 1971. Oxygen requirements of *Octopus briareus* Robson at different temperatures and oxygen concentrations. *J. Exp. Mar. Biol. Ecol.*, 7(3):263-269.

Bottazzi, F. 1916. Ricerche sulla ghiandola salivare posteriore dei Cefalopodi. *Pubbl. Staz, Zool. Napoli*, 1:59-146.

Bottke, W. 1974. The fine structure of the ovarian follicle of *Alloteuthis subulata* Lam. *Cell Tissue Res.*, 150(4):463-479.

Boucaud-Camou, E., R. Boucher-Rodoni, and K. Mangold. 1976. Digestive absorption in *Octopus vulgaris*. *J. Zool.*, 179(2):261-271.

Boucaud-Camou, E. and M. Yim. 1980. Fine structure and function of the digestive cell of *Sepia officinalis*. *Ibid.*, 191(1):89-105.

Boucher-Rodoni, R. 1973. Vitesse de la digestion d'*Octopus cyanea*. *Mar. Biol.*, 18(3):237-242.

Boucher-Rodoni, R. 1975. Vitesse de la digestion chez les Céphalopodes *Eledone cirrosa* (Lamarck) et *Illex illecebrosus* (Lesueur). *Cah. Biol. Mar.*, 16(2):159-175.

Boucher-Rodoni, R. and K. Mangold. 1977. Experimental study of digestion in *Octopus vulgaris*. *J. Zool.*, 183(4): 505-515.

Boycott, B. B. 1953. The chromatophore system of cephalopods. *Proc. Linn. Soc. London*, 164(2):235-240.

Boycott, B. B. 1960. The functioning of the statocysts of *Octopus vulgaris*. *Proc. R. Soc. London*, 152B(946):78-87.

Boycott, B. B. 1961. The functional organization of the brain of the cuttlefish, *Sepia officinalis*. *Ibid.*, 153B(953):503-534.

Boyle, P. R. 1983. Ventilation rate and arousal in the octopus. *J. Exp. Mar. Biol. Ecol.*, 69(2):129-136.

Boyle, P. R., K. Mangold, and D. Froesch. 1979. The organization of beak movements in *Octopus*. *Malacologia*, 18:423-430.

Branden, C. van den, M. Gillis, and A. Richard.

1980. Carotenoid producing bacteria in the accessory nidamental glands of *Sepia officinalis* L. *Comp. Physiol.*, 66B(2):331-334.

Brocco, S. L. and R. A. Cloney. 1980. Reflector cells in the skin of *Octopus dofleini*. *Cell Tissue Res.*, 205(2):167-186.

Budelmann, B.-U. 1979. The function of the equilibrium receptor systems of cephalopods. *Proc. Neurootol. Equilibriometric Soc.*, 6:15-63.

Budelmann, B.U. and J.Z. Young. 1985. Central pathways of the nerves of the arms and tentacles of Octopus. *Philos. Trans. R. Soc. London,* B310(1143): 109-122.

* Bullock, T. H. and G. A. Horridge. 1965. *Structure and function in the nervous systems of invertebrates.* 2 vols. San Francisco: Freeman, , 1719 pp.

Burukovsky, R. N. and A. N. Vovk. 1974. Some problems of the oogenesis in the North American squid (*Loligo pealei* Les.) of the Georges Bank. *Arkh. Anat. Hist. Embryol.,* 66(5):44-50(Russ., Eng. summ.).

Burukovsky, R. N., G. V. Zuev, Ch. M. Nigmatullin, and M. A. Tsymbal. 1977. Methodical bases for working out the scales of the reproductive system maturity in the squid female as exemplified by *Sthenoteuthis pteropus*. *Zool. Zh.,* 52(12):1781-1791(Russ. Eng. summ.).

Butcher, S., P. N. Dilly, and P. J. Herring. 1982. The comparative morphology of the photophores of the squid *Pyroteuthis margaritifera*. *J. Zool., London,* 196(1):133-150.

Caviello, L. and L. Zanetti. 1977. a- and ß-cephalotoxin: two paralyzing protein from posterior salivary glands of *Octopus vulgaris*. *Comp. Biochem. Physiol.,* 57C(2):169-174.

* Clarke, M. R. 1962. The identification of cephalopod "beaks" and the relationship between beak size and total body weight. *Bull. Brit. Mus. (Nat. Hist.), Zool.,* 8(10):419-480.

Clarke, M. R. 1978. The cephalopod statolith--an introduction to its form. *J, Mar. Biol. Assoc. U.K.,* 58(3):701-712.

Clarke, M. R., E. J. Denton, and J. B. Gilpin-Brown. 1979. On the use of ammonium for buoyancy in squids. *Ibid.,* 59(2):259-276.

Cloney, R. A. and E. Florey. 1968. Ultrastructure of cephalopod chromatophore organs. *Z. Zellforsch.,* 89:250-280.

Collewijn, H. 1970. Oculomotor reactions in the cuttlefish *Sepia officinalis*. *J. Exp. Biol.,* 52(2):369-384.

Corner, B. D. and H. T. Moore. 1980. Field observations on the reproductive behavior of *Sepia latimanus*. *Micronesia,* 16(2):235-260.

Cousteau, J.-Y. and P. Diolé. 1973. *Octopus and squid, the soft intelligence.* London: Cassell. 304 pp.

Cowden, R. R. 1968. Cytological and cytochemical studies of oocyte development and development of the follicular epithelium in the squid *Loligo brevis*. *Acta Embryol. Morphol. Experim.,*10(2):160-173.

Cowden, R. R. 1972. Some cytological and cytochemical observations on the leucopoietic organs, the "'white bodies,'" of *Octopus vulgaris*. *J. Invert. Pa-*

thol., 19(1):113-119.

* Denton, E. J. and J. B. Gilpin-Brown. 1973. Floatation mechanisms in modern and fossil cephalopods. *Adv. Mar. Biol.,* 11:197-268.

Denton, E. J. and M. F. Land. 1971. Mechanism of reflexion in silvery layers of fish and cephalopods. *Proc. R. Soc. London,* 178B(1050):43-61.

Dijkgraaf, S. 1963a. Versuche über Schallwahrnehmung bei Tintenfischen. *Naturwiss.* 50(2):50.

Dijkgraaf, S. 1963b. Nystagmus and related phenomena in *Sepia officinalis*. *Experientia.* 19(1):29-30.

Dilly, P. N. and P. J. Herring. 1981. Ultrastructural features of the light organs of *Histioteuthis macrohista*. *J. Zool., London,* 195(2):255-266.

Dilly, P. N. and M. Nixon. 1976a. The cells that secrete the beaks in octopus and squids. *Cell Tissue Res.,* 167(2):229-241.

Dilly, P. N. and M. Nixon. 1976b. The dermal tubercles of *Cranchia scabra*: surface structure and development. *J. Zool.,* 179(3):291-295.

Dilly, P. N., M. Nixon, and A. Packard. 1964. Forces exerted by *Octopus vulgaris*. *Pubbl. Staz. Zool. Napoli,* 34(1):86-97.

Drew, G. A. 1911, 1919. Sexual activities of the squid, *Loligo pealei* (Les.), I-II. *J. Morphol.,* 22(2):327-359, 32(2):379-435.

Emery, D. G. 1975a. The histology and fine structure of the olfactory organ of the squid *Lolliguncula brevis* Blainville. *Tissue & Cell,* 7(2):357-367.

Emery, D. G. 1975b. Ciliated sensory cells and associated neurons in the lip of *Octopus joubini* Robson. *Cell Tissue Res.,* 157(3):331-340.

Féral, J.-P. 1978, 1979. La régénération des bras de la seiche *Sepia officinalis* L. I-II. *Cah. Biol. Mar.,* 19(3):355-361, 20(1):29-42.

* Fields, W. G. 1965. The structure, development, food relations, reproduction, and life history of the squid *Loligo opalescens* Berry. *Calif. Div. Fish & Game, Fish Bull.,*No. 131:108 pp.

* Florkin, M. and B. T. Scheer. (eds.). 1972. *Chemical Zoology, Mollusca.* NY-Lond.: Acad. Press, 7:567 pp.

Fort, G. 1937, 1941. Le spermatophore des Céphalopodes, I-II. *Bull. Biol. France Belg.,* 71:353-373, 75:249-256.

Franzen, Aa. 1967. Spermiogenesis and spermatozoa of the Cephalopoda. *Ark. Zool.,* 19(4):323-334.

Freeman, S. E, and R. J. Turner. 1970. Maculotoxin, a potent toxin secreted by *Octopus maculosus* Hoyle. *Toxicol. Appl. Pharmacol.,* 16(3):681-690.

Froesch, D. 1979. Antigen-induced secretion in the optic gland of *Octopus vulgaris*. *Proc. R. Soc. London,* 205B(1160):379-384.

Froesch. D. and K. Mangold. 1976. On the structure and function of a neurohemal organ in the eye cavity of *Eledone cirrosa*. *Brain Res.,* 111(2):287-293.

Froesch, D. and H.-J. Marthy. 1975. The structure and function of the oviducal gland in octopods. *Proc. R. Soc. London.,* 188B(1090):95-101.

Froesch, D, and J. B. Messenger. 1978. On the leucophores and the chromatic unit of *Octopus vulgaris*. *J. Zool.,* 186(2):163-173.

Ghiretti, F. 1959. Cephalotoxin: the crab paralyzing agent of the posterior salivary glands of cephalopods. *Nature*, 183(4669):1192-1193.

Ghiretti-Magaldi, A., F. Ghiretti., and B. Salvato. 1977. The evolution of haemocyanin. *Symp. Zool. Soc. London*, No. 38:513-523.

Girsch, S. J., P. J. Herring, and F. McCapra, 1976. Structure and preliminary biochemical characterization of the bioluminescent system of *Ommastrephes pteropus* (Steenstrup). *J. Mar. Biol. Assoc. U. K.*, 56(3):707-722.

Giuditta, A. and N. Prozzo. 1974. Postembryonic growth of the optic lobe of *Octopus vulgaris* Lam. *J. Comp. Neurol.*, 157(2):109-116.

Gosline, J.M. and M.E. DeMont. 1984. Jet-propelled swimming in squids. *Sci. Amer.*, 252(1): 74-79.

Goto, T., S. Inoue, H. Kakoi et al. 1976. Squid bioluminescence, I-IV. *Tetrahedron Letters* No. 26:2321-2324, No. 34:2971-2974; 1975, *Chemistry Letters*, No. 2:141-144; 1977, No. 3:259-262.

★ Götting, K.-J. 1974. *Malakozoologie, Grundriss der Weichtierkunde*. Stuttgart: G. Fischer, 317 pp.

Graupneri, H. and J. Fischer. 1934. Das Tintendrüsenepithel von *Sepia* vor , während und nach der Pigmentbildung. *Z. Zellforsch.*, 21(3):329-341.

Graziadi, P. P. C. and H. T. Gagne. 1976. Sensory innervation in the rim of the octopus sucker. *J. Morphol.*, 150(3):639-679.

Hanlon, R. T. 1982. The functional organization of chromatophores and iridescent cells in the body patterning of *Loligo plei*. *Malacologia*, 23(1):89-119.

Hanson, D., T. Mann, and A. W. Martin. 1973. Mechanism of the spermatophoric reaction in the giant octopus of the North Pacific, *Octopus dofleini martini*. *J. Exp. Biol.*, 58(3):711-723.

Hara, T. and R. Hara. 1980. Retinochrome and rhodopsin in the extraocular photoreceptors of the squid, *Todarodes*. *J. Gen. Physiol.*, 75(1):1-19.

Hara, T., R. Hara, and J. Takeuchi. 1967. Vision in octopus and squid. *Nature*, 214(5088):572-573.

Harrison, F. M. and A. W. Martin. 1965. Excretion in the cephalopod, *Octopus dofleini*. *J. Exp. Biol.*, 42(1):71-98.

★ Herring, P. J. 1977. Luminescence in cephalopods. *Symp. Zool. Soc. London*, No. 38:127-159.

Herring, P. J. , M. R. Clarke, S. von Boletzky, and K.P. Ryan. 1981. The light organs of *Sepiola atlantica* and *Spirula spirula*:bacterial and intrinsic systems in the order Sepioidea. *J. Mar. Biol. Assoc. U.K.*, 61(4):901-916.

Herring, P.J., P.N. Dilly, and C. Cope. 1985. The photophore morphology of *Selenoteuthis scintillans* Voss and other lycoteuthids. *J. Zool.*, 206(4):567-589.

Hobbs, M. J. and J. Z. Young. 1973. A cephalopod cerebellum. *Brain Res.*, 55(2):424-430.

Hoffmann, H.-J. 1970. Tintenfische--ihre Präparation und microskopische Untersuchung, I-III. *Mikrokosmos*, 59(5-7):142-147, 171-177, 201-205.

Hotta, H. 1973. Identification of squid and cuttlefish in the adjacent waters of Japan, using the characteristics of beaks. *Bull. Seikai Reg. Fish. Res. Lab.*, No. 43:133-147.

Hubbard, S. J. 1960. Hearing and the octopus statocyst. *J. Exp. Biol.*, 37(4):845-853.

★ Isgrove, A. 1909. *Eledone. Liverpool Mar. Biol. Comm. Mems.*, 18:105 pp.

Ishikawa, M. 1929. On the statocyst of American cephalopod genera. *J. Morphol. Physiol. Philad.*, 48(2):563-584.

Ivanov, A. V. 1955. *Commercial water invertebrates*. Moscow:Sov. Nauka. 356 pp. (Cephalopods:pp. 179-189.)(in Russ.).

Ivanov, A. V. 1985. Class Cephalopoda. pp. 184-225 in: A. V. Ivanov, Yu. I. Polyansky, and A. A. Strelkov. *Great practicum in invertebrate zoology*, vol. 3. Moscow: Vys. Shkola. 390 pp.(in Russ.).

★ Ivanov, A. V. and A. A. Strelkov. 1949. *Commercial invertebrates of the Far Eastern Seas. Description of the structure and atlas of the anatomy*. Vladivostok:TINRO, 104 pp.(in Russ.).

Iverson, I. L. K., and L. Pinkas. 1971. A pictorial guide to the beaks of certain Eastern Pacific cephalopods. *Calif. Div. Fish & Game, Fish Bull.*,No. 152:83-105.

★ Jaeckel, S. G. A. 1958. Cephalopoden. *Tierwelt der Nord- und Ostsee*, 37(IXb₃):479-723.

Jaeckel, S. H. 1957. Kopffüsser (Tintenfische). *Neue Brehm-Bücherei*, No. 190. Wittenberg: A. Ziemsen, 81 pp.

Jander, R., K. Daumer, and T. H. Waterman. 1963. Polarized light orientation by two Hawaiian decapod cephalopods. *Z. vergl. Physiol.*,46(4):383-394.

Johansen, K., O. Brix, and G. Lykkeboe. 1982. Blood gas transport in the cephalopod, *Sepia officinalis*. *J. Exp. Biol.*, 99:331-338.

★ Kaestner, A. 1969. *Lehrbuch der speziellen Zoologie*, Bd. I, Teil. 1. 3. Aufl. Jena: G. Fischer, 898 pp. (Cephalopoda:424-451).

Kier, W. M. 1982. The functional morphology of the musculature of squid (Loliginidae) arms and tentacles. *J. Morphol.*, 172(2):179-192.

Kier, W. M. 1985. The musculature of squid arms and tentacles: ultrastructural evidence for functional differences. *J. Morphol.*, 185(2): 223-239.

★ Kondakov, N. N. 1940. Class Cephalopoda. In: *Manual of Zoology*, vol. 2. Moscow; Leningrad: Acad. Sci. USSR, pp. 548-609(in Russ.).

Kristensen, T. K. 1980. Periodical growth rings in cephalopod statoliths. *Dana*, No. 1:39-51.

★ Lane, F. W. 1957 *Kingdon of the octopus. The life history of Cephalopoda*, London: Jarrolds, 287 pp. 2nd ed., NY, 1960, 300 pp.

Lange, M. M. 1920. On the regeneration and finer structure of the arms of the cephalopods. *J. Exp. Zool.*, 31:1-57.

Lapan, E. 1975. Studies on the chemistry of the octopus renal system and an observation of the symbiotic relationship of the dicyemid Mesozoa. *Comp. Biochem. Physiol.*, 52A(4):651-658.

Leisman, G., D. H. Cohn, and K. H. Nealson. 1980. Bacterial origin of luminescence in marine animals. *Science*, 208(4449):1271-1273.

★ MacGinitie, G. E. and N. MacGinitie. 1968. *Natural*

history of marine animals. 2nd ed. NY, 523 pp.

Maddock, L. and J.Z. Young. 1984. Some dimensions of the angular acceleration receptor systems of cephalopods. *J. Mar. Biol. Assoc. U.K.,* 64(1): 55-79.

Maginnis, L. A. and M. J. Wells. 1969. The oxygen consumption of *Octopus cyanea. J. Exp. Biol.,* 51(3):607-613.

* Mangold-Wirz, K. 1963. Biologie des Céphalopodes benthiques et nectoniques de la mer Catalane. *Vie Milieu,* suppl. No. 13:285 pp.

Mangold, K. and R. Boucher-Rodoni. 1973. Role du jeûne dans l'induction de la maturation génitale chez les femelles d'*Eledone cirrosa. C. R. Acad. Sci. Paris,* 276D(13):2007-2010.

Mangold, K. and P. Fioroni. 1966. Morphologie et biométrie des mandibules de quelques Céphalopodes méditerranéens. *Vie Milieu,* 17(3A):1139-1196.

* Mangold-Wirz, K. and P. Fioroni. 1970. Die Sonderstellung der Cephalopoden. *Zool. Jahrb., Syst.,* 97(4):522-631.

Mangold, K. and D. Froesch. 1977. A reconsideration of factors associated with sexual maturation in cephalopods. *Symp. Zool. Soc. London,* No. 38:541-555.

Mangold, K., D. Froesch, R. Boucher-Rodoni, and V. L. Rowe. 1975. Factors affecting sexual maturation in cephalopods. *Pubbl. Staz. Zool. Napoli,* 31(suppl. 1):259-266.

Mangold, K. and A. Portmann. 1964. Dimensions et croissance relatives des Octopodides méditerranéens. *Vie Milieu,* No. 17:213-233.

Mann, T., A. W. Martin, and J. B. Thiersch. 1970. Male reproductive tract, spermatophores, and spermatophoric reaction in the giant octopus of the North Pacific, *Octopus dofleini martini. Proc. R. Soc. London,* 175B(1038):31-61.

Mann, T., A. W. Martin, and J. B. Thiersch. 1981. Changes in the spermatophoric plasma during spermatophore development and during the spermatophoric reaction in the giant octopus of the North Pacific, *Octopus dofleini martini, Mar. Biol.,* 63(2):121-127.

Marchand, W. 1907. Der männliche Leitungsapparat der Dibranchiaten. *Ztschr. wiss. Zool.,* 86(3):311-415.

Marchand, W. 1913. Über die Spermatophoren. *Zoologica, Stuttgart,* 26(1):171-200.

Marthy, H.-J., R. Hauser, and A. Scholl. 1976. Natural tranquilliser in cephalopod eggs. *Nature,* 261(5560):496-497.

* Martin, A. W. 1975. Physiology of the excretory organs of cephalopods. *Fortschr. Zool.,* 23(2-3):112-123.

Martin, A. W., J. B. Thiersch, H. M. Dott et al. 1970. Spermatozoa of the giant octopus of the North Pacific *Octopus dofleini martini. Proc. R. Soc. London,* 175B(1038):63-68.

Martin, R. 1977. The giant nerve fiber system of cephalopods. Recent structural findings. *Symp. Zool. Soc. London,* No. 38:261-275.

Matus, A. I. 1971. Fine structure of the posterior salivary gland of *Eledone cirrosa* and *Octopus vulgaris. Z. Zellforsch,* 122(1):111-121.

* Mauro, A. 1977. Extra-ocular photoreceptors in cephalopods. *Symp. Zool. Soc. London,* No. 38:287-308.

McCapra, F. M. and R. Hart. 1980. The origin of marine bioluminescence. *Nature,* 286(5774):660-661.

Messenger, J. B. 1967. Parolfactory vesicles as photoreceptors in deep-sea squid. *Nature,* 213(5078):836-838.

Messenger, J. B. 1974. Reflecting elements in cephalopod skin and their importance for camouflage. *J. Zool.,* 174(3):387-395.

Messenger, J. B. 1977. Evidence that octopus is colour blind, *J. Exp. Biol.,* 70(1):49-55.

Messenger, J. B. 1979a. The nervous system of *Loligo,* IV. The peduncle and olfactory lobes. *Philos. Trans. R. Soc. London,* 258B(1008):275-309.

Messenger, J. B. 1979b. The eyes and skin of octopus: compensating for sensory deficiencies. *Endeavour,* N. S. 3(3):92-98.

Messenger, J. B., E. O. Muzii, G. Nardi, and H. Steinberg. 1974. Haemocyanin synthesis and the branchial gland of octopus. *Nature,* 250(5462):154-155.

Meyer, W. T. 1906. Die Anatomie von *Opisthoteuthis depressa* (Ijima und Ikeda). *Z. wiss. Zool.,* 85(2):183-269.

* Meyer, W. T. 1913. Tintenfische. *Monog. einheim. Tiere,* Vol. 6. Leipzig: Klinkhardt, 148 pp.

Mochizuki, A. 1979. An antiseptic effect of cuttlefish ink. *Bull. Jap. Soc. Sci. Fish.,* 45(11):1401-1403.

Molluscs. *Abstracts of communications.* Leningrad: Nauka, vol. 2. 1965, 101 pp.; vol. 3, 1968, 96 pp.; vol. 4, 1971, 160 pp.; vol. 5, 1975, 244 pp.; vol. 6, 1979, 264 pp.(in Russ.).

Morales, E. 1973. Contribución al estudio de la morfologia, structura y anatomia microscópica de la región visceral de *Pteroctopus tetracirrhus* D. Ch. *Invest. Pesq.,*37(2):353-518.

Morishita, T. 1978. Studies on the protein digestive enzymes of octopus, *Octopus vulgaris* Cuvier. *Bull. Fac. Fish. Mie Univ.,* No. 5:179-282.

* Morton, J. 1967. *Molluscs.* 4th ed. London: Hutchinson, 244 pp.

Moynihan, M. and A. F. Rodaniche. 1982. The behavior and natural history of the Caribbean reef squid *Sepioteuthis sepioidea. Fortschr. Verhaltensforsch. (Suppl. Ztschr. Tierpsychol.),* No. 25:150 pp.

Muntz, W. R. A. and M. S. Johnson. 1978. Rhodopsin of oceanic decapods. *Vision Res.,* 18(5):601-602.

* Nesis, K. N. 1973d. Ecological classification(life forms) of cephalopods. *Itogi Nauki, ser. Invert. Zool.,* vol. 2, Moscow: VINITI, pp. 8-59(in Russ.).

Nesis, K. N. 1975b. Evolution of the life forms in recent cephalopods. *Trudy Inst. Okeanol. Acad. Sci. USSR,* 101:124-142(Russ., Eng. summ.).

Nesis, K. N. 1977b. Vertical distribution of pelagic cephalopods. *Zh. Obshch. Biol.,* 38(4):547-558(Russ., Eng. summ.).

Nesis, K. N. 1978b. Evolutionary history of the nekton. *Ibid.,* 39(1):53-65(Russ., Eng. summ.).

Nishioka, R. S., I. Yasumasu, A. Packard et al. 1966.

Nature of vesicles associated with the nervous system of cephalopods. *Z. Zellforsch.*, 75(1):301-316.

Nixon, M. 1969. Growth of the beak and radula of *Octopus vulgaris. J. Zool.*, 159(3):363-379.

Nixon, M. 1979. Hole-boring in shells by *Octopus vulgaris* Cuvier in the Mediterranean. *Malacologia*, 18(1-2):431-443.

Nixon, M. 1980. The salivary papilla of *Octopus* as an accessory radula for drilling shells. *J. Zool.*, 190(1):53-57.

Nixon, M. 1984. Is there external digestion by Octopus? *J. Zool.*, 202(3): 441-447.

Nixon, M. and P. N. Dilly. 1977. Sucker surfaces and prey capture. *Symp. Zool. Soc. London*, No. 38:447-511.

Nixon, M. and J. B. Messenger (eds.). 1977. The biology of cephalopods. *Symp. Zool. Soc. London*, No. 38:615 pp.

O'Dor, R. K. 1982. Respiratory metabolism and swimming performance of the squid, *Loligo opalescens. Can. J. Fish. Aquatic Sci.*, 39(4):580-587.

O'Dor, R. K. and M. J. Wells. 1978. Reproduction versus somatic growth: hormonal control in *Octopus vulgaris. J. Exp. Biol.*, 77(1):15-31.

Orlov, O. Yu and A. L. Byzov. 1962. Vision in cephalopods. *Priroda*, No. 2:115-118(in Russ.).

Packard, A. 1966. Operational convergence between cephalopods and fish: an exercise in functional anatomy. *Arch. Zool. Ital.*, 51(2):523-542.

Packard, A. 1969. Visual acuity and eye growth in *Octopus vulgaris* (Lamarck). *Monit. Zool. Ital.*, N.S., 3(1):19-32.

* Packard, A. 1972. Cephalopods and fish: the limits of convergence. *Biol. Rev.*, 47(2):241-307.

Packard, A. and V. Albergoni. 1970. Relative growth, nucleic acid content and cell numbers of the brain in *Octopus vulgaris* (Lamarck). *J. Exp. Biol.*, 52:539-552.

Packard, A. and F. G. Hochberg. 1977. Skin patterning in *Octopus* and other genera. *Symp. Zool. Soc. London*, No. 38:191-231.

Packard, A. and G. D. Sanders. 1971. Body pattern of *Octopus vulgaris* and maturation of the response to disturbance. *Anim. Behav.*, 19(4):780-790.

Person, P. 1969. Cartilaginous dermal scales in cephalopods. *Science*, 164(3886):1404-1405.

Peters, W. 1972. Occurrence of chitin in Mollusca. *Comp. Biochem. Physiol.*, 41B(3):541-550.

Philpott, D. E. and P. Person. 1970. The biology of cartilage, 2. Invertebrate cartilages: squid head cartilage. *J. Morphol.*,131(4):417-430.

Potts, W. T. W. and M. Todd. 1965. Kidney function in the octopus. *Comp. Biochem. Physiol.* 16(4):479-489.

Prosser, C. L. (ed.). 1973. *Comparative Animal Physiology. 3rd ed. Philadelphia e. a.:* W. B. Saunders, 3 vols.

* Purchon, R. D. 1977. *The biology of the Mollusca.* 2nd ed. Oxford e. a.: Pergamon, 560 pp.

Richard, A. 1970. Analyse du cycle sexuel chez les Céphalopodes: mise en évidence expérimentale d'un rythme conditionné par les variations des facteurs externes et internes. *Bull. Soc. Zool. France,* 95(3):461-469.

Richard, A., C. van den Branden, and W. Decleir. 1979. The cycle of activity in the accessory nidamental gland from cephalopods. In: *13th Europ. Mar. Biol. Symp.*, Oxford e. a.: Pergamon, pp. 173-180.

Richard, A. and J. Lemaire. 1975. Détermination et différenciation sexuelle chez la seiche *Sepia officinalis* L. *Pubbl. Staz. Zool. Napoli*, 39(suppl. 1):574-594.

Robison, B. H. and R. E. Young. 1981. Bioluminescence in pelagic octopods. *Pacif. Sci.*, 35(1):39-44.

Rodaniche, A.F. 1984. Iteroparity in the lesser Pacific striped octopus *Octopus chierchiae* (Jatta, 1889). *Bull. Mar. Sci.*, 35(1):99-104.

Robson, G. C. 1925. On seriation and asymmetry of the cephalopod radula. *J. Linn. Soc. London.* 36(241):99-108.

Rowe, V. L. and K. Mangold. 1975. The effect of starvation on sexual maturation in *Illex illecebrosus* (LeSueur). *J. Exp. Mar. Biol. Ecol.*, 17(2):157-164.

* Sanders, G. D. 1975. The Cephalopods. In: *Invertebrate learning*, vol. 3. NY-Lond.: Plenum, pp. 1-101.

Savage, I. V. E. and M. E. H. Howden. 1977. Hapalotoxin, a second lethal toxin from the octopus *Hapalochlaena maculosa. Toxicon*, 15(5):463-466.

* Schipp, R. and S. v. Boletzky. 1975. Morphology and function of the excretory organs in dibranchiate cephalopods. *Fortschr. Zool.*, 23(2-3):89-111.

Schipp, R. and S. v. Boletzky. 1976. The pancreatic appendages of dibranchiate cephalopods, I. *Zoomorphologie*, 86(1):81-98.

Schipp, R., S. Mollenhauger, and S. v. Boletzky. 1979. Electron microscópical and histochemical studies of differentation and function of the cephalopod gill (*Sepia officinalis* L.). *Ibid.*, 93(3):193-207.

Schipp, R. and K. Pfeiffer. 1980. Vergleichende cytologische und histochemische Untersuchungen an der Mitteldarmdrüse dibranchiater Cephalopoden. *Zool. Jahrb., Anat.*, 104(3):317-343.

Scheumack, D. D., M. E. H. Howden, I. Spence, and R. J. Quinn. 1978. Maculotoxin: a neurotoxin from the venom glands of the octopus *Hapalochlaena maculosa* identified as tetrodotoxin. *Science*, 199(4325):188-189.

Singley, C. T. 1982. Histochemistry and fine structure of the ectodermal epithelium of sepiolid squid *Euprymna scolopes. Malacologia*, 23(1):177-192.

Smith, P. J. S. 1982. The contribution of the branchial heart to the accessory branchial pump in the Octopoda. *J. Exp. Biol.*,98:229-237.

Solem, A. and C. F. E. Roper. 1975. Structures of recent cephalopod radulae. *Veliger*, 18(2):127-133.

Stephens, P. R. and J. Z. Young. 1976. The statocyst of *Vampyroteuthis infernalis. J. Zool.*, 180(4):565-588.

Stephens, P. R. and J. Z. Young. 1978. Semicircular canals in squids. *Nature*, 271(5644):444-445.

Stephens, P. R. and J. Z. Young. 1982. The statocyst of the squid *Loligo. J. Zool., London.* 197(2):241-266.

Stuart, A. E. 1967. The reticulo-endothelial apparatus of *Eledone cirrosa. Vie Milieu*, 18(1A):175-187.

Sutherland, N. S. 1969. Shape discrimination in rat,

octopus, and goldfish: a comparative study. *J. Comp. Physiol. Psychol.*, 67:160-176.

Sutherland, S. K. and W. R. Lane. 1969. Toxin and mode of envenomation of the common ringed or blue-banded octopus. *Med. J. Australia*, 1(18):893-898.

Takahashi, N. and T. Yahata. 1973. Histological studies of the maturation of the ovary in the squid, *Todarodes pacificus. Bull. Fac. Fish. Hokkaido Univ.*, 24(2):63-68.

Taki, I. 1936. Observations on autophagy in octopus. *Annotat. Zool. Jap.*, 15(3):352-354.

* Thore, S. 1939. Beiträge zur Kenntnis des zentralen Nervensystems der dibranchiaten Cephalopoden. *Pubbl. Staz. Zool. Napoli*, 17(3):313-506.

* Tompsett, D. H. 1939. *Sepia. Liverpool Mar. Biol. Comm. Mems.*, 32:184 pp.

Tsuji, F. I. 1985. ATP-dependent bioluminescence in the firefly squid, *Watasenia scintillans. Proc. Nat. Acad. Sci.* USA, 82(14): 4629-4632.

Tsuji, F. I. and G. B. Leisman. 1981. K^+/Na^+-triggered bioluminescence in the oceanic squid *Symplectoteuthis oualaniensis. Proc. Nat. Acad. Sci. USA*, 78(11):6719-6723.

Vinnikov Ya. A., O. G. Gazenko, L. K. Titova et al. Cephalopod statocysts, pp. 125-239 in: The gravitation receptor. *Prob. Space Biol.*, vol. 12, Leningrad: Nauka, 523 pp.(in Russ.).

Ward, D. V. 1972. Locomotory function of the squid mantle. *J. Zool.*, 167(4):487-499.

Ward, P.D. and S.v. Boletzky. 1984. Shell implosion depth and implosion morphologies in the species of *Sepia* from the Mediterranean Sea. *J. Mar. Biol. Assoc. U.K.*, 64(4): 955-966.

Ward, D. V. and S. A. Wainwright. 1972. Locomotory aspects of squid mantle structure. *Ibid.*, 167(4):437-449.

Weischer, M.-L. and H.-J. Marthy. 1983. Chemical and physiological properties of the natural tranquillizer in the cephalopod eggs. *Mar. Behav. Physiol.*, 9(2):131-138.

* Wells, M. J. 1962. *Brain and behaviour in cephalopods.* London: Heinemann, 171 pp.

* Wells, M. J. 1965. Learning by marine invertebrates. *Adv. Mar. Biol.*, 3:1-62.

* Wells, M. J. 1966. Cephalopod sense organs. The brain and behaviour of cephalopods. In: *Physiology of Mollusca*, vol. 2. NY-Lond.: Academic Press, pp. 523-590.

Wells, M. J. 1976a. Hormonal control of reproduction in cephalopods. In: *Perspectives experimental biology.* vol. 1. Oxford e. a.: Pergamon, pp. 157-166.

* Wells, M. J. 1976b. Proprioception and learning. In: *Structure and function of proprioceptors in the invertebrates.* London: Chapman & Hall, pp. 567-604.

* Wells, M. J. 1978. *Octopus. Physiology and behaviour of an advanced invertebrate.* London: Chapman & Hall, 424 pp.

Wells, M. J. 1979. The heartbeat of *Octopus vulgaris. J. Exp. Biol.*, 78:87-104.

Wells, M. J. 1980. Nervous control of the heartbeat in octopus. *Ibid.*, 85:111-128.

Wells, M. J., R. K. O'Dor, K. Mangold, and J. Wells. 1983. Diurnal changes in activity and metabolic rate in *Octopus vulgaris.* Oxygen consumption in movement by *Octopus.* Feeding and metabolic rate in *Octopus. Mar. Behav. Physiol.*, 9(4):275-287, 289-303, 305-317.

Wells, M.J. and P. J. S. Smith. 1985. The ventilation cycle in Octopus. *J. Exp. Biol.*, 116: 375-383.

Wells, M. J. and J. Wells. 1969. Pituitary analogue in octopus. *Nature*, 222(5190):293-294.

Wells, M. J. and J. Wells. 1982. Ventilatory currents in the mantle of cephalopods. *J. Exp. Biol.*, 99:315-330.

* Wilbur, K.M. (ed.). 1983, 1984. *The Mollusca.* London e.a.: Acad. Press. 7 vol.

* Wilbur, K. M. and C. M. Yonge (eds.). 1964, 1966. *Physiology of Mollusca.* NY-Lond.: Acad. Press, 1:473 pp.; 2:645 pp.

* Williams, L. 1909. *The anatomy of the common squid, Loligo pealeii LeSueur.* Leiden: Brill, 92 pp.

Wirz, K. 1959. Étude biométrique du système nerveux des Céphalopodes. *Bull. Biol. France Belg.*, 93(1):78-117.

Wodinsky, J. 1973. Mechanism of hole-boring in *Octopus vulgaris. J. Gen. Physiol.*, 88(2):179-183.

Wodinsky, J. 1977. Hormonal inhibition of feeding and death in octopus: control by optic gland secretion. *Science*, 198(4320):948-951.

Young, J. Z. 1960. The statocyst of *Octopus vulgaris. Proc. R. Soc. London*, 152B(946):3-29.

* Young, J. Z. 1961. Learning and discrimination in the octopus. *Biol. Rev.*, 36(1):32-96.

Young, J. Z. 1963. The number and sizes of nerve cells in octopus. *Proc. Zool. Soc. London*, 140(2):229-254.

* Young, J. Z. 1964. *A model of the brain.* Oxford: Clarendon, 348 pp.

Young, J. Z. 1965. The central nervous system of *Nautilus. Philos. Trans. R. Soc. London*, 249B(754):1-25.

Young, J. Z. 1966. *The memory system of the brain.* Oxford: Clarendon, 148 pp.

Young, J. Z. 1970. The stalked eye of *Bathothauma. J. Zool.*, 162(4):437-447.

* Young, J. Z. 1971. *The anatomy of the nervous system of Octopus vulgaris.* Oxford: Clarendon, 690 pp.

Young, J. Z. 1972. The organization of a cephalopod ganglion. *Philos. Trans. R. Soc. London.* 263B(854):409-429.

* Young, J. Z. 1974, 1976, 1977, 1979. The central nervous system of *Loligo.* I-III, V. *Ibid.*, 267B(885):263-302, 274B(930):101-167, 276B(948): 351-398, 285B(1009):311-354.

Young, J. Z. 1976. The "'cerebellum'" and the control of eye movements in cephalopods. *Nature*, 264(5586):572-574.

* Young, J. Z. 1977. Brain, behaviour and evolution of cephalopods. *Symp. Zool. Soc. London*, No. 38:377-434.

Young, J. Z. 1983. The distributed tactile memory system of *Octopus. Proc. R. Soc. London*, B218(1211):135-176.

Young, J.Z. 1984. The statocysts of cranchiid squids. *J. Zool.*, 203(1): 1-21.

Young, R. E. 1972. Function of extra-ocular photoreceptors in bathypelagic cephalopods. *Deep-Sea Res.*, 19(9):651-660.

Young, R. E, 1973. Information feedback from photophores and ventral countershading in mid-water squid. *Pacif. Sci.*, 27(1):1-7.

Young, R. E. 1975a. Function of the dimorphic eyes in the midwater squid *Histioteuthis dofleini. Ibid.*, 29(2):211-218.

Young, R. E. 1975b. Transitory eye shapes and the vertical distribution of two midwater squids. *Ibid.*, 29(3):243-255.

Young, R. E. 1975c. *Leachia pacifica:* spawning habitat and function of the brachial photophores. *Ibid.*, 29(1):19-25.

* Young, R. E. 1977. Ventral bioluminescent countershading in midwater cephalopods. *Symp. Zool. Soc. London*, No. 38:161-190.

* Young, R. E. 1978. Vertical distribution and photosensitive vesicles of pelagic cephalopods from Hawaiian waters. *Fish. Bull. U.S.*, 76(3):583-615.

Young, R. E. and J. M. Arnold. 1982. The functional morphology of a ventral photophore from a mesopelagic squid, *Abralia trigonura. Malacologia*, 23(1):135-163.

Young, R. E., E. M. Kampa, S. D. Maynard et al. 1980. Counterillumination and the uppermost limits of midwater animals. *Deep-Sea Res.*,27(9A):671-691.

Young, R. E. and F. M. Mencher. 1980. Bioluminescence in mesopelagic squid: diel color change during counterillumination. *Science*, 208(4449):1286-1288.

Young, R. E. and C. F. E. Roper. 1976. Bioluminescent countershading in midwater animals: evidence from living squid. *Ibid.*, 191(4231):1046-1048.

Young, R. E. and C. F. E. Roper. 1977. Intensity regulation of bioluminescence during countershading in living midwater animals. *Fish. Bull. U.S.*, 75(2):239-252.

Young, R. E., C. F. E. Roper, K. Mangold et al. 1979. Luminescence from non-bioluminescent tissues in oceanic cephalopods. *Mar. Biol.*,53(1):69-77.

Young, R. E., C. F. E. Roper, and J. F. Walters. 1979. Eyes and extraocular photoreceptros in midwater cephalopods and fishes: their roles in detecting downwelling light for counterillumination. *Ibid.*, 51(4):371-380.

Young, R. E., R. R. Seapy, K. Mangold, and F. G. Hochberg, Jr. 1982. Luminescent flashing in the midwater squids *Pterygioteuthis microlampas* and *P. giardi. Mar. Biol.*, 69(3):299-308.

Zalygalin, V. P., G. V. Zuev. and Ch. M. Nigmatullin. 1977. Peculiarities in spermatophore production and the male fecundity in the squid, *Sthenoteuthis pteropus*(Steenstrup). *Abstr. Commun. All-USSR Sci. Conf. Use Comm. Invert.*, Odessa, Nov. 22-25th, 1977, pp. 37-38(in Russ.).

* Zuev, G. V. 1966. *Functional bases of the external structure of cephalopods.* Kiev: Naukova Dumka, 140 pp.(in Russ.).

Zuev, G. V. 1969. Peculiarities of the mantle structure in cephalopods [The mantle of *Symplectoteuthis oualaniensis* (Lesson)]. *Biol. Morya (Kiev)*,No. 16:102-110(in Russ.).

Zuev, G. V. 1973. Allometric growth of the brain in cephalopods. *Ibid.*, No. 31:136-152(in Russ.).

Zuev, G. V. 1975. Growth and size of the brain in the ontogenesis of oceanic squids. *Ecologiya*, No. 4:70-73(in Russ.).

Zuev, G. V. and K. N. Nesis. 1971. *Squids (Biology and Fishery)*. Moscow: Pishchevaya Promyshlennost, 360 pp.(in Russ.).

Literature to Taxonomic Section

Adam, W. 1939a. The Cephalopoda in the Indian Museum, Calcutta. *Rec. Indian Mus.*, 41(1):61-110.

Adam, W. 1939b. Cephalopoda, I. Le genre *Sepioteuthis* Blainville,1824. *Siboga-Exped.*, 55a(134):1-34.

Adam, W. 1939c. Cephalopoda, II. Révision du espéces Indo-malaises du genre *Sepia* Linné, 1758. Révision du genre *Sepiella* (Gray) Steenstrup. *Ibid.*, 55b(135):35-122.

Adam, W. 1950. Un Céphalopode nouveau: *Pholidoteuthis boschmai* gen. et sp. nov. *Verh. Akad. Wet. Amsterdam*, 53(10):1592-1598.

* Adam, W., 1952. Céphalopodes. *Res. Sci. Expéd. Océanogr. Belge eaux côtiéres afric. Atlant. sud. (1948-49)*, 3(3):1-142.

Adam, W. E. 1954. Cephalopoda, III. *Siboga Exped.*, 55c(144):123-198.

* Adam, W. 1959. Les Céphalopodes de la mer Rouge. *Mission R. P. Dollfus en Egypte (déc. 1927-mars 1929), Rés. Sci.*, pt. 3(28):125-193.

Adam, W. 1960a. Cephalopoda from the Gulf of Aqaba. *Bull. Sea Fish. Res. Stat. Israel*, (26):1-27.

Adam, W. 1960b. Les Céphalopodes de l'Institut francaise d'Afrique noire, II. *Bull. IFAN*, 22(2A):465-511.

Adam, W. 1960c. Notes sur les Céphalopodes, 24. Contribution à la connaissance de l'hectocotyle chez les Ommastrephidae. *Bull. Inst. roy. Sci. natur. Belg.*, 36(19):1-10.

Adam, W. 1962. Céphalopodes de l'Archipel du Cap-Vert, de l'Angola et du Mozambique. *Mem. Junta Invest. Ultramar.*, sér. 2(33):7-64.

Adam, W. 1967. Cephalopoda from the Mediterranean Sea. *Bull. Sea Fish. Res. Stat., Israel*, (45):65-78.

Adam, W. 1972. Notes sur les Céphalopodes, 25. Contribution à la connaissance de *Chaunoteuthis mollis* Appellöf, 1891. *Bull. Inst. roy. Sci. natur. Belg.*, 48(12):1-7.

Adam, W. 1973. Cephalopoda from the Red Sea. *Contr. Knowl. Red Sea.* (47):9-47.

Adam, W. 1979. The Sepiidae (Cephalopoda, Decapoda) in the collection of the Western Australian Museum. *Rec. Aust. Mus.*, 7(2):109-212.

* Adam, W. and W. J. Rees. 1966. A review of the cephalopod family Sepiidae. *Sci. Repts. John Murray Exped. 1933-34*, 11(1):1-165.

Aldred, R. G. 1974. Structure, growth and distribution of the squid *Bathothauma lyromma* Chun. *J. Mar. Biol. Assoc. U. K.*, 54(4):995-1006.

Aldred, R. G., M. Nixon, and J. Z. Young. 1978. The blind octopus, *Cirrothauma*. *Nature*, 275(5680):547-549.

Aldred, R. G., M. Nixon, and J. Z. Young. 1983. *Cirrothauma murrayi* Chun, a finned octopod. *Phil. Trans. R. Soc. London*, B301:54 pp.

* Allan, J. 1945. Planktonic cephalopod larvae from the Eastern Australian coast. *Rec. Aust. Mus.*, 21:317-350.

Allan, J. 1959. *Australian Shells.* Melbourne: Georgian House, 487 pp.

Anderson, M. E. 1978. Notes on the cephalopods of Monterey Bay, California, with new records for the area. *Veliger*, 21(2):255-262.

Berry, S. S. 1911. A note on the genus *Lolliguncula*. *Proc. Acad. Nat. Sci. Philad.*, 63:100-105.

* Berry, S. S. 1912. A review of the cephalopods of western North America. *Bull. U. S. Bur. Fish.*, 30:267-336.

* Berry, S. S. 1914. The Cephalopoda of the Hawaiian waters. *Ibid.*, 32:255-362.

Berry, S. S. 1916. Cephalopoda of the Kermadec Islands. *Proc. Acad. Nat. Sci. Philad.*, 68(1):49-66.

Berry, S. S. 1918. Report on the Cephalopoda obtained by the F. I. S. "Endeavour" in the Great Australian Bight and other Southern Australian localities. *Biol. Res. Fish. Experiments "Endeavour" 1909-14*, 4(5):201-298.

Berry, S. S. 1920. Preliminary diagnoses of new cephalopods from the Western Atlantic. *Proc. U.S. Nat. Mus.*, 58(5335):293-300.

Berry, S. S. 1929. *Loliolopsis chiroctes*, a new genus and species of squid from the Gulf of California. *Trans. San Diego Soc. Nat. Hist.*, 5(18):263-282.

Berry, S. S. 1932. Cephalopods of the genera *Sepioloidea*, *Sepiadarium*, and *Idiosepius*. *Philippine J. Sci.*, 47(1):39-55.

Berry, S. S. 1952. The flapjack devilfish, *Opisthoteuthis*, in California. *Calif. Fish & Game*, 38(2):183-188.

Berry, S. S. 1953. Preliminary diagnoses of six West American species of *Octopus*. *Leafl. Malacol.*, 1(10):51-58.

Berry, S. S. 1955. The male flapjack devilfish. *Calif. Fish & Game.*, 41(3):219-224.

Boletzky, S. v. 1971. *Neorossia* n. g. pro *Rossia* (*Allorossia*) *caroli* Joubin, 1902, with remarks on generic status of *Semirossia* Steenstrup, 1887. *Bull. Mar. Sci.*, 21(4):964-969.

Boyle, P. R. (ed.). 1983. *Cephalopod life cycles. Vol.I.*

Species accounts. London: Acad. Press. 475 pp.

Brakoniecki, T, F. 1980. *Lolliguncula tydeus*, a new species of squid from the Pacific coast of Central America. *Ibid.*, *Bull. Mar. Sci.*, 30(2):424-430.

Brakoniecki, T.F. 1984. A full description of *Loligo sanpaulensis* Brakoniecki, 1984 and a redescription of *Loligo gahi* d'Orbigny, 1835, two species from the Southwest Atlantic. *Bull. Mar. Sci.*, 34(3): 435-448.

Brakoniecki, T. F. and C. F. E. Roper. 1985. *Lolliguncula argus*, a new species of loliginid squid from the tropical Eastern Pacific. *Proc. Biol. Soc. Wash.*, 98(1):47-53.

Bruun, A. F. 1943. The biology of *Spirula spirula* (L.). *Dana-Rept.*,No. 24:1-46.

* Bruun, A.F. 1945. Cephalopoda. *Zool. Iceland.* 4(pt. 64):1-15.

Bruun, A. F. 1955. New light on the biology of *Spirula*, a mesopelagic cephalopod. In: *Essays in the natural sicences in honor of Captain Allan Hancock.* Los Angeles: Univ. S. Calif. Press, pp.61-72.

Burgess, L. A. 1966. A study of the morphology and biology of *Octopus hummelincki* Adam, 1936. *Bull. Mar. Sci.*, 16(4):762-813.

Burgess, L. A. 1967. *Loliolus rhomboidalis*, a new species of loliginid squid from the Indian Ocean. *Ibid.*, 17(2):319-329.

Burgess, L. A. 1982. Four new species of squid (Oegopsida: *Enoploteuthis*) from the Central Pacific and a redescription of adult *Enoploteuthis reticulata*. *Fish. Bull. U.S.*, 80(4):703-734.

Cairns, S. D. 1976. Cephalopods collected in the Straits of Florida by the R/V "Gerda." *Bull. Mar. Sci.*, 26(2):233-272.

Castellanos, Z. J. A. de. 1964. Contribución biológico del calamar argentino, *Illex illecebrosus argentinus*. *Bol. Inst. Biol. marina*,No. 8:37 pp.

Castellanos, Z. J. A. de. 1967. Rehabilitación del genéro *Martialia* Roch. et Mab., 1887. *Neotropica.* 13(42):121-124.

Castellanos, Z. J. A de and N. Cazzaniga. 1979. Aclaraciones acerca de los Loliginidae del Atlántico sudoccidental. *Ibid.*, 25(73):59-68.

Castellanos, Z. J. A. de and R. C. Menni. 1968. Los Cefalópodos de la expedición 'Walther Herwig.' *Notas Com. Invest. Cient. Prov. Buenos Aires*, 6(2):1-31.

* Castellanos, Z. J. A. de and R. C. Menni. 1969a. Nota preliminar sobre distribución de los Cefalópodos del Atlántico sudoccidental. *An. Soc. cient. Argentina*, 188(5-6):205-226.

Castellanos, Z.J.A. de and R.C. Menni. 1969b. Sobre dos pulpos costeros de la Argentina. *Neotropica*, 15(47):89-94.

* Chun, C. 1910, 1915. Die Cephalopoden. I. Oegopsida. II. Myopsida, Octopoda. *Wiss. Ergeb. Dtsch. Tiefsee-Exped. "Valdivia" 1898-1899*, 18:552 pp. + Atlas.

Chun, C. 1913. Cephalopoda. *Rep. Sci. Res. "M. Sars" North Atlant. Deep-Sea Exped., 1910*, 3(1):21 pp.

Clarke, M. R. 1964. Young stages of *Lepidoteuthis grimaldii*. *Proc. Malacol. Soc. London*, 36(2):69-78.

* Clarke, M. R. 1966. A review of the systematics and

ecology of oceanic squids. *Adv. Mar. Biol.*, 4:91-300.

Clarke, M. R. 1967. A deep-sea squid, *Taningia danae* Joubin, 1931. *Symp. Zool. Soc. London*, No. 19:127-143.

Clarke, M. R. 1969. Cephalopoda collected on the SOND cruise. *J. Mar. Biol. Assoc. U. K.*, 49(4):961-976.

Clarke, M. R. 1970. Growth and development of *Spirula spirula*. *Ibid.*, 50(1):53-64.

* Clarke, M. R. 1980. Cephalopoda in the diet of sperm whales of the Southern Hemisphere and their bearing on sperm whale biology. *Discovery Repts.*, 37:324 pp.

Clarke, M. R. and C. C. Lu. 1974. Vertical distribution of cephalopods at 30° N, 23° W in the North Atlantic. *J. Mar. Biol. Asoc. U. K.*, 54(4):969-984.

Clarke, M. R. and C. C. Lu. 1975. Vertical distribution of cephalopods at 18° N, 25° W in the North Atlantic. *Ibid.*, 55(1):165-182.

Clarke, M. R. and G. E. Maul. 1962. A description of the "scaled" squid *Lepidoteuthis grimaldii* Joubin, 1895. *Proc. Zool. Soc. London*, 139(1):97-118.

Cohen, A. C. 1976. The systematics and distribution of *Loligo* in the Western North Atlantic, with description of two new species. *Malacologia*, 15(2):299-367.

* Cotton, B. C. and F. K. Godfrey. 1940. *The molluscs of South Australia*. Adelaide: F. Trygg, 2:317-600.

Degner, E. 1925. Cephalopoda. *Rep. Danish Oceanogr. Exped. 1908-10 Mediterranean*, 2(C1):1-94

* Dell, R. K. 1952. The recent Cephalopoda of New Zealand. *Bull. Dominion Mus.*, 16:1-157.

Dell, R. K. 1959a. Some additional New Zealand cephalopods from Cook Strait. *Zool. Publs. Victoria Univ. Wellington.* No. 25:1-12.

Dell, R. K. 1959b. Cephalopoda. *Rep. B.A.N.Z.A.R. Exped. 1929-1931*, 8B(4):89-106.

Dell, R. K. 1970. A specimen of the giant squid *Architeuthis* from New Zealand. *Rec. Dominion Mus.*, 7(4):25-36.

Dilly, P. N. and M. Nixon. 1976. Growth and development of *Taonius megalops*, and some phases of its life cycle. *J. Zool.*, 179(1):19-83.

Dilly, P. N., M. Nixon, and J. Z. Young. 1977. *Mastigoteuthis*, the whip-lash squid. *Ibid.*, 181(4):527-559.

* Dong, Zhenzhi. 1963. A preliminary taxonomic study of the Cephalopoda from the Chinese waters. *Stud. Mar. Sinica.*, No. 4:125-162.

Dong, Zhenzhi. 1976. On three new species of the genus *Octopus* from the Chinese waters. *Ibid.*, No. 11:211-215.

Dunning, M. and S.B. Brandt. 1985. Distribution and life history of deep-water squid of commercial interest from Australia. *Aust. J. Mar. Freshw. Res.*, 36)6): 343-359.

* Férussac, A. de and A. d'Orbigny. 1835-1848. *Histoire naturelle générale et particuliére des Céphalopodes acétabuliféres vivants et fossiles*. Paris, 2 vols. 361 pp. + Atlas.

Filippova, J. A. 1968. A new species of the genus *Cycloteuthis*. *Malacol. Rev.*, 1:119-124.

Filippova, J. A. 1969. On the squid fauna of the Southern Atlantic. *Zool. Zh.* 48(1):51-63(Russ., Eng. summ.).

Filippova, J. A. 1972. New data on the squids from the Scotia Sea (Antarctic). *Malacologia*, 11(2):391-406.

* Filippova, J. A. 1973. Distribution and biology of squids. *Itogi nauki, ser. Invert. Zool., Moscow, VINITI*, 2:60-101 (in Russ.).

Filipova, J. A. and V. L. Yukhov. 1979. Species composition and distribution of cephalopods in the meso- and bathypelagic zones of Antarctic waters. *Antarktika (Moscow)*, 18:175-187(in Russ.).

Filippova, J. A. and V. L. Yuhkov. 1982. New data on the genus *Alluroteuthis* Odhner, 1923. *Ibid.*, 21:157-168(in Russ.).

Garcia Cabrera, R. C. 1970. Espèces du genre *Sepia* du Sahara espagnol. *Rapp. Cons. int. Expl. Mer*, No. 159:132-139.

Golovan, G. A. and K. N. Nesis, 1975. Giant deepwater octopus. *Priroda*, No. 5:112-113(in Russ.).

Goodrich, E. C. 1896. Report on a collection of Cephalopoda from the Calcutta Museum. *Trans. Linn. Soc. London, Zool.*, 7(24):1-24.

* Grimpe, G. 1925. Zur Kenntnis der Cephalopodenfauna der Nordsee. *Wiss. Meeresunters. Helgoland*, N. F. 16(1):122 pp.

* Grimpe, G. 1933. Die Cephalopoden des arktischen Gebietes. *Fauna Arctica*, 6(5):489-514.

Guerra, A. 1982. Cefalópodos capturados en la campaña "Golfo di Cádiz-81." *Res. Exp. Cient., Barcelona*, 10:17-49.

* Hamada, T., I. Obata, and T. Okutani. (eds.). 1980. *Nautilus macromphalus in captivity*. Tokyo: Tokai Univ. Press, 80 pp.

Hochberg, F. G., Jr. 1980. Class Cephalopoda. p.201-204 in: R. C. Brusca, *Common Intertidal Invertebrates of the Gulf of California*. 2nd ed. Tucson: Univ. Arizona Press.

Hochberg, F. G., Jr. and W. G. Fields. 1980. Cephalopoda: the squids and octopuses. pp. 429-444 in: *Intertidal Invertebrates of California*. R. H. Morris, D. P. Abbott, and E. C. Haderlie (eds.). Stanford Univ. Press.

Homenko, L. P. and D. N. Khromov. 1984. A new species of the genus *Sepia* from the Arabian Sea. *Zool. Zh.*, 63(8):1150-1157 (Russ., Eng. summ.).

* Hoyle, W. E. 1886. Report on the Cephalopoda. *Rept. Sci. Res. Challenger*, 16(pt.44):246 pp. + Atlas.

Hoyle, W. E. 1904. Report on the Cephalopoda. *Repts. dredg. operat. "Albatross." Bull. Mus. Comp. Zool. Harvard*, 43(1):1-71.

* Hoyle, W. E. 1910. A list of generic names of dibranchiate Cephalopoda with their type species. *Senckenbergiana*, 32:407-413.

Imber, M. J. 1978. The squid families Cranchiidae and Gonatidae in the New Zealand area. *N. Z. J. Zool.*, 5(3):445-484.

Iredale, T. 1926. The cuttle-fish "bones" of the Sydney beaches. *Aust. Zool.*, 4:186-196.

Iredale, T. 1954. Cuttle-fish "bones" again. *Ibid.*, 12(1):63-82.

Iwai, E. 1956. Description of unidentified species of dibranchiate cephalopods, I-II. *Sci. Repts. Whales Res. Inst.*, No. 11:139-161.

Joubin, L. 1895. Contribution a l'étude des Céphalopodes de l'Atlantique Nord. *Rés. Camp. Sci. Monaco*, fasc.9:1-63.

Joubin,L. 1900. Céphalopodes provenant des campagnes de la "Princesse Alice" (1891-1897). *Ibid.*, fasc. 17:1-135.

Joubin, L. 1902. Revision des Sepiolides. *Mem. Soc. Zool. France*, 15(1):80-145.

Joubin, L. 1920. Contribution a l'étude des campagnes de la "Princesse Alice" (1898-1910). *Rés. Camp. Sci. Monaco*, fasc. 54:1-95 pp.

Joubin, L. 1924. Contribution a l'étude des Céphalopodes de l'Atlantique Nord, 4. *Ibid.*, fasc. 67:1-113.

Joubin, L. 1931, 1933. Notes préliminaires sur les Céphalopodes des croisiéres du "Dana" (1921-1922), 3, 4. *Ann. Inst. Oceánogr.*, N. S. 10(7):167-211, 13(1):1-49.

Joubin, L. 1937. Les Octopodes de la croisiére du "Dana" 1921-1922. *Dana Rept.*, No. 11:1-49.

Kawakami, T. and T. Okutani. 1981. A note on the identity of ommastrephid squids of the genus *Nototodarus* exploited in the New Zealand waters. *Bull. Tokai Reg. Fish. Res. Lab.*, No. 105:17-30.

Khromov, D. N. 1982. A new species of the genus *Sepia* from the southwestern Indian Ocean. *Zool. Zh.*, 61(1):137-140(Russ., Eng. summ.).

Klumov, S. K. and V. L. Yukhov. 1975. *Mesonychoteuthis hamiltoni* Robson, 1925 and its importance in the feeding of sperm whales in Antarctic waters. *Antarktika (Moscow)*, 14:159-189(in Russ.).

Kondakov, N. N. 1937. Cephalopoda of the Kara Sea. *Trudy Arctic Inst.*, No. 50:61-67(in Russ.).

* Kondakov, N. N. 1941. Cephalopoda of the Far Eastern Seas. *Issled. Dalnevost. Morei.* 1:216-255(Russ., Eng. summ.).

Kondakov, N. N., L. I. Moskalev, and K. N. Nesis. 1981. *Benthoctopus sibiricus* Løyning, an endemic octopod of the Eastern Arctic. In: *Ecological Investigations of the Shelf. Moscow: Inst. Okeanol. Acad. Sci. USSR*, pp. 42-56(Russ., Eng. summ.).

Korzun, Yu. V., K. N. Nesis, Ch. M. Nigmatullin, A. A. Ostapenko, and M. A. Pinchukov. 1979. New data on the distribution of squids, family Ommastrephidae, in the World Ocean. *Okeanologiya*, 19(4):729-733(Russ., Eng. summ.).

Kubodera, T. and K. Jefferts. 1984. Distribution and abundance of the early life stages of squid, primarily Gonatidae, in the northern North Pacific. *Bull. Nat. Sci. Mus., Tokyo*, A10 (3, 4): 91-106, 165-193.

Kubodera, T. and T. Okutani. 1977. Description of a new species of gonatid squid, *Gonatus madokai* n. sp. from the Northwest Pacific . . . *Venus* 36(3):123-151.

Kubodera, T. and T. Okutani. 1981a. *Gonatus middendorffi*, a new species of gonatid squid from the northern North Pacific, with notes on morphological changes with growth and distribution in immature stages. *Bull. Nat. Sci. Mus., Tokyo*, A7(1):7-26.

Kubodera, T. and T. Okutani. 1981b. The systematics and identification of larval cephalopods from the northern North Pacific. *Res. Inst. North Pacific Fish.*, Spec. Vol.:131-159.

Lipinski, M. A. 1983. A description of a new species of enoploteuthid cephalopod, *Abralia siedleckyi* spec. nov., with some remarks on *Abralia redfieldi* G. Voss, 1955. *Veliger*, 25(3):255-265.

Lönnberg, E. 1898. On the cephalopods collected by the Swedish Expedition to Tierra del Fuego 1895-96. *Svenska Exped. Magellansländerne*, 2(4):49-64.

Lu, C. C. 1977. A new species of squid, *Chiroteuthis acanthoderma*, from the Southwest Pacific. *Steenstrupiana*, 4(16):179-188.

Lu, C. C. and M. R. Clarke. 1975a. Vertical distribution of cephalopods at 40° N, 53° N and 60° N at 20° W in the North Atlantic. *J. Mar. Biol. Assoc. U. K.*, 55(1):143-163.

Lu, C. C. and M. R. Clarke. 1975b. Vertical distribution of cephalopods at 11° N, 20° W in the North Atlantic. *Ibid.*, 55(2):369-389.

Lu, C. C. and C. F. E. Roper. 1979. Cephalopods from the Deepwater Dumpsite 106 (Western Atlantic): vertical distribution and seasonal abundance. *Smithson. Contrib. Zool.*, No. 288:36 pp.

* Lu, C.C. and R.W. Tait. 1983. Taxonomic studies on *Sepioteuthis* Blainville from Australian region. *Proc. R. Soc. Victoria*, 95(4): 181-204.

Massy, A. L. 1909. The Cephalopoda Dibranchiata of the coasts of Ireland. *Fisheries, Ireland, Sci. Invest. for 1907.*, No. 1:1-39.

Massy, A. L. 1916a. Mollusca, 2. Cephalopoda. *Brit. Antarctic ("Terra Nova") Exped. 1910, Nat. Hist. Rept. Zool.*, 2(7):141-176.

Massy, A. L. 1916b. The Cephalopoda of the Indian Museum. *Rec. Indian Mus.*, 12(5):185-247.

Massy, A. L. 1928. The Cephalopoda of the Irish coast. *Proc. R. Irish Acad.*, 38B(2):25-37.

McSweeny, E. S. 1970. Description of the juvenile form of the Antarctic squid *Mesonychoteuthis hamiltoni* Robson. *Malacologia*, 10(2):323-332.

McSweeny, E. S. 1978. Systematics and morphology of the Antarctic cranchiid squid *Galiteuthis glacialis* (Chun). *Antarctic Res. Ser.*, No. 27:1-39.

Mercer, M. C. 1966. First record of *Pyrgopsis lemur* from the Northwest Atlantic. *J. Fish. Res. Bd. Canada*, 23(8):1257-1258

* Mercer, M. C. 1968. A synopsis of the recent Cephalopoda of Canada. *Proc. Symp. Mollusca*, 1:265-276.

Morales. E. and A. Guerra. 1977. Teuthoidea: Oegopsida del NW de Africa. *Invest. Pesq.*, 41(2):295-322.

Muus, B. J. 1956. Development and distribution of a North Atlantic pelagic squid, family Cranchiidae. *Medd. Danmarks Fisk.-og Havunders.*, N. S. 1(15):1-15.

* Muus, B. J. 1959. Skallus, søtaender, blaeksprutter. *Danmarks Fauna*, No. 65, Copenhagen: Gads. Forl. 239 pp.

Muus, B. J. 1962. Cephalopoda. The Godthaab-Expedition 1928. *Mddr. Grönland.* 81(5):1-23.

* Naef, A. 1921-1923, 1928. Die Cephalopoda. *Fauna und Flora des Golfes von Neapel*, Monogr. 35, 1:863 pp.; 2:357 pp.

Natsukari, Y. 1976. Description and new records of

Loligo sibogae Adam, 1954 from Formosa. *Venus*, 35(1):15-23.

Natsukari, Y. and T. Okutani. 1975. Identity of *Loligo chinensis* Gray, 1849, redescription of the type specimen and taxonomic review. *Ibid.*, 34(3-4):85-91.

Nesis, K. N. 1970. Biology of the Peruvian-Chilean giant squid *Dosidicus gigas*. *Okeanologiya*, 10(1):140-152(Russ., Eng. summ.).

Nesis, K. N. 1971. A new form of the squid, genus *Histioteuthis*. from the Eastern Pacific. *Zool. Zh.*, 50(10):1463-1471(Russ., Eng. summ.).

Nesis, K. N. 1972a. A revision of the squid genera *Taonius* and *Belonella*. *Ibid.*, 51(3):341-350(Russ., Eng. summ.).

Nesis, K. N. 1972b. Two new species of squids, family Gonatidae, from the North Pacific. *Ibid.*, 51(9):1300-1307(Russ., Eng. summ.).

* Nesis, K. N. 1973a. Taxonomy, phylogeny and evolution of squids of the family Gonatidae. *Ibid.*, 52(11):1626-1638(Russ., Eng. summ.).

Nesis, K. N. 1973b. Types of ranges in cephalopods of the North Pacific. *Trudy Inst. Okeanol. Acad. Sci. USSR*, 91:213-239(in Russ.)

Nesis, K. N. 1973c. Cephalopods of the Eastern Equatorial and Southeastern Pacific. *Ibid.*, 94:188-242(Russ., Eng. summ.).

Nesis, K. N. 1974a. Oceanic cephalopods of the Southwestern Atlantic Ocean. *Ibid.*, 98:51-75(Russ., Eng. summ.).

Nesis, K. N. 1974b. A revision of the squid genera *Corynomma, Megalocranchia, Sandalops,* and *Liguriella*. *Ibid.*, 96:5-22(Russ., Eng. summ.).

* Nesis, K. N. 1974c. The systematics of recent Cephalopods. *Bull. Mosk. Obshch. Ispyt. Prirody, sect. Biol.*, 79(5):81-93(Russ., Eng. summ.).

Nesis, K. N. 1974d. Giant squids. *Priroda*, No. 6:55-60(in Russ.).

Nesis, K. N. 1975a. Cephalopods of the American Mediterranean Sea. *Trudy Inst. Okeanol. Acad. Sci. USSR*, 100:259-288.

Nesis, K. N. 1977a. Geographical groups of pelagic cephalopods in the Western tropical Pacific. *Ibid.*, 107:7-14(Russ., Eng. summ.).

Nesis, K. N. 1977c. *Mastigoteuthis psychrophila* n. sp. from the Southern Ocean. *Zool. Zh.*, 56(6):835-841(Russ., Eng. summ.).

Nesis, K. N. 1977d. The biology of paper nautiluses, *Argonauta boettgeri* and *A. hians*, in the Western Pacific and the seas of the East Indian Archipelago. *Ibid.*, 56(7):1004-1014(Russ., Eng. summ.).

Nesis, K. N. 1978a. The subfamily Ancistrocheirinae (Enoploteuthidae). *Ibid.*, 57(3):446-449(Russ., Eng. summ.).

Nesis, K. N. 1979a. A brief review of zoogeography of the Australian-New Zealand pelagic realm (Cephalopoda). *Trudy Inst. Okeanol. Acad. Sci. USSR*, 106:125-139(Russ., Eng. summ.).

Nesis, K. N. 1979b. Squids of the family Ommastrephidae of the Australian-New Zealand region. *Ibid.*, 106:140-146(Russ., Eng. summ.).

Nesis, K. N. 1980a. Taxonomic position of *Chiroteu-*

this *famelica* Berry. *Bull. Mosk. Obshch. Ispyt. Prirody, sect. Biol.*, 85(4):59-66(Russ., Eng. summ.).

Nesis, K. N. 1980b. Sepiids and loliginids: A comparative review of distribution and evolution of neritic cephalopods. *Zool. Zh.*, 59(5):677-688(Russ., Eng. summ.).

Nesis, K. N. 1982a. Principles of the taxonomy of recent cephalopods. *Bull. Mosk. Obshch. Ispyt. Prirody, sect. Geol.*, 57(5):99-112(in Russ.).

Nesis, K. N. 1982b. Zoogeography of the World Ocean: comparison of the zonation of pelagic realm and regional subdivision of the shelf (by cephalopods). In: *Marine Biogeography. Moscow: Nauka*, pp. 114-134(in Russ.).

Nesis, K. N. 1982c. The zoogeographic position of the Mediterranean Sea. *Ibid.*, pp. 270-299(in Russ.).

Nesis, K.N. 1984. *Cephalopods*. In: *Field card manual of plankton*, pt. 3. Leningrad: Zool. Inst. Acad. Sci. USSR. 182 pp. (in Russ.).

Nesis, K.N. 1985a. Giant squid in the Sea of Okhotsk. *Priroda*, No. 10: 112-113 (in Russ.).

* Nesis, K.N. 1985b. *Oceanic cephalopods: Distribution, life forms, evolution.* Moscow: Nauka. 287 pp. (in Russ.).

Nesis, K.N. A.M. Amelekhina, A.R. Boltachev, and G.A. Shevtsov. 1985. Records of giant squids of the genus *Architeuthis* in the North Pacific and South Atlantic. *Zool. Zh.*, 64(4): 518-528 (Russ., Eng. summ.).

Nesis, K. N. and I. V. Nikitina. 1981. Macrotritopus, a planktonic larva of the benthic octopus, *Octopus defilippi;* identification and distribution. *Zool. Zh.*, 60(6):835-847(Russ., Eng. summ.).

Nesis, K.N. and I.V. Nikitina. 1984. Redescription of *Chiroteuthis joubini* Voss, 1967 (Chiroteuthidae). *Trudy Inst. Okeanol. Acad. Sci. USSR*, 119: 145-153 (Russ., Eng. summ.).

Nesis, K. N. and Ch. M. Nigmatullin. 1972. Near-bottom squids of the Patagonia-Falkland area. *Trudy AtlantNIRO*, 42:170-176(in Russ.)

Nesis, K. N. and Ch. M. Nigmatullin. 1979. Distribution and biology of the genera *Ornithoteuthis* Okada, 1927 and *Hyaloteuthis* Gray, 1849. *Bull. Mosk. Obshch. Ispyt. Prirody, sect. Biol.*, 84(1):50-63(Russ., Eng. summ.).

Nesis, K. N. and G. A. Shevtsov. 1977a. Neritic squids, family Loliginidae, in the waters of the Soviet Far East. *Biol. Morya (Vladivostok)*, No. 3:70-71(Russ., Eng. summ.).

Nesis, K. N. and G. A. Shevtsov. 1977b. First data on abyssal cephalopods of the Sea of Okhotsk. *Ibid.*, No.5:76-77(Russ., Eng. summ.).

Nigmatullin, Ch. M. 1972. Biology and fishery of cuttlefishes at the Northwestern African shelf. *Trudy AtlantNIRO*, 42:57-85.

Nigmatullin, Ch. M. 1979. Main stages of the evolution of squids, family Ommastrephidae. In: *Problems of evolutionary animal morphology. Kazan; Kazan State Univ.*, pp. 210-219(in Russ.).

Nishimura, S. 1966. Notes on the occurrence and biology of the oceanic squid, *Thysanoteuthis rhombus* Troschel, in Japan. *Publs. Seto Mar. Biol. Lab.*,

14:327-349.

Nishimura, S. 1968a. A preliminary list of the pelagic Cephalopoda from the Japan Sea. *Ibid.*, 16(1):71-83.

Nishimura, S. 1968b. Glimpse of the biology of *Argonauta argo* Linnaeus in the Japanese waters. *Ibid.*, 16(1):61-70.

Odhner, N. H. 1923. Die Cephalopoden. *Further Zool. Res. Swedish Antarctic Exped. 1901-1903.* 1(4):1-7.

Okiyama, M. 1969. A new species of *Gonatopsis* from the Japan Sea, with the record of a specimen referable to *Gonatopsis* sp. Okutani, 1967. *Publs. Seto Mar. Biol. Lab.*, 17(1):19-32.

Okutani, T. 1965, 1966, 1968, 1969. Studies on early life history of decapodan Mollusca. I-IV. *Bull. Tokai. Reg. Fish. Res. Lab.*, No. 41:29-31, No. 45:61-79, No. 55:9-57, No. 58:83-96.

★ Okutani, T. 1967. Preliminary catalogue of decapodan Mollusca from Japanese waters., *Ibid.*, No. 50:1-16.

★ Okutani, T. 1973, 1975. Guide and keys to squid in Japan. *Ibid.*, No. 74:83-111, No. 83:41-44.

Okutani, T. 1974. Epipelagic decapod cephalopods collected by micronekton tows during Eastropac Expedition, 1967-1968. (Systematic part). *Ibid.*, No. 80:29-118.

★ Okutani, T. 1980. *Useful and latent cuttlefish and squids of the World.* 3rd. ed., Tokyo Nat. Coop. Ass. Squid Processors, 67 pp.

Okutani, T. 1981. Two new species of the squid genus *Onykia* from the tropical Indian Ocean. *Bull. Nat. Sci. Mus. Tokyo.*, A7(4):155-163.

Okutani, T. and M. Hasegawa. 1979. A note on decapod cephalopods (squids) trawled from the Southwest Atlantic during May 1977 through March 1978. *Bull. Tokai Reg. Fish. Res. Lab.*, No. 99:9-21.

Okutani, T. and J. A. McGowan. 1969. Systematics, distribution, and abundance of the epiplanktonic squid larvae of the California Current, April 1954-March 1957. *Bull. Scripps. Inst. Oceanogr.*, 14:1-90.

Okutani, T. and Y. Satake. 1978. Squids in the diet of 38 sperm whales caught in the Pacific waters off Northeastern Honshu, Japan, February 1977. *Bull. Tokai Reg. Fish. Res. Lab.*, No. 93:13-27.

Okutani, T., Y. Satake, S. Ohsumi, and T. Kawakami. 1976. Squids eaten by sperm whales caught off Joban District, Japan, during January-February, 1976., *Ibid.*, No. 87:67-113.

Okutani, T. and K. Uemura. 1973. A new species of the genus *Nototodarus* from Japan. *Venus*, 32(2):39-47.

O'Sullivan, D.B., G.W. Johnstone, K.R. Kerry, and M.J. Imber. 1983. A mass stranding of squid *Martialia hyadesi* Rochebrune et Mabille at Macquarie Island. *Pap. Proc. R. Soc. Tasmania*, 117: 161-163.

Palacio, F. J. 1978. *Vosseledone charrua:* a new Patagonian cephalopod (Octopodidae) with notes on related genera. *Bull. Mar. Sci.*, 28(2):282-296.

Pearcy, W. G. and G. L. Voss. 1963. A new species of gonatid squid from the Northeast Pacific. *Proc. Biol. Soc. Wash..* 76:105-112.

Pereyra, W. T. 1965. New records and observations on the flapjack devilfish *Opisthoteuthis californiana*

Berry. *Pacif. Sci.*, 19(4):427-441.

Pérez-Gàndaras, G. and A. Guerra. 1978. Estudio sobre algunas especies del género *Bathypolypus* halladas en las costas de Galicia. *Invest. Pesq.*, 42(1):189-211.

★ Pfeffer, G. 1912. Die Cephalopoden der Plankton-Expedition. *Ergeb. Plankton-Exped. Humboldt-Stiftung*, 2:1-815 + Atlas.

Pickford, G. E. 1945. Le poulpe américaine: a study of the littoral Octopoda of the Western Atlantic. *Trans. Connecticut Acad. Arts Sci.*, 36:701-812.

★ Pickford, G. E. 1946, 1949. *Vampyroteuthis infernalis* Chun, an archaic dibranchiate cephalopod, I-II. *Dana Rept.*, No. 29:1-45, No. 32:1-132.

Pickford, G. E. 1959. Vampyromorpha. *Galathea-Rept.* 1:243-253.

Pickford, G. E. 1964. *Octopus dofleini* (Wülker), the giant octopus of the North Pacific. *Bull. Bingham Oceanogr. Coll.*, 19(1):70 pp.

Pickford, G. E. 1974. *Cistopus indicus* (Orbigny): a common Indo-Malayan species of octopus. *J. Mar. Biol. Assoc. India*, 16(1):43-48.

Pickford, G. E . and B. H. McConnaughey. 1949. The *Octopus bimaculatus* problem: a study in sibling species. *Bull. Bingham Oceanogr. Coll.*, 12(4):1-66.

★ Powell, A. W. B. 1960. Antarctic and Subantarctic Mollusca. *Rec. Auckland Inst. Mus.*, 5(3-4):117-193.

Rancurel, P. 1970. Les contenus stomacaux d'*Alepisaurus ferox* dans le sud-ouest Pacifique (Céphalopodes). *Cah. ORSTOM, sér. Océanogr.*, 8(4):3-87.

Rancurel, P. 1971. *Mastigoteuthis grimaldii* (Joubin, 1895), Chiroteuthidae peu connus de l'Atlantique tropical. *Ibid.*, 9(2):125-145.

Rancurel, P. 1972. *Mastigoteuthis inermis*, espéce nouvelle de Chiroteuthidae du Golfe de Guinée. *Bull. Soc. Zool. France*, 97(1):25-34.

Rancurel, P. 1973. *Mastigoteuthis hjorti* Chun, 1913. Description des trois echantillions provenant du Golfe de Guinée. *Cah. ORSTOM. sér. Océanogr.*, 11(1):27-32.

Rees, W. J. 1954. The *Macrotritopus* problem. *Bull. Brit. Mus. (Nat. Hist.) Zool.*, 2(4):67-100.

Rees, W. J. 1956. Notes on the European species of *Eledone* with special reference to eggs and larvae. *Ibid.*, 3(6):283-293.

★ Rees, W. J. and G. E. Maul. 1956. The Cephalopoda of Madeira. Records and distribution. *Ibid.*, 3(6):259-281.

Robson, G. C. 1924. On the Cephalopoda obtained in South African waters by Dr. J. F. D. Gilchrist in 1920-21. *Proc. Zool. Soc. London*, 39(1):589-686.

Robson, G. C. 1928. Céphalopodes des mers d'Indochine. *Note Serv. Océanogr. Pêches Indochine*, No. 10:53 pp.

★ Robson, G. C. 1929, 1932. *A monograph of the recent Cephalopoda based on the collections in the British Museum (Natural History).* London: Brit. Mus., pt. 1:236 pp., pt. 2:359 pp.

Robson, G. C. 1933. On *Architeuthis clarkei*, a new species of giant squid, with observations on the genus. *Proc. Zool. Soc. London*, No. 3:681-697.

Robson, G. C. 1948. The Cephalopoda Decapoda of the "Arcturus" oceanographic expedition 1925. *Zo-*

ologica, NY, 33, pt. 3(7):115-132.

* Roeleveld, M. A. 1972. A review of the Sepiidae of Southern Africa. *Ann. S. Afr. Mus.*, 59(10):193-313.

Roeleveld, M. A. 1975. A revision of Massy's checklist of "South African" Cephalopoda. *Ibid.*, 66(11):233-255.

Roeleveld, M. A. 1977. Cephalopoda from the tropical Eastern Atlantic Ocean. *Galathea-Rept.*, 14:123-132.

Roeleveld, M. A. 1982. Interpretation of tentacular club structure in *Sthenoteuthis oualaniensis* (Lesson, 1830) and *Ommastrephes bartrami* (LeSueur, 1821). *Ann. S. Afr. Mus.*, 89(4):249-264.

* Roper, C. F. E. 1966. A study of the genus *Enoploteuthis* in the Atlantic Ocean with a redescription of the type species, *E. leptura* (Leach, 1817). *Dana Rept.*, No. 66:1-46.

* Roper, C. F. E. 1969. Systematics and zoogeography of the worldwide bathypelagic squid *Bathyteuthis*. *Bull. U.S. Nat. Mus.*, 291:1-210.

Roper, C. F. E. and K. J. Boss. 1982. The giant squid. *Sci. Amer.*, 246(4):82-89.

Roper, C. F. E. and N. L. Brundage, Jr. 1972. Cirrate octopods with associated deep-sea organisms: new biological data based on deep benthic photographs. *Smithson. Contrib. Zool.*, No. 121:1-46.

Roper, C. F. E., C. C. Lu, and F. G. Hochberg (eds.). 1983. Proceedings of the Workshop on the Biology and Resources Potential of Cephalopods, Melbourne, 1981. *Mem. Nat. Mus. Victoria*, No. 44:311 pp.

Roper, C. F. E., C. C. Lu, and K. Mangold. 1969. A new species of *Illex* from the Western Atlantic and distributional aspects of other *Illex* species. *Proc. Biol. Soc. Wash.*, 82:295-322.

Roper, C. F. E. and M. J. Sweeney. 1976. The pelagic octopod *Ocythoe tuberculata* Rafinesque, 1814. *Bull. Amer. Malacol. Union for 1975.* pp.21-28.

* Roper. C.F.E., M.J. Sweeney, and C.E. Nauen. 1984. *Cephalopods of the World.* FAO Fish. Synopsis, No. 125, vol. 3. Rome: FAO. 277 pp.

* Roper, C. F. E. and R. E. Young. 1967. A review of the Valbyteuthidae and an evaluation of its relationship with the Chiroteuthidae. *Proc. U.S. Nat. Mus.*, 123(3612):1-9.

* Roper, C. F. E. and R. E. Young. 1968. The Promachoteuthidae, I: A reevaluation of its systematic position based on new material from the Antarctic and adjacent waters. *Antarctic Res. Series.* 11:203-214.

Roper, C. F. E. and R. E. Young. 1972. First record of juvenile giant squid, *Architeuthis. Proc. Biol. Soc. Wash.*, 85(16):206-222.

* Roper, C. F. E. and R. E. Young. 1975. Vertical distribution of pelagic cephalopods. *Smithson. Contrib. Zool.* No. 209:1-51.

Roper, C. F. E., R. E. Young, and G. L. Voss. 1969. An illustrated key to the families of the order Teuthoidea. *Ibid.*, No. 13:1-32.

Ruby, G. and J. Knudsen. 1972. Cephalopoda from the Eastern Mediterranean. *Israel J. Zool.*, 21:83-97.

Rudolph, H. 1932. Die Sepiolinen der Adria. *Zool. Anz.*, 101:112-120.

Sasaki. M. 1921. Report on cephalopods collected during 1906 by the U.S. Bureau of Fisheries steamer "Albatross" in the Northwestern Pacific. *Proc. U.S. Nat. Mus.*, 57(2310):163-203.

* Sasaki, M. 1929. A monograph of the dibranchiate cephalopods of the Japanese and adjacent waters. *J. Fac. Agric. Hokkaido Imp. Univ.*, suppl. 20:1-357.

Saunders, W. B. 1981. A new species of *Nautilus* from Palau. The species of living *Nautilus* and their distribution. *Veliger*, 24(1):1-7, 8-17.

Shevtsov, G. A. 1973. On the cephalopod fauna of the Southeastern and Central Pacific. In: *Tropical zone of the World Ocean and related global processes, Moscow: Nauka*, pp. 225-230(in Russ.).

Shevtsova, S. P. 1975. On the distribution and biology of the *Abraliopsis* squids from Kuroshio waters. In: *Complex studies in the World Ocean. Moscow: Inst. Okeanol. Acad. Sci. USSR*, pp. 351-352(in Russ.).

Silas, E. G. 1968. Cephalopoda of the West coast of India collected during the cruises of the R. V. "Varuna," with a catalogue of the species known from the Indian Ocean. *Proc. Symp. Mollusca*, 1:277-359.

Smith, P. J., P. E. Roberts, and R. J. Hurst. 1981. Evidence for two species of arrow squid in the New Zealand fishery. *N. Zeal. J. Mar. Freshwater Res.*, 15(3):247-253.

Starobogatov, Ya. I. and K.N. Nesis. (eds.). 1983. *Taxonomy and ecology of cephalopods.* Sci. Papers. Leningrad: Zool. Inst. Acad. Sci. USSR. 149 pp. (in Russ.).

Steenstrup, J. 1962. *The cephalopod papers of Japetus Steenstrup.* Translated into Eng., Copenhagen: Danish Sci. Press, 330 pp.

* Stenzel, H. B. 1964. Living *Nautilus.* Treatise on Invertebrate Paleontology, pt. K, Mollusca, 3:59-93.

Stephen, A. C. 1961. The species of *Architeuthis* inhabiting the North Atlantic. *Proc. R. Soc. Edinburgh*, 68B(2):147-161.

Taki, I. 1961. On two new eledonid octopods from the Antarctic Sea. *J. Fac. Fish. Anim. Husb. Hiroshima Univ.*, 3(2):297-316.

Taki, I. 1963. On four newly known species of Octopoda from Japan. *Ibid.*, 5(1):57-93.

Taki, I. 1964. On eleven new species of the Cephalopoda from Japan, including two new genera of Octopodinae. *Ibid.*, 5(2):277-343.

Taki, I. 1981. A catalogue of the Cephalopoda of Wakayama prefecture. *A catalogue of molluscs of Wakayama prefecture, the province of Kii*, vol. 1. Seto. Mar. Biol. Lab. Spec.Publ. Ser., 7(3):233-264.

Thiele, J. 1921. Die Cephalopoden der Deutschen Südpolar-Expedition 1901-1903. *Dtsch. Südpolar-Exped. 1901-1903*, 16(4):431-466.

* Thiele, J. 1934. *Handbuch der systematischen Weichtierkunde.* 3:779-1022, Jena: G. Fischer, (Cephalopoda:948-995).

* Thomas, R. F. 1977. Systematics, distribution, and biology of cephalopods of the genus *Tremoctopus.* *Bull. Mar. Sci.*, 27(3):353-392.

* Thore, S. 1949. Investigations on the "Dana" Octopoda, I. Bolitaenidae, Amphitretidae, Vitreledonellidae, and Alloposidae. *Dana-Rept.*, No. 33:1-85.

Thore, S. 1959. Cephalopoda. *Repts. Lunds Univ. Chile Exped. 1948-49*, No. 33, *Lunds Univ. Aarskr.*, N. F., Avd. 2, 55(1):19 pp.

Toll, R. B. 1981. *Benthoctopus oregonae*, a new species of octopod from the Southern Caribbean, with a redescription of *Benthoctopus januarii* (Hoyle, 1885). *Bull. Mar. Sci.*, 31(1):83-95.

Toll, R. B. and S. C. Hess. 1981. A small mature male *Architeuthis* with remarks on maturation in the family. *Proc. Biol. Soc. Wash.*, 94(3):753-760.

* Verrill, A. E. 1882. Report on the cephalopods of the northeastern coast of America. *Rep. U. S. Comm. Fish.*, 7:211-455.

Verrill, A. E. 1883. Supplementary report on the "Blake" cephalopods. *Bull. Mus. Comp. Zool. Harvard*, 11(5):105-115.

Voss, G. L. 1953. A new family, genus, and species of myopsid squid from the Florida Keys. *Bull. Mar. Sci. Gulf Carib.*, 2(4):602-609.

Voss, G. L. 1955. The Cephalopoda obtained by the Harvard-Havana Expedition off the coast of Cuba in 1938-39. *Ibid.*, 5(2):81-115.

* Voss, G. L. 1956. A review of the cephalopods of the Gulf of Mexico. *Ibid.*, 6(2):85-178.

Voss, G. L. 1957. Observations on *Ornihoteuthis antillarum* Adam, 1957, an ommastrephid squid from the West Indies. *Ibid.*,7(4):370-378.

Voss, G. L. 1958. The cephalopods collected by the R/V "Albatross" during the West Indian cruise of 1954. *Ibid.*, 8(4):369-389.

Voss, G. L. 1960. Bermudan cephalopods. *Fieldiana, Zool.*, 39(40);419-446.

* Voss, G. L. 1962a. A monograph of the Cephalopoda of the North Atlantic. I. The family Lycoteuthidae. *Bull. Mar. Sci. Gulf. Carib.*, 12(2):264-305.

Voss, G. L. 1962b. South African cephalopods. *Trans. R. Soc. S. Afr.*, 36(4):245-272.

* Voss, G. L. 1963. Cephalopods of the Philippine Islands. *Bull. U. S. Nat. Mus.*, No. 234:1-180.

Voss, G. L. 1967. Some bathypelagic cephalopods from South African waters. *Ann. S. Afr. Mus.*, 50(5):61-88.

Voss, G. L. 1968. Octopods from the R/V "Pillsbury" Southwestern Carribbean cruise, 1966, with a description of a new species, *Octopus zonatus. Bull. Mar. Sci.*, 18(3):645-659.

Voss, G. L. 1971. Cephalopods collected by the R/V "John Elliott Pillsbury" in the Gulf of Panama in 1967. *Ibid.*, 21(1):1-34.

Voss, G. L. 1974. *Loligo surinamensis*, a new species of loliginid squid from Northeastern South America. *Zool. Mededel.*, 48(6):43-53.

Voss, G. L. 1975. *Euaxoctopus pillsburyae*, a new species from the Southern Caribbean and Surinam. *Bull. Mar. Sci.*, 25(3):346-352.

Voss, G. L. 1976. Two new species of octopods of the genus *Graneledone* from the Southern Ocean. *Proc. Biol. Soc. Wash.*, 88(42):447-458.

Voss, G. L. 1982. *Grimpoteuthis bruuni*, a new species of finned octopod from the Southeastern Pacific. *Bull. Mar. Sci.*, 32(2):426-433.

Voss, G. L., L. Opresko, and R. Thomas. 1973. The potentially commercial species of octopus and squid of Florida, the Gulf of Mexico and the Caribbean Sea. *Univ. Miami Sea Grant Field Guide Series*, No. 2:33 pp.

* Voss, G. L. and G. R. Williamson, 1972. *Cephalopods of Hong Kong*, Hong Kong Govt. Press, 138 pp.

* Voss, N. A. 1969. A monograph of the Cephalopoda of the North Atlantic. The family Histioteuthidae. *Bull. Mar. Sci.*, 19(4):713-867,

Voss, N. A. 1974. Studies on the cephalopod family Cranchiidae. A redescription of *Egea inermis* Joubin, 1933. *Ibid.*, 24(4):939-956.

* Voss, N. A. 1980. A generic revision of the family Cranchiidae. *Ibid.*, 30(2):365-412.

Voss, N. A. and R. S. Voss. 1983. Phylogenetic relationships in the cephalopod family Cranchiidae. *Malacologia*, 23(2):397-426.

Wirz, K. 1955. *Bathypolypus sponsalis* (P. et H. Fischer), espéce commune dans la partie ouest de la Méditerranée. *Vie Milieu*, 6(1):129-147.

* Wirz, K. 1958. Céphalopodes. *Faune Marine des Pyrénées-Orientales*, fasc. 1. Paris, 59 pp.

* Wormuth, J. H. 1976. The biogeography and numerical taxonomy of the oegopsid squid family Ommastrephidae in the Pacific Ocean. *Bull. Scripps Inst. Oceanogr.*, 23:90 pp.

Yamamoto, K. and T. Okutani. 1975. Studies on early life history of decapodan Mollusca, V. *Bull. Tokai Reg. Fish. Res. Lab.*, No. 83:45-96.

Young, R. E. 1964. A note on three specimens of the squid *Lampadioteuthis megaleia* Berry, 1916 from the Atlantic Ocean, with the description of the male. *Bull. Mar. Sci.*, 14(3):444-452.

* Young, R. E. 1972. The systematics and areal distribution of pelagic cephalopods from the seas off Southern California. *Smithson. Contribs. Zool.*, No. 97:1-159.

Young, R. E. and C. F. E. Roper. 1968. The Batoteuthidae, a new family of squid from Antarctic waters. *Antarctic Res. Ser.*, 11:185-202.

Young, R. E. and C. F. E. Roper. 1969a. A monograph of the Cephalopoda of the North Atlantic. The family Cycloteuthidae. *Smithson. Contrib. Zool.*, No. 5:1-24.

Young, R. E. and C. F. E. Roper. 1969b. A monograph of the Cephalopoda of the North Atlantic. The family Joubiniteuthidae. *Ibid.*, No. 15:1-10.

Yukhov, V. L. 1974. Records of the giant squids. *Priroda*, No. 5:60-63(in Russ.).

* Zuev, G. V. 1971. *Cephalopods of the Northwestern Indian Ocean*. Kiev: Naukova Dumka, 223 pp.(in Russ.).

Zuev, G. V., K. N. Nesis, and Ch. M. Nigmatullin. 1975. Systematics and evolution of the genera *Ommastrephes* and *Symplectoteuthis*. *Zool. Zh.*, 54(10):1468-1479(in Russ.).

Zuev, G. V., K. N. Nesis, and Ch. M. Nigmatullin. 1976. Distribution of the genera *Ommastrephes* d'Orbigny, 1835, *Sthenoteuthis* Verrill, 1880, and *Todarodes* Steenstrup, 1880 in the Atlantic Ocean. *Bull. Mosk. Obshch. Ispyt. Prirody, sect. Biol.*, 81(4):53-63(Russ., Eng. summ.).

* Zuev, G.V., Ch. M. Nigmatullin, and V.N. Nikolsky. 1985. *Nektonic oceanic squids (genus Sthenoteuthis).* Moscow: Agropromizdat. 224 pp. (in Russ., Eng. contents).

Recent papers on revisions and new taxa not included in the keys.

Jefferts, K. 1985. *Gonatus ursabrunae* and *Gonatus oregonensis,* two new species of squids from the Northeastern Pacific Ocean. *Veliger,* 28(2):159-174.

Lu, C. C., C. F. E. Roper and R. W. Tait. 1985. A revision of *Loliolus,* including *L. noctiluca,* a new species of squid from Australian waters. *Proc. R. Soc. Victoria,* 97(2):59-85.

Nesis, K. N. and I. V. Nikitina. 1986a. A new family of deep-water squids from the Southeastern Atlantic. *Zool. Zh.,* 65(1):47-54 (Russ., Eng. summ.).

Nesis, K. N. and I. V. Nikitina. 1986b. New genus and species of squid of the family Neoteuthidae from the southeastern part of the Pacific Ocean. *Zool. Zh.,* 65(2):290-294 (Russ., Eng. summ.).

Riddell, D. J. 1985. Enoploteuthidae of the New Zealand Region. *Fish. Res. Bull. N.Z.,* No. 27:1-52.

Roeleveld, M. A. and W. R. Liltved. 1985. A new species of *Sepia* from South Africa. *Ann. S. Afr. Mus.,* 96(1):1-18.

Toll, R. B. 1985. The reinstatement of *Bathypolypus faeroensis* (Russell, 1909). *Proc. Biol. Soc. Wash.,* 98(3):598-603.

Voss, N. A. 1985. Systematics, biology and biogeography of the cranchiid cephalopod genus *Teuthowenia.* *Bull. Mar. Sci.,* 36(1):1-85.

Taxonomic Index

Valid scientific names are in *italic* type; higher taxa (orders, families, etc.) are in capital letters; and synonyms are in ordinary type. Page numbers with asterisk* refer to page(s) on which the description occurs; numbers in ordinary type refer to secondary references; and numbers in **bold** type refer to illustrations.

Index to Taxa Shown in Photographs